MOON HANDBOOKS®

'ELLOWSTONE
& GRAND TETON

D0027255

Old Bar BC Ranch, Grand Teton National Park

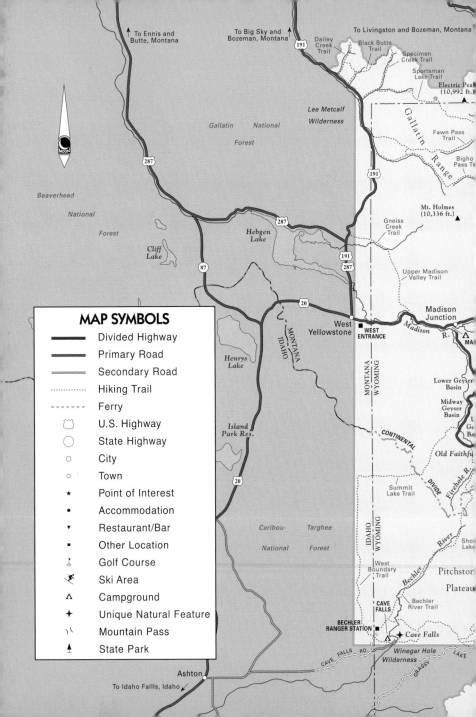

YELLOWSTONE NATIONAL PARK

Gallatin   National   Forest
Absaroka-
Beartooth
Wilderness

Jardine

Gardiner

Pebble Creek Trail
Silver Gate
Cooke City

NORTH ENTRANCE

MONTANA
WYOMING

Mammoth Hot Springs

Yellowstone

Yellowstone River Trail

Slough Creek Trail

NORTHEAST ENTRANCE

212

▲ Bunsen Peak

SLOUGH CREEK

Bliss Pass Trail

Abiathar Peak (10,928 ft.)

North Absaroka Wilderness

Gardner River

Petrified Tree

PEBBLE CREEK ▲

◆ Sheepeater Cliffs

ROOSEVELT LODGE

YELLOWSTONE INSTITUTE

The Thunderer (10,554 ft.) ▲

Shoshone National Forest

INDIAN CREEK

Tower Fall

TOWER FALL

Howard Eaton Trail

Specimen Ridge Trail

Cache Creek Trail

◆ Obsidian Cliff

Mt. Washburn (10,243 ft.) ▲

DUNRAVEN PASS

Grand Canyon of the Yellowstone

Mirror Plateau

Lamar River Trail

Roaring Mountain

▲▲ NORRIS

CANYON

▲ Norris

Canyon Village

Range

Norris Geyser Basin

Lower Falls

◆ Virginia Cascade

Howard Eaton Trail

Absaroka

Pelican Cone ▲

Hayden Valley

Lehardy Rapids

Pelican Valley

Mary Mountain Trail

MUD VOLCANO

FISHING BRIDGE RV PARK

North Absaroka Wilderness

Shoshone National Forest

Lake Village

Lake Butte

Avalanche Peak (10,566 ft.) ▲

EAST ENTRANCE

PAHASKA TEPEE ●

BRIDGE BAY

Bridge Bay

SYLVAN PASS

SLEEPING GIANT

14 16 20

Yellowstone Lake

Park Pt.

Mt. Doane (10,352 ft.) ▲

Mt. Langford (10,774 ft.) ▲

To Cody

GRANT VILLAGE

Frank Island

Mt. Stevenson (10,352 ft.) ▲

Washakie Wilderness

Eagle Creek Trail

West Thumb

Grant Village

Thorofare Trail

CONTINENTAL

Eagle Peak (11,358 ft.) ▲

EAGLE PASS

Delacy Creek Trail

shone Lake

Heart Lake

Table Mtn. (11,063 ft.) ▲

Shoshone National Forest

Lewis Lake

LEWIS LAKE

Mt. Sheridan (10,308 ft.) ▲

Trail Creek Trail

Mountain Creek Trail

is Falls

Heart Lake Trail

Snake River Trail

Two Ocean Plateau

Yellowstone

Moose Falls

Two Ocean Plateau Trail

DIVIDE

THOROFARE RANGER STATION

89 191 287

FLAGG RANCH ■

South Boundary Trail

Bridger-Teton National Forest

Teton Wilderness

River

To Jackson

0   10 mi

0   10 km

© AVALON TRAVEL PUBLISHING, INC.

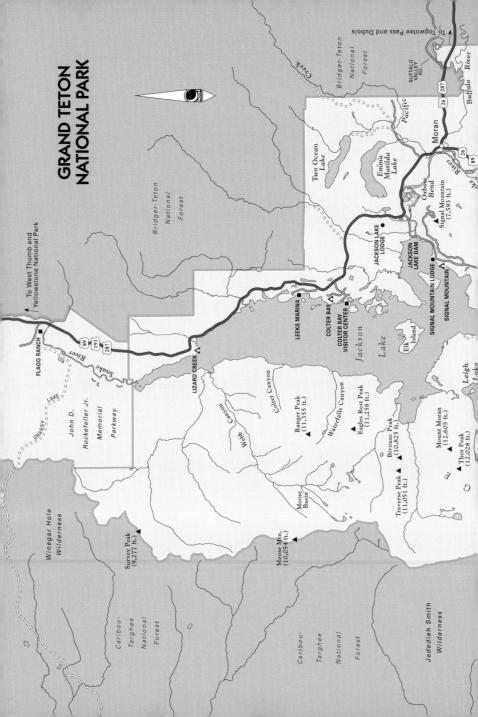

GRAND TETON NATIONAL PARK

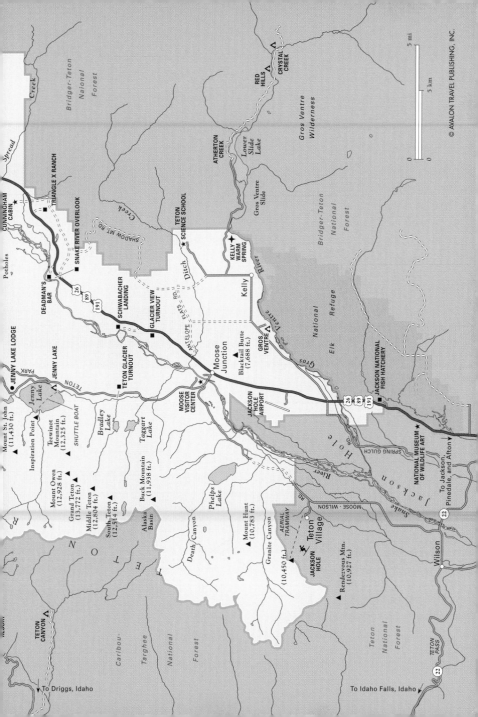

© AVALON TRAVEL PUBLISHING, INC.

5 mi
5 km

CRYSTAL CREEK

RED HILLS

Gros Ventre Wilderness

Bridger-Teton National Forest

Creek

Spread

Bridger-Teton National Forest

CUNNINGHAM CABIN

Potholes

TRIANGLE X RANCH

SNAKE RIVER OVERLOOK

ATHERTON CREEK

Lower Slide Lake

Gros Ventre Slide

TETON SCIENCE SCHOOL

Creek

SHADOW MT RD.

DEADMAN'S BAR

26
89
191

SCHWABACHER LANDING

GLACIER VIEW TURNOUT

KELLY WARM SPRING

Ditch

Kelly

JENNY LAKE LODGE

JENNY LAKE

ANTELOPE FLATS RD.

Moose Junction

River

Gros Ventre

PARK

TETON

Jenny Lake

Mount St. John (11,430 ft.)

Inspiration Point

Teewinot Mountain (12,325 ft.)

TETON GLACIER TURNOUT

SHUTTLE BOAT

Bradley Lake

Taggart Lake

Blacktail Butte (7,688 ft.)

MOOSE VISITOR CENTER

JACKSON HOLE AIRPORT

Gros Ventre

National

Elk Refuge

JACKSON NATIONAL FISH HATCHERY

26
89
191

Mount Owen (12,928 ft.)

Grand Teton (13,772 ft.)

Middle Teton (12,804 ft.)

South Teton (12,514 ft.)

Buck Mountain (11,938 ft.)

Alaska Basin

Phelps Lake

Death Canyon

Mount Hunt (10,783 ft.)

Granite Canyon

AERIAL TRAMWAY (10,450 ft.)

JACKSON HOLE

Teton Village

MOOSE-WILSON RD.

Snake River

Jackson Hole

SPRING GULCH

NATIONAL MUSEUM OF WILDLIFE ART

To Jackson, Pinedale, and Afton

22

Wilson

Rendezvous Mtn. (10,927 ft.)

TETON CANYON

Caribou-Targhee National Forest

TETON

Teton National Forest

TETON PASS

22

→ To Driggs, Idaho

→ To Idaho Falls, Idaho

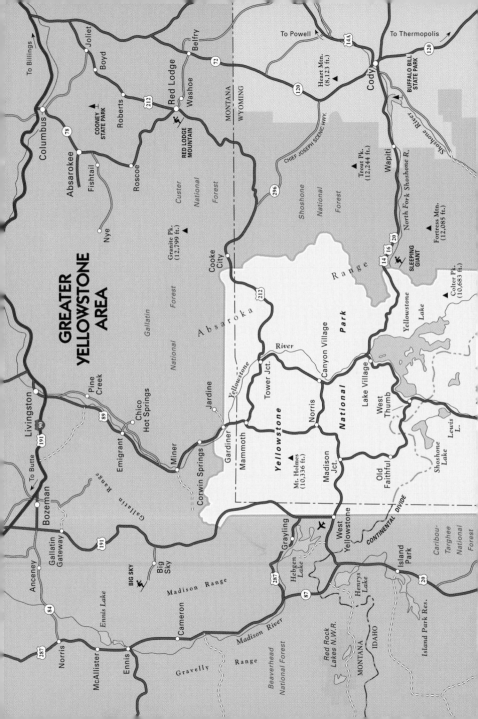

near Jackson Hole, Wyoming.

MOON HANDBOOKS®

YELLOWSTONE & GRAND TETON

SECOND EDITION

DON PITCHER

AVALON
TRAVEL

**Moon Handbooks Yellowstone & Grand Teton
Second Edition**

Don Pitcher

Editor: Amy Scott
Series Manager: Kevin McLain
Copy Editor: Ginjer L. Clarke
Graphics Coordinator: Melissa Sherowski
Production Coordinator: Amber Pirker
Freelance Layout Artist: Alvaro Villanueva
Cover Designer: Kari Gim
Interior Designers: Amber Pirker, Alvaro Villanueva, Kelly Pendragon
Map Editor: Naomi Adler Dancis
Cartographers: Kat Kalamaras, Mike Morgenfeld
Proofreader: Julie Leigh
Indexer: Kevin Millham

Please send all comments, corrections, additions, amendments, and critiques to:

**Moon Handbooks
Yellowstone & Grand Teton**
Avalon Travel Publishing
1400 65th Street, Suite 250
Emeryville, CA 94608, USA
atpfeedback@avalonpub.com
www.moon.com

Printing History
1st edition—2000
2nd edition—May 2003
5 4 3 2 1

ISBN: 1-56691-495-7
ISSN: 1542-8850

ABOUT THE AUTHOR
Don Pitcher

© DON PITCHER

Perhaps Don Pitcher's love of travel came about because he moved so much as a child; by age 15 he had lived in six states and two dozen East Coast and Midwest towns. Don's family hails from Maine, but being born in Atlanta made him a southerner with New England blood. He moved west for college, receiving a master's degree from the University of California, Berkeley, where his thesis examined wildfires in Sequoia National Park. When his first scientific paper was published, he appeared to be heading into the world of ecological research.

Shortly after graduate school Don landed the coolest job on the planet: being flown around Alaska's massive Wrangell-St. Elias National Park in a helicopter while conducting fire research. Wild places continued to beckon, and over the next 15 years Don built backcountry trails, worked as a wilderness ranger, mapped grizzly habitat, and operated salmon weirs—anything to keep away from an office job. After his first season in Alaska, he spent three months in the South Pacific, and quickly found himself addicted to travel. These explorations eventually took him to all 50 states and 35 countries.

Don started writing *Moon Handbooks Wyoming* after a summer of bear research in the Teton Wilderness and a winter of cleaning condos and skiing at Jackson Hole Ski Resort. *Moon Handbooks Yellowstone & Grand Teton* was a natural offshoot from that book, and this second edition expands considerably on the first iteration. Don's other titles include comprehensive Moon guides to Alaska, Washington, and the San Juan Islands. He has photographed two books on Wyoming and Alaska, and his images have appeared in a multitude of other publications and advertisements.

Don now works full time as a travel writer and photographer, basing his travels from Homer, Alaska, where he lives with his wife, Karen Shemet, and their children, Aziza and Rio. Find details on his latest projects at www.donpitcher.com.

*For Aziza Bali, who discovered rainbows, bison,
and chocolate cake in Jackson Hole.
May you always chase rainbows and snowflakes.
May you never lose your sense of wonder.*

Contents

Keeping Current

This is the second time around for *Moon Handbooks Yellowstone & Grand Teton,* and readers can play a role in keeping it up to date. I am not always able to check out all of the details hidden throughout this book, but I always appreciate any assistance in finding problems that appear. If a place I mention no longer exists, if certain statements are misleading (or flat out wrong), or if you've uncovered anything new, please contact me. I especially appreciate comments from local residents who have first-hand knowledge. Although I try to reply to all letters and emails, you may need to wait for a response because I'm often on the road or immersed in other projects. To learn more, visit my website, www.donpitcher.com.

Contact me at:
Don Pitcher
Moon Handbooks Yellowstone & Grand Teton
1400 65th St., Suite 250
Emeryville, CA 94608, USA
atpfeedback@avalonpub.com

Maps

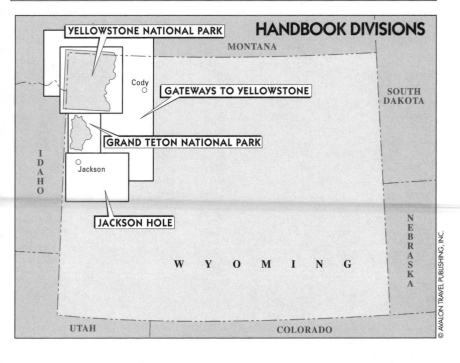

HANDBOOK DIVISIONS

© AVALON TRAVEL PUBLISHING, INC.

Here is your country. Cherish these natural wonders, cherish the natural resources, cherish the History and Romance as a sacred heritage, for your children and your children's children. Do not let selfish men or greedy interests skin your country of its beauty, its riches or its romance.

Theodore Roosevelt in 1903

Introduction

If ever a place deserved the term "Wonderland," it would have to be the northwest corner of Wyoming. In this spectacularly scenic region lies the nation's oldest and best-loved national park, Yellowstone, along with one of the most stunning mountainscapes on the planet, Grand Teton National Park. The valley beneath these peaks is Jackson Hole, recreation central for wintertime skiing and summertime whitewater rafting, horseback rides, day hikes, mountain biking, gourmet dining, and even shopping; it's one of the most sought-after vacation destinations in North America. Beyond these three justifiably famous areas are a wealth of attractions to please anyone who loves the great outdoors and the West, including a world-class museum complex in Cody, gorgeous badlands topography near the Old-West town of Dubois, and several delightful mountain settlements surrounding Yellowstone National Park. This book provides an introduction to the Greater Yellowstone area, a region that attracts more than three million visitors each year from around the globe.

© DON PITCHER

bison near Mormon Row, Grand Teton National Park

The Land

THE GREATER YELLOWSTONE ECOSYSTEM

The term Greater Yellowstone Ecosystem is broadly applied to the high plateau and mountain ranges inside and surrounding Yellowstone National Park. Covering approximately 19 million acres, this high-elevation country includes two national parks—Yellowstone and Grand Teton—along with portions of six surrounding national forests—Beaverhead-Deerlodge, Bridger-Teton, Caribou-Targhee, Custer, Gallatin, and Shoshone—plus other public lands managed by the Bureau of Land Management (BLM) and national wildlife refuges managed by the U.S. Fish & Wildlife Service. This vast landscape centers on the northwest corner of Wyoming but also includes parts of Montana and Idaho. All together, this is one of the largest relatively intact temperate-zone ecosystems on the planet.

The official websites for Yellowstone (www.nps.gov/yell) and Grand Teton (www.nps.gov/grte) National Parks are both packed with detailed information about plants, animals, geology, and other aspects of the Greater Yellowstone Ecosystem.

GEOGRAPHY

The Greater Yellowstone Ecosystem is a mountainous region, with several peaks topping

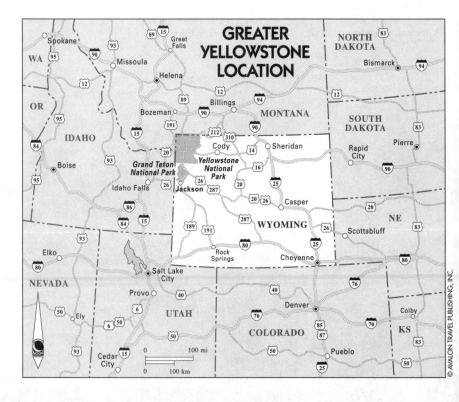

old barn in the shadow of Mormon Row, part of the Teton Range

The eastern and northern borders of Yellowstone National Park front on the Absaroka Range, which contains many peaks topping 12,000 feet. To the west and northwest of the park are the lower-elevation Gallatin, Madison, and Centennial ranges and the town of West Yellowstone, while the Caribou Range lies to the southwest. The Yellowstone gateway town of Cody sits at the eastern margin of the Absarokas within Bighorn Basin, and another gateway town, Dubois, occupies the upper end of protected Wind River Valley.

Grand Teton National Park and Jackson Hole lie just south of Yellowstone. The Teton Range creates an incredible western skyline, and the less grandiose, but still impressive Gros Ventre Range are to the east. Jackson Hole is a relatively flat intermountain basin through which the Snake River flows, with the town of Jackson on its southern margin. South of Jackson Hole are the Wyoming and Salt River ranges, while to the west of the Tetons lies Teton Valley, Idaho. The massive Wind River Mountains have many peaks over 13,000 feet and reach southeastward from Union Pass to South Pass, a distance of 100 miles. Areas south of Jackson Hole, including the Wind River Mountains, are beyond the scope of this book; for details see my *Moon Handbooks Wyoming* (www.moon.com).

13,000 feet. The nation's Continental Divide cuts diagonally across the region from the southeast to the northwest. Wyoming's highest summit, 13,804-foot Gannet Peak, is on the southern margin of the ecosystem in the Wind River Mountains, and the second-highest peak, Grand Teton (13,770 feet), forms the crown of the Tetons. Montana's tallest summit is 12,799-foot Granite Peak in the Absaroka-Beartooth Wilderness just northeast of Yellowstone. The little burgs of Cooke City and Silver Gate are not far away.

The heart of Yellowstone National Park is a high and rolling plateau that averages around 8,000 feet in elevation, but the eastern and northern portions of the park are considerably more rugged. The park's highest mountain is 11,358-foot Eagle Peak, on the southeastern border, and the lowest point (5,300 feet) is on the northwest corner near Gardiner, Montana.

CLIMATE

The complex and mountainous nature of the Greater Yellowstone Ecosystem creates widely varying microclimatic conditions. It may be a beautiful, sunny summer day in the town of Jackson, while backpackers 2,000 feet higher in the Tetons are getting drenched in a long and lightning-filled storm just a few miles away. The following overall weather description applies to Jackson Hole and the Yellowstone plateau (including the Old Faithful area). Temperatures may be a bit cooler along Yellowstone and Jackson lakes and are often warmer in the lower-elevation towns of Gardiner, Cody, and Dubois. Killing frosts are possible in any month of the year; I've awakened to new snow on the ground in late June! Total precipitation also varies across the region, from a low of just 11 inches annually at Gardiner to an estimated 70 inches or more in the Lewis Lake area of Yellowstone National Park. Most of the precipitation falls in the winter as snow; summers are relatively dry. (The exceptions to this are low-elevation areas on the north side of Yellowstone, where spring and early summer rains are more important.)

Get detailed climate data on the web at www.wrcc.dri.edu/summary/climsmwy.html. For daily weather forecasts, head to the National Weather Service's site for western and central Wyoming, www.crh.noaa.gov/riw. Most visitors centers inside and outside the parks have updated forecasts.

Summer

In general, summers are short but pleasant throughout the region, with warm, sunny days and cool nights. Lower-elevation hiking trails are usually free of snow from mid-June to mid-

October, but some high areas may not melt until late July. You may need both shorts and a light jacket in the same day. Midsummer daytime temperatures in Jackson Hole are typically in the upper 70s or low 80s F, with nighttime lows around 40°F. It's several degrees warmer in low-elevation places like Gardiner, and 5–10 degrees cooler in many road-accessible parts of Yellowstone. The warmest temperature recorded was 101°F for Jackson in 1934, and 103°F for Gardiner in 1960. Cody gets even hotter, and 90+°F summer days hit several times per month.

The air is generally dry, and most summer rain falls during afternoon thundershowers, when the rain can come down in torrents for brief periods, particularly in the mountains. Average rainfall for July and August in Jackson Hole is just one inch each month. All of this sunshine and showers makes for an abundance of rainbows. I've seen many days where a late afternoon storm over the Tetons tapers off to a glorious display of colors arching into the sky.

TROPICAL WYOMING

Sometimes I wish that Wyoming had more vegetation and less catarrh, more bloom and summer and fragrance and less Christmas and New Year's through the summer. I like the clear, bracing air of 7,500 feet above the civilized world, but I get weary of putting on and taking off my buffalo overcoat for meals all through dog days. I yearn for a land where a man can take off his ulster and overshoes while he delivers a Fourth of July oration, without flying into the face of Providence and dying of pneumonia. . . . As I write these lines I look out across the wide sweep of brownish gray plains dotted here and there with ranches and defunct buffalo craniums, and I see shutting down over the sides of the abrupt mountains, and meeting the foothills, a white mist which melts into the gray sky. It is a snow storm in the mountains.

I saw this with wonder and admiration for the first two or three million times. When it became a matter of daily occurrence as a wonder or curiosity, it was below mediocrity. Last July a snow storm gathered one afternoon and fell among the foothills and whitened the whole line to within four or five miles of town, and it certainly was a peculiar freak of nature, but it convinced me that whatever enterprises I might launch into here I would not try to raise oranges and figs until the isothermal lines should meet with a change of heart.

—*19th-century humorist Bill Nye*

Fall

Autumn provides a beautiful transition period from the warm summer days to the surprisingly cold winters. Nights are crisp and chilly, sending many folks scurrying for warmer climes. In Jackson Hole during September you can expect daytime highs around 55–65°F and nighttime lows around 25–30°F. Temperatures are 5–10 degrees cooler in the central portions of Yellowstone, where nighttime lows may reach into the single digits by late fall.

The peak of fall colors takes place around the first week of October in Jackson Hole and Grand Teton National Park, where aspens and cottonwoods turn a bright yellow (with a few orange trees). Although most of Yellowstone is covered with evergreen trees, you will find colorful deciduous stands in some areas, primarily on the north side of the park. You can expect to find snow on the ground anytime after late October, and earlier at high elevations.

Winter

Winter brings snow and cold weather throughout the Greater Yellowstone Ecosystem, although again, local microclimatic conditions vary widely. You'll face the coldest conditions in January, when a typical Jackson Hole day is in the 20s, with nights dropping to around 0–5°F. When the sky is clear, conditions can sometimes turn severely cold, with temperatures below zero for days at a time; the record low was recorded at West Yellowstone in 1933: –66°F. Fortunately, the relative humidity is quite low, making these temperatures easier to tolerate and creating fluffy powder snow conditions. The town of Jackson receives less summertime rain and wintertime snow than the nearby mountains. In a typical January you'll find a foot of snow on the ground, but nearby Jackson Hole Mountain Resort gets 38 feet of snow annually. Even more impressive is Grand Targhee Ski Resort on the west side of the Tetons, which gets an average of 42 feet of snow per year!

At Old Faithful in Yellowstone the snow is typically around 30–40 inches deep in midwinter, but in Mammoth Hot Springs (park headquarters) you're likely to see just 6–9 inches on the ground and much milder temperatures. At the other extreme, the Lewis Lake area may see 50 feet of snow in a typical winter! Temperatures at Old Faithful average in the 20s in the day but often drop well below zero at night. At Mammoth Hot Springs, day temperatures approach 30°F, with nights dropping to around 10°F.

One surprising winter feature is the presence of temperature inversions in intermountain valleys such as Jackson Hole. These often occur on cold, clear nights when the cold air sinks into the valley floors. Skiers who leave the lodge bundled in down parkas and polypro long johns are often surprised to find temperatures 20 degrees warmer at the top of the mountain.

Spring

Spring in the Greater Yellowstone Ecosystem is a transitional period as the snow gradually melts and the plants reappear after a long winter. For many locals this is the time to escape mud season for a week or two in southern Utah. Snow often remains on the ground until late April in Jackson Hole and doesn't melt from the higher mountains until late July. In addition, a few snowfields and glaciers remain year-round in the highest and most protected areas. Spring is when you'll meet the fewest travelers because the roads may not be plowed yet, snow blocks hiking trails, skiing gets worse by the day, and many summertime recreation operations haven't yet opened. Expect daytime temperatures in the 40s and 50s in early May, but warming up rapidly as the long days of June appear.

Vegetation

Several vegetation types predominate in the Greater Yellowstone Ecosystem. Within Grand Teton National Park, sagebrush flats cover the valley floor, with riparian corridors and wetlands lining the Snake River and smaller creeks. Northern Yellowstone National Park also has sagebrush-dominated areas, but much of Yellowstone and the surrounding mountain country is covered with forests dominated by lodgepole pine. Other common trees within the Greater Yellowstone Ecosystem include quaking aspens, whitebark and limber pine, Engelmann spruce, Douglas fir, and subalpine fir. The tree line is approximately 10,000 feet, and above this point, low-growing alpine species survive the harsh conditions and brief summers.

Wildlife

WATCHABLE WILDLIFE

The Greater Yellowstone Ecosystem is famous as a place to view wildlife, particularly elk, bison, wolves, moose, and grizzlies. Because of its abundant animal populations, you'll sometimes hear the term "America's Serengeti" applied to Yellowstone, which is the home of the largest concentration of large mammals in the Lower 48. During summer, the best times to see wildlife are from sunrise to early morning or from late afternoon to early evening. At other times of the year they tend to be equally visible in the middle of the day. Bring a pair of binoculars for a close-up view, but make sure your behavior isn't disturbing the animal or causing it to move away. This is particularly true in midwinter when any unnecessary movements lessen their chance for survival. Always stay at least 25 yards from wildlife and 100 yards from bears. See the Yellowstone chapter for additional wildlife information beyond that provided here, including details on bears, bighorn sheep, coyotes, deer, moose, and wolves.

PRONGHORN ANTELOPE

Antelope (biologists prefer the name pronghorn because they are not true antelopes) are sleek ungulates with beautiful reddish-brown coats accented by white throat patches and rumps. Antelope survive on grasses, forbs, and plants that other animals avoid, notably sagebrush—perhaps Wyoming's most abundant plant. They are almost never seen in wooded areas. Antelope are built for speed: oversized lungs and windpipes give them the ability to run for miles at 30 mph, and they can accelerate up to 45 mph for short bursts. To watch for predators, they have the largest eyes by body

© DON PITCHER

Pronghorn antelope are most often seen in the northern part of Yellowstone.

weight of any mammal. Despite this speed, antelope have an innate inquisitiveness that makes them relatively easy to hunt, an attribute that nearly drove them to extinction by market hunting early in this century. One surprising trait in antelope is their inability to jump fences; instead they crawl under them. Fences that are too low will completely halt their migrations.

Both males and females grow horns, and those on the males typically have a prong (hence the name). Dominant males (bucks) gather harems of females (does) and fawns, and fight off other bucks in the late summer rutting season. In May or June does give birth to one or two fawns.

Antelope are abundant in many parts of Wyoming, and more than 400,000 of them live in the state. They are not nearly as common in the northwest corner of Wyoming, where conditions are more marginal. You'll see small herds in open country within Grand Teton National Park and on the north side of Yellowstone National Park, particularly near Mammoth and Gardiner.

Because of its abundant animal populations, you'll sometimes hear Yellowstone called "America's Serengeti." Yellowstone is the home of the largest concentration of large mammals in the Lower 48.

ELK

A majestic member of the deer family, elk (some biologists prefer the term "wapiti") are a favorite with both tourists and hunters. In summer nearly 100,000 elk can be found within the Greater Yellowstone Ecosystem. With bulls weighing up to 900 pounds and cows up to 600 pounds, these are some of the largest antlered animals in the Americas.

Elk spend summers high in the mountains, feeding in alpine meadows and along forest edges. The young males and cows with their calves—generally born in late May and early June—group in large herds for protection. Meanwhile, the bachelor bulls hang out on their own, watching baseball games on TV while drinking Heineken (just kidding; they drink Teton Ale). When the fall rutting season arrives, bulls herd the cows and calves around, mating with cows when they come into estrus and defending their harems from other bulls. During this time of year the bugling of bull elk is a common sound in the mountains, a challenge to any bull within earshot. When a competitor appears, a dominance display often follows—complete with bugling, stomping, and thrashing of the ground—to show who is the baddest bull around. In a fight, bulls lock their massive antlers and try to push and twist until one finally gives in and retreats. These battles help ensure that the healthiest bulls produce the most offspring. Ironically, other bulls often wait in the wings for battles over harems to occur, then rush in to mate with the cows while the larger bulls are sparring. The snows of late fall push elk to lower-elevation winter ranges, notably at the National Elk Refuge in Jackson Hole, where they are fed. When spring comes, the bulls drop their antlers and immediately begin to grow new ones. The elk head back into the high country, following the melting snowline.

Elk and bison both can be infected with brucellosis, a bacterium causing spontaneous abortions. Brucellosis is transmitted to other animals by contact with the dead fetus or birthing material and can cause undulant fever in humans. Ranchers worry that brucellosis can spread from elk and bison to cattle, particularly around elk feeding grounds in western Wyoming. To lessen the incidence of brucellosis, state employees now routinely vaccinate elk at the feeding grounds, shooting them in the hindquarters with vaccine-loaded pellets.

MOOSE

The largest member of the deer family, moose are typically seen eating willow bushes in riparian areas. They are the loners of the deer world, and only during the fall mating season are you

© DON PITCHER

A female moose is called a "cow."

likely to see males (bulls) and females (cows) together or to see bulls jousting. Bulls can reach 1,300 pounds, while cows grow to 800 pounds and give birth to up to three calves. In addition to enormous racks, the bulls have a distinctive dewlap or "bell" that hangs below their throat but apparently serves no physical purpose. Both Yellowstone and Grand Teton support moose; look for them along streams and other wet places in the summer.

BISON

The bison is the definitive frontier animal and Wyoming's state mammal—its outline graces the state flag. Weighing up to 2,000 pounds, these are the largest land mammals in the New World. Bison live 45 years or more, with females bearing calves until they are in their forties. The calves weigh 30–40 pounds at birth and within minutes are standing and able to graze. Two races of bison exist: the plains bison, primarily east of the Rockies, and the mountain bison (sometimes called wood bison) in the higher elevations. Technically, these huge, hairy beasts are bison—the only true buffalo are the water buffalo of Southeast Asia—but the name buffalo is commonly used.

With their massive heads, huge shoulder humps, heavy coats of fur, and small posteriors, buffalo are some of the strangest animals in North America. They look so front-heavy as to seem unstable, ready to topple forward onto their snouts at any time. Despite this impression, buffalo are remarkably well adapted to life on the plains. A bison will use its strong sense of smell to find grass buried in a deep snowdrift and then sweep the snow away with a sideways motion of its head. The animals are also surprisingly fleet footed, as careless Yellowstone photographers have discovered. In addition, the buffalo is one very tough critter. In 1907, a buffalo was pitted against four of the meanest Mexican bulls at a Juarez, Mexico bullring. After knocking heads several times with the buffalo, the bulls fled and were saved only when bullfighters opened the chute gates to let them escape.

"Blackening the Plains"

When Europeans first reached the New World, they found massive herds of bison in the Appalachians and even more as they headed west. Daniel Boone hunted them in North Carolina in the 1750s; Pennsylvanians shot hundreds of buffalo that were invading their winter stores of hay. By 1820, settlers had nearly driven the buffalo to extinction in the east, but there were far more living to the west. As explorers, mountain men, and the first tentative settlers reached the "Great American Desert," they were awestruck by the numbers. Travelers told of slowly moving masses of buffalo blackening the plains and watched in astonishment as the herds stopped at rivers and literally drank them dry. A fair estimate of the original population of buffalo in North America is 75 million. Even in the middle 1860s, travelers through Wyoming's Wind River Valley reported seeing 10,000 bison at one time. A pioneer Kansas settler named William D. Street recalled a trip in which a herd roared past his camp for an entire night. The next morning, he climbed a nearby butte and saw buffalo covering the plains below. According to Street:

> *The herd was not less than 20 miles in width—we never saw the other side—at least 60 miles in length, maybe much longer; two counties of buffaloes! There might have been 100,000, or 1,000,000, or 100,000,000. I don't know. In the cowboy days in western Kansas we saw 7,000 head of cattle in one roundup. After gazing at them a few moments our thoughts turned to that buffalo herd. For a comparison, imagine a large pail of water; take from it or add to it a drop, and there you have it. Seven thousand head of cattle was not a drop in the bucket as compared with that herd of buffalo.*

Indians and Buffalo

The Plains Indians depended heavily on the buffalo for food and—like the proverbial hot dog, which "contains everything but the moo"—they used every part of the animal. Hooves were carved into spoons, skins became buffalo robes and covers for boats and tepees, rawhide was used for drumheads, calf skins became storage sacks, hair was turned into earrings, and horns were formed into cups and arrow points. Everything that remained—including the muzzle, penis, eyes, and cartilage—was boiled down to use as glue for arrowheads. Their dried testicles and scrotum were used for rattles, and the ubiquitous buffalo chips became a cooking fuel on the treeless prairies.

Hunting techniques varied depending on the terrain. When possible, the Indians drove herds of bison into arroyos with no exits, over cliffs, or into deep sand or snow, making them easier to kill. The arrival of Spanish horses in the 16th century made it far easier to hunt bison. In a surround, mounted hunters attacked from at least two sides, creating chaos in the herd and allowing buffalo to be shot with arrows or guns.

When whites first spread across the plains, they found the bison a plentiful food source, but they also viewed the massive herds as a hindrance to agriculture and cattle raising. But these were not the only reasons whites wanted to destroy the buffalo. Killing off the bison would starve the Indians into submission and force them to take a more "civilized" way of life. General Philip Sheridan, commenting in support of white buffalo hunters, said

> *Instead of stopping the [white] hunters they ought to give them a hearty, unanimous vote of thanks, and appropriate a sufficient sum of money to strike and present to each one a medal of bronze, with a dead buffalo on one side and a discouraged Indian on the other. They are destroying the Indian's commissary, and it is a well-known fact that an army losing its base of supplies is placed at a great disadvantage. Send them powder and lead, if you will, for the sake of a lasting peace, let them kill, skin and sell until the buffaloes are exterminated.*

This reckless slaughter did indeed endanger the Indians, but it also had an unwanted side effect: the Indians went on the warpath. The loss of their primary food source helped convince many Indians that their own extinction was next. The warriors who massacred Custer and his men at Little Big Horn had watched their people pushed to the brink of starvation by the destruction of the buffalo.

The Slaughter

Two factors propelled the slaughter to new heights in the 1870s: new railroads across the plains and a sudden international demand for buffalo robes and hides. Buffalo meat proved to be a readily available food source for railway construction workers, and hunters such as "Buffalo Bill" Cody provided a steady supply, generally taking just the hindquarters and hump and leaving the rest on the plains. Hundreds of thousands were killed. Once the railroads were completed in 1869, a new "sport" appeared—shooting buffalo from the moving railcars and leaving them to rot on the prairie. Wealthy gentry from the East Coast and Europe also discovered the joys of killing. One Irish nobleman had an entourage of 40 servants, with an entire wagon just for firearms; he killed 2,000 buffalo in a three-year carnage.

Conservationists tried to halt the buffalo slaughter through legislation in 1874, but President Grant's corrupt Secretary of the Interior, Columbus Delano, said, "I would not seriously regret the total disappearance of the buffalo from our western prairies, in its effect upon the Indians. I would regard it rather as a means of hastening their sense of dependence upon the products of the soil and their own labors." The legislation was pocket-vetoed by Grant.

In 1872, thousands of hide hunters spread throughout Kansas, Nebraska, and Colorado in search of buffalo. Over the next three years, they brought in more than three million buffalo hides, with Indians killing another

The Indian warriors who massacred Custer and his men at Little Big Horn had watched their people pushed to the brink of starvation by the destruction of the buffalo.

400,000 bison for meat and robes. Good hide hunters could bring down 25 to 100 buffalo in a typical day, keeping five skinners busy from sunup to sundown. One hunter, Jim White, killed at least 16,000 buffalo in his career. Only the hides, cured hams, and buffalo tongues (which could be salted and shipped in barrels) were saved. When Gen. Grenville M. Dodge toured Kansas in the fall of 1873, he noted that "the air was foul with a sickening stench, and the vast plain, which only a short twelvemonth before teemed with animal life, was a dead, solitary, putrid desert." Buffalo carcasses dotted the plains in such numbers that in later years bone pickers would collect massive piles of bones for knife handles, combs, and buttons or to be ground up for sugar refining, fertilizer, or glue.

When the buffalo of the central states approached extinction, hunters turned their attention elsewhere, reaching Wyoming, Montana, and the Dakotas in 1880. In 1882, more than 200,000 hides were taken, and another 40,000 the following year. By 1884, only 300 hides were shipped. The slaughter was nearly over; only a few private herds and scattered individual bison remained. The Indians who had once depended so heavily on buffalo for all the necessities of life were reduced to eating muskrats, gophers, and even grass. Some killed their horses, others stole settlers' cattle, and the rest had to beg the government for food. In only a couple of years, an entire culture had been devastated.

But the slaughter ruined the lives not just of the buffalo or the Indians; hide hunters often spiked buffalo carcasses with strychnine, returning later to skin the wolves that had come to feed on the meat. Coyotes, kit foxes, badgers, vultures, eagles, ravens, and anything else that ate the meat were also killed. With both the buffalo and the "vermin" out of the way, the West was safe for domestic sheep and cattle.

Protection

It wasn't until 1894 that Congress passed legislation protecting bison, and this was only inside Yellowstone National Park. The following year, only 800 buffalo remained in all of North America, one-thousandth of 1 percent of their original numbers. Despite this dismal picture, the population has rebounded dramatically; today an estimated 65,000 bison roam across America. A strong demand for buffalo meat has led some western ranchers to raise bison. Approximately 3,500 bison remain in Yellowstone (one of the few large wild populations in existence), with another 500 in Grand Teton National Park.

MOUNTAIN MEN

The era of the fur trapper is one of the most colorful slices of American history, a time when a rough and hardy breed of men took to the Rockies in search of furs and adventure. Romanticized in such films as *Jeremiah Johnson,* the trappers actually played but a brief role in history and numbered fewer than 1,000 individuals. Their real importance lay in acting as the opening wedge for the West, a vanguard for the settlers and gold miners who would follow their paths—often led by these same mountain men.

The Fur Business

Fashion sent men into the Rockies in the first place because the waterproof underfur of a beaver could be used to create the beaver hat, which was all the rage in the early part of the 19th century. (It cost a month's wages for a man in England to buy a fine beaver hat in the 1820s!) Beavers in the eastern United States were soon trapped out, forcing trappers to head farther and farther west. Several companies competed for the lucrative fur market, but John Jacob Astor's American Fur Company proved the most successful. In 1811, Astor sent a party of men across the Rockies to the mouth of the Columbia to build a trading post and then set up a chain of posts across the West. The men—known as the Astorians—were probably the first whites to follow the route that would later become the Oregon Trail.

John Jacob Astor's trappers went head to head against the Rocky Mountain Fur Company, which was owned at various times by some of the most famous mountain men—Jedediah Smith, David Jackson, William and Milton Sublette, Jim Bridger, Thomas Fitzpatrick, and others. Competition for furs became so intense that Astor's men began following Jim Bridger and Tom Fitzpatrick to discover their trapping grounds. After trying unsuccessfully to shake the men tailing them, Bridger and Fitzpatrick deliberately headed into the heart of Blackfeet country, where Indians killed the leader of Astor's party and managed to leave Bridger with an arrowhead in his shoulder that was not removed until three years later.

Many Indians (particularly from the Flathead and Nez Perce tribes) were also involved in the fur trade, and a standard Indian trade value was 240 beaver pelts for a riding horse. In the mountains, anything from the world back east had considerable value: guns sold for $100 each, blankets for $40 apiece, tobacco for $3 per pound, and alcohol (often diluted) for up to $64 per gallon. After just two years of such trading, William Ashley retired with an $80,000 profit. Control of the fur market continued to change hands as the Rocky Mountain Fur Company and the American Fur Company competed with each other and with a mysterious company headed by Capt. Benjamin Bonneville, which some believe was a front for the U.S. Army to explore the West.

Most of the men who trapped in the Rockies were hired and outfitted by the fur companies, but others worked under contract and traded furs for overpriced supplies. Many men

continued on next page

MOUNTAIN MEN (cont'd)

found themselves in debt to the company at the end of a season. At the top of the heap were the free trappers, men who worked either alone or with others but who sold their furs to whoever offered the highest prices. Some men, primarily those who brought trade goods to the rendezvous, became rich in the process. Others, such as John Colter, Jim Bridger, James Beckwourth, Jedediah Smith, Thomas Fitzpatrick, and Kit Carson, would achieve fame for their rich knowledge of the land and their ability to survive against insurmountable odds. Many trappers married Indian women, learned sign language and various Indian tongues, and lived in tepees.

Trappers worked throughout winter when the beaver pelts were their finest; most summers were spent hunting and fishing or hanging out with fellow trappers or friendly Indians. In his *Journal of a Trapper 1834-1843,* Osborne Russell described a campfire scene among fellow mountain men:

A large fire was soon blazing encircled with sides of Elk ribs and meat cut in slices supported on sticks down which the grease ran in torrents The repast being over the jovial tale goes round the circle the peals of loud laughter break upon the stillness of the night which after being mimicked in the echo from rock to rock it dies away in the solitary. Every tale puts an auditor in mind of something similar to it but under different circumstances which being told the "laughing part" gives rise to increasing merriment and furnishes more subjects for good jokes and witty sayings such as Swift never dreamed of Thus the evening passed with eating drinking and stories enlivened with witty humor until near Midnight all being wrapped in their blankets lying around the fire gradually falling to sleep one by one until the last tale is "encored" by the snoring of the drowsy audience The Speaker takes the hint breaks off the subject and wrapping his blanket more closely about him soon joins the snoring party—The light of the fire being supersed by that of the Moon just rising from behind the Eastern Mountains a sullen gloom is cast over the remaining fragments of the feast and all is silent except the occasional howling of the solitary wolf on the neighboring mountain whose senses are attracted by the flavors of roasted meat but fearing to approach nearer he sits upon a rock and bewails his calamities in piteous moans which are re-echoed among the Mountains.

A good trapper could take in more than 150 beaver in a year, worth $4–6 apiece. It was an arduous job, and the constant threat of attacks by the Blackfeet Indians made it even more difficult. The great letting-go came with the summer rendezvous, an event anticipated for months ahead of time.

The Rendezvous

William H. Ashley, founder of the Rocky Mountain Fur Company, was one of the most important figures in the fur trade. In 1822, he ran an ad in a St. Louis paper that read:

To Enterprising Young Men. The subscriber wishes to engage ONE HUNDRED MEN, to ascend the river Missouri to its source, there to be employed for one, two or three years.—For particulars enquire of Major Andrew Henry, near the Lead Mines, in the County of Washington, (who will ascend with, and command the party) or to the subscriber at St. Louis.

—Wm. H. Ashley

Ashley's company of men—along with $10,000 in supplies—made it into the Yellowstone River country, where he left them the following year, promising to resupply them in 1825 on the Henrys Fork near its confluence with the Green River, along the present-day Wyoming–Utah border. Thus began the first rendezvous. They would take place every summer until 1840. Ashley failed to bring booze that first summer and the rendezvous lasted only two days. In future years, however, the whiskey flowed freely and the festivities lasted for weeks.

The *rendezvous*—a French word meaning "appointed place of meeting"—was a time when both white and Indian trappers could sell their furs, trade for needed supplies and Indian squaws (the women had little say in the matter but most took considerable pleasure in the arrangement), meet with old friends, get rip-roaring drunk, and engage in storytelling, gambling, gun duels, and contests of all sorts. Horse racing, wrestling bouts, and shooting contests were favorites; Kit Carson killed Shunar, a big French bully, in a duel during one of the Green River rendezvous. Debauchery reigned supreme in these three-week-long affairs, and by the time they were over, many of the trappers had lost their entire year's earnings.

During the heyday of the fur trade, a common saying was "all trails lead to the Seedskeedee [Green River]." Six rendezvous were held here in the 1830s, others were held in the Wind River/Popo Agie River area, on Ham's Fork of the Green River, and in Idaho and Utah. Sites were chosen where there was space for up to 500 mountain men and 3,000 Indians, plenty of game, ample grazing for the thousands of horses, and good water. Not coincidentally, all were held in Shoshone country rather than farther east or north, where the hostile Sioux, Blackfeet, and Crow held sway. Despite such precautions, more than half of Ashley's men were scalped by Indians.

Changing Times

The end of the rendezvous system—and most of the Rocky Mountain fur trapping—came about for a variety of reasons: overtrapping, the financial panic of 1837, and the growing use of other materials—particularly the South American nutria and Chinese silk—for hats. In addition, permanent trading posts such as Fort Laramie drew Indians away from the mountains to trade for buffalo robes instead of beaver furs. By 1840, when the last rendezvous was held on the banks of the Green River near present-day Pinedale, it was obvious there would be no more. One of the longtime trappers, Robert Newell, said to his partner, Joseph Meek:

We are done with this life in the mountains—done with wading in beaver dams, and freezing or starving alternately—done with Indian trading and Indian fighting. The fur trade is dead in the Rocky Mountains, and it is no place for us now, if ever it was. We are young yet, and have life before us. We cannot waste it here; we cannot or will not return to the States. Let us go down to the Wallamet and take farms.

On the Road

Northwest Wyoming is famous for its year-round recreational opportunities. In the summertime, hiking, camping, horseback rides, river rafting, mountain biking, and other adventures top the charts, and winter brings out the skis, snowboards, skates, snowshoes, and snowmobiles. Each part of the region has its own attractions, from whitewater rafting through the Snake River Canyon, to mountain climbing within Grand Teton National Park, to family day hikes in Yellowstone. If outdoor adventure is what you crave, you've come to the right place!

FISHING

Outstanding fishing opportunities abound throughout the Greater Yellowstone Ecosystem, and several rivers have achieved an almost mythical status among fly-fishers.

Fishing Licenses

In **Wyoming,** nonresident fishing permits cost $10 for one day or $65 for a season. Resident fishing licenses are $15 for the year. Nonresident youths (ages 14–19) pay $15 for the year ($3 for resident youths). With the exception of the one-day rate, all of these prices include a mandatory $10 conservation stamp in addition to the cost

of the permit. Kids younger than 14 don't need a license if they're with an adult who has a valid fishing license. Purchase permits at most sporting-goods stores or from Game and Fish offices. For more fishing information, contact the **Wyoming Game and Fish Department,** 307/777-4600 or 800/548-9453, http://gf .state.wy.us.

Get **Montana** fishing information from the **Montana Fish, Wildlife and Parks Department,** 406/444-2535, www.fwp.mt.us/fishing. Nonresident two-day licenses cost $15 and season licenses are $60; these prices include a mandatory $4 conservation license. No license is required for children younger than age 12 if accompanied by an adult with a Montana fishing license (but special restrictions apply).

In **Idaho,** nonresident fishing licenses are $10.50 for one day plus $4 per day for additional days, or $74.50 for an annual license. Kids ages 14–18 pay $38 annually. Get details from the **Idaho Department of Fish and Game,** 208/334-3700 or 800/635-7820, www.state.id.us/fishgame.

Within **Grand Teton National Park** a Wyoming fishing license is required, but separate regulations apply in **Yellowstone National Park.** You don't need a state fishing license, but you will need to purchase a park license from a visitors center, ranger station, Yellowstone General Store, or fishing shops in surrounding towns. The adult fishing fee is $10 for a 10-day permit or $20 for a season permit. Kids ages 12–15 get permits for free, and younger children do not need a permit. Yellowstone visitors centers and ranger stations have copies of current fishing regulations.

Learning More

Several good books provide detailed information for fishing enthusiasts. Try one of the following: *Bud Lilly's Guide to Fly Fishing the New West,* by Bud Lilly and Paul Schullery (Frank Amato Publications); *Yellowstone Fishes; Ecology, History, and Angling in the Park,* by John Varley and Paul Schullery (www.stackpolebooks.com); *Fishing Yellowstone,* by Richard Parks (www.falcon books.com); or *Fishing the Beartooths* by Pat Marchuson (www.falconbooks.com). For broader coverage, see *Fishing Wyoming.* by Kenneth

Graham (www.falconbooks.com) or Ken Retallic's *Flyfisher's Guide to Wyoming* (Wilderness Adventures Press). Several other books detail the multitude of fishing options on surrounding lands in Montana and Idaho. In Jackson, stop by Jack Dennis' Outdoor Shop, 50 E. Broadway, 307/733-3270 or 800/570-3270, www.jack dennis.com, to pick up a copy of their free *Western Fishing Newsletter,* with descriptions of regional fishing areas and which lures to try.

An exceptionally helpful online source for fishing information is the **Wyoming Fishing Network,** www.wyomingfishing.net. Here you'll find details on where to fish, lures, local guides, and up-to-date fishing reports for various rivers and lakes.

ON THE WATER

Jackson Hole's most popular summertime recreational activity is floating Wyoming's largest river, the Snake. Almost 20 different rafting companies offer dozens of trips each day of the summer, and on a busy day you'll see several thousand folks floating the placid upper sections or blasting through the boiling rapids of Snake River Canyon. The Jackson Hole chapter has complete details on both float trips and whitewater rafting. Whitewater and float trips are also available from the towns of Cody, Gardiner, and West Yellowstone.

Two Jackson-based kayaking schools teach a full range of classes in river kayaking, sea kayaking, and canoeing. These and other companies also offer sea kayak trips on Jackson Lake in Grand Teton National Park and Lake Yellowstone within Yellowstone National Park. These are available in a variety of flavors, from quick half-day paddles to multinight kayaking and camping trips. Motor boat rentals are also available on Lake Yellowstone and Jackson Lake.

HORSEBACK AND WAGON RIDES

Horseback day-rides are available throughout the region, including within both Yellowstone and Grand Teton National Parks. These typically

© DON PITCHER

horses at the Triangle X Ranch, Grand Teton National Park

cost around $25 for a one-hour ride or $60 for a half-day trail ride.

Two companies lead overnight wagon-train rides into the country around Jackson Hole: **Wagons West,** 307/543-2418 or 800/447-4711, www.wagonswestwyo.com, and **Double H Bar,** 307/734-6101 or 888/734-6101, www.teton wagontrain.com.

In addition to these trips, very popular **chuck wagon cookouts** are offered in Jackson Hole and at Roosevelt Lodge within Yellowstone National Park. These outings combine a ride in a Conestoga-style wagon with a big Old West feast and cowboy entertainment. They offer great family fun.

BICYCLING

Bicycles are available for rent in Jackson, Cody, Moose (Grand Teton National Park), and West Yellowstone, but not inside Yellowstone Nation-

al Park. Excellent paved paths can be found around Jackson and within Teton Valley, and hiking/mountain-biking trails and dirt roads criss-cross the region, particularly on Forest Service lands. A few of these trails are described in this book; for others, contact local bike shops or get trail information from Forest Service or Park Service offices. Bikes are prohibited on backcountry trails in both Yellowstone and Grand Teton National Parks but are allowed on most main roads and certain other paths.

Bike Touring

Many cyclists ride through this part of Wyoming, Montana, and Idaho, but conditions are not the safest, particularly within Yellowstone, where traffic is heavy and the roads are narrow and winding with little or no shoulders. During summer, the best times to ride are in the morning before traffic thickens or late in the afternoon before the light begins to fade and you become less visible to motorists. September and October are far less crowded than midsummer. See the Yellowstone chapter for details on riding in the park.

Backroads, 800/462-2848, www.backroads .com, leads six-day tours of the Greater Yellowstone area that include biking, hiking, rafting, and kayaking.

The Wyoming Department of Transportation publishes a useful *Bicycle Guidance Map*—on waterproof paper—showing the amount of traffic on each paved road, the width of paved shoulders, profiles of the steeper road grades, and general wind patterns. Anyone touring on a bike will find this map immensely valuable. Get a copy by calling the WYDOT Bicycle Coordinator at 307/777-4719.

GETTING INTO THE WILDERNESS

To get a real feel for the Greater Yellowstone Ecosystem, you need to abandon your car, get away from the towns, and head out into the vast and undeveloped public lands. The region contains some of the most remote country in the Lower 48 and one of the largest intact temperate-zone ecosystems anywhere.

The Park Service recommends staying at least 25 yards from bison.

Many campers prefer to use horses for longer trips, but backpacking is popular on the shorter trails, especially in the national parks. Backcountry permits are required only within Yellowstone and Grand Teton National Parks. It is, however, a good idea to check in at a local Forest Service ranger station to get a copy of the regulations because each place is different in such specifics as how far your tent must be from lakes and trails and whether wood fires are allowed. Be sure to take insect repellent along on any summertime trip because mosquitoes, deerflies, and horseflies can be thick, especially early in the summer.

Trail Information

The **Wyoming State Trails Program,** 307/777-6560, has a useful website (http://wyotrails.state .wy.us/trails) with information on hiking, biking, cross-country skiing, snowmobiling, Volksmarch, and other trails around the state.

Several hiking trips, mostly two- or three-day

> *To get a real feel for the Greater Yellowstone Ecosystem, you need to abandon your car, get away from the towns, and head out into the vast and undeveloped public lands.*

hikes, are described for Yellowstone and Grand Teton National Parks, along with nearby Forest Service wilderness areas. Recommended hiking guides for the Tetons and Jackson Hole are *Jackson Hole Hikes* by Rebecca Woods (White Willow Publishing), and *Teton Trails* by Katy Duffy and Darwin Wile (www.grandtetonpark.org). For Yellowstone, there are two fine guidebooks: *Yellowstone Trails* by Mark Marschall (www.yellow stoneassociation.org), and *Hiking Yellowstone National Park* by Bill Schneider (www.falconbooks.com). The National Park Service and the U.S. Forest Service can also provide specific trail information, and they post much of this information on their websites.

The **Continental Divide National Scenic Trail** stretches for 3,100 miles from Mexico to Canada, including the Teton Wilderness and Yellowstone National Park. Learn more from the Continental Divide Trail Alliance, 303/838-3760 or 888/909-2382, www.cdtrail.org.

ON THE ROAD

Horses in the Backcountry

For many people, the highlight of a Western vacation is the chance to ride a horse into wild country. Although a few folks bring their own steeds, most visitors leave the driving to an expert local outfitter instead. (If you've ever worked around horses in the backcountry, you'll understand why.) Horse packing is an entirely different experience from backpacking. The trade requires years of experience in learning how to properly load horses and mules with *panniers* (large baskets), which types of knots to use for different loads, how to keep the packstrings under control, which horses to picket and which to hobble, and how to awaken when the horses decide to head down the trail on hobbles at three in the morning. Add to this a knowledge of bear safety, an ability to keep guests entertained with campfire tales and ribald jokes, a complete vocabulary of horse-cussing terms, and a thorough knowledge of tobacco chewing, and you're still only about 10 percent of the way to becoming a packer.

Get a complete listing of local backcountry outfitters from **Wyoming Outfitters and Guides Association,** 307/527-7453, www.wyoga.org; **Montana Outfitters and Guides Association,** 406/449-3578, www.moga-montana.org; or

Idaho Outfitters and Guides Association, 208/342-1919 or 800/494-3246, www.ioga.org. Not all of these guides and outfitters may be permitted in a given backcountry area; contact the Park Service or Forest Service to see which ones are licensed to use the place you plan to visit.

Although horses are far more common, **llamas** are used in some backcountry areas. You can't ride them, but they're easier to control than horses and do not cause as much damage to trails and backcountry meadows. Llamas are perfect for folks who want to hike while letting a pack llama carry most of the weight. Contact local Forest Service and Park Service offices for permitted llama packers.

Trail Etiquette

Because horses are so commonly used in the Yellowstone region, hikers should follow a few rules of courtesy. Horses and mules are not the brightest critters on this planet, and they can spook at the most inane thing, even a bush blowing in the breeze or a brightly colored hat. Hikers meeting a packstring should move several feet off the trail and not speak loudly or make any sudden moves. If you've ever seen what happens when just one mule in a string decides to act up, you'll appreciate the chaos that can result from sudden noises or

North Fork Meadows, Teton Wilderness

movements. Anyone hiking with a dog should keep it well away from the stock and not let it bark. Last of all, never walk close behind a horse, unless you don't mind spending time in a hospital. Their kick is *definitely* worse than their bite.

Backcountry Ethics

The wilderness areas of northwest Wyoming are places to escape the crowds, enjoy the beauty and peace of the countryside, and develop an understanding of nature. Unfortunately, as more and more people head into backcountry areas, these benefits are becoming endangered. To keep wild places wild, always practice "leave no trace" hiking and camping. This means using existing campsites and fire rings, locating your campsite well away from trails and streams, staying on designated trails, not cutting switchbacks, burning only dead and down wood, extinguishing all fires, washing dishes 200 feet from lakes and creeks, digging "catholes" at least 200 feet from lakes or streams, and hanging all food well above the reach of bears. Don't litter the ground with toilet paper; instead, bury it deep or burn it in your campfire. (Do not, however, try to burn toilet paper in the woods; more than one person has started a forest fire in this way.) Your tent site should be 100 yards from the food storage and cooking areas to reduce the likelihood of bear problems. Wood fires are not allowed in many areas, so be sure to bring along a portable gas stove. And, of course, haul your garbage out with you. Burning cans and tinfoil in the fire lessens their weight (and the odors that attract bears), but be sure to pick them out of the fire pit before you depart. And make sure that fire is completely out.

For a detailed brochure on minimizing your impact and treating the land with respect, call 800/332-4100, or visit the Leave no Trace website at www.lnt.org.

Backcountry Safety Tips

The most important part of enjoying—and surviving—the backcountry is to be prepared. Know where you're going; get maps, camping information, weather forecasts, and trail conditions from a ranger before setting out. Although I have often hiked alone, single hikers are at a greater risk of getting into trouble than those trekking with companions. Two are better than one, and three are better than two; if one gets hurt, one person can stay with the injured party and one can go for help. Bring more than enough food so hunger won't cause you to continue when weather conditions say stop. Tell a responsible person where you're going and when you'll be back. For additional precautions, see the Health and Safety section of this chapter.

Always carry the **10 essentials:** map, compass, water bottle, first-aid kit, flashlight, matches (or lighter) and fire starter, knife, extra clothing (a full set, in case you fall in a stream) including rain gear, extra food, and sunglasses—especially if you're hiking on snow. To this list, you might want to also add a cell phone. Most backcountry areas have no service, but in an emergency you might be able to find a high point where the phone can hit an antenna.

Check your ego at the trailhead; stop for the night when the weather gets bad, even if it's 2 P.M., or head back. And don't press on when you're exhausted; tired hikers are sloppy hikers, and even a small injury can be disastrous in the woods.

SAFETY IN BEAR COUNTRY

Bears seem to bring out conflicting emotions in people. The first is an almost gut reaction of fear and trepidation: What if the bear attacks me? But then comes that other urge: What will my friends say when they see these incredible bear photos? Both of these reactions can lead to problems in bear country. "Bearanoia" is a justifiable fear but can easily be taken to such an extreme that one avoids going outdoors at all for fear of running into a bear. The "I want to get close-up shots of that bear and her cubs" attitude can lead to a bear attack. The middle ground incorporates a knowledge of and respect for bears with a sense of caution that keeps you alert for danger without letting fear rule your wilderness travels. Nothing is ever completely safe in this world, but with care you can avoid most of the common pitfalls that lead to bear encounters.

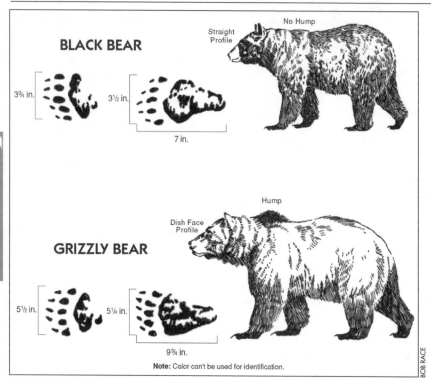

BLACK BEAR

No Hump

Straight Profile

3¾ in.   3½ in.

7 in.

GRIZZLY BEAR

Hump

Dish Face Profile

5½ in.   5¼ in.

9¾ in.

Note: Color can't be used for identification.

BOB RACE

Brown and Black Bears

Old-timers joke that bears are easy to differentiate: a black bear climbs up the tree after you, whereas a grizzly snaps the tree off at the base. Black bears live in forested areas throughout Wyoming, but grizzlies exist mainly in the northwest corner of the state, primarily within and around Yellowstone National Park. Both grizzlies and black bears pose potential threats to backcountry travelers, although you are considerably more likely to be involved in a car accident while driving to a wilderness area than to be attacked by a bear once you arrive.

Grizzlies once ranged across the entire Northern Hemisphere, from Europe across what is now Russia and through the western half of North America. When Europeans arrived, there were perhaps 50,000–100,000 grizzlies in what would become the Lower 48 states. Unfortunately, as white settlers moved in, they came to view these massive and powerful creatures (average adult

males weigh 500 pounds) as a threat to themselves and their livestock. The scientific name, *Ursus arctos horribilis,* says much about human attitudes toward grizzlies.

Grizzlies still have healthy populations in Alaska and western Canada, but elsewhere they were shot, trapped, and poisoned nearly to the brink of extinction. In the Lower 48 states grizzlies survive in only a few of the most remote parts of Montana, Wyoming, Idaho, and Washington. By 1975, when the U.S. Fish & Wildlife Service listed them as threatened, fewer than 1,000 grizzlies survived south of Canada. Since that time the population appears to have recovered somewhat and includes approximately 400–600 grizzlies in Wyoming's Greater Yellowstone Ecosystem.

Avoiding Bear Hugs

Surprise bear encounters are rare but frightening experiences. There were just 23 bear-caused injuries in Yellowstone National Park between 1980 and 1997—one injury for every 2.1 million visitors. Avoid unexpected encounters with bears by letting them know you're there. Most bears hear or smell you long before you realize their presence, and they hightail it away. Surprising a bear, especially a sow with cubs, is the last thing you want to do in the backcountry. Before heading out, check at a local ranger station to see whether there have been recent bear encounters. If you discover an animal carcass, be extremely alert because a bear may be nearby and may attack anything that appears to threaten its food. Get away from such areas. Do not hike at night or dusk, when bears can be especially active. Safety is also in numbers: the more of you hiking together, the more likely a bear is to sense you and stay away.

Make noise in areas of dense cover or when coming around blind spots on trails. If you're unable to see everything around you for at least 50 yards, warn any hidden animals by talking, singing, clapping your hands, tapping a cup, or rattling a can of pebbles. Some people tie bells to their packs for this purpose, but others regard this as an annoyance to fellow hikers. In general, bells are probably of little value because the sound does not carry far, and they might actually attract bears. If bears can't hear you coming, don't be shy—make a lot of noise! It might seem a bit foolish, but loud voices may prevent an encounter of the furry kind. Unfortunately, it will probably scare off other animals, so you're not likely to see many critters, and other hikers may not appreciate the noise. Personally, I reserve yelling "Hey Bear!" for situations where I'm walking in brushy bear country with low visibility and have to contend with other noises such as a nearby creek. I wouldn't recommend doing so while walking the paved path around Old Faithful Geyser; you might get carried off in a straitjacket.

Hunters and photographers are the main recipients of bear hugs. Never under any circumstances approach a bear, even if it appears to be asleep. Move away if you see bear cubs, especially if one comes toward you, because mom is almost always close by. Dogs create dangerous situations by barking and exciting bears—leave yours at home (dogs are not allowed in the back-

country in national parks). Never leave food around for bears. Not only is this illegal, but it also trains the bears to associate people with free food. Fed bears become garbage bears, and that almost inevitably means that the bear gets killed. Remember, bears are dangerous wild animals. This is *their* country, not a zoo. By going in you accept the risk—and thrill—of meeting a bear.

At the Campsite

Before camping, take a look around the area to see if there are recent bear tracks or scat and to make sure you're not on a game trail. Bears are attracted to odors of all sorts, including food, horse feed, soap, toothpaste, perfume, and deodorants. Your cooking, eating, and food storage area should be at least 50 yards away from your tent. Keep your campsite clean and avoid such smelly items as tuna, ham, sausage, and bacon; freeze-dried food is light and relatively odorless (although also relatively tasteless). Store food away from your sleeping area in airtight containers or several layers of plastic bags, and be sure to hang all food and other items that bears may smell at least 12 feet off the ground and four feet from tree trunks. Bring 50 feet of rope for this purpose. Tie two cups or pots to it so you will hear if it's moved. Some Forest Service and Park Service wilderness areas provide food storage poles at campsites. In the Teton and Bridger Wilderness Areas, you can also rent bear-resistant backpacker food tubes or horse panniers from Forest Service offices. Camping stores in Jackson, Cody, and elsewhere sell similar containers.

Good news: Researchers have reported no evidence that either sexual activity or menstrual odors precipitate bear attacks, despite reports to the contrary. It is, however, wise for menstruating women to use tampons instead of pads and to store soiled tampons in double ziplock bags above the reach of bears.

Encounters of the Furry Kind

If you do happen to suddenly encounter a bear and it sees you, try to stay calm and not make any sudden moves. Do not run because you could not possibly outrun a bear; they can exceed 40 mph for short distances. Bear researchers

Sleeping Area

100 yards

Hang at least 10' from the ground and 4' from the top and side supports

Cooking and Eating Area

BOB RACE

now suggest that quickly climbing a tree is also not a wise way to escape bears and may actually incite an attack. Instead, make yourself visible by moving into the open so the bear will (hopefully) identify you as a human and not something to eat. Never stare directly at a bear. Sometimes dropping an item such as a hat or jacket will distract the bear, and talking calmly (easier said than done) also seems to have some value in convincing bears that you're a human. If the bear sniffs the air or stands on its hind legs it is probably trying to identify you. When it does, it will usually run away. If a bear woofs and postures, don't imitate—this is a challenge. Keep retreating. Most bear charges are also bluffs; the bear will often stop short and amble off.

If a **grizzly bear** actually attacks, hold your ground and freeze. It may well be a bluff charge, with the bear halting at the last second. If the bear does not stop its attack, curl up facedown on the ground in a fetal position with your hands wrapped behind your neck and your elbows tucked over your face. Your backpack may help protect you somewhat. Remain still even if you are attacked because sudden movements may incite further attacks. It takes an enormous

amount of courage to do this, but often a bear will only sniff or nip you and leave. The injury you might sustain would be far less than if you tried to resist. After the attack, prevent further attacks by staying down on the ground until the grizzly has left the area.

Bear authorities now recommend against dropping to the ground if you are attacked by a **black bear** because they tend to be more aggressive in such situations and are more likely to prey on humans. If a black bear attacks, fight back with whatever weapons are at hand; large rocks and branches can be surprisingly effective deterrents, as can yelling and shouting. (This, of course, assumes you can tell black bears from brown bears. If you can't, have someone who knows—such as a park ranger—explain the differences before you head into the backcountry.)

In the rare event of a **nighttime bear attack** in your tent, defend yourself *very* aggressively. Never play dead under such circumstances because the bear probably views you as prey and may give up if you make it a fight. Before going to bed, try to plan escape routes should you be attacked in the night, and be sure to have a flashlight and pepper spray handy. Keeping your sleeping bag partly unzipped also allows the chance to escape should a bear attempt to drag you away. If someone is attacked in a tent near you, yelling and throwing rocks or sticks may drive the bear away.

Protecting Yourself

Cayenne pepper sprays (sold in camping goods stores) have sometimes proven useful in fending off bear attacks. Note, however, that these "bear mace" sprays are only effective at close range (10–30 feet). This is particularly true in open country where winds quickly disperse the mist or may blow it back in your own face. Another problem with bear mace is that you cannot carry it aboard commercial jets because of the obvious dangers if a canister explodes. If you do carry a pepper spray, make sure it is readily available by carrying it in a holster on your belt or across your chest. Also be sure to test-fire it to see how the spray carries. Although they *are* better than nothing, pepper sprays are not a cure-all or a replacement for caution in bear country. It's far better to avoid bear confrontations in the first place. A few clueless individuals have sprayed themselves with the pepper spray thinking it would work like mosquito repellent. Needless to say, this isn't much help, and there is some evidence it might even attract bears looking for a spicy meal!

Good web sources for up-to-date bear safety information are Yellowstone National Park, www.nps.gov/yell, and the Yellowstone Grizzly Foundation, www.yellowstonegrizzly.com. Two recommended safety books are *Bear Attacks: Their Causes and Avoidance* by Stephen Herrero (Lyons Press, www.lyonspress.com, 2002) and *Bear Aware: Hiking and Camping in Bear Country* by Bill Schneider (Globe Pequot/Falcon, www.falconbooks.com, 2001).

WINTER RECREATION
Downhill Skiing and Snowboarding

Jackson Hole is the primary skiing and snowboarding area in Wyoming. This area includes one of America's top winter destinations, **Jackson Hole Mountain Resort,** 307/733-2292 or 888/333-7766, www.jacksonhole.com, located in

Teton Village, 12 miles from the town of Jackson. For ease of access, it's hard to beat the smaller (but surprisingly steep) **Snow King Resort,** just seven blocks from Town Square. On the other side of Teton Pass—42 miles from Jackson—is **Grand Targhee Ski Resort,** 307/353-2300 or 800/827-4433, www.grandtarghee.com, famous for its deep powder skiing. **Sleeping Giant Ski Area** is a family area 50 miles west of Cody near Yellowstone. See the appropriate chapters for descriptions of each of these places. During winter, call the Wyoming Division of Tourism at 800/225-5996 for the statewide ski report, or visit their website, www.wyomingtourism.org.

Many more ski resorts can be found in Montana, including ones at Red Lodge (northeast of Yellowstone) and Big Sky (south of Bozeman and west of Yellowstone). For details on Montana resorts, see **Moon Handbooks Montana** by W. C. McRae and Judy Jewell (www.moon.com).

Cross-Country Skiing

Skinny-skiers have an overwhelming choice of places to ski in the Yellowstone-Grand Teton-Jackson Hole area. Developed Nordic areas are located in Jackson Hole, west of Cody, and at West Yellowstone, Montana. In addition, Yellowstone and Grand Teton National Parks have cross-country skiing with views to die for, although the trails are not groomed. Adjacent Forest Service lands provide deep snow and inexhaustible opportunities for those with backcountry skiing experience. See specific chapters for details on all of these cross-country skiing places. The Special Topic "Safety in Avalanche Country" includes precautions to take while cross-country skiing in the backcountry.

Snowmobiling

Snowmobiling is an exceptionally popular winter activity in the Yellowstone region, but it is also controversial. An extensive network of snowmobile trails leads through northwest Wyoming and nearby parts of Montana and Idaho. Best known is the 365-mile **Continental Divide Snowmobile Trail,** stretching around the south end of the Wind River Mountains northward through Grand Teton National Park

SAFETY IN AVALANCHE COUNTRY

Backcountry skiing is becoming increasingly popular in the mountains surrounding Jackson Hole. Unfortunately, many skiers fail to take the necessary precautions. Given the enormous snowfalls that occur, the steep slopes the snow piles up on, and the high winds that accompany many storms, it should come as no surprise that avalanches are a real danger.

Nearly all avalanches are triggered by the victims. If you really want to avoid avalanches, ski only on groomed ski trails or "bombproof" slopes that, because of aspect, shape, and slope angle, never seem to slide. Unfortunately, this isn't always possible, so an understanding of the conditions that lead to avalanches is imperative for backcountry skiers. The Forest Service produces a useful booklet called *Basic Guidelines for Winter Recreation,* available in many of its offices around Wyoming.

The best way to learn about backcountry safety is through an avalanche class. These are offered in the Jackson Hole area by **American Avalanche Institute,** 307/733-3315, www.avalanchecourse .com; **Exum Mountain Guides,** 307/733-2297, www.exumguides.com; **Jackson Hole Mountain Guides,** 307/733-4979 or 800/239-7642, www .jhmg.com; and **Yöstmark Backcountry Tours,** 208/354-2828, www.yostmark.com. Failing that, you can help protect yourself by following these precautions when you head into the backcountry:

• Before leaving, get up-to-date avalanche information. On the web, you can visit www .avalanche.org for links to avalanche forecasting sites throughout the western states. For the Jackson Hole area, call the Forest Service's 24-hour **Backcountry Avalanche Hazard & Weather Forecast** line at 307/733-2664, or find the forecasts on the web at www .jhavalanche.org. For areas around Yellowstone—including West Yellowstone and Cooke City on the margins and the Washburn Range inside the park—contact the **Avalanche Advisory Hotline** in Bozeman, 406/587-6981, www.mtavalanche.com. If the message says avalanche danger is high, ski on the flats instead. **Jackson Hole Snow Observations,** www.jhsnowobs.org, provides an online forum

to Yellowstone. Yellowstone National Park is the focal point for most snowmobile travel in Northwest Wyoming, with the primary entry points from West Yellowstone and through the South Entrance. The Park Service is currently reviewing its winter-use policy, so contact them for the current situation.

Snowmobile trail maps and listings of snowmobile rental companies are available from local visitors centers. For trail conditions around Wyoming, call 307/777-7777 or 800/225-5996, and ask for the snowmobile hotline. Find detailed snowmobile info—and current trail reports—on the web at http://wyotrails.state .wy.us/snow.

Snowcoaches

Yellowstone snowcoaches provide a fine alternative to snowmobiling through the park. These 10-passenger machines are old fashioned and gawky, but they provide a delightful way to explore the sights. The Yellowstone concessioner (Xanterra) runs a wide variety of snowcoach trips, including ones that drop you off to cross-country ski or explore. Another company (Yellowstone Expeditions) leads snowcoach trips to a remote yurt located near Grand Canyon of the Yellowstone. Here you stay overnight and can explore the winter wonderland at a slower pace.

Other Winter Fun

Several companies offer **dogsled** rides in the Greater Yellowstone area, including ones to delightful Granite Hot Springs and overnight trips to a remote yurt. You'll find them in Jackson, Dubois, and West Yellowstone. **Sleigh rides** are also available in Jackson Hole and at Grand Targhee, and some are combined with a meal at a remote cabin. The most unique sleigh rides take visitors among the elk on the National Elk Refuge.

Snowshoeing is popular and a good way to get

where backcountry users share observations on snowpack conditions and avalanche activity.
• Be sure to carry extra warm clothes, water, high-energy snacks, a dual-frequency avalanche transceiver (make sure it's turned on and that you know how to use it!), a lightweight snow shovel (for digging snow pits or excavating avalanche victims), an emergency snow shelter, first-aid supplies, a Swiss Army or Leatherman knife, a topographic map, an extra plastic ski tip, a flashlight, matches, and a compass. Many skiers also carry that cure-all, duct tape, wrapped around a ski pole. Let a responsible person know exactly where you are going and when you expect to return. It's also a good idea to carry special ski poles that extend into probes in case of an avalanche. Check with local ski shops or talk to Forest Service or Park Service folks for details on specific areas.
• Check the angle of an area before you ski through it. Slopes of 30–45 degrees are the most dangerous; lesser slopes do not slide as frequently.
• Watch the weather; winds over 15 mph can pile snow much more deeply on lee slopes, causing dangerous loading on the snowpack. Especially avoid skiing on or below cornices.
• Avoid the leeward side of ridges, where snow loading can be greatest.
• Be aware of gullies and bowls; they're more likely to slip than flat open slopes or ridgetops. Stay out of gullies at the bottom of wide bowls; these are natural avalanche chutes.
• Look out for cracks in the snow, and listen for hollow snow underfoot. These are strong signs of dangerous conditions.
• Look at the trees. Smaller trees may indicate that avalanches rip through an area frequently, knocking over the larger ones. Avalanches can, however, also run through forested areas.
• Know how much new snow has fallen recently. Heavy new snow over older weak snow layers is a sure sign of extreme danger on potential avalanche slopes. Most avalanches slip during or immediately after a storm.
• Learn how to dig a snow pit and how to read the various snow layers. Particularly important are the very weak layers of depth hoar or surface hoar that have been buried under heavy new snow.

ON THE ROAD

to places others don't go. Guided snowshoe hikes are offered in both Grand Teton and Yellowstone National Parks. **Ice-skating rinks** are located at the three big Jackson Hole ski areas and in the town of Jackson and at Mammoth Hot Springs within Yellowstone.

Accommodations

Lodging in the Yellowstone and Jackson Hole area is generally at a premium during summer and over the Christmas-New Year's holiday. Each chapter of this book details the local situation. During peak summer or winter seasons in Jackson Hole, you should expect to pay $90–120 for a decent room; even fairly basic rooms with older furnishings fetch $80 per night. Rates are somewhat lower in West Yellowstone, Gardiner, Cody, Driggs, Cooke City, and Dubois, but not nearly as cheap as in less-touristy towns in Wyoming, Montana, or Idaho.

Throughout this book I have typically listed only two prices for most accommodations: single, or s (one person), and double, or d (two people). Prices listed are the peak-season summertime rates, which are generally the highest of the year. These prices do not include state and local taxes, which typically run 4–8 percent. The prices are also, of course, not set in concrete and will certainly increase over time.

REGIONAL INFORMATION

For a complete listing of motels, hotels, bed-and-breakfasts, dude ranches, and places to camp in Wyoming, request a copy of the free *Wyoming Visitor Directory* by calling 307/777-7777 or

800/225-5996, or visiting the web at www
.wyomingtourism.org. Contact **Jackson Hole
Central Reservations,** 307/733-4005 or 800/
443-6931, www.jhsnow.com, for information
and a brochure detailing Jackson Hole's many
lodging options.

The *Montana Travel Plan-
ner* has helpful lodging information for towns in Montana. Get it
by calling 406/444-2978 or
800/847-4868, or visit them on
the web at www.visitmt.com.
They also produce a separate Yellowstone Country travel guide
that you may want to request.

For Idaho accommodation
choices, get the *Idaho State Travel Guide* at 208/334-2470 or
800/842-5858, or by clicking on
www.visitid.org.

*If you are visiting the
Greater Yellowstone
region and planning
to save money by
camping the entire
time, do book at
least one night in
Yellowstone's Old
Faithful Inn or Lake
Yellowstone Hotel.*

these places, especially if you're calling their 800
number; these "rack rates" are what they charge
if they can get away with it. Ask if they have
any promotional rates. You may also get better
prices by calling the motel directly to bargain
with a clerk; they're more likely to
be able to dicker over price than
the 800-number operators.

If in doubt about where to stay,
you may want to choose a place
that gets the American Automobile Association (AAA) seal of
approval. The annual *AAA Tour-
Book* for Idaho, Montana, and
Wyoming (free to AAA members)
is a helpful guide to the better hotels and motels, offering current
prices and accurate ratings. Members often get discounts on lodging rates and can find the same
information on the AAA website, www.aaa.com.

HOTELS AND MOTELS

The motel and hotel scene in the Greater Yellowstone area is geared to travelers with cash to
spend, although there are inexpensive hostels in
Jackson and West Yellowstone. If you are visiting the region and planning to save money by
camping the entire time, *do* make one or two
modifications to your plan by booking at least
one night in Yellowstone's Old Faithful Inn
or Lake Yellowstone Hotel. Both of these are
classics, and Old Faithful Inn occupies a league
of its own. Rates are surprisingly reasonable
if you're willing to walk down the hall for a
shower. Call far ahead for reservations at these
places. See specific chapters for other great
places to spend a night.

Every town in the area has its locally owned
small motels or cabins. These accommodations
vary widely in quality and price but tend to offer
the best rates and friendliest service.

If you're staying in one of the chain motels, always be sure to ask about the sometimes substantial discounts such as AAA-member rates,
senior discounts, corporate or government rates,
business travel fares, military rates, or other special deals. Try not to take the first rate quoted at

BED-AND-BREAKFASTS

Bed-and-breakfasts are found in every town described in this book. Favorites of 30- and 40-
something professional couples, bed-and-
breakfasts are a fine way to get acquainted with
a new area. They're also a good choice if you're
traveling alone because you'll have opportunities
to meet fellow travelers in the library, over tea,
and at breakfast. Note, however, that the single
person rate frequently differs little, if at all, from
the price for couples.

One problem with B&Bs is that they sometimes get a bit too homey and lack the privacy af-
forded by motels. I've stayed at places where the
owner sits by your table in the morning, feeling
it is his duty to hold a conversation. This may be
fine sometimes, especially if you want to learn
more about the local area, but it's not so great if
you're looking for a romantic place or you just
want to read the newspaper in peace. In some
places the intense personal attention and strict
rules (no hard-soled shoes, no noise after 10 P.M.,
and so on) get to be a bit much, making you
feel less a guest than an intruder. In others, hosts
serve breakfast at precisely 8 A.M., and guests

who sleep in miss out. Other B&Bs are more flexible, and some even offer separate cottages or suites for honeymooners seeking privacy.

Several regional B&Bs don't allow kids, and almost none allow pets or smoking inside. Most guest rooms have private baths, but if they don't, one is probably just a few steps away.

More Information

Get a detailed brochure listing many of Wyoming's B&Bs from **Wyoming Homestay & Outdoor Adventures (WHOA),** 307/237-3526. Their Internet site, www.wyomingbnb-ranchrec.com, has descriptions of each of these places, plus web links. For Montana listings, contact the **Montana Bed and Breakfast Association** at 406/449-7492, www.mtbba.com. Find connections to Idaho B&Bs on the web at www.visitid.org or www .idaho-lodging.com.

DUDE RANCHES

An old and respected Western tradition is the dude ranch, which began as a sideline to the business of raising cattle. Friends from back east would remember old Jake out there in wild Wyoming, where the buffalo roam and the antelope play, and would decide it was time for a visit. So off they would head, living in the rancher's outbuildings and helping with the chores. The "dudes," as they became known, soon told their friends, and Jake found his ranch inundated. After a couple of years of this arrangement, the next step was obvious: Get those eastern scoundrels to fork over some cash for the privilege of visiting. Pretty soon the dude ranching business was born. At its peak in the 1920s, dude ranching spread throughout much of the West. Dude ranching saved many cattle ranches from extinction by providing a second source of income and simultaneously brought these magnificent lands to the attention of people who had the money to prevent their development (most notably John D. Rockefeller, Jr. in Grand Teton National Park).

At the older ranches, generations of families have returned year after year for a relaxing and rejuvenating vacation in the "Wild West." Many dude ranches now call themselves guest ranches, a term that reflects both the suspicious way people view the word "dude" and the changing nature of the business. Most city folks today lack the desire or skill to actually saddle up their own horses, much less push cattle between pastures. As a result, guest/dude ranches tend to emphasize grand scenery, horseback riding—the centerpiece of nearly every ranch—campfires, hiking, fishing, hearty meals, chuck wagon cookouts, sing-alongs, and evenings around the fireplace. Some folks even camp overnight out there in the fearful wilderness, where the coyotes howl and the mice chew into your stash of potato chips. A few ranches still offer the chance to join in on such activities as cattle drives, branding, pregnancy testing, shot-giving, calving, and roundups. For some folks it's a great chance to learn about the real West; others view it as paying good money (sometimes a lot of good money!) to work as a cowhand.

What to Expect

Wyoming has literally dozens of dude ranches and ranch resorts offering accommodations ranging from spartan to so sumptuous that they bear absolutely no resemblance to ranch life. Not all dude ranches are created equal—some are slick and modern with tennis courts and hot tubs while others are funky and old-fashioned with delightful rough edges. The smaller ones offer more personalized service, but at larger ones you're more likely to find someone your own age (particularly important if there are teens in your entourage). Dudes normally sleep in log cabins. Conditions inside can vary widely, but don't expect TVs or phones in the rooms. The cabins are usually near a central lodge where meals are served family-style. Many also have large libraries, along with outdoor games such as volleyball and horseshoes. Fishing and photography are other big attractions.

Practicalities

Dude ranch stays generally cost around $2,500–3,500 for two people per week, with lower rates for kids and surcharges for those staying by themselves. The price includes all meals, lodging, and horseback rides, but you'll usually pay more for features such as airport shuttles, rafting trips, guided fishing, beer and wine, or backcountry pack trips, not to mention local taxes and tips. The fanciest Jackson Hole resort, Lost Creek Ranch, will set you back more than $12,000 for two people per week! Many guest ranches offer discounted rates in early June and late September and for repeat guests. A few also have special adults-only weeks. Most require that you stay a week, or at least three nights, although a few places offer overnight accommodations. To really get into the comfortably slow pace of ranch life, try to set aside at least a week.

Ask plenty of questions before you visit, such as what activities are available, what to bring in the way of clothing, what sort of meals to expect (vegetarians may have a hard time on some ranches), whether there are additional charges, whether they accept credit cards (many don't), what the living accommodations are like, and how many other guests will likely be there at the same time; some house more than a hundred, others fewer than a dozen. Upon request, the better ranches will provide lists of references from previous clients. Note that it is considered proper to tip the ranch hands, kitchen help, and others who work hard to keep the ranch running; the

standard total is 15 percent of your bill. For many of them, this is a way to fund their college education (or buy a winter in Belize).

Finding a Dude Ranch

Nearly all dude ranches have their own websites, filled with beautiful photos of their ranch, glowing reports from past clients, and details on the packages available and their costs. An outstanding source for detailed information about guest ranches in Wyoming (and elsewhere) is *Gene Kilgore's Ranch Vacations,* by Eugene Kilgore (www.travelmatters.com). Find Kilgore on the web at www.ranchweb.com.

Established in 1926, the **Dude Ranchers' Association** includes most of the nation's best-known guest ranches. Call 307/587-2339 to request their catalog, or visit their website (www.duderanch.org) for links to more than 30 Wyoming ranches. Another useful online source is www.guestranches.com/usa/wy, where you'll find links to 30 Wyoming dude ranches. Also worth a look is www.duderanches.com, which offers ranch descriptions along with employment info for would-be wranglers. Nearly all dude ranches have their own websites filled with beautiful photos of their ranch, glowing reports from past clients, and details on the packages available and their costs.

Camping

The Greater Yellowstone Ecosystem is dotted with several dozen Forest Service and Park Service campgrounds. Most of these have drinking water, garbage pickup, and outhouses, but they generally do not have showers. The fee is typically $5–12 per night, with a 14-day limit on camping at any location. It's generally legal to camp for free on undeveloped Forest Service land throughout the region, but check with local ranger district offices for any restrictions. Dispersed camping is not allowed in the Snake River Canyon south of Jackson or the North Fork of the Shoshone River west of Cody.

Campsite reservations are available for some Yellowstone National Park sites, but all of those

within Grand Teton National Park are on a first-come basis. In addition, several Forest Service campgrounds in the area are now on a reservation system; for an extra service charge of $9 you can reserve a site up to one year in advance. Get details at 518/885-3639 or 877/444-6777, or www.reserveusa.com.

RV PARKS

Every Yellowstone-area town of any size contains at least one private RV park and so-called campground. Most of these are little more than vacant lots with sewer and electrical hookups, showers, and toilet facilities, but a few are quite nice. These private campgrounds generally charge $3–5 for showers if you're not camping there. A better deal in many towns is to use the shower at the local public swimming pool, where you get a free swim thrown in for the entrance charge.

Food and Drink

Small towns in Wyoming, Montana, and Idaho are not known for their haute cuisine. This is cattle country, the land of the free and the home on the range, where juicy steaks and prime rib can be found everywhere. If you don't like that, try chicken-fried steak, the house specialty at many of these places. Wash it down with a beer and then sit back for a big hunk of apple pie. For breakfast, it's pretty much standard all-American fare, with the usual all-American burgers and fries for lunch.

Fortunately, towns in the Yellowstone region serve a much greater diversity of food, and Jackson is home to several restaurants that would stand out in even the largest American cities. Cody also has its share of fine restaurants, and other towns—even Dubois—have very respectable places serving gourmet meals. As might be expected, this high quality doesn't come cheap, and you'll pay substantially more for a dinner in Jackson than in most other Wyoming towns.

Several in-the-park places provide distinctive meals in a grand setting. Most notable is the dining room at Old Faithful Inn, with its classic log interior and good meals for a reasonable price. Jenny Lake Lodge within Grand Teton National Park is another favorite, serving gourmet meals in a cozy log building. Dinner reservations are required for both of these restaurants.

ON THE TOWN

The towns surrounding Yellowstone all provide ample opportunities for drinking and carousing, with country-and-western or rock bands that pull patrons onto the saloon dance floors. Jackson has a complete spectrum of such options, including the world-famous Million Dollar Cowboy Bar, with bar stools made from old saddles and Thursday-night swing dance lessons. The Mangy Moose in Teton Village attracts nationally known rock musicians and is the center of the party scene.

BEER AND WINE

Snake River Brewing Co., 307/739-2337, www.snakeriverbrewing.com, is a very popular brewpub and restaurant in downtown Jackson, with several of their award-winning beers on tap. **Grand Teton Brewing Company,** 208/787-4000, www.grandtetonbrewing.com, is located in Victor, Idaho, just over Teton Pass from Jackson Hole, and brews several beers, including Teton Ale, Old Faithful Ale, and Moose Juice Stout.

Jackson Hole is home to several of the finest wine shops in the Rockies, including **Dornan's Wine Shoppe,** with more than 1,700 different wines hidden away in the little settlement called Moose. Several Jackson wine shops offer weekly wine tastings.

Information and Services

INFORMATION SOURCES

Chambers of commerce information centers are described for each town in this book. A large **Wyoming State Information Center** is located in Jackson, and you'll also find helpful chambers of commerce in even the tiniest towns in the Yellowstone area.

Wyoming Information

For a helpful overall guide to Wyoming, along with a listing of events, chamber of commerce offices, lodging, and camping, request a copy of the free *Wyoming Visitor Directory* from the Wyoming Division of Tourism and State Marketing, 307/777-7777 or 800/225-5996. Both summer and winter versions are available. They also have free state maps, or pick them up at any local visitors center. You'll find complete Wyoming travel details—and web links—at www.wyomingtourism.org.

For additional information, head to the Wyoming state homepage: www.state.wy.us. See my *Moon Handbooks Wyoming* for the full story on the Cowboy State (www.moon.com).

Montana Information

Find Montana travel information, including a fat *Montana Travel Planner,* at 406/444-2654 or 800/847-4868, or get the same information on the web at www.visitmt.com. The maps in this publication are particularly revealing, showing Yellowstone as a green appendage of Montana! Request a free *Yellowstone Country Travel Guide* by calling 406/556-8680 or 800/736-5276, or find tourism details and links at www.yellowstone.visitmt.com. The state of Montana's homepage is www.state.mt.us. The most complete travel guide for the state is *Moon Handbooks Montana,* by W. C. McRae and Judy Jewell (www.moon.com).

Idaho Information

Contact the Idaho Department of Commerce

Tourism Division, 208/334-2470 or 800/842-5858 www.visitid.org, for the official *Idaho State Travel Guide* and a state map. The state of Idaho's homepage is www.state.id.us. Get complete Idaho details in *Moon Handbooks Idaho* by Don Root (www.moon.com).

On the Web

Internet addresses are listed in the text for local chamber of commerce offices and a multitude of businesses. Excellent places to begin your virtual voyage are the state tourism sites listed previously and land management agencies listed in the Land Management Agencies section of this chapter. See specific town descriptions for listings of chambers of commerce websites.

Two particularly useful websites with abundant links to local businesses are the Jackson Hole Chamber of Commerce's site, www.jacksonholechamber.com, and the Cody-based Park County Travel Council, www.yellowstone.org. Other websites worth browsing include www.jacksonholetraveler.com, www.jacksonholenet.com, www.jacksonnetwork.com, www.westyellowstonechamber.com, www.westyellowstonetraveler.com, www.westyellowstonenet.com, and www.yellowstonepark.com.

Looking for **web cameras** to see the Yellowstone-Grand Teton region in real time? The Wyoming Department of Transportation (www.wyoroad.info) has webcams in Alpine and Pinedale, and www.jacksonholenet.com/webcams shows a half-dozen more webcams scattered around Jackson Hole and Yellowstone (including Old Faithful). Find others at www.jacksonhole.com and www.codywy.org.

All local libraries have computers with free Internet access, although you may need to sign up for a terminal. Find a listing of Wyoming libraries and links to their homepages at www.publiclibraries.com/wyoming.htm. In addition, the towns of Jackson, Cody, Gardiner, and West Yellowstone all have Internet cafés or businesses with computers for rent by the hour.

LAND MANAGEMENT AGENCIES

The following phone numbers and websites provide contact information for major public land management agencies in the Greater Yellowstone Ecosystem:

Grand Teton National Park, Moose, 307/739-3399, www.nps.gov/grte

Yellowstone National Park, Mammoth, 307/344-7381, www.nps.gov/yell

National Elk Refuge, Jackson, 307/733-9212, http://nationalelkrefuge.fws.gov

Bridger-Teton National Forest, Jackson, 307/739-5500, www.fs.fed.us/btnf

Shoshone National Forest, Cody, 307/527-6241, www.fs.fed.us/r2/shoshone

Caribou-Targhee National Forest, Idaho Falls, Idaho, 208/524-7500, www.fs.fed.us/r4/caribou

Gallatin National Forest, West Yellowstone, Montana, 406/823-6961, or Gardiner, Montana, 406/848-7375, www.fs.fed.us/r1/gallatin

Beaverhead-Deerlodge National Forest, Dillon, Montana, 406/683-3900, www.fs.fed.us/r1/bdnf

Custer National Forest, Red Lodge, Montana, 406/446-2103, www.fs.fed.us/r1/custer

ON THE RADIO

Jackson, Cody, and other towns in the region have local radio stations of varying quality, offering the standard mix of top-40, rock, and country. For a bit more class, turn your dial to one of the **National Public Radio** stations that provide in-depth news, insightful call-in shows, and comedic relief. In Jackson, the local Wyoming Public Radio station is KUWJ 90.3 FM, http://uwadmnweb.uwyo.edu/wpr. In the Yellowstone area and Cody, you're also likely to hear "Yellowstone Radio" out of Bozeman, KBMC 102.1 FM. In Idaho's Teton Valley, listen to NPR on KRIC-FM 100.5 from Rexburg, Idaho.

NEWSPAPERS

Two respected daily tabloid-style papers are published in Jackson: the *Jackson Hole News* www.jacksonholenews.com, and the *Jackson Hole Guide* www.jhguide.com. Both of these papers publish weekly editions with local news, along with freebie versions on weekdays.

Wyoming's only statewide paper, the *Casper Star-Tribune,* www.trib.com, is ubiquitous throughout the area. Another paper you'll see in local racks (particularly within Yellowstone) is the *Billings Gazette,* www.billingsgazette.com.

MONEY AND BANKING

Travelers checks (in U.S. dollars) are accepted without charge at most stores and businesses throughout the Yellowstone region. It's not a good idea to travel with travelers checks in non-U.S. currency; they are accepted only at certain banks in Wyoming and are a time-consuming hassle. If you do arrive with pounds, yen, or Euros, several banks in Jackson, along with the park hotels inside Yellowstone, will exchange foreign currency for greenbacks.

Credit Cards and ATMS

When traveling, I pay for expenses by credit card whenever possible but also keep an automated teller machine (ATM) card as a backup. You'll find ATMs in all of the larger towns and increasingly in even the most remote settlements. Unfortunately, nearly all ATMs now tack on a charge—usually $1.50 per transaction—to your own bank's fees, making this an expensive way to get cash. The charges are posted on the machine. One way to avoid the charge is to buy something at a grocery store that takes ATM cards and simply ask to get cash back over the purchase amount. The state of Wyoming maintains an annual listing of ATMs and their charges online at http://audit.state.wy.us/banking.

The major credit cards, especially Visa and MasterCard, are accepted almost everywhere, even in many grocery stores. This is probably the easiest way to travel, especially if you can get airline mileage credit at the same time. The miles can quickly add up if you make all of your purchases in this way, but so can your credit card bill!

POST OFFICES

Post offices generally open between 7 and 9 A.M. and close between 5 and 6 P.M.; only a few are open on Saturday. Their outer doors are usually open, so you can go in to buy stamps from the machines. Some drug or card stores also operate a postal substation, where you can purchase stamps or mail packages within the United States (you'll have to go to a real post office for mailing to foreign addresses or other special services). Many grocery store checkout counters also sell books of stamps with no markup.

HEALTH AND SAFETY

Medical clinics can be found in most towns in the Yellowstone region, with good hospitals in Jackson and Cody, plus a smaller hospital in Driggs, Idaho. A summertime hospital is located near Lake Yellowstone Hotel within Yellowstone, with clinics at Old Faithful and Mammoth. Inside Grand Teton National Park there's a summertime clinic near Jackson Lake Lodge. See the Special Topics "Bear Country" and "Lightning Safety" for precautions while traveling in the Yellowstone region.

A common annoyance for travelers is insects, especially mosquitoes and blackflies. These pests are most prevalent in early summer in the mountains; by late August mosquito populations thin considerably. Use insect repellents containing DEET to help keep them away or wear a headnet.

Beaver Fever

Although the lakes and streams of the Greater Yellowstone Ecosystem may appear clean, you could be risking a debilitating sickness by drinking the water without treating it first. The protozoan *Giardia lambia* is found throughout the state, spread by both humans and animals (including beaver). The disease is curable with drugs, but it's always best to carry safe drinking water on any trip or to boil any water taken from creeks or lakes. Bringing water to a full boil for one minute

Mosquitoes and black-flies are a common annoyance for travelers. These pests are most prevalent in early summer in the mountains; by late August mosquito populations thin considerably.

is sufficient to kill Giardia and other harmful organisms. Another option—the one I much prefer—is to use one of the water filters sold in camping-goods stores. Make sure you buy one that filters out organisms such as *Campylobacter jejuni*, bacteria that are just 0.2 microns in size. Chlorine and iodine are not always reliable, taste foul, and can be unhealthy.

Hypothermia

Anyone who has spent much time in the outdoors will discover the dangers of exposure to cold, wet, and windy conditions. Even at temperatures well above freezing, hypothermia—the reduction of the body's inner core temperature—can prove fatal.

In the early stages, hypothermia causes uncontrollable shivering, followed by a loss of coordination, slurred speech, and then a rapid descent into unconsciousness and death. Always travel prepared for sudden changes in the weather. Wear clothing that insulates well and that holds its heat when wet. Wool and polypro are far better than cotton, and clothes should be worn in layers to provide better trapping of heat and a chance to adjust to conditions more easily. Always carry a wool hat because your head loses more heat than any other part of the body. Bring a waterproof shell to cut the wind. Put on rain gear *before* it starts raining; head back or set up camp when the weather looks threatening; eat candy bars, keep active, or snuggle with a friend in a down bag to generate warmth.

If someone in your party begins to show signs of hypothermia, don't take any chances, even if the person denies needing help. Get the victim out of the wind, strip off his clothes, and put him in a dry sleeping bag on an insulating pad. Skin-to-skin contact is the best way to warm a hypothermic person, and that means you'll also need to strip and climb in the sleeping bag. If you weren't friends before, this should heat up the relationship! Do not give the victim alcohol or hot drinks, and do not try to warm the person too quickly because it could lead to heart failure. Once the victim has recovered, get medical help as soon as possible. Actually, you're far better off keeping close tabs on everyone in the group and seeking shelter *before* exhaustion and hypothermia set in.

Frostbite

Frostbite is a less serious but painful problem for the cold-weather hiker; it is caused by direct exposure or by heat loss from wet socks, clothing, and boots. Frostbitten areas will look white or gray and feel hard on the surface, softer underneath. The best way to warm the area is with other skin: put your hand under your arm, your feet on your friend's belly. Don't rub it with snow or warm it near a fire. In cases of severe frostbite, in which the skin is white, quite hard, and numb, immerse the frozen area in water warmed to 99–104°F until it's thawed. Avoid refreezing the frostbitten area. If you're a long way from medical assistance and the frostbite is extensive, it is better to keep the area frozen and get out of the woods for help; thawing is painful, and it would be impossible to walk on a thawed foot.

West Nile Virus

This disease first appeared in New York during 1999 and spread rapidly across the nation in summer 2002. Most people who are infected with West Nile virus show mild (or no) symptoms, but the disease can be fatal. The virus is transmitted through mosquito bites, and it can infect not just humans, but also horses, many species of birds, and other animals—with potentially devastating impacts on wildlife populations. Reduce your chance of infection by applying insect repellents containing DEET. (A higher concentration lasts longer, but there's no benefit in using DEET in concentrations higher than 50 percent.) You can also spray your clothing with the repellent, wear long-sleeved shirts and long pants, and stay indoors at dusk and dawn when the mosquitoes are their most active. See the Centers for Disease Control website, www.cdc.gov, for details on the West Nile virus.

Hantavirus

This potentially fatal respiratory disease is spread by rodents, particularly deer mice. Contact with them or their droppings can lead to such symptoms as fever, muscle aches, coughing, and difficulty breathing resulting from fluid buildup in the lungs within 1–5 weeks. Once the symptoms appear, the disease progresses quickly, leading to hospitalization within 24 hours. More than one-third of those who come down with hantavirus die, and over the last decade, it has killed at least three Wyoming residents, including a young woman in 2002. Avoid contact with rodents and their feces or urine to minimize your chances of infection. Campers should never sleep on bare ground and avoid cabins if you find signs of rodents. Fortunately, the disease is not contagious from person to person. For additional information, visit www.cdc.gov.

Ticks

Ticks can be a bother in brushy and grassy areas in the spring and early summer. They drop onto unsuspecting humans and other animals to suck blood and can spread several potentially devastating diseases, including Rocky Mountain spotted fever, Ehrlichiosis, and Lyme disease. A few cases of these diseases have been reported in the Greater Yellowstone Ecosystem, but they are not common.

Avoid ticks by tucking pant legs into boots and shirts into pants, using insect repellents containing DEET, and carefully inspecting your clothes while outside. Light-colored clothing and socks are less attractive to ticks and make it easier for you to see them, while broad hats keep them out of your hair. Check your body while hiking and immediately after the trip. If possible, remove ticks before they become embedded in your skin. If one does become attached, use tweezers to remove the tick, making sure to get the head. Apply a triple-antibiotic ointment such as Neosporin to the area, and monitor the bite area for two weeks.

Lyme disease typically shows up as a large red spot with a lighter bulls-eye center and often causes muscle aches, fatigue, headache, and fever. Get medical help immediately if you show these symptoms after a tick bite. Fortunately, the disease can usually be treated with antibiotics. If untreated, it can cause a facial nerve palsy, memory loss, arthritis, heart damage, and other problems. A

ON THE ROAD

relatively effective vaccine has been developed for Lyme disease, but it requires a one-year regimen of doses and is expensive; check with your doctor for specifics. In northwest Wyoming, where the disease is relatively uncommon, the vaccine is probably not warranted, and it may give a false sense of security because ticks can still spread other—and more dangerous—diseases. There are no vaccinations available against either Rocky Mountain Spotted Fever or Erlichia, both of which sometimes kill people. The best action is to prevent tick bites in the first place. For more on tickborne diseases, see the Harvard Medical School's website at www.intelihealth.com.

Transportation

BY CAR

Most summer travelers to the Yellowstone-Grand Teton area—and a substantial number of winter visitors—arrive by car. Some fly into Jackson Hole, Salt Lake City, or Idaho Falls and rent a vehicle, whereas others head out on a grand road trip from home. The northwest corner of Wyoming is accessible from all sides in the summer, but most roads inside Yellowstone National Park are closed when the snow flies.

Travel Maps

Free state highway maps can be found at visitors centers in Wyoming, Montana, and Idaho, but map aficionados should also purchase one of the excellent statewide topographic map books published by DeLorme Mapping, 800/511-2459, www.delorme.com. These maps are indispensable for travelers heading off main routes and are sold in most local bookstores. National forest maps are also y helpful for mountain driving in many parts of Wyoming; buy them in local Forest Service offices.

Highway Conditions

A massive road project in the Snake River Canyon south of Jackson continues through 2004. Get the current status and information about delays at 307/733-3665, http://wyoroad .info. Extensive road work is also ongoing within Yellowstone National Park. Get road updates and delay information at 307/344-7381, www .nps.gov/yell.

For information on construction delays and current road conditions throughout Wyoming, call 307/772-0824 or 888/996-7623, or log onto www.wyoroad.info. Get Montana road information at 800/226-7623, www.mdt.state.mt.us /travinfo. For the Idaho road report, call 208/336-6600 or 888/432-7623, or head to www.state.id.us/itd.

Get today's regional weather forecast on the web at www.crh.noaa.gov/cys.

Car Rentals

You can rent cars in all of the larger towns, and those with airports generally have Hertz, Avis, and other national chains. See the Special Topic "Rental Car Contacts" in this chapter for more details. You'll find four-wheel-drive sport utility vehicles available in many locations, including Jackson Hole, but you will pay dearly for the privilege.

I've generally found the best car rental rates in the larger cities where there's more competition.

RENTAL CAR CONTACTS

Alamo, 307/733-0671 or 800/327-9633, www.alamo.com

Avis, 307/632-9371 or 800/831-2847, www.avis.com

Budget, 307/733-2206 or 800/527-0700, www.drivebudget.com

Dollar Rent A Car, 307/733-9224 or 800/800-4000, www.dollar.com

Enterprise, 307/632-1907 or 800/325-8007, www.enterprise.com

Hertz, 307/634-2131 or 800/654-3131, www.hertz.com

Thrifty, 307/739-9300 or 800/367-2277, www.thrifty.com

If you plan to rent a car for an extended period, it's worth your while to check travel websites such as www.travelocity.com, www.expedia.com, or www.orbitz.com to see which company offers the best rates. Note, however, that these quotes do not include taxes, which can be substantial, especially if you rent from the Salt Lake City airport. Even if you've made a reservation, it pays to call around once more after you arrive at the airport. On one visit I saved hundreds of dollars by getting a last-minute quote for a one-month rental. Cool tip: If you're visiting in the summer, try to get a light-colored car; the dark ones can get incredibly hot in the blazing sun!

Winter Road Closures

Jackson Hole remains accessible by highway year-round, but most roads in Yellowstone National Park close to cars when the first heavy snows block the passes. By the first of November, things are generally shut down all over except for the 56 miles between Gardiner and Cooke City. This is the only road within Yellowstone that remains open all year. The roads are groomed for snow-coaches (a delightfully old-fashioned way to travel) and snowmobiles from mid-December to mid-March. Plowing starts in March, but most park roads don't open for cars again until mid-May and sometimes not until early June. If you're planning a trip early or late in the season, contact the park for current road conditions; 307/344-7381, www.nps.gov/yell.

Within **Grand Teton National Park,** U.S. Hwy. 89/191/287 is plowed from Moran Junction to Flagg Ranch throughout the winter, providing a base for snowcoaches and snowmobiles heading into Yellowstone. Most other roads in Grand Teton are not plowed and are generally closed to cars November–April. Get current road conditions at 307/739-3399, www.nps.gov/grte.

Outside of the parks, most regional roads are plowed throughout the winter, including Teton Pass (west of Jackson), **Togwotee Pass** (northeast of Jackson), and U.S. Hwy. 14/16/20 from Cody to Pahaska Teepee near the East Entrance to Yellowstone. Two roads that are not plowed in winter are U.S. Hwy. 212 over **Beartooth Pass** (between Cooke City and Red Lodge, Montana) and an eight-mile stretch of **Chief Joseph Scenic Highway** east of Cooke City and northwest of Cody.

Winter Travel

Travelers need to take special precautions in winter. Snow tires are a necessity, but you should also have several emergency supplies on hand, including tire chains, a shovel and bag of sand in case you get stuck, a first-aid kit, booster cables, signal flares, a flashlight, a lighter and candle, a transistor radio, nonperishable foods (granola bars, canned nuts, or dried fruit), a jug of water, an ice scraper, blankets, winter clothes, and a sleeping bag. The most valuable tool may well be a **cell phone** to call for help, assuming you're in an area with reception.

If you become stranded in a blizzard, stay in your car. You're more likely to be found, and the vehicle provides shelter from the weather. Run the engine and heater sparingly, occasionally opening a window for ventilation. Don't run the engine if the tailpipe is blocked by snow, or you may risk carbon monoxide poisoning.

BY AIR

Commercial airline service is available to the towns of Cody, Jackson, and West Yellowstone in the region covered by this book. See the Special Topic "Airline Contacts" for complete details on major airlines.

If you're flying to Jackson from Seattle, Los Angeles, or San Francisco, you will either need to go through Salt Lake City or Idaho Falls. Many folks opt to fly to either Salt Lake (275 miles away) or Idaho Falls (90 miles away) and pick up a rental car for the drive to Jackson.

Great Lakes Aviation code shares with United and Frontier, so you can book flights and get airline miles through either of these airlines to fly into Cody or West Yellowstone.

Other Regional Airports

The airport at **Idaho Falls, Idaho** is a 90-mile drive from Jackson and is served by Horizon from Seattle via Boise or Pocatello, Sky West/Delta from Salt Lake City, and Big Sky Airlines

AIRLINE CONTACTS

American, 800/433-7300, www.aa.com: Summer and winter service from Dallas and Chicago.

Big Sky Airlines, 406/247-3910 or 800/237-7788, www.bigskyair.com: Serves Idaho Falls, Idaho via Denver.

Continental, 800/523-3273, www.continental.com: Serves Jackson Hole from Newark and Houston in the winter, and usually has service during summer to the same cities.

Delta/Skywest, 800/221-1212, www.deltaair.com: Year-round service from Salt Lake City to Jackson, Cody, and West Yellowstone, with additional winter flights out of Atlanta.

Great Lakes Aviation, 307/432-7000 or 800/554-5111, www.greatlakesav.com: Provides daily commuter service between Denver and Cody.

Northwest Airlines, 800/225-2525, www.nwa.com: Flies from Minneapolis/St. Paul in the summer and winter.

United/United Express, 800/241-6522, www.unitedairlines.com: Offers year-round turboprop service from Denver.

from Denver. Farther away are airports in Salt Lake City, Bozeman, and Billings.

Salt Lake City has service from most of the major carriers and is a 275-mile drive from Jackson. Because of its size, this is probably the least expensive regional airport to fly into and is a hub for Sky West/Delta.

It's an 84-mile drive from **Bozeman** to Mammoth Hot Springs on the northwest corner of Yellowstone or 225 miles from Bozeman to Jackson. Direct flights to Bozeman are offered by Delta from Salt Lake City, Horizon Air from Seattle and Los Angeles, Northwest Airlines from Minneapolis, and United from Denver.

Billings has the largest airport in Montana. It's a 127-mile drive from Billings to the Northeast Entrance to Yellowstone National Park, but this requires going over the 10,947-foot summit of

Beartooth Pass (closed in winter). From Billings to Gardiner, on the northwest corner of Yellowstone, it's 169 miles, and from Billings to Cody the drive is 104 miles (plus another 52 miles to the East Entrance of Yellowstone). Several airlines serve Billings: Sky West/Delta from Salt Lake City, Horizon Air from Seattle, Northwest Airlines from Minneapolis, and United Airlines from Denver.

BY BUS

To Jackson Hole

Greyhound buses don't come even close to Jackson; the nearest stopping places are Evanston, West Yellowstone, Idaho Falls, and the regional hub at Salt Lake City. **Alltrans/Jackson Hole Express,** 307/733-1719 or 800/652-9510, www.jacksonholealltrans.com, has daily bus connections to Jackson from Greyhound stations in Salt Lake City and Idaho Falls, with an additional stop in Pocatello, Idaho. They also provide a winter-only shuttle between Jackson and Grand Targhee Ski Resort.

Southern Teton Area Rapid Transit—better known as **START**—offers local bus service in the Jackson/Teton Village area; get details at 307/733-4521, www.startbus.com. As this book was being written, Grand Teton National Park was developing a new transportation plan that may include scheduled bus service from Jackson into the park.

Other Destinations

Greyhound, 800/231-2222, www.greyhound.com, operates along the I-80 corridor, including Salt Lake City and the southern Wyoming towns of Evanston and Rock Springs. Their buses also run north from Salt Lake City to Idaho Falls, West Yellowstone (the closest connection to Yellowstone National Park), Bozeman, and Billings, but not to Jackson, Cody, Gardiner, Driggs, Dubois, or other towns in the region.

Buses from **Powder River Transportation/Coach USA,** 307/682-0960 or 800/442-3682, provide service from Billings, Montana to Cody and other towns in Big Horn Basin, continuing east to Rapid City, South Dakota, and south all the way to Denver.

Community and Rural Transportation (CART), 208/354-2240 or 800/657-7439, has daily bus service between Driggs and Rexburg, Idaho.

Community Bus Service, 406/646-7600, provides bus service between West Yellowstone and Bozeman, Montana. Both **4x4 Stage,** 406/848-2224 or 800/517-8243, and **Karst Stage,** 406/388-2293 or 800/287-4759, www.karststage.com, also offer wintertime shuttles between the Bozeman airport and West Yellowstone.

A variety of options exist for tours and shuttles to Yellowstone and Grand Teton National Parks from surrounding towns; see the appropriate chapters for details.

BY TRAIN

Amtrak's *California Zephyr* runs between Chicago and Oakland but does not come close to Jackson Hole or Yellowstone. The nearest train station is in Salt Lake City, 275 miles from Jackson. Those traveling by train will need to take a bus, rental car, or plane from Salt Lake into Jackson. Get Amtrak details at 800/872-7245, www.amtrak.com.

ON THE ROAD

Jackson Hole

Jackson Hole is one of the most-visited slices of wild country in North America, attracting well more than three million travelers each year. They come here for a multitude of reasons: to camp under the stars in Grand Teton National Park, to play and shop in the New West town of Jackson, to hike flower-bedecked trails up forested valleys, to ride sleighs among thousands of elk, to raft down the Snake River, to ski or snowboard at one of the local resorts, or to simply stand in wonderment as the sun colors the sky behind the mountains. Many continue on north to Yellowstone National Park, another place on everyone's must-see list. Drive north from Jackson toward Yellowstone and you'll quickly discover the biggest reason so many people are attracted to this place—

its beauty. The Tetons act as a magnet, drawing your eyes away from the road and forcing you to stop and absorb some of their majesty. Welcome to one of the world's great wonderlands.

In the lingo of the mountain men, a "hole" was a large valley ringed by mountain ranges, and each was named for the trapper who based himself there. Jackson Hole, on Wyoming's far western border, is justifiably the most famous of all these intermountain valleys. Although Jackson Hole reaches an impressive 48 miles north to south and up to 16 miles across, the magnificent range of mountains to the west is what defines this valley. Shoshone Indians who wandered through this country called the peaks Teewinot (Many Pinnacles); later explorers would use such labels as

Conestoga wagons, Jackson

© DON PITCHER

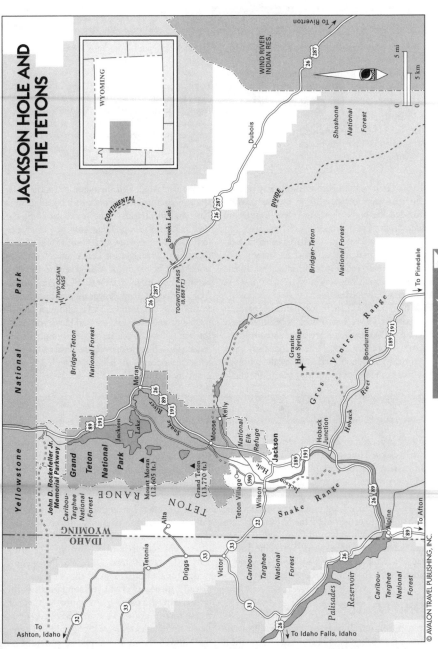

JACKSON HOLE AND THE TETONS

WYOMING

To Riverton

WIND RIVER INDIAN RES.

Shoshone National Forest

Dubois

CONTINENTAL

Brooks Lake

TWO OCEAN PASS

DIVIDE

Bridger-Teton National Forest

TOGWOTEE PASS (9,658 FT.)

Bridger-Teton National Forest

Yellowstone National Park

John D. Rockefeller Jr. Memorial Parkway

Caribou-Targhee National Forest

Grand Teton National Park

Granite Hot Springs

Gros Ventre Range

To Pinedale

Moran

Jackson Lake

Snake River

Kelly

National Elk Refuge

Hoback Junction

Hoback River

Bondurant

TETON RANGE

Mount Moran (12,605 ft.)

Grand Teton (13,770 ft.)

Moose

Jackson

IDAHO WYOMING

Alta

Tetonia

Teton Village

Wilson

Jackson Hole

Snake Range

Driggs

Victor

Caribou-Targhee National Forest

Alpine

To Afton

To Ashton, Idaho

Caribou-Targhee National Forest

Palisades Reservoir

To Idaho Falls, Idaho

© AVALON TRAVEL PUBLISHING, INC.

JACKSON HOLE

0 5 mi
0 5 km

JACKSON HOLE SIGHTSEEING HIGHLIGHTS

Town Square, art galleries, restaurants, and shoot-out in downtown Jackson

National Museum of Wildlife Art

National Elk Refuge

Snake River whitewater rafting and trout fishing

Horseback rides and chuck wagon cookouts

Jackson Hole Mountain Resort, Snow King Resort, and Grand Targhee Ski Resort for winter skiing and summertime lift rides

Grand Teton National Park for spectacular mountain vistas and hikes

Popular events: International Pedigree Stage Stop Sled Dog Race (January), Pole-Peddle-Paddle Race (April), Elk Antler Auction (May), Old West Days (Memorial Day), Grand Teton Music Festival (all summer), Jackson Hole Rodeo (all summer), Jackson Shoot-out (all summer), and Jackson Hole Fall Arts Festival (September)

Shark's Teeth or Pilot Knobs. But lonely French-Canadian trappers arriving in the early 1800s provided the name that stuck: les Trois Tetons (literally, the Three Tits).

Contrary to what you may have been told, Jackson Hole is *not* named for Michael Jackson. The valley, originally called Jackson's Hole, was instead named for likable trapper David E. Jackson, one of the men who helped establish the Rocky Mountain Fur Company. When Jackson and his partners sold out in 1830, they realized a profit of more than $50,000. Jackson's presence remains in the names of both Jackson Hole and Jackson Lake. Eventually, more polite folks began calling the valley Jackson Hole, in an attempt to end the ribald stories associated with the name Jackson's Hole. (It's easy to imagine the jokes with both Jackson's Hole and the Tetons in the same place.) By the way, in 1991, a group calling itself the Committee to Restore Decency to Our National Parks created quite a stir by suggesting that Grand Teton National Park be renamed. A letter sent to the Park Service and various members of Congress noted: "Though a great many Americans may be oblivious to this vulgarity, hundreds of millions of French people around the world are not! How embarrassing that these spectacular, majestic mountains are reduced to a dirty joke overseas." After a flurry of letters in response, the hoax was revealed; it was a prank by staff members of *Spy* magazine.

History

The first people to cross the mountain passes into Jackson Hole probably arrived while the last massive glaciers were still retreating. Clovis stone arrowheads—a style used 12,000 years ago—have been found along the edges of the valley. These early peoples were replaced in the 16th and 17th centuries by the Shoshone, Bannock, Blackfeet, Crow, and Gros Ventre tribes, who hunted bison from horses. When the first fur trappers tramped into Jackson Hole, they found Indian paths throughout the valley.

JOHN COLTER

Transport yourself back to the early 19th century, a time when people from the new nation called America saw the world west of the Mississippi River as just a blank spot on the map. In 1803, Thomas Jefferson purchased the Louisiana Territory from France, and to learn more about this gigantic piece of real estate he sent Meriwether Lewis and William Clark on a military expedition to the Pacific coast, a trip that took nearly 2.5 years. Although the expedition skirted around Wyoming—heading across Montana instead—it proved the opening wedge for the settlement of the West and, indirectly, the discovery of Jackson Hole. On the return trip, the party met two fur trappers en route to the upper Missouri River. One of Lewis and Clark's respected scouts, John Colter, was allowed to join the trappers, "provided no one of the party would ask or expect a Similar permission."

After a winter of trapping with his partners, Colter headed alone down the Platte River, but before he could get back to civilization he met up with a company of trappers led by Manuel Lisa. They were on their way to the Rockies, determined to cash in on the huge demand for beaver furs by trapping the rich beaver streams that Lewis and Clark had described. Wealth beckoned, and John Colter gladly turned around again, guiding Lisa's men up to the mouth of the Big Horn River, where they built a small fort. From there Colter was sent on a mission: contact Indians throughout the region, trading beads and other items for beaver furs.

His wanderings in the winter of 1807–1808 were the first white exploration of this region. A map produced by William Clark in 1814 and based on Colter's recollections shows an incredible midwinter journey around Yellowstone and Jackson Lakes, across the Tetons twice, and up through Jackson Hole. He did not get back to the fort until the following spring, telling tales of huge mountain ranges and a spectacular geothermal area that others quickly laughed off as "Colter's Hell."

Because of the abundance of beavers along tributaries of the Snake River, Jackson Hole became an important crossroads for the Rocky Mountain fur trade. Many of the most famous mountain men spent time here.

Colter went on to become one of the most famous of all mountain men, and his later harrowing escape from the Blackfeet in Montana has become the stuff of legend. After being captured and stripped naked, he was forced to literally run for his life. Somehow he managed to outdistance his pursuers for six miles before hiding in a pile of logs until dark. He walked barefoot the 300 miles back to Manuel Lisa's fort, surviving on roots and tree bark. Shortly thereafter, Colter was reported to have thrown his hat on the ground, declaring, "I'll be damned if I ever come into [this country] again." He returned to St. Louis, married, and established a farm near that of fellow explorer Daniel Boone. Colter lived long enough to give William Clark a description of the country he had visited, but he died from jaundice just three years later, in 1813.

Because of the abundance of beavers along tributaries of the Snake River, Jackson Hole became an important crossroads for the Rocky Mountain fur trade. Although no rendezvous was ever held in the valley, many of the most famous mountain men spent time here. They first trapped beavers in Jackson Hole in 1811, but it was not until the 1820s that fur trapping really

JACKSON HOLE IN 1835

This Valley is called "Jackson Hole" it is generally from 5 to 15 mls wide: the southern part where the river enters the mountain is hilly and uneven but the Northern portion is wide smooth and comparatively even the whole being covered with wild sage and Surrounded by high and rugged mountains upon whose summits the snow remains during the hottest months in Summer. The alluvial bottoms along the river and streams inter sect it thro. the valley produce a luxuriant groth of vegetation among which wild flax and a species of onion are abundant. The great altitude of this place however connected with the cold descending from the mountains at night I think would be a serious obstruction to growth of most Kinds of cultivated grains. This valley like all other parts of the country abounds with game.

—From Journal of a Trapper 1834–1843, *by Osborne Russell*

came into its own as mountain men fanned throughout the wilderness in search of the "soft gold." This quest continued for the next two decades, finally dying out when overtrapping made beavers harder to find and silk hats replaced fur hats. After the last rendezvous in 1840, most of the old trappers headed on to new adventures, the best becoming guides for those en route to Oregon and California. Because Jackson Hole was not near the Oregon Trail or other routes west, the area remained virtually deserted until the late 19th century.

SETTLERS

The first Jackson Hole homesteaders arrived in 1884, followed quickly by a handful of others fleeing the law. The settlers survived by grazing cattle, harvesting hay, and acting as guides for rich hunters from Europe and eastern states. Gradually they filled the richest parts of the valley with homesteads. Conflicts soon arose between the Bannock Indians, who had been hunting in Jackson Hole for more than a hundred years, and the new settlers who made money guiding wealthy sportsmen.

By 1895, Wyoming had enacted game laws prohibiting hunting during 10 months of the year. Claiming that the Indians were taking elk out of season, Constable William Manning and 26 settlers arrested a group of 28 Indians (mostly women and children) who had been hunting in Hoback Canyon. When the Bannocks attempted to flee, an elderly Indian was shot four times in the back and died. Most of the others escaped. Settlers in Jackson Hole feared revenge and called in the cavalry, but the Indians who had been hunting in the area all returned peaceably to their Idaho reservation. Astoundingly, *The New York Times* headlined its report of the incident, "Settlers Massacred—Indians Kill Every One at Jackson's Hole—Courier Brings the News—Red Men Apply the Torch to All the Houses in the Valley." Absolutely none of this was true, but the attack by whites succeeded in forcing the Indians off their traditional hunting grounds, an action eventually upheld in a landmark U.S. Supreme Court case.

THE WHITE SHOSHONE

The little Jackson Hole town of Wilson is named for one of Wyoming's most fascinating characters, "Uncle Nick" Wilson. Born in 1842, Wilson grew up in Utah, where he made friends with a fellow sheepherder, an Indian boy, and learned to speak his language. Then, suddenly, Nick's life took a strange twist. The mother of Chief Washakie (from Wyoming's Wind River Reservation) had recently lost a son, and in a dream she was told that a white boy would come to take his place. Unable to convince her otherwise, Washakie sent his men out to find the new son. They came across Nick and offered him a pinto pony and the chance to fish, hunt, and ride horses all he wanted. It didn't take much persuading, and for the next two years he lived as a Shoshone, learning to hunt buffalo, to use a bow and arrow, and to answer to his new name, Yagaiki. He became a favorite of Chief Washakie, but when word came (falsely) that Nick's father was threatening to attack the Shoshones with an army of men to retrieve his son, the chief reluctantly helped Nick return home.

At age 18, Nick Wilson became one of the first Pony Express riders, a job that nearly killed him when he was struck in the head during a Paiute Indian attack. A doctor managed to remove the arrow point, but Wilson remained in a coma for nearly two weeks. Thereafter, Wilson always wore a hat to cover the scar, even inside buildings. He went on to become an army scout and a driver for the Overland Stage before returning to a more sedate life as a farmer. Many years later, in 1889, Nick Wilson led a party of five Mormon families over steep Teton Pass and down to the rich grazing lands in Jackson Hole. The town that grew up around him became Wilson. In later years, "Uncle Nick" recounted his adventures in *The White Indian Boy*.

JACKSON HOLE COMES OF AGE

By the turn of the 20th century, the Jackson Hole settlements of Jackson, Wilson, Kelly, and Moran had all been established. The towns grew slowly; people survived by ranching, guiding, and engaging in the strange new business of tending to wealthy "dudes" from back east. Eventually, tourism would vastly eclipse raising cattle in importance, but even today Teton County has nearly as many cattle as people.

Jackson, Jackson Hole's primary settlement, was named by Maggie Simpson, who opened a post office here in 1894. Three years later Grace Miller—wife of a local banker known derisively as "Old Twelve Percent"—bought a large plot of land and planned a townsite, but the town wasn't officially incorporated until 1914. In an event that should come as no surprise in "The Equality State," Jackson later became the first town in America to be entirely governed by women. The year was 1920, and not only was the mayor a woman (Grace Miller), but so were all four council members, the city clerk, the treasurer, and even the town marshal. They remained in office until 1923.

Over the years Jackson has grown, spurred on by the creation of Grand Teton National Park and the development of Jackson Hole Mountain Resort. In the last 25 years, Jackson Hole has seen almost continuous growth; tourists have

flooded the region to play, investors have built golf courses and ostentatious hotels, and wealthy families have snatched up their own parcels of paradise. Today, Teton County has the highest per capita income of any county in America (around $70,000), and locals quip that the billionaires are buying land so fast that they're driving the millionaires out of Jackson Hole.

Although much of the area is public land and will remain undeveloped, rapid growth on private land is transforming Jackson Hole into the Wyoming version of Vail or Santa Fe. Even the formerly quiet town of Wilson failed to fight off the development onslaught, with a massive new grade school and a collection of modest new homes that locals call Whoville (after those in the Dr. Seuss book). As a former resident of Wilson, I can appreciate the joke going the rounds: How many Wilsonites does it take to change a light bulb? Seven. One to screw it in, and the other six to talk about how good the old one used to be.

Growth in Jackson Hole has forced land values sky-high, and affordable housing has become an oxymoron. Despite all of the problems brought on by growth, the area is still remarkably beautiful, and the surrounding public lands will remain wild. Locals like to point out that this is more than a place to visit; for them it is a place to live surrounded by the best of the old (and new) West.

Jackson

The town of Jackson (pop. 9,000) lies near the southern end of Jackson Hole, hemmed in on three sides by Snow King Mountain, the Gros Ventre Range, and East Gros Ventre Butte. At 6,200 feet in elevation, Jackson experiences cold snowy winters, wet springs, delightfully warm and sunny summers, and crisp but color-filled falls. Jackson is unlike any other place in Wyoming; on a typical summer day more than 35,000 tourists flood the town. Sit on a bench in Town Square on a summer day and you're likely to see cars from every state in the Union. Tourists dart in and out of the many gift shops, art galleries, fine restaurants, Western-style saloons, and trendy boutiques. The

cowboy hats all look as if the price tags just came off. This sure isn't Rock Springs!

In other parts of Wyoming, Jackson is viewed with a mixture of awe and disdain—awe over its booming economy, but disdain that Jackson is not a "real" town, just a false front put up to sell things to outsiders. Yes, Jackson is almost wholly dependent on the almighty tourist dollar, but as a result it enjoys a cultural richness lacking in other parts of the state. Besides, if you don't like all the commercial foolishness, it's easy to escape to a campsite or remote trail in the wonderful countryside of nearby Grand Teton National Park or Bridger-Teton National Forest.

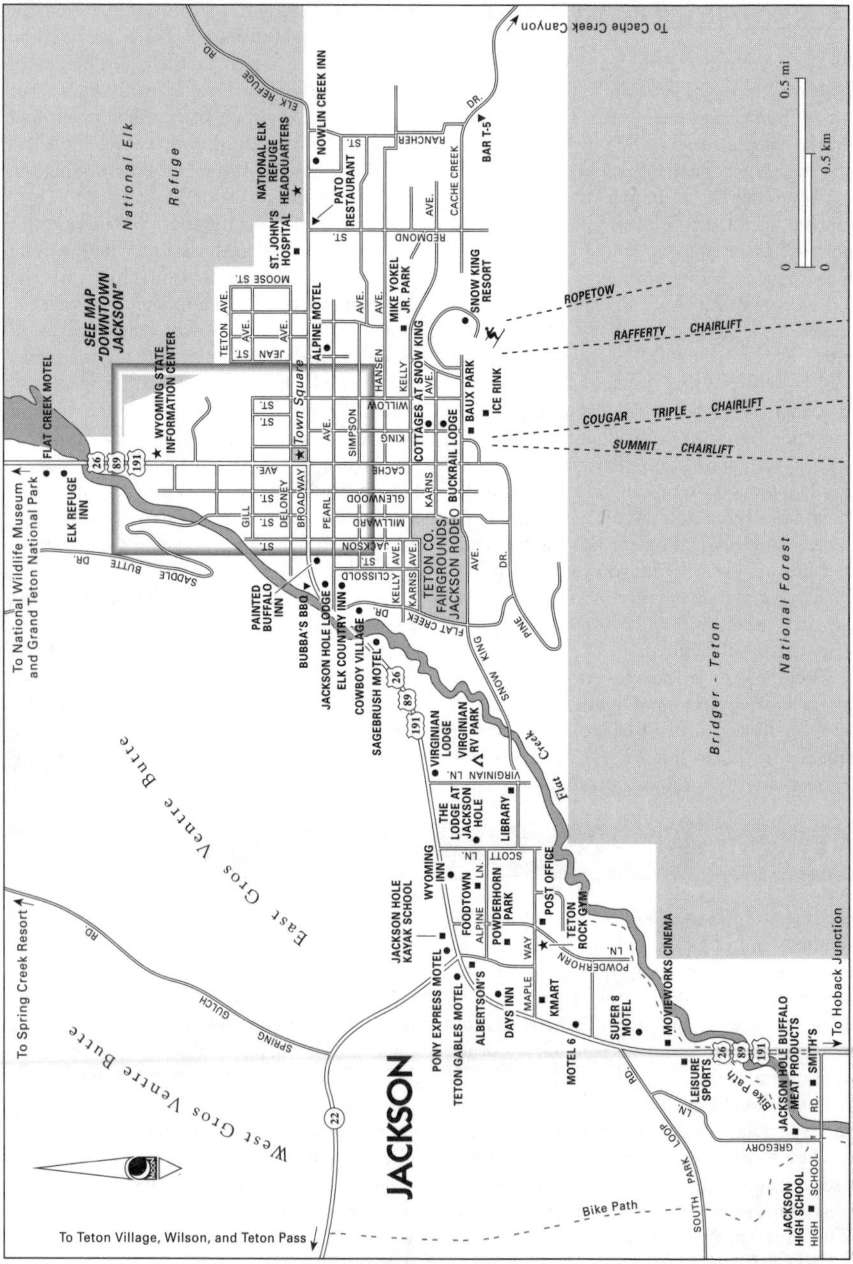

JACKSON HOLE

To Cache Creek Canyon

NOWLIN CREEK INN
National Elk Refuge
RANCHER ST.
BAR T-5
CACHE CREEK DR.
NATIONAL ELK REFUGE HEADQUARTERS
PATO RESTAURANT
REDMOND AVE.
CACHE CREEK AVE.
National Elk Refuge
ST. JOHN'S HOSPITAL
MOOSE ST.
MIKE YOKEL JR. PARK
SNOW KING RESORT
ROPETOW
TETON AVE.
ALPINE MOTEL
JEAN ST.
KELLY AVE.
RAFFERTY CHAIRLIFT
SEE MAP "DOWNTOWN JACKSON"
HANSEN AVE.
COTTAGES AT SNOW KING
ICE RINK
BAUX PARK
WYOMING STATE INFORMATION CENTER
WILLOW ST.
KING ST.
SIMPSON AVE.
BUCKRAIL LODGE
COUGAR TRIPLE CHAIRLIFT
SUMMIT CHAIRLIFT
FLAT CREEK MOTEL
Town Square
CACHE ST.
BROADWAY
PEARL AVE.
GLENWOOD ST.
KARNS AVE.
MILLWARD ST.
ELK REFUGE INN
26 89 191
GILL AVE.
DELONEY AVE.
SADDLE BUTTE DR.
To National Wildlife Museum and Grand Teton National Park
PAINTED BUFFALO INN
JACKSON ST.
CLISSOLD
KARNS AVE.
TETON CO. FAIRGROUNDS JACKSON RODEO
PINE DR.
Bridger - Teton
BUBBA'S BBQ
JACKSON HOLE LODGE
ELK COUNTRY INN
COWBOY VILLAGE
FLAT CREEK DR.
SNOW KING AVE.
East Gros Venture Butte
SAGEBRUSH MOTEL
26 89 191
VIRGINIAN LODGE
VIRGINIAN RV PARK
VIRGINIAN LN.
Flat Creek
National Forest
THE LODGE AT JACKSON HOLE
LIBRARY
SCOTT LN.
To Spring Creek Resort
SPRING GULCH RD.
WYOMING INN
FOODTOWN
ALPINE LN.
POWDERHORN PARK
POST OFFICE
POWDERHORN LN.
TETON ROCK GYM
West Gros Venture Butte
JACKSON HOLE KAYAK SCHOOL
PONY EXPRESS MOTEL
TETON GABLES MOTEL
ALBERTSON'S
DAYS INN
MAPLE WAY
KMART
SUPER 8 MOTEL
MOVIEWORKS CINEMA
22
JACKSON
MOTEL 6
LEISURE SPORTS
26 89 191
JACKSON HOLE BUFFALO MEAT PRODUCTS
SMITH'S
Bike Path
To Hoback Junction
GREGORY LN.
SOUTH PARK LOOP RD.
JACKSON HOLE HIGH SCHOOL
HIGH SCHOOL RD.
Bike Path
To Teton Village, Wilson, and Teton Pass

0   0.5 mi
0   0.5 km

© AVALON TRAVEL PUBLISHING, INC.

Keep your eyes open around Jackson and you're likely to see well-known residents such as Hollywood stars Harrison Ford, Danny DeVito and his wife Rhea Perlman, Connie Stevens, and Sandra Bullock, along with former Secretary of the Interior James Watt (who resigned in disgrace in 1983), attorney Gerald Spence (of Karen Silkwood and Imelda Marcos notoriety), Yvon Chouinard (mountaineer and founder of Patagonia), industrial heir Charles DuPont, and members of the extended Rockefeller family. Vice President Dick Cheney also has a luxury home in Jackson Hole and is a frequent visitor, which explains all of the Blackhawk helicopters, Secret Service agents, and Suburbans with dark-tinted windows.

SIGHTS

Town Square

In 1932, the local Rotary Club planted trees in the center of Jackson, adding four picturesque arches made from hundreds of elk antlers in the 1950s and '60s. Today the trees offer summertime shade, and at any time of day or night you'll find visitors admiring or posing for photos in front of the arches that mark the corners of Town Square. During winter, the snow-covered arches and trees are draped with lights, giving the square a festive atmosphere. Surrounded by dozens of board-walk-fronted galleries, bars, restaurants, factory outlets, and gift shops, the square is the focal point of tourist activity in Jackson.

During summer, stagecoaches wait to transport you on a leisurely ride around town, and each evening "cowboys" put on a free **shoot-out** for throngs of camera-happy tourists. The shoot-out starts every summer night (except Sunday) at 6:15 P.M. They've been killing each other like this since 1957. With stereotypical players and questionable acting, the "mountain law" system seems in dire need of reform. Most folks love the sham; Kodak and Fuji love it even more. Warning: The sound of blanks is surprisingly loud and can be frightening for small children.

National Museum of Wildlife Art

Jackson is home to the magnificent National Museum of Wildlife Art, which lies two miles north of town along U.S. Hwy. 26/89, directly across from the National Elk Refuge. Built from brown Arizona sandstone, the exterior

the National Museum of Wildlife Art

JACKSON HOLE

To National Museum of Wildlife Art,
Grand Teton and Yellowstone National Parks

DOWNTOWN JACKSON

National

Elk

Refuge

26
89
191

WAGON WHEEL
RV PARK

WAGON WHEEL
VILLAGE

DAVY JACKSON
INN

WYOMING STATE
★ INFORMATION CENTER

■ WYOMING GAME AND FISH

PERRY   ST.

CACHE CREEK
MOTEL

ROSECRANZ

■ BRIDGER-TETON
NATIONAL FOREST
OFFICE

SNAKE RIVER
KAYAK AND CANOE
SCHOOL

WILD FLOUR
BAKERY

JACKSON HOLE
HISTORICAL
CENTER ★

AVE.

INN ON
THE CREEK ●

MERCILL

● KUDAR'S MOTEL

WOLF MOON
INN

ALPINE HOUSE
COUNTRY INN ●

ANGLERS
INN

NANI'S
PASTA
HOUSE

TRAPPER
INN ●

NIKAI

PUBLIC   PARKING

TETON INN

EL RANCH
MOTEL

PUBLIC
RESTROOMS

JACKSON
RECREATION CENTER
■

RUSTY PARROT
LODGE

GILL

ANVIL MOTEL
AND BUNKHOUSE

AVE.

Miller

TETON
CYCLERY

■ TETON MOUNTAINEERING
■ IMAGES OF NATURE GALLERY

PROSPECTOR
INN

Park

JACKSON HOLE
MOUNTAIN GUIDES

▼ BLUE LION
RESTAURANT

RIPLEY'S
BELIEVE IT OR NOT ■

BROWSE 'N BUY ■

MERRY
▼ PIGLETS

THE
BUNNERY ■

■ ROBERT DEAN GALLERY

PARKWAY
INN ●

FOUR WINDS ▼
MOTEL

WILD BY
NATURE SKINNY VALLEY
GALLERY SKIS BOOKS

TETON THEATRE

■ MEYER GALLERY

■ LIGHT REFLECTIONS
GALLERY

PUBLIC
RESTROOMS

■ ■ TRAILSIDE GALLERIES

PUBLIC
PARKING

DELONEY

PUBLIC
PARKING

JACKSON
HOLE
PLAYHOUSE

JACKSON
HOLE
MUSEUM

CADILLAC GRILLE/
BILLY'S BURGERS

AVE.

CENTER ST. GALLERY

HUFF HOUSE
INN B&B ●

NEW YORK
SUB SHOP ▼

MOUNTUNES

SUNDANCE
INN

SILVER DOLLAR
BAR AND WORT
HOTEL

Town

Square

COWBOY
BAR

JEDEDIAH'S
▼

CASWELL
GALLERY

GOLDEN
EAGLE
MOTEL

W. BROADWAY

HARVEST
NATURAL
FOODS ▼

26 89 191

E. BROADWAY

BROADWAY BOTTLE CO ▼

HOBACK SPORTS

MT. HIGH
PIZZA PIE

MAINSTAGE
THEATRE

RANCHER ▼
BAR

■ JACK DENNIS'

PUBLIC
RESTROOMS

▼ SNAKE RIVER
GRILL

■ TETON
KIDS

BETTY
ROCK
CAFE ▼

JACKSON
HOLE
CINEMA

RAWHIDE
MOTEL

TETON BOOKSHOP ▼

PEARL ST.
BAGELS

▼ ANTHONY'S
ITALIAN
RESTAURANT

TETON
STEAKHOUSE ▼

SHADES ▼
CAFE

■ RAWSON
GALLERIES

THAI ME UP ▼

SWEETWATER RESTAURANT

PEARL

LE JAY'S ▼
CAFE

RANCH INN ●

ST.

49ER ●
INN

ART
ASSOCIATION

POST
OFFICE
■

PONY EXPRESS
MOTEL

ANTLER
INN

CITY HALL
■

SIMPSON

AVE.

SNAKE RIVER BREWING ▼
COMPANY & RESTAURANT

SIMPSON   AVE.

0   100 yds

0   100 m

© AVALON TRAVEL PUBLISHING, INC.

blends in with nearby rock outcroppings. Step inside the doors of this 51,000-square-foot museum to discover a marvelous interior space. As visitors enter the main gallery, a larger-than-life bronze mountain lion crouches above, ready to pounce. Kids will have fun in the hands-on Children's Gallery. Adults will appreciate the artwork spread throughout a dozen galleries, along with the video theater, Rising Sage Cafe (delicious lunches), 200-seat auditorium, and gift shop.

The museum collection features pieces by Carl Rungius, George Catlin, Albert Bierstadt, Karl Bodmer, Alfred Jacob Miller, N. C. Wyeth, Conrad Schwiering, John Clymer, Charles Russell, Robert Bateman, and many others. Of particular interest are the reconstructed studio of John Clymer and the spacious Carl Rungius Gallery, where you'll find the most complete collection of his paintings in the nation. Also of note is the exhibit on the American bison, which documents these once vastly abundant animals and their slaughter. Six galleries contain changing exhibitions of photography, painting, and other art. Spotting scopes in the lobby and the cozy members' lounge (open to the public) are useful for watching residents of the adjacent National Elk Refuge.

Admission to the museum costs $8 adults, $7 seniors and students, $16 families; kids under six get in free. It's open daily 9 A.M.–5 P.M. year-round, with the exception of April, May, and November, when the hours are Sunday 1–5 P.M. and Monday–Saturday 9 A.M.–5 P.M. Free museum tours are sometimes offered; ask at the front desk is a docent is available. Call 307/733-5771 for details on the museum, or visit their website, www.wildlifeart.org.

Wildlife films, slide lectures, talks, concerts, kids' programs, and other activities take place throughout the year in the auditorium and galleries; pick up a schedule of upcoming events at the entrance desk. One of the most popular events is the **Miniature Show and Sale** in mid-September; it attracts more than a hundred of the country's leading artists.

During winter, come to the museum to purchase tickets for sleigh rides on the refuge. A combination museum entrance and Elk Refuge sleigh ride costs $15 adults, $11 ages 6–12, free for kids under six.

Historical Museums

The small **Jackson Hole Museum,** 105 N. Glenwood, 307/733-2414, www.jacksonhole history.org, has a surprising homespun charm. Inside are displays and collections illustrating the days when Indians, trappers, cattlemen, and dude ranchers called this magnificent valley home. Check out the Paul Bunyan–size bear trap, the old postcards, and a replica of the "Colter stone." Admission costs $3 adults, $2 seniors, $1 students, and $6 families. Hours are Monday–Saturday 9:30 A.M.–6 P.M. and Sunday 10 A.M.–5 P.M. from Memorial Day to early October; closed the rest of the year. The museum sponsors hour-long **historical walking tours** of Jackson's downtown on Tuesday, Thursday, Friday, and Saturday at 10 A.M. Memorial Day to Labor Day. These cost $2 adults, $1 seniors and students, or $5 families.

Also managed by the local historical society, the **Jackson Hole Historical Center,** 105 Mercill Ave., 307/733-9605, is a small research facility housing photo archives, a library of old books from the area, and rotating exhibits throughout the year. Hours are Monday–Friday 8 A.M.–5 P.M. year-round; free admission.

Information Center

Anyone new to Jackson Hole should be sure to visit the spacious **Wyoming State Information Center** on the north end of town at 532 N. Cache Drive, 307/733-3316, www.jackson holechamber.com. Hours are daily 8 A.M.–7 P.M. between Memorial Day and Labor Day, and daily 8 A.M.–5 P.M. the rest of the year. (The phone is answered only on weekdays, but on weekends you can leave a message and they'll mail you an information packet.)

The information center is a two-level, sod-roofed wooden building (jokingly called the "little prairie on the house") with natural-history displays, a blizzard of free leaflets extolling the merits of local businesses, a gift shop selling books and maps, and an upstairs rear deck overlooking the National Elk Refuge. Ducks and trumpeter swans are visible on the marsh in the summer, and elk can be seen in the winter. The information center is staffed by the Jackson Hole Chamber of Commerce, along with Fish & Wildlife Service and Forest Service personnel in the summer. Free naturalist talks are generally given daily at 10 A.M. and 2 P.M. in the summer.

In addition to the main information center, you'll find racks of brochures at the airport, outside the Pink Garter Plaza on the corner of W. Broadway and Glenwood, at the stagecoach stop on Town Square, at the Mangy Moose in Teton Village, and at the Do Jackson office next to Albertson's.

NATIONAL ELK REFUGE

Immediately north of Jackson is the National Elk Refuge, winter home for thousands of these majestic animals. During summer, the elk range up to 65 miles away to feed on grasses, shrubs, and forbs in alpine meadows. But as the snows descend each fall, the elk move downslope, wintering in Jackson Hole and the surrounding country. The chance to view elk up close from a

horse-drawn sleigh makes a trip to the National Elk Refuge one of the most popular wintertime activities for Jackson Hole visitors.

History

When the first ranchers arrived in Jackson Hole in the late 19th century, they moved onto land that had long been an elk migration route and wintering ground. The ranchers soon found elk raiding their haystacks and competing with cattle for forage, particularly during severe winters. The conflicts peaked early in the 20th century when three consecutive severe winters killed thousands of elk, leading one settler to claim that he had "walked for a mile on dead elk lying from one to four deep."

Fortunately, local rancher and hunting guide Stephen N. Leek had been given a camera by one of the sportsmen he had guided, George Eastman (founder of Kodak). Leek's disturbing photos of starving and dead elk found a national audience and helped pressure the state of Wyoming to appropriate $5,000 to buy hay in 1909. Two years later the federal government began purchasing land for a permanent

The National Elk Refuge north of Jackson is a winter home for thousands of elk.

© DON PITCHER

winter elk refuge that would eventually cover nearly 25,000 acres. Today it's administered by the U.S. Fish & Wildlife Service. Famed biologist, illustrator, and conservationist Olaus Murie came to Jackson Hole in 1927 to begin his studies of the elk, remaining here until his death in 1963. Murie and his wife, Margaret "Mardy" Murie, chronicled their adventures in *Wapiti Wilderness*. Conservationist Mardie Murie—now older than 100—still lives in Moose, holding near-sainthood status among conservationists.

Today more than 7,000 elk (two-thirds of the local population) spend November–May on the refuge. Because development has reduced elk habitat in the valley to one-quarter of its original size, refuge managers try to improve the remaining land through seeding, irrigation, and prescribed burning. In addition, during the most difficult foraging period, the elk are fed alfalfa pellets paid for in part by sales of elk antlers collected on the refuge. During this time, each elk eats more than seven pounds of supplemental alfalfa per day, or 30 tons per day for the entire herd. Elk head back into the mountains with the melting of snow each April and May; during summer you'll see few (if any) on the refuge.

Visiting the Refuge

The National Elk Refuge, 307/733-9212, http://nationalelkrefuge.fws.gov, is primarily a winter attraction, although it's also an excellent place to watch birds and other wildlife in summer. Trumpeter swans nest and winter here. The refuge has staff members on duty year-round in the Wyoming State Information Center. Find them on the web at www.jacksonholechamber.com.

The main winter attraction here is the chance to see thousands of elk up close from one of the **horse-drawn sleighs** that take visitors through the refuge. The elk are accustomed to these sleighs and pay little heed, but people on foot would scare them. A tour of the National Elk Refuge is always a highlight for wintertime visitors to Jackson Hole. In December and January the bulls have impressive antlers that they start to shed by the end of February. The months of January and February are good times to see sparring matches. You might also catch a glimpse of a wolf or two because a pack now resides in the area year-round and hunts elk in winter. Morning is the best time to look for wolves.

Begin your wintertime visit to the refuge at the National Museum of Wildlife Art (see previous description). Purchase your sleigh ride tickets here; $12 adults, $8 ages 6–12, free for kids under age six. A better deal is the combination ticket that includes museum entrance and an Elk Refuge sleigh ride for $15 adults, $11 ages 6–12, and free for younger kids. For reservations, contact Bar-T-Five (they run the sleighs) at 307/733-5386 or 800/772-5386, www.bart5.com. The museum shows an interpretive slide show about the refuge while you're waiting for a shuttle bus to take you downhill to the sleighs. The sleighs run daily 10 A.M.–4 P.M. mid-December through March (closed Christmas), heading out as soon as enough folks show up for a ride—generally just long enough for the early-comers to finish watching the slide show. The rides last 45–60 minutes. Be sure to wear warm clothes or bring extra layers because the wind can get bitterly cold.

Four miles north of town and next to the elk refuge is the **Jackson National Fish Hatchery,** 307/733-2510, which rears a half million cutthroat and lake trout annually. It's open daily 8 A.M.–4 P.M. year-round.

Shopping

If you have the money (or a credit card), Jackson is a great place to buy everything from artwork to mountain bikes. Even if you just hitchhiked in and have no cash to spare, it's always fun to wander through the shops and galleries surrounding Town Square.

ART

Artists have long been attracted by the beauty of Jackson Hole and the Tetons. Mount Moran, the 12,605-foot summit behind Jackson Lake, is named for Thomas Moran, whose watercolors helped persuade Congress to set aside Yellowstone as the first national park. The late Conrad Schwiering's paintings of the Tetons have attained international fame; one was even used on the Postal Service's Wyoming Centennial stamp in 1990. Ansel Adams's photograph of the Tetons remains etched in the American consciousness as one of the archetypal wilderness images. A copy of the image was included in the payload of the *Voyager II* spacecraft currently en route out of our solar system. Today many artists live or work in Jackson Hole, and locals proclaim it "Art Center of the Rockies," ranking it with New York, San Francisco, Santa Fe, and Scottsdale.

More than 30 galleries crowd the center of Jackson, their collections covering the spectrum from Indian art of questionable authenticity to impressive photographic exhibits and shows by nationally acclaimed painters. Unfortunately, many of these galleries offer recycled ideas now manufactured in mass quantity with every possible cliché thrown in. Particularly egregious examples are the Southwestern-style pastel pottery, the campy cowboy sculptures, and the prints of sexy Indian maidens with windblown hair and strategically torn garments. See the local free newspapers for a complete rundown of current exhibitions and displays, along with maps showing gallery locations, but don't believe everything the galleries say about themselves in their ads. For descriptions of local artists and galleries, visit the **Jackson Hole Gallery Association's** website, www.jacksonholearts.com.

Art Galleries

Several Jackson galleries are worth a visit, most notably the outstanding National Museum of Wildlife Art. For physical sustenance with your visual nourishment, don't miss the weekly **Gallery Walks** that take place every Thursday 5–8 P.M. in the summer. Many downtown galleries serve appetizers and wine for these fun and low-key events.

The nonprofit **Art Association,** 260 W. Pearl, 307/733-6379, www.artassociation.org, offers art classes of all types throughout the year and displays changing exhibitions by local and national artists in its **ArtWest Gallery,** open Mon.–Fri. 9 A.M.–5 P.M.

Just off Town Square at the corner of Center and Deloney, **Trailside Galleries,** 307/733-3186, www.trailsidegalleries.com, focuses on Western works, but you'll also find everything from impressionism to wildlife art in this big gallery. Two other Western-themed galleries worth a visit are **Mountain Trails Gallery,** 150 N. Center St., 307/733-8150, www.mtntrails.net; and **Legacy Gallery,** 75 N. Cache, 307/733-2353, www. legacygallery.com. More unusual is **Center Street Gallery,** 30 Center St., 307/733-1115 or 888/733-1115, www.centerstreetgallery.com, where the emphasis is on vivid contemporary art and jewelry.

Also downtown, the **Caswell Gallery & Sculpture Garden,** 145 E. Broadway, 307/734-2660, www.caswellgallery.com, is home to Jackson's only outdoor sculpture garden, with wildlife bronzes by Rip Caswell. These are not my cup of tea (or espresso for that matter), but you may appreciate the innovative sculptures from other artisans displayed in this gallery.

Jack Dennis' Wyoming Gallery, 50 E. Broadway, 307/733-7548, www.jackdennis.com, specializes in wildlife and traditional landscape paintings and photography. **Rawson Galleries** features traditional watercolors, displayed in a crowded space at 50 King St., 307/733-7306. They're open July–October. **Meyer Gallery,** 155 N. Center St., 307/733-0905 or 877/681-8900, www.meyergallery.com, presents beautifully passionate oil paintings and bronzes by respected Western artists at 155 Center Street. These artworks are well worth seeing, but they're priced for serious art patrons only. **Robert Dean Gallery,** 172 Center St., 307/733-9290, is known for its quality Indian artwork, with pottery, silver and gold jewelry, leather belts, and more.

For a different kind of art, head to **Dancer's Workshop,** downstairs in the Pink Garter Plaza at 49 W. Broadway, 307/733-6398, which offers country-and-western, modern, ballroom, hip-hop, ballet, tap, jazz, and even belly dance classes throughout the year, with nationally known guest artists on occasion.

Nearby Galleries

The **Hennes Studio & Gallery,** 5850 N. Larkspur Dr. (off Spring Gulch Rd. near the Jackson Hole Golf and Tennis Club), 307/733-2593, features oil and watercolor paintings of the Tetons by Joanne Hennes. Two of her commissioned works hang in the Moose Visitor Center and Jenny Lake Lodge.

One of Jackson's largest private exhibition spaces is **Wilcox Gallery,** one mile north of town on U.S. Hwy. 26/89, 307/733-6450, www.wilcoxgallery.com. Inside are traditional oil paintings by Jim Wilcox, along with works by other prominent Western painters and sculptors.

SAVING JACKSON HOLE

The Jackson Hole economy has been stuck in permanent high gear for the last few decades as Jackson has grown from a sleepy burg to a national focal point for outdoor fun. From 1990 to 2000, the population nearly doubled, and today the area is home to almost 9,000 people. Expensive homes now spread across old ranch lands, retailers such as Kmart have moved in, and development reaches for miles south from Jackson itself. Surrounding towns such as Alpine and Driggs have become bedroom communities for those willing to endure the long commute to Jackson, and their growth spreads the problems outward from Jackson.

Although 97 percent of the land in Teton County is in the public domain, the 70,000 acres of private land that remain are rapidly being developed, and Jackson Hole is in grave danger of losing the wild beauty that has attracted visitors for more than a century. This dilemma is immediately obvious to anyone arriving in Jackson. Instead of the wide-open spaces that remain protected by public land ownership, the edges of Jackson are falling under a proliferation of trophy homes, real-estate offices, chain motels, fast-food outlets, megamarts, gas stations, and elaborate banks, all competing beneath a thicket of signs. Summertime traffic jams are becoming all too common in this once-quiet place, where more than 35,000 visitors can be found on a summer afternoon.

In 1994, Jackson voters got fed up with the pace of development and voted to scrap the town's 2 percent lodging tax, which had provided more than $1 million per year in funding to promote Jackson Hole around the world. Despite this lack of promotional effort, growth shows no signs of slowing down. A large new Albertson's store went up in 1999, followed by an equally impressive Smiths in 2002, located next to the sprawling new high school. Housing costs continue to spiral upward, pushed by a wealthy clientele willing to drop $1 million or more for a Jackson Hole home. Antigrowth sentiment remains strong, however. In 2002, Jackson voters overturned the town council's efforts to annex the 822-acre Jackson Hole Hereford Ranch just south of town by a two-to-one margin.

The **Jackson Hole Conservation Alliance,** 307/733-9417, www.jhalliance.com, is a 1,600-member environmental group that works to preserve the remaining natural areas of Jackson Hole. Membership starts at $25 per year and includes a bimonthly newsletter and a chance to help control the many developments that threaten this still-beautiful valley.

Another influential local group is the **Jackson Hole Land Trust,** 307/733-4707, www.jhlandtrust.org. Established in 1980, this nonprofit organization obtains conservation easements to maintain ranches and other land threatened by development. The group has protected more than 10,000 acres in the valley in this way, including the 1,740-acre Walton Ranch, visible along the highway between Jackson and Wilson.

JACKSON HOLE

For art from the natural world, head six miles south of town on U.S. Hwy. 89 to **Fossilworks.** Inside are beautifully prepared fish fossils from the Kemmerer area (where the Ulrich's have a fossil quarry), including tabletops, flooring tiles, wall pieces, and other prepared specimens. The gallery is open by appointment only; call 307/733-1019 or 307/733-3613, or take a virtual visit at www.fossilportal.com.

Photo Galleries

Many nationally known photographers live or work in Jackson Hole and exhibit their prints in Jackson galleries. Tom Mangelsen displays his outstanding wildlife and landscape photos at **Images of Nature Gallery,** 170 N. Cache Dr., 307/733-9752 or 888/238-0177, www.mangelsen.com, and has galleries at 14 other locations around the country.

Inside **Light Reflections,** 35 E. Deloney, 307/733-4016 or 800/346-5223, www.lightreflections.com, are many of Fred Joy's large-format visions of the American West. Also well worth a visit is **Wild by Nature Gallery,** 95 W. Deloney, 307/733-8877 or 888/494-5329, www.wildbynature.com, where photographer Henry H. Holdsworth shows prints of his strikingly beautiful wildlife and nature imagery.

Located in Gaslight Alley at 125 N. Cache **Brookover-Muench Fine Art Photography,** 307/733-3988, www.davidbrookoverphotos.com, exhibits beautiful (and big) landscapes by photographers David Brookover and David Muench. **Wild Exposures Gallery,** 60 E. Broadway Ave. (upstairs next to Snake River Grill), 307/739-1777, www.wildexposuresgallery.com, shows works from a half-dozen local photographers.

OUTDOOR GEAR

Outdoor enthusiasts will discover several excellent shops in Jackson. Climbers, backpackers, and cross-country skiers head to America's oldest climbing shop, **Teton Mountaineering,** 170 N. Cache Dr., 307/733-3595 or 800/850-3595, www.tetonmtn.com, for quality equipment, maps, and travel guides. They also rent tents, sleeping bags, backpacks, cookstoves, climbing shoes, ice axes, cross-country skis, and even climbing and skiing videos. Check the bulletin board for used items.

Jack Dennis' Outdoor Shop, 50 E. Broadway, 307/733-3270 or 800/570-3270, www.jackdennis.com, is a large upscale store with fly-fishing and camping gear in summer and skis and warm clothes during winter. They also rent almost anything: tents, stoves, lanterns, cookware, sleeping bags, fishing poles, fly rods, waders, float tubes, backpacks, skis, snowshoes, and more.

Skinny Skis, 65 W. Deloney Ave., 307/733-6094 or 888/733-7205, www.skinnyskis.com, has more in the way of high-quality clothing and supplies, especially cross-country ski gear. Rent sleeping bags, tents, climbing shoes, ice axes, inline skates, baby carriers, and backpacks here. Another place to rent outdoor gear of all types—including volleyball sets, fishing gear, float tubes, tents, sleeping bags, backpacks, campstoves, and lanterns—is **Leisure Sports,** 1075 South U.S. Hwy. 89, 307/733-3040, www.leisuresportsadventure.com.

Moosely Seconds Mountaineering, in Moose, 307/739-1801, sells climbing and outdoor gear and rents trekking poles, ice axes, crampons, rock shoes, approach shoes, plastic boots, day packs, and snowshoes. It's open summers only.

Gart Sports, 485 W. Broadway, 307/733-4449, www.gartsports.com, is a large store with a variety of outdoor and sports gear. Purchase used outdoor gear of all types from **Gear Revival,** 854 W. Broadway, 307/739-8699. The least expensive place to buy rugged outdoor wear, cowboy boots, and cowboy hats is **Corral West,** 840 W. Broadway, 307/733-0247.

BARGAINS

Buy used clothing and other items at **Browse 'N Buy Thrift Shop,** 139 N. Cache Dr., 307/733-7524, or the more chaotic **Orville's,** 285 W. Pearl, 307/733-3165. Hint: Browse 'N Buy puts out new items on Wednesday, attracting a queue of discount shoppers for their 1 P.M. opening. Get there early for the real deals! Orville's sometimes sells old Wyoming license plates—a big hit with European tourists.

BOOKS

Unlike many Wyoming towns where the book selection consists of a few bodice-buster romance novels in the local pharmacy, Jackson is blessed with several fine bookstores. **Valley Bookstore,** 125 N. Cache Dr., 307/733-4533, www.valleybook.com, is the largest local bookshop, with a great choice of regional titles. The store has occasional author signings and readings. **Teton Bookshop,** 25 S. Glenwood, 307/733-9220, is a small downtown shop with a knowledgeable owner. **Main Event,** in the Powderhorn Mall at 980 W. Broadway, 307/733-7112, sells new books and CDs and rents a wide choice of videos. A few doors away in the mall is **Jackson Hole Book Trader,** 307/734-6001 or 800/722-2710, www.wy -biz.com/jacksonholebook, where you'll find a surprising choice of used and rare books. Up in Grand Teton National Park, find natural-history books and maps at the **Moose Visitor Center,** 307/739-3399, and **Colter Bay Indian Arts Museum,** 307/543-2467.

KITSCH

If you're a fan of the *National Enquirer,* check out the weird and wacky collection at **Ripley's Believe It or Not,** 140 N. Cache, 307/734-0000, www.ripleys.com/jac.htm. Here you'll discover a shrunken head, six-legged buffalo calf, six-foot-long cigar, antique bedpan collection, and even art created from dryer lint. Who says art is only for the elite? Entrance costs a steep $8 adults, $5 ages 5–12; free for kids under five. The family rate is $28, a bargain price for families of 10 from Salt Lake City. Ripley's is open daily 9 A.M.–10 P.M. in summer and daily 10 A.M.– 6 P.M. the rest of the year.

For more foolishness, have the kids drag you to the **Teton Maze,** across from the Snow King chairlift, 307/734-0455. As the ads proclaim, it's a-Maze-ing.

Accommodations

As one of the premier centers for tourism in Wyoming, Jackson Hole is jam-packed with more than 70 different motels, hotels, and B&Bs, plus many more condominiums and guest ranches. Other lodging can be found just to the north within or near Grand Teton National Park; these are detailed in the Grand Teton National Park chapter. The Jackson Hole Chamber of Commerce's website (www.jacksonholechamber.com) has brief descriptions and web links for most local places to stay.

Because of the town's popularity, Jackson accommodations command premium prices—a marked contrast to rates in other parts of Wyoming. With a few exceptions, you'll pay at least $90 s or d during the peak visitor seasons of July–August and late December to early January. Rates can drop more than 50 percent in the off-season, so if you can visit March–May or late September to mid-December, you'll save a lot of cash. (The same Super 8 Motel rooms that go for $100 in July cost just $46 in April!) In the town of Jackson, the highest rates are usually in July and August, while at Teton Village, skiers and snowboarders send room rates to their peak between mid-December and early January.

Reservations are highly recommended. For midsummer, make reservations at least two months ahead, or longer if you really want to be certain of a place. During the Christmas-to-New Year's period you should probably reserve six months in advance to ensure a spot. Summer weekends tend to be the most crowded, with many families driving up from Salt Lake City for a cooling break in the mountains.

UNDER $50

Jackson's least-expensive option, the **Bunkhouse,** 307/733-3668 or 800/234-4507, www.anvil motel.com, is in the basement of the Anvil Motel at 215 N. Cache Drive. Right in town, the hostel almost always has space. It costs $21 per person and includes a TV room and a kitchen with a refrigerator and microwave (but no stove or dishes). The big sleeping room contains 27 bunk beds with linen and adjacent storage lockers; bring your own lock. Alhough men's and women's showers and restrooms are separate, the sleeping space is coed. It can get pretty noisy with all those snoring bodies in one room at night, so earplugs are a smart purchase. Check in after 3 P.M. and be out by 11 A.M. Alcohol is not allowed. Folks who aren't staying here can take showers for $5.

Despite the name, **Hostel X,** 307/733-3415, www.hostelx.com, really isn't a hostel, but it does provide budget rates in a scenic location. Private rooms cost $50 s or d, or $63 for up to four people. The very small plain-vanilla rooms lack TV or phones, but there's a central lounge for camaraderie. The lounge includes a TV, pay phones, a pool table, table tennis, a children's play area, a fireplace, a microwave, games, Internet access, and a ski-waxing room. Because of its Teton Village location at the foot of Jackson Hole Mountain Resort, Hostel X is very popular with skiers on a budget; reserve three months ahead for midwinter rooms.

$50-100
Downtown Accommodations
Alpine Motel, 70 S. Jean St., 307/739-3200, is in a quiet part of town but just a few blocks from Town Square. The furnishings may not be the newest in town, but the rooms are clean and start at $64 s or d or $72 for four people. Kitchenettes with two queen beds sleep up to four for $90. A small outdoor pool (heated but seasonal) is also on the premises.

Despite its name, **The Cottages at Snow King,** 470 King St., 307/733-3480, doesn't have cottages, but it does rent modest but comfortable motel rooms in a residential part of town. These range from rooms with one queen bed for $68 s or d, up to full-kitchen units that sleep four for $106. All rooms have microwaves and fridges, and a continental breakfast is served in the lobby each morning. Winter rates provide skiers with some of the best deals in Jackson: $175 d for a week! The motel is entirely nonsmoking.

Sagebrush Motel, 550 W. Broadway, 307/733-0336 or 888/219-0900, has a variety of units, all for the same prices: $75 for one bed or $90 for two beds. This includes motel rooms and cabins, some of which have kitchenettes. The cabins with kitchenettes are generally your best bet. Sagebrush Motel is open May–October only.

Kudar's Motel, 260 N. Cache Dr., 307/733-2823, offers rather plain motel rooms with "antique" furnishings and microscopic televisions for reasonable prices: $75 d. Of more interest are their rustic log cabins built in 1938. These go for $85–110 d, and the larger ones can sleep five. Open mid-May to mid-Oct.

A recommended place is **Anvil Motel,** 215 N. Cache Dr., 307/733-3668 or 800/234-4507, www.anvilmotel.com, where the modern rooms are $94 d or $119 for two beds (four people). All rooms here have microwaves and small fridges, plus access to the outdoor hot tub. Just around the corner at 240 N. Glenwood is **El Rancho Motel,** with the same owners and phone number as the Anvil. The small rooms here contain older furnishings, fridges, microwaves, and ceiling fans, but no air conditioning. Rooms with one bed cost $75 d; larger rooms with two beds are $112 for up to four people. Guests can use the Anvil Motel's hot tub.

One of the nicer reasonably priced Jackson motels is **Wolf Moon Inn,** 285 N. Cache Dr., 307/733-2287 or 800/964-2387, www.jak -biz.com/wolfmooninn. Clean and spacious rooms feature log furnishings, fridges, microwaves, and ceiling fans (but no air-conditioning). Rates are $85–89 d in standard rooms (some with hot tubs); $159 for six people in two-room suites.

Teton Inn, 165 W. Gill St., 307/733-3883 or 800/429-8873, www.jacksonlodging.com, is a small and friendly motel with rustic interiors and nonsmoking rooms for $89–109 d. No air conditioning.

Ranch Inn, 45 E. Pearl St., 307/733-6363 or 800/348-5599, www.ranchinn.com, offers a wide variety of accommodations just one block from Town Square, all with fridges and microwaves. These include newly remodeled standard rooms ($98 d), tower rooms with balconies facing Snow King, fridges, and microwaves ($155 d), and suites with king beds, wood-burning fireplaces, balconies, and hot tubs ($175–185 d). Extra guests are $5 per person. Other amenities include indoor and outdoor hot tubs and a continental breakfast. Some of the tower rooms are wheelchair accessible.

Nearby Accommodations
One of Jackson's better deals for standard motel rooms is—not surprisingly—**Motel 6,** 1370 W. Broadway, 307/733-1620 or 800/466-8356, www.motel6.com, but even here the summertime rates are $88 s or $94 d. You'll find humdrum rooms and an outdoor pool, but reserve six months in advance for July and August. The off-season rates ($36 s or $42 d) are a much better bargain.

Twelve miles south of Jackson in Hoback Junction, **Hoback River Resort,** 307/733-5129, www.hobackriverresort.com, has large motel rooms and cabins for up to six people on attractive grounds facing the Hoback River. The rooms are very clean and well maintained, but the location—away from busy downtown Jackson—is the real draw here. Rates are $75–85 s or d in motel rooms with decks, or $110–145 d in rustic cabins with full kitchens (but no maid service). Modern cottages (also with full kitchens) are $135–155 for up to four guests. A three-night minimum stay is required in the cabins and cottages.

Located on the south end of Jackson at the "Y" intersection of highways 89 and 22, **Pony Express Motel,** 1075 W. Broadway, 307/733-3835 or 800/526-2658, www.ponyexpress.com, has a seasonal heated outdoor pool, along with standard motel rooms ($85 d or $95 for units with a queen bed and bunks for kids) and units with full kitchens ($130–160).

Right across the highway from Pony Express Motel, **Teton Gables Motel,** 1140 W. Broadway, 307/733-3723, www.tetongables.com, is another recently renovated place with rooms for $100 d. They also have a couple of suites, plus an outdoor hot tub.

$100–150
Many Jackson accommodations fall in the $100–150 range, with pricing factors being location, type of room, quality of furnishings, and presence of amenities such as pools and hot tubs. Several comfortable midrange options are described as follows. These are not the corporate lodging giants, but they offer good value and down-home friendliness.

Downtown Accommodations
Elk Country Inn, 480 W. Pearl, 307/733-2364 or 800/483-8667, www.townsquareinns.com, is popular with families and small groups of travelers. The spacious motel rooms (a bit old-fashioned but nicely maintained) all have three beds and cost $102 d. Also available are loft units that sleep six for $126; add $6 for a kitchenette unit. Modern log cabins with kitchenettes and lodgepole furnishings go for $144 d or $152 for four.

Prospector Inn, 155 N. Jackson, 307/733-4858 or 800/429-8835, www.jacksonlodging.com, offers updated but modest rooms for a decent price: $99–119 d for one or two queen beds (but no air-conditioning), or $169 d for air-conditioned suites with a hot tub and gas fireplace. An outdoor hot tub is available, and the motel is right across the street from a kid-friendly park. A continental breakfast is available each morning.

The rooms are a bit small, but guests appreciate the friendly service and extra touches at **Sundance Inn,** 135 W. Broadway, 307/733-3444 or 888/478-6326, www.sundanceinnjackson.com. The motel is close to Town Square and serves a light homemade breakfast plus evening cookies and lemonade. Guests can also use the outdoor hot tub (with alleyway ambience, alas). Standard rooms cost $104 s or $114 d, while two-room suites are $154 for four people. The hotel does not have air-conditioning.

Antler Inn, 50 W. Pearl Ave., 307/733-2535 or 800/522-2406, www.townsquareinns.com, is a large property with 110 rooms just one block off Town Square. Most contain two queen beds and cost $104 for up to four, but also available are a dozen large family rooms/suites ($130) with three beds and space for six people. Some of these contain wood-burning fireplaces or jetted tubs. Rounding out the options here are some attractive (but small) log-walled rooms for $92 d. All guests have access to an exercise room, sauna, and a big indoor hot tub.

Anglers Inn, 265 N. Millward St., 307/733-3682 or 800/867-4667, www.anglersinn.net, has attractive rooms with Western-style fixtures, lodgepole beds and chairs, and small baths. This cozy motel is right on Flat Creek but just a couple of blocks from Town Square. Rates are $105–115 s or d, and all rooms contain fridges and microwaves.

Four Winds Motel, 150 N. Millward St., 307/733-2474 or 800/228-6461, www.jackson holefourwinds.com, is just a few blocks from Town Square and across the street from a city park (with a popular children's playground). The rooms are not fancy, but they are exceptionally clean and affordably priced: $107 s or d for air-conditioned rooms in this entirely non-smoking motel.

Jackson Hole Lodge, 420 W. Broadway, 307/733-2992 or 800/604-9404, www.jackson holelodge.com, has a diverse mixture of rooms, but the featured attractions are a large indoor swimming pool, wading pool, hot tub, sauna, and game room on attractive grounds. Standard motel rooms are a bit dated but clean and in good condition for $109–134 d. Condo-type units are much nicer, with an upscale decor that includes log furniture; $184 for a studio unit, $219 for a one-bedroom unit (sleeps four) with a living room, fireplace, and full kitchen. Two-bedroom units cost $394 for up to eight people.

Another very comfortable option is **Trapper Inn,** 235 N. Cache Dr., 307/733-2648 or 800/341-8000, www.trapperinn.com, where the spacious standard rooms are $103–137 s or d. Family rooms are $169 for four people, and some have hot tubs and king-size beds. Also available are two-bedroom units that sleep four guests for $231. The motel features indoor and outdoor hot tubs, along with fridges and microwaves in many rooms.

Buckrail Lodge, 110 E. Karns Ave., 307/733-2079, www.buckraillodge.com, is in a quiet part of town six blocks from Town Square. The immaculate grounds include an outdoor hot tub, and the 12 motel rooms are all in faux-log-cabin style. The well-maintained rooms have two queen beds and are decorated with Western-style furnishings. Rates are $110 d or $120 for four people. No air-conditioning or phones in the rooms, and Buckrail is closed mid-October through April.

On the quiet north side of town, **Cache Creek Motel,** 390 N. Glenwood, 307/733-7781 or 800/843-4788, www.cachecreekmotel.com, is a good moderately priced lodging choice. All rooms include full kitchens, and an outdoor hot tub is available. Standard rooms are $110 d or $130 for four people. One-bedroom suites cost $175, and two-bedroom suites are $190; the suites sleep up to six for the same price.

A large heart-of-town place is **49'er Inn & Suites (Quality Inn),** 330 W. Pearl, 307/733-7550 or 800/483-8667, www.townsquare inns.com, with 148 rooms spread across several buildings. Standard rooms have two queen beds and a nothing-special decor for $115 s or d. Newer and considerably nicer are the large kitchenettes for $189 d ($4 per person extra for additional guests); some include fireplaces. Two luxury suites (with hot tub and fireplace) are available for $269 d. All guests have access to an indoor hot tub, sauna, and exercise room, plus a continental breakfast.

Rawhide Motel, 75 S. Millward, 307/733-1216 or 800/835-2999, www.rawhidemotel.com, is a fine place with large rooms containing handmade lodgepole furniture. Rates are $113 s or $117 d; $127 for four.

Golden Eagle Inn, 325 E. Broadway, 307/733-2042 or 888/748-6937, www.golden eagleinn.com, is a quiet family motel with standard rooms for $95–123 d, and larger rooms for $141–175 d. All include microwaves and small refrigerators, plus access to the heated seasonal pool. Adjacent is a two-bedroom house with a full kitchen for $267 d.

Nearby Accommodations

With 170 units, **Virginian Lodge,** 750 W. Broadway, 307/733-2792 or 800/262-4999, www.virginianlodge.com, is one of the larger local motels. The rooms cluster around a grassy central space with a seasonal heated pool and hot tub. A variety of ho-hum rooms are available, including standard units for $95 s or d, kitchenette suites for $135 d, and two-bedroom suites for $185 d. Virginian RV Park is right behind the motel.

Super 8 Motel, 750 South U.S. Hwy. 89, 307/733-6833 or 800/800-8000, www.super8 .com, offers predictable chain-motel rooms (some with fridges and microwaves). Weekend rates are $100–150 d; $10 less on weekdays.

Two midpriced motels are adjacent to each other and one mile north of Jackson on U.S. 89. Both face the Elk Refuge (and the busy highway). **Elk Refuge Inn,** 307/733-3582 or 800/544-3582, www.elkrefugeinn.com, is the smaller and more homey of the two, with a mixture of rooms and friendly management, plus corrals where horses can be boarded at no additional charge. Rates are $105 s or d ($10 per person for extra guests), and all rooms contain fridges, microwaves, and a small deck. A family room ($125 for six) and kitchenettes ($115 d) are also available. All rooms have drive-up access, but no air-conditioning. **Flat Creek Inn,** 307/733-5276 or 800/438-9338, www.flatcreekinn.com, is a large two-level motel just a few hundred feet north of Elk Refuge Inn. The rooms are functionally furnished, and all include microwaves and small fridges. Standard rooms cost $95–114 for up to four guests, and spacious kitchenettes are $140 for up to five. Motel amenities include a hot tub, sauna, and ski-waxing room.

In the heart of Teton Village action, and right next to the tram, **Village Center Inn,** 307/733-3990 or 800/443-8613, www.jhresortlodging.com, charges $110–125 s or d for studio or loft units and $165 for two-bedroom units that sleep six. All units include full kitchens. Peak season winter rates rise to $175 d for a one-bedroom unit, up to $230 for two bedrooms. The decor is fairly utilitarian, but other than Hostel X, this is the cheapest Teton Village accommodation.

It's quite a distance from Jackson, but **Hatchet Resort,** 307/543-2413 or 877/543-2413, www.hatchetresort.com, has clean accommodations and a friendly staff in a delightful country setting. Located in Buffalo Valley, 39 miles northeast of Jackson (eight miles east of Moran Junction) on U.S. Hwy. 26/287, the motel is open year-round. Well-maintained log-walled motel rooms go for $95–105 d, and modern log suites with vaulted ceilings, fridges, microwaves, and hot tubs are $215 d. Hatchet also has five simple "hostel" rooms with shared baths for $65 d. A restaurant, bar/pizzeria, general store, and gas station are also on the premises.

Log Cabin Motels

Several local motels offer log cabin accommodations for a step back to the Old West while keeping such newer amenities as televisions and private baths. Set amid tall cottonwood trees, **Wagon Wheel Village,** 435 N. Cache Dr., 307/733-2357 or 800/323-9279, www.wagonwheelvillage.com, has well-maintained and cozy log cabins and log motel units. These go for $100–170 d, depending on the amenities. The most luxurious are modern log cabin–style suites ($170 for up to six people), each with a fireplace, fridge, microwave, and small deck facing Flat Creek. All guests have access to two outside hot tubs at this friendly, family-run place.

Near a busy Jackson intersection, **Cowboy Village Resort,** 120 Flat Creek Dr., 307/733-3121 or 800/962-4988, www.townsquareinn.com, has 82 modern, but jammed-together cabins with kitchenettes. The cabins start at $135 d ($145 for four) in a cabin with two queen bunkbeds, up to $169 d ($179 for four) with one queen bed and a sleeper sofa. Guests have access to two enclosed hot tubs.

Other places with log units are described earlier: Elk Country Inn, Sagebrush Motel, Hoback River Resort, Kudar's Motel, and Hatchet Resort.

$150 AND UP

It should come as no surprise that tony Jackson Hole has several elaborate, pricey, and sumptuous places to stay, with rooms starting around $150 and hitting the stratosphere at more than $1,000 per night.

JACKSON HOLE

Downtown Accommodations

Close to Town Square, the **Wort Hotel,** 50 N. Glenwood St., 307/733-2190 or 800/322-2727, www.worthotel.com, has been a Jackson favorite since 1941 and is the only downtown hotel earning a four-diamond rating from AAA. A disastrous 1980 fire—started by a bird that built a nest too close to a neon sign—destroyed the roof and upper floor. The hotel was completely restored within a year, and today it's better than ever, with such modern amenities as a fitness center and two hot tubs. The lobby, with its grand central staircase and stone fireplace with crackling fire, makes a fine place to meet friends. The Silver Dollar Bar & Grill serves meals, or you can sidle up to the famous curving bar—inlaid with 2,032 uncirculated silver dollars from 1921. The Wort's spacious rooms are attractively decorated with a New West motif that includes lodgepole-pine beds, creative fixtures, and barbed-wire-patterned wallpaper. Rates are $235 d for standard rooms (with two queens or one king bed), or $260 d for larger and more luxurious rooms. Spacious junior suites with king beds and wet bars cost $325, while the three-bedroom luxury suite will set you back $485 d.

An outstanding in-town choice is **Parkway Inn,** 125 N. Jackson St., 307/733-3143 or 800/247-8390, www.parkwayinn.com. This midsize lodge has a delightful Victorian ambience with antique furniture and quilts in every room. The rooms are immaculate, and guests will also enjoy a small indoor lap pool, two hot tubs, two saunas, and a gym in the basement. A light breakfast is served in the lobby each morning. Rates are $169 d for standard rooms with two queen beds or a king bed, $199 for larger suites, or $209 d for two-room suites; $12 each for additional guests (maximum of four in a room).

An excellent nine-room lodge just a few blocks from Town Square, **Inn on the Creek,** 295 N. Millwood, 307/739-1565 or 800/669-9534, www.innonthecreek.com, has a peaceful location beside Flat Creek. Standard rooms ($179–199 s or d) feature designer furnishings, down comforters, and VCRs. The deluxe rooms ($209–229 s or d) also include balconies, fireplaces, and in-room hot tubs, while a gorgeous suite ($379) sleeps four and has a full kitchen, hot tub bath, and private patio. A light breakfast is served in the lounge, and all guests have access to the outdoor hot tub facing the creek.

Downtown's Wort Hotel, rebuilt after a disastrous fire, is better than ever.

A very attractive downtown lodging option is **Davy Jackson Inn,** 85 Perry Ave., 307/739-2294 or 800/584-0532, www.davyjackson.com, where modern rooms ($199 d) come in a variety of styles, including some with old-fashioned clawfoot tubs. A full breakfast is delivered to your room each morning, and guests can relax in the outdoor hot tub. The two honeymoon suites ($249 d) include steam showers, gas fireplaces, and king-size canopy beds.

Rusty Parrot Lodge and Spa, 175 N. Jackson, 307/733-2000 or 800/458-2004, www.rustyparrot.com, offers outstanding accommodation just two blocks from Town Square. The 31 rooms feature handcrafted furniture, original artwork, oversize tubs, and goose-down comforters; some also contain fireplaces and hot tubs. A gourmet breakfast (it's never the same) is served each morning in the luxurious dining room, and guests can relax in the hot tub on a deck overlooking Jackson, borrow a book from the library, or enjoy a massage, aromatherapy session, or facial from Body Sage Day Spa (extra charge). Rates are $284–329 s or d for standard rooms, or $500 d for the luxurious suite. No children under age 12 are allowed. The lodge also serves gourmet dinners each evening to its guests (and others).

Other Jackson Hotels

Days Inn of Jackson Hole, 1280 W. Broadway, 307/739-9010 or 800/329-7466, www.daysinnjacksonhole.com, has comfortable and modern rooms at the south end of town. Standard rooms cost $159 s or d, while suites with fireplaces and hot tubs go for $209–229. Amenities include a light breakfast, large hot tub, sauna, and in-room safes, plus microwaves and fridges in some rooms.

Wyoming Inn (Red Lion), 930 W. Broadway, 307/734-0035 or 800/844-0035, www.wyoming-inn.com, is a corporate-style hotel with a ludicrously ostentatious lobby and southside location. It isn't downtown, but you'd never know it by the prices. Most of the large rooms go for $239 d, including a light breakfast and access to the hot tub. The nicest rooms have fireplaces and hot tubs, with a luxury suite for $419 d.

Guests have free access to the health club across the street, and a free airport shuttle.

The Lodge at Jackson Hole (Best Western), 80 S. Scott Lane, 307/739-9703 or 800/458-3866, www.lodgeatjh.com, is a three-story building sandwiched between strip malls on the south end of Jackson. The large guest rooms feature mini-bars, microwaves, safes, and two queen beds (or a king) for $229 d. Hotel guests are treated to a buffet breakfast, a distinctive indoor/outdoor heated pool, hot tubs, and a sauna, plus access to the Jackson Hole Athletic Club and a free winter shuttle to Teton Village.

Snow King Resort

Located at the base of Jackson's in-town ski hill, and just a few blocks from downtown, Snow King Resort, 400 E. Snow King, 307/733-5200 or 800/522-5464, www.snowking.com, includes more than 200 hotel rooms and 58 condos, plus such amenities as a year-round heated outdoor pool and two hot tubs, a sauna, an exercise facility, restaurants, a bar, a concierge, a business center, a game room, and a spa. A free shuttle provides connections to the airport and Teton Village (winters), and guests receive discounted passes for Snow King Ski Area. When the snow is gone, Snow King is a popular destination for meetings, offering 40,000 square feet of conference space. A winter ice rink is close by, and in summer a slide and miniature golf course attract the kids. Hotel rooms at Snow King cost $200–210 d, and two-room suites are $200–400 d. Condos start at $200 d, up to an ultra-luxurious four-bedroom unit that will set you back $600 per night; this is where the Secret Service agents stay when Vice President Dick Cheney is in town.

Spring Creek Ranch

Some of the most dramatic vistas of the Tetons are from the luxurious Spring Creek Ranch, 307/733-8833 or 800/443-6139, www.springcreekranch.com. Located on a thousand-acre estate, the resort sits high atop Gros Ventre Butte four miles west of Jackson and includes a wide range of lodging options. Hotel rooms are $250 d, and suites cost $310 for four people. Studio units run $275; one- to three-bedroom condos are $375–695 and sleep four to six. Also available are executive four-bedroom homes that sleep eight and cost a mere $2,200 per night. All rooms at Spring Creek Ranch contain fireplaces and lodgepole furnishings, and the condos and studios have full kitchens. Other amenities include a private pond, tennis courts, an outdoor pool, a hot tub, a fitness center, and a day spa with massage and other offerings.

Teton Pines Resort

Located four miles south of Teton Village, Teton Pines Resort & Country Club, 307/733-1005 or 800/238-2223, www.tetonpines.com, features the amenities you'd expect in a year-round resort, including an 18-hole golf course, tennis center, and classy restaurant. The accommodations are varied, but all include a continental breakfast, access to the outdoor pool and hot tub, athletic-club privileges, concierge service, and an airport shuttle. One-bedroom units (with separate his and hers baths) are $395 d, while two-bedroom and living-room suites cost $750 d ($40 per person extra for additional guests). The resort also has two furnished three-bedroom townhouses, each with a kitchen, two decks, a fireplace, washer and dryer, and garage. These sleep up to eight for $950 per night.

Amangani

Atop Gros Ventre Butte near Spring Creek Ranch is stunning **Amangani,** 307/734-7333 or 877/734-7333, www.amanresorts.com, the only representative of Amanresorts in America. (Most of the company's other lavish resorts are in Southeast Asia.) Aman groupies and business travelers know to expect the utmost in luxury, and they will certainly not be disappointed here, starting with a knowledgeable staff and spare-no-expenses construction. The three-story sandstone-faced hotel contains 40 suites, each with a patined-metal fireplace, mountain-facing balcony, king-size bed, deep soaking tub (with a window view), minibar, and terrazzo dining table. Amangani's central lobby is particularly impressive, blending sandstone columns, redwood accents, custom furnishings, and soaring

two-story windows. Outside, those soaking in a whirlpool and heated 35-meter pool enjoy a remarkable view of the Tetons. Among other amenities are a complete health center (exercise facility, gym, steam rooms, yoga and meditation classes, and massage), a gourmet restaurant (The Grill) that specializes in steaks, chops, and seafood, and a lounge. Amangani's accommodations include suites ($700 d), six deluxe suites ($825 d), four large luxury suites with two baths and spacious balconies ($900 d), and the premier Sena suite ($1,100) for the utmost in luxury.

Teton Village Lodges

If you're looking for beautifully appointed accommodations in Teton Village instead of downtown Jackson, you can't go wrong at **Snake River Lodge & Spa,** 307/733-3657 or 800/445-4655, www.snakeriverlodge.com. The lodge features a New West–style lobby with stone fireplaces and whimsically carved bears, plus rooms that continue the theme with rustic lamps, pine furniture, and colorful prints. A gorgeous free-form indoor/outdoor heated pool has a cascading waterfall, and other attractions include indoor and outdoor hot tubs, a sauna, ski lockers, a ski-in concierge service, and a five-story spa and health club with exercise equipment, facials, manicures, hydrotherapy, massages, soaking tubs, and steam baths. Rates are $200–500 d in the guest rooms or $350–1,500 d in the condominiums.

Also in Teton Village, **Alpenhof Lodge,** 307/733-3242 or 800/732-3244, www.jacksonhole.com/alpenhof, exudes a European ambience, and its owners come from Switzerland and Germany. Some of the recently remodeled rooms follow through with Bavarian furnishings, and all guests have access to the heated year-round outdoor pool, hot tub, and sauna. Summertime rates start at $134 d for the simplest rooms, up to $418 for four people in their nicest suite. Winter ski-season rates are $193–538 d.

Jackson Hole's newest upmarket lodging option, **Teton Mountain Lodge,** 307/734-7111 or 800/801-6615, www.tetonlodge.com, sits at the base of the mountain in Teton Village. The lodge offers an array of amenities and services, including indoor and outdoor heated pools, hot tubs, a fitness center/spa, and underground parking. Guests can choose rooms or studios for $275–375 d, or one-, two-, or three-bedroom suites for $350–800.

Another Teton Village option is **The Inn at Jackson Hole (Best Western),** 307/733-2311 or 800/842-7666, www.innatjh.com, where standard rooms (recently renovated with log furniture) cost $189–209 d. Family-friendly loft suites with kitchenettes are $249 d (plus $10 per person for additional guests). The hotel also has an outdoor heated pool, three outdoor hot tubs, a sauna, and ski lockers.

Four Seasons Resort, 307/734-5040 or 800/819-5053, www.fourseasons.com/jackson-hole, opens in time for the 2003–2004 ski season and includes a 124-room luxury hotel with ski-in access, 57 condos (most with fractional ownership), a fine-dining restaurant and après ski bar, and an outdoor heated pool and hot tub, health club, and spa. They're all under one roof in Wyoming's third-largest building.

BED-AND-BREAKFASTS

Jackson hosts many fine B&Bs, where those who can afford it can relax in comfort at the homes of locals. Be sure to reserve space far ahead during the peak summer season, although you might get lucky at the last minute if someone cancels. The **Jackson Hole Bed & Breakfast Association's** website, www.jacksonholebnb.com, has links to a half-dozen local B&Bs, all of which are described as follows.

Teton View

On the way to Teton Village, Teton View B&B, 2136 Coyote Loop, 307/733-7954 or 866/504-7954, www.tetonview.com, features two guest rooms that share a bath ($115 d) and one with its own bath ($150 d). Guests enjoy a full breakfast and a dramatic view of the Tetons from the indoor hot tub. A five-night minimum stay is required in winter and two nights in summer. The owners also rent out a comfortable cabin with space for six, a kitchen, and private yard; $175 d plus $20 per person for additional guests.

Breakfast is not included, and the cabin is available only in the summer.

Alpine House Country Inn

You'll find outdoorsy owners at Alpine House Country Inn, 285 N. Glenwood, 307/739-1570 or 800/753-1421, www.alpinehouse.com; both Hans and Nancy Johnstone were skiers for U.S. Olympic teams. The modern timber-frame lodge is just two blocks from Jackson's Town Square and has 21 guest rooms in two connected buildings. Both are bright and modern, accented by Swedish-style stenciling on the walls. All rooms have private baths and balconies, plus access to the outdoor hot tub. A healthy full breakfast is served, along with evening wine and cheese. Rates are $155 d in the original rooms, and $170–215 d in the new building, which also features TVs and air-conditioning, along with gas fireplaces and hot tubs in most rooms. Suites cost $265 for up to four guests. Children are welcome for $25 extra.

Huff House Inn

For quiet close-to-downtown accommodations, another fine option is The Huff House Inn, 240 E. Deloney Ave., 307/733-4164, www.jackson wyomingbnb.com. Built in 1916, this was for many years the home of one of Jackson's first doctors, Charles Huff. Today it is a gracious place with a feminine sense of style. The three guest rooms ($139 d) are attractive, and all have private baths. Also available are four modern cottages with cathedral ceilings, king-size beds, sleeper-sofas, VCRs, and hot tubs. These go for $215 d. An outdoor hot tub is on the premises, and a creative full breakfast is served family-style each morning. Kids are welcome in the cottages. A three-night minimum is generally required, but shorter stays may be available.

The Painted Porch

On the road to Teton Village, The Painted Porch, 3755 N. Moose-Wilson Rd., 307/733-1981, www.jacksonholebedandbreakfast.com, was built in 1901 in Idaho and moved here many years later. Located on three acres and surrounded by a white picket fence and tall aspen trees, this rambling red farmhouse has a guest room ($160 d) with a king bed, and a two-room suite ($225 d) with space for the kids. Each has a microwave, fridge, TV/VCR, private bath with jetted tub, and access to the game room that includes a pool table. For more privacy, stay in the adjacent cottage for $180 d. The fridge has juice and fruit, or you can join breakfast in the house for an extra $20. An outdoor hot tub and game room with pool table are available for guests, and children are welcome ($25 extra) in the suite and cabin. A two-night minimum stay is required; closed Nov. to late Dec. and Apr. to mid-June.

Teton Treehouse

A personal favorite—it gets high marks from all who visit—is Teton Treehouse B&B, 307/733-3233, www.cruising-america.com/tetontreehouse, a gorgeous four-story hillside home in Wilson. This spacious open-beam B&B sits up 95 steps (needless to say, it's not accessible for disabled people) and contains six guest rooms with private baths. It really does offer the feeling of living in a treehouse, and it's a great place for birdwatchers. Decks provide impressive views across the valley below, and you can soak in the outdoor hot tub each evening and enjoy a healthy full breakfast each morning. Rooms cost $165–200 d. No young children, but ages 10 and older are welcome. There's a three-night minimum stay in July and August.

Sassy Moose Inn

Near the Aspens along the road to Teton Village, The Sassy Moose Inn, 307/733-1277 or 800/356-1277, www.sassymoose.com, is a modest log house with five guest rooms, each with private bath, TV, and VCR. A full breakfast is served each morning, along with complimentary wine and fruit in the evening. An indoor hot tub is also available. Rates are $129–189 d. Family rooms provide space for kids, and pets are welcome (a rarity for B&Bs).

Wildflower Inn

A recommended place is Wildflower Inn, 307/733-4710, www.jacksonholewildflower .com. This spacious log house sits on three acres of country land along Teton Village Road and contains five bright guest rooms. Four rooms have their own private decks, and all contain private baths and handcrafted lodgepole beds. One of the rooms is actually a suite with a separate sitting room, hot tub, and gas fireplace. Wildflower's hot tub occupies a plant-filled solarium. The owner/builders are an Exum climbing guide and a former ski instructor. Rates are $220–260 d ($340 d in the suite) including an earthy breakfast served family-style. Children are welcome.

Bentwood

One of the most impressive local lodging options is Bentwood B&B, just north of the junction on the road to Teton Village, 307/739-1411, www.bentwoodinn.com. This 6,000-square-foot log home sits amid tall cottonwood trees and is a favorite place for weddings and receptions. The grand living room is centered on a three-story stone fireplace, and each of the five luxurious guest rooms has its own fireplace, TV, deck or balcony, and jetted tub. The loft room is perfect for families. The interior is filled with Western styling and English antiques, not to mention gracious hosts and the enormous chocolate Lab. Drinks and hors d'oeuvres are served each evening, and morning brings a creative breakfast. Rates are $255–325 d. Children are welcome in this very special place. A three-night minimum stay is sometimes required in the summer.

Don't Fence Me Inn

This 5,000-square-foot custom log home sits on six acres along Teton Village Road, 307/733-7979, www.dontfencemeinn.com. The home is set back from the road, with a pond in the back and an active osprey nest nearby. Four large bedrooms ($199 d) and a suite ($259 for up to four guests) are available, all with private baths. Relax in the large common area with its crackling fire or soak in the outdoor hot tub. A gourmet breakfast is served each morning, and children are welcome.

CONDOMINIUM RENTALS

Condominiums provide a popular option for families and groups visiting Jackson Hole. These privately owned places are maintained by several local property-management companies and range from small studio apartments to spacious five-bedroom houses. All are completely furnished (including dishes) and have fireplaces, cable TV, phones, and midstay maid service. The nicest also include access to pools and hot tubs and have balconies overlooking the spectacular Tetons. Many of the condominiums are in Teton Village (adjacent to the ski area) or just to the south in Teton Pines or the Aspens; others are scattered around Jackson Hole.

Condo prices vary widely, but during the winter holiday season (Christmas to early January), expect to pay $160–185 per night for studios (one or two people). Two-bedroom units (up to four people) cost $275–425 per night, and full four-bedroom condos (these sleep eight and also have a private hot tub and stone fireplace) are $720–800. The most sumptuous places, such as those at the base of the tram, will set you back $1,500 per night in the peak winter season! Summer and off-peak winter rates are typically 35–45 percent lower, with spring and fall rates 50–75 percent less than peak-season prices. In fall or spring, condos offer a real bargain for traveling families looking to stay several nights in the area. Minimum stays of 2–7 nights are required throughout the year, with the longest minimum stays required in the peak winter season. Midstay maid service is generally offered if you stay more than five nights.

If you have the luxury of time, do a little comparison shopping before renting a condo. Things to ask include whether you have access to a pool and hot tub, how close you are to the ski slopes, how frequent the maid service is, and whether the units include such amenities as VCRs and washing machines. Also be sure to find out what beds are in the rooms because couples might not enjoy sleeping in twin bunk beds.

Condo Companies

For condo rental information, including prices and available dates, you can go to www.jackson holenet.com and click on lodging for connections to most of the larger condo companies. You can also contact the following companies directly:

Black Diamond Vacation Rentals, 307/733-6170 or 800/325-8605, www.blackdiamond vrre.com

Ely & Associates, 307/733-8604 or 800/735-8310, www.jackson-hole-vacations.com

Jackson Hole Lodge, 307/733-2992 or 800/604-9404, www.jacksonholelodge.com

Jackson Hole Resort Lodging, 307/733-3990 or 800/443-8613, www.jhresortlodging.com

Jackson Home Management, 307/739-3000 or 800/739-3009, www.wy-biz.com/jacksonhome

Mountain Property Management, 307/733-1684 or 800/992-9948, www.mpmjh.com

MTA Resorts of Jackson Hole, 307/733-0613 or 800/272-8824, www.mtaresorts.com

Rendezvous Mountain Rentals, 307/739-9050 or 888/739-2565, www.rmrentals.com

Snow King Resort Condominiums, 307/733-5200 or 800/522-5464, www.snowking.com

Spring Creek Ranch, 307/733-8833 or 800/443-6139, www.springcreekranch.com

Teton Pines Resort & Country Club, 307/733-1005 or 800/238-2223, www.tetonpines.com

The largest of these companies—and a good place to begin your search—is Jackson Hole Resort Lodging. Owned by Jackson Hole Mountain Resort, it manages more than 260 units, more than all of the other companies combined. Among the largest of the other management companies on the list are Black Diamond Vacation Rentals, Jackson Hole Lodge, and Snow King Resort Condominiums.

In contrast to the condo rental companies, **Teton Club** has the only fractional-ownership condos in Jackson Hole, located in Teton Pines and available for 2–5 weeks per year. Get details at 307/734-7679 or 877/838-6677, www.teton club.com.

CABINS

Several Jackson Hole places offer log cabin accommodations for a taste of old-time living. These small places are generally rented for several days or a week at a time and are favorites of families and groups. They may or may not have TVs and phones, and maid service may not be on a daily basis. In addition to these places, several log cabin motels were described previously, with others available in Grand Teton National Park and at Teton Village KOA.

North of Jackson

Out in the quiet town of Kelly (12 miles northeast of Jackson), **Anne Kent Cabins,** 307/733-4773, www.annekentcabins.com, offers rustic accommodations with an unbeatable Teton view. These cabins are perfect for those who want a real taste of Wyoming from a family with a long local history. Two rental options are available. Your best bet is to request the very comfortable log house, which has bedrooms in the loft and basement, two baths, a complete kitchen, washer, and dryer. The home could sleep 12 people in a pinch and goes for $200 per night (plus $25 per person for more than four guests). Next door are two cabins that rent together and sleep four guests for $150. The front one (built in 1939) includes a bedroom and kitchen, while the back cabin contains a second bedroom plus bath. The Anne Kent Cabins feature handmade lodgepole furniture created by co-owner Ron Davler, who crafts them at the adjacent Jackson Hole Log & Rawhide Furniture. Kids under 12 are free.

Moulton Ranch on Historic Mormon Row, 307/733-3749, www.moultonranchcabins.com, offers several cabins in one of Jackson Hole's most majestic locations. This is the only private property on Mormon Row inside Grand Teton National Park, and the much-photographed Moulton Barn—one of the prototypical Wyoming images—is just a few hundred feet away. The four cabins are cozy but not at all elaborate. Nevertheless, where else might you awake to a spectacular Teton vista with bison grazing outside your window? Rates start at $85 for a two-person cabin with a separate bathhouse, up to $135 for four people in the bunkhouse. The latter is especially poplar and features a kitchenette, deck, and picture window facing the Tetons.

Budges' Slide Lake Cabins, 307/733-9061, www.jacksonholecabins.com, are four secluded but modern cabins along Slide Lake, six miles east of Kelly. Each has a woodstove, full kitchen, VCRs, and phone. Rates are $215 d,

© DON PITCHER

The Anne Kent Cabins in Kelly offer a great view of the Tetons and a taste of old-time Wyoming.

plus $10 each for each additional guest (maximum of eight). Weekly rates are $1,300 d. Open year-round.

Split Creek Ranch, 307/733-7522, www.split creekranch.com, is seven miles north of Jackson and right along the Snake River. The ranch covers 25 acres of land and is a good place to see elk, moose, and other animals. Nine rooms are available. Eight of these are attractive log motel–type units ($95–110 d; plus $10 per person for additional guests) with either kitchenettes or microwaves and fridges. A separate honeymoon cabin ($250 d) includes a fireplace, full kitchen, and private hot tub. Evening campfires are a favorite of guests, and other amenities include a stocked fishing pond and continental breakfasts. There's a two-night minimum stay, and Split Creek is open mid-May through September.

Buffalo Valley

Buffalo Valley Ranch, 307/543-2026 or 888/543-2477, www.heartsix.com, has six cabins with fine views across Buffalo Valley to the Tetons. Three of these cabins are basic older units that share a bathhouse and cost a very reasonable $60 d. A separate triplex log building houses a one-bedroom unit ($100 d), along with a pair of two-bedroom units ($150 for up to four guests), all with kitchenettes and private baths. They're next to Heart Six Ranch in Buffalo Valley, 45 miles northeast of Jackson.

You'll discover spectacular views of the Tetons from **Luton's Teton Cabins,** 36 miles northeast of Jackson (five miles east of Moran Junction), 307/543-2489, www.tetoncabins.com. The modern duplex cabins have full kitchens, private baths, and front porches facing the mountains. One-bedroom units cost $162 d, and two-bedroom units are $250–285 for up to six people. They're open May–November and have horse boarding facilities.

South of Jackson

Camp Creek Inn, 16 miles south of Jackson in quiet Hoback Canyon, 307/733-3099 or 877/338-4868, www.camp-creek-inn.com, has nine A-frame cabins costing $89 for up to four people, or $134 for a unit with three double beds. No TVs or phones in the rooms, but a bar and restaurant are on the grounds. Camp Creek also offers horseback rides, pack trips, fishing trips, and wintertime snowmobiling.

HOUSE RENTALS

Jackson Hole home rentals are available from **Ely & Associates,** 307/733-8604 or 800/735-8310, www.jackson-hole-vacations.com; **Mountain Property Management,** 307/733-1684 or 800/992-9948, www.mpmjh.com; **Prime Properties of Jackson Hole,** 307/733-7440 or 800/800-6455, www.jackson-hole-wyoming-real-estate.com; **Rendezvous Mountain Rentals,** 307/739-9050 or 888/739-2565, www.rm-rentals.com; and **Rocking-V Lodge,** 307/733-7319, www.rocking-v.com.

Rancho Alegre Lodge, 3600 S. Park Loop Rd., 307/733-7988, www.ranchoalegre.com, offers Jackson's most expensive lodging. On a 50-acre spread facing the Tetons, this 10,000-square-foot structure houses seven bedrooms (each with its own TV, phone, feather bed, and fridge) and offers an upscale hunting lodge decor along with such amenities as concierge service, a private chef (additional fee for meals), seven fireplaces, extensive decks, a hot tub, and a pool table. Full house rentals are $2,250 per night, with a five-night minimum stay in the summer. Up to 14 people can stay for this price, or save money and rent it all month for the bargain rate of $50,000! At these prices, the lodge is primarily used for weddings, corporate retreats, large (and wealthy) families, and ski groups.

HOME SWAPS

In addition to the lodging places described, visitors to Jackson Hole may want to investigate a house exchange. Several online companies list homeowners in Jackson who are interested in a trade if you have an upscale home, especially one on the beach in midwinter! If you live in Hawaii or Florida and want to go skiing, your home might be a hot property. If you live in North Dakota, good luck. Companies worth investigating include **Home Exchange** 310/798-3864

or 800/877-8723, www.homeexchange.com;
Home Link, 813/975-9825 or 800/638-3841,
www.swapnow.com; **Intervac,** 800/756-4663,
www.intervacus.com; and **Holi-Swaps,** www
.holi-swaps.com.

GUEST RANCHES

Several of Wyoming's best-known and most luxurious dude ranches are in Jackson Hole, providing wonderful places for families who are
looking to rough-it in style. In addition to the
local places listed alphabetically, many more guest
ranches are just over Togwotee Pass in the Dubois
area and to the south in the Pinedale area; get details on these ranches in the Wind River Mountains Country chapter.

Flat Creek Ranch

Located at the base of Sheep Mountain, Flat
Creek Ranch, 307/733-0603 or 866/522-3344,
www.flatcreekranch.com, is packed with history. The land was originally homesteaded by
cowboy, hunting guide, and rustler Cal Car-
rington, but he sold it to his close friend,
"Countess" Cissy Patterson in 1923. Previously married to a Polish count, Cissy came from a
wealthy Chicago newspaper family, but her love
of the West and horses matched Cal's. For two
decades Cissy and Cal were grist for the gossip
mill, mostly during her trips to Wyoming, but
also when she took him along on a grand tour of
Europe. Cissy died in 1948, and her relatives
now own the ranch. After a long hiatus and extensive improvements in 2001, this historic
ranch in a gorgeous setting is once again open
for guests. The emphasis is on fly-fishing in legendary Flat Creek; the ranch owns 1.5 miles
along the stream. Other activities include horseback rides and hikes into the Gros Ventre
Wilderness, boating, and a wood-fired sauna
for chilly evenings. There's a three-night minimum stay in the summer; $420 for two people
per night, all-inclusive. There are separate family periods and times when kids aren't allowed.
The ranch is 15 miles up a bumpy dirt road, but
the ranch provides transportation if you don't
have a four-wheel-drive with high clearance.

Goosewing Ranch

Looking for a peaceful place to relax? Twenty
miles up a dirt road in undeveloped Gros Ventre
Valley (30 miles northeast of Jackson), Goosewing Ranch, 307/733-5251 or 888/733-5251,
www.goosewingranch.com, is one of the most remote guest ranches in Jackson Hole. The well-
appointed modern log cabins have fireplaces,
private baths, and decks. Guests can use the outdoor hot tub all year and the outdoor heated
pool in the summer. Popular summertime activities include horseback excursions, riding in-
struction, fishing, and hiking. All-inclusive
weekly summertime rates are $3,260 for two
people. There's a three-night minimum stay.
When winter arrives, the ranch becomes a favorite destination for snowmobiling, with a variety of packages available.

Gros Ventre River Ranch

This small ranch has accommodations for up to
34 guests in modern log cabins and a homestead
house and is known for its delicious meals. The
ranch sits up undiscovered Gros Ventre River
Valley, 18 miles northeast of Jackson near Slide
Lake. The main activities are horseback riding,
world-class fly-fishing, cookouts, canoeing, and
mountain biking. The lodge has a pool table,
table tennis, and a large-screen television. A one-
week minimum stay is required May–October,
and summertime weekly all-inclusive rates are
$2,720 for two people. Contact Gros Ventre
River Ranch at 307/733-4138, www.grosventre
riverranch.com.

Heart Six Ranch

This classic family dude ranch is in the heart of
Buffalo Valley, 12 miles east of Moran Junction
and 43 miles northeast of Jackson. Horseback
rides are a star attraction, along with kids' programs, day trips to Yellowstone National Park
and the Jackson Hole rodeo, and a range of
evening activities including cookouts, nature
programs, and country music. All-inclusive weekly rates are $2,900 for two people. The ranch
takes in up to 50 guests at a time and is open
year-round. Only weekly stays are available
June–August, but at other times of the year the

ranch offers nightly lodging. This is a favorite base for snowmobilers mid-December through March. Contact Heart Six Ranch at 307/543-2477 or 888/543-2477, www.heartsix.com.

Lost Creek Ranch

Wyoming's most elaborate—and expensive—guest ranch, Lost Creek Ranch, 307/733-3435, www.lostcreek.com, is 21 miles north of Jackson. This showplace resort emphasizes fitness, with a spa facility that includes exercise classes, a weight room, steam room, sauna, and hot tub, along with massage and facials (extra charge). Guests stay in modern duplex log cabins and enjoy gourmet meals in the main lodge's patio overlooking the Tetons. Amenities include such nontraditional items as a heated swimming pool, tennis courts, and a skeet range, in addition to more standard horseback riding, kids' programs, float trips, hiking, Yellowstone tours, and fly-fishing. It's all a bit too Disneyesque for my tastes, and the prices are too Madison Avenue. Weekly all-inclusive rates run $5,400 for two people in a duplex cabin or an astounding $12,425 for four people (even if two of these are children!) in a luxurious two-bedroom, two-bath cabin with a living room and fireplace. Some consider this a small price to pay for such pampering. The ranch hosts up to 60 guests at a time and is open late May to mid-October. A one-week minimum stay is required except after Labor Day, when it drops to a three-night minimum.

Moose Head Ranch

You may get lucky and find a space at historic Moose Head Ranch, 13 miles north of Moose, 307/733-3141 in summer or 850/877-1431 the rest of the year. This family ranch has space for 45 guests, and it receives so many repeat customers that it's almost always booked up. The ranch is entirely surrounded by Grand Teton National Park and features modern log cabins, horseback riding, private trout ponds, fly-fishing lessons, and excellent meals. There's a five-night minimum stay, and all-inclusive rates are $3,750 per week for two people. The ranch is open mid-June through late August.

R Lazy S Ranch

Another historic dude ranch is R Lazy S Ranch, 13 miles northeast of Jackson, 307/733-2655, www.rlazys.com. The ranch has space for 45 guests, who enjoy horseback rides, fishing, and other Western adventures. Tykes under age seven are not allowed, but teenagers can take advantage of a special program just for them. A one-week minimum stay is required. All-inclusive rates are $2,225–3,110 for two people per week, and the ranch is open early June through September.

Red Rock Ranch

Located along the rolling Gros Ventre River, Red Rock Ranch, 307/733-6288, www.theredrock ranch.com, faces spectacular orange-red badlands. The ranch is 32 miles northeast of Jackson, and the quiet location and drop-dead-gorgeous scenery are reason enough to stay here. Guests settle into comfortable log cabins with woodstoves, and they can take part in horseback riding, cattle drives, cookouts, and other activities. The ranch also features kids' programs, stocked fishing ponds, a swimming pool, and a hot tub. There's space for a maximum of 30 guests, and a six-night minimum stay is required. Open June to early Sept. All-inclusive weekly rates are $3,170 for two adults.

Spotted Horse Ranch

Located on the banks of the Hoback River, 16 miles south of Jackson, this ranch exudes a comfortable rusticity. The main lodge and cabins contain lodgepole furniture, and guests stay in log cabins with modern conveniences. Activities include horseback riding (some Appaloosas), fly-fishing, and cookouts, and you can unwind in the hot tub or sauna. All-inclusive weekly rates are $3,800 for two adults. A three-night minimum stay is required. Contact Spotted Horse Ranch at 307/733-2097 or 800/528-2084, www.spotted horseranch.com.

Triangle X Ranch

Located within Grand Teton National Park, 25 miles north of Jackson, Triangle X Ranch, 307/733-2183 or 888/860-0005, www.trianglex.com, is a classic family-oriented ranch with unmatched

Teton views. The ranch has been in the Turner family for more than six decades, and the acclaimed author Barry Lopez once worked as a wrangler here. Horseback riding is the main focus, but they also offer kids' programs and nightly events such as Dutch-oven cookouts, naturalist presentations, square dancing, and campfire sing-alongs. All-inclusive weekly rates are $2,600 for two adults. The ranch is open May–October and January–March. In winter Triangle X goes upscale, with fewer guests (maximum of 35 versus 80 in the summer), a hot tub, and three gourmet meals a day. The nightly winter rate is $200 d, including lodging, meals, and use of cross-country skis and snowshoes. There's a two-night minimum stay in winter and a one-week minimum stay in summer.

Turpin Meadow Ranch

A longtime favorite—it began taking guests in the 1920s—is Turpin Meadow Ranch, 307/543-2496 or 800/743-2496, www.turpinmeadow ranch.com. The ranch's Buffalo Valley location provides impressive Teton vistas, along with all of

the traditional ranch activities: horseback riding, cookouts, fishing, and pack trips, plus weekly nature programs by Forest Service naturalists. Guests stay in modern cabins and have access to an indoor hot tub. Summertime all-inclusive rates are $175 per day for two adults, with a three-night minimum stay. The ranch is open year-round and is a favorite snowmobile spot in winter.

MOUNTAIN RESORTS

Two noteworthy mountain resorts are east of Moran Junction off U.S. Hwy. 26/287. At Togwotee Pass (9,658 feet) the highway tops the Continental Divide and then slides eastward towards Dubois and the Wind River Valley. The Togwotee Pass area is famous for luxuriously deep snow all winter and is a destination for snowmobilers, cross-country skiers, and dogsledding enthusiasts. Just north of the pass is Teton Wilderness, a place to discover what solitude means. Facing west from the pass, the Teton Range offers a jagged horizon line. This entire area provides a delicious escape from hectic Jackson and is home to two attractive high-elevation resorts: Cowboy Village Resort at Togwotee and Brooks Lake Lodge.

Cowboy Village Resort at Togwotee

Forty-eight miles northeast of Jackson and just a few miles west of Togwotee Pass is Cowboy Village Resort at Togwotee, 307/733-8800 or 800/543-2847, www.cowboyvillage.com, a pleasantly rustic place to spend a night or a week. The resort is a busy place, offering horseback rides, mountain-bike tours, fly-fishing, a ranger-naturalist program, and backcountry pack trips in summer, along with snowmobiling (the primary winter activity), dogsledding, and cross-country skiing when the snow flies. Togwotee has a variety of accommodations, and guests will enjoy the sauna and four large hot tubs. Summer rates are $109 d for rooms in the lodge, $129 d for mini-suites, and $159 d for cabins. The mini-suites and cabins sleep up to six people ($10 per person for more than two). In winter, the resort has package deals that include lodging, breakfast and dinner, snowmobile use, a guide, and

© DON PITCHER

Triangle X Ranch

free airport shuttle. There's a four-night minimum stay in winter. The resort also houses a steak house, bar, gas station, and convenience store. Togwotee is closed from early April to mid-May, and from mid-October to late November.

Brooks Lake Lodge

This lodge may have the finest location of any Wyoming resort, with a placid lake in front and the cliffs of Pinnacle Buttes nearby. Built in 1922, it has long served travelers en route to Yellowstone, and its enormous great hall contains big-game trophies from all over the world. The lodge was completely restored in the late 1980s and is now on the National Register of Historic Places. Six guest rooms are available in the main lodge, and six private cabins are hidden in the trees; all are furnished with handmade lodgepole furniture. In addition, three luxurious suites are available, along with a recently added spa that features a workout room, sauna, and a large outdoor hot tub; massages are extra. Guests can ease into the hot tub or pull on hiking or cowboy boots to explore the magnificent country nearby.

The turnoff for Brooks Lake Lodge is 65 miles northeast of Jackson (34 miles east of Moran Junction) and another five miles off the highway via Brooks Lake Road. The lodge is open late June to mid-September and late December to early March. There's a three-night minimum stay, and the two-person rates are $500 per day in the lodge, $560 per day in the cabins, or $600 in the luxury suites. Weekly rates are also available, but be sure to reserve far ahead. These rates include gourmet meals, horseback riding, canoeing, and fishing in summer, or meals, cross-country skis, and snowshoes in winter. Snowmobile rentals are also available for guests, and dogsled tours are offered. Contact Brooks Lake Lodge at 307/455-2121, www.brookslake.com.

Camping

PUBLIC CAMPGROUNDS

Both the National Park Service and the U.S. Forest Service maintain campgrounds around Jackson Hole. The Jackson Hole/Grand Teton Public Campgrounds chart shows two-dozen public campgrounds within 50 miles of Jackson. For more specifics on public sites, contact Bridger-Teton National Forest in Jackson at 340 N. Cache Dr., 307/739-5500, www.fs.fed.us/btnf, or Grand Teton National Park in Moose, 307/739-3603, www.nps.gov/grte. In addition to these sites, many people camp for free on dispersed sites on Forest Service lands; see the Forest Service for locations and restrictions.

RV PARKS

Jackson has several RV parks scattered around town and in surrounding areas, but the rates are shockingly high in midsummer. Additional privately run campgrounds are located at Colter Bay and Flagg Ranch Resort inside Grand Teton National Park.

None of the private RV parks in the town of Jackson is really noteworthy; "parking lots" would be a better term. They can also be surprisingly expensive: Some places charge more for a tent space than it would cost to stay in a motel room in many Wyoming towns! Even more expensive is a ticket for parking RVs overnight on Jackson city streets. It's illegal to do so, and local police strictly enforce the ordinance.

Virginian RV Park, 750 W. Broadway, 307/733-7189 or 800/321-6982 (summer) or 800/262-4999 (winter), www.virginianlodge .com, is the biggest RV parking lot in the area, with more than 100 sites (including many pull-through sites) on the south end of town. Full hookups cost $40–50; no tents. Guests at the RV park can use the Virginian Lodge's outdoor pool and hot tub. The park is open May to mid-October.

Wagon Wheel RV Park & Campground, 525 N. Cache, 307/733-4588, www.wagon wheelvillage.com, is along Flat Creek on the north end of town. Located behind the motel of the same name, it has both RV hookups

JACKSON HOLE PUBLIC CAMPGROUNDS

The following public campgrounds are available on a first-come, first-served basis with no reservations. They are listed by distance and direction from Jackson. Get details for each from Bridger-Teton National Forest (BTNF; 307/739-5400; www.fs.fed.us/btnf/teton), Grand Teton National Park (GTNP; 307/739-3603; www.nps.gov/grte), or Caribou-Targhee National Forest (CTNF; 208/354-2312; www.fs.fed.us/r4/caribou). See the text for private RV campgrounds in the area.

Campgrounds North of Jackson

Curtis Canyon Campground; seven miles northeast of Jackson; open late May–Sept.; $12; BTNF; six miles of gravel road with a fine view of the Tetons

Gros Ventre Campground; 10 miles northeast of Jackson; open May to mid-Oct.; $12; GTNP; along Gros Ventre River; dump station; campground often fills by evening in midsummer

Atherton Creek Campground; 18 miles northeast of Jackson; open Memorial Day to Sept.; 12; BTNF; six miles up Gros Ventre Rd. near Gros Ventre River

Jenny Lake Campground; 20 miles north of Jackson; open mid-May to late Sept.; $12; GTNP; tents only (no RVs); campground fills by 8 A.M. in midsummer

Red Hills Campground; 22 miles northeast of Jackson; open late May–Sept.; $10; BTNF; 12 miles up Gros Ventre Rd. (partly dirt) along Gros Ventre River

Crystal Creek Campground; 23 miles northeast of Jackson; open late May–Sept.; $10; BTNF; five miles up Gros Ventre Rd. (gravel) along Gros Ventre River

Signal Mountain Campground; 32 miles north of Jackson; open mid-May to mid-Oct.; $12; GTNP; on Jackson Lake; dump station; no vehicles over 30 feet; campground fills by 10 A.M. in midsummer

Colter Bay Campground; 40 miles north of Jackson; open mid-May to mid-Sept.; $12; GTNP; on Jackson Lake; coin-operated showers and laundry nearby, dump station; campground fills by noon in midsummer

Hatchet Campground; 40 miles northeast of Jackson; open June–Sept.; $10; BTNF; in Buffalo Valley eight miles east of Moran Junction

Box Creek Campground; 46 miles northeast of Jackson; open mid-June through Sept.; $10; BTNF; on Buffalo Valley Rd., no potable water

Pacific Creek Campground; 46 miles north of Jackson; open mid-June through Sept.; $5;

($42 d) and grassy tent spaces ($24 d) and is open May–September.

Teton Village KOA, 307/733-5354 or 800/562-9043, www.koa.com, is five miles south of Teton Village and six miles from Jackson. The location is out of the way and quiet, with trees providing shade (lacking in other local RV parks). Full RV hookups cost $40 d, tent sites are $30 d, and basic camping cabins run $50–57 d. Also here are a game room and playground. It's open May to mid-October.

Grand Teton Park RV Resort is 37 miles northeast of Jackson (six miles east of Moran Junction) along Hwy. 26/287, 307/733-1980 or 800/563-6469, www.yellowstonerv.com. There are fine views of the Tetons, and facilities include a heated seasonal pool and hot tub, recreation room, and grocery store. The cost is $42 d for RVs with hookups, $30 d for tents. Simple camping cabins go for $52–58 d, and tepees run $39–43. Open year-round.

Two private campgrounds are in the Hoback Junction area, 12 miles south of Jackson. **Lazy J Corral,** 307/733-1554, is right on the highway at Hoback Junction, but the rates are low: RV sites with full hookups for $22. They do not have tent spaces and are open May–October. **Snake River Park KOA,** 307/733-7078 or 800/562-1878, www.koa.com, is one mile north of Hoback Junction and has RV spaces for $40 d, tent sites for $30 d, and simple "kamping kabins" for $52–62 d. Open Apr. to mid-Oct. The KOA has a little riverside beach and a game room.

BTNF; nine miles up Pacific Creek Rd. (enter through Grand Teton National Park)

Lizard Creek Campground; 48 miles north of Jackson; open early June to early Sept.; $12; GTNP; on Jackson Lake; no vehicles over 30 feet; campground fills by 2 P.M. in midsummer

Turpin Campground; 48 miles northeast of Jackson; open June –Sept.; $10; BTNF; in Buffalo Valley 10 miles east of Moran Junction

Angles Campground; 49 miles north of Jackson; open mid-June through Sept.; $10; BTNF; small site one-half mile northeast of Cowboy Village Resort on U.S. 287

Sheffield Creek Campground; 55 miles north of Jackson; open mid-June through Sept.; $5; BTNF; small campground off Hwy. 89/191/287 near Flagg Ranch Resort; poor road access until late summer

Campgrounds South of Jackson

Cabin Creek Campground; 19 miles south of Jackson; open late May–Sept.; $10; BTNF; along Snake River Canyon five miles from Hoback Junction

Elbow Campground; 22 miles south of Jackson; open late May–Sept.; $10; BTNF; along Snake River Canyon six miles from Hoback Junction

Hoback Campground; 22 miles southeast of Jackson; open late May–Sept.; $12; BTNF; along Hoback River seven miles east of Hoback Junction

East Table Creek Campground; 24 miles south of Jackson; open late May–Sept.; $15; BTNF; along Snake River 8.5 miles southwest of Hoback Junction

Kozy Campground; 19 miles southeast of Jackson; open late May–Sept.; $12; BTNF; along Hoback River seven miles southeast of Hoback Junction

Granite Campground; 35 miles southeast of Jackson; open late May–Sept.; $15; BTNF; near Granite Hot Springs, nine miles up Granite Creek Rd. (gravel)

Campgrounds West of Jackson

Trail Creek Campground; 20 miles west of Jackson; open mid-May to mid-Sept.; $8; CTNF; on the west side of Teton Pass. Reservations ($9 extra charge) at 518/885-3639 or 877/444-6777

Mike Harris Campground; 21 miles west of Jackson; open mid-May to mid-Sept.; $8; CTNF; on the west side of Teton Pass

Food

Jackson stands out from the rest of Wyoming on the culinary scene: chicken-fried steak may be available, but it certainly isn't the house specialty! You won't need to look far to find good food; in fact, the town seems to overflow with memorable (and even more memorably priced) eateries. If you stood in Town Square and walked in any direction for a block you would find at least one restaurant that would be a standout in any other Wyoming town. More than 70 local restaurants do business here—in a town that contains just 9,000 people.

To get an idea of what to expect at local restaurants, pick up a copy of the free *Jackson Hole Dining Guide* at the visitors center or local restaurants. You'll find the same information online at www.focusproductions.com/jhdining. The guide includes sample menus and brief descriptions of many local establishments. If you don't find a place to your liking among those listed here or in the dining guide, be assured that all of the major fast-food outlets line Jackson's streets, ready to grease your digestive tract.

BREAKFAST

The best breakfast place in Jackson isn't in Jackson, but in Wilson, where **Nora's Fish Creek**

Inn, 307/733-8288, www.jacksonholenet.com/noras, attracts a full house each morning. The food is great, the setting is authentically rustic, and the waitresses are friendly and fast. Nora's also serves tried-and-true lunches and dinners at very good prices, from tuna fish sandwiches for $4.50 to 16-ounce steaks for $19. Highly recommended, but you may have to contend with a smoky atmosphere at the counter in the morning.

Very popular for breakfast and lunch is **Jedediah's House of Sourdough,** 135 E. Broadway, 307/733-5671, www.wy-biz.com/jedediahsourdough, where, as the name implies, sourdough pancakes are the morning specialty. Housed in a 1910 log cabin, the restaurant gets noisy and crowded in the morning, making it perfect for families with young kids. The lunch menu stars burgers, sandwiches, and salads, while the summer-only dinners include steaks, chicken, trout, and burgers. A half-dozen tables are on the deck, shaded by tall cottonwoods.

Another longtime breakfast and lunch standout is **The Bunnery,** 130 N. Cache Dr., 307/733-5474, with good omelets and delicious lunch sandwiches on freshly baked breads, along with fresh salads and homemade soups.

The old-time crowd heads to **LeJay's Sportsman's Cafe,** 72 S. Glenwood St., 307/733-3110, a greasy spoon that's open 24 hours a day. This is the place to go when no other restaurant is open and your stomach is demanding all-American grub. But be ready for clouds of cigarette smoke.

One of the cheapest breakfast deals in town can be found at **Teton Steakhouse,** 40 W. Pearl St., 307/733-2639, www.tetonsteakhouse.com; $5 for their stuff-a-gut buffet, with pancakes, bacon, sausage, potatoes, fruits, and more. This place is very popular with hogs who park their Hogs (Harleys) and waddle in. **Bubba's Bar-B-Que Restaurant,** 515 W. Broadway, 307/733-2288, is another cheap and tasty option, with a worker's special for $3.75, including filling biscuits and gravy. Other local breakfast places are listed under Espresso and Light Meals.

LUNCH

One of the most popular noontime spots in Jackson is **Sweetwater Restaurant,** 85 King St., 307/733-3553, where the lunch menu includes dependably good salads, homemade soups, and a variety of earthy sandwiches. For dinner, try Moroccan lamb over couscous or the roasted eggplant and leek lasagna. Dinner entrées are $13–28. Recommended.

Get delicious sub sandwiches on tangy homemade bread at **New York City Sub Shop,** 20 N. Jackson St., 307/733-4414. It's a little pricey ($6 for a half hoagie or more than $10 for a whole), but the service is fast, and the hot sandwiches are always vastly better than Subway. Definitely recommended.

Pearl Street Bagels, 145 Pearl St., 307/739-1218, serves home-baked bagels (they're on the small side, however) along with good espresso and juices. Open daily until 6 P.M. in summer. They have a second shop in Wilson, 307/739-1261. The latter is *the* groovy place to be seen in Wilson (OK, so are Nora's and the 'Coach). **Bagal Jax,** 145 N. Glenwood, 307/733-9148, is another popular grab-a-bagel-and-run place, with a covered side deck for those with time to relax. The same building houses **Jamba Juice** with a variety of healthy smoothies.

If you're in search of a substantial vegetarian breakfast or lunch, try the café at **Harvest Natural Foods,** 130 W. Broadway, 307/733-5418. The salad-and-soup bar in the back is a favorite lunch break for locals. Great sandwiches, fruit smoothies, and baked goods are offered, too. You won't go wrong here.

Much to the chagrin of locals (and visitors), Jackson's famous corner drug store closed in 2001, and the historic stone building is now occupied by a rug gallery. Fortunately, **Jackson's Original Soda Fountain,** 307/733-5260, has opened a half-block away at 85 Cache Street, with the same old backbar and a similar menu that includes sandwiches, homemade ice cream, shakes, banana splits, floats, sundaes, inexpensive sandwiches, and chili.

For lunches in the Teton Village area, stop by **Westside Store & Deli,** 307/733-6202, located in the Aspens. The deli will be glad to pack you a big picnic lunch, and it also sells such dinner entrées as lemon dijon chicken, lasagna, and ribs.

ESPRESSO AND LIGHT MEALS

The hip crowd heads for breakfast and lunch to two excellent local cafés: Betty Rock and Shades. **Betty Rock Cafe and Coffeehouse,** 325 W. Pearl, 307/733-0747, is a great and noisy place for lunch, with delectable homemade breads, paninis, wraps, salads, soups, and espresso. Highly recommended. You'll find similar food and service at the oft-crowded **Shades Cafe,** 82 S. King St., 307/733-2015. This tiny log cabin has a shady summer-only patio on the side. Breakfasts feature waffles, egg dishes, fruit, and yogurt, plus lattes, mochas, and other coffee drinks. At lunch, the standouts are salads, quiches, burritos, and paninis. Shades is a relaxing place to hang out with the latte habitués, although it does close early in the fall, winter, and spring.

Out in Teton Village across from the tram, **Village Cafe,** 307/733-2233, serves very good breakfasts, baked goods, sandwiches, wraps, pizza by the slice, espresso, and microbrewed beer. Open summers and winters only.

The National Museum of Wildlife Art, two miles north of Jackson on U.S. Hwy. 26/89, houses a delightfully bright little restaurant with vistas across the National Elk Refuge. Called **Rising Sage Cafe,** 307/733-8649, it has a lunch menu of paninis, pita and hummus, homemade soups served in a bread bowl, salads, and espresso.

AMERICAN

Jackson's most popular family eatery is **Bubba's Bar-B-Que Restaurant,** 515 W. Broadway, 307/733-2288. Each evening the parking lot out front is jammed with folks waiting patiently for a chance to gnaw on barbecued spare ribs, savor the spicy chicken wings, or fill up at the salad bar. Get there before 6:30 for shorter lines. Lunch is a real bargain, with specials for less than $6. Drinks come in recycled Mason jars, but they don't serve alcohol, so BYOB (no corkage fee). Cheap breakfasts are served, too. Al-though based in Jackson, Bubba's now has restaurants in five other locations around Wyoming, Colorado, and Idaho.

Get great all-American burgers at the '50s-style **Billy's Burgers,** 55 N. Cache Dr., 307/733-3279, adjacent to the more upscale Cadillac Grille. The Billy burger is a half-pound monster. It's not on the menu, but recommended if you aren't absolutely famished is the one-third-pound Betty burger. Ask for it.

Next door to Billy's and in the basement of the bar of the same name, the **Million Dollar Cowboy Steakhouse,** 307/733-4790, www.milliondollarcowboybar.com, offers "casual Western elegance" and great steaks, from porterhouse to filet mignon. In addition, the menu includes salads, rack of lamb, seafood, pasta, ribs, and vegetarian specials. The bar features a dozen different single-malt scotches. Not for kids, and not cheap: entrées are $20–32. Reservations are advised.

Also popular is **Gun Barrel Steakhouse,** 862 W. Broadway, 307/733-3287, www.gunbarrel.com, where the mesquite-grilled steaks, elk, and buffalo are served in a hunting-lodge atmosphere with trophy game mounts; they came from a wildlife museum that previously occupied the site. You'll find lots of historic guns and other Old West paraphernalia around the Gun Barrel too, making this an interesting place to explore even if you aren't hungry. It's a bit on the pricey side, with dinner entrées for $16–26. The bar has a wide choice of beers on tap. Another recommended place is **Camp Creek Inn,** 16 miles south of Jackson in Hoback Canyon, 307/733-3099 or 800/228-8460, www.camp-creek-inn.com. The cozy fireplace and rustic setting make this a good place to escape the Jackson Hole crowds. Very good steaks and prime rib, and "no mercy" one-pound burgers enough to fill even Rush Limbaugh's lardbelly. Friday and Saturday nights bring St. Louis style BBQ ribs.

The classic Wort Hotel at 50 N. Glenwood St., 307/733-2190, www.worthotel.com, is home to **Silver Dollar Bar & Grill,** with chop house fare, including buffalo prime rib, elk chops, fresh mahi-mahi, and seafood linguini in a white-linen setting. Very good Caesar salads are served, too.

The bar next door is a fun place for an after-dinner drink, and the Plug Nickel Cafe features home-style family dining.

Horse Creek Station, 10 miles south of Jackson, 307/733-0810, serves delicious smokehouse meats, including pork chops, baby back ribs, chicken, elk medallions, and shrimp in a casual Old West atmosphere with stuffed animal heads on the walls.

A very popular place with both locals and ski bums is the **Mangy Moose** in Teton Village, 307/733-4913, where you'll find a big salad bar and fair prices on steak, prime rib, pasta, chicken, and fresh fish (dinner entrées $12–36). It's a fun and lively place. Downstairs is The Rocky Mountain Oyster (don't ask), offering killer breakfasts and inexpensive burgers, pizza, and sandwiches for lunch.

Get chicken atchaflaya, seafood gumbo, and other Cajun specialties at **The Acadian House,** 180 N. Millward, 307/739-1269. The menu has broadened lately and now includes a diversity of other entrées, including ginseng tea–basted duck, grilled tuna, and Thai curry vegetable sauté. Don't miss the Louisiana bread pudding for dessert.

The menu and setting at **Teton Steakhouse,** 40 W. Pearl St., 307/733-2639, www.teton steakhouse.com, reflect this restaurant's previous incarnation as a Sizzler, but that doesn't faze anyone. The central location (one block off Town Square), inexpensive stuff-yourself meals, and noisy, kid-friendly setting bring a crowd every day. Line up to put in your order for steaks, ribs, or chicken, or just sidle up to the big salad, soup, and dessert bar to fill your plate. Steaks are $10–20, and they also have a cheap breakfast buffet. No booze is sold here, but bring your own beer or wine and they'll provide the glasses (no corkage fee).

Housed in an old Denny's building at 380 South U.S. Hwy. 89, **Rendezvous Bistro,** 307/739-1100, has a strong local following for meat-loaf, pan-seared halibut, confit of duck, and a rather pricy oyster bar. Entrées are $12–20.

See **Chuck Wagon Cookouts** section for outfits that combine cowboy cookery with Old West entertainment.

PASTA AND PIZZA

One of the tried-and-true local eateries is **Anthony's Italian Restaurant,** 62 S. Glenwood St., 307/733-3717. In business since 1977, Anthony's has built a reputation for simple food (a bit heavy for some tastes) and attentive, efficient service. Vegetarians will find several good menu items. Meals come with homemade soup, salad, and fresh-baked garlic bread—guaranteed to fill you up and then some. Open for dinner only.

Hidden away on the north end of town, **Nani's Genuine Pasta House,** 242 N. Glenwood, 307/733-3888, www.nanis.com, is Jackson's gourmet Italian restaurant. Meals are served in a charming little home with an old-country ambience and friendly service. Prices are surprisingly reasonable, with most entrées for $10–20. Many vegetarian and vegan dishes are available, and be sure to ask about the nightly specials. Nani's is open for dinner year-round, plus lunch in the summer.

Several pizza places stand out in Jackson. You'll find **Calico Italian Restaurant & Bar,** 307/733-2460, www.calicorestaurant.com, in a garish red-and-white building three-quarters of a mile north on Teton Village Road. The menu has gone a bit upscale, but prices are still reasonable: $11–19 entrees. Thursday means tapas night. During the summer, be sure to get a side salad, fresh from the big house garden. The bar at Calico is a very popular locals' watering hole. Kids love the 2.5-acre lawn/playground.

Mountain High Pizza Pie, 120 W. Broadway, 307/733-3646, www.mountainhighpizza.com, is a favorite downtown place offering free delivery in Jackson. In the winter Mountain High also serves pizza by the slice.

For other notable pizza places, see Yellowstone Garage and Grand Teton Brewing Company.

CONTINENTAL/ NOUVELLE CUISINE

If you want fine continental dining and aren't deterred by entrées costing $20 or more, Jackson has much to offer you.

Just off Town Square, **Snake River Grill,**

upstairs at 84 E. Broadway, 307/733-0557, www.snakerivergrill.com, is one of Jackson's finest gourmet restaurants—with prices to match (most entrées $18–35). The meals are exquisite, and the seasonal menu typically contains a variety of seafood, free-range beef, and organic vegetables that are artfully presented. The wine list is equally impressive, and a few outside tables face the square. Reservations are a must; reserve one week in advance for prime-time seatings in the summer. Try the fallen chocolate soufflé for dessert. Snake River Grill is a good place to watch for Jackson's best-known resident, Harrison Ford. Closed Nov. and Apr.

For views so spectacular they make it difficult to concentrate on your meal, don't miss **The Granary,** 307/733-8833 or 800/443-6139, www.springcreekranch.com, located atop East Gros Ventre Butte west of Jackson. This is also a very popular place for evening cocktails. Dinner entrées run $22–32 and include rack of lamb, fresh seafood, and a very popular elk tenderloin.

An excellent in-town continental restaurant is **The Blue Lion,** 160 N. Millward St., 307/733-3912. The front patio makes for delightful summertime dining. Try the Southwestern tempeh crepes or the Thai shrimp linguine.

Jackson's most popular nouvelle cuisine restaurant is **Cadillac Grille,** 55 N. Cache (on the square), 307/733-3279. The food is artfully prepared and includes a changing menu of seafood, grilled meats, and game. The art deco decor of the Cadillac helps make it one of the most crowded tourist hangouts in town. The restaurant includes a bar and rear patio for summertime dining under the stars. Dinner entrées run $14–30.

Old Yellowstone Garage, 115 Center St., 307/734-6161, serves exceptional Italian meals that can be matched with their Italian wines. There's outside dining in the summer, and most entrees cost $16–36. The restaurant was formerly located in an old garage in Dubois, hence the name. Yellowstone Garage is famous for their all-you-can-eat Sunday pizza fest. Servers come around as each pie emerges from the oven, offering slices to diners. Don't come here expecting to eat and run because the pizzas are served at a leisurely pace that can be annoying to

some folks. The owners say this is in keeping with the Italian ambience, but it also means you'll probably be ordering drinks and salads while you wait. The restaurant is open for dinners only and closed Mondays.

Inside the ultra-luxurious Amangani Resort atop Gros Ventre Butte, **Amangani Grill,** 307/734-7333 or 877/734-7333, www.aman resorts.com, is open to the public for three meals a day, with a menu that includes seared ahi tuna, grilled filet of beef, venison loin, and a wonderful Caesar salad. Great breakfasts are served, too; try the smoked trout eggs Benedict. Reservations are advised, and this is decidedly *not* a place for T-shirts or shorts. Dinner entrées run $27–32.

Out in the Aspens on Teton Village Road, **Stiegler's,** 307/733-1071, has a menu with names big enough to eat—you could start with *leberknödel suppe,* before a main course of veal sweetbreads *forestiere,* followed by a *topfen*

© DON PITCHER

The luxurious Amangani Resort houses the popular Amangani Grill.

JACKSON HOLE

palatschinken. The dense Austrian cuisine is outstanding, and the service is exceptional. If you're around in the fall, make reservations for their popular Oktoberfest, a celebration of Austrian food and beer.

Alpenhof, 307/733-3462, is another fine Teton Village dining experience, with a changing menu that often features rack of lamb, tenderloin of venison, Barbarie duck, and some wonderful appetizers, not to mention an award-winning wine list. The **Alpenhof Bistro** upstairs has a more casual setting and a less-expensive dinner menu. People come to the bistro for balcony dining with a close-up view of Teton Village.

Jenny Lake Lodge, inside Grand Teton National Park, is famous for gourmet American cuisine served in an elegantly cozy log lodge. Open June–Sept. only; call 307/733-4647 for reservations (required). Jackets are recommended. Breakfast and dinner are fixed-price affairs, while lunch is served à la carte.

MEXICAN AND CARIBBEAN

For the fastest Mexican food in town (with the possible exception of Taco Bell), drop by **Pica's Mexican Taqueria,** 307/734-4457. You'll find tasty tacos, burritos, quesadillas, enchiladas, and tortas in a hip setting. The shop is in the Buffalo Junction strip mall at 1160 Alpine Lane (near the Albertson's store).

In business since 1969, **The Merry Piglets,** 160 N. Cache Dr., 307/733-2966, serves very good Mexican meals, including their specialty, the cheese crisp. Excellent margaritas, pitchers of beer, and an open front section add to the appeal.

Chili Pepper Grill, 380 W. Pearl, 307/734-6574, has fill-you-up servings of Mexican cooking, including quesadillas, burritos, fajitas, and enchiladas. The largest and most popular Mexican restaurant is **Vista Grande,** 307/733-6964, on the road to Teton Village. The biggest drawing cards here are the pitchers of margaritas; the food itself is reasonably priced ($10–13 entrées) but nothing special.

Pato Restaurant, 680 E. Broadway, 307/739-9191, is an out-of-the-way place with eclectic offerings inspired by Central American and Caribbean cookery. I suppose you could think of it as World Beat food. On the menu are such items as shrimp Cubano, spice-rubbed ribeye, achiote chicken, fish tacos, and even Vietnamese spring rolls. They use locally grown organic vegetables when possible and have a great Sunday brunch.

ASIAN
Chinese
Chinatown Restaurant, 850 W. Broadway, 307/733-8856, makes good Chinese dishes—particularly the mu shu vegetables, lemon chicken, and pot stickers—and offers $5.50 weekday lunch specials.

Looking for a fast and filling Chinese meal? **Hong Kong Buffet,** in Grand Teton Plaza at 826 W. Broadway, 307/734-8988, is popular and cheap.

Japanese
Nikai, 225 N. Cache, 307/734-6490, is open for dinner only, and reservations are advised. Creatively prepared sushi is the main attraction, but the restaurant also has a menu of Asian fusion items from the open kitchen, including tuna ume, miso-crusted pork, and wakame seaweed salad. The atmosphere is contemporary and stylish. Most items cost $10–19.

Get freshly rolled sushi, including a variety of vegetarian rolls, at **Masa Sushi,** 307/733-2311, located inside The Inn at Jackson Hole in Teton Village.

Thai
In the previous edition of this book I bemoaned the lack of Thai restaurants in Jackson. Fortunately, two local places have stepped up for those of us who love food from Thailand. **Thai Me Up,** 75 E. Pearl St., 307/733-0005, has a gimmicky name and chefs born in the United States, but the food is spicy and delicious. They're open for dinners only seven days a week and have a few sidewalk tables. The location is a bit quieter than places on the Square, but the entrées aren't cheap: $10–18. The restaurant is closed in April and May. Recommended.

For the downscale version, check out **Teton Thai Restaurant,** across the street from Teton Theater at 135 N. Cache Drive, 307/733-0022, with a handful of plastic tables and seats under a covered deck. The food is simple and authentic, with lunch specials such as chicken satae or tom yum koong for $7–8.

BREWERIES

Before Prohibition in 1920, nearly every town in Wyoming had its own brewery, making such local favorites as Hillcrest, Schoenhofen, and Sweetwater. After repeal of "the noble experiment," breweries again popped up, but competition from industrial giants such as Anheuser-Busch and Coors forced the last Wyoming operation—Sheridan Brewing—out of business in 1954. It was another 34 years before commercial beermaking returned. In 1988, Charlie Otto started a tiny backyard operation in Wilson. His **Grand Teton Brewing Company,** 208/787-4000, www.grandteton brewing.com, now brews just over Teton Pass in Victor, Idaho, where you can sample Teton Ale, Old Faithful Ale, Moose Juice Stout, Teton Golden Ale, Teton Huckleberry Wheat, and Sweetgrass IPA. You'll find them on tap at many Jackson-area bars and restaurants and for sale in six-pack bottles.

An old downtown warehouse has been beautifully transformed into **Snake River Brewing Co. & Restaurant,** 265 S. Millward, 307/739-2337, www.snakeriverbrewing.com. The bright and spacious setting fills with a convivial crowd of young outdoors enthusiasts most evenings, and the bar generally has seven of their award-winning beers on tap. Particularly notable—they've all won gold medals at various brew festivals—are Zonker Stout, Snake River Lager, and Snake River Pale Ale. The lunch and dinner café menu includes delicious thin-crust pizzas and calzones baked in their cherrywood-fired oven, flavorful appetizers, daily pasta specials, sandwiches, and salads. It's great food in a lively atmosphere, and one of *the* places to be seen in Jackson. Most dinner entrées run $9–11, but they have a variety of $6 lunch specials.

WINE SHOPS

The most complete local wine and beer shops are **Westside Wine & Spirits,** in the Aspens along Teton Village Rd., 307/733-5038; **The Liquor Store,** next to Albertson's on W. Broadway, 307/733-4466, www.wineliquorbeer.com; and **Dornan's Wine Shoppe** in Moose, 307/733-2415, ext. 202, www.dornans.com. The Liquor Store features an impressive upstairs wine department and a wine bar with free wine tastings Friday and Saturday evenings. You can even use their computer to check your email. **Jackson Hole Wine Company,** 200 W. Broadway, 307/739-9463, also has a fine selection and offers free Friday evening wine tastings all summer long, with a different choice of wines each week. It's a great way to learn about various vintages from wine experts. You'll generally find the lowest wine prices from **Jackson's Original Discount Liquor Store at Sidewinders,** on West Broadway, 307/734-5766.

BAKERIES

The Bunnery, 130 N. Cache Dr., 307/733-5474, bakes a big variety of treats and sweets, but it's best known for its hearty-flavored OSM (oat, sunflower, and millet) bread—on the pricey side at around $4.50 a loaf. Another place for fresh-baked—and organic—goods is **Harvest Natural Foods,** 130 W. Broadway, 307/733-5418.

The location is a bit out of the way, but a visit to **Wildflour Bakery,** 345 N. Glenwood, 307/734-2455, is a must if you're in search of French baguettes and other breads (different choice every day). Tasty pastries, cookies, and muffins are served, too. You can also find the company's goods in several local grocers, and they bake the house bread for several of Jackson's gourmet restaurants.

GROCERIES AND NATURAL FOODS

Get groceries from the large **Albertson's,** on the south end of town at the corner of Buffalo Way and Broadway, 307/733-5950. Inside you'll find a bakery, pharmacy, deli, one-hour photo lab, bank branch, and coffee bar. This is the most lucrative Albertson's in the entire chain of 2,300 stores; sales are said to be three times higher than the second most successful store! A few blocks farther south (right in front of the high school) is the new **Smith's,** 1425 South U.S. Hwy. 89, 307/733-8908, www.smithsfoodanddrug.com, with the same features as Albertson's.

Meet the locals at the less ostentatious (and generally cheaper) **Food Town,** in the Powderhorn Mall at 970 W. Broadway, 307/733-0450. The best spot for fresh vegetables and fruit is the little **market stand** next to the Maverik gas station on the south end of town. It's open Thursday–Saturday only in the summer, and it has better prices and higher quality than local grocers.

In business since 1947, **Jackson Hole Buffalo Meat,** 1655 Berger Lane, 307/733-8343 or 800/543-6328, www.buybuffalomeat.com, sells smoked buffalo salami, jerky, sausage, steaks, and burgers, along with buffalo meat gift packs and New Zealand elk steaks.

For health foods, head downtown to **Harvest Natural Foods,** 130 W. Broadway, 307/733-5418, or to the smaller **Here & Now Natural Foods,** 1925 Moose-Wilson Rd., 307/733-2742.

Jackson's popular **Farmers Market** comes to Town Square Saturdays 8–11 A.M. in the summer. Shop for fresh veggies, fruits, and other farm products, including flowers. Live music and cooking demonstrations add to the attraction.

Entertainment and the Arts

NIGHTLIFE

Barflies will keep buzzing in Jackson, especially during midsummer and midwinter, when visitors pack local saloons every night of the week. At least one nightclub always seems to have live tunes; check Jackson's free newspapers to see what's where. Cover charges are generally $3–5 on the weekends, and most other times you'll get in free.

The famous **Million Dollar Cowboy Bar,** on the west side of Town Square, 307/733-2207, www.milliondollarcowboybar.com, is a favorite of real cowboys and their wannabe cousins. Inside the Cowboy you'll discover burled lodgepole pine beams, four pool tables (nearly always in use), display cases with stuffed dead bears and other cuddly critters, bars inlaid with old silver dollars, and barstools made from old saddles. Until the 1950s, the Cowboy was Jackson's center for illegal gambling. Bartenders kept a close eye on Teton Pass, where messengers used mirrors to deliver warnings of coming federal revenuers, giving folks at the bar time to hide the gaming tables in a back room. Today the dance floor fills with honky-tonking couples as the bands croon lonesome cowboy tunes six nights a week. Looking to learn swing and two-step dancing? Every Thursday you can join an excellent free beginners' class at 7:30 P.M., then dance up a storm when the band comes on at 9.

Just across the square and up the stairs is **Rancher Spirits & Billiards,** 307/733-3886, where the room is filled with a half dozen tables for billiards aficionados.

Silver Dollar Bar & Grill, in the Wort Hotel at 50 N. Glenwood St., 307/733-2190, offers a setting that might seem more fitting in Las Vegas: gaudy pink neon lights curve around a bar inlaid with 2,032 (count 'em!) silver dollars. It tends to attract an older crowd (best martinis in Jackson), and the music is generally of the piano or acoustic variety.

Right next to the tram in Teton Village is **Mangy Moose Saloon,** 307/733-4913, Jackson Hole's jumpingest pickup spot and *the* place to rock out. The Moose attracts a hip skier/outdoorsy crowd with rock, blues, or World Beat bands Wednesday–Saturday both summer and winter. This is also where you'll hear nationally known acts.

Sidewinders Tavern & Sports Grill, on West Broadway, 307/734-5766, is filled with big-screen TVs for sports enthusiasts. Smokers head to the cigar bar, but there's also a big smoke-free section.

The **Shady Lady Saloon** at Snow King Resort, 400 E. Snow King Ave., 307/733-5200, typically serves up live music most Wednesday nights, along with a Tuesday DJ and open mike Fridays. More popular is the Monday night **Jackson Hole Hootenanny,** held in the lodge room of the Snow King Center throughout the summer, or at the nearby ice rink in spring and fall. Local and visiting musicians get together to jam in an all-acoustic set, and anyone can join the onstage fun if they have musical talent—or can pretend.

Over in Wilson, **The Stagecoach Bar,** 307/733-4407, is *the* place to be on Sunday nights 6–10 P.M. (Wyoming bars close their doors at 10 P.M. on Sunday.) In the early '70s, when hippies risked getting their heads shaved by rednecks at Jackson's Cowboy Bar, they found the 'Coach a more tolerant place. Today tobacco-chewing cowpokes show their partners slick moves on the tiny dance floor as the Stagecoach Band (jokingly known as the "worst country-western band in the U.S.") runs through the country tunes one more time; the band has performed here every Sunday since February 16, 1969! Outside you'll find picnic tables and a volleyball court for pickup games in the summer, or pick up a cue stick and show off you billiard skills indoors. The bar food is notable, especially the buffalo burgers.

Other spots with occasional live music (or DJs) are the **Spur Bar,** at Dornan's in Moose, 307/733-2415, ext. 200; **The Granary,** atop East Gros Ventre Butte, 307/733-8833; **Log Cabin Saloon,** 307/733-7525; and **Leek's Marina Restaurant,** along Jackson Lake, 307/543-2494.

CLASSICAL MUSIC

In existence since 1962, the **Grand Teton Music Festival** takes place at Walk Festival Hall in Teton Village, with performances of classical and modern works by a cast of 200 world-renowned symphony musicians. Concerts take place evenings late June to mid-August each year, with chamber music on Tuesday and Wednesday, small ensembles on Thursday, and festival orchestra concerts on Friday

and Saturday. They also perform a free outdoor "Music in the Hole" concert on the Fourth of July, plus special young people's concerts in July and August. The three-hour-long Friday morning rehearsals are just $10. Call 307/733-3050 for a schedule of events and ticket prices, or get details on the web at www.gtmf.org.

MUSICALS AND MOVIES

In addition to the bar scene, summers bring several lighthearted acting ventures to Jackson. For family musicals such as *Paint Your Wagon, The Unsinkable Molly Brown,* or *Oklahoma,* head to **Jackson Hole Playhouse,** 145 W. Deloney, 307/733-6994, www.jhplayhouse.com. Shows take place Monday–Saturday evenings in a campy 1890s-style setting. A family saloon (no alcohol) and restaurant are next door.

Productions of Broadway and Western musical comedies play throughout the summer at **Mainstage Theatre,** in Pink Garter Plaza at 50 W. Broadway, 307/733-3670, www.jacksonhole theatre.com. The rest of the year, the Mainstage puts on more serious plays from the Performing Arts Company of Jackson Hole and attracts national touring productions. Both Mainstage and Jackson Hole Playhouse are very popular with families, and reservations are strongly recommended.

Watch flicks at **Teton Theatre,** 120 N. Cache Dr., **The Cinema,** 295 W. Pearl St., or **MovieWorks Cinema Four-plex,** 860 South U.S. Hwy. 89. All three of these have the same ownership, phone number, and website: 307/733-4939, www.jhmovies.com.

RODEO

On Wednesday and Saturday nights in summer you can watch bucking broncs, bull riders, barrel racers, rodeo clowns, and hard-riding cowboys at the **Jackson Hole Rodeo** on the Teton County Fair Grounds. Kids get to join in the amusing calf scramble. The rodeo starts at 8 P.M. and costs $10 adults, $8 ages 4–12, free for kids under four, or $30 for the whole family. Rodeos take place Memorial Day to Labor Day, with Saturday

JACKSON HOLE

night rodeos all summer and Wednesday night rodeos starting in mid-June. Get details at 307/733-2805, www.jhrodeo.com.

CHUCK WAGON COOKOUTS

Jackson Hole is home to several chuck wagon affairs offering all-you-can-eat barbecue cookouts and Western musical performances in the summer. Each has its own advantages, but reservations are highly recommended at all of these.

Bar-T-Five

Run by the Thomas family since 1973, Bar-T-Five, 790 Cache Creek Rd., 307/733-5386 or 800/772-5386, www.bart5.com, is one of the best chuck wagon feeds. Horse-drawn Conestoga-style wagons depart just east of Snow King, carrying visitors along Cache Creek past costumed mountain men, cowboys, and Indians. At the in-the-trees cookout site, cowboys serenade your meal, tell stories, and crack corny jokes that aren't entirely politically correct. It's great fun for families and busloads of Japanese tourists. Rates are $30 adults, $23 ages 6–12, and free for kids under six. Open mid-May through September, with departures at 5:30 and 6:30 P.M. Monday–Saturday. Recommended.

A/OK Corral

Located 10 miles south of Jackson near Hoback Junction, A/OK Corral, 307/733-6556, www.horsecreekranch.com, has 45-minute horseback or wagon rides that end at an outdoor cookout. Big ranch breakfasts and steak suppers are on the menu. Breakfasts cost $33 adults, $12 kids; dinners are $51 adults with the horseback ride, $38 with a covered-wagon ride. For kids, a covered-wagon ride and dinner are $16. Western musical entertainment is provided with the evening meals.

Bar J

Along the Teton Village Road near Teton Pines, the Bar J, 307/733-3370 or 800/905-2275, www.barjchuckwagon.com, does a land office business throughout the summer, with seating for up to 750 people in a cavernous building, including busloads of gray-haired Gray Liners. In existence for more than 25 years, Bar J is famous for its first-rate musicians who fiddle (one is a two-time national fiddle champion), sing, yodel, and regale the audience with cornball jokes and dollops of cowboy poetry. Before the show everyone queues up for heaping servings of barbecued beef, roast chicken, or ribeye steak served with baked potatoes, beans, biscuits, applesauce, spice cake, and lemonade (no alcohol). Amazingly, they manage to feed the entire crowd in a half hour. The picnic-table seating is cramped, but after dinner you're treated to 90 minutes of rollicking entertainment. The cost is $16–24 for adults (depending on your meal), $6 for kids under eight, or free for tots. Bar J is open Memorial Day to late September, with dinner at 7:30 P.M.; many folks arrive earlier to get front-row seats for the show. It's a good idea to make reservations at least one week ahead. The Bar J does not offer wagon or horseback rides.

Castagno Outfitters

Located in beautiful Buffalo Valley, 45 miles northeast of Jackson, Castagno Outfitters Covered Wagon Cookouts start with a 30-minute ride in covered wagons. The wagons stop at an isolated aspen grove, where guests enjoy a dinner of steak, beans, baked potato, salad, and dessert. Dinners cost $25 adults, $20 kids, and run mid-June to late August. They also have breakfast rides for $15 adults, $12 kids. Get details at 307/543-2407, www.castagnooutfitters.com.

Events

Jackson Hole is packed with entertaining events almost every day of the year. Some of these are homegrown affairs such as the county fair, whereas others attract people from near and far. Of particular note are the International Pedigree Stage Stop Sled Dog Race (IPSSSDR), the Pole-Peddle-Paddle Race, the Elk Antler Auction, the Grand Teton Music Festival, and the Jackson Hole Fall Arts Festival. (In addition to the events listed, see Grand Targhee Ski Resort later in this chapter for a year-round calendar of events on the other side of the Tetons.)

WINTER

December is a particularly beautiful time in downtown Jackson. Lights decorate the elk antler arches, and a variety of events take place. Buy

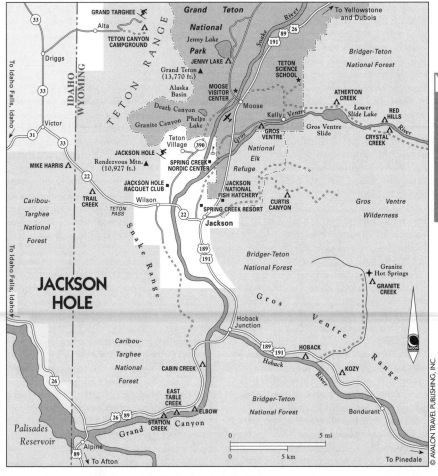

JACKSON HOLE

arts and crafts during the **Christmas Bazaar** early in the month, or take the kids to visit Saint Nick and his elves on Town Square starting in mid-December; they're there daily 5–7 P.M.

Kick the year off by watching (or participating in) the annual **torchlight ski parades** at all three local ski areas. They take place on Christmas evening and New Year's Eve at both Jackson Hole Mountain Resort and Grand Targhee Ski Resort, and on New Year's Eve at Snow King.

In existence since 1996, the **International Pedigree Stage Stop Sled Dog Race** (IPSSS-DR; pronounced IPS-der) is the largest sled dog race in the lower 48 states and a qualifying event for the Iditarod. Unlike the Iditarod and most other mushing events, this one is run in short 30- to 60-mile legs, with teams operating from a different town each day. As with the Tour de France, it's the total time that counts in this stage race. The race is the creation of Iditarod musher Frank Teasley and nurse Jayne Ottman, who came up with the idea as a way to raise awareness of the need to immunize children; it's unofficially called "The Race to Immunize." IPSSSDR starts in Jackson and then goes on to Dubois, Lander, Evanston, Kemmerer, Alpine, and Pinedale, before a final day out of Teton Village. The race boasts a $100,000 purse and has attracted some of the top names in dog mushing, including Iditarod winners Jeff King, Rick Swenson, and Susan Butcher. It's held over eight days in late January. Get the complete story at 307/734-1163, www.wyomingstagestop.org.

Each February, local Shriners hold horse-drawn **cutter races**—essentially a wild chariot race on one-quarter mile of ice—at Melody Ranch, six miles south of Jackson. Call 307/733-1938 for more info.

In February, the **Cowboy Ski Challenge** provides a different kind of race, with skiers pulled behind a horse and rider at speeds of up to 40 miles per hour. The race takes place at the base of Jackson Hole Mountain Resort.

Ski and snowboard races take place all winter long, ranging from elegant "Powder Eight" Championships in early March to blazingly fast downhill races. (Volunteer to work one of the gates at a downhill race and you get to ski free the rest of the day.)

One of the most popular (and dumbest) Jackson events is the **World Championship Snowmobile Hillclimb,** in which man (or woman) and machine churn up the slopes at Snow King Resort. The event takes place in late March.

The ski season ends the first weekend of April with the **Pole-Pedal-Paddle Race,** combining alpine skiing, cross-country skiing, cycling, and canoeing in a wild, tough competition. It's the largest such event in the West and great fun for spectators and contestants, many of whom dress up in goofy costumes. Get the full story at 307/733-6433, www.polepedalpaddle.com.

SPRING

Spring in Jackson Hole is the least favorite time of the year for many locals. The snow is going, leaving behind brown grass and trees; biking and hiking trails aren't yet passable; and the river is too cold to enjoy. For many folks, this is the time to load up the car and head to Utah for a desert hike in Canyonlands. Despite these conditions, April and May can be a good time to visit, especially if you want to avoid the crowds, need to save money on lodging, or are planning to stay for the summer and need a job and a place to live. (Housing gets progressively more difficult to find after April.)

On the third Saturday in May, the world's only public **elk antler auction** takes place at Town Square, attracting hundreds of buyers from all over the globe. Local Boy Scouts collect five tons of antlers from the nearby National Elk Refuge each spring, with 80 percent of the proceeds helping to fund feeding of the elk. This may sound like an odd event, but the take is more than $100,000! Prices average $10 per pound, and the bidding gets highly competitive; perfectly matched pairs can go for more than $2,000. The antlers are used in taxidermy, belt buckles, furniture, and most important, to satisfy the high demand for antlers in the insatiable (pun intended) South Korean and Chinese aphrodisiac markets. There's more than a touch of irony in the Boy Scouts making money from the sale of sexual stimulants! Call 307/733-5935 for more info.

SUMMER

Memorial Day weekend brings **Old West Days,** complete with a parade, street dance, barbecue dinner, cowboy poetry, bed races, pony rides, children's rodeo and games, and **mountain-man rendezvous.** Call 307/733-3316 for details. The **Fourth of July** is another big event in Jackson, with a parade, rodeo, and an impressive fireworks show from Snow King Mountain. Another very popular Fourth of July event is the free **Music in the Hole** outdoor classical concert by the Grand Teton Music Festival orchestra; details at 307/733-1128, www.gtmf.org.

The **Jackson Hole Rodeo** (307/733-2805; www.jhrodeo.com) brings spills and thrills to town, with Saturday night rodeos all summer and Wednesday night rodeos starting in mid-June. Another ongoing event is the **Grand Teton Music Festival,** www.gtmf.org, providing summertime classical music at Teton Village. These latter two activities are detailed in the preceding Entertainment and the Arts section.

The **Mountain Artists' Rendezvous Art Fair** is a great late July event, with more than 100 artisans displaying their works at Miller Park. Contact the Art Association for details, 307/733-8792, www.artassociation.org.

The last week of July brings an always fun **Teton County Fair,** 307/733-5289, www.tetonwyo.org/fai, with 4-H exhibits (from lambs to photography), pig wrestling in the mud, a horse show, free pony rides and a petting zoo, watermelon- and pie-eating contests, live music and comedy acts, a carnival, rodeos, monster trucks, and everyone's favorite: a bang-up demolition derby ($10) on the final Sunday night.

On second weekend of September, the invitation-only **Jackson Hole One-Fly Contest** attracts anglers from all over, including several celebrity competitors. For details, call 307/733-3270 or 800/570-3270.

FALL

Jackson Hole is at its most glorious in the fall, as aspens and cottonwoods turn into a fire of yellow and orange against the Teton backdrop. Most tourists have fled back home, leaving locals and hardier visitors to savor the cool autumn nights. The peak time for **fall colors** is generally the first week of October—considerably later than most people expect.

The primary autumn event is the **Jackson Hole Fall Arts Festival,** featuring exhibits at the National Museum of Wildlife Art and local galleries, a juried art fair, a miniature art show, art and cooking demonstrations, silent auctions, cowboy poetry and old-time cowboy music, and other events over a 10-day period from mid- to late September. Also fun is a "quickdraw" in which artists paint, draw, and sculpt while you watch; the pieces are then auctioned off. For more information and a schedule of the many events, call 307/733-3316, or head to www.jacksonholechamber.com on the web. The festival's **Arts for the Parks National Art Competition** attracts thousands of paintings representing scenes from America's national parks. This isn't for amateurs; the top prize is $50,000. The banquet and silent auction seats fill by mid-August; call 307/733-2787 or 800/553-2787 for reservations (required), or get additional details at www.artsfortheparks.com.

In early October, **Quilting in the Tetons** brings a week of exhibits, classes, workshops, and quilting demonstrations. Get details at 307/733-3087, www.quiltthetetons.org.

Summer Recreation

RIVER RAFTING

Jackson Hole's most popular summertime recreational activity is running Wyoming's largest river, the Snake. Each year more than 150,000 people climb aboard rafts, canoes, and kayaks to float down placid reaches of the Snake or to blast through the boiling rapids of Snake River Canyon. (As an aside, the name "Snake" comes from the Shoshone Indians, who used serpentine hand movements as sign language for their tribal name—a motion trappers misinterpreted as a snake and applied to the river flowing through Shoshone land.)

Almost 20 different rafting companies offer dozens of raft trips each day of the summer. Although you may be able to walk up and get a raft trip the same day, it's a good idea to reserve ahead for any river trip in July and August. In general, try to book a trip three or four days in advance if possible and at least one week ahead if you need a specific time, prefer an overnight float trip, or are traveling with a larger group. One or two people are more likely to get onboard at the last minute.

You may want to ask around to determine the advantages of each company. Some are cheaper but require you to drive a good distance from town; others offer more experienced crews; still others provide various perks such as fancy meals, U-paddle trips, overnight camps along the river, interpretive trips, or boats with fewer (or more) people. Several operators also lead seven-hour combination trips that include a lazy float followed by a meal break and a wild whitewater run.

The rafting companies generally operate from mid-May to late September, and river conditions change throughout the season. Highest flows—and the wildest rides—are generally in May and June. Get a complete listing of floating and boating outfits, along with descriptive brochures, from the Wyoming State Information Center in Jackson.

Float Trips

The gentlest way to see the Snake is by taking one of the many commercial float trips. Along the way, you'll be treated to stunning views of the Tetons and glimpses of eagles, ospreys, beavers, and perhaps moose or other wildlife along the riverbanks. Several companies—Fort Jackson, Barker-Ewing, Grand Teton Lodge Co., Heart Six, Signal Mountain, Solitude, and Triangle X—offer five- or 10-mile scenic float trips along the quiet stretch within Grand Teton National Park, putting in at Deadman's Bar (10 miles) or Schwabacher Landing (five miles) and taking out in Moose. Flagg Ranch Resort has float and whitewater rafting on the Snake River above Jackson Lake.

Jackson Hole's most popular summertime recreation is running Wyoming's largest river, the Snake. Each year more than 150,000 people raft, canoe, and kayak, floating down placid reaches of the Snake or blasting through the boiling rapids of Snake River Canyon.

Several other rafting operations offer 13-mile South Park float trips *outside the park* (these typically include a lunch), putting in at the bridge near Wilson and taking out above Hoback Junction. Companies offering this trip include Barker-Ewing, Dave Hansen, Flagg Ranch, Lewis & Clark, Sands, Snake River Kayak & Canoe School, and Teton Expeditions. The in-the-park trips are considerably more scenic, so know what you are getting before you sign up because the differences are not usually emphasized by the rafting companies (at least not by those who don't operate inside the park).

Float trip prices on the longer 13-mile runs outside the park typically cost $35–40 for adults and $25–35 for children. Expect to pay around $40 ($25 kids) for the 10-mile trips inside the park, or $25 (18 for kids) for the five-mile in-the-park floats. Age limits vary, but kids must generally be at least eight to float the river. Raft companies usually have folks meet up in either Jackson or Moose, but Heart Six departs from their ranch in Buffalo Valley, 45 miles northeast of Jackson. A wide variety of special voyages are also available from the various companies, including overnight camping and fish-and-float trips.

Call one of the following rafting outfits for details or pick up their slick brochures at the visitors center or from their offices scattered around town: **Barker-Ewing Float Trips,** 307/733-1000 or 800/448-4202, www.barker-ewing.com; **Dave Hansen Whitewater,** 307/733-6295 or 800/732-6295, www.davehansenwhitewater .com; **Fort Jackson Scenic Snake River Float Trips,** 307/733-2583 or 800/735-8430, www .scenicfloats.com; **Grand Teton Lodge Float Trips,** 307/543-2811 or 800/628-9988, www .gtlc.com; **Heart Six Ranch,** 307/543-2477 or 888/543-2477, www.heartsix.com; **Lewis & Clark Expeditions,** 307/733-4022 or 800/824-5375, www.lewisandclarkexpeds.com; **Sands Wild Water,** 307/733-4410 or 800/358-8184,

www.sandswhitewater.com; **Signal Mountain Lodge & Marina,** 307/733-5470 or 307/543-2831, www.signalmountainlodge.com; **Mad River Boat Trips,** (a.k.a. Snake River Expeditions), 307/733-6203 or 800/458-7238, www .mad-river.com; **Snake River Kayak & Canoe School,** 307/733-9999 or 800/529-2501, www.snakeriverkayak.com; **Solitude Scenic Float Trips,** 307/733-2871 or 888/704-2800, www.solitudefloattrips.com; **Teton Expeditions** (a.k.a. Jackson Hole Whitewater), 307/733-1007 or 888/700-7238, www.tetonexpeditions .com; and **Triangle X Float Trips** (a.k.a. National Park Float Trips), 307/733-5500 or 888/860-0005, www.trianglex.com.

Flagg Ranch Rafting, 307/543-2861 or 800/443-2311, www.flaggranch.com, leads 10-mile float trips down the upper Snake River ($40 adults; $27 kids), starting at Flagg Ranch Resort and heading downriver to Jackson Lake.

You can also float the river with any of the local fishing outfitters and combine angling with drifting downriver. One good company—they give a really personalized tour—is **Wooden Boat River Tours,** 307/732-2628, www.wood-boattours.com, which has classic wooden dories.

JACKSON HOLE

© DON PITCHER

floating the Snake River

Note that a few of the raft operators are regarded as "training grounds" for other companies; recommended outfits with good records include Barker-Ewing, Solitude, Grand Teton Lodge Co., and Triangle X.

Whitewater Trips

Below Jackson, the Snake enters the wild Snake River Canyon, a stretch early explorers labeled "the accursed mad river." The usual put-in point for whitewater "rapid-transit" trips is West Table Creek Campground, 26 miles south of Jackson. The take-out point is Sheep Gulch, eight miles downstream. In between, the river rocks and rolls through the narrow canyon, pumping past waterfalls and eagle nests and then over the two biggest rapids, Big Kahuna and Lunch Counter, followed by the smaller Rope and Champagne Rapids. For a look at the action from the highway, stop at the paved turnout at milepost 124, where a trail leads down to Lunch Counter. The river changes greatly throughout the season, with the highest water and wildest rides in June. By August the water has warmed enough for a quick dip. Be sure to ask your river guide about the Jeep that sits in 60 feet of water below Lunch Counter!

Whitewater trips last around 3.5 hours (including transportation from Jackson) and cost around $40 adults, $31 children (age limits vary). Seven-hour combination trips that include a float trip, meal, and whitewater run are around $69 adults, $53 kids. You'll find discounted rates early or late in the summer and with operators who use Titanic-size 16-person rafts. The U-paddle versions are more fun than letting the guide do all the work in an oar raft, and the smaller eight-person rafts provide the most challenging (and wettest) runs. Most companies include round-trip transportation from Jackson.

Expect to get wet, so wear lightweight clothes and bring a jacket for the return ride. Most rafting companies provide wetsuits and booties. Note that this is not exactly a wilderness experience, especially in mid-July, when stretches of the river look like a Los Angeles freeway with traffic jams of rafts, kayaks, inner tubes, and other flotsam and jetsam. The river isn't as crowded on weekdays and early in the morning; take an 8 A.M. run for the fewest people.

Don't take your own camera along unless it's waterproof; bankside float-tographers are positioned along the biggest rapids to shoot both commercial and private rafters. Stop by **Float-O-Graphs,** 130 W. Broadway, 307/733-6453 or 888/478-7427, www.floatographs.com, for a photo from your run. Another company with a similar service is **Whitewater Photos & Video,** 140 N. Cache Dr., 307/733-7015 or 800/948-3426, www.snakeriverphotos.com. Both companies also post photos online.

For details on whitewater raft trips, contact one of the following companies: **Barker-Ewing Whitewater,** 307/733-1000 or 800/448-4202, www.barker-ewing.com; **Dave Hansen Whitewater,** 307/733-6295 or 800/732-6295, www.davehansenwhitewater.com; **Jackson Hole Whitewater,** 307/733-1007 or 800/700-7238, www.jhww.com; **Lewis & Clark Expeditions,** 307/733-4022 or 800/824-5375, www.lewisandclarkexpeds.com; **Mad River Boat Trips,** 307/733-6203 or 800/458-7238, www.mad-river.com; **Sands Wild Water,** 307/733-4410 or 800/358-8184, www.sandswhitewater.com; **Snake River Kayak & Canoe School,** 307/733-9999 or 800/529-2501, www.snakeriverkayak.com; or **Snake River Park Whitewater,** 307/733-7078 or 800/562-1878, www.srpkoa.com. In addition to these, **Flagg Ranch Rafting,** 307/543-2861 or 800/443-2311, www.flaggranch.com, guides three-hour scenic floats down the upper Snake River (above Jackson Lake) for $40 adults, $27 kids.

Recommended companies with good safety records and well-trained staff include Barker-Ewing, Dave Hansen, and Sands. The largest local rafting company, Mad River, has a reputation as a proving ground for novice guides. It's your choice, but I personally would not raft with Snake River Park Whitewater.

Float It Yourself

Grand Teton National Park in Moose, 307/739-3602, www.nps.gov/grte, has useful information on running the park portions of the river; ask for a copy of *Floating the Snake*

River. Note that life jackets, boat permits ($5 for a seven-day permit), and registration are required to run the river through the park, and that inner tubes and air mattresses are prohibited. Floating the gentler parts (from Jackson Lake Dam to just above Pacific Creek) is generally easy for even novice boaters and canoeists, but below that point things get dicier. The water averages two or three feet deep, but it sometimes exceeds 10 feet and flow rates are often more than 8,000 cubic feet per second, creating logjams, braided channels, strong currents, and dangerous sweepers. Peak flows are between mid-June and early July. Inexperienced rafters or anglers die nearly every year in the river. Flowrate signs are posted at most river landings, the Moose Visitor Center, and the Buffalo Ranger Station in Moran. If you're planning to raft or kayak on the whitewater parts of the Snake River, be sure to contact the Bridger-Teton National Forest office in Jackson, 307/739-5500, for additional information, including their *Snake River Floater's Guide.*

Excellent waterproof maps of the Grand Canyon of the Snake River are sold at the Wyoming State Information Center, 532 N. Cache. In addition to showing the rapids, these maps describe local geology and other features.

Rent rafts from **Leisure Sports** in Jackson at 1075 South U.S. Hwy. 89, 307/733-3040, www.leisuresportsadventure.com; **Riding & Rafts** in Alpine (35 miles southwest of Jackson), 307/654-9900, www.jacksonholeout fitters.com; **Rent-A-Raft** in Hoback Junction (12 miles south of Jackson), 307/733-2728 or 800/321-7328; or **Snake River Kayak & Canoe School,** 307/733-9999 or 800/529-2501, www.snakeriverkayak.com. Rent whitewater kayaks from Leisure Sports, Snake River Kayak & Canoe School, and **Jackson Hole Kayak School,** 307/733-2471 or 800/733-2471, www.jhkayakschool.com. Both **Alltrans,** 307/733-4325 or 800/443-6133, www.jackson holealltrans.com, and **Teton Taxi & Backcountry Shuttle,** 307/733-1506, www.tetontaxi .com, offers a shuttle service; around $18 to transport your car from the put-in point to your take-out spot.

FISHING

Jackson Hole has some of the finest angling in Wyoming, with native Snake River cutthroat (a distinct subspecies) and brook trout in the river, along with Mackinaw (lake trout), cutthroat, and brown trout in the lakes. The Snake is a particular favorite of beginning fly-fishing enthusiasts; popular shoreside fishing spots are just below Jackson Lake Dam and near the Wilson Bridge. Jackson Lake may provide higher odds for catching a fish, but you'll need to rent a boat from one of the marinas. This is the place parents take kids. Another very popular fishing hole is just below the dam on Jackson Lake. Flat Creek on the National Elk Refuge is an acclaimed spot for fly-fishing. Note that Wyoming fishing licenses are valid within Grand Teton National Park but not in Yellowstone, where you'll need a separate permit.

Fishing Guides

Many local companies offer guided fly-fishing float trips down the Snake River and other area waterways. Two people (same price for one person) should expect to pay $350 per day for a guide, rods and reels, lunch, and boat. Your fishing license and flies are extra. The visitors center has a listing of local fishing guides and outfitters, and its racks are filled with their brochures.

On Your Own

If you'd rather do it yourself, pick up a copy of the fat and free *Western Fishing Newsletter,* which offers descriptions of regional fishing areas and advice on which lures to try. Find it at **Jack Dennis' Outdoor Shop,** 50 E. Broadway, 307/733-3270 or 800/570-3270, www.jackdennis.com. While there, you may want to buy a regional guide to fishing such as *Flyfisher's Guide to Wyoming* by Ken Retallic (Wilderness Adventures Press; www.wildav.com) or *Fishing Wyoming* by Kenneth Lee Graham (Globe Pequot Press; www.falconbooks.com).

Jackson has several excellent fly-fishing shops, including the aforementioned Jack Dennis' Outdoor Shop. **Westbank Anglers,** 3670 Teton Village Rd., 307/733-6483 or 800/922-3474, www.westbank.com, is a nationally known fly-fishing dealer with a slick mail-order catalog, excellent fishing clinics, and float trips. Both **High Country Flies,** 185 N. Center St., 307/733-7210, www.highcountryflies.com, and **Orvis Jackson Hole,** 485 W. Broadway, 307/733-5407, offer fly-fishing classes and sell quality gear. Rent fishing rods, fly rods, float tubes, and waders from Jack Dennis, High Country Flies, or **Leisure Sports,** 1075 South U.S. Hwy. 89, 307/733-3040, www.leisure sportsadventure.com.

BOATING
Kayaking and Canoeing

In business for more than 25 years, **Snake River Kayak & Canoe School,** 365 N. Cache, 307/733-9999 or 800/529-2501, www.snake riverkayak.com, offers a wide variety of river kayaking and canoeing classes for all levels of ability, plus fishing trips and raft trips. Full-day private lessons—including transportation, boats, paddles, wetsuit, rubber booties, and lifejackets—cost $330 for two students. Beginners may want to start out with one of the three-hour "rubber duckie" inflatable kayak river trips for $49. In addition, the school has sea kayak tours of all lengths in Yellowstone National Park. They rent practically anything that floats: canoes, sea kayaks, whitewater kayaks, inflatable kayaks, driftboats, and rafts, all with paddles and roof racks included. Also available are dry bags and life jackets.

The folks at **Rendezvous River Sports/Jackson Hole Kayak School,** 945 W. Broadway, 307/733-2471 or 800/733-2471, www.jhkayak school.com, teach a wide range of kayaking courses from the absolute beginner level to advanced "hairboating" for experts. Classes include kayak roll clinics ($80), river rescue ($135), and special women's and kids' classes. Two-day introductory classes cost $245; four days of instruction is $475. Private lessons are available, and the company rents sea kayaks and whitewater kayaks, plus inflatable kayaks.

Leisure Sports, 1075 South U.S. Hwy. 89, 307/733-3040, www.leisuresportsadventure.com,

rents rafts, canoes, inflatable kayaks, water skis, wet suits, dry bags, life jackets, and all sorts of other outdoor equipment (including jet skis). **Adventure Sports** in Moose, 307/733-3307, also rents canoes and kayaks.

Windsurfing

Jackson Lake is a popular sailboarding place with moderate winds (good for beginners) and an impressive Teton backdrop. Advanced windsurfers looking for stronger wind conditions head to Slide Lake east of Kelly or to blow-me-down Yellowstone Lake. Equipment rentals are not available locally.

HORSEBACK RIDING
Trail Rides

Think of the Wild West and one animal always comes to mind—the horse. A ride on Old Paint gives city slickers a chance to saunter back in time to a simpler era and to simultaneously learn how ornery and opinionated horses can be. If it rains, you'll also learn why cowboys are so enthralled with cowboy hats. In Jackson Hole you can choose from brief half-day trail rides in Grand Teton National Park all the way to weeklong pack trips into the rugged Teton Wilderness. The visitors center has a brochure listing more than a dozen local outfitters and stables that provide trail rides and pack trips.

For rides by the hour or day (approximately $25 for a one-hour ride or $60–65 for a half-day), try **Scott's Jackson Hole Trail Rides** in Teton Village, 307/733-6992; **Snow King Stables,** behind Snow King Resort, 307/733-5781, www.snowking.com; **Spring Creek Ranch,** atop Gros Ventre Butte off Spring Gulch Rd., 307/733-8833 or 800/443-6139, www.spring creekranch.com; **A/OK Corral,** in Hoback Junction, 307/733-6556, www.horsecreek ranch.com; **Mill Iron Ranch,** 10 miles south of Jackson, 307/733-6390 or 888/808-6390, www.millironranch.net; or **Goosewing Ranch,** 25 miles east of Kelly near the Gros Ventre Wilderness, 307/733-5251 or 888/733-5251, www.goosewingranch.com. Of these, Scott's Jackson Hole Trail Rides, Spring Creek Ranch, and Mill Iron Ranch are the most popular, but you probably won't go wrong with any of these companies. Spring Creek Ranch and A/OK Corral also offer rides that include breakfast or dinner cookouts. Farther afield are several companies offering trail rides, including four that operate out of Buffalo Valley (45 miles northeast of Jackson): **Buffalo Valley Ranch,** 307/543-2026 or 888/543-2477; **Castagno Outfitters,** 307/543-2407, www.castagnooutfitters.com; **Two Ocean Pass Ranch & Outfitting,** 307/543-2309 or 800/726-2409; and **Yellowstone Outfitters/Wagons West,** 307/543-2418 or 800/447-4711, www.yellowstoneoutfitters .com. More trail rides are offered at **Cowboy Village Resort at Togwotee,** 307/733-8800 or 800/543-2847, www.cowboyvillage.com, 48 miles northeast of Jackson on the way to Togwotee Pass. The minimum age for horseback riding is typically five or six; these young children typically ride while the horse is being led around by a parent.

Rides of all sorts are available in Grand Teton

trail rides at Teton Village

© DON PITCHER

National Park at **Jackson Lake Lodge** and **Colter Bay Corral;** get specifics at 307/543-2811 or 800/628-9988, www.gtlc.com. In Alpine (35 miles southwest of Jackson), **Riding & Rafts,** 307/654-9900, www.jacksonholeoutfitters.com, offers unguided horse rentals for $15 for the first hour and $12 for subsequent hours; it's the only place for do-it-yourselfers in the area.

Jackson Hole Llamas, 307/739-9582 or 800/830-7316, www.jhllamas.com, offers backcountry treks with these fascinating and gentle animals.

Chuck wagon cookouts are a very popular family option in Jackson Hole during the summer. Guests travel in horse-drawn wagons (or by horseback) and are treated to a delicious all-you-can-eat meal and entertainment. See Chuck Wagon Cookouts (in Entertainment and the Arts) for details.

Equestrian Center

Experienced riders head out Spring Creek Road to **Spring Creek Equestrian Center,** 307/739-9062, www.springcreekequestrian.com. Facilities at the center (not connected with Spring Creek Ranch) include a heated indoor arena, three outdoor arenas, a cross-country course, and a small tack store. The public is welcome to attend their shows, most notably the Jackson Hole Horse Trials in August and a pair of summertime hunter-jumper shows. They do not offer general horse boarding or riding lessons.

Wagon Trains

Two local companies lead overnight wagon-train rides (in wagons with rubber tires) into the country around Jackson Hole. Guests split their time between riding in the wagons and riding on horseback. **Wagons West,** 307/543-2418 or 800/447-4711, www.wagonswestwyo.com, heads up into the Mt. Leidy Highlands for 2–6 days. The shortest trips (two days and one night) are $340 adults, $300 kids under 14. Four-day, three-night trips are $650 adults, $575 kids; and six-day, five-night trips run $875 adults, $775 kids. **Double H Bar,** 307/734-6101 or 888/734-6101, www.tetonwagontrain.com, charges $745 adults ($695 ages 9–14, and $645

JACKSON HOLE

for younger kids) for a three-night package that includes horseback and wagon riding, meals, and camping gear.

DAY HIKES

The country around Jackson abounds with hundreds of miles of hiking trails, providing recreation opportunities for all levels of ability. Many of the most popular local trails are within nearby **Grand Teton National Park.** Notable in-the-park hikes are found in the Taggart Lake and Jenny Lake areas, at Colter Bay, and off the Moose-Wilson Road. The Information Center in Jackson has a brochure detailing these hikes.

For a fast trip to the alpine, take the **tram at Jackson Hole Ski Resort** to the summit Rendezvous Mountain ($15), where trails fan out in various directions and the bird's-eye view is hard to beat. See the Alpine Rides section in this chapter for specifics.

A local outdoors shop, Skinny Skis, 65 W. Deloney Ave., 307/733-6094 or 888/733-7205, www.skinnyskis.com, produces an excellent free summertime guide to hiking in the area called *Trailhead.* Another good free source (for Forest Service trails) is *Top Ten Trails,* available from the Bridger-Teton National Forest office at 340 N. Cache Dr. 307/739-5500, www.fs.fed.us/btnf /teton. Several of the best Forest Service hikes are briefly described as follows.

Snow King

Closest to town are the trails at **Snow King,** where you can either hike up the mountain or ride the chairlift ($8) to the summit and hike back down. Once on top, you'll find a half-mile nature trail and wonderful across-the-valley views of the Tetons. Nearby is the **Cache Creek Trail,** which follows this pretty creek uphill for six miles along an old road that's closed to motor vehicles. It's a great family hike or mountain-bike ride. For an alternate loop back (four miles round-trip), turn onto the **Putt-Putt Trail** two miles up. Cyclists often use Cache Creek Trail to connect with Game Creek Trail for a loop around Snow King Mountain. All of the trails in the Snow King area are

open to mountain bikes, and you can transport bikes on the chairlift.

Teton Pass

Ski Lake is a more challenging hike, but spectacular views await. It starts west of Wilson on Wyoming 22 at Phillips Canyon. Walk up the dirt road one-half mile and take the left fork in the road to the start of the trail. It side-slopes around to a viewpoint and then climbs through the forest to Ski Lake, nestled high in the alpine and three miles from your starting point. The **Black Canyon Overlook Trail** starts from the parking area at the top of Teton Pass, 10 miles west of Jackson. It follows Pass Ridge for two miles, with an abundance of wildflower meadows and forest along the way. You can continue from here down Black Canyon to the end of Trail Creek Road at the base of the pass for a longer hike, but you will need a shuttle ride back up the pass.

Snake River Canyon

The Snake River Canyon south of Jackson is best known as a river rafting destination, but a couple of good hikes are a landlubber's option. The **Cabin Creek Trail** begins one-half mile up a dirt road behind Cabin Creek Campground (17 miles from Jackson). The trail follows the creek uphill to a pass that is filled with late summer wildflowers, and from here you'll be treated to delightful views of the Snake River drainage. Return the same way, or head back downhill along the **Dog Creek Trail** that ends near the junction of Wilson-Fall Creek Road with U.S. Hwy. 89/26. Either way, it's about six miles of hiking, but if you head back via Dog Creek Trail you'll need a shuttle back to your car.

Granite Creek

This beautiful valley has good hiking, a quiet out-of-the-way location, and the added bonus of a hot spring. Get here by driving south from Jackson 12 miles to Hoback Junction and then another 12 miles east on U.S. Hwy. 189 to the turnoff for Granite Hot Springs. The **Granite Creek Falls Trail** starts at the junction of Swift Creek and Granite Creek, eight miles up the road.

It follows the creek upstream to impressive Granite Falls and then on to **Granite Hot Springs,** where you can soak in the wonderful mineral pool for $5.50. Towel and swimsuit rentals are available. The trail is two miles long and quite easy, and camping is available in the area.

For a more challenging hike, try the **Shoal Falls Trail** which starts from the same trailhead eight miles up Granite Creek Road and leads five miles to an overlook near Shoal Falls. Get trail details from the Forest Service.

Guided Hikes

The **Teton County Parks and Recreation Department,** inside the Recreation Center at 155 E. Gill St., 307/739-9025, www.tetonwyo.org/parks, sponsors a wide range of outdoor activities throughout the summer. Adult hikes ($7–10) take place every Tuesday from May–October, plus on Thursdays from June–August. Longer hikes (including an overnighter) take place several times a summer, and free senior walks are offered on Monday mornings during May and June. For a break from the younguns, take them to the kids outings on Wednesdays (for age five and up; $10–12 for half-day) or Fridays (ages eight and up with more strenuous activities; $26 for all day). You don't need to be a local resident to take part in any of these activities, but reserve ahead because some fill up. The Parks and Rec office also rents out volleyballs, horseshoes, and croquet sets.

Educational nature walks into the mountains around Jackson are offered by **The Hole Hiking Experience,** 307/690-4453 or 866/733-4453, www.holehike.com. Rates start at $55 ($45 for kids) for a four-hour hike. For a free version, Grand Teton National Park offers guided walks and nature talks throughout the year.

Get a geologist's perspective from **Earth Tours,** 307/733-4261, www.earth-tours.com. These outstanding day hikes are led by Dr. Keith Watts and include a ride on the Jackson Hole Resort tram. He also guides full-day trips into Yellowstone.

For a different sort of guided hike, check out the excellent **historical walking tours** offered by the Jackson Hole Museum; they're described under Sights.

MOUNTAIN BIKING

Jackson Hole offers all sorts of adventures for cyclists, particularly those with mountain bikes. Most local bike shops provide maps of local mountain-bike routes, or you can purchase a waterproof Jackson Hole mountain-biking map. Note that mountain bikes are not allowed on hiking trails in Grand Teton National Park or in Forest Service wilderness areas. If you visit Jackson early in the season, check out the Jenny Lake road inside the park; in April it's plowed but closed to cars. It's great for an easy and scenic ride.

Bike Paths

The easiest local places to ride are the **Jackson Hole Community Pathways,** an expanding series of paved paths that may eventually continue for 50 miles. There are ongoing efforts to put a bike path over Teton Pass via the Old Pass Road, thus allowing riders to go all the way to Driggs, Idaho. Get details from the Teton County, 307/733-4609, www.tetonwyo.org /pathways, or from the Friends of Pathways website, www.jhpathways.com.

Currently a seven-mile path connects Wilson with Teton Village, and a second seven-mile paved trail heads south of town, paralleling the highway to the Snake River bridge. It provides a connection to the very popular Game Creek Trail, which meets the Cache Creek Trail, circling back to Jackson behind Snow King. In addition, the trails at Snow King are open to mountain bikers, and you can either peddle uphill or ride the chairlift with your bike ($8). Jackson Hole Mountain Resort has seven miles of bike trails on the lower sections of the mountain for all levels of ability, although you can't ride the road to the summit or take a bike on the tram.

A four-mile path starts behind the main post office on Maple Way, crosses U.S. Hwy. 89, and continues past the high school before turning north to meet the road to Wilson (State 22). This road has wide shoulders but gets lots of traffic.

JACKSON HOLE

Bike Rentals and Tours

Rent mountain bikes from **Teton Cycle Works,** 175 N. Glenwood St., 307/733-4386, www .tetoncycleworks.com; **Hoback Sports,** 40 S. Millward St., 307/733-5335, www.hoback sports.com; **The Edge Sports,** 490 W. Broadway, 307/734-3916; **Wilson Backcountry Sports,** in Teton Village, 307/733-5228; and **Adventure Sports** in Moose, 307/733-3307. All of these places rent bikes and helmets for around $30–40 per day, $20–25 per half day, and several also rent bike trailers, car racks, and kid bikes. Most also sell and repair bikes.

Half-day mountain-bike tours are available for $40–55 per day from **Fat Tire Tours/Hoback Sports,** 307/733-5335, www.hobacksports.com; one of the tours includes a chairlift ride to the top of Snow King. **Teton Mountain Bike Tours,** 307/733-0712 or 800/733-0788, www.teton mtbike.com, offers scenic half- or all-day bike trips through Grand Teton and Yellowstone National Parks as well as Bridger-Teton National Forest and the National Elk Refuge. These trips are for all levels of ability, with prices starting at $45 for a four-hour ride.

ALPINE RIDES

Jackson Hole Resort

Take a fast and scenic ride to the top of Rendezvous Mountain (10,450 feet) aboard the **aerial tram** at Teton Village. The tram ride takes 10 minutes, gains more than 4,000 feet in elevation, and costs $15 adults, $13 seniors, $5 ages 6–12, and free for kids under six. Details at 307/733-2292 or 888/333-7766, www.jacksonhole.com. Open daily late May to late September, this is a sensational way to reach the alpine. Dogs and bikes aren't allowed on the tram.

On top is a small snack shop, but you should bring a lunch because the choices are limited and pricey. Several trails provide enjoyable hikes from the summit, and naturalists lead free two-hour walks twice daily. Be sure to pack drinking water and a warm jacket.

Rendezvous Mountain is a favorite place for paragliders to launch. Tandem paragliding flights

($200) are available from **Jackson Hole Paragliding,** 307/739-2626, www.jhparagliding.com. No experience is needed for these half-hour flights.

Snow King

At Snow King Mountain right on the edge of Jackson, the resort's main **chairlift** operates during summer, taking folks for a 20-minute ride to the summit of the 7,751-foot mountain for $8 round-trip. The chairlift runs daily 9 A.M.–8 P.M. in midsummer. On top you'll find a short nature trail and panoramic views of the Tetons.

Also at Snow King is the 2,500-foot-long **Alpine Slide,** a favorite of kids. For anyone older than six, the cost is $8 for one ride or $22 for three rides. For children under six (riding with an adult) it's just $1 per ride. Get details on both the chairlift and slide at 307/733-7680 or 800/522-5464, www.snowking.com.

Grand Targhee

On the other side of the Tetons at **Grand Targhee Ski Resort,** 307/353-2300 or 800/827-4433, www.grandtarghee.com, you can ride the chairlift for $8 ($5 for kids) to the 10,200-foot summit of Fred's Mountain, where Grand Teton stands just seven miles away. The lift operates daily July to mid-August, plus Wednesdays, Saturdays, and Sundays in June, and from mid-August to Labor Day.

SWIMMING AND GYMS

Jackson is home to the marvelous **Teton County/Jackson Recreation Center,** 155 E. Gill St., 307/739-9025, www.tetonwyo.org/parks, which includes an indoor aquatics complex with a lap pool, 185-foot corkscrew water slide, and hot tub, plus a wading pool featuring a waterfall, slide, and water geyser. Basketball and volleyball courts are also inside the Rec Center, and after your workout, relax in the sauna and steam room. Nonresident prices are a steep (but worth it!) $6 adults, $4.75 ages 13–17, $3.50 seniors and ages 3–12, and $16 families; free for tots under three. The rec center also offers a variety of courses and activities, including yoga, toddler swimming, basketball, volleyball, and aerobics. It's open Monday–Friday 6 A.M.–9 P.M., Saturday noon–9 P.M., and Sunday noon–7 P.M.

Out of the way is the wonderful hot mineral pool (93°F in summer and 112°F in winter) at **Granite Hot Springs,** 307/733-6318. Head south 12 miles to Hoback Junction and then 12 miles east on U.S. Hwy. 189 to the turnoff for Granite. The pool is another 10 miles out a well-maintained gravel road—a total of 35 miles from Jackson. Entrance is $5.50 adults, $3.50 ages 3–12, free for infants. Towel and swimsuit rentals are available. The springs are open 10 A.M. until dusk (around 8 P.M.) in summer, and 11 A.M.–5 P.M. in winter; closed fall and spring. No showers or running water at the pool, but vault toilets are nearby.

Take exercise and yoga classes at **Jackson Hole Athletic Club,** 875 W. Broadway, 307/733-8830, which also houses a full gymnasium with all of the usual workout equipment, weights, and a steam room. Day passes are $12. **Teton Sports Club,** 4030 W. Lake Creek Dr., 307/733-7004, is near the Aspens (south of Teton Village) and offers aerobic classes, cardio machines, free weights, hot tubs, a sauna, and a seasonal outdoor pool. Day passes are $10. Massage therapists and personal trainers are available. **Teton Rock Gym,** 1116 Maple Way, 307/733-0707, www.jacksonholenet.com/tetonrockgym, has large indoor climbing walls, a weight room, and gear rentals. An **outdoor climbing wall** is located in the heart of Teton Village next to the pond. See the Grand Teton National Park chapter for mountain-climbing options.

BALLOON RIDES

Two local companies offer hot air balloon rides in the summer. **Wyoming Balloon Co.,** 307/739-0900, www.wyomingballoon.com, takes off from the Jackson Hole side of the mountains. An hourlong flight is $195 adults, $125 kids (six and older). **Grand Teton Balloon Flights,** 307/733-0470 or 800/378-0470, www.hometown.aol.com/tetonballooning, picks people up in Jackson and transports them over the mountains to Teton Valley, Idaho, for a one-hour flight; $189 per person.

GOLF AND TENNIS

Jackson Hole Golf & Tennis Club, one mile north of town, 307/733-3111, www.gtlc.com, has an 18-hole golf course designed by Robert Trent Jones, Jr. and rated one of the 10 best in America. Also here are a private swimming pool, tennis courts, and The Strutting Grouse Restaurant and Lounge, a perfect place for patio dining in the summer.

Teton Pines Country Club, on Teton Village Rd., 307/733-1773 or 800/238-2223, www.tetonpines.com, is Jackson Hole's other golf spot. Its Arnold Palmer–designed 18-hole championship course is very challenging; 14 of the holes require over-water shots. The club also features a grand clubhouse, tennis courts, a large (and private) outdoor pool, and fine dining at The Pines restaurant. Both Teton Pines and Jackson Hole Golf & Tennis Club have rentals and lessons for golfers and tennis aficionados. **Public tennis courts** are located on the east end of the rodeo grounds along Snow King Drive, and within Miller Park at Deloney and Gill streets.

For the truly serious professional golfer, **Alpine Miniature Golf,** 307/733-5200 or 800/522-5464, www.snowking.com, has a Lilliputian 18-hole hillside course next to the Alpine Slide at Snow King Resort.

TOWN PARKS

Eight parks are scattered around Jackson, including the famous Town Square described previously. Several others are of note, particularly if you have children in tow. The largest, **Miller Park,** covers a grassy city block at Deloney and Gill streets and includes basketball and tennis courts, a picnic shelter, restrooms, and a delightful playground. **Powderhorn Park,** on the west side of town near Powderhorn Lane and Alpine Lane, has additional playground equipment, a picnic shelter, and restrooms. **Mike Yokel Jr. Park,** on E. Kelly Ave. near Snow King, features a sand volleyball court, horseshoe pits, a playground, a picnic shelter, and restrooms. **Baux Park** at the base of Snow King Mountain is similar, with a playground, horseshoe pits, and picnic tables. **Home Ranch Park** is next to the parking lot at Cache and Gill and has picnic tables and restrooms. **Owen Bircher Park** in Wilson includes a summertime roping arena (a good place to watch budding cowboys and cowgirls on summer afternoons) that becomes a wintertime ice rink. The park also has a sand volleyball court, a softball/soccer field, picnic tables, and restrooms.

In addition to those mentioned in the town parks, **public restrooms** can also be found one-half block south of Town Square on Cache Drive.

Downhill Skiing and Snowboarding

Jackson Hole has an international reputation as a winter destination. As access has become easier and the facilities more developed, many people have discovered the wonders of a Jackson Hole winter, especially one centered on a week of skiing or snowboarding. Three very different ski resorts attract the crowds: Grand Targhee for downhome, powder-to-the-butt conditions; Snow King for steep, inexpensive, edge-of-town slopes; and Jackson Hole for flashy, world-class skiing. All three places have rental equipment, ski schools, and special programs for kids. Snowboarders and telemarkers are welcome on the slopes. These resorts combine with an incredible abundance of developed and wild places to ski cross-country to make Jackson Hole one of the premier ski and snowboard destinations in America.

See your travel agent for package trips to any of the Jackson-area resorts. For daily ski reports, including information on both downhill and Nordic areas and the backcountry, listen to KMTN (FM 96.9) in the morning.

Ski Club

If you plan to spend more than a couple of days in the area, it is probably worth your while to join the **Jackson Hole Ski Club,** 307/733-6433, www.jhskiclub.com. In return for a $30 annual membership, you receive an impressive number of premiums, including reduced rates for lift tickets and season passes at all three local ski areas, plus discounted lodging, meals, drinks, snowmobile trips, and shopping at dozens of local stores. Join up at any local ski shop.

Ski and Snowboard Rentals

Rent or buy downhill skis and snowboards from **Hoback Sports,** 40 S. Millward St., 307/733-5335, www.hobacksports.com; **Gart Sports,** 485 W. Broadway, 307/733-4449, www.gartsports .com; **Jack Dennis' Outdoor Shop,** 50 E. Broadway, 307/733-3270 or 800/570-3270, www.jackdennis.com, and in Teton Village, 307/733-6838; **Pepi Stiegler Sports** in Teton Village, 307/733-4505; **Wildernest Sports,** Teton Village, 307/733-4297; or **Teton Village Sports,** 307/733-2181 or 800/874-4224, www .skitvs.com. Rentals are also available at all three ski areas.

Snowboarders will find the latest gear at **Boardroom of Jackson Hole,** 245 W. Pearl, 307/733-8327; **Hole in the Wall Snowboard Shop,** 307/739-2689; **Low Rider Board Shop** at Pepi Stiegler Sports in Teton Village, 307/733-4505; and **Village Board Shop,** at Teton Village Sports, 307/733-2181 or 800/874-4224, www.skitvs.com. At Grand Targhee Ski Resort, rent or buy boards from **Phat Fred's,** 307/353-2300 or 800/827-4433, www.grandtarghee.com.

GRAND TARGHEE SKI RESORT

On the west side of the Tetons 42 miles from Jackson, Grand Targhee Ski Resort offers the friendliness of a small resort with the amenities and snow you'd expect at a major one. To get here you'll need to drive into Idaho and turn east at Driggs. The resort sits at the end of a beautiful road (recently rebuilt) 12 miles east of Driggs and just six miles inside Wyoming. Their motto says it all: "Snow from heaven, not from hoses." With an annual snowfall topping 500 inches (42 feet!)—most of which is champagne powder—Targhee became the spot where powderhounds got all they could ever want. Ski magazines consistently rank it as having North

America's best (or second-best) snow. In fact, the resort guarantees its snow: If you find conditions not to your liking, you can turn in your ticket within an hour of purchase and get a "snow check" good for another day of skiing. By the way, the official name is Grand Targhee Ski and Summer Resort, but most folks call it Grand Targhee, or simply Targhee.

Now owned by George Gillett—he previously owned Vail Resort—Grand Targhee has seen some changes in the last few years, including a quad chairlift that opened 500 acres of intermediate skiing terrain on adjacent Peaked Mountain. A second quad chairlift is expected to open for the 2003–2004 winter season, and additional hotel rooms are on the drawing boards. The resort is negotiating a land swap with the Forest Service to gain ownership of the public land on which the resort sits. If this happens (and it is controversial), it could lead to several major developments at Targhee. But some things won't change: the beautifully groomed slopes, the uncrowded and relaxed setting, the dramatic Teton backdrop, and the friendly staff, including at least one cowboy-hatted potato farmer who doubles as a lift operator.

The biggest drawback to Grand Targhee Ski Resort is the same thing that makes it so great—the weather. Lots of snow means lots of clouds and storms, and because it snows so much there are many days when the name cynics apply—"Grand Foghee"—seems more appropriate. Many folks who have returned to Targhee year after year have still not seen the magnificent Grand Teton backdrop behind the ski area! Be sure to bring your goggles. The quad lift up Peaked Mountain provides intermediate skiing on slopes that are more protected and suffer less wind and fog.

Skiing and Snowboarding

Get details for Grand Targhee at 307/353-2300 or 800/827-4433, www.grandtarghee.com. The resort has two quads, one double chairlift, and a surface lift on Fred's Mountain, plus a quad on adjacent Peaked Mountain. The top elevation is 10,230 feet, with the longest run dropping 2,822 feet over almost three miles. Some 750 acres are

groomed, but you'll always find track-free skiing on the remaining 2,250 acres of ungroomed powder, so bring your snorkel. In addition, snow-cat skiing ($299 per day including lunch and guide) is offered on a 1,000-acre section of Peaked Mountain reserved for powderhounds.

Lift tickets at Grand Targhee cost $49 per day ($36 half day) for adults and $31 per day for children ages 6–14 and seniors (free under age six). Substantial discounts are offered for multi-day lift tickets or lodging-and-ski packages.

Fully 70 percent of Targhee's groomed runs are intermediate to advanced-intermediate, but advanced skiers will find an extraordinary number of deep-powder faces to explore. Snowboarders can play at the half-pipe. The ski school offers lessons for all abilities, and children's programs make it possible for parents to leave their kids behind. Cross-country skiers enjoy the Nordic center (described later), and ski and snowboard rentals are available at the base of the mountain. The ski area usually opens in mid-November and closes in late April, although some years you may be able to ski even into July. Lifts operate 9:30 A.M.–4 P.M. daily.

Other Winter Activities

Moon Mountain Ranch (www.sharplink.com /dogsled) leads **dogsled tours** from the lodge in winter, starting with a half-day trip for $115 per adult for single riders or $200 for two riders. Lunch trips and moonlight rides are also available. Guided **snowshoe wildlife tours** ($16) will appeal to amateur naturalists, and on the **sleigh ride dinner** ($32 adults, $15 kids), you'll ride in a horse-drawn sleigh to a yurt where a Western-style meal is served. Targhee's **tubing park** ($8 per hour; opens at 5 P.M.) is a fun place for kids to slide down a snowy hill, and the resort also has an outdoor **skating pond** and skate rentals ($5). A **Kid's Club** at Targhee provides supervised child care.

Summer Activities

Not far from Grand Targhee are several popular summertime hiking trails within the Jedediah Smith Wilderness. The resort is a popular place to relax in the summer and offers many activities.

The quad chairlift ($8 adults, $5 ages 6–14) takes you up the 10,200-foot summit of Fred's Mountain for strikingly close views of the Tetons. The lift operates daily July to mid-August, plus Wednesdays, Saturdays, and Sundays in June, and from mid-August to Labor Day. A Forest Service naturalist leads **guided walks** on weekends, or by request Wednesday–Friday.

Horseback rides and lessons are a favorite Targhee summertime activity; one-hour rides are $24. The area is also a fun mountain-biking destination, with bike rentals and guided tours; you can also take them up the ski lift. The climbing wall ($6) is open to all abilities and is a good place to learn some basic—or advanced—moves. Even more challenging is the adventure ropes course, for those who have always wanted to walk the high wire. There's a special Science Explorers program for older kids, and a Camp Targhee for ones under six, both with tons of fun activities. Other summer activities and facilities at Targhee include a zip line, basketball courts, an outdoor swimming pool and hot tubs, a fitness center, horseshoes, teatherball, tennis, and volleyball. The nine-hole **Targhee Village Golf Course** is just down the road. After all this excitement, you'll probably want to relax with a massage, aromatherapy, facial, or steam bath from the on-site spa.

Based at the resort, the nonprofit **Targhee Institute,** 307/353-2233, directs four-day science programs for ages 6–13 in summer, including a range of fun classes. The institute also offers weeklong Elderhostel programs, covering everything from snowshoeing to photography.

Targhee Accommodations

Call Targhee at 307/353-2300 or 800/827-4433 for details on lodging options at or near the resort, or visit their website: www.grandtarghee.com. The three lodges at the base of the mountain—Targhee Lodge, Teewinot Lodge, and Sioux Lodge—offer ski-in, ski-out access, a large heated outdoor pool, a hot tub, and a workout room. Rates quoted are for the winter holiday season; they're approximately 40 percent lower in summertime. Most lodging places are closed from early September to mid-November, and from mid-April to mid-June.

Get standard motel accommodations at **Targhee Lodge** with holiday winter rates of $181 d. Deluxe hotel rooms with lodgepole furnishings and access to an indoor hot tub are $231 d at **Teewinot Lodge.** The lobby here is a fine place to relax in front of the fire on winter evenings. **Sioux Lodge** continues the Western theme with lodgepole furnishings, but also has kitchenettes, adobe-style fireplaces, and small balconies. Studio units are $331 for up to four people, loft units $436 for four people, and two-bedroom units run $610 for up to eight.

Summer packages are good bargains, including two nights of lodging with breakfast, a scenic chairlift ride, and a one-hour horseback ride; $215 d in the high season. A wide variety of wintertime package deals are also available for stays longer than three nights. One that provides seven nights of lodging and six days of skiing costs $1,700 for two people during the holiday season at Targhee Lodge; rates are considerably higher at Teewinot or Sioux Lodge. You can cut these rates substantially if you ski in the "value" season before mid-December and after late March, with a complete seven-night package for just $1,000 d.

The resort also has off-site condo lodging available approximately 10 miles down the hill at **Teton Creek Resort** and **Powder Valley Condominiums.** Choose from one-, two-, and three-bedroom condominiums, each with a fireplace, kitchen, private patio, and VCR. Outdoor hot tubs are also available. Nightly holiday-season rates start at $210 d for the one-bedroom units, up to $536 for eight people in a three-bedroom unit. Most people rent these condos on a weekly basis; four people can stay in a two-bedroom unit for $3,300 per week during the peak winter holiday season. Rates are, of course, lower if you can come at other times.

In addition to the places at the base of the resort, lodging is available just down the hill in Alta, Wyoming, and in the nearby Idaho towns of Driggs, Victor, and Tetonia. These are described in the Teton Valley, Idaho section of this chapter.

Food and Entertainment

At the base of Grand Targhee is a compact cluster of shops and places to stay. You won't have to walk far to find a cafeteria, pizza place, and burger joint. The nicest place is **Parghee's Steakhouse,** serving hearty breakfasts and lunches, along with cozy dinners. Grand Targhee's social center is the **Trap Bar,** with live music on winter weekends and pub grub on the menu all the time. Guests at Targhee can also take a **horse-drawn sleigh** on a 15-minute ride to a Mongolian-style yurt for a home-cooked steak or chicken dinner. The price is $32 ($15 for kids ages 7–12), and reservations are required. Other shops here sell groceries, ski and snowboard gear, clothing, and gifts. **Lost Horizon Dinner Club,** 307/353-8226, five miles below the resort in the town of Alta, is highly recommended for a relaxing formal dinner with an Asian flair.

Getting There

Grand Targhee is 42 miles northwest of Jackson on the western side of the Tetons in Alta, Wyoming. Get there by driving over Teton Pass (occasionally closed by winter storms), north through Victor and Driggs, Idaho, and then east back into Wyoming.

The **Targhee Express/Alltrans** bus makes daily wintertime trips (90 minutes each way) to Grand Targhee from Jackson Hole. Buses pick up skiers from Jackson and Teton Village hotels shortly after 7 A.M., returning from Targhee at 4:30 P.M. for a round-trip fare of $61, including a full-day lift ticket. Round-trip bus fare without a lift ticket costs $20. Reservations are required; make them before 9 P.M. on the night before by calling 307/733-4325 or 800/443-6133, or on the web at www.jacksonholealltrans.com. Van service is also available year-round to airports in Jackson or Idaho Falls, Idaho.

Events

End the year—and start a new one—with **Torch Light Parades** at Grand Targhee on the evenings of December 25 and 31. Also on New Year's Eve is a fireworks display over the mountain. Each March, the resort celebrates telemark skiing with **Nordic Fest.** Ski races of all sorts take place, and Targhee rocks to great music, an outdoor barbecue, and fun events.

The resort pulls out the stops for the always popular **Targhee Bluegrass Festival** in mid-August, with nationally known acts. Bring your dancin' shoes! The music attracts hundreds of people, so call the resort well ahead of time for camping or lodging reservations. Other big summertime events at Targhee include the **Grand Teton Summer Festival** around Fourth of July and the **WYDAHO Mountain Bike Race,** at the same time.

JACKSON HOLE MOUNTAIN RESORT

Just 12 miles northwest of Jackson is Jackson Hole Mountain Resort, the largest and best-known Wyoming ski area. A true skiers' and snowboarders' mountain, Jackson Hole is considered the most varied and challenging of any American ski area. The powder is usually deep (average snowfall is 38 feet), lift lines are short, the slopes are relatively uncrowded, and the vistas are unbelievable. First opened in 1965, Jackson Hole Mountain Resort has become one of the nation's favorite ski areas. The resort has invested many millions of dollars over the last decade or so, upgrading facilities, adding lifts, expanding snowmaking, completing a spacious children's center, and building an ice rink and snowboarding half-pipe. These improvements have helped expand the resort's reputation as an expert's paradise to also include facilities that are more friendly to families and intermediate skiers.

The mountain has one unusual feature that occurs in midwinter: A temperature inversion frequently develops over the valley, meaning that when it's bitterly cold at the base of the mountain, the top is 15–20°F warmer. Skiers often remain on the upper slopes all day to enjoy these warmer temperatures.

Contact Jackson Hole Mountain Resort at 307/733-2292 or 888/333-7766, www.jacksonhole.com. It is owned by the Kemmerer family, whose ancestors founded the town of Kemmerer, Wyoming, and is one of the few major American ski resorts that is still independently owned.

Superlatives

With an unsurpassed 4,139-foot vertical drop (longest in the United States), 2,500 acres of terrain

JACKSON HOLE

spread over two adjacent mountains, runs that exceed four miles in length, and 24 miles of groomed trails, Jackson Hole Mountain Resort is truly a place of superlatives. Half of the resort's 60 runs are in the advanced category—including several of the notorious double-diamonds—but it is so large that even rank beginners will find plenty of bunny slopes on which to practice. (As a trivial aside, Montana's Big Sky Resort also claims the longest vertical drop of any American mountain—4,300 feet—but this involves taking three lifts and ending your run below where you start.)

The only way to the summit of 10,450-foot **Rendezvous Mountain** is aboard one of the 63-passenger aerial tram cars. Powered by 500-horsepower engines, they climb nearly 2.5 miles in 10 minutes, offering jaw-dropping views across Jackson Hole. Rendezvous Mountain is where experts strut their stuff on these steep and fast slopes, and if you're not at least close to the expert status you'll find your blood pressure rising as the tram heads up the mountain. More than a few skiers and boarders have taken the tram back down after seeing what lies below. Yes, those death-defying cliff-jumping shots are real; from the tram, check out infamous **Corbet's Couloir,** a rocky gully that requires a leap of faith and suicidal urges.

Fortunately, intermediate skiers and boarders are not given short shrift at Jackson Hole Mountain Resort, particularly on the friendlier slopes of 8,481-foot **Apres Vous Mountain.** Intermediate (and advanced) downhillers could spend all day playing on these slopes, and a high-speed quad here means that riders can blast to the summit of Apres Vous in just five minutes. Because of the speed of this and other lifts, the wait at the base is now usually just a few minutes.

In addition to these lifts, you can ride a gondola, three other quad chairs, a triple chair, double chair, and poma lift. Snowboarders will appreciate the half-pipe and boarders' terrain trail. The resort's Kids Ranch provides supervised day care, including a spacious play area. Not far away is a special "magic carpet" (a conveyer belt of sorts) for children learning to ski or snowboard.

Rates and Services

Get to Teton Village from the town of Jackson by hopping on the START bus ($3 each way; 307/733-4521, www.startbus.com). This is the only inexpensive part of a visit to Jackson Hole Resort because prices for lift tickets approach the stratosphere. Single-day tickets for all lifts (including the tram) are $61 adults ($45 per half day), $48 ages 15–21 ($34 per half day), and $31 kids under 14 and seniors older than 65 ($23 per half day). Multiday all-lift tickets—the most common kind bought—are $280 per week (five days of skiing) for adults, $210 for ages 15–21, and $140 for younger kids under 14 and seniors. Lifts are open 9 A.M.–4 P.M. daily (last tram departs at 3:30 P.M.) from Thanksgiving until early April.

Skis and snowboards can be rented at shops in Jackson or Teton Village. The ski school offers a special Kinderschule program for children, and beginning snowboarders can learn from the pros. Jackson Hole Resort even has special steep snowboarding and skiing camps, where you learn from extreme downhill fanatics. Tommy Moe—gold and silver medalist at the 1994 Winter Olympics—teaches a "Steep and Deep" ski camp

© DON PITCHER

and is a ski ambassador for the resort. Jackson Hole's director of skiing (he headed the ski school here for 30 years) is Pepi Stiegler, the Austrian winner of a silver medal in the 1960 Olympics and a gold medal in the 1964 Olympics. You can ski with Pepi on weekdays at 1 P.M.; meet him at the Bridger Gondola.

Ski hosts are scattered around the mountain, ready to provide information and free hourly tours of the slopes from the top of Rendezvous Mountain. Racers and spectators will enjoy NAS-TAR events each Tuesday, Friday, Saturday, and Sunday, along with various other competitions throughout the winter. (The acronym NASTAR is derived from National Standard Race. In NAS-TAR, ski racers of all ages and abilities compete against each other, using a handicap system that helps you gauge your progress through the season. See www.nastar.com for complete details.)

For more information on Jackson Hole Mountain Resort, call 307/733-2292 or 888/333-7766. Get recorded snow conditions by calling 307/733-2291; the messages are changed each morning before 5 A.M. Their website, www.jacksonhole .com, is packed with additional details, including the current weather and snow conditions.

Teton Village

At the base of the mountain is the Swiss-style Teton Village—alias "the Vill." Everything skiers and boarders need is crowded together here: lodges, condominiums, espresso stands, restaurants, après-ski bars, gift shops, groceries, ski, snowboard, and snowshoe rentals and lessons, storage lockers, car rentals, a skating pond, child care, personal trainers, dogsled tours, and even a travel agency for escapes to Hawaii.

On-the-mountain facilities include Casper Restaurant at the bottom of Casper Bowl and snack bars at the top of the tram, the bottom of Thunder chairlift, and the top of Apres Vous chairlift. Casper Restaurant serves a barbecue picnic most days and is a popular place to join friends for lunch.

Into the Backcountry

If you're looking for untracked powder, call **Jackson Hole Guide Service,** 307/739-2663 or 800/450-0477, which leads small groups of downhill skiers to parts of the mountain that are off-limits to mere mortals.

Located in lower Rock Springs Canyon, two miles south of the resort, **Rock Springs Yurt** has a backcountry location that's accessible by cross-country skis or snowshoes. It's a two-mile trek, but you gain 1,000 feet along the way, making this a challenging trip. The yurt is available for guided day trips and overnight stays (it sleeps nine) and may eventually be part of a series of European-style backcountry huts. Call the resort for details.

Powder-hound skiers with a ton of cash will find unparalleled outback conditions accessed via **High Mountain Heli-Skiing,** 307/733-3274, www.skitvs.com. Note, however, that the areas where the choppers land are under consideration for wilderness status, and as this book was being written, the company's Forest Service permit was still in contention.

SNOW KING RESORT

Snow King Resort has three things that other local ski areas lack: location, location, and location. The resort sits directly behind town and just seven blocks from Town Square. This is the locals' place, Jackson's "town hill," but it also offers surprisingly challenging runs. It may not be the largest or fanciest place around, but the King's ski runs make up in difficulty what they lack in size. From below, the mountain (7,808 feet at the summit) looks impossibly steep and narrow. High atop the big chairlift, the vista provides a panoramic tour of Jackson Hole and the Tetons.

Snow King was the first ski area in Wyoming—it opened in 1939—and one of the first in North America. The original chapter of the National Ski Patrol was established here in 1941. The mountain has a 1,571-foot vertical drop. You'll find more than 400 acres of skiable terrain at Snow King, with the longest run stretching nearly a mile. A triple chair, two double chairs, and a Poma lift climb the mountainside. Other features include snowmaking, a tubing park, and a very popular 300-foot half-pipe and terrain park for

JACKSON HOLE

snowboarders. It's the only local resort with lights for nighttime skiing.

Rates and Services

Prices for lift tickets at Snow King are well below those at other Jackson Hole resorts: $32 per day ($20 per half day) for adults and $22 per day ($14 per half day) for kids under 15 and seniors. Hours of operation are 9:30 A.M.–4:30 P.M., with **night skiing** (Mon.–Sat. 4:30–8:30 P.M.) available on the lower sections of Snow King for an additional $15 adults or $10 kids and seniors. In addition, the King has special two-hour rates for lift tickets ($15 adults, $10 kids and seniors); these are perfect for skiers and boarders who arrive late in the afternoon and want to hit the slopes for a bit. With some of the best snowmaking in Wyoming, the resort usually opens by Thanksgiving and remains in operation through March.

At the base of Snow King you'll discover a lodge with reasonable ski-and-stay packages, starting at $199 for three nights of lodging, plus breakfasts and two days of skiing. Also at Snow King are two restaurants, the Shady Lady Saloon, ski and snowboard rentals and lessons, plus a variety of other facilities, including an indoor ice rink and mountaintop snack shack. A plethora of lodging options are scattered around the adjacent town of Jackson. Jackson's START buses (307/733-4521, www.startbus.com) offer frequent service to town (free) or Teton Village ($3). For more information on Snow King Resort, call 307/733-5200 or 800/522-5464, or find them on the web at www.snowking.com.

Cross-Country Skiing

For many Jackson Hole residents the word "skiing" means heading across frozen Jenny Lake or telemarking down the bowls of Teton Pass rather than sliding down the slopes of the local resorts. Jackson Hole has become a center for cross-country enthusiasts and offers an impressive range of conditions—from flat-tracking along summertime golf courses where a gourmet restaurant awaits to remote wilderness settings where a complete knowledge of snowpack structure, avalanche hazards, and winter survival techniques is essential. Beginners will probably want to start out at a Nordic center, progressing to local paths and the more gentle lift-serviced ski runs with experience. More advanced skiers will quickly discover incredible snow in the surrounding mountains.

Ski Rentals

Rent or buy cross-country skis from **Skinny Skis,** 65 W. Deloney Ave., 307/733-6094 or 888/733-7205, www.skinnyskis.com; **Teton Mountaineering,** 170 N. Cache Dr., 307/733-3595 or 800/850-3595, www.tetonmtn.com; **Wilson Backcountry Sports,** Wilson, 307/733-5228; or **Leisure Sports,** 1075 South U.S. Hwy. 89,

307/733-3040, www.leisuresportsadventures.com. All of the local Nordic centers also rent equipment. Most places rent both classical cross-country skis and skate skis (much faster and a better workout), along with telemarking and randonnée (alpine touring) skis.

NORDIC CENTERS
Jackson Hole Nordic Center

Nordic skiing enthusiasts will find three different developed facilities near Jackson and others at Grand Targhee and near Togwotee Pass. The largest is Jackson Hole Nordic Center, 307/739-2629, www.jacksonhole.com/skiing, with 17 km of groomed trails—both set track and skating lanes—that cover a wide range of conditions. Call 307/733-2291 for the snow report. Located in Teton Village, this is the best place to learn cross-country skiing. Daily trail passes are $8 per day for adults or $4 per day for children and seniors. Traditional cross-country skis, skate skis, and telemarking equipment are available for rent, and the center offers a wide spectrum of lessons and tours. Hours are daily 8:30 A.M.–4:30 P.M. You can exchange your alpine lift ticket at Jackson

Hole Mountain Resort for one at the Nordic center (but, hey, it better be for no extra charge since you've already dropped $61!).

Teton Pines Cross-Country Ski Center
Located along Teton Village Road, Teton Pines, 307/733-1005 or 800/238-2223, www.teton pines.com, features 14 km of groomed track (both classical and skating) on a summertime golf course. Daily trail passes cost $10 adults or $5 children, and ski rentals and lessons are available. Hours are daily 9 A.M.–5 P.M. The clubhouse here has a restaurant for gourmet après-ski lunches and dinners.

Spring Creek Ranch Nordic Center
Three miles north of State Hwy. 22 on Spring Gulch Road, Spring Creek Ranch, 307/733-1004 or 800/443-6139, www.springcreekranch.com, is open 9:30 A.M.–4:30 P.M. daily. If you're staying in town, you can catch the free shuttle bus at the Wort Hotel; call the Nordic center for specifics. Guests of Spring Creek Ranch ski free here. The center has 15 km of gentle groomed trails with skating lanes, making this perfect for beginners. Trail passes are $10 per day for adults or $7 per day for seniors or kids. Ski rentals and lessons are available.

Grand Targhee Nordic Center
On the west side of the Tetons 42 miles out of Jackson, Grand Targhee Nordic Center, 307/353-2300 or 800/827-4433, www.grandtarghee.com, has 15 km of groomed cross-country ski trails covering rolling terrain. Trail passes are $10 adults and $5 seniors and kids. Lessons and ski rentals are also available. Hours are daily 9:30 A.M.–4 P.M. Guests with Targhee lodging packages can ski free on the cross-country tracks.

ON YOUR OWN
Nordic skiers who would rather explore Jackson Hole and the mountains that surround it on their own will discover an extraordinary range of options, from beginner-level treks along old roads to places where only the most advanced skiers dare venture. Because Jackson has so many

cross-country fanatics (and visiting enthusiasts), tracks are quickly broken along the more popular routes, making it easier for those who follow. For complete coverage of all these options, pick up a copy of the helpful free winter outdoors guide *Trailhead* at Skinny Skis, 65 W. Deloney Ave., 307/733-6094 or 888/733-7205, www.skinnyskis.com. The store also rents cross-country, skating, and telemark skis, and snowshoes. If you're heading out on your own, be prepared for deep snow (four feet in the valley) and temperatures that often plummet below zero at night.

The **Teton County Parks and Recreation Department,** 155 E. Gill, 307/739-9025, www.tetonwyo.org/parks, leads a variety of all-day cross-country ski outings most Tuesdays from mid-December to mid-March for $7 per person. Bring your own skis and a lunch; they provide the guide and transportation. The department also offers a full-moon ski tour once each winter.

Ski Tours
Jackson Hole Mountain Guides, 307/733-4979 or 800/239-7642, www.jhmg.com, runs winter ascents of Grand Teton, plus safety and avalanche courses and ski mountaineering trips. Longer winter trips, including a six-day Teton Crest tour, are also available.

Over on the western slopes of the Tetons, **Rendezvous Ski Tours,** 208/787-2906 or 877/754-4887, www.skithetetons.com, maintains three Mongolian-style yurts in the Jedediah Smith Wilderness, each located several hours of skiing (or hiking) from the next. The huts can sleep up to eight and have kitchens, bunks, sleeping bags, and woodstoves. Rates are $180 per night, but you need to be experienced in backcountry skiing and have the necessary safety equipment and avalanche training. If you don't quite measure up, they can provide guided backcountry ski tours to the huts. These start at $340 per person for a two-day and one-night tour.

Both Spring Creek Ranch Nordic Center and Jackson Hole Nordic Center offer guided ski tours into Grand Teton National Park; $45 for a half-day.

Jackson Area

Even rank beginners will enjoy exploring several local spots. Get to **Moose-Wilson Road** by heading one mile north of Teton Village to where the plowing ends. The nearly level road continues for two scenic miles across a creek and through groves of aspen. For more adventure, turn off at the **Granite Canyon Trailhead** (one mile up the unplowed Moose-Wilson Rd.) and follow the trail along the moraine, which offers a range of skiing conditions. Just don't ski into the canyon, where avalanches are a hazard.

The closest place to Jackson for on-your-own cross-country skiing is **Cache Creek Canyon.** The trailhead is at the east end of Cache Creek Drive, where the plowing ends at a parking lot. Snowmobiles and skiers have packed the route. For a longer trip, take the Rafferty ski lift at Snow King and then ski west through the trees and down to Cache Creek, returning via the road. Ask at Snow King Resort for specifics. Another popular local place is along the **Snake River dikes,** where State Hwy. 22 crosses the river one mile east of Wilson. The dikes extend along both sides of the river for several miles, making for easy skiing. This is also a good place to watch ducks, moose, and other critters or to listen to the river rolling over the rocks.

Grand Teton National Park

A bit farther afield, but well worth the detour, are several trails in Grand Teton National Park. Orange markers denote the paths, but these are not machine-groomed—just tracks laid down by other skiers. Park at the Cottonwood Creek bridge (the road isn't plowed beyond this point) and head out for **Jenny Lake** (nine miles round-trip) or **Taggart Lake** (three miles round-trip). Just three miles south of Moose on Moose-Wilson Road, you may also want to try the trail to **Phelps Lake** (five miles round-trip). Or, if you have more ambition and skill (along with avalanche beacons and other gear), longer routes could take you far up into the canyons of the Tetons. Be sure to stop at the Moose Visitor Center for current conditions and a copy of their trail map. Overnight ski tourers must also register here.

For unsurpassed vistas of the Tetons, try skiing to the top of 8,252-foot **Shadow Mountain,** 14 miles northeast of Jackson. From the town of Kelly, drive another five miles north to a parking area (the road isn't plowed beyond this point), and then ski up the nearby Forest Service road that snakes up the mountain. It's fairly steep in places and seven miles round-trip. Snowmobilers also use this road, so be ready to move out of the way quickly.

Granite Hot Springs

One of the most popular ski- and snowmobile-in sites is Granite Hot Springs, 307/734-7400, a delightful hot-spring-fed pool on Forest Service land. Get there by driving 25 miles southeast of Jackson into Hoback Canyon and then skiing 10 miles in from the signed parking area. The route is not difficult, but because of the distance it isn't recommended for beginners unless they're prepared for a 20-mile round-trip trek. The pool costs $5.50 adults, $3.50 ages 3–12, and free for infants. It's open 11 A.M.–5 P.M. in winter. Bring your swimsuit or rent a suit and towel here. Ask the attendant about places to snow camp nearby.

Teton Pass

Locals head to 8,429-foot Teton Pass when they really want to test their abilities. The summit parking area fills with cars on fresh-snow mornings as everyone from advanced beginners to world-class ski mountaineers heads out for a day in the powder or a week of wilderness trekking in the Tetons. Snow depths of eight feet or more are not uncommon in midwinter. (The snow once became so deep on the pass that it took plows two weeks to clear the road!) The slopes around Teton Pass cover the full spectrum, but be sure you know your own ability and how to avoid avalanches. Check the previously mentioned Skinny Skis *Trailhead* guide for specifics on Teton Pass, or talk to folks at Skinny Skis or Teton Mountaineering. This is the backcountry, so you won't see any signs at the various bowls; ask other skiers if you aren't sure which is which. Avalanches do occur in some of these bowls, and it's possible to get lost up here during a storm, so come prepared.

Those without backcountry experience

should contact **Rendezvous Ski Tours,** 208/787-2906 or 877/754-4887, www.skithe tetons.com; **Jackson Hole Mountain Guides,** 307/733-4979 or 800/239-7642, www.jhmg .com; or **Jackson Hole Nordic Center,** 307/739-2629, www.jacksonhole.com/skiing, for guided ski tours at Teton Pass and elsewhere. Expect to pay around $150 per person.

Other Winter Recreation

ICE SKATING

Each winter, the town of Wilson floods a hockeyrink-sized part of the town park for skating, hockey, and broomball. A warming hut stands next to the rink. Jackson maintains a smaller ice rink at 155 E. Gill Avenue, plus a rink in Snow King Ballpark which is used for hockey and broomball. All three of these rinks are free to the public and are lighted 6–10 P.M. Call 307/733-5056 for details.

All three local ski resorts have ice skating and skate rentals. You'll find skating ponds in Teton Village at the base of **Jackson Hole Mountain Resort** and over in Alta at **Grand Targhee Ski Resort.** For the out-of-the-elements version, skate over to **Snow King Resort,** where the indoor ice-skating rink is open in the winter and offers skate rentals and lessons.

SNOWSHOEING

Snowshoeing began as a way to get around in the winter, but the old-fashioned wood-and-rawhide snowshoes were bulky and heavy. In recent years snowshoeing has become a popular form of recreation, as new technology created lightweight and easily maneuverable snowshoes. Snowshoeing requires no real training: Just strap them on, grab a pair of poles, and start walking. But be careful where you walk; see the Special Topic "Safety in Avalanche Country" for tips.

Rent snowshoes from **Skinny Skis,** 65 W. Deloney Ave., 307/733-6094 or 888/733-7205, www.skinnyskis.com; **Teton Mountaineering,** 170 N. Cache Dr., 307/733-3595 or 800/850-3595, www.tetonmtn.com; **Gart Sports,** 485 W. Broadway, 307/733-4449, www.gartsports.com; **Wilson Backcountry Sports,** Wilson, 307/733-5228; **Leisure Sports,** 1075 South U.S. Hwy. 89,

307/733-3040, www.leisuresportsadventure.com; **Jackson Hole Mountain Resort,** 307/733-2292 or 888/333-7766, www.jacksonhole.com; and **Grand Targhee Ski Resort** in Alta, 307/353-2300 or 800/827-4433.

Guided Trips

Grand Teton National Park has excellent naturalist-led **snowshoe hikes** several times each week during winter. Snowshoes are provided at no charge, and no experience is necessary. These trips generally depart at 2 P.M. from the visitors center in Moose, but for specifics call 307/739-3399. Reservations are required; no kids under eight are permitted. Free naturalist-led snowshoe tours are offered at **Grand Targhee Ski Resort'** details at 307/353-2300 or 800/827-4433, www.grandtarghee.com.

Snowshoe walks into the mountains around Jackson are also offered by **The Hole Hiking Experience,** 307/690-4453 or 866/733-4453, www.holehike.com, the only company permitted to guide snowshoeing trips in nearby national forests. Their most popular trips go to Shadow Mountain north of Kelly. Rates start at $60 ($45 for kids) for a four-hour snowshoe trek.

The Saddlehorn Activity Center at **Jackson Hole Mountain Resort** has snowshoe rentals ($12 per day), along with guided snowshoe tours within Grand Teton National Park: $80 for a half-day or $160 for a full-day tour with lunch. In addition, a snowshoe trail ($5) parallels the ski tracks at the Nordic Center at the resort, and Forest Service naturalists lead occasional snowshoe hikes in the area. Get details at 307/733-2292 or 888/333-7766, www.jacksonhole.com. Snowshoe trails and tours are also available at **Spring Creek Ranch Nordic Center,** three miles north of State 22 on Spring Gulch Rd., 307/733-1004 or 800/443-6139, www.springcreekranch.com.

SLEIGH RIDES

Several companies offer romantic dinner horse-drawn sleigh rides in the Jackson Hole area mid-December through March. Make reservations well in advance for these popular trips. If you don't have the cash for one of these, take a day-time sleigh ride at the National Elk Refuge (described earlier in this chapter).

Jackson Hole Mountain Resort picks up Teton Village guests for a romantic 30-minute ride to a rustic log cabin where they are served a four-course roast prime-rib or broiled salmon dinner (vegetarian options available) with nightly entertainment. Prices are $57 adults, $35 children under 11, and $16 infants. There are two seatings each night, and reservations are required; call 307/739-2603. Additional details are on the web at www.jacksonhole.com.

Spring Creek Ranch, 307/733-8833 or 800/443-6139, www.springcreekranch.com, has 45-minute afternoon sleigh rides at the top of Gros Ventre Butte for $15 per person. They also have packages that combine a sleigh ride with a meal at the Granary Restaurant. This is one of Jackson's finer restaurants, so bring dress clothes.

Mill Iron Ranch, 307/733-6390 or 888/808-6390, www.millironranch.net, is a friendly family-run operation with evening sleigh rides in a down-home setting 10 miles south of Jackson. Guests get a 30-minute ride that takes you past an elk herd to the lodge for a big T-bone steak dinner; $57 adults, $48 kids. This is the most authentic of the local sleigh rides, but access may require a 4WD vehicle, so call ahead for road conditions.

Dinner sleigh rides are also offered at **Grand Targhee Ski Resort,** 307/353-2300 or 800/827-4433, www.grandtarghee.com, where a horse-drawn sleigh transports you to a remote yurt for a Western-style meal; $32 adults, $15 kids.

TUBING

Two local ski areas have sliding parks with customized inner tubes and rope tows. At Snow King Resort it's called **King Tubes,** 307/734-8823 or 800/522-5464, www.snowking.com,

and is available on weekday evenings and weekends after noon. Rates are $10 per hour for adults, $7 per hour for kids. The **Grand Targhee tube park** is open for après-ski fun only (after 5 P.M.) and costs $8 per hour; 307/353-2300 or 800/827-4433, www.grandtarghee.com.

DOGSLEDDING

Founded by Iditarod musher Frank Teasley, **Jackson Hole Iditarod Sled Dog Tours,** 307/733-7388 or 800/554-7388, www.jhsleddog.com, offers half-day trips ($135 per person including lunch) and all-day trips ($225 per person including a big dinner). The main destination is wonderful Granite Hot Springs, but when snow conditions are right, the teams also run in the Grays River, Shadow Mountain, and Gros Ventre areas. All trips include round-trip transportation from Jackson. Overnight trips to remote lodges are also available for $450–600 per person, depending on the lodge.

Washakie Outfitting, 307/733-3602 or 800/249-0662, www.dogsledwashakie.com, leads a variety of dogsled tours in the Jackson Hole area, using Alaskan husky racing dogs. Rides out of Teton Village are $120 ($80 for kids) and take 1.5 hours. For a more remote experience, join their trips from Cowboy Village Resort at Togwotee (48 miles north of Jackson) or Brooks Lake Lodge (65 miles northeast of Jackson). On these trips, Iditarod veteran Billy Snodgrass offers half-day ($140 adults, $90 kids), full-day ($210 adults, $115 kids), overnight ($450 adults, $280 kids), and trips that combine time behind the dogs with time on a snowmobile.

Continental Divide Dogsled Adventures, 307/739-0165 or 800/531-6874, www.dogsledadventures.com, also leads dogsled tours of the Brooks Lake area, starting with a half-day trip for $175 adults or $80 kids. A variety of longer trips are available, including a three-night adventure with lodging in a surprisingly comfortable yurt; $1,920 per person, with meals. All trips include round-trip transportation from Jackson.

Grand Targhee Ski Resort, 307/353-2300 or 800/827-4433, www.sharplink.com/dogsled, has dogsled trips on the west side of the Tetons. Half-day rates are $115 for one person or $200 for two riders on a sled.

SNOWMOBILING

One of Jackson Hole's most popular—and controversial—wintertime activities is snowmobiling. Hundreds of miles of packed and groomed snowmobile trails head into Bridger-Teton National Forest as well as Yellowstone and Grand Teton National Parks. Some of the most popular places include the Togwotee Pass area 48 miles north of Jackson, Cache Creek Road east of town, and Granite Hot Springs Road 25 miles southeast. More than a dozen different Jackson companies offer guided all-day snowmobile trips into Yellowstone and elsewhere. Yellowstone tours (including breakfast and lunch) typically cost $190–205 for one rider or $250–300 for two

riders. Tours to other areas are usually less expensive, and some motels offer package deals. You can also rent machines for self-guided trips for around $120 per day for one person or $170 for two riders. The visitors center has a complete listing of local snowmobile-rental companies and maps of snowmobile trails.

The 365-mile-long **Continental Divide Snowmobile Trail** passes through the heart of Grand Teton National Park, connecting the Yellowstone road network with snowmobile trails that reach all the way to Atlantic City at the southern end of the Wind River Mountains. Unfortunately, this means that snowmobiles now roar into two of America's great national parks. Don't be a part of this desecration; instead, enjoy these parks in quieter, less hurried ways such as on snowshoes or cross-country skis. If you must use a snowmobile, make sure it is one of the new less-polluting four-stroke versions.

Information and Services

INFORMATION SOURCES

Jackson's big **Wyoming State Information Center** is detailed earlier in this chapter. Find it on the north end of town at 532 N. Cache Dr., 307/733-3316, www.jacksonholechamber.com. It's open daily all year. Immediately south of the Information Center is an impressive building housing the **Wyoming Game & Fish** offices, 307/733-2321.

The **Bridger-Teton National Forest** supervisor's office is at 340 N. Cache Drive, 307/739-5500, www.fs.fed.us/btnf, and is open Monday–Friday 8 A.M.–4:30 P.M. Get information and Forest Service maps from the Wyoming State Information Center.

On the Radio

Find **National Public Radio** KUWJ on your dial at 90.3 FM, http://uwadmnweb.uwyo.edu/wpr. The locals' station is **KMTN** at 96.9 FM. Other Jackson hole radio stations are KZJH 95.3 FM and KSGT 1340 AM. See www.jacksonholeradio.co for details on the commercial stations.

JACKSON HOLE ON THE WEB

A great place to begin your web tour is the chamber of commerce site: www.jacksonhole chamber.com. Also very useful are www.jackson holetraveler.com, from Circumerro Publishing; and www.jacksonholenet.com, sponsored by *Jackson Hole Magazine.* All three of these sites contain links to dozens of local businesses of all types. You may also want to check out another local site, www.jacksonnetwork.com. The **Teton County** website, www.tetonwyo.org, has additional local information. Federal government websites for the local area include Grand Teton National Park at www.nps.gov/grte, Yellowstone National Park at www.nps.gov/yell, Bridger-Teton National Forest at www.fs.fed.us/btnf, and Caribou-Targhee National Forest at www.fs.fed.us/r4/caribou.

Internet Access

To keep in touch with folks via email, use the free terminals in the library. Another option is **Mountunes,** 265 W. Broadway, 307/733-4514 or 800/982-2241, www.mountunes.com. In addition to a big and diverse collection of CDs for sale, they have an Internet café where computer time costs $5 per half-hour.

TRIP PLANNING

Several local travel agencies offer reservation services for those who prefer to leave the planning to someone else. They can set up airline tickets, rental cars, lodging, horseback riding, fishing trips, whitewater rafting, ski vacations, and all sorts of other packages. The biggest is **Jackson Hole Central Reservations,** 307/733-4005 or 800/443-6931, www.jhsnow.com. Central Reservations will also send out big glossy brochures describing local ski areas and lodging. **Do Jackson,** 307/739-1500 or 866/500-3654, www.dojacksonhole.com, has an office next to the Albertson's store with lots of visitor information. Also helpful for trip planning are **Jackson Hole Reservations,** 307/733-6331 or 800/329-9205, www.jacksonholeres.com, and **Llama Lou's Reservations,** 307/733-1617 or 800/709-1617, www.jhsummerfun.com.

POST OFFICES

Jackson's main post office is at 1070 Maple Way, near Powderhorn Lane, 307/733-3650; open Mon.–Fri. 8:30 A.M.–5 P.M., Sat. 10 A.M.–1 P.M. Other post offices are downtown at 220 W. Pearl Ave., 307/739-1740; in Teton Village, 307/733-3575; in Wilson, 307/733-3335; and in Kelly, 307/733-8884.

RECYCLING

Just because you're on vacation doesn't mean you should just throw everything away. Jackson has a good recycling program and accepts newspaper, aluminum cans, glass, tin cans, plastic milk jugs, magazines, catalogs, cardboard, and office paper. The recycling center, 307/733-7678, www.teton wyo.org/recycling, is the big brown building two miles south of the high school on U.S. Hwy. 89. Bins are accessible 24 hours a day.

MEDICAL HELP

Because of the abundance of ski and snowboard accidents, orthopedic specialists are in high demand in Jackson and are some of the best around. The specialists at Orthopaedics of Jackson Hole are official physicians for the U.S. and French national ski teams! Head to **St. John's Hospital,** 625 E. Broadway, 307/733-3636, www.teton hospital.org, for emergency medical attention.

Medical service by appointment or on a walk-

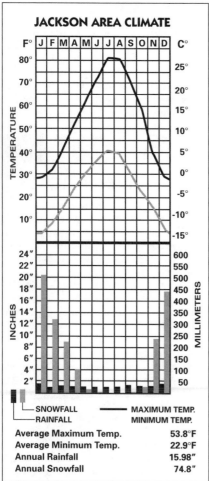

JACKSON AREA CLIMATE

	Average Maximum Temp.	53.8°F
	Average Minimum Temp.	22.9°F
	Annual Rainfall	15.98"
	Annual Snowfall	74.8"

© AVALON TRAVEL PUBLISHING, INC.

in basis is available at **Gooder Family Care,** 545 W. Broadway, 307/733-7003; **Emerg-A-Care,** 975 W. Broadway (Powderhorn Mall), 307/733-8002; and **Jackson Hole Medical Clinic,** 988 South U.S. Hwy. 89, 307/739-8999. Unfortunately, none of these facilities will bill your insurance company; you'll have to fork out the cash and hope for a refund later.

BANKING AND CURRENCY EXCHANGE

Get fast cash from **ATMs** at many locations around town, including banks, Albertson's, downtown in front of Sirk Shirts, at the airport, and in Teton Village and the Aspens.

International travelers will appreciate the **currency exchange** where you can swap those Euros or colorful Canadian bills at all three Jackson State Bank locations: 112 Center Street, 50 Buffalo Way, and in the Aspens on Teton Village Road. Call 307/733-3737 for details.

LIBRARY

The spacious **Teton County Library,** 125 Virginian Lane, 307/733-2164, http://will.state.wy.us/teton/home, is the kind of library every town should have. Inside this modern building is a large collection of books about Wyoming and the West, plus a great kids' section (complete with a fenced-in children's garden with a tepee). Computers provide free **Internet access** and are available by reservation or on a walk-up-and-wait basis. In the summer the queue can get long if you don't have a reservation. They take reservations up to one week in advance. Library hours are Monday–Thursday 10 A.M.–9 P.M., Friday 10 A.M.–5:30 P.M., Saturday 10 A.M.–5 P.M., and Sunday 1–5 P.M. If you plan to be in the Jackson area for a week or more, it may be worth your while to get a visitor's library card. For a one-time fee of $5 you can check out up to four books at a time.

NEWSPAPERS

Jackson has not just one but two thick local newspapers, each produced in tabloid format.

The **Jackson Hole News** (307/733-2047; www.jacksonholenews.com) and the **Jackson Hole Guide** (307/733-2430; www.jhguide.com) both publish weekly editions with local news for 50 cents, as well as weekday freebies found in local shops. The *Guide* typically represents more traditional Wyoming views (i.e., it's basically Republican) while the *News* has more liberal leanings. Despite any leanings, both are excellent sources of information and strive for balanced news coverage.

TRAVELING WITH CHILDREN

Those traveling with children will find an abundance of kid-friendly options in Jackson Hole. A few noteworthy examples include:
• the hands-on Children's Gallery at the National Museum of Wildlife Art
• playgrounds at Mike Yokel Jr. Park (Kelly and Hall streets) and Miller Park (Powderhorn Lane and Maple Way)
• the excellent swimming pool and corkscrew water slide at the Teton County Recreation Center
• the fine children's section of the library
• chuck wagon dinners at Bar-T-Five or Bar J
• pizzas at the Calico (where the lawn is great for kids)
• comedies and melodramas at Jackson Hole Playhouse or Mainstage Theatre
• the Alpine Slide at Snow King Resort
• the aerial tram up Rendezvous Mountain at Jackson Hole Resort
• the evening shoot-outs at Town Square
• horseback or wagon rides
• a trip to the fish hatchery
• a night at the rodeo (including the kids-only calf chase)
• and a boat ride and hike at Jenny Lake inside Grand Teton National Park.
During summer, older kids will also enjoy hiking, mountain-biking, Snake River float and whitewater trips, and the putting course at Alpine Miniature Golf. In winter, snowboarding and skiing are favorites of older kids, but sleigh rides, dogsledding, ice skating, and snowshoeing are also fun.

JACKSON HOLE

For those traveling with tots, **Baby's Away**, 307/733-0387 or 888/616-8495, rents all sorts of baby supplies, including car seats, cribs, gates, backpacks, swings, and high chairs. You'll find more stroller and backpack rentals—along with kids' clothing—at **Teton Kids**, 130 E. Broadway, 307/739-2176. Just down the street is a large toy shop, **Broadway Toys and Togs**, 48 E. Broadway, 307/733-3918. But don't come here looking for Wal-Mart prices; the last time I visited, they were selling a toddler's overalls (with cute rodeo decorations) for $80! **Second Helpings**, 141 E. Pearl Ave., 307/733-9466, has an excellent selection of quality used baby and children's clothes. For child care, contact **Babysitting by the Tetons**, 307/733-0754, www.babysittingbythetetons.com, or **Jackson Hole Babysitting**, 307/733-7720, www.jacksonholebabysitting.com.

PHOTOGRAPHY

Photographers will find several good small photo shops in Jackson, including **D. D. Camera Corral**, 60 S. Cache, 307/733-3831; **Mountain Camera Supply**, 180 W. Broadway, 307/733-7998; and **Grand Teton Photo Center**, in the Pink Garter Plaza at 150 West Broadway, 307/733-3198. The last of these places processes not only print film but also transparencies (E-6 chemistry), with a one-day turnaround, and has a good reputation for quality.

Serious professional or semi-pro photographers will be interested in **Photography at the Summit**, an extraordinary five-day series of workshops led by internationally famous photographers and photo editors. The staff always includes a contingent from *National Geographic.* Evening talks—held at the National Museum of Wildlife Art—are open to the public. Get workshop details at 303/295-7770 or 800/745-3211, www.richclarkson.com. Highly recommended.

WEDDINGS

Jackson Hole makes a wonderful spot for a mountain wedding, with a grand setting, an abundance of fine lodging places and upscale caterers, plus easy access from anywhere in the nation. You can choose the simple back-to-nature version with a couple of family members along Jenny Lake or the full-blown variety at such places as Rancho Alegre Lodge ($2,250 per night, with a five-night minimum). A local company produces a slick 60-page free publication called *A Grand Wedding,* filled with details on Jackson Hole caterers, locations, musicians, photographers, wedding consultants, tent and carriage rentals, limos, and lots more. The same information is available online at www.jacksonhole wedding.com.

DOG KENNELS

Thinking of bringing a dog to Jackson but not sure what to do if the hotel won't allow pets? Several local kennels will keep an eye on Fido for you. Try **Kindness Kennels**, 1225 S. Gregory Lane, 307/733-2633; **Critter Camp** (Jackson Hole Veterinary Clinic), Rafter J Subdivision, 307/733-4279; or **Happy Tails Pet Resort** (Spring Creek Animal Hospital), 1035 W. Broadway, 307/733-1606.

LAUNDRY AND SHOWERS

Wash clothes at **Soap Opera Laundry**, 850 W. Broadway, 307/733-5584, or **Ryan Cleaners**, 545 N. Cache Dr., 307/733-2938. You'll find public lockers at Jackson Hole Mountain Resort during winter. **Showers** ($5 with towel) are available in the Bunkhouse portion of Anvil Motel, 215 N. Cache Dr., 307/733-3668 or 800/234-4507, www.anvilmotel.com.

LIVING IN JACKSON HOLE

Jackson Hole is an increasingly popular place to live and work—a fact that angers many long-time residents who came here to escape crowds elsewhere. The surrounding country is grand, with many things to do and places to explore, the weather is delightful, and you're likely to meet others with similar interests, not to mention the great-looking babes and snowboard studs. Jobs such as waiting tables, operating ski lifts, driving tour buses, cleaning hotels and condos, and doing construction work are plentiful. The unemployment rate generally hovers around 2 percent, and housing is so scarce—and jobs so plentiful—that the local rescue mission kicks folks out after a week if they don't find work. Wages are not high but have improved with the rising demand for workers. Get to Jackson in mid-May and you'll find the papers filled with half a dozen pages of employment ads and Help Wanted signs at virtually every shop. Even in midsummer, many places are looking for workers.

Finding Work

The best jobs are those that either offer such perks as housing or free ski passes or give you lots of free time to explore the area. To get an idea of available jobs, check local classified ads or stop by the Wyoming Job Service Center, 155 W. Gill, 307/733-4091. You can also search for jobs on the state's Job Bank homepage: http://wyjobs .state.wy.us. Other good web sources are www .jacksonholejobs.com, www.jacksonholenews .com, and www.jhguide.com.

Navigating the Housing Maze

Because of Jackson Hole's popularity, finding a place to live is extremely difficult, especially during the peak summer and winter tourist seasons. As the moneyed class has moved in, those who work in service jobs find it tougher and tougher to obtain affordable housing. Many Jackson workers now suffer long commutes from Victor or Driggs in Idaho, or the Wyoming towns of Alpine, Afton, or Pinedale. Land prices (and consequently housing costs) have been rising an average of 15 percent per year over the past decade or so, and because of this, the median home price is now twice what the median household income will buy! Two-bedroom apartments rent for $900–1,100 per month. The median single-family home in Jackson costs $400,000, and the average home in the area sells for a cool $1 million. More prestigious local homes sell for $2–3 million, and the very finest log mansions ("log cabins on steroids") can fetch more than $6 million. The inflation of real estate has attracted the major players: both Christie's and Sotheby's (the auction folks) have offices in Jackson. As a side note, Teton County is the wealthiest county in America, with the highest average taxable income anywhere in the nation. (These figures are, of course, skewed by a relatively small number of ultra-rich individuals; you'll find many folks working at $8-an-hour jobs.)

Because of the extreme difficulty in finding rental housing, many Jackson-area businesses include this perk as a way to lure workers. Those workers who are not so lucky are often forced to jam into too-small apartments or to join the commuters from Driggs. The best times to look for a place to live are in April and October. Check the local newspapers (or their online versions if you haven't yet arrived in the area) as well as local laundromat and grocery-store bulletin boards for apartments or cabins. The *Trash and Treasure* morning program on radio station KMTN (96.9 FM; www.jacksonholeradio.com/kmtn.htm) is another place to try.

Transportation

Access to Jackson Hole has become easier in recent years, with several airlines and daily buses now serving the valley. Most summer visitors arrive by car, although a few more adventurous souls pedal in on bikes. If you're looking for or offering a ride, KMTN (96.9 FM), 307/733-4500, www.jacksonholeradio.com/kmtn.htm, has daily ride-finder announcements during its Trash and Treasure radio program. Tune in weekdays 9:30–9:50 A.M.

Road Work

The highway through the Snake River Canyon has been undergoing a $75-million highway reconstruction that began in 1998, with completion scheduled for 2004. Get the current status and information about expected delays at 307/733-3665, http://wyoroad.info.

BY AIR

Jackson Hole Airport is eight miles north of Jackson inside Grand Teton National Park. It's the only commercial airport within any national park. The airport is small and cozy but offers daily jet service to several U.S. cities. The tarmac is often crowded with Lear and Gulfstream jets and other noisy transportation symbols of the elite. See the Special Topic "Airline Contacts" in the On the Road chapter for information on all major airlines.

Delta/Skywest, has year-round service from Salt Lake City, with additional winter flights out of Atlanta. Some of the Salt Lake flights are in smaller turboprops, others in jets; all of the Atlanta flights are in 757s. **American,** has summer and winter service from Dallas and Chicago. **Northwest Airlines,** flies from Minneapolis/St. Paul in summer and winter. **United/United Express,** offers year-round turboprop service from Denver. **Continental,** serves Jackson Hole from Newark and Houston in the winter and usually has service during summer to the same cities.

If you're flying in from Seattle, Los Angeles, or

San Francisco, you will need to go through either Salt Lake City or Idaho Falls. The latter airport is served by Horizon Air (Alaska Airlines). Many folks opt to fly to either Salt Lake (275 miles away) or Idaho Falls (90 miles away) and pick up a rental car for the drive to Jackson.

Jackson Hole Aviation, 307/733-4767 or 800/437-5387, www.jhaviation.com, offers scenic flights over the valley as well as charter air service.

AIRPORT SHUTTLES AND TAXIS

Alltrans/Gray Line of Jackson Hole, 307/733-4325 or 800/443-6133, www.jacksonholealltrans.com, provides airport shuttle service to and from motels in Jackson ($13 one-way or $23 round-trip per person) and Teton Village ($20 one-way or $35 round-trip per person). The shuttles meet nearly all commercial airline flights in winter and most summertime flights, but you should make advance reservations to be sure of an airport pickup. Make outgoing reservations for a motel pickup 24 hours in advance.

Local taxis also provide direct service from the airport to Jackson; $12 for one or two people. To Teton Village you're best off getting a roundt-rip ticket for $35 per person. The taxi companies are **A Snake River Taxi,** 307/732-2221; **Airport Taxi/Alltrans,** 307/733-1700 or 800/443-6133, www.jacksonholealltrans.com; **Airport Shuttle Service,** 307/730-3900; **All Star Taxi,** 307/733-2888; **Buckboard Transportation,** 307/733-1112 or 877/791-0211, www.buckboardtrans.com; **Bullseye Taxi,** 307/730-5000; **Cowboy Cab,** 307/734-8188; **Elks Country Cab,** 307/733-8181; and **Teton Taxi & Backcountry Shuttle,** 307/733-1506, www.tetontaxi.com.

CAR RENTALS

Most of the national and regional chains offer rental cars in town or at the airport. See the

"Rental Car Contacts" Special Topic in the On the Road chapter for national companies. Local companies include **Eagle Rent-A-Car,** 307/739-9999 or 800/582-2128, www.jacksonholenet .com/eagle, and **Leisure Sports,** 307/733-3040, www.leisuresportsadventure.com. Of the national chains, Alamo, Avis, Budget, and Hertz all have counters at the airport, while the others provide a free shuttle bus to town. You may be better off getting a car in town, where you don't have to pay the additional taxes imposed at the airport. Most of these companies also rent 4WD cars and minivans. The best deals are often from Dollar or Thrifty, but check one of the online reservation sources (www.travelocity.com or www.expedia.com) to see who currently has the best rates. Note that peak-season car rental rates in Jackson are on the high side; expect to pay at least $55 per day or $360 and up per week for a midsize car. Taxes and fees (especially for airport rentals) can add another 20 percent to these rates, so read the fine print! Reserve cars at least one month ahead during summer and two months ahead for midsummer or Christmas to New Year's. Be sure to mention any discounts; a AAA membership always seems to cut 10 percent from the bill.

START BUSES

Local buses are operated by Southern Teton Area Rapid Transit (START) and serve Jackson and Teton Village all year. START fares are free within town and $3 to Teton Village (cheaper for seniors and children). Discount coupons are available for multiple rides. Hours of operation are generally 6 A.M.–10 P.M. During summer, buses run seven days a week, with in-town service every 15 minutes from noon to 6:45 P.M. Service to Teton Village is eight times a day in summer and more often in winter. Reduced bus service is available in fall and spring. Get bus schedules and route maps in the visitors center. Buses stop near most Jackson hotels and motels and are equipped to carry skis (in winter) and bikes (in summer) on outside racks. Wintertime service is also offered to the National Museum of Wildlife Art and National Elk Refuge.

LONE HIGHWAYMAN OF YELLOWSTONE

Because of its remote location, Teton Valley became a rendezvous place for rustlers and outlaws in the 1880s. Horses stolen from the soldiers at Fort Hall, along with cattle "liberated" from Wyoming and Montana ranches made their way through Pierre's Hole to the railroads. Hiram C. Lapham was the first to try his hand at ranching in the valley, but his cattle quickly disappeared. With the help of a posse from Rexburg, Lapham tracked down the culprits, one of whom was killed in the ensuing gunfight. The others surrendered but escaped from jail when the wife of bandit Ed Harrington smuggled a gun to her husband in clothing worn by his baby. Harrington and partner Lum Nickerson were eventually tracked down and sent to jail.

Although Harrington was sentenced to 25 years, the governor pardoned him after just three. Harrington went on to become Teton Valley's first postman, but his criminal activity continued. Using the alias Ed Trafton, Harrington went on to rob stores throughout Teton Valley and eventually spent another two years behind bars. After getting out, he turned his attention to the tourism business in Yellowstone, but not in the standard way. Although it was never proven, he was suspected of being behind a string of stagecoach robberies in 1908 where cash and jewelry were taken from tourists at gunpoint. Harrington's most brazen feat came on July 29, 1914, when he single-handedly robbed 15 stages, earning the nickname "the lone highwayman of Yellowstone." The tourists were particularly impressed with his gentlemanly manner as he asked them to "please" hand over all their cash and jewelry. Harrington made off with $915.35 in cash and $130 in jewelry, but he made the mistake of posing for photos in the process. He was caught the following year and spent five years in Leavenworth Prison.

When Harrington died, a letter in his pocket claimed that he had been Owen Wister's model for the Virginian in the famous novel of the same name. Others suspected that he was more likely to have been Wister's model for the villain, Trampas.

JACKSON HOLE

Unfortunately, START buses do not run to the airport, Kelly, or Moose, but winter service is available to Wilson. Call 307/733-4521 for more information, or find them on the web at www.startbus.com.

As this book was being written, the Park Service was developing a new transportation plan for Grand Teton National Park that may include scheduled bus service from Jackson. Get the latest information at 307/739-3399, www .nps.gov/grte.

LONG-DISTANCE BUSES

Greyhound buses don't come even close to Jackson; the nearest stopping places are Evanston, West Yellowstone, Idaho Falls, and the regional hub at Salt Lake City. **Alltrans/Jackson Hole Express,** 307/733-1719 or 800/652-9510, www.jacksonholealltrans.com, provides daily bus or van connections between Salt Lake City ($54 one-way), Idaho Falls ($31 one-way), Pocatello ($42 one-way), and Jackson.

TOURS AND SHUTTLES

Grand Teton Lodge Company, 307/543-2811 or 800/628-9988, www.gtlc.com, has five-times-daily summer shuttle buses between Jackson and Jackson Lake Lodge for $20 one-way (plus a $10 park entrance fee), and on to Colter Bay Village for an additional $4 one-way. Transportation to the airport is $30 from the airport to Jackson Lake Lodge or $20 in the other direction. Reservations are required for all of these. and N. Cache Drive. The company also offers three-hour bus tours of Grand Teton National Park and eight-hour tours of Yellowstone National Park.

Park Tours

Summertime bus tours of Grand Teton and Yellowstone National Parks are available several times a week from **Alltrans/Gray Line of Jackson Hole,** 307/733-4325 or 800/443-6133, www.jacksonholealltrans.com. Yellowstone tours last 11 hours and cost $80 plus park entrance fees. Eight-hour Grand Teton tours are $69 plus the park entrance. Those without vehicles can use these tours for access to the parks; reserve ahead to schedule a pickup in Jackson, Grand Teton, or Yellowstone. In Yellowstone, travelers can connect with other buses to West Yellowstone (Montana), Gardiner (Montana), or Cody. Gray Line's four-day tours of the Yellowstone and Grand Teton areas start at $900 for one person or $1,200 for two, including lodging (but only one meal). During winter, Alltrans/Gray Line has daily bus runs to Flagg Ranch Resort for $40 one-way ($60 round-trip), arriving in time to meet the snowcoach departures for Yellowstone. Reservations are required. Jackson taxi companies also offer shuttle services within the park and guided tours.

Operated by Teton Science School, **Wildlife Expeditions,** 307/733-2623 or 888/945-3567, www.tetonscience.org/wildlife, leads a variety of wildlife-viewing safaris throughout the region, including half-day Grand Teton trips for $85, and all-day jaunts for $145. Multiday wildlife tours into Yellowstone are also available. Other companies with guided van tours of the area include **Callowishus Park Touring Company,** 307/733-9521, www.callowishus .com; **Jackson's Hole Adventure,** 307/654-7849 or 800/392-3165, www.jacksonhole-adventure.com; and **Upstream Anglers and Outdoor Adventures,** 307/739-9443 or 800/ 642-8979, www.upstreamanglers.com.

Bridger-Teton National Forest

One of the largest national forests in the Lower 48, Bridger-Teton ("the B-T") National Forest stretches southward for 135 miles from the Yellowstone border and covers 3.4 million acres. Portions of the forest are described elsewhere (see Bridger Wilderness in the Wind River Mountains Country chapter and Greys River Area in the Southwest chapter). In Jackson Hole, the two areas of most interest for recreation are the Teton Wilderness and the Gros Ventre Wilderness. Much of the remaining nonwilderness land managed by the Forest Service is multiple-use, meaning a mix of recreation, logging, cattle grazing, and oil and gas leasing.

> *The 585,468 acres of the Teton Wilderness offer a diverse mixture of rolling lands carpeted with lodgepole pine, spacious grassy meadows, roaring rivers, and dramatic mountains.*

The Bridger-Teton National Forest **supervisor's office** is at 340 N. Cache Drive in Jackson, 307/739-5500, www.fs.fed.us/btnf. The Wyoming State Information Center, a couple of blocks north on Cache, usually has a Forest Service worker on duty who can provide recreation information. The center also sells Bridger-Teton maps and has a good choice of outdoor books. Local ranger stations are the **Jackson Ranger District,** also at 340 N. Cache Drive, 307/739-5400, and the **Blackrock Ranger Station,** nine miles east of Moran Junction, 307/543-2386.

Short Hikes

Forest Service lands around Jackson provide an amazing array of hiking and mountain-biking options. Pick up a copy of *Top Ten Trails* from the Forest Service office in town for descriptions of the most popular trails, or find the same information on their website. Some of these hikes are detailed in the Day Hikes section under Summer Recreation.

TETON WILDERNESS

The Teton Wilderness covers 585,468 acres of mountain country, bordered to the north by Yellowstone National Park, to the west by Grand Teton National Park, and to the east by the Washakie Wilderness. Established as a primitive area in 1934, it was declared one of the nation's first wilderness areas upon passage of the 1964 Wilderness Act. The Teton Wilderness offers a diverse mixture of rolling lands carpeted with lodgepole pine, spacious grassy meadows, roaring rivers, and dramatic mountains. Elevations range from 7,500 feet to the 12,165-foot summit of Younts Peak. The Continental Divide slices across the wilderness, with headwaters of the Yellowstone River draining the eastern half and headwaters of the Buffalo and Snake Rivers flowing down the western side. Teton Wilderness has a considerable amount of bear activity, so make sure you know how to avoid bear encounters and bring pepper spray.

One of the most unusual places within Teton Wilderness is **Two Ocean Creek,** where a creek abruptly splits at a rock and the two branches never rejoin. One branch becomes Atlantic Creek, and its waters eventually reach the Atlantic Ocean, while the other becomes Pacific Creek and its waters flow to the Snake River, the Columbia River, and thence into the Pacific Ocean! Mountain man Osborne Russell described this phenomenon in 1835:

> *On the South side about midway of the prairie stands a high snowy peak from whence issues a Stream of water which after entering the plain it divides equally one half running West and other East thus bidding adieu to each other one bound for the Pacific and the other for the Atlantic ocean. Here a trout of 12 inches in length may cross the mountains in safety. Poets have sung of the "meeting of the waters" and fish climbing cataracts but the "parting of the waters and fish crossing mountains" I*

Granite Hot Springs is nestled in the Bridger-Teton National Forest south of Jackson.

believe remains unsung yet by all except the solitary Trapper who sits under the shade of a spreading pine whistling blank-verse and beating time to the tune with a whip on his trap sack whilst musing on the parting advice of these waters.

Two natural events have had a major effect on the Teton Wilderness. On July 21, 1987, a world-record high-elevation tornado created a 10,000-acre blowdown of trees around the Enos Lake area, and it took years to rebuild the trails. In 1988, extreme drought conditions led to a series of major fires in Yellowstone and surrounding areas. Within the Teton Wilderness, the Huck and Mink Creek Fires burned (in varying degrees of severity) approximately 200,000 acres. More than half of the wilderness remained untouched. Don't let these incidents dissuade you from visiting; this is still a marvelous and little-used area. Herds of elk graze in alpine areas, and many consider the Thorofare country abutting Yellowstone National Park the most remote place in the Lower 48. This is prime grizzly habitat, so be very cautious at all times. Poles for hanging food have

been placed at most campsites, as have bear-resistant boxes or barrels. Local Forest Service offices have brochures showing the locations of these poles. You can rent bear-resistant backpacker food tubes or horse panniers from the Blackrock Ranger District, 307/543-2386, but it's a good idea to make reservations for these items before your trip.

Access

Three primary trailheads provide access to the Teton Wilderness: Pacific Creek on the southwestern end, Turpin Meadow on the Buffalo Fork River, and Brooks Lake just east of the Continental Divide. Campgrounds are located at each of these trailheads. Teton Wilderness is a favorite of Wyomingites, particularly those with horses, and in the fall elk hunters from across the nation come here. Distances are so great and some of the stream crossings so intimidating that few backpackers head into this wilderness area. No permits are needed, but it's a good idea to stop in at the **Blackrock Ranger District,** 307/543-2386, nine miles east of Moran Junction on U.S. Hwy. 26/287, for topographic maps and information on current trail conditions, bear problems, regulations, and a list of permitted outfitters offering horse or llama trips.

For a shorter trip, you could take a guided horseback ride with one of two companies based at the Turpin Meadow Trailhead: **Two Ocean Pass Outfitting,** 307/543-2309 or 800/726-2409, www.twooceanpass.com; **Yellowstone Outfitters,** 307/543-2418 or 800/447-4711, www.yellowstoneoutfitters.com. Additional rides are available from nearby **Turpin Meadow Ranch,** 307/543-2496 or 800/743-2496, www.turpinmeadow.com, **Buffalo Valley Ranch,** 307/543-2026 or 888/543-2477. All four of these have horses available for hourly or all-day rides into the Teton Wilderness. **Teton Horseback Adventures,** 307/856-3628 or 307/739-7176, www.horsebackadv.com, has horseback rides and wilderness trips out of the Pacific Creek Trailhead.

Unfortunately, the U.S. Geological Survey maps don't show the many Teton Wilderness trails built and maintained (or not maintained) by private outfitters and hunters. These can make hiking confusing. A few of the many possible hikes are described as follows.

Whetstone Creek

Whetstone Creek Trail begins at the Pacific Creek Trailhead, on the southwest side of Teton Wilderness. An enjoyable 20-mile round-trip hike leaves the trailhead and follows Pacific Creek for 1.5 miles before splitting left to follow Whetstone Creek. Bear left when the trail splits again another three miles upstream and continue through a series of small meadows to the junction with Pilgrim Creek Trail. Turn right here and follow this trail two more miles to Coulter Creek Trail, climbing up Coulter Creek to scenic Coulter Basin and then dropping down along the East Fork of Whetstone Creek. This rejoins the Whetstone Creek Trail and returns you to the trailhead, passing many attractive small meadows along the way. The upper half of this loop hike was burned in 1988; some areas were heavily scorched, while others are patchy. Flowers are abundant in the burned areas, and this is important elk habitat.

South Fork to Soda Fork

A fine loop hike leaves Turpin Meadow and follows South Buffalo Fork River to South Fork Falls. Just above this point, a trail splits off and climbs to Nowlin Meadow (excellent views of Smokehouse Mountain) and then down to Soda Fork River, where it joins the Soda Fork Trail. Follow this trail back downstream to huge Soda Fork Meadow (a good place to see moose and occasionally grizzlies) and then back to Turpin Meadow, a distance of approximately 23 miles round-trip. For a fascinating side trip from this route, head up the Soda Fork into the alpine at Crater Lake, a six-mile hike above the Nowlin Meadow–Soda Fork Trail junction. The outlet stream at Crater Lake disappears into a gaping hole, emerging as a large creek two miles below at Big Springs. It's an incredible sight.

Cub Creek Area

The Brooks Lake area just east of Togwotee Pass is a popular summertime camping and fishing place with magnificent views. Brooks Lake Trail follows the western shore of Brooks Lake and continues past Upper Brooks Lakes to Bear Cub Pass. From here, the trail drops down to Cub Creek, where you'll find several good campsites. You can make a long and scenic loop by following the trail up Cub Creek into the alpine country and then back down along the South Buffalo Fork River to Lower Pendergraft Meadow. From here, take the Cub Creek Trail back up along Cub Creek to Bear Cub Pass and back out to Brooks Lake. Get a topographic map before heading into this remote country. Total distance is approximately 33 miles round-trip.

GROS VENTRE WILDERNESS

The 287,000-acre Gros Ventre Wilderness was established in 1984 and covers the mountain country just east of Jackson Hole. This range trends mainly in a northwest-southeast direction and is probably best known for Sleeping Indian Mountain (maps now call it Sheep Mountain, but locals never use that appellation), the distinctive rocky summit visible from Jackson Hole. Although there are densely forested areas at lower elevations, the central portion of the wilderness lies above timberline, and many peaks top 10,000 feet. The tallest is Doubletop Peak at 11,682 feet. The Tetons are visible from almost any high point in the Gros Ventre, and meadows line the lower-elevation streams. Elk, mule deer, bighorn sheep, moose, and black bears are found here, and a few grizzlies have been reported. The Forest Service office in Jackson has more information on the wilderness, including brief trail descriptions and maps.

Access and Trails

Several roads provide good access to the Gros Ventre Wilderness: Gros Ventre River Rd. on the northern border; Curtis Canyon Rd. on the western margin; and Granite Creek Rd. to the south. Flat Creek is rough and only accessible in a 4WD vehicle. Hikes beginning or ending in the Granite Creek area have the added advantage of nearby Granite Hot Springs, a great place to soak tired muscles.

For a beautiful hike, follow **Highline Trail** from the Granite Creek area across to Cache Creek, a distance of 16 miles. This route passes just below a row of high and rugged mountains, but because it isn't a loop route, you'll need to hitchhike or set up a shuttle back. Plan on three days for this hike. The area is crisscrossed with game and cattle trails, making it easy to get lost, especially on the headwaters of Little Granite Creek. Talk with Forest Service folks before heading out, and make sure that you know how to read a map and compass.

A third hike begins at the **Goosewing Ranger Station,** 12 miles east of Slide Lake on Gros Ventre River Road. Take the trail from here to Two Echo Park (a fine camping spot) and then continue up to Six Lakes. You can return via the same trail or take the Crystal Creek Trail back to Red Rock Ranch and hitch back to Goosewing. The trail distance is approximately 23 miles round-trip.

Caribou-Targhee National Forest

Covering nearly three million acres, Caribou-Targhee National Forest extends from Montana to Utah. Most of the forest lies within Idaho, but it also includes the western edge of Wyoming along the Tetons. Much of the forest is heavily logged, but two wilderness areas protect most of the Wyoming portion. Cattle and sheep graze many backcountry areas; contact the Forest Service office in Driggs, Idaho, 208/354-2312, www.fs.fed.us/r4/caribou, for areas where you can avoid running into livestock.

Day Hikes

Many short hiking options are available on the west side of the Tetons, and the Forest Service office in Driggs has a handout that describes more than 20 of these hikes. A few of the best include the following. From Darby Canyon Trailhead, you can choose either the **Aspen Trail** (3.6 miles one-way; especially pretty in the fall) or the **South Darby Trail** (2.7 miles one-way; with nice waterfalls and flowered meadows).

From the South Teton Trailhead, you can opt to climb **Table Mountain** (6.4 miles one-way), visit gorgeous **Alaska Basin** (7.7 miles one-way), or ascend the **Devil's Stairs** to Teton Shelf (6.8 miles one-way). All three of these hikes take you high into the alpine, but many families just hike until the kids get tired, eat lunch, and then head back to the car.

Several trails take off from the Teton Pass area along Wyoming 22/Idaho 33, including **Moose Creek Trail,** which accesses Moose Meadows (5.4 miles one-way), and the Teton Crest Trail if you're feeling very ambitious (nine miles one-way). It joins up with another popular hiking route, the **Coal Creek Trail** for an alternative return route to the highway.

JEDEDIAH SMITH WILDERNESS

The 123,451-acre Jedediah Smith Wilderness lies on the west side of the Teton Range, facing Idaho but lying entirely within Wyoming. Access is primarily from the Idaho side, although trails breach the mountain passes at various points, making it possible to enter from Grand Teton National Park. This area was not declared a wilderness until 1984. A second wilderness area, the 10,820-acre **Winegar Hole Wilderness** (pronounced WINE-a-gur), lies along the southern border of Yellowstone National Park. Grizzlies love this country, but hikers will find it uninteresting and without trails. In contrast, the Jedediah Smith Wilderness contains nearly 300 miles of paths and some incredible high-mountain scenery.

Several mostly gravel roads lead up from the Driggs and Victor areas into the Tetons. Get a map ($7) showing wilderness trails and access points from the Caribou-Targhee National Forest ranger station in Driggs, Idaho, 208/354-2312, or from the Forest Service offices in Jackson. Be sure to camp at least 200 feet from lakes and 100 feet from streams. Group size limits are also in place; check with the Forest Service for specifics on these and other backcountry regulations. In addition, anyone planning to cross into Grand Teton National Park from the west side will need to get a park camping permit in advance. Wilderness permits are not required for the Jedediah Smith Wilderness. Both grizzly and black bears are present throughout the Tetons, so all food must be either hung out of reach or stored in bear-resistant containers.

Hidden Corral Basin

At the northern end of the wilderness, Hidden Corral Basin provides a fine loop hike. Locals (primarily those on horseback) crowd this area on late-summer weekends. Get to the trailhead by driving north from Tetonia on Idaho 32 to Lamont, then turn north on a gravel road. Follow it one mile and then turn right (east) onto Coyote Meadows Road. The trailhead is approximately 10 miles up, where the road dead-ends. An eight-mile trail parallels South Bitch Creek (the name Bitch Creek comes from the French word for a female deer, *biche*) to Hidden Corral, where you may see moose. Be sure to bring a fishing pole to try for the cutthroats.

Above Hidden Corral you can make a pleasant loop back by turning north onto the trail to

Nord Pass and then dropping down along the Carrot Ridge and Conant Basin Trails to Bitch Creek Trail and then on to Coyote Meadows, a distance of 21 miles round-trip. Note that this is grizzly and black bear country, and bear-resistant containers are required. By the way, Hidden Corral received its name in the outlaw days, when rustlers would steal horses in Idaho, change the brands, and hold the horses in this natural corral until the branding wounds healed. The horses were then sold to Wyoming ranchers. Owen Wister's *The Virginian* describes a pursuit of horse thieves through Bitch Creek country.

Alaska Basin

The most popular hiking trail in the Jedediah Smith begins near the **Teton Canyon Campground** ($8; open late May to mid-Sept.; reservations at 518/885-3639 or 877/444-6777, www.reserveusa.com) and leads through flower-bedecked meadows to mountain-rimmed Alaska Basin. It's great country, but don't expect a

© DON PITCHER

breathtaking Alaska Basin in the Jedediah Smith Wilderness

JACKSON HOLE

true wilderness experience because many others will also be hiking and camping here. Get to the campground by following the Grand Targhee Ski Resort signs east from Driggs, Idaho. A gravel road splits off to the right approximately three miles beyond the little settlement of Alta. Follow it to the campground. (If you miss the turn, you'll end up at the ski area.) For an enjoyable loop, follow Alaska Basin Trail up the canyon to Basin Lakes and then head southwest along the Teton Crest Trail to the Teton Shelf Trail. Follow this trail back to its junction with the Alaska Basin Trail, dropping down the Devils Stairs—a series of very steep switchbacks. You can then take the Alaska Basin Trail back to Teton Campground, a round-trip distance of approximately 19 miles. You could also use these trails to access the high peaks of the Tetons or to cross the mountains into Death Canyon within Grand Teton National Park (camping permit required). Campfires and horse camping are not allowed in Alaska Basin.

Moose Meadows

For a somewhat less crowded hiking experience, check out the Moose Meadows area on the southern end of the Jedediah Smith Wilderness. Get to the trailhead by going three miles southeast of Victor on Idaho State Hwy. 33. Turn north (left) on Moose Creek Road and follow it to the trailhead. The trail parallels Moose Creek to Moose Meadows, a good place to camp. You'll need to ford the creek twice, so this trail is best hiked in late summer. At the meadows, the trail dead-ends into Teton Crest Trail, providing access to Grand Teton National Park through some gorgeous alpine country. A nice loop can be made by heading south along this trail to flower-covered Coal Creek Meadows. A trail leads from here past 10,068-foot Taylor Mountain (an easy side trip with magnificent views), down to Taylor Basin, through lodgepole forests, and then back to your starting point. This loop hike will take you 15 miles round-trip.

Teton Valley, Idaho

The west side of the Tetons differs dramatically from nearby Jackson Hole. As the road descends from Teton Pass into Teton Valley, Idaho (a.k.a. Pierre's Hole), the lush farming country spreads out before you, reaching 30 miles long and 15 miles across. This, the "quiet side" of the Tetons, offers a slower pace than bustling Jackson, but the Teton Range vistas are equally dramatic.

In recent years the growth in Jackson Hole has spilled across the mountains. The potato farms, horse pastures, and country towns are now undergoing the same transformation that first hit Jackson in the 1970s. As land prices soar and affordable housing becomes more difficult to find in Jackson, more people have opted to move over the pass and commute from the Idaho side. Glossy ads now fill *Teton Valley Magazine,* offering ranchland with a view, luxurious log homes, cozy second homes, balloon flights, espresso coffee, mountain-bike rentals, and handmade lodgepole furniture. Despite these changes, Teton Valley remains a laid-back place, and spud farming is still a part of the

local economy. The primary town here—it's the county seat—is Driggs, with tiny Victor nine miles south and even more insignificant Tetonia eight miles north.

See Don Root's *Moon Handbooks Idaho* (www.moon.com) for excellent coverage of eastern Idaho, including the Swan Valley to the south and the Island Park area to the north.

HISTORY

The area now known as Teton Valley was used for centuries by various Indian tribes, including the Bannock, Blackfeet, Crow, Gros Ventre, Shoshone, and Nez Perce. John Colter—a member of the Lewis and Clark expedition—was the first white man to reach this area, wandering through in the winter of 1807–1808. In 1931, an Idaho farmer claimed to have plowed up a stone carved into the shape of a human face, with "John Colter 1808" etched into the sides. The rock later turned out to be a hoax created by a man anxious to obtain a horse concession with

Grand Teton National Park. He got the concession after donating the rock to the park museum.

Vieux Pierre, an Iroquois fur trapper for the Hudson's Bay Company, made this area his base in the 1820s, but was later killed by Blackfeet Indians in Montana. Many people still call the valley Pierre's Hole. Two fur trapper rendezvous took place in Pierre's Hole, but the 1832 event proved pivotal. Some 1,000 Indians, trappers, and traders gathered for an annual orgy of trading, imbibing, and general partying. When a column of men on horseback appeared, two white trappers headed out for a meeting. The column turned out to be a group of Gros Ventre Indians, and the meeting quickly turned sour. One trapper shot the Gros Ventre chief point-blank, killing him. A battle quickly ensued that left 38 people dead on both sides and forced rendezvous participants to scatter. Later rendezvous were held in valleys where the animosities were not as high. For the next 50 years, virtually the only whites in Pierre's Hole were horse thieves and outlaws. Hiram C. Lapham was the first to try his hand at ranching in the valley, but his cattle were rustled by three outlaws, including Ed Harrington, alias Ed Trafton.

In 1888, a lawyer from Salt Lake City, B. W. Driggs, came to the valley and liked what he found. With his encouragement, a flood of Mormon settlers arrived over the next few years, establishing farms along the entire length of Teton Valley. By the 1940s the valley was home to a cheese factory, sawmills, a railroad line, and numerous sprawling ranches. Teton Valley's population plummeted in the 1960s, but in 1969 development began at Grand Targhee Ski Resort, and the economy started to turn around. Recent years have seen the area come into its own as tourism-related businesses began to eclipse farming and ranching. In the last decade the valley was positively booming, and Teton County, Idaho, has been one of the fastest-growing counties (on a percentage basis) in the nation.

VICTOR

Twenty-four miles west of Jackson, the town of Victor, Idaho, is little more than the proverbial wide spot in the road. It does, however, have several places that make it worth visiting.

Pierre's Playhouse, on Main St. in Victor, 208/787-2249, www.pierresplayhouse.com, puts on old-fashioned melodramas twice weekly from mid-June to early September. A Dutch-oven chicken dinner is served before the show. You know you're in for a serious production when the villain is named Gustavo Scumsuckler.

Accommodations

Built in the 1940s, **Timberline Inn,** 38 W. Center St., 208/787-2772 or 800/711-4667, has an attractive log-cabin exterior, with standard motel rooms for $60–65 s or d. Open June–Sept. **Trails End Motel,** 208/787-2973, rents four-person log cabin units for $49. Open May–Oct.

Kasper's Kountryside Inn, 208/787-2726, www.tetonvalleychamber.com/kountrysideinn.htm, has two modern apartments in a barn-style building for $75. These include full kitchens, private baths, and one sleeps four. **Fin Spring Cottage,** 208/787-2771, www.tetonvalleychamber.com/finspring.htm, is a cozy waterside place on a wooded lot west of Victor. The cottage rents for $225 d or $250 for four people, and has a full kitchen. **Teton Mountain Hideaways,** 208/787-3094, www.tetonmountainhideaway.com, has several vacation rental houses scattered around Teton Valley.

Four miles southeast of Victor at the foot of Teton Pass, **Moose Creek Ranch,** 208/787-2784 or 800/676-0075, www.moosecreekranch.com, has guest ranch accommodations on a weekly basis; $2,300 for two people. This rate includes lodging, meals, horseback lessons and rides, children's programs, whitewater float trips, chuck wagon dinners, and other ranch activities. Accommodations are cozy cabins with private baths, and the ranch also has an outdoor pool and hot tub.

Teton Springs, 208/787-8000 or 866/445-3328, www.tetonsprings.com, is more evidence of the spillover effect from Jackson. This private club for the moneyed class includes 500 homes and condos, a golf course, spa, tennis courts, fly-fishing school, swimming pool, and an "old town village" with shopping, dining, lodging, and more. The entire development should be completed by 2005. A heliport waits for those who can afford the helicopter flight over to Jackson for the evening.

Camping

The Forest Service's pleasant **Trail Creek Campground** ($8; open mid-May to mid-Sept.) is six miles southeast of Victor and just across the Wyoming state line. Make reservations ($9 fee) at 518/885-3639 or 877/444-6777, www.reserve usa.com. **Teton Valley Campground,** one mile west of Victor on Idaho Hwy. 31, 208/787-2647, www.tetonvalleycampground.com, has RV hookups ($32–34), tent sites ($22), basic cabins ($42), and a small outdoor pool. The campground also rents canoes, mountain bikes, and fishing gear.

Food

For the finest meals in Teton Valley, make dinner reservations at **The Old Dewey House Restaurant,** 37 S. Main St., 208/787-2092, www.odh .com. Everything is made from scratch by the owners, and the entrées ($13–30) are accompanied by freshly baked breads, salads with homemade dressings, fresh vegetables, and spicy appetizers. The menu changes frequently at this eight-table restaurant, but house favorites include blackened chicken and jalapeño pistachio sauce, and charbroiled rack of lamb. Delectable desserts are offered, too. No young children are permitted to dine here in the evening, and the menu warns: "Undisciplined children will be impounded and sent to the local taxidermist or fed to the Yellowstone wolves!" Closed Tuesday. The same characters also run tiny Grumpy's Goat Shack next door, with wines, beers, and appetizers, including wonderful roasted garlic with homemade goat cheese from their own goats.

Victor Emporium, 208/787-2221, houses an old-fashioned soda fountain with good fish tacos and famous shakes, especially their huckleberry shakes in season. They've been in business for more than 50 years and also sell fishing supplies and Idaho souvenirs.

Also in Victor is **Knotty Pine Restaurant,** 208/787-2866, considered one of the better local places for ribs and steaks, but be ready for clouds of cigarette smoke with your meal. It's an old-fashioned place with low ceilings and log walls, plus a large deck for outside dining. Live bands crank out the dance tunes most summer weekends.

Brewery

Grand Teton Brewing Company, 208/787-4000, www.grandtetonbrewing.com, is on the east side of Victor at 430 Old Jackson Highway. Drop by weekdays for a free tour or to sample Teton Ale, Old Faithful Ale, Moose Juice Stout, Teton Huckleberry Wheat, or Sweetgrass IPA. The gift shop sells T-shirts, glasses, and beer to go.

DRIGGS

Driggs (pop. 1,000) is an odd conglomeration, mixing an old-time farming settlement and newfangled recreation mecca. It's also fast becoming a bedroom community for commuters to Jackson Hole. A major development on the south end of town will bring many more homes and businesses. There isn't much to downtown Driggs, so it's pretty easy to find your way around. But don't expect things to stay small for long because the area has been discovered; in 2002, *Men's Journal* put Driggs at the top of their list for best small towns in America.

Sights

Driggs is perhaps best known as home to the delightfully amusing **Spud Drive-In,** here since 1953. You can't miss the big truck out front with a flatbed-sized "potato" on the back. The drive-in even attracts folks from Jackson, who cross the pass for an evening of fun beneath the stars. Call 208/354-2727 or 800/799-7783 for upcoming flicks. The drive-in is locally famous for Gladys burgers and Spud buds—served by carhops.

The spacious **Teton Valley Museum** opened in 2003 and houses historical displays from the valley's past. It's located on the north side of town just beyond the Super 8 Motel. Call 208/354-2200 or 208/456-2652 for details.

Located at the airport just north of town, **Warbirds Museum** is an interesting collection of nicely restored historic planes in a hanger at the Teton Aviation Center, 208/354-3100 or 800/472-6382, www.tetonaviation.com. No charge, and they're open daily 7 A.M.–7 P.M. in summer and daily 8 A.M.–5 P.M. the rest of the year. They have several unusual fighter aircraft—including a T-28 Trojan and a Mig-15—but only five or six are displayed at any given time. Warbirds Cafe is adjacent.

Accommodations

For a town this small, Driggs offers a surprising number of places to stay. In addition to those listed, you'll find others just east in Alta, Wyoming. **The Pines Motel Guest Haus,** 105 S. Main St., 208/354-2774 or 800/354-2778, is a delightful European-style guest house built in 1900. Run by the Nielson family, the home has seven rooms, each different but all nicely appointed with tasteful touches such as handmade quilts. A hot tub is available outside. Rates are very reasonable: $40 s or $50 d, and children are welcome. Breakfasts cost $10 per person.

Super 8 Motel, on the north side of Driggs at 133 Hwy. 33, 208/354-8888 or 800/800-8000, www.super8.com, has standard rooms for $78 d, including an indoor pool, sauna, hot tub, and continental breakfast.

Intermountain Lodge, 34 Ski Hill Rd. (one mile east of Driggs), 208/354-8153, offers modern log cabin lodging with an outdoor hot tub. All rooms include kitchenettes. Rates are $69 s or d, plus $5 per person for additional guests.

Best Western Teton West, 476 N. Main St., 208/354-2363 or 800/252-2363, www.best western.com, features a continental breakfast, indoor pool, and hot tub. Rates are $80–90 d in standard rooms. Closed Oct. to mid-Dec. and Apr. to mid-May.

Teton Ranch, 208/456-2010 or 888/456-2012, www.tetonranch.com, has two log homes on a working ranch. Each contains two bedrooms, a fireplace, and kitchenette and costs $175–250 for four people. The cabins are six miles northeast of Driggs; reserve 3–6 months ahead for the peak summer season. There's a two-night minimum stay.

Short-term bookings for townhouses, homes, cabins, and condos in the area are provided by two property management companies: **Grand Valley Lodging,** 208/354-8890 or 800/746-5518, www.grandvalleylodging.com; and **Teton Valley Property Management,** 208/354-8881 or 888/354-8881, www.tetonvalleyidaho.com. Rates range from $125 to $500 per night during the peak season. These accommodations are popular with families and ski groups heading to Grand Targhee Ski Resort.

Bed-and-Breakfasts

Teton Sunrise Inn, 208/456-2777 or 888/456-2777, www.tetonsunriseinn.com, is a recently built B&B halfway between Driggs and Tetonia (three miles in either direction). The lodge-style home contains five large guest rooms, each with a private bath. An enclosed hot tub faces the Tetons, and a full breakfast is served, along with evening snacks. Rates are $80 s or d, and children are welcome.

Willowpine B&B, 136 E. Little Ave., 208/354-2735, has two guest rooms that share a bath in a refurbished 1940s home. It's right in town. Rates are $65 s or d, including a full breakfast. No kids under 12 are allowed, and the B&B is only open on weekends and holidays.

Camping

The nearest public campsites are at **Teton Canyon Campground** ($8; open mid-May to mid-Sept.), 11 miles east of Driggs in the Tetons. This is a delightful camping spot, and the trailhead into beautiful (and very popular) Alaska Basin is nearby. Make reservations ($9 fee) at 518/885-3639 or 877/444-6777, www.reserveusa.com.

Food

One benefit of Teton Valley's rapid growth is a dramatic improvement in the local restaurant scene. Driggs now has several good dining places. (The best local meals, however, are Dewey's in Victor and Lost Horizon in Alta.)

Bunk House Bistro, 285 N. Main St., 208/354-3770, emphasizes "cowboy" breakfasts and lunches all week, with Friday and Saturday dinners starring pasta, seafood, and prime rib. The kitchen is small, so you may need to wait for your meal, but the servings are substantial. Reservations recommended.

Auntie M's Sweet Shoppe & Coffee, 189 N. Main St., 208/354-2010, is not a place for fast food or young children. The owner makes virtually everything from scratch, and the menu exists only in Auntie's head. Just ask her for today's sandwich, soup, and dessert specials, or get an espresso and check out her collection of homemade jams, jellies, and fruit butters for sale. It's a friendly and classy little spot.

Miso Hungry Cafe, 165 N. Main St., 208/354-8015, is a hip spot with several covered tables on the front porch and a small art gallery in the back room. The food is flavorful, with an ethnic twist, and they bake their own breads and pastries. Check the chalkboard for today's specials.

Warbirds Cafe, 208/354-2550, www.teton aviation.com, is an aviation-themed restaurant located—appropriately enough—at the airport just north of town. The à la carte menu includes such treats as buffalo burgers, blackened catfish, vegetable fettuccini alfredo, or beef stew served over garlic mashed potatoes. Their wonderful Sunday brunch is $14—and worth it. Several restored planes are in the adjacent hanger. Warbirds Cafe is popular with pilots who can fly in for lunch with a view. Or, as one local pointed out, it represents "all the things we ran away from when we moved here from Jackson."

According to locals, **The Grand Ole Grill,** 95 S. Main St., 208/354-8294, makes the best Philly cheesesteaks west of the Mississippi. Also on the menu are burgers, steaks, and various sandwiches. In the evening, stop by **O'Rourke's Sports Bar & Grille,** 42 E. Little Ave., 208/354-8115, where you can watch sports on the tube while you munch pizzas, sandwiches, fish & chips, and burgers.

Inside a 1916 home off the main drag, **Royal Wolf,** 208/354-8365, is another place with a big choice of beers on tap, plus a diverse dinner menu in a smoke-free setting. A pool table, dartboards, and sports on the TVs provide for extra-culinary fun.

Tony's Pizza & Pasta, 364 N. Main St., 208/354-8829, serves hand-tossed New York–style pizzas, plus focaccia, calzone, and Italian meals. Choose from a big choice of microbrewed beers, with many on draught. Tony's flavorful "Avalanche" pizza comes with ricotta, mozzarella, and garlic—but no tomato sauce. No smoking allowed here.

Get malts, shakes, and hot fudge sundaes at the old soda fountain inside **Corner Drug,** 10 S. Main St., 208/354-2334. Lime freezes are their claim to fame. Where can you find the best local espresso? Try **Java the Hut,** next to the bike shop on Main Street.

Latino's Delights, 190 N. Main St., 208/354-2718, is the real thing, with tamales, enchiladas, guaraches, gorditos, flautas, and Mexican pastries, along with a TV blaring Spanish-language broadcasts. It's a good place to bone-up on your Spanish skills.

The main place for groceries is **Broulim's,** 52 S. Main St., 208/354-2350. Right next door is tiny **Barrels and Bins,** 208/354-2307, selling health foods and freeze-dried backcountry meals.

Teton Valley Events

The main summer event comes on Fourth of July weekend, the **Grand Teton Summer Festival.** Highlights include hot air balloon launches (more than 20 balloons) and tethered rides for the kids at the airport, a parade and crafts fair in Victor, a rodeo in Tetonia, arts exhibits, a pig roast, live music, evening fireworks in Driggs, and barbecue lunches at Grand Targhee Resort. That same weekend, the resort puts on the **WYDAHO Mountain Bike Race,** a cross-country event that attracts everyone from beginners to pros. In early August, Driggs is home to a half-marathon race, the **John Colter Run.**

Grand Targhee Ski Resort pulls out the stops for the always popular **Targhee Bluegrass Festival** in mid-August, with nationally known acts. The music attracts a throng, so make camping or lodging reservations well ahead of time. Get details at 307/353-2300 or 800/827-4433, www.grandtarghee.com.

Heritage Days in late July celebrates the area's Mormon settlers; featured attractions are a parade through the center of Driggs, art shows, and a theatrical production. **Taste of the Tetons**

arrives in early August, with local restaurants showing off their fare to raise funds for the nonprofit Teton Regional Land Trust. Call 208/354-8939 for information on the event and this organization.

In mid-August, the **Teton County Fair** brings down-home fun with livestock judging, arts and crafts, quilts, pies, jams, and other fare on display. Call 208/354-2961 for details.

Teton Valley Recreation

Outdoor enthusiasts will discover an array of activities at all times of the year in the Driggs area. The Teton River runs the entire length of Teton Valley and is renowned among fly-fishing enthusiasts. A plethora of hikes can be found both to the east in the Tetons and to the west in the Big Hole Mountains. See Caribou-Targhee National Forest earlier in this chapter for details on Alaska Basin; it's one of the most popular day (or multinight) hikes in the area. The Forest Service office in Driggs has details on other hiking options if you're looking for a less crowded experience.

The **National Outdoor Leadership School** (NOLS) has an office off the main road south of Driggs at 166 E. 200 S., 208/354-8443, www .nols.edu. This is one of nine regional NOLS offices scattered around the globe; headquarters is in Lander, Wyoming. The Driggs office runs summertime backpacking and whitewater training, plus backcountry skiing classes in the winter. Classes last two weeks to three months.

A paved **bike path** parallels Hwy. 33 between Victor and Driggs, providing a pleasant running, cycling, or in-line skating opportunity. A new section of the path continues east from Driggs to the Wyoming border at Alta, and the path may eventually continue over Teton Pass to Wilson. Get details at 208/353-2252, www.tetonvalley-chamber.com/pathways.html. Kids and their parents will appreciate the **Driggs Town Park,** with an attractive playground and sprinklers that make for impromptu summer fun. It's located on Ashley Street.

Peaked Sports, 70 E. Little Ave., 208/354-2354 or 800/705-2354, rents mountain bikes, bike trailers, and in-line skates, but **Big Hole Mountain Sports,** 65 S. Main St., 208/354-

2209 or 877/574-3377, is for the real biking enthusiast. The store rents high-quality mountain bikes in the summer, along with skis and snowboards in winter. You can join locals for a ride out local trails most afternoons, but this is for advanced riders only—unless you want to get left in the dust.

High Peaks Health & Fitness Center, on Little Ave., 208/354-3128, has guest passes for $10 per day. **The Links at Teton Peaks,** 208/456-2374, is a Scottish-style nine-hole golf course at 127 N. 400 West.

For horseback rides, contact **Dry Ridge Outfitters,** 208/354-2284, www.dryridge.com, or **Bar H Ranch,** 888/216-6025, www.tetontrail rides.com. Trail rides are also available at Grand Targhee Ski Resort.

Bagley's Teton Mountain Ranch, 265 W. 800 South, 208/787-9005 or 866/787-9005, www.elkadventures.com, raises 130 elk as breeding stock and for their antlers. They offer summertime wagon rides and wintertime sleigh rides among the elk for $8 ($5 for ages 4–9), plus horseback rides (starting at $35 for a one-hour ride).

Teton Aviation Center, 208/354-3100 or 800/472-6382, www.tetonaviation.com, is best known for their scenic glider flights past the Tetons, but they also offer airplane rides and have an impressive collection of vintage military aircraft. **Rainbow Balloon Flights,** 307/733-0470 or 800/378-0470, www.hometown.aol.com/rain-bowballoons, offers one-hour hot air balloon flights over Teton Valley for $189 per person.

Shopping

For a unique shopping experience at "the cultural hub of the universe," drop by **Mountaineering Outfitters,** 62 N. Main St., 208/354-2222 or 800/359-2410. Inside the jam-packed aisles are hiking boots, sleeping bags, Patagonia clothing (good prices), army-surplus wool pants, and maps. Owner Fred Mugler opened his shop in 1971 and has been cramming it with supplies ever since. Stop for a chat and a laugh.

Considerably more organized is **Yöstmark Mountain Equipment,** 12 E. Little Ave.,

208/354-2828, www.yostmark.com, which sells a wide range of outdoor equipment. They also rent fishing gear, drift boats, backpacks, tents, sleeping bags, boots, inflatable kayaks, rafts, and all sorts of other summer gear, along with snow-shoes, cross-country skis, skate skis, snowboards, and telemark and alpine touring skis in winter. Open daily 8 A.M.–7 P.M. Ask them about guided backcountry ski tours.

Browse the eclectic selection of regional books at the friendly **Dark Horse Books,** 76 N. Main St., 208/354-8882 or 888/434-8882, www.dark horsebooks.com.

Bergmeyer Manufacturing Co., 229 N. Hwy. 33, 208/354-8611 or 800/348-3356, www .bergmeyermfg.com, creates quality log furniture in traditional and modern styles.

Information and Services

The **Teton Valley Chamber of Commerce,** 208/354-2500, www.tetonvalleychamber.com, is in downtown Driggs at 81 N. Main Street. Their hours are officially Monday–Friday 10 A.M.–3 P.M., but call first to make sure someone is there. Another source for information—with links to local businesses—is on the web at www.tetonguide.com.

Get Caribou-Targhee National Forest information from the **Teton Basin Ranger District Office,** just south of town at 525 S. Main St., 208/354-2312, www.fs.fed.us/r4/caribou. Wash clothes at the appropriately named **Coin Laundry** next to Latino's Delight, 190 N. Main Street.

Teton Valley Hospital is at 283 N. 1st East, 208/354-2383. Also here is **Teton Valley Medical Center,** 208/354-2302, for nonemergency care.

Transportation

Community and Rural Transportation (CART), 208/354-2240 or 800/657-7439, has daily bus service between Driggs and Rexburg. Rent cars from **Basin Auto,** 208/354-2297.

TETONIA

Tiny Tetonia is eight miles north of Driggs. The town is surrounded by farming country and grand old barns; it's a good place to see kids rid-ing horseback. The crest of the tourist wave is just starting to lap at the shores of Tetonia, and at last check no local place sold espresso, focaccia, or cell phones.

Accommodations

Teton Mountain View Lodge, 208/456-2741 or 800/625-2232, www.tetonmountainlodge.com, has large and modern rooms with rustic furnishings; some also have fireplaces. Other amenities include a continental breakfast and an enclosed hot tub. Rates are $60–100 s or d.

Locanda di Fiori (The Inn of Flowers), 208/456-0909, www.rpgwebs.com/locanda, is a modern log cabin with masses of wildflowers (hence the name) and stunning views of the Tetons to the east. Two comfortable guest rooms are available, both with private baths and entrances, plus access to an outdoor hot tub. A full breakfast is served each morning, along with wine and cheese in the afternoon. Rates are $95 d. The inn is open June–mid-October; no kids under age 15.

East of Tetonia in the Teton foothills inside Wyoming, **Beard's Mountain Ranch,** 307/576-2694, www.beardoutfitters.com, rents a cozy two-bedroom cabin with kitchenette for $100 and has a new and much larger two-bedroom cabin with loft, balcony, and full kitchen for $225 d. Additional guests are $5 per person (maximum of six). The ranch also offers horseback riding and guided fishing trips.

Occupying a 4,000-acre spread five miles northeast of Tetonia, **Teton Ridge Ranch,** 200 Valley View Rd., 208/456-2650, www.teton ridge.com, provides guest ranch accommodations. The modern 10,000-square-foot log lodge forms a central focal point, but a cottage is also available for guests. Rates are a stiff $630 for two people per day, including excellent meals, horseback riding, and fishing in their stocked ponds. A three-night minimum stay is required, and the ranch has space for 14 guests. During winter they provide groomed cross-country ski trails. Winter rates are $500 d per day, including lodging, meals, and guided skiing. Open mid-June through Oct., and mid-Dec. to mid-Mar.

Other Practicalities

Trail's End Cafe, 208/456-2202, attracts local farmers and ranchers from all around for home-cooked meals of turkey, gravy, mashed Idaho potatoes, burgers, and other hearty fare. The homemade pies are worth the visit. This is where you'll meet the hardworking good ol' boys. Open at 6 A.M. daily.

A Tetonia company called **Drawknife,** 516 N. Hwy. 33, 800/320-0527, www.drawknife.com, creates one-of-a-kind billiard tables using hand-carved lodgepole bases and top-quality tabletops.

ALTA, WYOMING

The little place called Alta sits right along the Wyoming border and just six miles northeast of Driggs, Idaho. There are no stores in Alta, but the settlement does have a stellar restaurant and several places to stay. East from Alta, the road climbs through heavily timbered country, with periodic views of the Big Hole Mountains to the west and up-close looks at the Teton Range. Also in Alta is the nine-hole **Targhee Village Golf Course,** 208/354-8577 or 307/353-8577.

Grand Targhee Ski Resort, 307/353-2300 or 800/827-4433, www.grandtarghee.com—just five miles above Alta—is the main attraction for the entire Teton Valley area. The resort offers excellent skiing and snowboarding in winter, along with a wide range of summer activities. Get the complete scoop, including details for on-mountain lodging and meals, in the Downhill Skiing and Snowboarding section.

Accommodations

Alta Lodge B&B, 307/353-2582, www.pdt .net/altalodge, is a large modern home with tall picture windows framing the Tetons. Four guest rooms are here (two with private baths), and a hot tub is available. Rates are $65–85 d, including a full breakfast. No kids are allowed.

Teton Teepee Lodge, 470 W. Alta Rd., 307/353-8176 or 800/353-8176, www.teton teepee.com, is a winter-only place with a spa-cious common area at the center of a tepee-shaped building. Twenty-one guest rooms (no TV or phones in rooms) surround it, and two large dorm rooms—primarily used by kids—occupy a lower level. The lodge is a favorite of skiers and snowboarders, with a large central stone fireplace, dining area, pool table, game room, TV room, and outdoor hot tub. The rooms are rented on a package basis only: $864 for three days for two people, including private room, breakfast, dinner, drinks, transportation to Grand Targhee, and lift tickets. In other words, everything but your lunch and skis. For five days, the all-inclusive rate is $1,340 for two people. The packages are also available in dorm rooms: $384 per person for a complete three-day stay ($296 for ages 15–18; $156 for ages 6–14). The lodge is only open during ski season, mid-November through April.

Also in Alta is **Wilson Creekside Inn B&B,** 130 Alta North Rd., 307/353-2409, where you'll find a century-old home on a 200-acre sheep farm. Four guest rooms are available and all contain family heirlooms. One costs $90 d and includes a king-size bed and private bath; the others share a bath and run $80 d. Guests are served an ample country breakfast. Kids are welcome, but no credit cards are accepted. The owner's son raises some 150 ewes on the ranch.

Food

Lost Horizon Dinner Club, 307/353-8226, is one of two standout places in the Teton Valley area (the other being the Dewey Restaurant in Victor). The restaurant/home has space for just a dozen guests, who sit down to a memorable 10-course Japanese and Chinese meal ($40 plus wine) prepared by co-owner and chef Shigako Irwin. This isn't for vegetarians or for those in a hurry; expect to be here for three leisurely hours. Dinners are served Friday and Saturday nights at 7 P.M., and reservations are required. No credit cards are accepted. Formal dress isn't necessary, but don't come in shorts, sandals, or T-shirts. Recommended.

Grand Teton National Park

Grand Teton National Park remains one of the preeminent symbols of American wilderness. The Tetons rise abruptly from the valley floor, their bare triangular ridges looking like broken shards of glass from some cosmic accident of creation. With six different summits topping 12,000 feet, plus some of the finest climbing and hiking in Wyoming, the Tetons are a paradise for lovers of the outdoors. They have long been a favorite of photographers and sightseers and once even appeared in an ad promoting Colorado tourism! The Tetons change character with the seasons. In summer the sagebrush flats are a garden of flowers set against the mountain backdrop. When autumn arrives, the cottonwoods and aspens become swaths of yellow and orange. Winter turns everything a glorious, sparkling white, set against the fluorescent blue sky.

the majestic Tetons

© DON PITCHER

Geology

BUILDING A MOUNTAIN RANGE

The precipitous Teton Range contains perhaps the most complex geologic history in North America. Although the Tetons are ancient by any human scale, they are the youngest mountains in the Rockies, less than 10 million years old (versus 60 million years for the nearby Wind River Mountains). The Tetons are a fault-block range, formed when the earth's crust cracked along an angled fault. Forces within the earth have pushed the western side (the Tetons) up, while the eastern portion (Jackson Hole) dropped down like a trapdoor. Geologists believe the fault could slip up to 10 feet at a time, producing a violent earthquake. All this shifting has created one of the most dramatic and asymmetric mountain faces on earth.

Unlike typical mountain ranges, the highest parts are not at the center of the range but along the eastern edge, where uplifting continues. The western slope, which drops gently into Idaho, is much less dramatic, although the views are still impressive. This tilting-and-subsidence process is still going on today, pushed by the movement of a plume of magma beneath Yellowstone as the continental plate slides over the top. Because of this subsidence, the town of Wilson in Jackson Hole now lies 10 feet below the level of the nearby Snake River; only riverside dikes protect the town from flooding.

As the mountains rose along this fault, millennia of overlying deposits were stripped away by erosion, leaving three-million-year-old Precambrian rock jutting into the air above the more recent sedimentary deposits in the valley. Because of this shifting and erosion, sandstone deposits atop Mt. Moran match those 24,000 feet below Jackson Hole. Although the most recent major earthquake on the Teton Fault was at least 2,000 years ago, geologists are convinced that Jackson Hole could experience a major temblor at any time.

RIVERS OF ICE

In counterpoint to the uplifting actions that created the general outline of the Tetons, erosional forces have been wearing them down again. Glaciers, which are created when more snow falls than melts off, have proven to be one of the most important of these erosional processes. After a period of several years and under the weight of additional snow, the accumulated snow crystals change into ice. Gravity pulls this ice slowly downhill, creating essentially a frozen river that grinds against whatever lies in the way, plucking loose rocks and soil and polishing hard bedrock. This debris moves slowly down the glacier as if on a conveyer belt, eventually reaching the glacier's terminus.

When a glacier remains the same size for a long period, large piles of glacial debris accumulate at its end, creating what glaciologists call a terminal moraine. One of these created Jackson Lake, when a huge glacier dumped tons of rock at its snout. After the glacier melted back, this terminal moraine became a natural dam for the waters of the Snake River. Similar mounds of glacial debris dammed the creeks that formed Jenny, Leigh, Bradley, Taggart, and Phelps Lakes within Grand Teton National Park.

The earth has experienced cyclical periods of glaciation for hundreds of thousands of years, probably due to changes in the earth's orbit around the sun. During the colder portions of these cycles, glaciers appear and advance. The entire Yellowstone region has undergone a series of massive glaciations, the last of which is called the Pinedale Glaciation. It began around 70,000 years ago and had essentially disappeared by 15,000 years ago. At its peak, the Pinedale Glaciation covered all of Yellowstone and reached well into Jackson Hole.

Streams flowed from the ends of these glaciers, carrying along gravel, sand, silt, and clay. The cobbles and sands from these streams were dropped on the flat valley below, while the finer silts and clays continued downstream, leaving behind soils too rocky and nutrient-poor to support trees. Only sagebrush grows on this plain today, while the surrounding hills and mountain slopes (which were spared this rocky deposition) are covered with lodgepole and subalpine fir forests. Trees can also be found covering the silty terminal moraines that ring the lakes.

Other reminders of the glacial past are the "potholes" (more accurately termed "kettles") that dot the plain south of Signal Mountain. These depressions were created when large blocks of ice were buried under glacial outwash. When the ice melted, it left a kettle-shaped pond surrounded by glacial debris. Only a dozen or so small glaciers remain in the Tetons; the largest is the 3,500-foot-long Teton Glacier, visible on the northeastern face of Grand Teton. For a far more detailed picture of Teton geology, read *Interpreting the Landscape: Recent and Ongoing Geology of Grand Teton & Yellowstone National Parks,* by John Good and Kenneth Pierce (Moose, WY: Grand Teton Natural History Association, 1996).

Wildlife

Grand Teton National Park is an excellent place to look for wildlife. Moose are often seen in the willow meadows along Jackson Lake, south of the settlement of Moose, and along the Snake River. The best times to see animals are in the early morning or at dusk. Herds of pronghorn antelope are common on the sagebrush flats near Kelly. Elk are frequent sights in fall as they migrate down from the high country to the elk refuge near Jackson, but smaller numbers are in the park during summer. (Grand Teton is the only national park outside of Alaska that allows hunting. The rules are pretty strange, however, requiring elk hunters to become temporarily deputized park rangers before they head out!) Grizzlies are currently found only on the park's northern margins, but black bears are present in wooded canyons and riverbeds, so be careful when hiking or camping in the park. Moose are often seen along the Snake River, at Oxbow Bend, and at Willow Flats. Other animals to look for are bald eagles and ospreys along the Snake River and trumpeter swans and Canada geese in ponds and lakes. Look for mule deer in meadow areas and at forest edges, such as those near Colter Bay.

BISON

Herds of bison (buffalo) are commonly seen in the Moran Junction area and in the Mormon Row area. They were present historically (hence the name Buffalo River) but had been extinct for perhaps a century when eight bison were released into Grand Teton National Park in 1969. The population grew slowly for the first decade until they discovered the free alfalfa handout at the elk refuge north of Jackson. Partly because of this winter feeding, the population has grown

About 600 bison live in Grand Teton National Park.

to almost 600 animals—much to the chagrin of the elk-refuge managers. A few bison are hunted outside the park to control their numbers.

WOLVES

Wolves were reintroduced to Yellowstone National Park starting in 1995, and they continue to spread into new territory. By the winter of 1998–1999, they had moved into Grand Teton National Park and are now denning in the park. They're most easily seen in winter, particularly on the adjacent National Elk Refuge where they prey on elk, but they may sometimes be seen during summer inside the park.

Park History

Once the wonders of Yellowstone came to widespread public attention, it took only a few months for Congress to declare that area a national park. But the magnificent mountain range to the south proved an entirely different story. Early on, there were suggestions that Yellowstone be expanded to include the Tetons, but it would take decades of wrangling before Jackson Hole would finally be preserved.

"DAMNING" JACKSON LAKE

Jackson Lake represents one of the sadder chapters in the history of northwestern Wyoming. Jackson Lake Dam was built in the winter of 1910–1911 to supply water for Idaho potato and beet farmers. The town of Moran was built to house construction workers for Jackson Lake Dam and at one time included more than a hundred ramshackle structures. Virtually nothing remains of the town. The 70-foot-tall dam increased the size of the natural lake, flooding out more than 7,200 acres of trees and creating a tangle of floating and submerged trunks and stumps. To some, the dam seemed like the serpent in the Garden of Eden, a symbol of the development that would destroy the valley if not stopped. The trees remained in Jackson Lake for many years, creating an eyesore until the Park Service and the CCC finally launched a massive cleanup project in the 1930s. The dam was completely rebuilt in 1988–1989, and while the lake now looks attractive, it remains yet another example of how Wyoming provides water for farmers in surrounding states. Late in the fall, especially in dry years, the lake can drop to a large puddle with long stretches of exposed bottom at the upper end. Fortunately, Idaho irrigators did not succeed in their planned dams on Jenny, Leigh, and Taggart Lakes in what is now Grand Teton National Park.

DUDES AND DEVELOPMENT

Because of the rocky soils and long winters, Jackson Hole has always been a marginal place for cattle ranching, and only in the southern end of the valley are the soils rich enough to support a decent crop of hay. This poor soil and harsh climate saved Jackson Hole from early development and forced the ranchers to bring in dudes to supplement their income. (One old-timer noted, "Dudes winter better than cattle.")

Louis Joy established the first Jackson Hole dude ranch, the JY, in 1908 along Phelps Lake. It was followed a few years later by the Bar BC Ranch of Struthers Burt, an acclaimed East Coast author who had come west as a dude but learned enough to go into the business for himself. The dude ranchers were some of the first to realize the value of Jackson Hole and to support its preservation. Burt proposed that the valley and mountains be saved not as a traditional park but as a "museum on the hoof," where ranching and tourism would join hands to stave off commercial developments. The roads would remain unpaved, all homes would be log, and Jackson would stay a frontier town. Needless to say, that didn't happen.

The movement to save Jackson Hole coalesced in a 1923 meeting at the cabin of Maude Noble. Horace Albright, superintendent of Yellowstone

GRAND TETON

National Park, was there, along with local dude ranchers, businessmen, and cattlemen who were eager to save the remote valley from exploitation. To accomplish this goal, they proposed finding a wealthy philanthropist who might be willing to invest the $2 million that would be needed to buy the land. Fortunately, one of Struthers Burt's friends happened to be Kenneth Chorley, an assistant to John D. Rockefeller, Jr. Burt used this contact to get Rockefeller interested in the project.

ROCKY TO THE RESCUE

In 1926, Rockefeller traveled west for a 12-day trip to Yellowstone. Horace Albright used the chance to take him on a side trip into Jackson Hole and to proselytize for protection of the valley. What they saw portended badly for the future: the Jenny Lake dance hall, roadside tourist camps and hot dog stands, rusting abandoned cars, and a place that billboards proclaimed "Home of the Hollywood Cowboy." Rockefeller was angered by the prospect of crass commercial developments blanketing Jackson Hole and quickly signed on to the idea of purchasing the land and giving it to the Park Service.

To cover his tracks as he bought the land, Rockefeller formed the Snake River Land Company; if ranchers had known that the Rockefeller clan was behind the scheme, they would have either refused to sell or jacked up the price. Only a few residents—mostly supporters—knew of the plan. The local banker, Robert Miller, served as land-purchasing agent, although even he opposed letting the Park Service gain control of the valley. Miller used his position to buy out ranches with delinquent mortgages at his Jackson State Bank and then resigned, claiming the whole thing was part of a sinister plot to run the ranchers out and halt "progress." In 1929, Congress voted to establish a small Grand Teton National Park that would encompass the mountains themselves, which stood little chance of development, but not much else. Conservationists knew that without preservation of the valley below, the wonderful vistas would be lost.

A NATIONAL BATTLEGROUND

Rockefeller and Albright finally went public with their land-purchasing scheme in 1930, releasing a tidal wave of outrage. Antipark forces led by Sen. Milward Simpson (father of recently retired Sen. Alan Simpson) spent the next decade fighting the park tooth and nail, charging that it would destroy the economy of Jackson Hole and that ranchers would lose their livelihood. Rockefeller's agents were falsely accused of trying to intimidate holdouts with strong-arm tactics. Congress refused to accept Rockefeller's gift, and local opposition blocked the bill for more than a decade.

Finally, in 1943, President Roosevelt made an end run around the antipark forces; he accepted the 32,000 acres purchased by Rockefeller, added 130,000 acres of Forest Service land, and declared it the Jackson Hole National Monument. The move outraged those in the valley, prompting more hearings and bills to abolish the new national monument. Wyoming's politicians attacked Roosevelt's actions. A bill overturning the decision was pocket-vetoed by the president, but for the next several years, the Wyoming delegation kept reintroducing the measure.

Things came to a head when Wallace Beery—a Reaganesque Hollywood actor—threatened to "shoot to kill" park officials. Beery, who had to use a stepladder to climb on his horse, organized a cattle drive across the monument. Unable to find anyone to fire on in the new monument, his cadres sat on a creek bank and drank a case of beer, cussing out the damn bureaucrats. So much for the Wild West.

By 1947, the tide had turned as increasing postwar tourism revitalized the local economy. Finally, in 1950, a compromise was reached granting ranchers lifetime grazing rights and the right to trail their cattle across the park en route to summer grazing lands. The new-and-improved Grand Teton National Park had finally come to fruition.

POSTMORTEM

Some of the early fears that Rockefeller would use the new park for his own gain seem at least partly justified. His descendants still own the old JY

Ranch and use Phelps Lake as something of a semiprivate playground, while most of the other dude ranches have long since been taken over by the Park Service. Rockefeller also built the enormous Grand Teton Lodge along Jackson Lake and facilities at Colter Bay Village and Jenny Lake, leading some to accuse the family of attempting to monopolize services within the park. The company, Grand Teton Lodge Company, is now owned by Vail Resorts, which manages Jackson Lake Lodge, Jenny Lake Lodge, and Colter Bay Village, along with Jackson Hole Golf & Tennis Club (near Jackson).

Looking back on the controversial creation of Grand Teton National Park, it's easy to see how wrong park opponents were. Teton County has Wyoming's most vibrant economy, and millions of people arrive each year to enjoy the beauty of the undeveloped Tetons. As writer Nathaniel Burt noted, "The old enemies of the park are riding the profitable bandwagon of unlimited tourism with high hearts and open palms." Park opponents' claims that the Park Service would "lock up" the land ring as hollow as similar antiwilderness claims today by descendants of the same politicians who opposed Grand Teton National Park half a century ago. Without inclusion of the land purchased by Rockefeller, it is easy to imagine the valley covered with all sorts of summer-home developments, RV campgrounds, souvenir shops, motels, billboards, and neon signs. Take a look at the town of Jackson to see what might have been.

Exploring the Park

Grand Teton National Park has fewer "attractions" than Yellowstone—its big sister to the north—and an easy day's drive takes you past the road-accessible portions of the park. The real attractions are the mountains and the incomparable views one gets of them from Jackson Hole. This is one backdrop you will never tire of seeing.

ROADS

Grand Teton National Park is bisected by the main north-south highway (U.S. Hwy. 26/89/191) and by the road heading east over Togwotee Pass (U.S. Hwy. 26/287). Both of these routes are kept open year-round, although wintertime plowing ends at Flagg Ranch Resort, just south of the Yellowstone boundary. In addition, a paved park road cuts south from Jackson Lake Dam to Jenny Lake and Moose. Only the southern end of this road is plowed in winter; the remainder becomes a snowmobile and cross-country ski route. South of Moose, a narrow, winding road (the Moose-Wilson Road) connects the park to Teton Village, nine miles away. It is rough dirt in places—no trailers or RVs— and is closed in winter.

As this book was being written, the Park Service was developing a new transportation plan for Grand Teton National Park that may include the closure of some roads to motorized vehicles and the addition of a scheduled bus service from Jackson to the park.

MOOSE

The following tour takes you past points of interest along the main roads. The route follows a general clockwise direction beginning at the **Moose Visitor Center,** 307/739-3399, www.nps.gov/grte. Before heading out, step inside the center (open daily year-round) for a fine introduction to the park and a look at the natural-history videos, books, and oil paintings. A large three-dimensional map here reveals the lay of the land.

The commercial center at Moose is across the Snake River bridge and just east of the visitors center. Here you'll find a plethora of operations run by **Dornan's,** 307/733-2415, www .dornans.com: a general store, gift shop, lodging, restaurant and bar, wine shop, bike shop, canoe and kayak rentals, and a chuck wagon eatery. Also here is a sporting-goods store (Moosely Seconds, 307/739-1801) and fishing shop (Snake River Anglers, 307/733-3699). Moose has pretty much everything you might need for a day in the park.

GRAND TETON NATIONAL PARK
SIGHTSEEING HIGHLIGHTS

Menor's Ferry/Chapel of
    the Transfiguration
Jenny Lake
Signal Mountain
Jackson Lake Lodge
Colter Bay Indian Arts Museum

Mormon Row
Gros Ventre River Valley
Schwabacher Landing
Snake River Overlook
Moose-Wilson Road
Cascade Canyon

MENOR'S FERRY AREA

Just inside the South Entrance to Grand Teton National Park, a side road leads to **Chapel of the Transfiguration** and Menor's Ferry. The rustic log church (built in 1925) is most notable for its dramatic setting. Episcopal services are held on summer Sundays, with Eucharist at 8 and 10 A.M.

The back window faces directly toward the Tetons, providing ample distractions for worshippers. The bell out front was cast in 1842. Nearby **Menor's Ferry** is named for William D. Menor, who first homesteaded here in 1894 and later built a cable ferry to make it easier to cross the river. His old whitewashed store still stands. You can cross the river in a reconstructed version of the old ferry when the water level is low enough; check out the ingenious propulsion mechanism that uses the current to pull it across. For many years, Menor's ferry served as the primary means of crossing the river in the central part of Jackson Hole. Wagons were charged 50 cents, while those on horseback paid 25 cents. (William Menor's brother, Holiday, lived on the opposite side of the river, but the two often feuded, yelling insults across the water at each other and refusing to acknowledge one another for years at a time.)

Also here is the half-mile **Menor's Ferry Trail;** a brochure describes historic points of interest along the path. Bill Menor's cabin houses a small country store that sells the old-fashioned supplies he stocked at the turn of the 20th century. It is open daily 9 A.M.–4:30 P.M. from late May to late September; closed the rest of the year.

Menor sold out to Maude Noble in 1918, and she ran the ferry until 1927, when a bridge

was built near the present one in Moose. Her cabin now houses an excellent collection of historical photos from Jackson Hole. Maude Noble gained a measure of fame in 1923 when she hosted the gathering of residents to save Jackson Hole from development (see Park History).

TAGGART AND BRADLEY LAKES

Heading northwest beyond the Menor's Ferry area, the main road climbs up an old river bench, created by flooding from the rapid melting of the glaciers, and passes the trailhead to the turquoise waters of Taggart Lake. The land around here was burned in the 1,028-acre Beaver Creek lightning fire of 1985, and summers find a riot of wildflowers. A very popular day hike leads from the parking lot at the trailhead to Taggart Lake and then back via the Beaver Creek Trail, a distance of 4.4 miles round-trip. A side loop to Bradley Lake adds about two miles to this journey. These trails provide a fine way to explore the dam-like glacial moraines that created these lakes. You can also continue beyond Bradley Lake on a trail that climbs to beautiful Amphitheater Lake, the primary access point for climbs up Grand Teton. (Climbers generally begin from Jenny Lake, however.)

JENNY LAKE

The most loved of all Grand Teton lakes is Jenny Lake, nestled at the foot of Cascade Canyon and surrounded by a luxuriant forest of Engelmann spruce, subalpine fir, and lodgepole pine. Jenny Lake is named for Jenny Leigh, the Shoshone wife of Beaver Dick Leigh. A one-way loop road leads south past Jenny and String Lakes, providing excellent views of the **Cathedral Group:** Teewinot, Grand Teton, and Mt. Owen. This is the most popular part of the park, and day-hikers will find a plethora of trails to sample, along with crowds of fellow hikers. Paths lead around both Jenny and String Lakes, while another nearly level trail follows the east shore of **Leigh Lake** to several pleasant sandy beaches. **String Lake** is narrow but very pretty and makes a fine place for canoeing or swimming. Get supplies from the small store at Jenny Lake and information or guidebooks from the **Jenny Lake Visitor Center** (open June to early Labor Day). Coin-operated storage lockers are next to the store.

Beautiful **Jenny Lake Lodge** sits on the

BEAVER DICK LEIGH

Around 1863, Richard "Beaver Dick" Leigh became the first white man to attempt a permanent life in Jackson Hole. An Englishman by birth, Beaver Dick lived in a log cabin with his Shoshone wife, Jenny, and their four children, scraping out the barest existence by hunting, trapping, and guiding. As guide for the 1872 Hayden Survey of the Jackson Hole area, Beaver Dick gained the respect of the surveyors, who named Leigh Lake for him and Jenny Lake for his wife. Today a local bar denigrates this remarkable man by calling itself Beaver Dick's and using a cartoonish image of him in its ads. The real man was nothing like this, and reading his diaries and letters is a lesson in how difficult life was for early Wyoming settlers. On one terrible Christmas in 1876, Beaver Dick watched his entire family—Jenny, their newborn baby, and the four other children—all slowly die from smallpox. Their deaths left him badly shaken, as he related in a letter to a friend:

i got Dick in the house and to bed and Tom went over to get Mr. Anes. Wile Tom and Anes was sounding the ice to see if a horse could cross my wife was struck with Death. she rased up and looked me streaght in the face and then she got excited . . . and she sade she was going to die and all our childron wold die and maby i wold die . . . she was laying very quiet now for about 2 hours when she asked for a drink of water. i was laying downe with one of my daughters on eatch arme keeping them quiet because of the fevor. i told Anes what she wanted and he gave hur a

drink and 10 minuts more she was ded . . . i can not wright one hundreth part that pased thrue my mind at this time as i thaught deth was on me. i sade Jinny i will sone be with you and fell asleep. Tom sade i ad beene a sleep a half hour when i woke up everything was wet with presperation i was very weak. i lade for 10 or 15 minuts and saw William and Anne Jane had to be taken up to ease themselves every 5 minuts and Dick Juner very restlas . . . Anne Jane died about 8 o clock about the time every year i used to give them a candy puling and thay menchond about the candy puling many times wile sick . . . William died on the 25 about 9 or 10 o clock in the evening . . . on the 26th Dick Juner died . . . Elizabeth was over all danger but this, and she caught cold and sweled up agane and died on the 28 of Dec about 2 o clock in the morning. this was the hardist blow of all . . . i shall improve the place and live and die near my famley but i shall not be able to do enything for a few months for my mind is disturbed at the sights that i see around me and [the] work that my famley as done wile thay were liveing.

But the human spirit is remarkably resilient. Beaver Dick later married a Bannock girl, raised another family, and guided for others, even meeting Theodore Roosevelt on one of his hunting trips. Beaver Dick Leigh died in 1899 and was buried on a ridge overlooking Idaho's Teton Basin.

GRAND TETON

© DON PITCHER

Jenny Lake rests at the foot of Cascade Canyon.

boat cruises and fishing-boat rentals are also available at Jenny Lake; call 307/734-9227. Boats operate early June to early September.

From the boat dock on the west side, the trail climbs one-half mile to picturesque **Hidden Falls,** then continues steeply another one-half mile to Inspiration Point, which overlooks Jackson Hole from 400 feet above Jenny Lake. Avoid the crowds on the way down from Inspiration Point by following a second trail back to Jenny Lake. If you miss the last boat at 6 P.M., it's a 2.4-mile hike around the lake to the parking area.

Many day-hikers continue at least part of the way up Cascade Canyon from Inspiration Point. The trail climbs gradually, gaining 640 feet in the next 3.6 miles, and provides a good chance to fish for trout or watch for moose and other animals along Cascade Creek. Those with strong legs can make a *very* long day hike all the way up to Lake Solitude (18.4 miles round-trip) or even Hurricane Pass (23.2 miles round-trip and gaining almost 3,600 feet on the way up). If you're into hiking that far, it probably makes more sense to reserve a backcountry campsite and take things a bit more leisurely. See Backcountry Hiking for details.

SIGNAL MOUNTAIN AREA

As the road approaches Jackson Lake, a paved but narrow side road (no RVs or trailers) turns east and leads to the summit of Signal Mountain, 800 feet above Jackson Hole. On top are panoramic views of the Tetons, Jackson Lake, the Snake River, and the long valley below. To the south lies **The Potholes,** a hummocky area created when retreating glaciers left behind huge blocks of ice. The melting ice created depressions, some of which are still filled with water. Signal Mountain was burned by a massive 1879 fire and offers a good opportunity to see how Yellowstone may look in a century.

Hugging the southeast shore of Jackson Lake, **Signal Mountain Lodge,** 307/733-5470 or 307/543-2831, www.signalmountainlodge.com, includes cabins and campsites, plus a gift shop, convenience store, gas station, marina with boat rentals, restaurant, and bar. Just east of the lodge is **Chapel of the Sacred Heart,** a small Roman

northeast end of the lake and provides the finest lodging in the park. The gourmet meals are legendary, but reservations are necessary; call 307/733-4647.

INSPIRATION POINT AND CASCADE CANYON

One of the most popular attractions in the area is Inspiration Point, on the west side of Jenny Lake. It's 2.4 miles by trail from the Jenny Lake Ranger Station on the east side, or you can ride one of the summertime shuttle boats that cross the lake every 20 minutes or so for $7 round-trip ($5 for ages 7–12, free for younger kids). In midsummer, the shuttle boat lines lengthen around 11 A.M., so get here early in the morning to avoid the crush and to better your odds at finding a parking spot. Afternoon thunderstorms frequently build up over the Tetons, which is another good reason to start your hike early. Boat tickets are not available in advance. Scenic

JENNY AND
LEIGH LAKES

Grand Teton
National Park

Cleaver Pk.
(11,055 ft.)

Maidenform Pk.
(11,137 ft.)

Cirque
Lake

Little Pk.
(10,712 ft.)

Caribou-
Targhee
National
Forest

Teton   Range

Table Mtn.
(11,106 ft.)

Mink Lake

Lake
Solitude

Petersen Glacier

Mica Lake

The
Wigwams

(10,855 ft.)

Leigh   Canyon

Falling Ice
Glacier

Grizzly
Bear Lake

Holly
Lake

Mt. Woodring
(11,590 ft.)

(11,012 ft.)

The Jaw
(11,400 ft.)

Mt. Owen
(12,928 ft.)

Teewinot Mtn.
(12,325 ft.)

Valhalla Canyon

Cascade   Canyon

Teton   Crest   Trail

Rock of Ages
(10,895 ft.)

Lake of the
Crags

Mt. St. John
(11,430 ft.)

Rockchuck Pk.
(11,144 ft.)

Paintbrush   Canyon   Trail

Trapper Lake

Bearpaw
Lake

Mystic Isle

Leigh   Lake

Boulder
Island

Leigh Lake

String Lake

String Lake/
Picnic Area

Jenny Lake Lodge

Two-way

One-way

Teton Park Rd.

To N. Jenny Lake Jct., Jackson Lake, and Yellowstone

Jenny   Lake

Shuttle Boat

West Shore
Boat Dock

East Shore
Boat Dock

Jenny Lake
Visitor Center,
Ranger Station, and
Store

Inspiration Pt.

Hidden
Falls

Moose Ponds

To Lupine
Meadows Trailhead

S. Jenny Lake Jct.
To Moose Junction
and Jackson

Canyon   Trail

0   0.5 mi

0   0.5 km

N

GRAND TETON

© AVALON TRAVEL PUBLISHING, INC.

Catholic church that has summer services on Saturdays at 5:30 P.M. and Sundays at 10 A.M. The road then crosses **Jackson Lake Dam,** which raises the water level by 39 feet, alters the river's natural flow, and inundates a large area upstream. Many conservationists fought to have Jackson Lake excluded from the park, concerned that it would establish a bad precedent for allowing reservoirs in other parks. Nevertheless, once you get away from the dam, the lake appears relatively natural today.

ALONG JACKSON LAKE

A turnout near Jackson Lake Junction provides views over **Willow Flats,** where moose are frequently seen, especially in the morning. Topping a bluff overlooking the flats is **Jackson Lake Lodge,** built in the 1950s with the $5 million financial backing of John D. Rockefeller, Jr. Architects are not thrilled about the design (one author termed it "the ugliest building in Western Wyoming"), but the 60-foot-tall back windows frame an unbelievable view of the Tetons and Jackson Lake. Immediately across from the lodge is a trail leading to **Emma Matilda** and **Two Ocean** Lakes. It is 14 miles round-trip around both lakes, with lots of wildlife along the way, including moose, trumpeter swans, pelicans, and ducks. You may have to contend with large groups on horseback.

COLTER BAY

Colter Bay Village is one of the most developed parts of Grand Teton National Park, with a full marina, stores, a gas station, cabins, a campground, restaurants, and acres of parking. The main attraction here is the visitors center, which houses the **Colter Bay Indian Arts Museum,** 307/739-3594. It's open daily 8 A.M.–5 P.M. mid-May to Memorial Day and Labor Day to September; daily 8 A.M.–8 P.M. from early June to Labor Day. The museum is closed the rest of the year. Admission is free. Inside you will find the extraordinary David T. Vernon collection of Indian arts, the finest of its kind in any national park and one of the best in Wyoming. The collection

spreads through several rooms on two floors and includes exquisitely beaded buckskin dresses, moccasins, masks, ceremonial pipes, war clubs, shields, bows, baskets, headdresses, and other decorated items. Stop to chat with Native artisans as they work on paintings, beaded items, wood carvings, pottery, and weaving. They're at the museum daily Memorial Day to Labor Day. This museum should not be missed! Step out back to join the shoreside fun or to rent a canoe or boat from the nearby marina.

A mostly level trail leads from the marina out to **Hermitage Point** before looping back again, a distance of nine miles round-trip. Along the way you pass beaver ponds and willow patches where trumpeter swans, moose, and ducks are commonly seen. Get a map of Colter Bay trails from the visitors center. Shorter loop paths include the two-mile **Lakeshore Trail** and the three-mile **Swan Lake-Heron Pond Trail.**

ROCKEFELLER MEMORIAL PARKWAY

North of Colter Bay, the highway cruises along the shore of Jackson Lake for the next nine miles, providing some fine vantage points of the Tetons. The burned area on the opposite shore was ignited by lightning in the 1974 Waterfalls Canyon Fire, which consumed 3,700 acres. By late fall each year, Idaho spud farmers have drawn down water in the lake, leaving a long, barren shoreline at the upper end.

Shortly after the road leaves the upper end of Jackson Lake, a signboard announces your entrance into **John D. Rockefeller Jr. Memorial Parkway.** This 24,000-acre parcel of land was transferred to the National Park Service in 1972 in commemoration of Rockefeller's unstinting work in establishing Grand Teton National Park. The land forms a connection between Grand Teton and Yellowstone and is managed by Grand Teton National Park. Much of this area was severely burned by the 1988 Huck Fire, which began when strong winds blew a tree into power lines. Despite immediate efforts to control the blaze, it consumed 4,000 acres in the first two hours and later grew to cover nearly 200,000 acres, primarily within the Forest Service's Teton Wilderness. Dense young lodgepole pines now carpet much of the land.

On the northern end of Rockefeller Parkway is **Flagg Ranch Resort,** 307/543-2861 or 800/443-2311, www.flaggranch.com, where the modern facilities include a gas station, convenience store, gift shop, cabins, restaurant, and campground with RV hookups. The park service operates the **Flagg Ranch Information Station** here from early June to Labor Day. During the winter, Flagg Ranch is the jumping-off point for snowcoach and snowmobile trips into Yellowstone, and snowmobiles are available for rent.

Two nearby trails provide easy day hikes. The nearly level **Polecat Creek Loop Trail** is 2.3 miles round-trip and follows a ridge overlooking a marsh and through conifer forests. **Flagg Canyon Trail** is five miles round-trip and provides views of a rocky canyon cut through by the Snake River.

GRASSY LAKE ROAD

Grassy Lake Road takes off just north of Flagg Ranch Resort and continues 52 miles to Ashton, Idaho. It's a scenic drive, but don't attempt this narrow and rough dirt road with a trailer or an RV. This route provides a shortcut to the Bechler River area of Yellowstone and is a popular wintertime snowmobile route. Huckleberry Hot Springs, a short hike north from the Grassy Lake Road bridge over the Snake River, was the site of a public swimming pool until 1983, when the facility was razed by the Park Service. The hot springs are accessible via an unmaintained trail, but you'll need to wade Polecat Creek to reach them. Although they remain popular with hikers and cross-country skiers, it's worth noting that the springs may pose a risk from dangerously high radiation levels.

A few miles east of the Idaho–Wyoming border on Grassy Lake Road is **Squirrel Meadows,** where Caribou-Targhee National Forest has a two-room guard station with three sets of bunkbeds, a hand pump for water, and an outhouse. The cabin sleeps six and costs $35; details at 208/652-7442, www.fs.fed.us/r4/caribou.

During the winter, access is via snowmobile or skis for the last 12 miles to the cabin from the Idaho side. Lodging is also available just across the Idaho border at **Squirrel Creek Guest Ranch,** 208/652-3972, www.idahoranch.com.

JACKSON LAKE TO MORAN JUNCTION

Heading east and south from Jackson Lake, the road immediately passes **Oxbow Bend,** where the turnout is almost always filled with folks looking for geese, ducks, moose, and other animals. The oxbow was formed when the meandering river cut off an old loop. The calm water here is a delightful place for canoes, although the mosquitoes can be a major annoyance in midsummer. Come fall, photographers line the shoulder of the road for classic shots of flaming aspen trees with Grand Teton and **Mt. Moran** in the background. Mt. Moran is the massive peak with a flattened summit, a skillet-shaped glacier across its front, and a distinctive black vertical diabase dike that looks like a scar from some ancient battle. It rises 12,605 feet above sea level and is named for Thomas Moran, whose beautiful paintings of Yellowstone helped persuade Congress to set aside that area as the world's first national park.

At **Moran Junction** you pass the park's Buffalo Entrance Station and meet the road to Togwotee Pass and Dubois. A post office and school are the only developments remaining here. The epic Western *The Big Trail* was filmed nearby in 1930, starring an actor named John Wayne in his first speaking role. (Wayne had never ridden a horse before this.) An interesting side trip is to head east from Moran on U.S. Hwy. 26/287 for three miles to **Buffalo Valley Road.** This narrow and scenic road leads to Turpin Meadow, a major entryway into the Teton Wilderness (see the Jackson Hole chapter). It is very pretty, especially in early summer when flowers carpet the fields. Buck-and-rail fences line the road, and the pastures are filled with horses and cattle. Beyond Turpin Meadow, the road turns to gravel and climbs sharply uphill, rejoining the main highway a couple of miles below Cowboy Village Resort at

Togwotee. The Blackrock Ranger Station of Bridger-Teton National Forest is eight miles east of Moran Junction on U.S. Hwy. 26/287. Nearby is historic **Rosie's Cabin,** built early in the 20th century by Rudolph Rosencrans, an Austrian emigrant who was the first forest ranger in this part of the Tetons.

MORAN JUNCTION TO MOOSE

Heading south from Moran, U.S. Hwy. 26/89/191 immediately crosses the Buffalo River (a.k.a. Buffalo Fork of the Snake River), where bison were once abundant. With a little help from humans, bison have been reestablished and are now often seen just south of here along the road. The turnoff to the **Cunningham Cabin** is six miles south of Moran Junction. The structure actually consists of two sod-roofed log cabins connected by a covered walkway called a "dogtrot." Built around 1890, it served first as living quarters and later as a barn and smithy. A park brochure describes the locations of other structures on the property.

Pierce Cunningham came here as a homesteader and, with his wife Margaret, settled to raise cattle. Although this was some of the better land in this part of the valley, the soil was still so rocky that they had a hard time digging fencepost holes. Instead, they opted to build the buck-and-rail fences that have become a hallmark of Jackson Hole ranches. Cunningham Ranch gained notoriety in 1893 when a posse surrounded two suspected horse thieves who were wintering at Cunningham's place while he was away. Vigilantes shot and killed George Spencer and Mike Burnett in an example of "mountain justice." Later, however, suspicions arose that hired killers working for wealthy cattle barons had led the posse and that the murdered men may have been innocent. **Spread Creek** is just north of the Cunningham cabin; it gained its name by having two mouths, separated by a distance of three miles.

The highway next rolls past **Triangle X Ranch,** one of the most famous dude ranches in Jackson Hole. Although it's on park land, the Turner family has managed Triangle X for more than 60 years. (One of the owners, John Turner, was director of the U.S. Fish & Wildlife Service under the first President Bush.) Stop by just after sunup to watch wranglers driving 120 head of horses to the corrals. It's a scene straight out of an old Marlboro ad.

Southwest from Triangle X, the road climbs along an ancient river terrace and passes **Hedrick Pond,** where the 1963 Henry Fonda movie *Spencer's Mountain* was filmed. Although the book on which the movie was based was set in Virginia, the producers found the Tetons a considerably more impressive location. Trumpeter swans are often seen on the pond. Hedrick Pond isn't really visible from the road and there are no signs pointing it out, but you can get there by parking near the S-curve road sign 1.4 miles south of Triangle X. The pond is a good example of a kettle pond, created when retreating glaciers left behind a block of ice covered with gravel and other deposits. The ice melted, leaving behind a depression that filled to become Hedrick Pond.

Several turnouts provide popular photo-opportunity spots, the most famous being **Snake**

horseback riders from Triangle X Ranch

© DON PITCHER

River Overlook. Ansel Adams's famous shot of the Tetons was taken here and has been repeated with less success by generations of photographers. Throughout the summer, a progression of different flowers blooms in the open sagebrush flats along the road, adding brilliant slashes of color. They're prettiest in late June; in the high country, the peak comes a month or more later than elsewhere.

Just north of Snake River Overlook is the turnoff to **Deadman's Bar.** A steep partially dirt road (not for RVs) drops down to one of the primary river-access points used by river rafters. The river bar received its name from an incident in 1886. Four German prospectors entered the area, but only one—John Tonnar—emerged. Bodies of the other three were found along the Snake River, and Tonnar was charged with murder. The jury in Evanston believed his claim of self-defense, and he was set free, an act that so angered locals that they vowed to take care of future Jackson Hole criminals with a shotgun. A skull from one of the victims is on display in the Jackson Hole Museum.

Another popular put-in for river runners is **Schwabacher Landing,** at the end of a one-mile gravel road that splits off just north of the Glacier View Turnout. This is a pleasant place for riverside picnics. Some of the most famous Teton Range photos—the ones you see in local galleries—were taken just a few hundred yards upstream from the parking area.

BLACKTAIL BUTTE AND MORMON ROW

One mile north of the turnoff to Moose, Antelope Flats Road heads east along Ditch Creek. Just south of here lies Blacktail Butte, a timbered knoll rising over the surrounding sagebrush plains. It's a favorite of rock climbers and has a hiking trail up the back (east) side. You will want to stop at the much-photographed old farm buildings known as Mormon Row. The farmland here was homesteaded by predominantly Mormon settlers in the early 1900s but was later purchased by Rockefeller's Snake River Land Company and transferred

THE MAGIC OF THE TETONS

Somewhere at the eastern base of the Tetons did those hoofprints disappear into a mountain sanctuary where many crooked paths have led. He that took another man's possession, or he that took another man's life, could always run here if the law or popular justice were too hot at his heels. Steep ranges and forests walled him in from the world on all four sides, almost without a break; and every entrance lay through intricate solitudes. Snake River came into the place through canyons and mournful pines and marshes, to the north, and went out at the south between formidable chasms. Every tributary to this stream rose among high peaks and ridges, and descended into the valley by well-nigh impenetrable courses. . . . Down in the bottom was a spread of level land, broad, and beautiful, with the blue and silver Tetons rising from its chain of lakes to the west and other heights residing over its other sides.

—*from Owen Wister's* The Virginian

to the Park Service. Only one set of buildings—an acre of the Moulton Ranch—is still in private hands. The other buildings were allowed to decay until the 1990s when the Park Service recognized their value and stepped in to preserve the structures. Herds of bison often wander past the old farmsteads in summer, providing one of the best places to view them. Also keep your eyes open for small groups of pronghorn antelope in the vicinity.

TETON SCIENCE SCHOOL

Hidden away in a valley along upper Ditch Creek is Teton Science School (TSS), a fine hands-on school for both young and old. Founded in 1967 as a summer field-biology program

GRAND TETON

for high-school kids, it has grown into a year-round program with classes that run the gamut from elementary-school level all the way up to intensive college courses and a residency program. Summertime visitors will enjoy their one- to four-day adult seminars on such diverse subjects as entomology for fly-fishers, bird-watching, the biology of bugs, wildflower identification, river channels, and grizzly bear biology. These classes are limited to 12 students and fill up fast, so make reservations in the spring to be sure of a spot. The school's excellent month-long wilderness emergency medical technician (EMT) course in early winter ($2,400 per person) is one of the few programs of its kind in the nation. TSS also offers a fine **winter speaker series** at the National Museum of Wildlife Art covering a spectrum of scientific, environmental, and social issues. In addition, the school operates **Wildlife Expeditions,** 307/733-2623 or 888/945-3567, www.tetonscience.org/wildlife, with wildlife-viewing safaris throughout the Grand Teton and Yellowstone area.

Based at the old Elbo dude ranch (started in 1932), TSS includes two dormitories, a central kitchen, a dining area, and other log structures. Visitors to the school should visit the **Murie Natural History Museum,** which displays thousands of specimens of birds, mammals, and plants. Included are casts of animal tracks used by famed wildlife biologist Olaus Murie in producing his *Peterson's Guide to Animal Tracks.* It's open to the public, but call ahead to arrange an appointment. Get a copy of the course catalog by contacting TSS at 307/733-4765, www.tetonscience.org.

SHADOW MOUNTAIN AREA

North from the TSS turnoff, the paved road splits. Turn left (west) on Antelope Flats Road to head back to Mormon Row and the main highway, or continue straight ahead to climb up Shadow Mountain (8,252 feet). The name comes from the shadows of the Tetons that fall across the mountain's face each evening. The road is paved for the first mile or so, but turns to gravel as it snakes rather steeply up the mountain. The road is definitely not recommended for RVs or trailers,

Kelly Warm Spring

© DON PITCHER

or for any vehicles after rains when some sections turn to slippery mud. The views from the top of Shadow Mountain are truly amazing, with the Tetons in all their glory. Several dispersed campsites can be found along this route on Forest Service land.

KELLY AND VICINITY

The small settlement of Kelly borders on the southeastern end of Grand Teton National Park and has log homes and a cluster of Mongolian-style yurts—certainly the most unusual dwellings in Wyoming. Folks living in the yurts share a common bathhouse and rent the land. The town has a shoebox-size post office and a couple of rental cabins. The Park Service's **Gros Ventre Campground** is three miles west of here.

Gros Ventre Road leads east from the Kelly area, passing **Kelly Warm Spring** on the right. Its shallow and warm waters are a favorite place for local kayakers to practice their rolls or for families to swim on a summer afternoon. A short distance up the road and off to the north (left) are the collapsing remains of the *Shane* **cabin,** where a scene from the classic 1951 Western was filmed. Beyond this point, the road enters Bridger-Teton National Forest and the Slide Lake area, where there is a Forest Service campground.

GROS VENTRE SLIDE

One of the most extraordinary geologic events in recent Wyoming history took place in the Gros Ventre (pronounced GROW-vont—"Big Belly" in French trapper lingo) Canyon, named for the Gros Ventre Indians of this area. Sheep Mountain, on the south side of the canyon, consists of sandstone underlain by a layer of shale that becomes slippery when wet. Melting snow and heavy rains in the spring of 1925 lubricated this layer of shale, and on June 23 the entire north end of the mountain—a section 2,000 feet wide and one mile long—suddenly slid 1.5 miles downslope, instantly damming the river below and creating Slide Lake. A rancher in the valley, Guil Huff, watched in amazement as the mountain began to move, but he managed to gallop his

horse out of the way as the slide roared within 30 feet. Huff's ranch floated away on the new lake several days later.

For two years folks kept a wary eye on the makeshift dam of rock and mud. Then, on May 18, 1927, the dam suddenly gave way, pushing an enormous wall of water through the downstream town of Kelly. Six people perished in the flood, and when the water reached Snake River Canyon nine hours later it filled the canyon to the rim with boiling water, trees, houses, and debris. Today a smaller Slide Lake still exists, and the massive landslide that created it more than 75 years ago remains an exposed gouge visible for miles around. Geologists say that, under the right conditions, more of Sheep Mountain could slide. Dead trees still stand in the upper end of Slide Lake. The Forest Service has a **Gros Ventre Geological Trail** 10 miles up Gros Ventre Road. This quarter-mile path leads to an incredible viewpoint overlooking the slide and is marked with interpretive signs.

GROS VENTRE RIVER VALLEY

Above Slide Lake (six miles up), the road turns to gravel, becoming quite rutted in places. Surprising scenery makes the sometimes bone-jarring route easier to take. The landscape here is far different from that of the Tetons, with brilliant red-orange badland hills rising sharply above the Gros Ventre River. Two more Forest Service campgrounds (Red Hills and Crystal Creek) are four miles above Slide Lake, or you can camp in dispersed sites off the road. **Grizzly Lake Trail** starts at the Red Hills Campground and continues for 3.5 miles to this small mountain lake. There are wonderful vistas of the Red Hills and Gros Ventre River valley below.

The road continues another 15 beautiful miles along the river above the lake, getting rougher at the upper end. Several remote guest ranches are up here. Beyond Cow Creek Trailhead (29 miles from Kelly) the route is virtually impassable unless you have a high-clearance 4WD and are ready to get stuck. Hard-core mountain-bikers sometimes continue up this road/trail and then drop down into the Green

River watershed north of Pinedale. Cow Creek Trail and other paths lead into the Gros Ventre Wilderness, which borders the south side of the road. On the drive back down the Gros Ventre River valley you will discover some fine views across to the Tetons.

MOOSE-WILSON ROAD

This narrow and winding road heads south from park headquarters in Moose, continuing nine miles to Teton Village. It is paved most of the way, but a sometimes bone-jarring middle section is dirt. Keep your speed down to reduce the amount of dust in the air. No trailers or RVs are allowed, and the road is not plowed in the winter. It is especially pretty in the fall when the aspens are turning. This is also a good place to watch for moose and other animals in summer or for easy cross-country ski adventures on a sunny winter day. Note: As this book was being written, the Park Service was considering closing the Moose-Wilson Road to most vehicles. If this happens, it will still be open to bicycles and foot traffic.

Two backcountry trailheads—Death Canyon Trailhead and Granite Canyon Trailhead—are accessed from the Moose-Wilson Road. A long loop hike up Death Canyon is described as an overnight hike later. For something less challenging, start from Death Canyon Trailhead (three miles south of Moose) and hike about one mile to **Phelps Lake Overlook,** where you get a view across this beautiful mountain lake 600 feet below. The historic JY Ranch (built in 1908) sits back from Phelps Lake and still belongs to the Rockefeller family; any motorboats you see are probably theirs. This is one of the only remaining private inholdings within Grand Teton National Park. From Phelps Lake Overlook you can hike steeply down for a lakeside picnic on the sandy beach (four miles round-trip from the trailhead). An alternative day-hiking option is to continue from the overlook to **Death Canyon Patrol Cabin.** Getting to the cabin requires losing 400 feet in elevation and then climbing 1,000 feet higher. The small log cabin was built by the Civilian Conservation Corps in the 1930s and is still used by trail maintenance crews. Continue one-half mile beyond the cabin up the trail to Fox Creek Pass for a dramatic vista into Death Canyon. It's a bit more than eight miles round-trip between this viewpoint and Death Canyon Trailhead.

Backcountry Hiking

The precipitous Tetons that look so dramatic from the roads are even more impressive up close and personal. Grand Teton National Park is laced with 200 miles of trails, and hikers can choose anything from simple day treks to weeklong trips along the crest of the range. Unlike nearby Yellowstone, where most of the country is forested, the Tetons contain extensive Alpine scenery. This means, however, that many of the high passes won't be free of snow until late July and may require ice axes before then. Check at the visitors centers or Jenny Lake Ranger Station for current trail conditions. In addition, this high country can be dangerous when frequent thunderstorms roll through in summer. Several people have been killed by lightning strikes in the Tetons.

The most popular hiking area centers on the crest of the Tetons and the lakes that lie at its feet, most notably Jenny Lake. **Teton Crest Trail** stretches from Teton Pass north all the way to Cascade Canyon, with numerous connecting paths from both sides of the range. Three relatively short (two- to three-day) loop hikes are described later. For more complete descriptions of park trails, see *Jackson Hole Hikes* by Rebecca Woods (Jackson: White Willow Publishing) or *Teton Trails* by Katy Duffy and Darwin Wile (Grand Teton Natural History Association, www.grandtetonpark.org). Get topographic maps at the Moose Visitor Center or Teton Mountaineering in Jackson. Best is the waterproof version produced by Trails Illustrated.

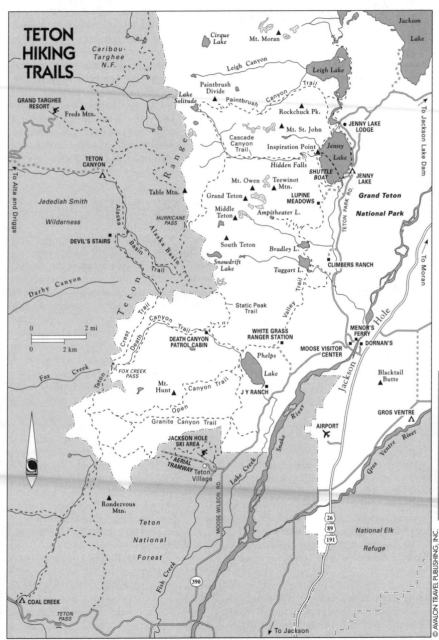

TETON HIKING TRAILS

Caribou-Targhee N.F.

Jackson Lake

Cirque Lake

Mt. Moran

Leigh Canyon

Leigh Lake

GRAND TARGHEE RESORT

Freds Mtn.

Paintbrush Divide

Lake Solitude

Paintbrush Canyon Trail

To Jackson Lake Dam

Rockchuck Pk.

JENNY LAKE LODGE

Mt. St. John

Cascade Canyon Trail

Inspiration Point

Hidden Falls

Jenny Lake

JENNY LAKE

TETON CANYON

Table Mtn.

HURRICANE PASS

Mt. Owen

Teewinot Mtn.

SHUTTLE BOAT

Grand Teton

LUPINE MEADOWS

Grand Teton National Park

Jedediah Smith Wilderness

Middle Teton

Ampitheater L.

TETON PARK RD.

South Teton

Bradley L.

DEVIL'S STAIRS

Snowdrift Lake

Taggart L.

CLIMBERS RANCH

To Moran

Darby Canyon

Static Peak Trail

Valley Trail

WHITE GRASS RANGER STATION

MENOR'S FERRY

DEATH CANYON PATROL CABIN

MOOSE VISITOR CENTER

DORNAN'S

0   2 mi

0   2 km

FOX CREEK PASS

Phelps Lake

Blacktail Butte

Fox Creek

Mt. Hunt

Canyon Trail

J Y RANCH

Jackson Hole

GROS VENTRE

Open Granite Canyon Trail

Snake River

AIRPORT

JACKSON HOLE SKI AREA

AERIAL TRAMWAY

Teton Village

MOOSE-WILSON RD.

Lake Creek

Gros Ventre River

Rondezvous Mtn.

Teton National Forest

26
89
191

National Elk Refuge

Fish Creek

390

COAL CREEK

TETON PASS

To Jackson

GRAND TETON

© AVALON TRAVEL PUBLISHING, INC.

REGULATIONS AND PERMITS

The hiking trails of Grand Teton National Park are some of the most heavily used paths in Wyoming, and strict regulations are enforced. Backcountry-use permits are required of all overnight hikers, and you'll need to specify a particular camping zone or site for each night of your trip. Get permits and detailed backcountry brochures from the visitors centers in Moose or Colter Bay or the Jenny Lake Ranger Station. Get there early in the morning during summer for permits to popular trails. A limited number of backcountry permits can be reserved in advance from January 1 to May 15 by writing the Permits Office, Grand Teton National Park, P.O. Drawer 170, Moose, WY 83012. For faster service, send a fax to 307/739-3438. You'll need to pick the permit up in person and pay a $15 service fee for reservations. There's no charge for permits if you get them the day of your trip. Get more information on permits and reservations by calling 307/739-3309 or 307/739-3397. Be sure to also request their Backcountry Camping publication, with details on regulations, snow conditions, minimizing impacts, and bear safety issues. On the back is a trail map that shows camping zones and access. The same information is available on the web at www.nps.gov/grte.

SAFETY IN THE BACKCOUNTRY

Grizzlies are primarily found in the northern end of Grand Teton National Park, but you still need to hang all food because black bears roam throughout the park, particularly in the forested areas along the lakes. Special boxes are provided for food storage at some backcountry campsites. Campfires are not allowed at higher elevations, so be sure to bring a cooking stove. Bikes are not permitted on trails anywhere in the park.

Backcountry hikers (and day-hikers for that matter) need to be aware of the dangers from summertime thunderstorms in the Tetons. A common weather pattern is for clear mornings to build to blustery thunderstorms in late after-

noon, followed by gradual clearing as evening arrives. Lightning is a major threat in the park's exposed alpine country, and rain showers can be surprisingly heavy at times. Make sure all of your gear is wrapped in plastic (garbage bags work well), and carry a rain poncho or other rainwear. Many hikers carry cell phones for emergencies, but coverage is spotty in the mountains. Unfortunately, the phones can also create a false sense of security for those who are not familiar with backcountry travel. Don't head unprepared into the mountains thinking you can always call for a rescue if you sprain your ankle.

CASCADE CANYON TO PAINTBRUSH CANYON

One of the most popular hikes in Grand Teton National Park is this 19-mile loop trip up Cascade Canyon, over Paintbrush Divide, and down Paintbrush Canyon (or vice versa). The trip offers a little of everything: dense forests, alpine lakes, flower-covered meadows, and magnificent views of the Tetons. This trip is best done in late summer because a cornice of snow typically blocks Paintbrush Divide until the latter part of July. Most folks do it as an overnight trip, but it's possible to do the entire loop in a single very long day if you're in good shape and have a masochistic streak. Be sure to bring plenty of water along.

Begin at the String Lake Trailhead and head south around Jenny Lake, stopping to enjoy the views (and crowds) at Inspiration Point before heading up along Cascade Creek. The trail splits at the upper end of this canyon; turning left takes you to Hurricane Pass and the Teton Crest Trail, where you'll discover wonderful views of the back side of Grand Teton. Instead, turn right (north) and head up to beautiful Lake Solitude. Behind you, Teewinot, Mt. Owen, and Grand Teton are framed by the glacially carved valley walls. Above Lake Solitude, the trail climbs sharply to Paintbrush Divide and then switchbacks even more quickly down into Paintbrush Canyon. The trail eventually leads back to String Lake. Be sure to stop at beautiful Holly Lake on the way down.

LIGHTNING SAFETY

Lightning is a significant hazard for travelers on foot or horseback in Wyoming, particularly in the high mountains such as the Tetons, Wind River Range, Snowy Range, or the Big Horns. Three people were killed by lightning strikes in 1998 and 1999 in the Snowy Range west of Laramie, and others are struck almost every year around the state. Perhaps the most famous incident came in the 1990s, when acclaimed writer Gretel Ehrlich was struck while riding a horse on her ranch at the foot of the Big Horns. Her long and excruciating recovery is detailed in *A Match to the Heart* (Random House, www.randomhouse.com, 1994).

Creating a Thunderhead

Thunderstorms are created by a combination of convective forces, moisture, and unstable air. On sunny days as the ground warms, heat begins to rise convectively. When the air above is unstable (much cooler at higher altitudes than closer to the ground), the warm air rises rapidly. As it rises, the air cools enough that tiny droplets of moisture precipitate out, forming clouds that may grow into thunderheads if there is enough moisture and atmospheric instability. This rapid development of thunderheads generates enormous amounts of energy that is released as lightning, wind, hail, and rain. During a lightning strike, an electrical charge reaches toward the ground and is met by an opposite charge rising from the earth. They connect in a brilliant flash of light, heat, and noise as 35,000 amperes of charge are released.

Protecting Yourself

Nearly 100 people die each year from lightning strikes in the United States, and hundreds of others are injured. Statistically speaking, golfers are the most likely to get zapped because they are often in open areas carrying metal golf clubs when a storm rolls in. Others at risk include softball and soccer players, mountain climbers, horseback riders, swimmers, and hikers.

Several factors are important in protecting yourself from lightning. One is to pay attention to building storms, even distant ones, and especially those that build quickly. Mountain thunderstorms—created when winds push air masses upslope against a mountain range—are five times more likely to occur than storms over adjacent valleys. The color of thunderheads is another factor to watch; black bases mean significant amounts of moisture and may portend a more violent thunderstorm.

The most dangerous times are—surprisingly—before a thunderstorm comes directly overhead. Strikes can hit up to five miles in front of a fast-moving thunderstorm. In 1999, a Boy Scout was struck in the Tetons while watching a distant thunderstorm; overhead it was mostly blue sky! To determine your distance from an approaching storm, count the number of seconds between a lightning strike and the subsequent thunderclap, then divide by five to get the approximate distance in miles. If thunder arrives within five seconds, the storm is dangerously close, just one mile away.

If you see a storm approaching, get off ridgetops and other high places, move out of open fields, away from single trees or other tall objects, and out of the water. Lightning follows the path of least resistance, which usually means taller objects or those containing metal. Safer places are inside a car or house, or in a stand of even-sized trees. If those options aren't possible, lie down and stay as low as possible—preferably in a *dry* ditch (stay away from wet areas). If you're caught on an open ridge, crouch on an insulated pad or a backpack. Metallic objects attract lightning, so stay away from fence posts, golf clubs, climbing gear, or metal objects in your backpack. Don't stand in a group of people. If you're indoors when a storm hits, move away from windows, doors, appliances, pipes, and telephones.

Lightning strikes are sometimes preceded by a tingling sensation, and your hair may stand on end. If this happens, immediately crouch down (but don't lie down or put your hands on the ground) and cover your ears. If someone near you is struck by lightning, get immediate help and be ready to perform CPR. For additional lightning safety information, contact the **Lightning Protection Institute,** 800/488-6864, www.lightning.org.

GRAND TETON

DEATH CANYON LOOP

Another fine loop trip departs from the Death Canyon Trailhead, approximately three miles south of park headquarters on the Moose-Wilson Road. Many hiking options are available here, with trails leading to Phelps Lake, up Open Canyon, or into Death Canyon. (The name came about when a survey party was in the area in 1899 and one of the men disappeared. He was never seen again.) Despite the name, Death Canyon provides a wonderful 26-mile loop hike that takes you over three high passes and into spectacular alpine country. From the trailhead, hike to Phelps Lake Overlook before dropping down to a junction, where you turn right to hike up Death Canyon. Bear left at a patrol cabin built in the 1930s, and continue climbing all the way to Fox Creek Pass (9,520 feet). After this the going is fairly easy for the next three miles along Death Canyon Shelf to Mt. Meek Pass, where you drop into famous **Alaska Basin** (described in the Jackson Hole chapter). Return to your starting point by climbing east from Alaska Basin over Static Peak Divide (10,800 feet) and then switchbacking downhill to the CCC cabin and the trailhead. This is a late-season trek because snow often blocks the passes until July; get snow conditions at the Jenny Lake Ranger Station.

AMPHITHEATER LAKE

A relatively short but very steep hike begins at the Lupine Meadows Trailhead just south of Jenny Lake. Amphitheater Lake is only five miles up the trail but is 3,000 feet higher, making this the quickest climb to the Teton treeline. Many folks day hike this trail to savor the wonderful vistas across Jackson Hole along the way. Camping is available at Surprise Lake, one-half mile below Amphitheater Lake. More adventurous folks may want to climb **Disappointment Peak,** the 11,618-foot summit directly in front of Grand Teton. (It was named by climbers who mistakenly thought they were on the east face of Grand Teton.) If you plan to do so, first talk to the climbing rangers at Jenny Lake—and only attempt it if you're able to handle a few areas of Class 3 moves.

RENDEZVOUS MOUNTAIN TO DEATH CANYON

This 23-mile-long loop hike is different in that much of the way is downhill. Begin at the Jackson Hole tram in Teton Village, where a $15 ticket takes you to the top of Rendezvous Mountain. From the summit, the trail leads down to a saddle, across the South Fork of Granite Creek, and up to Teton Crest Trail. Head north on this trail to Marion Lake—a popular camping site—and then over Fox Creek Pass. The trail splits, and the right fork drops sharply down into scenic Death Canyon. At the lower end of Death Canyon, cliffs rise nearly 3,000 feet on both sides. The trail forks at Phelps Lake, and from here you can either hike back to Teton Village via the Valley Trail or head to the trailhead at White Grass Ranger Station, 1.5 miles northeast of Phelps Lake. Note: If you reverse the direction of this hike you can save your money because there is no charge for riding the tram down to Teton Village.

Mountain Climbing

The Tetons are considered some of the premier mountaineering country in the nation, with solid rock, good access, and a wide range of climbing conditions. Hundreds of climbing routes have been described for the main peaks, but the goal of many climbers is Grand Teton, better known as "the Grand." At 13,772 feet, this is Wyoming's second-highest summit, exceeded only by 13,804-foot Gannett Peak in the Wind River Mountains.

FIRST TO THE TOP

In the climbing trade, first ascents always rate highly, but the identity of the first climbers to have scaled Grand Teton has long been a matter of debate. The official record belongs to the party of William Owen (as in nearby Mt. Owen), Bishop Spalding (as in nearby Spalding Peak), John Shive, and Frank Petersen, who reached the summit in 1898. Today, however, it appears that they were preceded by two members of the 1872 Hayden Expedition: Nathaniel P. Langford (first superintendent of Yellowstone National Park) and John Stevenson. In addition, another party apparently made it to the top in 1893. Owen made a big deal out of his climb and spent 30 years trying to work himself into the record books by claiming the Langford party never reached the top. The whole thing got quite nasty, with Owen even accusing Langford of bribing the author of a history book to gain top honors. In 1929, Owen convinced the Wyoming Legislature to declare his group the first on top. Few people believe it today, and the whole thing looks pretty foolish because even seven-year-old kids have made it up the Grand.

Several thousand people climb the mountain each summer, many with no previous climbing experience (but with excellent guides and a cou-

The Tetons provide some of the best mountaineering in the nation. Hundreds of climbing routes have been described for the main peaks, but many climbers' goal is Grand Teton, better known as "the Grand."

ple days of training). The record time is an unbelievable three hours, six minutes, and 25 seconds for Bryce Thatcher in 1983. This time includes starting—and returning—to the parking lot at the foot of the mountain! And just to prove that it could be done, in 1971 one fanatic actually skied the Grand (he's the ski-school director at Snow King Resort), followed in 1989 by a snowboarder. Both lived to tell the tale.

GETTING THERE

Most climbing takes place after the snow has melted back (mid-July) and before conditions again deteriorate (late September). Overnight mountain climbing or off-trail hiking requires a special permit available from the **Jenny Lake Ranger Station,** staffed daily June to mid-September. There's no need to register if you're climbing or doing off-trail hiking for the day only, just for overnight trips. (Still, it's a good idea to leave a detailed trip itinerary with a responsible person in case of an emergency.) Winter climbers should register at the Moose Visitor Center. The climbing rangers—one of the most prestigious and hazardous jobs in the park—are all highly experienced mountaineers and can provide specific route information for the various summits. Call 307/739-3604 for recorded climbing information, or talk to folks at the Jenny Lake Ranger Station, 307/739-3343, for weather conditions, route information, and permits.

Many climbers who scale Grand Teton follow the Amphitheater Lake Trail from Lupine Meadows to its junction with the Garnet Canyon Trail. This leads to the **Lower Saddle,** which separates Grand Teton and Middle Teton. Exum and the Park Service have base-camp huts and steel storage boxes here, along with an outhouse. (The park is experimenting with high-tech

GRAND TETON

carry-out bags for human waste—complete with a system that breaks down feces. They have been optional but may become mandatory for climbers.) Other folks pitch tents behind boulders in this extraordinarily windy mountain gap. See Park Service handouts for camping restrictions and recommendations in this fragile alpine area where heavy use by 4,000 climbers each year has caused considerable damage. The final assault on the summit of Grand Teton requires technical equipment and expertise. No motorized drills are allowed for placing climbing bolts.

Mountaineers who have registered to climb the Grand can stay at **Climbers' Ranch,** near Taggart Lake, for $8 per night. Lodging is in small log cabins with four to eight bunks; hot showers and a cooking shelter are close by, but you'll need to bring your own sleeping bag and food. The ranch is open mid-June to mid-September. Call 307/733-7271 after June 1 for reservations, or visit the American Alpine Club's website, www.americanalpineclub.org, for details.

CLIMBING SCHOOLS

Jackson Hole is blessed with two of the finest climbing schools in North America: **Jackson Hole Mountain Guides,** 165 N. Glenwood, 307/733-4979 or 800/239-7642, www.jhmg .com; and **Exum Mountain Guides,** 307/733-2297, www.exumguides.com, with a summertime office at the south end of Jenny Lake near the boat dock. Both are authorized concessions of the National Park Service and the U.S. Forest Service and offer a wide range of classes, snow training, and climbs in the Tetons and elsewhere—even as far away as Alaska and the Himalayas. Exum has been around since 1931, when Glenn Exum pioneered the first solo climb of what has become the most popular route to the top of the Grand, the Exum Route. It's the only company permitted to guide all Teton peaks and routes throughout the year. Exum's base camp is in the busy Lower Saddle area, while Jackson Hole Mountain Guides' base camp is 450 feet lower in elevation in a more secluded location (it takes an extra hour of climbing on the day of your ascent). Exum has some of the most experienced guides in the world, but they take up to four clients in a group, while Jackson Hole limits its Grand Teton ascent parties to three clients.

During midsummer, you'll pay around $600–900 (depending on the number of people in the group) for an ascent of Grand Teton; this includes two days of basic and intermediate training followed by a two-day climb up the Grand and back. Food, gear, and shelter are also included. If you're planning to climb the Grand during the peak summer season, be sure to make reservations several months in advance to be assured of a spot. For July and August, make Grand Teton climbing reservations before the end of March.

Reservations generally are not needed for the companies' one-day basic ($95) and intermediate ($120) climbing schools. Also available are climbs of other faces, such as Baxter's Pinnacle, Symmetry Spire, and Cube Point, along with more advanced classes and climbs in the Wind River Mountains and up Devils Tower and other precipices throughout the western states. In addition, both companies offer many winter classes, such as avalanche safety and ski or snowboard mountaineering.

ON YOUR OWN

If you already have the experience and want to do your own climbing, the most accessible local spot is **Blacktail Butte,** just north of Moose near Ditch Creek. The parking lot here fills on warm summer afternoons as hang-dogging enthusiasts try their moves on the rock face. Get climbing supplies at **Moosely Seconds Mountaineering** in Moose, 307/739-1801, or in Jackson at **Teton Mountaineering,** 170 N. Cache Dr., 307/733-3595 or 800/850-3595, www.tetonmtn.com. Both stores rent climbing shoes and other gear. **Teton Rock Gym,** 1116 Maple Way, 307/733-0707, has challenging indoor climbing walls where you can practice your moves. They also rent climbing gear and have special kid's climbing classes in the summer.

For complete details on local climbing, see Reynold Jackson's *A Complete Guide to the Teton*

Range (The Mountaineers Books, www.mountaineerbooks.org, or the smaller but well-written *Teton Classics,* by Richard Rossiter (Chockstone Press). Online, check out **Way Wired Mountaineer,** www.way-wired.com for details on climbing and skiing in the Tetons.

Other Park Recreation

DAY HIKES

Short hikes are detailed in the Exploring the Park section of this chapter. Notable ones are found in the Taggart Lake and Jenny Lake areas (particularly the hike to Inspiration Point), at Colter Bay, and off the Moose-Wilson Road (Granite Canyon). All are described previously, or get the day hikes pamphlet from park visitors centers. In addition, the tram at Jackson Hole Ski Resort provides instant gratification for folks looking to get into the alpine; it's described under Backcountry Hiking. Start your hike early in the day or you may well find all of the trailhead parking spaces filled, especially on warm summer weekends. Besides, afternoon thunderstorms often build over the mountains.

For the guided version, get a schedule of free **ranger walks and hikes** (including special ones for kids) from visitors centers or in the park newspaper. These are offered daily throughout the summer.

FLOATING THE RIVER

Several rafting companies lead scenic half-day float trips down the Snake River inside the park, generally putting in at Deadman's Bar or Schwabacher Landing and taking out in Moose. Four of these companies are based in the park: **Grand Teton Lodge Company,** 307/543-3100 or 800/628-9988, www.gtlc.com; **Flagg Ranch Rafting,** 307/543-2861 or 800/443-2311, www.flaggranch.com; **Signal Mountain Lodge & Marina,** 307/733-5470 or 307/543-2831, www.signalmountainlodge.com; and **Triangle X Float Trips** (a.k.a. National Park Float Trips), 307/733-5500 or 888/860-0005, www.trianglex.com. Other rafting companies with trips inside the park are **Barker-Ewing Float Trips,** 307/733-1000 or 800/448-4202, www.barker-ewing.com; **Fort Jackson Scenic Snake River Float Trips,** 307/733-2583 or 800/735-8430, www.scenicfloats.com; **Heart Six Ranch,** 307/543-2477 or 888/543-2477, www.heartsix.com; and **Solitude Scenic Float Trips,** 307/733-2871 or 888/704-2800, www.solitudefloattrips.com. Expect to pay around $40 ($25 kids) for the 10-mile trips from Deadman's Bar, or $25 ($18 kids) for the five-mile floats from Schwabacher Landing. Flagg Ranch has rafting down the upper the Snake River above Jackson Lake. Their one-hour whitewater trips are $25 adults or $20 kids, while three-hour scenic floats cost $40 adults or $27 kids. For full details—including do-it-yourself floats—see River Rafting in the Jackson Hole chapter.

BOATING

Canoeists will discover several excellent places to paddle within Grand Teton, particularly the Snake River Oxbow Bend, String Lake, and Leigh Lake. Canoes are available for rent both in the park at Colter Bay Marina and Signal Mountain Lodge, and in Jackson.

Boaters within Grand Teton will need to purchase a permit; seven-day permits cost $10 for motorboats, $5 for nonmotorized craft. Motorboats are only allowed on Jackson Lake, Jenny Lake (10-horsepower max), and Phelps Lake. Sailboarding, water-skiing, and sailing are permitted on Jackson Lake, but no personal watercraft are allowed anywhere in the park. Get the park boating brochure for details.

Jackson Lake has three marinas, all of which are generally open from sometime in May to late September. At **Signal Mountain Lodge Marina,** 307/733-5470 or 307/543-2831, www.signalmountainlodge.com, can rent water-ski boats and skis, life jackets, deck cruisers,

GRAND TETON

fishing boats, pontoon boats, and canoes. **Colter Bay Marina,** 307/543-2811 or 800/628-9988, www.gtlc.com, is near a Park Service campground, cabins, and the Colter Bay Indian Arts Museum. It's an exceptionally busy place in the summer, with motorboat, rowboat, and canoe rentals, along with guides to take you to the hot fishing spots. Scenic **Jackson Lake cruises** ($15 adults, $7.50 kids under 12) are also available from Colter Bay Marina, as are breakfast or evening cruise-and-dine trips ($28 for breakfast; $46 for dinner). A short distance north of Colter Bay is **Leek's Marina,** 307/543-2494, a simple place with a couple of docks, a pizza restaurant, and gas pumps.

FISHING

Grand Teton National Park rivers and lakes contain cutthroat, lake, and brown trout, along with whitefish. Park anglers must have a valid Wyoming state fishing license, available for $10 for one day if you aren't a resident. Pick up a handout describing fishing regulations from park visitors centers. Fishing licenses and supplies are available at park marinas and stores. For more on fishing in the park, see the Jackson Hole chapter.

SEA KAYAKING

O.A.R.S., 209/736-4677 or 800/346-6277, www.oars.com, offers one- to four-day sea kayaking trips around Jackson Lake—perfect for beginning kayakers and families. You don't need any paddling experience for these trips, which are supported by a motorized skiff. One-night overnight trips cost $216 adults or $175 youths; four-day kayak trips will set you back $637 adults or $546 kids. O.A.R.S. also has combination trips that include kayaking on the lake and rafting down the Snake River. Their two-day combo trips cost $366 adults or $304 youths; five-day trips run $817 adults or $700 kids. They supply kayaks, a guide, and dry bags, and have tents and sleeping bags available for rent. Reserve well ahead for these popular trips.

BIRDING

The diversity of habitat types within Grand Teton National Park means that birdwatchers can find everything from trumpeter swans to calliope hummingbirds. The park produces a free *Bird-Finding Guide* with descriptions of birding hot spots. A couple of the best places are Willow Flats and Blacktail Ponds. A checklist of park birds is also available from visitors centers.

BICYCLING

The main roads through Grand Teton get heavy traffic, and the shoulder width varies (although it is wide from Moose to Jenny Lake). Pick up the park's bicycling pamphlet for details on cycling options. Bikes are not allowed on any trails within Grand Teton National Park, but you *can* ride mountain bikes on several wonderful dirt roads, including Two-Ocean Lake Road (three miles), Grassy Lake Road (52 miles from Flagg Ranch to Ashton, Idaho), and the River Road (15 surprisingly remote miles in the heart of the park). In addition, the paved secondary roads in the Antelope Flats–Mormon Row–Kelly area see less traffic and provide the opportunity to see bison and spectacular mountain vistas. Shadow Mountain Road is an off-the-beaten-path dirt road that takes off from the Antelope Flats area and climbs through Forest Service land to splendid vistas.

TRAIL RIDES

Horseback and wagon rides, including popular breakfast and dinner rides, take place at **Jackson Lake Lodge Corral** and **Colter Bay Village Corral.** Trail rides start at $25 for 1.5 hours, with dinner wagon rides for $32. Get details on both of these activities from Grand Teton Lodge Company, 307/543-2811 or 800/628-9988, www.gtlc.com. In the Rockefeller Parkway between Grand Teton and Yellowstone, **Flagg Ranch Resort,** 307/543-2861 or 800/443-2311, www.flaggranch.com, offers hour-long horseback trail rides in the summer for $25.

SWIMMING

Swimming is allowed in all park lakes, but they can be quite cold. Jenny, String, and Leigh lakes all have delightful spots for swimming on the east side, including some sandy or gravelly beaches. The Snake River is dangerous and swimming isn't recommended. Jackson Lake Lodge has a large outdoor pool, but it's only open for guests at the lodge or nearby Colter Bay Village. In addition, the town of Jackson has a wonderful recreation center with pools, and the pond at Kelly Warm Spring is a fun spot to splash around.

WINTER RECREATION

The snow-covered landscape of Grand Teton National Park draws cross-country skiers, snowshoers, and snowmobilers throughout the winter.

Skiing

Cross-country skiing is possible on several trails within the lower reaches of the park, but the high country is dangerous because of extreme avalanche hazards. Park ski trails are not machine-groomed but are generally well packed by other skiers. After a new snowfall you'll need to break trail as you follow the orange markers. See Cross-Country Skiing in the Jackson Hole chapter for information on Nordic skiing in the park, or pick up a brochure describing ski trails from the Moose Visitor Center. If you're planning to camp overnight in the park, you'll need to get a free permit here as well. Skiers and snowshoers are not allowed on the Continental Divide Snowmobile Trail for safety reasons. Unfortunately, snowmobilers ride on Teton Park Road, so your peace and solitude may be broken by the roar of distant machines.

Snowshoeing

Park naturalists lead two-hour **snowshoe hikes** from late December through March and provide snowshoes at no charge. No experience is necessary. The hikes generally depart from the Moose Visitor Center at 2 P.M. several times a week. Reservations are required; no kids under age eight. Call 307/739-3399 for details on these and other winter activities in the park.

Snowmobiling

The controversial 365-mile-long **Continental Divide Snowmobile Trail** cuts through 33 miles of Grand Teton National Park, providing a link between the Wind River Mountains and Yellowstone National Park. Within Grand Teton the trail is generally open from early January to mid-March and essentially parallels U.S. Hwy. 26/287 from the east park boundary to Moran Junction and then along U.S. Hwy. 89 north to Yellowstone. A spur trail connects the trail with other snowmobile routes along the Teton Park Road and up Signal Mountain. Snowmobiles are allowed only on designated routes, and specific regulations are enforced within the park. Get a copy of the park snowmobiling handout from the Moose Visitor Center, or call 307/739-3612 for recorded information on the Continental Divide Snowmobile Trail.

Winter Access

During winter, **Alltrans/Gray Line of Jackson Hole,** 307/733-4325 or 800/443-6133, www .jacksonholealltrans.com, has daily bus runs between Jackson and Flagg Ranch Resort for $40 one-way or $60 round-trip, arriving in time to meet the snowcoach departures for Yellowstone. Reservations are required. Taxi companies in Jackson can also provide shuttles to Flagg Ranch in the winter, including **Buckboard Transportation,** 307/733-1112 or 877/791-0211, www.buckboardtrans.com, and **All Star Taxi,** 307/733-2888.

GRAND TETON

Camping

Grand Teton National Park has five camp-grounds, with sites in all of these costing $12 ($6 for Golden Age/Golden Access cardhold-ers). These are available on a first-come, first-served basis with no reservations, and by midafternoon in the peak summer season all park campgrounds may well be full. The maxi-mum stay is seven days at Jenny Lake or 14 days at other campgrounds. Camping (or overnight parking) is not allowed along roadsides, over-looks, or parking areas within the park. Off-the-road camping is restricted to specific sites and requires a special permit; see Backcountry Hiking for specifics.

Grand Teton rangers lead popular evening campfire programs at all five campgrounds throughout the summer. All campgrounds have running water but no utility hookups. Showers and a laundromat are available at Colter Bay Village. Several special hiker/biker sites are at Jenny Lake and Colter Bay for $5. Group sites can be found at Colter Bay and Gros Ventre campgrounds, but advance reservations are required. All Grand Teton Na-tional Park campgrounds are closed in winter, but limited tent camping and RV parking ($5; restrooms and water but no hookups) is avail-able near the Colter Bay Visitor Center. Get recorded park campground information at 307/739-3603, or on the web at www .nps.gov/grte.

GROS VENTRE CAMPGROUND

With 372 sites, Gros Ventre Campground is both the largest campground in the park and the last to fill (if at all). The campground is lo-cated on the southern edge of the park along the Gros Ventre River near Kelly and is 10 miles from Jackson. It's open May to mid-October and has a dump station and five group sites. There are no stores or restaurants nearby; the closest are in Jackson or Moose.

JENNY LAKE CAMPGROUND

First to fill is always Jenny Lake Campground, with 51 tent sites (no RVs) near this wonderful-ly scenic lake in the heart of the park. The camp-ground is open mid-May to late September and usually fills by 8 A.M. in midsummer. Not far away is a little general store, plus Jenny Lake Lodge with gourmet meals.

SIGNAL MOUNTAIN CAMPGROUND

Located on the south shore of Jackson Lake, Signal Mountain Campground has 86 sites, a trailer dumping station, and room for RVs up to 30 feet long. It fills by 10 A.M. in midsummer and is open mid-May to mid-October. The campground is close to Signal Mountain Lodge, which has a restau-rant and general store. It's 32 miles from Jackson.

COLTER BAY CAMPGROUND

Located on the east side of Jackson Lake, Colter Bay Campground is one of the largest in the park, with 350 sites, a dump station, and nearby coin-operated showers and laundry facilities. Also close by are the famous Indian Arts Museum, a general store, a pair of eateries, and rustic cabins for rent. Leeks Marina with a popular pizzeria and Jackson Lake Lodge is just a few miles down the road. Colter Bay Campground is open mid-May to mid-Sep-tember and typically fills by noon in midsummer.

LIZARD CREEK CAMPGROUND

This campground has 60 quiet campsites on the north end of Jackson Lake and is open early June to early September. These sites usually fill by 2 P.M. in the peak season, and RVs must be less than 30 feet. The nearest food and supplies are in Flagg Ranch or Colter Bay, both approximately eight miles away.

OTHER CAMPING OPTIONS

In addition to the five NPS campgrounds, park concessioners maintain two seasonal RV parks with full hookups, showers, washers, and driers. **Flagg Ranch Resort** in Rockefeller Parkway, 307/543-2861 or 800/443-2311, www.flaggranch.com, has 100 pull-through RV sites with full hookups for $38, and 75 tent sites for $22. The resort is open early to mid-May till early October, but reservations are highly recommended.

On the south shore of Jackson Lake, **Colter Bay RV Park,** 307/543-3100 or 800/628-9988, www.gtlc.com, charges $38 for RV hookups and is open late May to mid-September. No tent spaces are available here. Evening nature programs are offered in summer.

Not far from the park is **Grand Teton Park RV Resort** six miles east of Moran Junction along Hwy. 26/287, 307/733-1980 or 800/563-6469, www.yellowstonerv.com. Facilities include a heated seasonal pool and hot tub, recreation room, and grocery store; $42 per day for RVs with hookups, $30 per day for tents. Simple camping cabins go for $52–58 per day, and tepees run $39–43. Open year-round.

The Forest Service has quite a few campgrounds in the surrounding country, and several private RV parks are available in Jackson.

Accommodations

Several places provide concessioner lodging inside Grand Teton National Park. As in all national parks, none of the lodge rooms contains TVs or radios. Reserve at least nine months ahead to be sure of getting a room in the peak summer season. Dozens of additional accommodations are south of the park in Jackson, and the pleasant **Hatchet Resort,** 307/543-2413 or 877/543-2413, www.hatchetresort.com, has cozy and moderately priced rooms in the heart of Buffalo Valley.

JACKSON LAKE LODGE

Built on a grand scale, the 385-room Jackson Lake Lodge, 307/543-2811 or 800/628-9988, www.gtlc.com occupies a bluff above Willow Flats on the southeast side of Jackson Lake. Sixty-foot-high windows look across to the Tetons, and fireplaces flank the spacious central hall. Outside is a large swimming pool and kiddie pool (major attractions for families), and inside you'll find restaurants, a lounge, a gift shop, a newsstand, a clothing shop, and an ATM. All rooms contain two double beds and phones; some also have small fridges. Rooms in the lodge without a view (unless you count the parking lot) are $124 d, while those with big windows fronting the Tetons are $225 d. Cottages cost $154 d ($164 d with a patio), or $220 d for ones with mountain vistas. Luxury suites in the lodge are $394–564 d. Extra guests (beyond two) in any of these rooms are $9.50 per person. The lodge is open mid-May to mid-October.

JENNY LAKE LODGE

For four-star accommodations a stone's throw from the Tetons, stay at Jenny Lake Lodge, 307/733-4647 or 800/628-9988, www.gtlc.com, where 37 comfortably appointed cabins surround a cozy Old West main lodge. This is a marvelous honeymoon or big-splurge place, and the $348 s or $429 d price includes horseback rides, bikes, breakfast, and a marvelous six-course dinner. (Note, however, that the meals are only served at specific times, so you'll need to adjust your schedule accordingly.) For the ultimate in extravagance, choose the lodge's luxurious suites; $579–619 d. Jenny Lake Lodge is open June to early October.

COLTER BAY VILLAGE

Family-oriented Colter Bay Village, 307/543-2811 ext. 1080 or 800/628-9988, www.gtlc.com, has 166 rustic cabins of varying sizes and types, some of which sleep six people. There are no phones or cooking facilities in any of these cabins. The most basic are canvas-and-log structures with outdoor

GRAND TETON

the marina at Colter Bay Village on Jackson Lake

grills and picnic tables, indoor woodstoves, and bring-your-own-linen bunk beds. Restrooms are nearby, and the showers are coin-operated. These tent cabins cost just $34 d ($4.50 for each additional person up to six). Sleeping bags and other camping supplies are available for rent. The tent cabins are open early June to early September.

A bit nicer are little one-room cabins that share a bath for $34 d. Cabins with a private bath start at $69 d for ones with a double bed, up to $104 d for those with two double beds and a twin bed. Two-room cabins with a bath are $109 d or $129 for up to four. Additional guests are $4.50 each in all of these, and the cabins are open late May to late September. Guests at Colter Bay Village can use the big swimming pool at nearby Jackson Lake Lodge.

DORNAN'S

Near park headquarters in Moose, Dornan's Spur Ranch Cabins, 307/733-2522, www.dornans.com,

has a dozen modern log cabins filled with handcrafted lodgepole pine furniture. One-bedroom cabins are $140 s or d or $170 for up to four people, and two-bedroom cabins cost $210 for up to six people. There's a three-night minimum stay in the summer. All cabins include full kitchens and are open year-round.

SIGNAL MOUNTAIN LODGE

On the south shore of Jackson Lake, Signal Mountain Lodge, 307/733-5470 or 307/543-2831, www.signalmountainlodge.com, offers a variety of lodging options. Simple and rustic log cabins start at $95 d, up to $135 for a room that sleeps six. Motel-style rooms with fridges and microwaves are $114 for up to four people or $163 for a nicer room with a fireplace and king bed. The lodge's finest options include suites for $182, cozy bungalows with kitchens and private decks for $137–195 d, and a three-room cabin with fireplace in the living room, full kitchen, and laundry for $225. Signal Mountain Lodge is open early May to mid-October.

FLAGG RANCH RESORT

In Rockefeller Parkway just three miles south of Yellowstone, Flagg Ranch Resort, 307/543-2861 or 800/443-2311, www.flaggranch.com, has modern four-plex log cabins with patios and two queen beds or a king bed. Rates are $139–145 d in summer or $110 d in winter, and kids stay free. Additional adults are $10 each. Flagg Ranch is open late May–September and mid-December to mid-March. The main lodge houses a convenience store, restaurant, deli, gift shop, and central area with couches and a large fireplace.

Food

RESTAURANTS AND BARS

Several dining options exist at **Jackson Lake Lodge,** including the Mural Room with its 60-foot windows fronting the Tetons. The restaurant serves three meals a day, while the nearby Blue Heron Lounge offers up equally impressive views and musicians provide accompaniment for your cocktails. Dinner reservations are required in summer; call 307/543-2811 ext. 1911. Casual meals are available at Pioneer Grill, also inside Jackson Lake Lodge, or the very popular Pool Grill and BBQ, next to the big outdoor swimming pool. The latter is an all-you-can-eat buffet with steaks, barbecue chicken and ribs, and other Western grub; it's open daily in July and August, and costs $15 adults or $8 kids.

Marvelous old **Jenny Lake Lodge** has impeccable service, windows that face the mountains, and a cozy setting. Six-course dinners are the featured attractions, and the wine list is extensive. Lunch is à la carte, but breakfast and dinner are fixed price (and pricey: $48 for dinner, $16 for breakfast). Jenny Lake Lodge is open June to early October, and reservations are required; call 307/733-4647. This is a dress-up place, so a jacket is recommended for dinner. For details on Jackson Lake Lodge and Jenny Lake Lodge, visit the Grand Teton Lodge Company's website, www.gtlc.com.

Colter Bay Village has two dining choices: the Chuckwagon for steaks and pasta and the John Colter Cafe Court for chicken, pizza, deli sandwiches, salads, and snacks.

An old favorite with an egalitarian setting (look for the tepees) is **Dornan's Chuck Wagon Restaurant,** 307/733-2415, www.dornans.com, offering reasonable meals every summer since 1948. The all-you-can-eat breakfasts include pancakes, ham, bacon, and eggs. Sandwiches are the main lunch attraction, and dinners include grilled-to-order barbecue ribs, chicken, steaks, salmon, or trout, plus a big outdoor salad bar. The Chuck Wagon is open mid-June through Labor Day.

Across the street—and open all year—is Dornan's **Spur Bar/Moose Pizza & Pasta Co.,** 307/733-2415, offering a wide range of superb homemade pizzas ($13–15), sandwiches, calzones, and pastas. Dining is available on two outside decks with can't-beat-the-view Teton vistas, and folk musicians perform once or twice a month. The bar puts on monthly wine tastings ($5) on the first Sunday of the month, October–May. Check out the club on the wall. In 1944, local resident Farney Cole used it to defend himself from a bear attack. He survived, as did the bear.

Signal Mountain Lodge, 307/733-5470 or 307/543-2831, www.signalmountainlodge.com, houses both Trapper Grill with casual fare and a popular deck for al fresco dining, along with Peaks Restaurant with an upscale menu and spectacular vistas of the Tetons. Deadman's Bar at Signal Mountain is famous for blackberry margaritas and also serves a pub menu.

Leek's Marina 307/543-2494, is home to a very popular pizzeria that also serves calzones, sandwiches, salads, and beer on tap. Musicians drop by every other Wednesday evening for an open mic session.

The main lodge at **Flagg Ranch Resort,** 307/543-2861 or 800/443-2311, www.flag granch.com, houses Bear's Den Restaurant, serving three meals a day. Also here is a deli, saloon, and grocery store.

GROCERIES AND SUPPLIES

The best in-the-park store is **Dornan's Trading Post,** 307/733-2415, located near park headquarters in Moose. The store is open all year and stocked with groceries, tasty deli sandwiches, fresh baked goods, and camping supplies. The cart out front has espresso, and next door is

Dornan's Wine Shoppe with the biggest selection of fine wine and beer in Jackson Hole, including more than 1,700 different wines. Other nearby Dornan's operations include Moose Pizza & Pasta Co. and the Chuck Wagon (both described previously), and a gift shop. In winter, the gift shop rents cross-country skis, snowshoes, and pull-behind sleds.

Colter Bay General Store, 307/543-2811, has a good choice of groceries and supplies, and convenience stores operate at Signal Mountain, Flagg Ranch Resort, and Jenny Lake. The store at Flagg Ranch Resort is open in both summer and winter seasons (mid-May to mid-Oct., and mid-Dec. to mid-Mar.). All of the others are only open for summer.

Practicalities

GETTING IN

Entrance to Grand Teton National Park is $20 per vehicle or $10 for individuals entering by bicycle, foot, or as a bus passenger. Motorcycles and snowmobiles are $15. *The pass covers entrance to both Yellowstone and Grand Teton National Parks and is good for seven days.* If you're planning to be here longer or to make additional visits, get an annual pass covering both parks for $40, or the National Park Pass—good for all national parks—for $50 per year. A Golden Age Passport for all national parks is available to anyone over 62 for a one-time fee of $10, and people with disabilities can get a free Golden Access Passport. Both of these also give the holders 50 percent reductions in most camping fees. Call 307/739-3600 for additional park information, or visit the park on the web at www.nps.gov/grte.

At the entrance stations, park visitors receive a copy of *Teewinot,* the park newspaper. It lists park facilities and services, along with interpretive programs, nature walks, and other activities. Family favorites for generations are the evening **campfire programs** held at campground amphitheaters throughout the summer. The park

also produces a helpful **Easy Access** brochure with details on wheelchair-accessible visitors centers, trails, sights, picnic areas, activities, campsites, and accommodations.

VISITORS CENTERS

Grand Teton National Park headquarters is in the settlement of Moose near the southern end of the park. **Moose Visitor Center,** 307/739-3399, is open daily 8 A.M.–7 P.M. from early June to early September, and daily (except Christmas) 8 A.M.–5 P.M. the rest of the year. **Jenny Lake Visitor Center** is open daily 8 A.M.–7 P.M. from early June to early September; closed the remainder of the year.

On the east side of Jackson Lake, **Colter Bay Visitor Center,** 307/739-3594, is open daily 8 A.M.–8 P.M. from early June to early September, and daily 8 A.M.–5 P.M. from mid-May to early June and for most of September; closed the rest of the year.

Just north of Grand Teton inside John D. Rockefeller Jr. Memorial Parkway is **Flagg Ranch Information Station,** open daily 9 A.M.–5:30 P.M. between early June and early September, and with varying hours from mid-December to mid-March.

SUPPORT ORGANIZATIONS

The **Grand Teton Natural History Association** operates bookstores in park visitors centers and the store at Menor's Ferry. They also have a mail-order service for books about the park. For a catalog, call 307/739-3403, or find everything on the web at www.grandtetonpark.org.

The nonprofit **Grand Teton National Park Foundation,** 307/739-0629, www.gtnpf.org, provides support for park projects that would not otherwise be funded, and all contributions are tax-deductible. Their big project is to help fund the much-needed construction of a new visitors center at Moose.

The **Murie Center,** www.muriecenter.org, 307/739-2246, is named for Olaus and Mardy Murie. The grande dame of the conservation movement, Mardy grew up in Alaska and was the first woman to graduate from the University of Alaska. She later married the famous naturalist (and founder of the Wilderness Society) Olaus Murie and went on to write several books and to play an important role in passing the Alaska National Interest Lands Conservation Act. She received the Presidential Medal of Freedom from President Clinton for her conservation work in both Alaska and Wyoming. Mardy turned 100 years old in 2002 and lives at her little log cabin in Moose. Her ranch is now also home to the Murie Center, which puts on a variety of conservation seminars and programs throughout the year.

MEDICAL HELP

Get emergency medical assistance at the **Grand Teton Medical Clinic,** 307/543-2514, near the Chevron station at Jackson Lake Lodge. It's open daily 10 A.M.–6 P.M. mid-May to mid-October. The nearest hospital is in Jackson.

OUTDOOR GEAR

The little settlement of Moose has several businesses in addition to the Dornan's shops and eateries described previously. **Adventure Sports,** 307/733-3307, www.dornans.com, rents mountain bikes, recumbents, canoes, and kayaks. Next door is **Moosely Seconds,** 307/739-1801, with good deals on outdoor clothing and climbing gear; open mid-May through September. They also rent ice axes, crampons, rock shoes, trekking poles, approach shoes, plastic boots, day packs, and snowshoes. **Snake River Anglers,** 307/733-3699, sells and rents fishing supplies and camping equipment.

OTHER PRACTICALITIES

Gas is available year-round at Dornan's in Moose and Flagg Ranch Resort, and summers only at Colter Bay Village, Signal Mountain Lodge, and Jackson Lake Lodge. You'll find gift shops at Signal Mountain, Flagg Ranch Resort, Jackson Lake Lodge, Moose, and Colter Bay. Year-round **post offices** are located in Moran, Moose, and Kelly. Get cash from **ATMs** located at Dornan's in Moose, Jackson Lake Lodge, Colter Bay Village, Flagg Ranch Resort, and Signal Mountain Lodge.

TRANSPORTATION AND TOURS

As this book was being written, the Park Service was developing a new **transportation plan** for Grand Teton, and it could have a major impact on access to certain areas. Some of the options being considered were to provide transit bus service between Jackson and the park and to close some roads to most motorized vehicles, including the Moose-Wilson Road. Contact the park for the latest at 307/739-3399, www.nps.gov/grte.

Grand Teton Lodge Company, 307/543-2811 or 800/628-9988, www.gtlc.com, has five-times-daily summer shuttle buses connecting Jackson with Jackson Lake Lodge for $20 one-way, and on to Colter Bay Village for an additional $4 one-way. Transportation is $30 from the airport to Jackson Lake Lodge or $20 in the other direction. Reservations are required for all of these shuttles. In Jackson, the buses depart from the Home Ranch parking lot on the corner of Gill Street and N. Cache Drive. The company also offers three-hour bus tours of Grand Teton National Park on Mondays, Wednesdays, and Fridays for $30 ($15

GRAND TETON

kids under 12) and eight-hour tours of Yellowstone National Park on Tuesdays, Thursdays, and Saturdays for $50 ($30 kids). Tours depart from Jackson Lake Lodge at 8:30 A.M.

Summertime bus tours of Grand Teton and Yellowstone National Parks are available several times a week from **Alltrans/Gray Line of Jackson Hole,** 307/733-4325 or 800/443-6133, www.jacksonholealltrans.com. Yellowstone tours last 11 hours and cost $80 plus park entrance fees. Eight-hour Grand Teton tours are $69 plus the park entrance. Those without vehicles can use these tours for access to the parks; reserve ahead to schedule a pickup in Jackson, Grand Teton, or Yellowstone. In Yellowstone, travelers can connect with other buses to West Yellowstone (Montana), Gardiner (Montana), or Cody. Gray Line's four-day tours of the Yellowstone and Grand Teton areas start at $900 for one person or $1,200 for two, including lodging (but only one meal).

Operated by the respected Teton Science School, the nonprofit **Wildlife Expeditions,** 307/733-2623 or 888/945-3567, www.tetonscience.org/wildlife, leads wildlife-viewing safaris throughout the region. Half-day Grand Teton trips are $85, and all-day jaunts cost $145. Multiday wildlife tours into Yellowstone are also offered. Other companies offering guided van tours of the park include **Callowishus Park Touring Company,** 307/733-9521, www.callowishus.com; Jackson's Hole Adventure, 307/654-7849 or 800/392-3165, www.jacksonholeadventure.com; and Upstream Anglers and Outdoor Adventures, 307/739-9443 or 800/642-8979, www.upstreamanglers.com.

Yellowstone National Park

The words "national park" seem to stimulate an almost Pavlovian response: Yellowstone. The geysers, canyons, and bears of Yellowstone National Park are so intertwined in our collective consciousness that even 1960s American cartoons used the park as a model—Jellystone Park, where Yogi Bear and Boo Boo were constantly out to thwart the rangers. One source estimated that nearly one-third of the U.S. population has visited the park, and each year three million people roll through its gates.

Yellowstone has always been a place of wonder. There is considerable evidence that

the Indians who first lived in this area viewed it as a place of great spiritual power and treated it with reverence. Yellowstone was to later become the birthplace for the national-park movement, and Americans today still love the park, although they don't always treat it with reverence.

There is something about Yellowstone National Park that calls people back again and again, something more than simply the chance to see the curiosities of the natural world. Generations of parents have brought their

© DON PITCHER

Morning Glory Pool in Upper Geyser Basin, Yellowstone National Park children to see the place that they recall from their own childhood visits. Other cultures have the Ganges River, Rome, or Mecca as places with deep spiritual meaning. In America, our national parks have become places for similar renewal, and as the nation's first national park, Yellowstone remains one of our most valued treasures.

So, into the park we come in our cars with our crying babies in the back—babies who suddenly quiet down at the sight of a bison or elk. I recall bringing relatives to Yellowstone after I had worked in the vicinity all summer and had become a bit jaded. Their emotional reaction surprised me, and more than a decade later they still tell stories of the bison calves, the astounding geysers, the rush of the waterfalls, and the night they spent at Old Faithful Inn. Yellowstone is a collective religious experience that sends us back to our roots in the natural world. The smell of wood smoke from a campfire, the picnic lunch on the shore of Yellowstone Lake, the backcountry horseback ride, the hike down to the lip of Lower Falls, the quick strike of a trout on the line, the gasp of the crowd as the first spurt of Old Faithful jets upward, the herds of bison wading Firehole River, the evening piano tunes drifting through the air at Lake Hotel, the howl of a distant wolf, and even the cheesy Yellowstone trinkets—all of these things combine to leave an indelible mark on visitors to Yellowstone National Park.

THE SETTING

On a map, Yellowstone appears as a gigantic box wedged so tightly against the northwest corner of Wyoming that it squeezes over into Montana and Idaho. The park measures 63 by 54 miles and covers 2.2 million acres, making it one of the largest national parks in the Lower 48 (although it is dwarfed by Alaska's Wrangell-St.

Elias National Park and Preserve, which covers almost six times as much land). The United Nations has declared Yellowstone both a World Biosphere Reserve and a World Heritage Site.

The park is accessible from all four sides, and a loop road provides easy access to all of the best-known sights. Because of its popularity as a destination, tourist towns surround Yellowstone: Jackson to the south, Cody to the east, Gardiner and Cooke City on the northern margin, and West Yellowstone on its western border. Also because so many people visit the park, there is a well-developed network of facilities inside the park, including visitors centers, campgrounds, hotels, restaurants, a hospital, gift shops, ATMs, one-hour photo shops, espresso stands, and other supposed necessities of modern life. Although less than 2 percent of the park is developed, Yellowstone contains more than 2,000 buildings of various types. In some spots (most egregiously

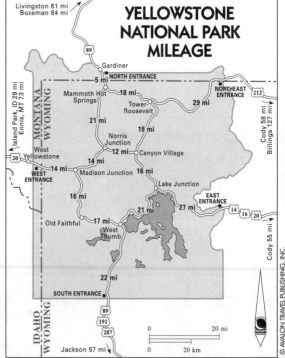

around Old Faithful), these developments have grown to the point that the natural world seems simply a backdrop for the human world that pulls visitors in to buy T-shirts or to watch park slide shows on wildlife or geysers while missing the real thing just outside the door.

More than any other national park, Yellowstone seems to provide the oddities of nature, creating, as historian Aubrey L. Haines noted, "a false impression that the park is only a colossal, steam-operated freak show." Yellowstone is a mix of the real and the unreal, a place where our fantasies of what nature should be blend with the reality of crowds of fellow travelers and the impact we have on the place we love so much. In midsummer, a trip into Yellowstone can be something less than a natural experience. Long lines of cars back up behind RVs creeping up the narrow roads, and throngs of visitors crowd the benches around Old Faithful Geyser waiting for an eruption, while dozens of others cluster around bewildered elk to get photos to email their friends. Despite this crowding—or perhaps because most folks prefer to stay on paved paths—many parts of the park remain virtually uninhabited. In the Yellowstone backcountry, one can still walk for days without seeing more than a handful of other hardy hikers.

A PLACE OF CONTROVERSY

Yellowstone National Park evokes a torrent of emotions in anyone with a knowledge of and concern for the natural world. Perhaps more than any other wild place in America, the park seems to be in a perpetual state of controversy, be it over fire policies, bison and wolf management, snowmobile use, or some other issue; there's always something getting folks stirred up. Perhaps it is because so many Americans have visited the park that we feel a vested interest in what it means to us. Writer Paul Schullery in his wonderful book *Searching for Yellowstone* put it best when he noted, "Caring for Yellowstone National Park brings to mind all the metaphors of growth and change; it is a process more organic than political; a crucible of ideas, ambitions, dreams, and belief systems; a cultural, intellectual, and spiritual crossroads at which we are forever debating which way to turn." As visitation has risen in recent decades, more and more folks have begun to suggest some sort of limits on numbers to preserve the experience and protect the park. Don't-tread-on-me Westerners consider the idea of limits an example of environmental extremism for the elite, but as visitation increases, conflicts and controversies are a natural outcome.

Geology

Yellowstone is, without a doubt, the most geologically fascinating place on this planet. Here the forces that elsewhere lie deep within the earth seem close enough to touch. They're palpable not only in the geysers and hot springs but also in the lake that fills part of an enormous caldera, the earthquakes that shake this land, the evidence of massive glaciations, and the deeply eroded Grand Canyon of the Yellowstone.

FIRE AND ICE
The Yellowstone Hotspot

When geologists began to study the Yellowstone area in depth, they found a surprising pattern. Extending far to the southwest was a chain of volcanic fields, the most ancient of which—16 million years old—lay in northern Nevada. In addition, geologic fault lines created a hundred-mile-wide semicircle around the Yellowstone area, as if some deep-seated force were pushing the land outward and upward the way a ripple moves across a pond.

Both the volcanic activity and the wavelike pattern of faults are caused by the same source: a plume of superheated material moving up from the core of the planet through a narrow tube, creating a hotspot beneath the earth's crust. As the North American continent has slid to the southwest over the eons, this plume has traced a line of volcanoes across the West, and as the land continues to move, the plume causes massive deformations in the crust that show up as mountain ranges, fault lines, and earthquakes. It's a little like somebody tugging a piece of cloth across a candle. Approximately 40 such hotspots are known to exist around the globe, but most are beneath the seas. Other than Yellowstone, the best-known example is the chain of Hawaiian Islands. The earth has been moving over the Yellowstone hotspot at the rate of 15 miles per million years for the last 10 million years, and on the present track, the spot might eventually end up in Hudson Bay in 100 million years or so. Don't hold your breath.

Tambora on Steroids

The volcanic activity revealed by Yellowstone's geysers, hot springs, and fumaroles is not always benign. Within the last two million years there have been three stupendous volcanic eruptions in the area, the most recent taking place 650,000 years ago. The largest of these eruptions took place two million years ago and created an event beyond the realm of imagination: 600 cubic miles of ash were blasted into the atmosphere! This eruption—probably one of the largest to ever occur on earth—ejected 17 times more material than the massive Tambora eruption of 1815, an explosion that was heard 1,600 miles away. Compared to an explosion that is better known to Americans, the 1980 eruption of Mt. St. Helens, the first Yellowstone event was 2,400 times as large. Ash from this first Yellowstone eruption carried east to Iowa, north to Saskatchewan, south to the Gulf of Mexico, and west to California. This titanic infusion of ash into the atmosphere undoubtedly affected the global climate for years to follow.

The process that creates these explosions starts when molten rock pushes up from the center of the earth, bulging the land upward into an enormous dome. Eventually the pressure becomes too great and fractures develop around the dome's margins, sending hot gases, ash, and rock blasting into the atmosphere. After the most recent eruption (650,000 years ago), the magma chamber collapsed into a gigantic, smoldering pit reaching 28 by 47 miles

in surface area and perhaps several thousand feet deep. Over time, additional molten rock pushed up from underneath and flowed as thick lava over the land. The most recent of these lava flows was 70,000 years ago.

Two resurgent domes—one near Old Faithful and the other just north of Yellowstone Lake near LeHardy Rapids—have been discovered by geologists. Measurements at LeHardy Rapids showed that the land rose almost three feet from 1923 to 1985, although it has since been subsiding. This upsurge raised the outlet of Yellowstone Lake, causing the water level to increase and flooding trees along the lake's margins. Obviously, Yellowstone's volcanism is far from dead, and scientists believe another eruption is possible or even likely, although nobody knows when it might occur.

Glaciation

Not everything in Yellowstone is the result of volcanic activity. The entire Yellowstone region has undergone a series of at least eight major glaciations over the last million years, the last of which—the Pinedale Glaciation—began around 70,000 years ago. At its peak, the Pinedale Glaciation covered almost all of Yellowstone and reached southward into Jackson Hole and north much of the way to Livingston, Montana. Over Yellowstone Lake the icefield was 4,000 feet thick and covered 10,000-foot mountains. This period of glaciation ended about 15,000 years ago, but trees did not appear in the Yellowstone area until 11,500 years ago, and it wasn't until around 5,000 years ago that the landscape began to appear as it does today.

GEYSERS

Yellowstone is famous for geysers, and geyser-gazers will not be disappointed. At least 60 percent of the world's geysers are in the park, making this easily the largest and most diverse collection in existence. Yellowstone's more than 300 geysers are spread over nine different basins, with half of these in Upper Geyser Basin, the home of Old Faithful.

Geysers need three essentials to exist: water, heat, and fractured rock. The water comes from snow and rain falling on this high plateau, while the heat comes from molten rock close to the earth's surface. Massive pressures from below have created a ring of fractures around the edge of Yellowstone's caldera. This is one of the hottest places on the planet, with heat flows more than 60 times the global average.

How They Work

Geysers operate because cold water is dense and sinks, while hot water is less dense and rises. The periodic eruption of geysers is caused by constrictions in the underground channels that prevent an adequate heat exchange with the surface. Precipitation slowly moves into the earth, eventually contacting the molten rock. Because of high pressures at these depths, water can reach extreme temperatures without vaporizing (as in a pressure cooker). As this superheated water rises back toward the surface, it emerges in hot springs, fumaroles, mud pots, and geysers. The

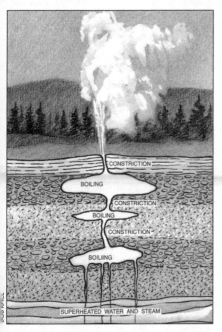

most spectacular of these phenomena are geysers. Two general types of geysers exist in Yellowstone. Fountain geysers (such as Great Fountain Geyser) explode from pools of water and tend to spray water more widely, whereas cone-type geysers (such as Old Faithful) jet out of nozzlelike formations.

In a geyser, steam bubbles upward from the superheated source of water and expands as it rises. These bubbles block the plumbing system, keeping hot water from reaching the surface. Eventually, however, pressure from the bubbles begins to force the cooler water above out of the vent. This initial release triggers a more violent re-action as the sudden lessening of pressure allows the entire column to begin boiling, explosively ex-pelling steam and water to produce a geyser. Once the eruption has emptied the plumbing system, water gradually seeps back into the chambers to begin the process anew. Some of Yellowstone's geysers have enormous underground caverns that fill with water; in its rare eruptions, massive Steamboat Geyser can blast a million gallons of water into the air!

As an aside, the term "geyser" is one of the few Icelandic terms in the English language; it means to "gush forth." There are probably 30 active geysers in Iceland, many more on Russia's Kamchatka Peninsula, and a few in New Zealand, where geothermal development has greatly less-ened geyser activity. A fine online source with details about Yellowstone's geysers—and others around the globe—is maintained by the non-profit **Geyser Observation and Study Association,** www.geyserstudy.org.

Protecting the Geysers

Unfortunately, some of Yellowstone's geysers have been lost because of human stupidity or vandalism. At one time, it was considered great sport to stuff logs, rocks, and even chairs into the geysers for a little added show. Others poured chemicals into them to make them play. As a result of such actions, some geysers have been se-verely damaged or destroyed, and some hot springs have become collection points for coins, rocks, sticks, and trash. It shouldn't be neces-sary to point out that such actions ruin these thermal areas for everyone and destroy something that may have been going on for hundreds of years.

OTHER GEOTHERMAL ACTIVITY

Although geysers are Yellowstone's best-known features, they make up only a tiny fraction of perhaps 10,000 thermal features in the park. **Hot springs** appear where water can reach the ground surface relatively easily, allowing the heat that builds up in the chambers of geysers to dissipate. When less groundwater is present, you may find **fumaroles,** vents that shoot steam, carbon dioxide, and even hydrogen sulfide gas. **Mud pots** (also called paint pots) are essentially wet fumaroles. Hydrogen sulfide gas combines with water to produce hydrosulfuric acid. This acid breaks down surrounding rocks to form clay, and the clay combines with water to create mud. As gas passes through the mud, it creates the bubbling mud pots. Probably the best examples of these different forms are at Fountain Paint Pot in Lower Geyser Basin, where geysers and hot springs are found in the wetter areas below, while mud pots and fumaroles sit atop a small hill.

The colors in Yellowstone's hot springs come from a variety of sources, including algae and bacteria as well as various minerals, particularly sulfur, iron oxides, and arsenic sulfide. The algae and bacteria are highly temperature-specific and help create the distinct bands of colors around many hot springs. Interestingly, many of these algal species are found only in hot springs, although they exist around the world. The bacteria have proven of considerable interest to science because of their ability to survive such high temperatures. One such organism, *Thermus aquaticus,* was discovered in a Yellowstone hot springs in 1967, and scientists extracted an enzyme that was later used to develop the increasingly important technique of DNA fingerprinting. Above 190°F, even these hot-water bacteria and algae cannot survive, so the hottest springs may appear a deep blue because of the water's ability to absorb all wavelengths of light except blue, which is reflected back into our eyes.

More Terminology

A couple of other terms are worth learning before heading out to see the sights of Yellowstone. **Sinter** (also called "geyserite") is a deposit composed primarily of silica. The silica is dissolved by hot water deep underground and brought to the surface in geysers or hot springs. At the surface the water evaporates, leaving behind the light gray sinter, which can create large mounds (up to 30 feet high) around the older geysers. The rate of accumulation is very slow, and some of the park's geysers have obviously been active for many thousands of years. The other precipitate that is sometimes deposited around Yellowstone's hot springs and geysers is **travertine,** consisting of calcium carbonate that has been dissolved underground. (See Mammoth Hot Springs for more on this process.)

A Note of Warning

The surface around many of the hot springs and geysers is surprisingly thin, and people have been killed or seriously injured by falling through into the boiling water. Stay on the boardwalks in developed areas, and use extreme caution around backcountry thermal features. If in doubt, stay away!

The Greater Yellowstone Ecosystem

One of the largest intact temperate-zone ecosystems on the planet, Yellowstone was for decades viewed as an island of nature surrounded by a world of human development. Unfortunately, this attitude has led to a host of problems. Despite its size, Yellowstone alone is not large enough to support a viable population of all the animals that once existed within its borders, and developments outside the park pose threats within. In recent years, there have been increasing calls to treat the park as part of the larger Greater Yellowstone Ecosystem—18 million acres of land at the juncture of Wyoming, Montana, and Idaho covering both public and private lands. With each year that passes it has become more obvious that Yellowstone can never be simply an island. Most of the issues that have made headlines in the last decade or so—from fisheries problems to snowmobile use—have been ones that spread beyond the artificial park boundaries.

Within surrounding lands, conflicts between development and preservation are even more obvious than within the park itself. Logging is one of the most apparent of these, and along the park's western border aerial photos reveal a perfectly straight line, with lodgepole pines on the park side and old clearcuts on the Forest Service side. One of these was the largest timber sale ever made outside of Alaska! Near the park boundaries, housing developments, the massive growth of the tourism industry, oil and gas drilling, mining, a grizzly bear and wolf theme park and other activities all create potential problems within the park and for the Yellowstone ecosystem as a whole.

The way everything is tied together is perhaps best exemplified by two seemingly unrelated issues that have been on the front burner in recent years: bison and snowmobiles. I talk more about both later, but needless to say, environmentalists think there are far too many snowmobiles heading into the park, and Montana ranchers think there are far too many bison coming out of the park about the same time of year. As a result, bison are being sent to slaughter,

sometimes in large numbers. But these two problems are partially linked; some bison exit the park on roads kept smooth for the snowmobiles. If the roads were not groomed it is possible that more of the bison would remain inside the park in heavy snow years. The point here is not that we should immediately ban all snowmobiles in Yellowstone (though I wish that would happen), but that our actions can have unforeseen ramifications both outside and inside the park.

PLANTS

Yellowstone National Park is primarily a series of high plateaus ranging from 7,500 to 8,500 feet in elevation. Surrounding this gently rolling expanse are the Absaroka Mountains along the east and north sides and the Gallatin Range in the northwestern corner. Elevations are lowest along the northern end of the park, where the Yellowstone River and other rivers cut through, and highest on the eastern and northwestern margins. The plants that carpet Yellowstone are predominantly determined by the amount of precipitation and the type of soils in which they grow: areas underlain by Absaroka volcanic bedrock have more nutrient-rich soils than areas with Yellowstone rhyolites.

Sagebrush-Steppe

These habitats dominate dry areas of Yellowstone, particularly on the northern portion of the park in Lamar Valley and along the Yellowstone River. Here the precipitation totals less than 20 inches annually, and one finds open country with sagebrush, grasses, and shrubs, along with pockets of aspen and Douglas fir. Other similarly open country is found in the Hayden and Pelican valleys.

Lodgepole Pine

Forests of lodgepole pine cover more than half of Yellowstone, including much of the central plateau. In these forests lodgepoles dominate, although you may find a sprinkling of whitebark pine, spruce, and fir trees. Lodgepole forests are mostly even-aged, having been established after a forest fire that destroyed the previous generation of trees. Some lodgepole cones are serotinous, meaning that they can hang on the tree for years, only opening to release the seeds when a fire melts the gluelike material holding them shut. After a fire, the seedlings grow rapidly if conditions are right. Young trees established after the 1988 fires are dense in many areas, with some already topping 20 feet. Lodgepole roots are shallow, making them susceptible to being blown over in windstorms.

Spruce-Fir

Higher elevations in the park have cooler temperatures and forests dominated by Englemann spruce and subalpine fir. These sites get more precipitation than lodgepole forests and are underlain by better soils.

Subalpine

On mountain slopes between 8,000 and 10,000 feet you'll find whitebark pine trees. Although these trees seldom top 40 feet high, their seeds are an important food source for red squirrels, Clark's nutcrackers, and more surprisingly, grizzlies. Above timberline (approximately 10,000 feet), even these trees give way, and only low-growing forbs, grasses, and shrubs survive. Mount Washburn is a good place to find an easily accessible subalpine area.

Other Habitat Types

Although they don't cover large areas of the park, several other types of vegetation exist in Yellowstone. Small areas are dominated by **Douglas fir** trees within the sagebrush-steppe and along the Madison River. **Aspen** stands are present on the north end of the park, near the Snake River, and in the Bechler region. In addition, a **dry sagebrush-steppe** vegetation type can be seen in the Gardiner area, where you'll even find prickly pear cactus. The park also contains extensive areas of **wet meadows** in the Bechler region and along the upper Yellowstone River. Willows are common in these moist areas, and cottonwoods line **riparian** areas. Yellowstone's geyser basins have given rise to plants that are specially adapted to heat and disturbance, including a species of grass (Ross' bentgrass) that grows where the temperature is 100°F just an inch below the surface!

Wildlife

Yellowstone is world-famous for its wildlife and provides a marvelous natural setting in which to view bison, elk, moose, wolves, coyotes, pronghorn antelope, bighorn sheep, and other critters. One of the easiest ways to find wildlife is simply by watching for the brake lights, the cars pulled half off the road, and the cameras all pointed in one direction. Inevitably, you'll find an elk or a bison placidly munching away, trying to remain oblivious to the chaos that surrounds it. Be sure to bring binoculars for your trip to Yellowstone. A spotting scope is also helpful in searching for distant bears and wolves.

FINDING WILDLIFE

The Park Service has a free brochure showing where you're most likely to see wildlife in Yellowstone. Pick one up at any visitors center. During summer, the best wildlife-viewing hours are early in the morning and in the late afternoon to early evening.

The park contains some 60 species of resident mammals, ranging from shrews and bats to bison and grizzlies. In addition, 309 species of birds have been recorded, along with 18 species of fish (five of which are nonnative), four amphibians, and six reptiles. The only poisonous animal is the prairie rattlesnake, found at low elevations in the northern end of Yellowstone. Oh yes, countless insect species live here, too. Some Yellowstone critters are more friendly than others, most notably the mosquitoes that show up in large numbers early in the summer. By mid-August they're much less of a hassle, and winter visitors will have no problems at all.

Safety

Because of the constant parade of visitors and the lack of hunting, many of Yellowstone's animals appear to almost ignore the presence of people, and it isn't uncommon to see visitors approach an animal without respecting its need for space. Although they may appear tame, Yellowstone's animals really are wild, and attacks are not uncommon. Those quiet bison can suddenly erupt with an enormous ferocity if provoked by photographers who come too close. Between 1983 and 1994, four people were killed by bison in Yellowstone and Grand Teton National Parks. **Stay at least 25 yards away from bison and elk and at least 100 yards away from bears.** Do not under any circumstances feed the park's animals. This creates an unnatural dependency, is unhealthy for the animal, and may even lead to its death.

Wildlife Tours

Several nonprofits, companies, and individuals guide wildlife tours in the park. Of particular note is the nonprofit **Yellowstone Association Institute,** 307/344-2294, www.yellowstone association.org, whose naturalists lead two- to five-day programs that blend education,

recreation, and lodging. They also can act as private guides. Tours from **Wildlife Expeditions,** 307/733-2623 or 888/945-3567, www .tetonscience.org/wildlife, are run by guides from the Teton Science School, another highly respected nonprofit.

Tory and Meredith Taylor, 307/455-2161, provide personalized wildlife package tours and have a good reputation. Other wildlife guiding companies include **Callowishus Park Touring Company,** 307/733-9521, www.callowishus .com; **Jackson's Hole Adventure,** 307/654-7849 or 800/392-3165, www.jacksonholeadventure .com; **Upstream Anglers and Outdoor Adventures,** 307/739-9443 or 800/642-8979, www.up-streamanglers.com; and **Yellowstone Country Adventures,** 406/994-0422, www.yellowstone country-adventures.com. Get a complete list of licensed tour operators from the Park Service at 307/344-7381, www.nps.gov/yell.

BIRDS

Trumpeter swans—beautiful white birds with seven-foot wingspans—are a fairly common sight in Yellowstone, particularly on the Madison and Yellowstone Rivers and on Yellowstone Lake. Many trumpeter swans winter in hot spring areas. These are some of the largest birds in America, weighing 20–30 pounds. Another large white bird here is the ungainly looking and bulbous-billed **white pelican,** a common sight on Yellowstone Lake and near Fishing Bridge. More than 350 pairs of pelicans nest on the Molly Islands in Yellowstone Lake; this is one of the largest white-pelican breeding colonies in the Rockies. **Bald eagles**—America's national bird—and **ospreys** have managed comebacks in recent years and are frequently seen along the Yellowstone River and above Yellowstone Lake. Look for **golden eagles** flying over the open grasslands of Lamar Valley or Hayden Valley.

KILLING THE PREDATORS

Wildlife has always been one of the big drawing cards at Yellowstone, and early on there were

constant charges of mass slaughter by poachers and market hunters. It was not until 1894 that Congress passed the Lacey Act, finally making it illegal to hunt within the park. Unfortunately, predators such as wolves, coyotes, mountain lions, and wolverines were regarded as despoilers of the elk, deer, and moose and became fair targets for poisoning and shooting by early park managers. (This happened throughout the West, not just in the park.) The campaign proved all too successful, devastating the wolf and mountain lion populations. In recent years, wolves have returned in a spectacular way, although mountain lion numbers remain low.

CONTROVERSY ON THE NORTHERN RANGE

A recurring area of strife in Yellowstone has been the suggestion that elk and bison are overgrazing and destroying the Lamar and Yellowstone River basins, an area known as the northern range. The issue periodically flares up, fed in part by the efforts of Montana ranchers and others who suffer from bison and elk that migrate out of Yellowstone onto their land each winter. They—and some researchers—believe that the Park Service has allowed too many animals to survive and that overgrazing is damaging the land. Most research, however, points in the opposite direction—that the land is not overgrazed, and that ecological processes are working fine in a system termed "natural regulation." The populations of elk and bison fluctuate over time; some years numbers are up, and other years they drop because of harsh winters, predation, hunting outside the park, or other factors.

BEARS

During Yellowstone's early years, bears were commonly viewed as either pets or nuisances. Cubs were tethered to poles in front of the hotels, and other bears fed on the garbage piles that grew up around the camps and hotels. Older folks still recall the bear-feeding grounds at the garbage dumps, where visitors might see 50 bears pawing through the refuse. The feeding shows continued until 1941, but it wasn't until 1970 that the park's open-pit dumps were finally sealed off and the garbage cans bear-proofed. Closure of the dumps helped create confrontations between "garbage bears" and humans; the bears nearly always lost. Between 1970 and 1972, dozens of grizzlies died in showdowns with humans in the park or surrounding areas. Fortunately, careful management in the intervening years has helped the population rebound. Today there are believed to be at least 400 grizzlies in the Greater Yellowstone Ecosystem, and their numbers have been increasing fairly steadily since the 1980s. (Some scientists believe there are more than 600 grizzlies.)

One unusual aspect of the Yellowstone grizzlies was just discovered in recent years: the importance of moths as a food source in the grizzly diet. Millions of army cutworm moths congregate on Yellowstone's high alpine slopes during summer, where they feed on nectar from the abundant flowers. Bears are attracted to this food source because of the insect's abundance and high fat content. Researchers have sometimes seen two dozen bears feeding on a single slope!

Bear Viewing

Both black and grizzly bears are found throughout Yellowstone, but the days of bear jams along the park roads are long past because rangers actively work to prevent bears from becoming habituated to people. Most bears have returned to their more natural ways of living, although problems still crop up with individuals wandering through campgrounds in search of food. You're more likely to encounter a bear in the backcountry areas, and some places are closed to hiking for extended periods each year for this reason. The best places to watch for grizzlies along the road system are in the Hayden and Lamar Valleys, near Mt. Washburn, and in the Antelope Creek drainage (just south of Tower Fall).

Safety in grizzly country is always a concern, but statistically you are considerably more likely to be hurt in a traffic accident than to be mauled by a bear. There were just 22 bear-caused injuries in the park between 1980 and 1997—one injury for every 2.1 million visitors! Most of these injuries took place in backcountry areas and involved female bears with cubs or yearlings, and nearly all attacks took place following a surprise encounter with a bear. Three people were killed by Yellowstone bears in the last three decades of the 20th century, the most recent being a 1986 fatality caused when a photographer approached an adult female grizzly too closely. For details on staying safe around bears, see the section Safety in Bear Country in the On the Road chapter.

Protecting the Bears

The **Yellowstone Grizzly Foundation,** 307/734-8643, www.yellowstonegrizzly.com, is an excellent nonprofit organization dedicated to conserving grizzlies within the Greater Yellowstone Ecosystem. Established by Steve and Marilynn French—who have been studying grizzly bears since 1983—the foundation emphasizes nonintrusive observations. One of their groundbreaking projects involved collecting hair samples as bears crawled under barbed wire. DNA analysis of these hairs led to a new understanding of how grizzly bears in Yellowstone are related to other bears. It turns out that more than 90 percent of Yellowstone grizzlies originated from the same maternal lineage, a fact that may have important ramifications for management. The research also showed that the grizzlies of Yellowstone differ markedly from Alaskan grizzlies such as those found at the wildlife park in West Yellowstone.

The **Sierra Club** is also deeply involved in the politics of grizzly bear management around the park. For their take on the issues, see www.grizzly.sierraclub.org.

BIGHORN SHEEP

These stocky mountain dwellers are named for the massive curling horns of the males (rams) and can be seen in several parts of Yellowstone. They have a tan-colored coat with a white rump patch. Bighorns were once abundant throughout the western United States, and early trappers in the mountains east of Yellowstone reported finding thousands of sheep in and around the pre-

sent-day park. They were also an important source of food for the Sheepeater Indians who lived in Yellowstone before the arrival of whites. Bighorn sheep were virtually wiped out by hunters in the late 19th century, and domestic sheep overran their lands and brought deadly diseases. Within a few decades, the millions of sheep that had roamed the West were reduced to a few hundred survivors.

Both the rams and ewes (females) have horns that remain for life, but only the rams get the massive curl for which bighorn sheep are known. Rams are 125–275 pounds in size, with ewes 75–150 pounds. During the mating season in November and December you're likely to see the original head-bangers in action as rams clash to establish dominance. The clashes can be surprisingly violent, and to protect the brain, bighorns have a double cranium that absorbs much of the shock. Those with the larger horns are typically the dominant bighorns and the primary breeders. The young lambs are born in May and June. In summer the sexes separate, with the ewes and lambs remaining lower while the bachelor herds climb higher into the mountains. Bighorns use their ability to climb steep and rocky terrain as protection from predators such as coyotes, wolves, and mountain lions. Winter often finds bighorns in mixed herds at lower elevations. Around 250 bighorns live within Yellowstone National Park, with much larger populations in the surrounding national forests.

Finding Bighorns

Look for bighorn sheep on cliffs in the Gardner River Canyon between Mammoth Hot Springs and the town of Gardiner. Ewes and lambs are also frequently seen just off the road on Dunraven Pass north of Canyon, and day-hikers commonly encounter rams up-close on the slopes of Mt. Washburn. Another place where bighorns may be seen is along Specimen Ridge.

BISON

Before their virtual annihilation in the 19th century, around 60 million bison were spread across America. When Yellowstone was established in

1872, hundreds of mountain bison (also called wood bison) still ranged across this high plateau. Sport and meat hunting—legal until 1894—and later poaching reduced the population so that by 1902 perhaps fewer than 25 remained. That year, 21 plains bison were brought in from private ranches in Montana and Texas to help restore the Yellowstone herd, and today there are approximately 2,500 in the park, making this the largest free-ranging herd of bison anywhere on earth. Unfortunately, interbreeding between the mountain and plains bison means that the animals in Yellowstone today are genetically different from the original inhabitants.

Bison are typically found in open country throughout the park, including Hayden, Lamar, and Pelican Valleys, along with the Firehole River Basin (including Old Faithful). A favorite time to see bison in Yellowstone is late May, just after the new calves have been born. The calves' antics are always good for laughs. Be sure to use caution around bison; many people have been gored when they've come too close. Always stay at least 25 yards away, preferably farther.

Cattle Versus Bison

Bison are carriers of brucellosis, a disease that causes cows to abort calves and is the source of undulant fever in humans. Brucellosis can be spread when other animals lick a contaminated fetus or birthing material, a situation that is unlikely given the timing of bison movements. In 1985, Yellowstone's bison began wandering north into the Gardiner area for the winter. Montana and Wyoming are certified as "brucellosis-free" states, and although there is absolutely no evidence that wild bison have ever transmitted the disease to cattle, ranchers feared that the bison might threaten Montana's brucellosis-free status. If cattle become infected with brucellosis, ranchers might be prohibited from shipping livestock out of state.

A highly controversial "hunt" during the late 1980s let hunters shoot bison when they wandered outside the park. After a public outcry, the job was turned over to the Montana state Division of Livestock (DOL), an agency accustomed to dealing with cattle, not wildlife. Things came to a head in the heavy-snow winter of 1996–1997 when nearly 1,100 Yellowstone bison were sent to slaughter, cutting the park bison herd by one-third. It was one of the largest killings of bison anywhere since their destruction on the Great Plains in the 1880s. Smaller numbers of bison have been killed in recent winters, although it topped 200 in 2002 (out of a population now numbering 4,000).

Today, the Park Service, Montana DOL, and U.S. Forest Service operate under a controversial bison management plan that attempts to simultaneously maintain a free-ranging bison population while reducing the risk of transmission of brucellosis to cattle. Under this plan, some bison are tolerated on outside lands when cattle aren't present, and if the population continues to be high, others can be captured in pens and slaughtered when they wander outside the park, even if they haven't been tested for brucellosis. It's not a pleasant situation, especially for a national park that was established in part to help protect wild bison. Even a Yellowstone publication admits, "Many park visitors are confused about why the National Park Service is a partner in a plan that can result in killing bison, a natural resource the National Park Service goes to great lengths to protect within the boundaries of the park and an animal so representative of the agency's successful protection of wildlife that it is prominently featured on the National Park Service's familiar 'arrowhead' logo." You can find much more about this issue on the Yellowstone National Park website, www.nps.gov/yell.

Ironically, Yellowstone's far more numerous elk also carry brucellosis, and during 2002, elk infected an Idaho cattle herd with the disease, leading to their destruction. Although elk migrate each fall out from Yellowstone, you won't hear Montana authorities talking about slaughtering all of the elk that wander across the park's borders! The state of Wyoming has managed to keep its brucellosis-free status despite the presence of cattle, bison, and elk in Jackson Hole. There, most ranchers vaccinate their cattle and work with the Park Service to keep bison and elk separate from livestock. Why won't it work in Montana? The answer probably has far more to do with Montana politics than biology.

Buffalo Field Campaign is a nonprofit environmental group that has been at loggerheads with the Park Service and DOL over bison management for years. You may meet their outspoken activists handing out literature at Old Faithful. Get their take on the issue at www.wildrockies.org/buffalo.

COYOTES

Although wolves get the media attention, visitors to Yellowstone are probably more likely to see another native of the dog family: the coyote. Keep your eyes open for coyotes anywhere in Yellowstone but especially in open grassy areas where they are more easily spotted. During summer, they're often seen in small packs or alone as they hunt small mammals such as mice, voles, and pocket gophers. At other times of the year they prey on larger animals, including the calves of elk and pronghorn antelope, and scavenge carrion.

Differentiating coyotes from wolves can be a bit tricky, especially from a distance without binoculars. Coyotes are considerably smaller animals; adult male coyotes weigh around 30 pounds, whereas wolves are far more massive, with many weighing 100 pounds or more. The wolf has a large head, short and rounded ears, and a broad and blocky muzzle, whereas the coyote has a small head, large and pointy ears, and a narrow, pointy nose. From a distance coyotes are more delicate in appearance, with smaller feet and thin legs.

The coyotes within Yellowstone generally live in packs containing six or seven animals led by a dominant pair called the alpha male and female. Most packs have a long family lineage and a well-defined territory; some coyote packs have been using the same denning areas for at least 50 years! The average coyote lives around six years. The alphas mate in early February, and pups are born in early April. Other members of the pack guard the den from wolves and other predators and regurgitate food to feed the pups.

Top Dog No More

Before the reintroduction of wolves, coyotes were the big dogs (so to speak) in northern Yellowstone, and the primary predators of elk calves, killing about 1,200 each year. Wolves occupy a similar ecological niche to coyotes, and their return has led to a 50 percent reduction in coyote numbers in northern Yellowstone. Some of this decrease comes from outright killing of coyotes by the far larger wolves, particularly alpha coyotes. The ever-resourceful coyotes have responded by banding together in larger packs, denning in rocky areas, becoming more wary, and staying on the margins of wolf territories. Despite competition, coyotes remain common and are certainly in no danger of being displaced from Yellowstone; after all, both species were here for thousands of years before the extermination of wolves in the 20th century. Good places to look for coyotes are in the Blacktail Plateau area and Lamar Valley, along with the Upper and Lower Geyser Basins near Old Faithful.

Deer

Mule deer (also known as black-tailed deer) are common in many parts of Yellowstone during summer, but most migrate to lower elevations when winter comes. They are typically found in open areas containing sagebrush or grass. Mule deer are named for their long mulelike ears. They also have black-tipped tails and a peculiar way of pogoing away when frightened. Adult males (bucks) grow antlers each summer, and mating season arrives in November and December. Fawns are born in May or June.

The smaller **white-tailed deer** are occasionally seen within Yellowstone but are far less common. You are most likely to find them along rivers or in brushy areas at low elevations, such as around Mammoth Hot Springs or in Lamar Valley. Other places to watch for them are along Yellowstone Lake and in the Upper Geyser Basin.

Elk

One animal virtually every visitor to Yellowstone sees is elk. About 30,000 of these regal animals summer in the park, and approximately 15,000 remain through the winter, primarily on the north end of Yellowstone. In summer, look for elk in Mammoth Hot Springs, Elk Park, and Gibbon Meadows, but you're certain to also see them

Elk relax on the terraces at Mammoth Hot Springs.

© DON PITCHER

elsewhere in Yellowstone. Bull elk can top 700 pounds, whereas the cows (females) weigh around 500–525 pounds, making elk the second-largest members of the deer family after moose. Each summer, adult bulls grow massive antlers that can weigh 30 pounds or more, which prove useful in the fall mating season as bulls spar with each other. Dominant bulls herd females into harems during the rut and may sometimes control 25 or so cows, mating with those that come into estrus and battling with rivals intent on taking over their harems. The bugling of bull elk is a common autumn sound in Yellowstone, as anyone who visits Mammoth Hot Springs at that time of year can attest. It's a strange sound that starts out low, followed by a trumpetlike call and then a series of odd grunts. Approximately 90 percent of the elk cows become pregnant each year.

The mating season ends by mid- to late November, and winter snows push the elk to lower elevations on the north side of Yellowstone or out of the park into surrounding areas. With the arrival of spring, bulls lose their antlers, and elk start moving back toward the high country.

Calves are born in late May or early June (sometimes during the migration) and weigh 25–40 pounds at birth. Elk—particularly young calves—are an important food source for predators in Yellowstone; almost one-third of the calves are killed each year by wolves, grizzly and black bears, coyotes, and golden eagles.

MOOSE

The largest members of the deer family, moose are typically seen eating willow bushes in riparian areas inside Yellowstone National Park. During winter, these moose migrate into high-elevation forests where the snow isn't as deep (tree branches hold the snow) or as crusty as in the open. In these forests they browse on subalpine fir and Douglas fir. The fires of 1988 burned through many of these forests, and the loss of cover has hurt the Yellowstone moose population. The best places to look for moose are Hayden Valley, around Yellowstone Lake, the Willow Park area north of Norris, the southwestern corner along the Bechler and Falls Rivers, and along the Gallatin, Lamar, and Lewis River drainages.

PRONGHORN ANTELOPE

These speedy and colorful ungulates (hoofed mammals) are common sights on the plains of Wyoming, but most of Yellowstone doesn't provide adequate habitat for them. Pronghorn antelope are only found in sagebrush and grassy areas on the northern end of the park from Lamar Valley to the Gardiner area. Their populations declined sharply in the 1990s within the park, and as of 2000 pronghorn numbered around 200. Coyotes and other predators take many newborn fawns each spring and may be a significant factor in the decline, combined with several other factors such as inbreeding caused by the small population; changes in vegetation; loss of habitat to development in their Paradise Valley wintering area north of the park; increasing numbers of fences across their range; and hunting.

WOLVES

The wolves are back! One of the most exciting developments for visitors to Yellowstone has been the reintroduction of wolves to the park, making this one of the few places in the Lower 48 where they can be viewed in the wild. Wolves once ranged across nearly all of North America, but white settlers regarded them—along with mountain lions, grizzly bears, and coyotes—as threats to livestock and unwanted predators on game animals. Even in Yellowstone, wolves were hunted and poisoned by both the army and the Park Service. By 1940, the wolf was probably gone from the park, although a few lone animals turned up briefly again in the early 1970s.

In the United States, until 1995 wolves could only be found in Alaska, in northern Minnesota, and in Isle Royale and Glacier National Parks. With the more enlightened public attitude evident in recent years, ecologists and conservationists began pushing for the reintroduction of wolves to Yellowstone, considered one of the few remaining areas in the Lower 48 that could support a viable wolf population.

The proposal to return wolves to Yellowstone set off a firestorm from ranchers (with ardent support from Wyoming's Republican senators), who feared that the wolves would wander outside the park to destroy sheep and cattle. Opponents said hundreds of livestock would be killed each year around the park and that the reintroduction cost might reach $1.8 million per wolf, a figure that proved grossly inflated. Despite these dire predictions, the U.S. Fish & Wildlife Service began reintroducing wolves to Yellowstone in 1995, initially releasing 14 gray wolves that had been captured in British Columbia. Additional wolves were set free the following spring. During subsequent years things have gone far better than anyone had predicted. By 2002, biologists estimated that 24 groups of wolves totaling 216 individuals inhabited the Greater Yellowstone Ecosystem from north of Yellowstone to the Pinedale area on the south and eastward into Shoshone National Forest. Because of the successful reintroduction, it's only a matter of time until wolves are removed from the endangered species list (which will inevitably create still more controversy and lawsuits).

Finding Wolves

The return of the wolf to Yellowstone has created a buzz of excitement as visitors gather to watch for them in the distance. The best place to look is the open terrain of Lamar Valley, where the **Druid Peak Pack** has taken up residence and are visible at many times of the year. Visit early in the morning or near dusk to increase your odds of seeing them. You may well hear their plaintive cry from your campground late at night, particularly at Slough Creek or Pebble Creek campgrounds. Binoculars or spotting scopes are helpful for roadside wolf watching. Do not follow the wolves around because this may disturb them and affect their survival. Denning activity typically takes place early April to early May, with active denning areas closed to humans; check with the Park Service for currently closed areas.

Wolves are the largest members of the canids (dog family), with males averaging 70–120 pounds and stretching up to six feet long from head to tail. They are much more massive than coyotes, although the two are sometimes confused. Wolves live in packs of two to eight, led by an alpha male and female, and establish territories to exclude other wolf packs. Most pack members are from an extended family, but they may include outside members. The alphas are the only ones that generally mate, and a litter of six or so pups is born in early spring. Once they are weaned, the pack feeds pups regurgitated meat until they are large enough to join the hunt. Wolves hunt primarily in the evening and morning hours when their prey—elk, deer, moose, bison, and pronghorn—are feeding.

The park website, www.nps.gov/yell, has additional details on wolves, or visit www.wolf tracker.com (not affiliated with the Park Service).

Park History

Yellowstone National Park has a rich and fascinating history that reaches back through thousands of years of settlement. The most thorough source for history is *The Yellowstone Story* (University Press of Colorado, www.upcolorado.com), an excellent two-volume set by former park historian Aubrey L. Haines. For an engaging and personal journey through the past, read *Searching for Yellowstone* by Paul Schullery (Houghton Mifflin, www.hmco.com).

SHEEPEATER INDIANS

The last major glaciation ended around 15,000 years ago, and the first peoples may have reached Yellowstone while the ice was still retreating. There is good evidence that the country was occupied for at least 10,000 years, although the tribes apparently changed over time. By the mid-19th century, the country was surrounded by Blackfeet to the north, Crow to the east, and Shoshone and Bannock to the south and west. These tribes all traveled through and hunted in Yellowstone, building temporary shelters, called *wickiups,* made of aspen poles covered with pine boughs; a few of these still exist in the park. The primary inhabitants of this high plateau were the Sheepeater Indians, who may have been here for more than 2,000 years. Of Shoshone stock, the Sheepeaters hunted bighorn sheep (hence the name) and made bows from the sheep horns, but their diet also included other animals, fish, roots, and berries. Because they did not have horses, the Sheepeaters used dog-pulled travois to carry their few possessions from camp to camp. Summers were spent in high alpine meadows and along passes, where they hunted migrating game animals or gathered roots and berries. They wintered in protected canyons.

The Sheepeaters were smaller than other Indians and have achieved an aura of mystery because so little is known of their way of living. Yellowstone was at the heart of their territory, but with the arrival of whites came devastating diseases, particularly smallpox. The survivors joined their Shoshone brothers on the Wind River Reservation or the Bannock Reservation in Idaho. The last of the tribe left Yellowstone in the 1870s.

FUR TRAPPERS

The word "Yellowstone" appears to have come from the Minnetaree Indians, who called the river "Mi tse a-da-zi," a word French-Canadian trappers translated into "Rive des Roche Jaunes"—literally, "Yellow Rock River." The Indians apparently called it this because of the yellowish bluffs along the river near Billings, Montana (not because of the colorful Grand Canyon of the Yellowstone). The term "Yellow Stone" was first used on a map made in 1797. When the Lewis and Clark Expedition traveled through the country north of Yellowstone in 1805–1806, the Indians told them tales of this mysterious place: "There is frequently heard a loud noise like thunder, which makes the earth tremble, they state that they seldom go there because children Cannot sleep—and Conceive it possessed of spirits, who were adverse that men Should be near them." (This certainly was not the attitude of all the native peoples, for the park had long been inhabited.) The first white man to come through Yellowstone is believed to be John Colter, a former member of the Lewis and Clark Expedition who wandered through the region in the winter of 1807–1808. A map based on Colter's recollections shows Yellowstone Lake ("Eustis Lake"), along with an area of "Hot Spring Brimstone."

YELLOWSTONE

As fur trappers spread through the Rockies in the 1820s and '30s, many discovered the geysers and hot springs of Yellowstone, and stories quickly spread around the rendezvous fires. The word of the trappers was passed on to later settlers and explorers but not entirely believed. After all, mountain man Jim Bridger described not just petrified trees, but petrified birds singing petrified songs! His tales of a river that "ran so fast that it became hot on the bottom" could well have referred to the Firehole River. When Bridger tried to lead a party of military explorers into Yellowstone, they were stymied by deep snows. Still, word gradually got out that something very strange could be found in this part of the mountains. Little remains today from the mountain-man era, although in 1880 the letters "J.O.R. Aug. 19, 1819" were found carved in a tree near the Upper Falls of the Yellowstone, and later a cache of iron beaver traps similar to those used by the Hudson's Bay Company was discovered near Obsidian Cliff.

EXPEDITIONS

National attention finally came to Yellowstone with a series of three expeditions to check out the wild claims of local prospectors. In 1869, David E. Folsom, Charles W. Cook, and William Peterson headed south from Bozeman, finding the Grand Canyon, Yellowstone Lake, and the geyser basins. When a friend pressured them to submit a description of their travels for publication, the *New York Tribune* refused to publish it, noting that the paper "had a reputation that they could not risk with such unreliable material."

The adventures of this first expedition led another group of explorers into Yellowstone the following year, but this time money was the motive. Jay Cooke's Northern Pacific Railroad needed investors for a planned route across Montana. A good public-relations campaign was the first step, and it happened to coincide with the visit of a former Montana tax collector named Nathaniel P. Langford, who had heard of the discoveries of Folsom, Cook, and Peterson. The party of 19 soldiers and civilians, including Langford, headed out in August of 1870 under Gen. Henry D. Washburn. They were thrilled by what they dis-

> ## FIREHOLE RIVER AREA, 1839
>
> *At this place there is also large numbers of hot Springs some of which have formed cones of limestone 20 feet high of a Snowy whiteness which make a splendid appearance standing among the ever green pines Some of the lower peaks are very serviceable to the hunter in preparing his dinner when hungry for here his kettle is always ready and boiling his meat being suspended in the water by a string is soon prepared for his meal without further trouble. . . .*
> *Standing upon an eminence and superficially viewing these natural monuments one is half inclined to believe himself in the neighborhood of the ruins of some ancients City whose temples had been constructed of the whitest marble.*
>
> —*mountain man Osborne Russell*

covered and proceeded to give the geysers names—Old Faithful, Castle, Giant, Grotto, Giantess—which became permanently attached to the features. The joy of the trip was marred when one man—Truman Everts—became separated from the others and then lost his horse. He was not found until 37 days later, by which time he weighed just 50 pounds. His rescuer did not even recognize him as human. Amazingly, Everts survived and recovered.

With the return of the Washburn Expedition, national newspapers and magazines finally began to pay attention to Yellowstone, and Langford began lecturing in the East on what they had found. One of those listening was Dr. Ferdinand V. Hayden, director of the U.S. Geological Survey. Hayden asked Congress to fund an official investigation. With the help of Representatives James G. Blaine (coincidentally a supporter of the Northern Pacific Railroad) and conservationist Henry M. Dawes, Congress appropriated $40,000 for an exploration of "the sources of the Missouri and Yellowstone Rivers." Thus began the most famous and influential trip into Yellowstone—the 1871

ESTABLISHING THE PARK

When Hayden returned to Washington to prepare his report, he found a letter from railroad promoter Jay Cooke. In the letter, Cooke proposed that "Congress pass a bill reserving the Great Geyser Basin as a public park forever—just as it has reserved that far inferior wonder the Yosemite valley and big trees." (Abraham Lincoln had established Yosemite earlier as a state park.) In an amazingly short time, a bill was introduced to set aside the land, and Hayden rushed to arrange a display in the Capitol rotunda of geological specimens, sketches by Moran, and photos by Jackson. The bill easily passed both houses of Congress and was signed into law on March 1, 1872, by Pres. Ulysses S. Grant. The first national park had come into existence, a culmination not just of the discoveries in Yellowstone but also of a growing appreciation for preserving the wonders of the natural world.

Congress saw no need to set aside money for this new creation because it seemed to be doing fine already. Besides, it was thought that Jay Cooke's new railroad would soon arrive, making it easy for thousands of vacationers to explore Yellowstone. In turn, concessioners would build roads and hotels and pay the government franchise fees. The park was placed under the control of the Secretary of the Interior, with Nathaniel P. Langford as its unpaid superintendent. Meanwhile, the planned railroad fizzled when Jay Cooke & Co. declared bankruptcy, precipitating the panic of 1873.

ROADS AND RAILROADS

Because of the difficult access, fewer than 500 people visited in each of Yellowstone's first few years as a park, most to soak in tubs at Mammoth Hot Springs. Not a few decided to take home souvenirs, bringing pickaxes and shovels for that purpose. Meanwhile, hunters—including some working for the Mammoth Hotel—began

Hayden Expedition. The troop included 34 men, an escort of cavalry, painter Thomas Moran, and photographer William H. Jackson.

shooting the park's abundant game. Two brothers who had a ranch just north of the park killed 2,000 elk in a single year. Superintendent Langford did little to stop the slaughter and only bothered to visit the park twice. Finally, in 1877, the Secretary of the Interior fired him, putting Philetus W. Norris in charge instead. Norris proved a good choice, despite a knack for applying his name to everything in sight. (Most of his attempts at immortality have been replaced by other titles, but Norris Geyser Basin, Norris Road, and even the town of Norris, Michigan, remain.)

Norris oversaw construction of the first major road in Yellowstone, a rough 60-mile route built in just 30 days to connect Upper Geyser Basin with Mammoth and the western entrance. All of this was precipitated by the raids of the Nez Perce Indians earlier that summer and threats that the Bannock Indians would strike next. In addition, Norris began, but never completed, the Queen's Laundry, a bathhouse that is considered the first government building built for the public in any national park. The log walls are still visible in a meadow near Lower Geyser Basin.

By 1882, Norris had managed to alienate the company that helped found the park, the Northern Pacific Railroad. The company announced plans to build a railroad line to the geysers and construct a large hotel, "being assured by the Government of a monopoly therein." Norris's opposition led to his being fired and replaced by railroad man Patrick H. Conger. Soon, however, the scheme began to unravel. The Yellowstone Park Improvement Company—whose vice-president happened to be construction superintendent for the Northern Pacific's branch line into Gardiner—had planned not just a lodging monopoly but also a monopoly on all transportation, timber rights, and ranching privileges in the park. Later it was discovered that the company had contracted for 20,000 pounds of venison (killed in the park) to feed the construction crews. As one newspaper writer commented, "It is a 'Park Improvement Company' doing this, and I suppose they consider it an improvement to rid the park, as far as possible, of game."

Finally, in 1884 Congress acted by limiting the land that could be leased—thus effectively ending

THE NEZ PERCE WAR

One of the saddest episodes in the history of Yellowstone took place in 1877 and involved the Nez Perce Indians of Oregon's Wallowa Valley. When the government tried to force the people of Chief White Bird and Chief Joseph onto an Idaho reservation so that white ranchers could have their lands, the Indians stubbornly refused. A few drunken young Indians killed four whites, and subsequent raids led to the deaths of at least 14 more. The army retaliated but was turned back by the Nez Perce. Rather than face government reinforcements, more than 1,000 Nez Perce began an 1,800-mile flight in a desperate bid to reach Canada. A series of running battles followed as the Indians managed to confound the inept army using their geographic knowledge and battle skills. The Nez Perce entered Yellowstone from the west, and a few hotheads immediately attacked vacationing tourists and prospectors. Two whites were killed in the park, others were kidnapped, and another man nearly died from his wounds.

The Nez Perce exited Yellowstone two weeks after they arrived, narrowly missing an encounter with their implacable foe, Gen. William T. Sherman, who just happened to be vacationing in Yellowstone at the time. East of the park, the Indians plotted a masterful escape from two columns of army forces, feinting a move down the Shoshone River and then heading north along a route that left their pursuers gasping in amazement—straight up the narrow Clarks Fork Canyon, "where rocks on each side came so near together that two horses abreast could hardly pass." Finally, less than 40 miles from the international border with Canada, the army caught up with the Nez Perce, and after a fierce battle the tribe was forced to surrender (although 300 did make good their escape).

Chief Joseph's haunting words still echo through the years: "Hear me, my chiefs, I am tired; my heart is sick and sad. From where the sun now stands, I will fight no more forever." Despite promises that they would be allowed to return home, the Nez Perce were hustled onto reservations in Oklahoma and Washington while whites remained on their ancestral lands. Chief Joseph spent the rest of his life on Washington's Colville Reservation and died in 1904, reportedly of a broken heart. Yellowstone's Nez Perce Creek, which feeds the Firehole River, is named for this desperate bid for freedom.

---

the railroad's plans—and adding funding to hire 10 assistants to patrol Yellowstone. Unfortunately, they neglected to include any penalties for the poachers and despoilers other than expulsion, so even the few assistants who did decent work found the culprits quickly returning. The problems were myriad. Cooke City miners were fishing with spears, seine nets, and even dynamite. Guides were throwing rocks into the geysers, squatters had ensconced themselves on prime land in Lamar Valley, and visitors were leaving fires unattended and breaking off specimens from the geysers.

Superintendent Conger was later replaced by Robert E. Carpenter, a man about whom historian Hiram Chittenden noted, "In his opinion, the Park was created to be an instrument of profit to those who were shrewd enough to grasp the opportunity." Carpenter lobbied Congress to remove lands from the park so that the Northern Pacific could construct a railroad along the Yellowstone and Lamar Rivers to Cooke City. In return, friends promised to locate claims in his name along the route so that he too might profit from the venture. The landgrab fell apart when the Senate vetoed the move, and Carpenter was summarily removed from office. Not long thereafter, Congress flatly refused to fund the civilian administration of Yellowstone, and the Secretary of the Interior was forced to request the aid of the military in 1886. It proved a fortuitous step.

THE ARMY YEARS

The U.S. Army finally brought a semblance of order to Yellowstone, eliminating the political appointees who viewed the park as a place to get rich. That first year, a temporary fort—Camp Sheridan—was thrown up and a troop of soldiers arrived, but it wasn't until 1891 that work began on a permanent Fort Yellowstone at Mammoth. By

1904, the fort consisted of some 26 buildings housing 120 men. The soldiers had clear objectives—protecting wildlife (or at least bison and elk) from poachers, fighting fires, stopping vandalism, and generally achieving order out of chaos. These goals were accomplished with a fervor that gained widespread respect, and in a way that would later influence the organization of the National Park Service. One of the major accomplishments of the soldiers was completion of the Grand Loop Road, which passes most of Yellowstone's attractions. The basic pattern was completed by 1905.

Fort Yellowstone was a favorite station for soldiers, and it was considered something of an honor to be sent to such a setting. The life of the soldiers was not always easy, however, and some died in the bitter winters or in accidents. A series of 16 soldier stations—actually little more than large cabins—was established around the park, and each was manned year-round, usually by four soldiers.

Before the arrival of cars, many visitors to Yellowstone were wealthy people from the East Coast or Europe intent on doing the grand tour of the West. The railroads (Northern Pacific to the north, Union Pacific to the west, and the Burlington to the east) deposited them near park borders, where they were met by carriages, Tallyhos (26-passenger stagecoaches), and surreys. In 1915, some 3,000 horses were in use within the park! Most "dudes" paid approximately $50 for a six-day tour that included transportation, meals, and lodging at the hotels. They paid another $2.50 for the privilege of sailing across Yellowstone Lake on the steamship *Zillah*. By contrast, another group, the "sagebrushers," came to Yellowstone in smaller numbers, arriving in their own wagons or hiring a coach to transport them between the "Wylie Way" campgrounds. These seasonal tent camps were scattered around the park, providing an inexpensive way to see the sights—just $35 for a seven-day tour. Even as early as 1908, Yellowstone was being seen by 18,000 visitors per year.

The Northern Pacific was still intent on carving Yellowstone into a moneymaking resort, even going so far as to propose an electric railroad, to be powered by a dam at the falls of the Yellowstone River. Fortunately, equally powerful forces—notably Gen. Philip Sheridan and naturalist Joseph Bird Grinnell—saw through their designs and thwarted each attempt to bring railroads into Yellowstone. Still, the Northern Pacific's interests were represented by its indirect control of many of Yellowstone's hotels, stagecoaches, wagons, and other vehicles used to transport tourists.

All of this changed when the first car was allowed through the gate on August 1, 1915. (Entrance fees were a surprisingly stiff $5 for single-seat vehicles and $7.50 for five-passenger cars.) Almost immediately, it became clear that horses and cars could not mix, and motor buses replaced the old coaches. From then on, the park would be increasingly a place for "autoists." Interestingly, within a year the park would come under the jurisdiction of the newly created National Park Service.

THE PARK SERVICE TAKES OVER

After years of army control, supporters of a separate National Park Service finally had their way in 1916. The congressional act created a dual role for the new park system: to "conserve the scenery" and to "provide for the enjoyment of the same," a contradictory mandate that would later lead to all sorts of conflicts. The first couple of years were tenuous, as management flip-flopped between the army and civilians; the final changeover came in 1918 and ended three decades of military supervision. The management of Yellowstone fell on the shoulders of two men, Horace M. Albright and his mentor, Stephen Mather, both of whom had been heavily involved in lobbying to create the new agency. Mather became the Park Service's first director, while Albright served as superintendent at Yellowstone and later stepped into Mather's shoes to head the agency.

Albright quickly upgraded facilities to meet the influx of motorists who demanded more camping facilities but also cabins, lodges, cafeterias, and bathhouses. Forty-six camps of one sort or another were constructed (only 12 survive today), fulfilling Albright's dream of "a motorist's paradise." The focus of the new Park Service was clearly visitation rather than preservation. Albright assembled a first-rate force of park rangers and instituted the environmental-education programs that have been the agency's hallmark ever since.

As the automobile took over Yellowstone, the railroads gradually lost their sway, and the final passenger train to the park's gateway towns stopped in 1960. In the 1950s, the Park Service initiated "Mission 66," a decade-long project to upgrade facilities and add more lodging. By the late '60s, a growing appreciation for the natural world was shifting public opinion away from such developments, and the 1973 master plan scaled back proposed developments. From day one, Yellowstone National Park had been set up for what Edward Abbey called "industrial tourism." The park had come into existence in part because of a railroad promoter who hoped to gain from its development, and it grew to maturity on a diet of roads, hotels, and curio shops. In recent years, Americans have taken a second look at this heritage and have begun to wonder which matters more: providing a public playground or preserving an area that is unique on this planet.

The inherent conflict between the need for public facilities and services in Yellowstone and the survival of a functioning ecosystem will continue to create a tug-of-war between various factions.

Certainly the most famous recent event was the series of massive fires that swept across nearly half of Yellowstone in 1988. The land has recovered surprisingly well since then, and in recent years other issues came to the fore: wolf reintroduction, bison being killed on the park boundaries, snowmobile and other winter use, and problems caused by exotic species and fish disease. There's always something stewing in the mud pots of Yellowstone! Some things have been improving in recent years, including efforts to repair aging roads and to replace outdated buildings in the park. Despite any problems and controversies, the park is just as fascinating as ever. The geysers never cease to amaze visitors, the scenery remains majestic, the Grand Canyon of the Yellowstone is still just as stunning, and the superb wildlife viewing continues to make this the Serengeti of America.

THE YELLOWSTONE FIRES OF 1988

Many will long remember the summer of 1988 as the year that fires seared Yellowstone National Park. TV reporters flocked to the park, pronouncing the destruction of America's most famous national wonder as they stood before trees turned into towering torches and 27,000-foot-high clouds of black smoke. Newspaper headlines screamed, "Park Sizzles," "Winds Whip Fiery Frenzy Out of Control," and "Firestorms Blacken Yellowstone." Residents of nearby towns complained of lost tourism dollars, choking smoke, and intentionally lit backfires that threatened their homes and businesses; Wyoming politicians berated the Park Service's "Let Burn" policy; President Reagan expressed astonishment that fires were ever allowed to burn in the national parks, although the policy had been in place for 16 years. Perhaps the most enduring image is from a forest that had been blown down by tornado-force winds in 1984 and then burned by the wind-whipped fires of 1988. The media ate it up, with one headline reading, "Total Destruction: Intense Heat and Flames from the Fires in Yellowstone Left Nothing but Powdered Ash and Charcoal Near Norris Junction." Unfortunately, the real story behind the fires of '88 was lost in this media feeding frenzy.

A Century of Change

In reality, these fires were not unprecedented; we were just fortunate enough to witness a spectacle of nature that may not occur for another 300 years. When Yellowstone National Park was established in 1872, most of the land was carpeted with a mixture of variously aged stands of lodgepole pine established following a series of large fires. Fewer large fires, partly because of a fire-suppression policy in effect until 1972, meant that by the 1980s one-third of the park's lodgepole stands were more than 200 years old. Yellowstone was ripe to burn.

Since the early 1950s, Smokey the Bear had drummed an incessant message: "Only You Can Prevent Forest Fires." Forest fires were viewed as dangerous, destructive forces that had to be stopped to protect our valuable public lands. Unfortunately, this immensely effective and generally valid ad campaign convinced the public that *all* fires were

continued on next page

THE YELLOWSTONE FIRES OF 1988 (cont'd)

bad. Ecological research has shown not only that this is wrong, but also that putting out all fires can sometimes create conditions far more dangerous than if fires had been allowed to burn in the first place. Fire, like the other processes that have affected Yellowstone—cataclysmic volcanic explosions, geothermal activity, and massive glaciation—is neither good nor evil. It is simply a part of the natural world that national parks are attempting to preserve. Unfortunately, national parks are no longer surrounded by similarly undeveloped land, so when fires burned in Yellowstone and on adjacent Forest Service lands, they also affected nearby towns and the people who made a living from tourism or logging.

Fire in Lodgepole Forests

Fire has played an important role in lodgepole pine forests for thousands if not millions of years, and as a result the trees have evolved an unusual adaptation. Some of the cones are sealed with a resin that melts in a fire, thus releasing the seeds. The parent trees are killed, but a new generation is guaranteed by the thousands of pine seeds released to the bare, nutrient-rich soil underneath the blackened overstory. Within five years the landscape is dotted with thousands of young pines, competing with a verdant cover of grasses and flowers.

Although some animals are killed in the wildfires (including, in 1988, at least 269 of Yellowstone's 30,000 elk), and others, weakened by the lack of food available immediately after the fire, succumb to the rigors of the next succeeding winter, the early decades following major fires create conditions that are unusually rich for many animals. Wildlife diversity in lodgepole forests reaches a peak within the first 25 years after a fire as woodpeckers, mountain bluebirds, and other birds feed on insects in the dead trees, and elk and bears graze on the lush grasses.

As the forest ages, a dense thicket of trees develops, keeping light from reaching the forest floor and making it difficult for understory plants to survive. These trees are eventually thinned by disease and windthrow, creating openings in the forest, but after 200–300 years without fire, lodgepole forests become a tangle of fallen trees that are difficult to walk through, are of lesser value to many

animals, and burn easily. They also become susceptible to attacks by bark beetles, such as those that killed thousands of acres of trees in Yellowstone starting in the 1960s and continuing through the 1980s. These beetle-killed trees added to the fuel available to burn once a fire started.

Yellowstone in 1988

Yellowstone's 1988 fires were caused by not just the heavy fuel loading from aging forests but also by weather conditions that were the driest and windiest on record. The winter of 1987–1988 had been a mild one, and by spring there was a moderate-to-severe drought in the park, lessened only by above-normal rainfall in April and May. Since 1972, when Yellowstone Park officials first began allowing certain lightning fires to burn in backcountry areas, the acreage burned had totaled less than 2 percent of the park. (Mistakenly called a "Let Burn" policy, the natural fire program actually involved close monitoring of these lightning-ignited fires to determine when and if a fire should be suppressed. All human-caused fires were immediately suppressed, as were any that threatened property or life.)

When the first lightning fires of the 1988 season began in late May, those in the backcountry areas were allowed to burn, as fire management officials anticipated normal summer weather conditions. Many fires went out on their own, but when June and July came and the rains failed to materialize, the fires began to spread rapidly. Alarmed park officials declared them wildfires and sent crews to put them out. (Ironically, the largest fire, the North Fork/Wolf Lake Complex, was started by a logger outside the park who tossed a lit cigarette to the ground. Although firefighters immediately attacked the blaze, it consumed more than 500,000 acres.) As the summer progressed, more and more firefighters were called in, eventually totaling more than 25,000 personnel, at a cost exceeding $120 million. Firefighters managed to protect most park buildings but had little effect on the forest fires themselves. Experts say that conditions in summer 1988 were so severe that even if firefighters had immediately responded to all of the natural fires, it would likely have made little difference. Yellowstone has experienced these massive fires in the past and will again in the future, no matter what humans do.

Out of Control

August brought worsening conditions with each passing day. Winds blew steadily at 20–40 miles per hour, and gusts up to 70 mph threw firebrands two miles in beyond the firefront, across fire lines, roads, and even over the Lewis River Canyon. The amount of moisture in the large logs was less than that in kiln-dried wood. By mid-August, more than 25 fires were burning simultaneously across the park and in surrounding national forests, with many joining together to create massive complexes, such as the Clover-Mist Fire, the Snake River Complex, and the North Fork/Wolf Lake Complex. On a single day—September 7—more than 100,000 acres burned. Also torched that day were 20 cabins and outbuildings in the vicinity of Old Faithful (out of the more than 400 structures there). Fortunately, all of the major historical buildings were spared. The fires seemed poised to consume the remainder of Yellowstone, but four days later the season's first snow carpeted the park. Within a few days firefighters had the upper hand.

A Transformed Landscape

The fires had burned nearly 800,000 acres—more than one-third of the park—plus another 600,000 acres on adjacent Forest Service lands. Of the park total, 41 percent was consumed in canopy fires in which all of the trees were killed, and another 35 percent burned in a mixture of ground fires and canopy fires. The remaining acreage suffered lighter burns. Less than one-tenth of 1 percent of the land was burned hot enough to sterilize the soil. The fires killed countless small mammals, along with at least 269 elk, nine bison, six black bears, four deer, and two moose. The drought of 1988 followed by the severe winter of 1988–1989 led to a large die-off of elk and bison, but their carcasses provided food for predators. Since then, wildlife populations have rebounded and may even exceed prefire levels.

It's been more than 15 years since the massive fires were put out, and much has changed, including the park's natural-fire program. It was replaced by a somewhat more conservative version that requires managers to provide daily certifications that fires are controllable and that they will remain "in prescription" for another 24 hours. Visitors to Yellowstone today will find dense thickets of young lodgepole pines in many areas that burned, and the first seedlings of other evergreen species are starting to emerge. In other places, grasses, colorful wildflowers, forbs, and other plants dominate. Not everything burned, of course, so you'll also see many green older forests next to burned stands, creating a complex mosaic of habitats that supports a high diversity of animal life. Once you grow accustomed to the burned areas and understand that they are a part of the natural process, they actually add interest to the park and help you appreciate Yellowstone as a functioning ecosystem rather than a static collection of plants and animals.

Take a hike through one of the burned areas to discover the wealth of new life within Yellowstone. Vistas that were long blocked by forests are now more open and will gradually become more so; by the end of this decade most of the standing dead trees will have fallen. The Park Service has placed informative signboards at sites around Yellowstone describing the fires of 1988 and the changes they brought about. The Grant Village Visitor Center offers an informative exhibit and film about the fires.

© DON PITCHER

new lodgepole pines from the 1988 Yellowstone fire

YELLOWSTONE

Exploring the Park

Yellowstone is perhaps the most accessible large national park in America. Nearly all of the famous sights are within a couple hundred feet of the Grand Loop Road, a 142-mile figure-eight through the middle of the park. The speed limit on all park roads is a vigilantly enforced 45 mph (or less); exceed the limit and you're likely to get a ticket! (Be especially cautious on the south side of the park where rangers seem to await most evenings and the relatively straight road makes it easy to speed.) Whatever you do, *don't* see Yellowstone at 45 miles per hour; that's like seeing the Louvre from a passing train.

For all too many visitors, Yellowstone becomes a checklist of places to visit, geysers to watch, and animals to see. This tends to inspire an attitude that treats this great national treasure as a drive-through theme park, where the animals come out to perform and the geyser eruptions are predicted so everyone can be there on time. If you're one of this crowd, give yourself a giant kick in the rear and take a walk, even if it is just around Upper Geyser Basin where you see something beyond Old Faithful.

The following loop tour of Yellowstone begins in the south and traces a clockwise path around the Grand Loop with several side trips. Although it is possible to follow this sequence (or some variation) the entire distance, a far bet-

ter way to learn about Yellowstone is to stop for a while in the places that are the most interesting to you and really explore them, rather than trying to see everything in a cursory way. If you have the time, the entire park is well worth visiting, but if you only have a day or two, pick a couple of spots and see them right. Don't just check out the views everyone else sees; find a nearby trail and do a little exploring on your own. If you are planning a trip to the area, try to set aside a bare minimum of three days in Yellowstone.

PARK ACCESS

Entrance to Yellowstone costs **$20 per vehicle,** or $10 for individuals entering by bicycle, foot, or as a bus passenger. Motorcycles and snowmobiles are $15. The pass covers both Yellowstone and Grand Teton National Parks and is good for seven days. If you're planning to be here longer or to make additional visits, get an annual pass covering both parks for $40, or the National Park Pass—good for all national parks—for $50 per year. A Golden Age Passport for all national parks is available to anyone older than 62 for a one-time fee of $10, and people with disabilities can get a free Golden Access Passport. Both of these passes also give you 50 percent reductions in most camping fees.

YELLOWSTONE NATIONAL PARK SIGHTSEEING HIGHLIGHTS

Upper Geyser Basin, including Old Faithful, Old Faithful Inn, Morning Glory Pool, Giant Geyser, and Riverside Geyser

Grand Prismatic Spring in Midway Geyser Basin

Great Fountain Geyser

Fountain Paint Pot

Norris Geyser Basin, including Echinus Geyser

Mammoth Hot Springs and the Albright Visitor Center

Lamar Valley

Roosevelt Lodge

Tower Fall

Mount Washburn

Grand Canyon of the Yellowstone, including Brink of the Lower Falls, Uncle Tom's Trail, Artist Point, and Inspiration Point

Hayden Valley

Mud Volcano

Yellowstone Lake, Fishing Bridge, and Lake Yellowstone Hotel

Wildlife viewing, particularly bison, elk, wolves, grizzlies, and moose

the south entrance to Yellowstone National Park

Upon entering the park, you'll receive a Yellowstone map and a copy of *Yellowstone Today,* a quarterly newspaper that describes facilities and services and provides camping, fishing, and backcountry information. This is the best source for up-to-date park information. It's also packed with enough warnings to scare off a platoon of Marines. Examples include cautions against falling trees, bathing in thermal pools (infections and/or amoebic meningitis), unpredictable wildlife, improper food storage, health problems from the altitude, narrow roads, theft, spotlighting elk, and scalding water. And, oh yes, "swim at your own risk." Pets are prohibited on trails or boardwalks anywhere in Yellowstone. Kennel facilities are not available in the park but can be found in Jackson and Cody.

Visitors Centers

The Park Service maintains visitors centers at Mammoth Hot Springs, Norris Geyser Basin, Old Faithful, Canyon Village, Fishing Bridge, and Grant Village. All of these sell maps and natural-history books covering the park and surrounding areas. In addition, you'll find smaller

information stations at Madison and West Thumb. Hours, seasons, and phone numbers for all of these are listed in the sections that follow. Get complete Yellowstone National Park information on the web at www.nps.gov/yell, or call 307/344-7381 for additional details and publications.

Seasonal Road Closures

Most roads in Yellowstone close with the first heavy snows of early November and usually open again by mid-May. The roads connecting Mammoth to West Yellowstone open first, while Dunraven Pass is plowed last. Only the road between Mammoth and Cooke City is kept open all year. If you're planning a trip early or late in the season, call the park for current road conditions; 307/344-7381.

SOUTH ENTRANCE ROAD

The South Entrance Station consists of several log structures right along the Snake River. Just 1.5 miles beyond the entrance is an easily missed turnout where you can walk down to

YELLOWSTONE

30-foot-high **Moose Falls.** Beyond this point, the road climbs up a long, gentle ramp to Pitchstone Plateau, passing green forests of lodgepole pine. Stop at a turnout to look back at the majestic Tetons. Abruptly, this gentle country is broken by the edge of **Lewis River Canyon,** with rhyolite walls that rise up to 600 feet. The fires of 1988 burned hot throughout much of this area, and dead trees line both sides of the canyon in all directions, although young trees are now carpeting many areas.

The road parallels the river for the next seven miles. Nearly everyone stops for a look at 29-foot-high **Lewis Falls.** Camping is available at the south end of **Lewis Lake,** which—like the lake, falls, river, and canyon—was named for the Lewis and Clark expedition's Meriwether Lewis. Lewis Lake is the park's third-largest body of water (after Yellowstone Lake and Shoshone Lake) and is popular with canoeists, kayakers, and anglers. The clear waters contain brown trout and Mackinaw (lake trout). Approximately four miles north of Lewis Lake, the highway tops the Continental Divide, 7,988 feet above sea level. This is one of three such crossings that roads make within Yellowstone.

Day Hikes in the Lewis Lake Area

Two trailheads one mile north of Lewis Lake provide access west to Shoshone Lake and east to Heart Lake. At the Dogshead Trailhead you can choose between two trails to Shoshone Lake, both of which cross land burned in the 1988 fires. The four-mile-long **Dogshead Trail** is more direct, while the seven-mile **Lewis Channel Trail** takes a much more scenic trek via the channel that connects Shoshone and Lewis Lakes. This slow-flowing channel is popular with anglers who come to fish for brown and cutthroat trout during the fall spawning season, and it's also used by canoeists and kayakers heading into Shoshone Lake. Once you reach Shoshone Lake, follow Delacy Creek Trail northward along the shore for fine vistas. The area gets considerable overnight use, and campsites are scattered around the lake.

Heart Lake Trailhead is on the opposite side of the road and south a few hundred feet from Dogshead Trailhead. Heart Lake is a scenic and interesting area that gets considerable day-use, but it's probably best visited on a backpacking trip of several days or longer because it's an eight-mile (one-way) hike to the lake. Be sure to bring water with you. Hard-core hikers may want to attempt a day trip all the way to the summit of Mt. Sheridan, but this is 22 miles round-trip, and you gain (and lose) 2,700 feet in elevation along the way. The Heart Lake area is closed to access before July because of grizzly activity. For details on longer hikes in the Heart Lake and Shoshone Lake areas, see Into the Backcountry later in this chapter.

Grant Village

This odd scattering of buildings is named for Pres. Ulysses S. Grant, who signed the act establishing Yellowstone, and whose terms in office were marked by massive corruption scandals. Grant Village was built in the 1980s to replace facilities at Fishing Bridge, an area of important grizzly habitat. Unfortunately, instead of one bad development, Yellowstone now has two because some of the buildings at Fishing Bridge still stand. Unlike some of the more historic places in Yellowstone where a natural rusticity prevailed, Grant Village has less charm than most Wal-Marts. An ugly steakhouse restaurant and waterside cafeteria face Yellowstone Lake, but the marina that was once here is closed. Also sprawled around Grant Village are a campground, rows of chintzy condos, a Yellowstone General Store, a gas station, and post offices. Much of the area around here was consumed in the 1988 Snake River Fire; unfortunately, the fire missed this scar on the Yellowstone landscape.

Grant Village Visitor Center, 307/242-2650, houses an informative exhibit and film on the fires of 1988. These provide a good background to help understand the changes taking place as the burned areas recover. The visitors center is open daily 8 A.M.–7 P.M. Memorial Day to Labor Day, and daily 9 A.M.–6 P.M. for the rest of September. It's closed the rest of the year. The visitors center at Grant is scheduled for a major revamping, but it probably won't be completed until 2005.

West Thumb

If you look at a map of Yellowstone Lake, it's possible to imagine the lake as a giant hand with three mangled fingers heading south and a gnarled thumb hitching west. Hence the name West Thumb. This portion of Yellowstone Lake is the deepest (to 390 feet) and is actually a caldera that filled with water after erupting 150,000 years ago. There is still considerable heat just below the surface, as revealed by **West Thumb Geyser Basin.** Get a Park Service booklet (50 cents) from the box for details on the area's geothermal origins and attractions.

A short loop trail leads past steaming hot springs and pools at West Thumb. Right on the shore is **Fishing Cone,** where tourists once caught fish and then plopped them in the cone to be cooked; after several clowning tourists were injured, the Park Service put a stop to this stunt. The **West Thumb Information Station** is open daily 8 A.M.–7 P.M. from Memorial Day to Labor Day, and daily 8 A.M.–7 P.M. for the rest of September. A small bookstore is housed here, and in winter the station is used as a warming hut.

A fine day hike takes off across the road from the entrance to West Thumb Geyser Basin and climbs for one mile to **Yellowstone Lake Overlook.** The two-mile loop trail gains 400 feet in elevation, enough for a commanding vista across the lake, with the Absaroka Mountains behind.

WEST THUMB TO UPPER GEYSER BASIN

Heading west from West Thumb, the highway climbs over the Continental Divide twice. Most of these forests escaped the 1988 fires. A few miles beyond the eastern crossing of the divide is a turnout at **Shoshone Point,** where you catch glimpses of Shoshone Lake and the Tetons. In 1914, highwayman Ed Trafton (his real name was Ed Harrington) held up 15 stagecoaches as they passed by this point carrying tourists. He got away with $915.35 in cash and $130 in jewelry but made the rather obvious mistake of posing for photos. He was caught the following year and spent five years in Leavenworth. When he died, a letter in his pocket claimed that he had been

Owen Wister's model for the Virginian. Others suspected that he was more likely to have been Wister's model for the villain, Trampas.

DeLacy Creek Trail provides access to Shoshone Lake—Yellowstone's largest backcountry lake—and begins at the picnic area between the two passes. It's three miles to the lake, which is circled by more trails. Keep your eyes open for moose and other animals in the meadows along the way. The western crossing of the Continental Divide is at **Craig Pass,** where a tiny pond (Isa Lake) empties into both the Atlantic and Pacific Oceans through its two outlet streams.

Approximately 14 miles beyond West Thumb, pull off to see the Firehole River as it drops over **Kepler Cascades.** Just to the east, a wide and partly paved trail (actually an old road) leads five miles round-trip to **Lone Star Geyser.** This is a popular route for bicyclists in the summer and skiers in the winter. Bikes are not allowed beyond the geyser. Lone Star Geyser erupts every three hours from a distinctive nine-foot-high cone, with eruptions generally reaching 45 feet and lasting for 30 minutes. Hikers can also get to Lone Star via the Howard Eaton Trail out of Old Faithful. For a longer hike, you can continue south from Lone Star on **Shoshone Lake Trail** to Shoshone Lake, eight fairly easy miles from the main road. (See Into the Backcountry later in this chapter for other Shoshone Lake hikes.)

UPPER GEYSER BASIN

As you approach Old Faithful from either direction, the two-lane road suddenly widens into four, and a cloverleaf exit takes you to Yellowstone's most fabulous sight. Welcome to Upper Geyser Basin, home of Old Faithful, some 400 buildings of all sizes, and a small town's worth of people. For many folks, this is the heart of Yellowstone, and a visit to the park without seeing Old Faithful is like a baseball game without the national anthem. If you came to Yellowstone to see the wonders of nature, you're going to see more than your share here, but you'll probably have to share your share with hundreds of other folks. On busy summer days more than 25,000

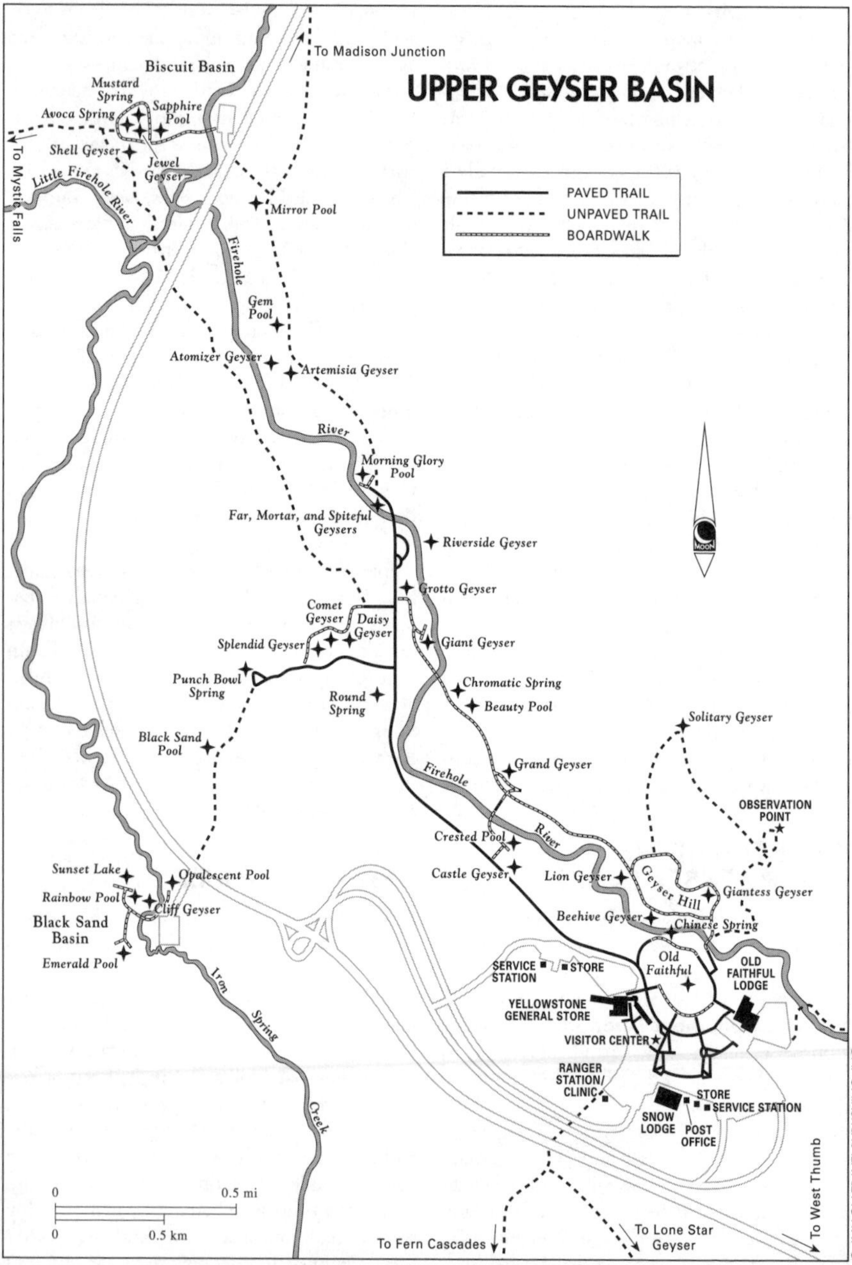

UPPER GEYSER BASIN

To Madison Junction

Biscuit Basin

Mustard
Spring
Avoca Spring
Sapphire
Pool
Shell Geyser
Jewel
Geyser

To Mystic Falls

Little Firehole River

Firehole

Mirror Pool

Gem
Pool

Atomizer Geyser
Artemisia Geyser

River

Morning Glory
Pool

Far, Mortar, and Spiteful
Geysers

Riverside Geyser

Grotto Geyser

Comet
Geyser
Daisy
Geyser

Splendid Geyser

Giant Geyser

Punch Bowl
Spring

Round
Spring

Chromatic Spring

Beauty Pool

Black Sand
Pool

Solitary Geyser

Firehole

Grand Geyser

OBSERVATION
POINT

River

Crested Pool

Castle Geyser

Lion Geyser

Geyser Hill

Giantess Geyser

Sunset Lake
Opalescent Pool

Rainbow Pool
Cliff Geyser

Black Sand
Basin

Emerald Pool

Beehive Geyser

Chinese Spring

Iron

Spring

Creek

SERVICE
STATION   STORE

Old
Faithful

OLD
FAITHFUL
LODGE

YELLOWSTONE
GENERAL STORE

VISITOR CENTER

RANGER
STATION/
CLINIC

STORE
SERVICE STATION

SNOW
LODGE

POST
OFFICE

To Fern Cascades

To Lone Star
Geyser

To West Thumb

	PAVED TRAIL
- - - -	UNPAVED TRAIL
▪▪▪▪▪▪	BOARDWALK

N

0   0.5 mi

0   0.5 km

YELLOWSTONE

visitors come through the Old Faithful area! Fortunately, the Upper Geyser Basin contains the largest concentration of geysers in the world, and the adventurous will even discover places almost nobody ever visits. But be very careful: The crust can be dangerously thin around some of the hot springs and geysers, and people have been badly scalded and even killed by missteps. Stay on the boardwalks and trails.

Old Faithful

The one sight seen by virtually everyone who comes to Yellowstone is Old Faithful Geyser, easily the most visited geyser in the world. Old Faithful is neither the tallest nor the most frequently erupting geyser in Yellowstone, but it always provides a great show and is both highly accessible and fairly predictable. Contrary to the rumors, Old Faithful never erupted "every hour on the hour," but for many years its period was a little more than an hour. It has slowed in recent years and is now averaging around 92 minutes per cycle, but varies from 45 to 120 minutes. In general, the longer the length of the eruption, the longer the interval until the next eruption. Check at the visitors center for the latest prognostications on this and other geysers in the basin.

An almost level paved path circles Old Faithful, providing many different angles from which to view the eruptions, although none of these is particularly close to the geyser because of the danger from hot water. Along the north side is **Chinese Spring,** named in 1885 for a short-lived laundry operation. Apparently, the washman had filled the spring with clothes and soap, not knowing that soap can cause geysers to erupt. One newspaper correspondent claimed—although the tale obviously suffered from embellishment and racism—that,

The soap awakened the imprisoned giant; with a roar that made the earth tremble, and a shriek of a steam whistle, a cloud of steam and a column of boiling water shot up into the air a hundred feet, carrying soap, raiment, tent and Chinaman along with the rush, and dropping them at various intervals along the way.

Yellowstone's most famous geyser, Old Faithful, erupts about once every 90 minutes.

Old Faithful provides a textbook example of geyser activity. The first signs of life are when water begins to splash out of the vent in what is called preplay. This splashing can last up to 20 minutes, but it's generally only a few minutes before the real thing. The water quickly spears into the sky, reaching 100–180 feet for 2–5 minutes before rapidly dropping down. During a typical eruption, between 3,700 and 8,400 gallons of water are sent skyward.

On any given summer day, the scene at Old Faithful is almost comical. Just before the predicted eruption time, the benches encircling the south and east sides are jammed with hundreds of people waiting expectantly for the geyser to erupt, and with each tentative spray the camera shutters begin to click. Listen closely and you'll hear half the languages of Europe and Asia. Once the action is over, there's a mad rush back into the visitors center, the stores, and Old Faithful Inn, and within a few minutes the benches are virtually empty. A tale is told of two concessioner

YELLOWSTONE

employees who once decided to have fun at Old Faithful by placing a large crank atop a box and putting the contraption near the geyser. When they knew it was ready to erupt, they ran out and turned the crank just as Old Faithful shot into the air. Their employer failed to find humor in the prank, and both were fired, or so the story claims.

Geyser Hill Area

Upper Geyser Basin is laced with paved trails that lead to dozens of nearby geysers and hot springs. The easiest path loops around Geyser Hill, just across the Firehole River from Old Faithful. Here are more than 40 different geysers. Check at the visitors center to get an idea of current activity and predicted eruptions, and while you're there pick up the excellent Upper Geyser Basin map (50 cents), which describes some of them. Several geysers are particularly noteworthy. When it plays, **Beehive Geyser** (it has a tall, beehive-shaped cone) vents water as high as 180 feet into the air. These spectacular eruptions vary in frequency; one time you visit they may be 10 days apart, while the next time you come they may be happening twice daily. **Lion Geyser Group** consists of four different interconnected geysers with varying periods of activity and eruptions up to 50 feet. Listen for the roar when Lion is ready to erupt. **Giantess Geyser** may not be active for years at a time—or may erupt several times a year—but the eruptions are sensationally powerful, sending water 100–200 feet skyward. **Doublet Pool** is a beautiful deep-blue pool that is a favorite of photographers. Not far away is **Sponge Geyser,** which rockets water an astounding 2.29 billion angstroms into the air (that's nine inches for the nonscientific crowd). It's considered the smallest named geyser in Yellowstone and gets its title by sending up a spurt of water big enough to be mopped up with a sponge.

Observation Point Loop Trail splits off shortly after you cross the bridge on the way to Geyser Hill and climbs to an excellent overlook where

> *Old Faithful is neither the tallest nor the most frequently erupting geyser in Yellowstone, but it always provides a great show and is both highly accessible and fairly predictable, with an average cycle of about 92 minutes.*

you can watch eruptions of Old Faithful. This is also a good place to view the effects of, and recovery from, the 1988 North Fork Fire. It's two miles round-trip to Observation Point from the visitors center. Another easy trail splits off from this path to **Solitary Geyser,** which is actually just a pool that periodically burps four-foot splashes of hot water. This is not a natural geyser. In 1915, the hot spring here was tapped to provide water for Old Faithful Geyser Bath, a concession that lasted until 1948. The lowering of the water level in the pool completely changed the plumbing system of the hot springs and turned it into a geyser that at one time shot 25 feet in the air. The system still hasn't recovered, although water levels have been restored for many decades.

More Geyser-Gazing

Another easy, paved path follows the Firehole River downstream from Old Faithful, looping back along the other side for a total distance of three miles. Other trails head off from this loop to the Fairy Falls Trailhead, Biscuit Basin, and Black Sand Basin. The loop is a very popular wintertime ski path, and portions are open to bikes in the summer. Twelve-foot-high **Castle Geyser** does indeed resemble a ruined old castle. Because of its size and the slow accretion of sinter (silica) to form this cone, it is believed to be somewhere between 5,000 and 50,000 years old. Castle sends up a column of water and steam 90 feet into the air and usually erupts every 10–12 hours. Check at the visitors center for a guess at the next eruption.

Daisy Geyser is farther down the path and off to the left. It is usually one of the most predictable of the geysers, erupting to 75 feet approximately every 90–125 minutes. The water shoots out at a sharp angle and is visible all over the basin, making this a real crowd pleaser.

Just east of Daisy is **Radiator Geyser,** which isn't much to look at—eruptions to two feet— but was named when this area was a parking lot and the sudden eruption under a car led people to think its radiator was overheating. A personal favorite, **Grotto Geyser** is certainly the weirdest of all the geysers, having formed around a tangle of long-petrified tree stumps. It is in eruption one-third of the time, but most eruptions only reach 10 feet.

Look for **Riverside Geyser** across the Firehole from the path and not far downstream from Grotto. This picturesque geyser arches spray 75

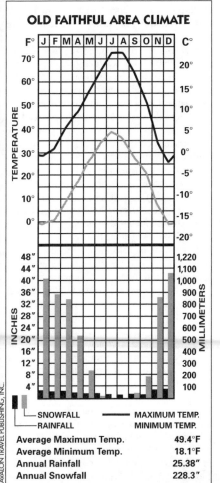

OLD FAITHFUL AREA CLIMATE

- SNOWFALL — MAXIMUM TEMP.
- RAINFALL — MINIMUM TEMP.

Average Maximum Temp.	49.4°F
Average Minimum Temp.	18.1°F
Annual Rainfall	25.38"
Annual Snowfall	228.3"

feet over the river and is one of the most predictable, with 20-minute-long eruptions approximately every six hours. The paved trail crosses the river and ends at famous **Morning Glory Pool.** For many years, the main road passed this colorful pool, which became something of a wishing well for not just coins but also trash, rocks, logs, and other debris. Because of this junk, the pool began to cool, and the beautiful blue color is now tinged by brown and green algae, despite efforts to remove the debris.

Turning back at Morning Glory, recross the bridge and head left where the path splits at Grotto Geyser. **Giant Geyser** is on the left along the river. Years may pass between eruptions of Giant (or it might erupt every week or so), but when it does go, the name rings true because the water can reach 250 feet. Cross the river again and pass **Beauty Pool** and **Chromatic Pool,** which are connected below the ground so that one declines as the other rises. Very pretty.

Grand Geyser is a wonderful sight. The water column erupts in a towering burst every 7–15 hours, with a series of bursts lasting 10 minutes or so and sometimes reaching 200 feet. It's the tallest predictable geyser on the planet; see the visitors center for the next eruption. When Grand isn't playing, watch for smaller eruptions from nearby **Turban Geyser.** Two little fun geysers are a short distance to the south: **Sawmill** and **Tardy Geysers.** The latter is just 10 feet or so from the trail, providing an up-close look at a small but active geyser. Cross the river again just beyond these two geysers and pass **Crested Pool** on your way back to Castle Geyser. The pool contains deep-blue water that is constantly boiling, preventing the survival of algae.

Black Sand Basin

Just one mile west of Old Faithful is Black Sand Basin, a small cluster of geysers and hot springs. Most enjoyable is unpredictable **Cliff Geyser,** which often sends a spray of hot water 25–30 feet over Iron Spring Creek. Three colorful pools are quite interesting in the basin: **Emerald Pool, Rainbow Pool,** and **Sunset Lake. Handkerchief Pool** is now just a small spouter but was famous for many years as a place where visitors

YELLOWSTONE'S FIRST "TOURIST"

From the surface of a rocky plain or table, burst forth columns of water of various dimensions, projected high in the air, accompanied by loud explosions, and sulphurous vapors, which were highly disagreeable to the smell. . . . The largest of these wonderful fountains, projects a column of boiling water several feet in diameter, to the height of more than one hundred and fifty feet. . . . After having witnessed three of them, I ventured near enough to put my hand into the water of its basin, but withdrew it instantly, for the heat of the water in this immense couldron, was altogether to great for comfort, and the agitation of the water, disagreeable effluvium continually exuding, and the hollow unearthly rumbling under the rock on which I stood, so ill accorded with my notions of personal safety, that I retreated back precipitately to a respectful distance.

—Angus Ferris, in 1833

could drop a handkerchief in one end and then recover it later at another vent. In 1929, vandals jammed logs into the pool, destroying this little game. The pool was covered with gravel in subsequent eruptions of Rainbow Pool.

Biscuit Basin and Mystic Falls

Three miles north of Old Faithful, this basin is named for biscuitlike formations that were found in one of the pools; they were destroyed in an eruption following the 1959 Hebgen Lake earthquake. From the parking lot, the trail leads across the Firehole River to pretty **Sapphire Pool** and then past **Jewel Geyser**, which typically erupts every 7–10 minutes to a height of 15–20 feet. The boardwalk follows a short loop through the other sights of Biscuit Basin.

From the west end of the boardwalk, a one-mile trail leads to where the Little Firehole River

cascades 100 feet over **Mystic Falls.** You can switchback farther up the trail to the top of the falls and then connect with another trail for the loop back to Biscuit Basin (three miles round-trip). This is a very nice short hike and can be lengthened into a trip to **Little Firehole Meadows** (10 miles round-trip), where bison are often seen in the summer.

Old Faithful Inn

Matching one of the great sights of the natural world is one of America's most majestic hotels, Old Faithful Inn. The largest log structure of its kind in existence, the inn has delighted generations of visitors and continues to enthrall all who enter. The building was designed by Robert Reamer and built in the winter of 1903–1904. Its steeply angled roofline reaches seven stories high, with gables jutting out from the sides and flags flying from the roof. Surprisingly, the hotel does not face the geyser. Instead, it was built facing sideways to allow newly arriving visitors the opportunity to view the geyser as they stepped from carriages. As you open the rustic split-log front doors with their hand-wrought hardware, you enter a world of the past. The central lobby towers more than 75 feet overhead and is dominated by a massive four-sided stone fireplace that required 500 tons of stone from a nearby quarry. Four overhanging balconies extend above, each bordered by posts made from gnarled lodgepole burls found within the park. Above the fireplace is an enormous clock designed by Reamer and built on the site by a blacksmith. Reamer also designed the two wings that were added in 1913 and 1928.

On warm summer evenings, visitors stand out on the porch, where they can watch Old Faithful erupting, or sit inside at the handcrafted tables to write letters as music spills from the grand piano. It's enough to warm the heart of even the most cynical curmudgeon. A good restaurant is on the premises, along with a rustic but comfortable bar, a gift shop, fast-food eatery, ice cream shop, and ATM. Free 45-minute **tours** of Old Faithful Inn are given daily at 9:30 A.M., 11 A.M., 2 P.M., and 3:30 P.M. from mid-May to late September. Meet at the fireplace in the lobby. Old

YELLOWSTONE

Faithful Inn closes during the winter; it would be hard to imagine trying to heat such a cavern when it's 30° below zero outside!

Another nearby building of interest is **Old Faithful Lodge.** Built in 1928, this is the large stone-and-log building just south of the geyser of the same name. The giant fireplace inside is a joy on frosty evenings, and cafeteria windows face the geyser—unlike those at the Inn.

Much newer, but an instant classic, is the award-winning **Old Faithful Snow Lodge,** which opened in 1999. This large building offers a sense of rustic elegance, with heavy timbers, a window-lined main entrance, a large stone fireplace, overstuffed couches, and handmade wrought-iron light fixtures and accents. It is one of just two places (the other being Mammoth Hot Springs Hotel) open in winter.

Old Faithful Services

The Park Service's **Old Faithful Visitor Center,** 307/545-2750, is generally open mid-April to early November and mid-December to mid-March. It's open daily 8 A.M.–7 P.M. from Memorial Day to Labor Day, daily 8 A.M.–6 P.M. the rest of September. During the fall, winter, and spring when park gates are open, the visitors center operates daily 9 A.M.–5 P.M. Among the films about Yellowstone shown throughout the day here is a fascinating production (narrated by Walter Cronkite) on the lifeforms that survive in Yellowstone's hot springs. The center has a big selection of books, maps, and other Yellowstone publications. In summer, be sure to check the board for the predicted eruptions of six major geysers in the area: Old Faithful, Grand, Daisy, Riverside, Great Fountain, and Castle. The rangers can provide you with all sorts of other information, from where to see bighorn sheep to where to find the restrooms. A much-needed new visitors center is in the planning stages for Old Faithful, but don't expect to see it until at least 2005 because the Park Service needs to raise $15 million for its construction.

Backcountry permits are available from the ranger station, while food, supplies, and postcards can be purchased at either of the two Yellowstone General Stores. Old Faithful Inn has a

gift shop, restaurant, snack bar, ice cream parlor, lounge, and ATM. Cafeteria meals, espresso, and baked goods are available at Old Faithful Lodge, and Old Faithful Snow Lodge houses a restaurant and snack bar. Both of these also have gift shops. In addition, the Old Faithful area has two gas stations, a post office, photo shop, and medical clinic. See the Camping and Hotels, Lodges, and Cabins sections later in this chapter for lodging details. Note that camping is *not* available in the Old Faithful area, and it's illegal to stay overnight in the parking lots. The closest campgrounds are in Madison (16 miles north) and Grant Village (19 miles southeast).

MIDWAY AND LOWER GEYSER BASINS

Heading north from Upper Geyser Basin, the road follows the Firehole River past Midway and Lower Geyser Basins, both of which are quite interesting. This stretch of the river is popular with fly-fishing enthusiasts, and several side roads provide access to a variety of hot springs and other sights.

Fairy Falls

Just south of Midway Geyser Basin (or 4.5 miles north of the Old Faithful Interchange) is a turnoff that leads to the southern end of Fountain Freight Road. This four-mile-long trail is closed to cars, but it's a great place for mountain bikers and those out for a relatively level walk. A steel bridge crosses the Firehole River at the trailhead, and the road soon passes the west side of Grand Prismatic Spring; rough trails lead up the hillside for a better view. One mile up from the trailhead you'll come to **Fairy Falls Trail** on your left. It's an easy 1.5-mile walk to the falls, a 200-foot ribbon of water that cascades into a large pool. The hike to Fairy Falls can be combined with longer treks to Little Firehole Meadow and Mystic Falls (both described earlier) or to a pair of small peaks called Twin Buttes. One-half mile beyond Fairy Falls is **Imperial Geyser,** which was active in the 1920s and from 1966–1984, but is now just a boiling pool. Nearby **Spray Geyser** erupts frequently, sending water six feet in the air. For a longer version of the hike to Fairy Falls (10 miles round-trip), start from the north end, where Fountain Flat Drive ends.

Midway Geyser Basin

Midway is a large and readily accessible geyser basin with a loop path leading to most of the sights. **Excelsior Geyser** is actually an enormous hot spring that pours 4,000 gallons per minute of steaming water into the Firehole River. The water is a deep turquoise. During the 1880s, this geyser was truly stupendous, with explosions that reached 380 feet in the air and almost as wide. These violent eruptions apparently damaged the plumbing system that fed them, and the geyser was dormant for nearly a century until smaller

eruptions took place in 1985. At 370 feet across, **Grand Prismatic Spring** is Yellowstone's largest hot spring. The brilliant reds and yellows around the edges of the blue pool are from algae and bacteria that can tolerate temperatures of 170°F. It's difficult to get a good perspective on this spring from the ground; see aerial photos to really appreciate its pulchritude.

Firehole Lake Drive

This road (one-way heading north) goes three miles through Lower Geyser Basin, the park's most extensive geyser basin. **Great Fountain Geyser** is truly one of the most spectacular geysers in Yellowstone. Charles Cook, of the 1869 Cook-Folsom-Peterson Expedition, recalled his impression of the geyser: "We could not contain our enthusiasm; with one accord we all took off our hats and yelled with all our might." Modern-day visitors would not be faulted for reacting similarly.

Great Fountain erupts every 8–12 hours (although it can be irregular) and usually reaches 100 feet, but has been known to blast more than 200 feet. Eruptions begin an hour or so after water starts to overflow from the crater and last for 45–60 minutes in a series of decreasingly active eruptive cycles; but don't leave too early or you may miss the real show! Eruption predictions are posted at the geyser and in the Old Faithful Visitor Center. While you're waiting, watch the periodic eruptions of **White Dome Geyser** just a hundred yards down the road. Because of its massive 30-foot cone, this is believed to be one of the oldest geysers in the park. Eruptions occur every 10 minutes to three hours and spray 30 feet into the air.

Another mile ahead, the road literally cuts into the mound of **Pink Cone Geyser,** which now erupts every 6–20 hours and reaches a height of 30 feet. The pink color comes from manganese oxide. Just up from here at the bend in the road is **Firehole Lake,** which discharges 3,500 gallons of water per minute into Tangled Creek, which in turn drains across the road into **Hot Lake. Steady Geyser** is unusual in that it forms both sinter (silica) and travertine (calcium carbonate) deposits. The geyser is along the edge

---

GRAND PRISMATIC SPRING, 1839

At length we came to a boiling Lake about 300 ft in diameter forming nearly a complete circle as we approached on the south side The steam which arose from it was of three distinct Colors from the west side for one third of the diameter it was white, in the middle it was pale red, and the remaining third on the east light sky blue Whether it was something peculiar in the state of the atmosphere the day being cloudy or whether it was some Chemical properties contained in the water which produced this phenomenon I am unable to say and shall leave the explanation to some scientific tourist who may have the Curiosity to visit this place at some future period—The water was of deep indigo blue boiling like an imense caldron running over the white rock which had formed the edges to the height of 4 or 5 feet from the surface of the earth sloping gradually for 60 or 70 feet. What a field of speculation this presents for chemist and geologist.

—mountain man Osborne Russell

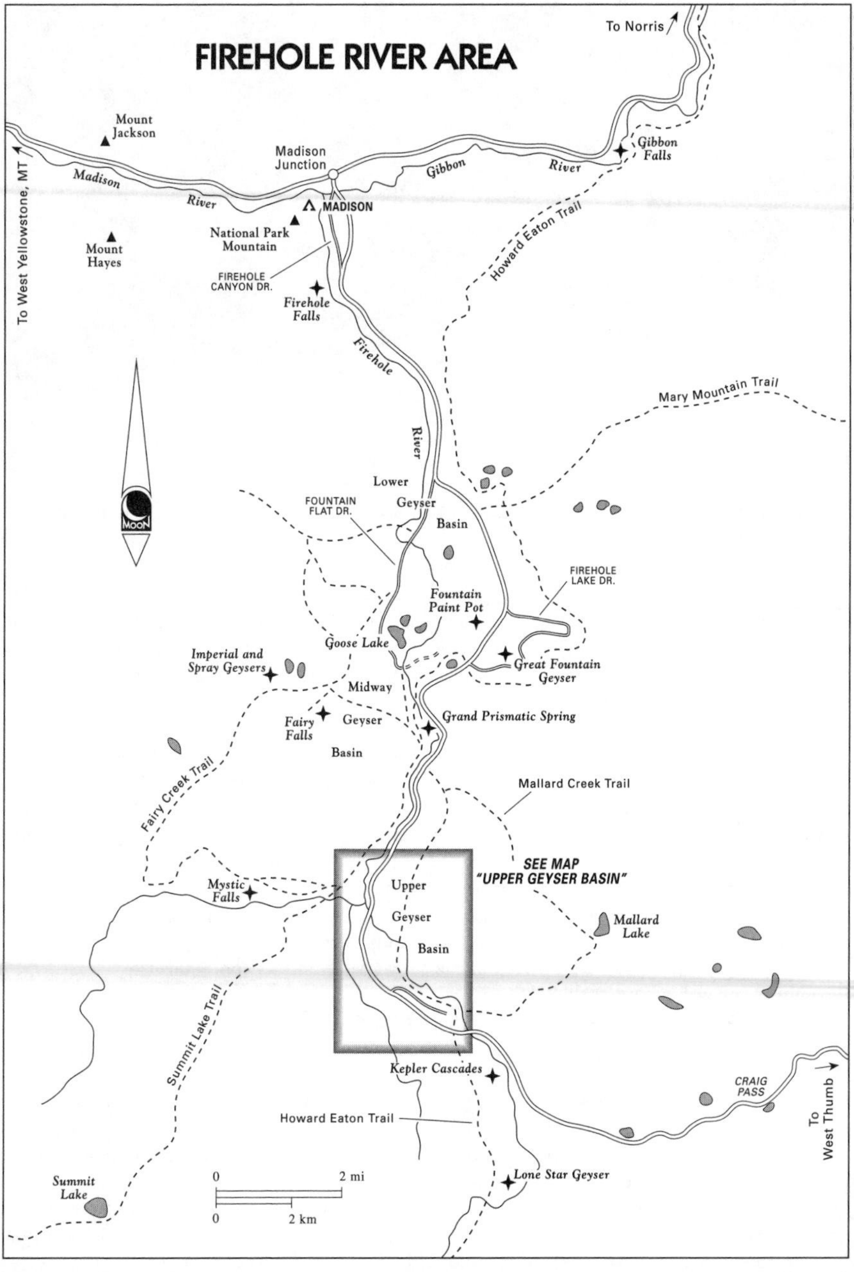

FIREHOLE RIVER AREA

© AVALON TRAVEL PUBLISHING, INC.

To Norris

Mount Jackson

Madison Junction

Gibbon River

Gibbon Falls

Madison River

MADISON

To West Yellowstone, MT

Mount Hayes

National Park Mountain

FIREHOLE CANYON DR.

Firehole Falls

Howard Eaton Trail

Firehole River

Mary Mountain Trail

Lower Geyser Basin

FOUNTAIN FLAT DR.

Fountain Paint Pot

FIREHOLE LAKE DR.

Goose Lake

Imperial and Spray Geysers

Great Fountain Geyser

Midway

Fairy Creek Trail

Fairy Falls

Geyser Basin

Grand Prismatic Spring

Mallard Creek Trail

Mystic Falls

Upper Geyser Basin

SEE MAP "UPPER GEYSER BASIN"

Mallard Lake

Summit Lake Trail

Kepler Cascades

CRAIG PASS

To West Thumb

Howard Eaton Trail

Summit Lake

0   2 mi

0   2 km

Lone Star Geyser

YELLOWSTONE

taking the plunge at Firehole Cascades

of Hot Lake and, true to its name, erupts almost continuously, although the height is only five feet. Firehole Lake Drive continues another mile to its junction with the main road right across from the parking area for Fountain Paint Pot. In the winter, Firehole Lake Drive is popular with skiers but is closed to snowmobiles.

Fountain Paint Pot

Always a favorite of visitors, Fountain Paint Pot seems to have a playfulness about it that belies the immense power just below the surface. Pick up a trail guide (50 cents) as you head up the walkway for the full story. **Silex Spring,** off to the right as you walk up the small hill, is colored by different kinds of algae and bacteria. The spring has been known to erupt as a geyser (to 20 feet) but is currently dormant. The famous **Fountain Paint Pot** is a few steps up the boardwalk and consists of colorful mud that changes in consistency throughout the season depending on soil moisture. The pressure from steam and gases under the Paint Pot can throw gobs of mud up to 20 feet into the air. Just north of here are fumaroles that spray steam, carbon dioxide, and hydrogen sulfide into the air. Continuing down the boardwalk, you come upon an impressive overlook above a multitude of geysers that change constantly in activity, including **Morning Geyser,** which has been known to erupt more than 200 feet. The most active is **Clepsydra Geyser,** which is in eruption much of the time. **Fountain Geyser** explodes in a stunning display that can last 30 minutes and reach up to 50 feet. Eruptions are unpredictable but impressive, particularly at sunset. The rest of the loop trail passes dead lodgepole pines that are being petrified as the silica is absorbed, creating a bobby-socks appearance.

Fountain Flat

Fountain Flat Drive provides access to meadows along the Firehole River and is a good place to see bison and elk. The paved road ends after one mile at a parking area, but hikers and cyclists (or skiers in winter) can continue another four miles on Old Fountain Freight Road to its junction with the main road again near Midway Geyser Basin. The road ends in a parking area near **Ojo Caliente**—a small hot springs with a big odor—

right along the river. Several more hot springs are upstream from here, and the **Fairy Falls Trail** starts three miles south of the parking area. See Midway Geyser Basin for details on this scenic and popular day hike.

Firehole Canyon Drive

This one-way road (south only) curves for two miles through Firehole Canyon, where dark rhyolite cliffs rise hundreds of feet above the river. The road begins just south of Madison Junction and was intensely burned in the 1988 North Fork Fire, giving the canyon's name a dual meaning. **Firehole Falls,** a 40-foot drop, is worth stopping to see, as is **Firehole Cascades** a bit farther up. Kids of all ages enjoy the popular hot-springs-warmed swimming hole a short distance up the road. It's one of the few places along the Yellowstone road system where swimming is openly allowed (albeit not encouraged). No lifeguard is provided, of course.

MADISON JUNCTION TO WEST YELLOWSTONE

At Madison Junction, the Gibbon and Firehole Rivers join to form the Madison River, a major tributary of the Missouri River. The 14-mile drive from Madison Junction to the West Entrance closely parallels this scenic river, in which geese, ducks, and trumpeter swans are commonly seen. Bison and elk are other critters to watch for in the open meadows. The 406,359-acre North Fork Fire of 1988 ripped through most of the Madison River country, so be ready for many blackened trees, but also expect to see many flowers in midsummer. The river is open only to fly-fishing and is considered one of the finest places in the nation to catch trout (although they can be a real challenge to fool). On warm summer evenings, you're likely to see dozens of anglers casting for wily rainbow and brown trout and mountain whitefish. **West Entrance** is the busiest of all the park entry stations, handling more than one-third of the more than 3 million people who enter Yellowstone each year. The tourist town of West Yellowstone, Montana, is right outside the boundary.

Madison Canyon is flanked by mountains named for two photographers who had a marked influence on Yellowstone. To the north is 8,257-foot **Mt. Jackson** (as in William H. Jackson, whose photos helped bring the area to national attention), and to the south is distinctive, 8,235-foot **Mt. Haynes,** named for the man who held the park photo concession for nearly four decades. These mountains and the surrounding slopes were created by rhyolite lava flows.

THE NORTHWEST CORNER

Highway 191 heads north from West Yellowstone, Montana, to Bozeman, passing through a small corner of Yellowstone National Park en route. There are no entrance stations or developed facilities here, but the area provides backcountry access for hikers and horsepackers from several trailheads. The drive itself is scenic, and the road is wide and smooth. The road enters the park approximately 10 miles north of West Yellowstone and gradually climbs through stretches that were burned in the fires of 1988 before emerging into unburned alpine meadows near tiny Divide Lake. North of here, U.S. Hwy. 191 follows the growing Gallatin River downhill through a pretty mix of meadows, sagebrush, rocky outcrops, and forested hillsides with grassy carpets beneath. Approximately 31 miles north of West Yellowstone, the road exits Yellowstone and enters Gallatin National Forest. It's another 17 miles from here to the turnoff for Big Sky Resort or 60 miles from the park boundary to Bozeman.

Bighorn Peak Hike

If you're up for a long and challenging day hike, climb Bighorn Peak on the northern boundary of Yellowstone. Start from the Black Butte Creek Trailhead just south of milepost 29 on U.S. Hwy. 191. The hike is steep, rising 3,100 feet in just seven miles and providing spectacular views. Look for pieces of petrified wood along the way, but leave them in place; it's illegal to take them from the park. As an added bonus, this country was untouched by the 1988 fires. Be sure to bring plenty of water because it is nonexistent on the upper portion of this hike. It is possible to do an overnight loop trip (21 miles round-trip) by continuing north from Bighorn Peak along the beautiful **Sky Rim Trail** and dropping back down Dailey Creek Trail to Black Butte Cutoff Trail. (A backcountry permit is required for this, however.) This connects to Black Butte Trail and your starting point. See one of the Yellowstone hiking guides for details on this hike.

MADISON JUNCTION TO NORRIS

The **Madison Information Station,** near Madison Junction, is open daily 8 A.M.–7 P.M. Memorial Day to Labor Day and daily 9 A.M.–5 P.M. from early September to early October. Closed the rest of the year. A small bookstore is also here. Directly behind Madison Campground is 7,500-foot **National Park Mountain,** named in honor of a fabled incident in 1870. Three explorers were gathered around the campfire, discussing the wonders that they had found in this area, when one suggested that rather than letting all of these wonders pass into private hands, they should be set aside as a national park. Thus was born the concept that led to the world's first national park. The tale was passed on as the gospel truth for so long that the mountain was named in honor of this evening. Unfortunately, the story was a complete fabrication. Cynics may read something into the fact that National Park Mountain was torched by the fires of 1988.

North of Madison Junction, the road (in very poor condition in 2002) follows the Gibbon River nearly all of the 14 miles to Norris. It crosses the river five times and hangs right on the edge through Gibbon Canyon. The pretty, 84-foot-high **Gibbon Falls** is approximately five miles up the road and situated right at the edge of the enormous caldera that fills the center of Yellowstone. The 1988 fires consumed most of the trees around the falls. Another five miles beyond this point, the road emerges from the canyon into grassy **Gibbon Meadows,** where elk and bison are commonly seen. The prominent peak visible to the north is 10,336-foot Mt. Holmes. On the west end of Gibbon Meadows is a barren area that contains **Sylvan Springs Geyser Basin.**

No maintained trail leads to this small collection of pools and springs, but hikers sometimes head across the north end of the meadows at the Gibbon River Picnic Area. The path is wet most of the summer.

An easy half-mile trail leads to **Artist Paint Pots,** filled with colorful plopping and steaming mud pots and hot springs. Although it's a short hike, the paint pots see far fewer visitors than roadside sites, making it a nice place to escape the crowds. The forest was burned in the North Fork Fire, so it's also a good place to see how the lodgepole pines are regenerating. Just south of the parking area for Artist Paint Pots is a trail to **Monument Geyser Basin,** where there isn't much activity, but the tall sinter cones form all sorts of bizarre shapes, including Thermos Bottle Geyser. The mile-long hike climbs 500 feet and provides views of the surrounding country. Another attraction is **Chocolate Pots,** found along the highway just north of Gibbon Meadows. The reddish-brown color comes from iron, aluminum, and manganese oxides. Just before you reach Norris, the road crosses through the appropriately named **Elk Park.**

NORRIS GEYSER BASIN

Although Old Faithful and the Upper Geyser Basin are more famous, many visitors to Yellowstone find Norris Geyser Basin equally interesting. Norris sits atop the junction of several major fault lines, providing conduits for heat from the molten lava below. Because of this, it is apparently the hottest geyser basin in North America, if not the world; a scientific team found temperatures of 459°F at 1,087 feet underground and was forced to quit drilling when the pressure threatened to destroy the drilling rig! Because of considerable sulfur (and hence sulfuric acid) in the springs and geysers, the water at Norris is acidic; most of the world's acid geysers are here. The acidic water kills lodgepole trees in the basin, creating an open, nearly barren place. Norris Basin has been around at least 115,000 years, making it the oldest of any of Yellowstone's active geyser basins. It is a constantly changing place, with small geysers seeming to come and go on an almost daily basis.

The paved trail from the often crowded parking area leads to **Norris Museum,** 307/344-2812, built of stone in 1929–1930. The small museum houses exhibit panels on hot springs and geothermal activity and is open daily 10 A.M.–5 P.M. from Memorial Day to early October. Closed the rest of the year. Be sure to pick up the detailed brochure (50 cents) describing the various features at Norris. Ranger-led walks are given several times a day in the summer, and there's usually one in the area ready to answer your questions. A little bookstore is housed in a nearby building. From the museum, the Norris Basin spreads both north and south, with two rather different trails to hike. Take the time to walk along both. The Norris Campground is only one-quarter mile from the geyser basin.

Porcelain Basin

Just behind the museum is an overlook that provides an impressive view across the always changing Porcelain Basin. The path descends into the basin, passing hissing steam vents, bubbling hot pools, and small geysers, including **Constant Geyser,** with frequent and sudden bursts to 20 feet or more. **Big Whirligig Geyser** is another one that is often active, spraying a noisy fan of water. (Watch your glasses and camera lenses in the steam; silica deposits can be difficult to remove.) For an enjoyable short walk, follow the boardwalk around the mile-long loop through Porcelain Basin. Stop to admire the bright colors in the steaming water, indicators of iron, arsenic, and other elements, along with algae and cyanobacteria.

Back Basin

A mile-long loop trail takes you to the sights within the Back Basin south of the museum. Before heading out, check at the museum for the latest on geyser activity. Most people follow the path in a clockwise direction, coming first to **Emerald Spring,** a gorgeous green pool with acidic water just below boiling. A little ways farther down the path is **Steamboat Geyser.** Wait a few minutes and you're likely to see one of its minor eruptions, which may reach 40 feet. On rare occasions, Steamboat erupts with a fury that

is hard to believe, blasting more than 300 feet into the air—more than twice the height of Old Faithful—making this the world's tallest geyser. Eruptions can last up to 20 minutes or more, enough time to pour out a million gallons of water, and the explosions have been heard up to 14 miles away. Steamboat's unforgettable eruptions cannot be predicted; a 50-year span once passed between eruptions, while several eruptions may occur in one year. If you ever see this one erupt, consider yourself incredibly lucky!

The path splits just below Steamboat; on the right is **Cistern Spring,** whose deep blue waters are constantly building deposits of sinter and have flooded the nearby lodgepole-pine forests, killing the trees. If you turn left where the trail splits, you come to **Echinus Geyser,** a personal favorite. (It's pronounced e-KI-nus.) The name—Greek for "spiny"—comes from the pebbles that lie around the geyser; resembling sea urchins, they are a result of sinter accumulation. The eruptions of Echinus have varied in recent years. Sometimes it settles into a regular pattern, with eruptions every hour or two, but at other times you may wait four hours for an eruption. Whatever the case, it's certainly worth the wait. When Echinus does erupt, the geyser sends explosions of acidic steam and water (pH 3.5) 40–60 feet. These generally last 3–5 minutes but sometimes continue for much longer. Unlike Old Faithful, this is one geyser where you can get up close and personal. Bench-sitters may get splashed, although the water is not hot enough to burn.

Continue along this trail beyond Echinus to see many more hot springs and steam vents. **Porkchop Geyser** was in continuous eruption for several years, but in 1989 it self-destructed in an explosion that threw rocks more than 200 feet, leaving behind a bubbling hot spring.

NORRIS JUNCTION TO CANYON

From Norris Geyser Basin to Canyon, the road cuts across the center of the park on the high Solfatara Plateau. This dozen-mile stretch of road is best known for what looks like a scene from an atomic blast, with the blackened remains of a forest seemingly blown down by the ferocity of the 1988 North Fork Fire. This is the place the news media focused on after the fires, making it appear as if it were typical of the park as a whole. In reality, the lodgepole pines were all uprooted in a wild 1984 windstorm that flattened many miles of forest both here and farther south in the Teton Wilderness. The dead trees dried out over the next four years, and when the wind-whipped fires arrived, the trees went up in a holocaust. In 50 years, this may well be a meadow. **Virginia Cascades Road** is a 2.5-mile-long, one-way road that circles around this blowdown area and provides a view of the 60-foot-tall Virginia Cascade of the Gibbon River. Back on the main highway heading east, keep your eyes open for elk and bison as the road approaches Canyon. Also note the thick young forest of lodgepole pines that was established after a fire burned through in 1955.

NORRIS JUNCTION TO MAMMOTH

The park road between Norris and Mammoth Hot Springs provides some interesting sights, although much of this country burned in the 1988 North Fork Fire. Just beyond the highway junction is the **Norris Soldier Station.** Built by the army in 1897 and modified in 1908, it is one of just three stations still standing in the park. The attractive log building now houses the small **Museum of the National Park Ranger,** 307/344-7353, with displays and a video on the history of park rangers. It is open daily 9 A.M.–6 P.M. from Memorial Day to Labor Day, and daily 9 A.M.–5 P.M. the rest of September. Closed the rest of the year.

Just up the road is **Frying Pan Spring** (named for its shape), where the water is actually not that hot. The bubbles are from pungent-smelling hydrogen-sulfide gas. **Roaring Mountain** is a bleak, steaming mountainside four miles north of Norris. In 1902, the mountain erupted into activity with fumaroles that made a roar audible at great distances. It is far less active today and is best seen in winter, when the temperature difference results in much more steam.

Obsidian Cliff

Stop at Obsidian Cliff to see the black glassy rocks formed when lava cooled rapidly. One mountain man (not, as many sources claim, Jim Bridger) told tall tales of "Glass Mountain," where his shots at an elk kept missing. When he got closer, he found he had actually been firing at a clear mountain of glass. The elk was 25 miles away, but the mountain was acting as a telescope to make the animal appear close. Obsidian Cliff was an important source of rock for Indians in making fine arrowheads and other tools. The obsidian from here was of such value that Indians traded it extensively; obsidian points made from this rock have even been found in Ohio and Ontario. (It is illegal to remove obsidian; leave it for future generations to enjoy.) North of here the countryside opens up along Obsidian Creek at **Willow Park,** one of the best places to see moose, especially in the fall.

Sheepeater Cliff and Golden Gate

Approximately 13 miles north of Norris, the road passes Indian Creek Campground (one of the quietest in the park) and the basalt columns of Sheepeater Cliff, named for the Indian inhabitants of these mountains. North of this point, the country opens into Swan Lake Flats, where you get a fine gander at 10,992-foot Electric Peak nine miles to the northwest.

At Golden Gate the road suddenly enters a narrow defile, through which flows Glen Creek. Stop to look over the edge of **Rustic Falls** and to note how the road is cantilevered over the cliff edge. Acrophobics should *not* stop here. Instead, have someone else drive, close your eyes, and say three Hail Marys.

Bunsen Peak

Just south of Mammoth is Bunsen Peak, an 8,564-foot inactive volcanic cone. Any chemistry student will recognize the name because Robert Wilhelm Eberhard von Bunsen not only first explained the action of geysers but also invented the Bunsen burner. Parts of Bunsen Peak look like a chemistry experiment run amok. The North Fork Fire of 1988 swept through this area in a patchy mosaic, leaving long strips of unburned trees next to those that are now just blackened telephone poles.

Bunsen Peak Road is a dirt track open to hikers and mountain bikers but closed to cars. Starting approximately five miles south of Mammoth and just beyond the Golden Gate, it circles the east side of the mountain, connecting with the main road six miles later. Approximately four miles in on the road is a side trail to **Osprey Falls.** This steep trail drops 800 feet in less than a mile to the base of a stunning 150-foot waterfall, but you'll need to climb back out the same way, so don't get too late of a start. Trails also lead to the summit of Bunsen Peak from both the east and west sides. Most folks choose the west trail (four miles round-trip with an elevation difference of 1,300 feet), which begins a short way up the road from the Golden Gate entrance. From the mountaintop you can drop down the east side and hike back along the road, making a total of nine miles round-trip.

The Hoodoos

North of Golden Gate, the main road soon passes the Hoodoos, a fascinating jumble of travertine boulders leaning in all directions. The rocks were created by hot springs thousands of years ago and toppled from the east face of Terrace Mountain. Just before Mammoth, turn left onto Upper Terrace Drive, a half-mile loop road providing access to the upper end of Mammoth Hot Springs. (No trailers or large RVs.)

MAMMOTH HOT SPRINGS VICINITY

Mammoth Hot Springs lies at an elevation of 6,239 feet near the northern border of Yellowstone, just five miles from the town of Gardiner, Montana. Here you'll find park headquarters, a variety of other facilities, and delightfully colorful hot springs. The Mammoth area is an important wintering spot for elk, pronghorn antelope, deer, and bison. During the fall, at least one bull elk and his harem can be seen wandering across the green lawns, while lesser males bugle challenges from behind the buildings or over the hill. The bugling

may even keep you awake at night if you're staying in the Mammoth Hotel.

Origins

Mammoth Hot Springs consists of a series of multihued terraces down which hot, mineral-laden water trickles. This water originates as snow and rain that falls on the surrounding country, although some is believed to come from the Norris area, 20 miles to the south. As it passes through the earth, the water comes into contact with volcanic magma containing massive amounts of carbon dioxide, creating carbonic acid. The now-acidic water passes through and dissolves the region's sedimentary limestone, and the calcium carbonate remains in solution until it reaches the surface at Mammoth. Once at the surface, the carbon dioxide begins to escape into the atmosphere, reducing the acidity and causing the lime to precipitate out, forming the travertine terraces that are so prominent here. As the water flows over small obstructions, more carbon dioxide is released, causing accumulations that eventually grow into the lips that surround the terrace pools. The rate of accumulation of travertine (calcium carbonate) is astounding: more than two tons a day at Mammoth Hot Springs. Some terraces grow by eight inches per year. The first explorers were fascinated by these terraces; mountain man Jim Bridger noted that they made for delightful baths. A later operation—long since ended—coated knickknacks by dipping them in the hot springs!

The springs are constantly changing as underground passages are blocked by limestone deposits, forcing the water in new directions. As a result, old dried-out terraces stand on all sides, while new ones grow each day. Areas that were active just a few years ago may now be simply gray masses of crumbling travertine rock, and new areas may appear and spread in a matter of days. Mammoth is guaranteed to be different every time you visit. One of the most interesting aspects of the hot springs here is the variety of colors, results of the many different species of algae and bacteria that live in the water. Various factors, including temperature and acidity, affect the survival of different species;

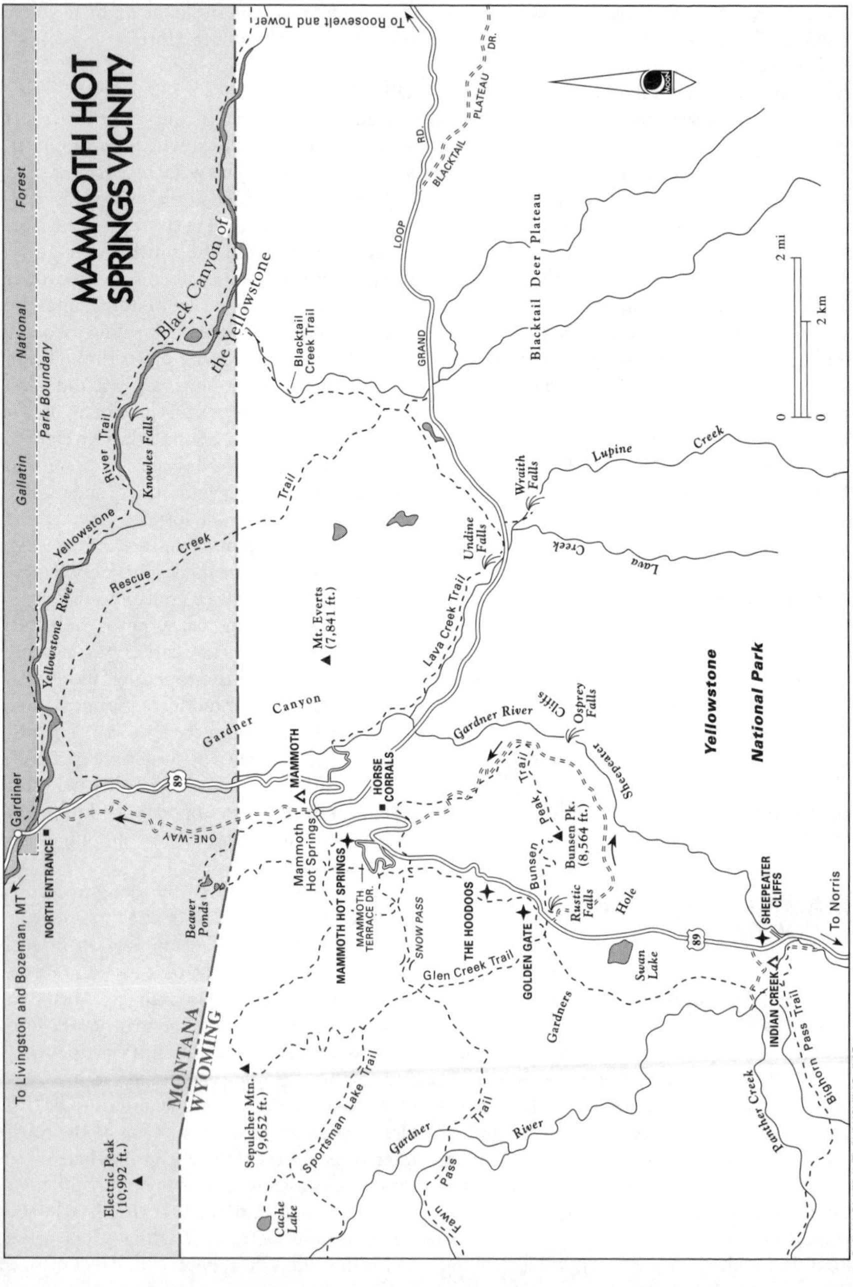

MAMMOTH HOT SPRINGS VICINITY

To Livingston and Bozeman, MT

Gallatin   National   Forest

Park Boundary

Black Canyon of the Yellowstone

Yellowstone River Trail

Knowles Falls

Yellowstone River

Rescue   Creek   Trail

Gardiner

NORTH ENTRANCE

Gardner Canyon

MAMMOTH

HORSE CORRALS

Mammoth Hot Springs

MAMMOTH HOT SPRINGS

MAMMOTH TERRACE DR.

Beaver Ponds

ONE-WAY

MONTANA
WYOMING

Electric Peak
(10,992 ft.)

Sepulcher Mtn.
(9,652 ft.)

Cache Lake

Sportsman Lake Trail

Gardner

Pass

Trail

River

Fawn

Pass

Trail

SNOW PASS

Glen Creek Trail

THE HOODOOS

GOLDEN GATE

Gardners

Bunsen Peak Trail

Bunsen Pk.
(8,564 ft.)

Rustic Falls

Hole

Swan Lake

Gardner River

Osprey Falls

Sheepeater Cliffs

Mt. Everts
(7,841 ft.)

Lava Creek Trail

Undine Falls

Wraith Falls

Lupine   Creek

Lava   Creek

Blacktail Creek Trail

To Roosevelt and Tower

BLACKTAIL PLATEAU DR.

GRAND   LOOP   RD.

Blacktail Deer Plateau

Yellowstone

National Park

SHEEPEATER CLIFFS

INDIAN CREEK

Panther Creek

Bighorn Pass Trail

To Norris

2 mi

2 km

0

0

YELLOWSTONE

N

© AVALON TRAVEL PUBLISHING, INC.

bright yellow algae live in the hottest areas, whereas cooler waters are colored orange and brown by other algae.

Visiting the Springs

Mammoth Hot Springs covers a steep hillside and consists of a series of colorful springs in various stages of accretion or decay. The area is accessible by road from below or above (Upper Terrace Dr.), and a boardwalk staircase connects the two. At the bottom of Mammoth Hot Springs and off to the right is a 37-foot-tall mass of travertine known as **Liberty Cap** for its faint similarity to the caps worn in the French Revolution. The spring that created this formation no longer flows. (You may well find the Liberty Cap shows a striking similarity to something else.)

The springs at Mammoth change continuously, and every visit brings something new. For details on currently active areas, pick up the Park Service's informative brochure (50 cents) from the box at the parking area. When I last visited, the most interesting areas were **Angel Terrace** along Upper Terrace Drive, along with **Palate Spring** near the base, and **New Blue Spring** and **Canary Spring** in the vicinity of the overlook.

All of the water flowing out of Mammoth terraces quickly disappears into underground caverns. In front of the Mammoth Hotel are two sinkholes from which steam often rises. Caverns above the terraces were once open to the public but later were closed when it became apparent that they contained poisonous gases. Dead birds are sometimes found around one of the small pools in this area appropriately named Poison Spring.

Albright Visitor Center

The Albright Visitor Center, 307/344-2263, is named for Horace Albright, the first National Park Service superintendent at Yellowstone. The center is housed in the army's old bachelor officers' quarters and is open daily 8 A.M.–7 P.M. from Memorial Day to Labor Day, daily 9 A.M.–5 P.M. the rest of the year. Spread over the two floors are exhibits on park wildlife and history, but the real treats are the works of two artists who helped bring Yellowstone's magnifi-

Liberty Cap

© DON PITCHER

cent scenery to public attention. Twenty-three of painter Thomas Moran's famous Yellowstone watercolors line the walls, and his studio has been re-created in one corner. Equally impressive are 26 classic photographs—including one of Thomas Moran at Mammoth Hot Springs—taken by William H. Jackson during the 1871 Hayden Survey. The paintings and photos are must-sees for anyone with an artistic bent. The center also has an information desk, racks of books, and films about the park and Moran. Check at the information desk for schedules of wildlife talks and frequent ranger-led walks to surrounding sights in the summer.

Other Buildings

Mammoth contains several other historic structures built during the army's tenure at **Fort Yellowstone.** The most distinctive are the six buildings (all in a row) constructed between 1891 and 1909 as quarters for the officers and

YELLOWSTONE

captains. Most of the grunt soldiers lived just behind here in barracks, one of which is now the park administration building. The U.S. Engineers Department was housed in an odd stone building with obvious Asian influences; it's right across from the visitors center. The visitors center has an informative pamphlet (50 cents) that describes the Fort Yellowstone Historic District in detail. Displays around the grounds provide additional details.

Although one wing survives from a hotel built in 1911, most of the **Mammoth Hot Springs Hotel** was constructed in 1937. Step inside to view the large map of the United States built from 15 different types of wood. Mammoth also features a Yellowstone General Store, post office, gas station, restaurant, fast-food eatery, and medical clinic. Mammoth Campground is just down the road. Just up the hill—less than one mile from the hotel—is the Mammoth corral, where horseback rides are offered. Also here is a small **cemetery** populated mostly by infants and a few civilians who died here in the early 1900s.

North to Montana

The main road north from Mammoth Hot Springs follows the Gardner River, dropping nearly 1,000 feet in elevation before reaching the town of Gardiner, Montana. (Both the river and the misspelled town are named for Johnson Gardner, a ruthless trapper from the 1820s.) The river is a favorite of fly-fishing enthusiasts. A turnout near the Wyoming–Montana border notes the "boiling river" section of the Gardner River; it's well worth a stop. Sometimes during the winter you can spot bighorn sheep on the mountain slopes just north of the river as you head down to Gardiner.

The "back way" to Gardiner is the Old Gardiner Road, a five-mile gravel road (great for mountain bikes, but not for RVs or trailers) that starts behind Mammoth Hot Springs Hotel. Traffic is downhill only, so you'll need to take the main road for your return into the park; mountain bikes can go in both directions. This is one of the best places to spot pronghorn antelope in the park, and it also provides a fine escape from the crowds at Mammoth.

Day Hikes

For a relatively easy loop hike, try the five-mile (round-trip) **Beaver Ponds Trail,** which begins between Liberty Cap and the stone house. It gains 500 feet in elevation, passing through spruce and fir forests along the way and ending at several small beaver ponds. The path then drops down to join Old Gardiner Road, which you can follow back to Mammoth. This trail provides a good opportunity to see mule deer, elk, pronghorn antelope, and moose, but is best hiked in the spring or fall when temperatures are cooler. Black bears are sometimes seen along the way, so be sure to make noise while you walk.

A longer (12 miles round-trip) hike is the **Sepulcher Mountain Trail,** which climbs to the top of this 9,652-foot peak just northwest of Mammoth. There are several possible routes to the top, and any of them can be combined into a nice loop hike. One begins at the same place as the Beaver Ponds Trail. You'll find many flowers in the expansive meadows on the south side of Sepulcher Mountain (named for several strange rocks at its summit). From Mammoth, it is a 3,400-foot elevation gain, so be ready to sweat. Before heading out, check at the visitors centers to see if there are any major bear problems in the area and to get a topographic map and hiking tips.

MAMMOTH TO TOWER JUNCTION

The 18-mile drive from Mammoth to Tower Junction takes visitors through some of the driest and most open country in Yellowstone. Two waterfalls provide stopping places along the way. Beautiful **Undine Falls** is a 60-foot-high double falls immediately north of the road. Just up the road is a gentle half-mile path to the base of **Wraith Falls,** where Lupine Creek cascades 90 feet. Look for ducks and trumpeter swans in **Blacktail Pond,** a couple of miles farther east.

Blacktail Plateau Drive, approximately nine miles east of Mammoth, turns off from the main road. The rough seven-mile dirt road is a one-way route that loosely follows the Bannock Trail, a path used by the Bannock tribe on their way to buffalo-hunting grounds east of here. Their travois trails are still visible. The Bannocks used this route from 1838 to 1878, but it was probably used for hundreds or thousands of years by various tribes crossing the high plateau. Much of Blacktail Plateau Drive is through open sagebrush, grass, and aspen country, where you're likely to see deer and pronghorn antelope. The trees are very pretty in the fall. On the east end, the road drops back into a forest burned by a severe crown fire in 1988 but now containing young aspen and lodgepole trees and abundant summertime flowers.

The Park Service has developed a two-thirds-mile boardwalk **Forces of the Northern Range Self-Guiding Trail** approximately six miles east of Mammoth Hot Springs. Trailside exhibits describe the natural world. One-half mile beyond where Blacktail Plateau Drive rejoins the main road is the turnoff to the **petrified tree.** The 20-foot-tall stump of an ancient redwood tree (50 million years old) stands behind iron bars; a second petrified tree that used to stand nearby was stolen piece by piece over the years by thoughtless tourists. The **Tower Ranger Station,** originally occupied by the U.S. Army, is located just before Tower Junction where the road splits, leading to either Northeast Entrance Road or Canyon.

NORTHEAST ENTRANCE ROAD

Of the five primary entryways into Yellowstone, Northeast Entrance is the least traveled, making this a great place to escape the hordes in midsummer. It is also one of the best places to see tall mountains in Yellowstone. The road heads east from Tower Junction and immediately enters **Lamar Valley,** an area of grass and sage along the sinuous Lamar River. Osborne Russell, who trapped this country in the 1830s, described it with affection:

We descended the stream about 15 mls thro. the dense forest and at length came to a beautiful valley about 8 Mls. long and 3 or 4 wide surrounded by dark and lofty mountains. The stream after running thro. the center in a NW direction rushed

down a tremendous canyon of basaltic rock apparently just wide enough to admit its waters. The banks of the stream in the valley were low and skirted in many places with beautiful Cotton wood groves. Here we found a few Snake indians comprising 6 men 7 women and 8 or 10 children who were the only Inhabitants of this lonely and secluded spot. They were all neatly clothed in dressed deer and Sheep skins of the best quality and seemed to be perfectly contented and happy. . . . We stopped at this place and for my own part I almost wished I could spend the remainder of my days in a place like this where happiness and contentment seemed to rein in wild romantic splendor surrounded by majestic battlements which seemed to support the heavens and shut out all hostile intruders. . . . There is something in the wild romantic scenery of this valley which I cannot . . . describe; but the impressions made upon my mind while gazing from a high eminence on the surrounding landscape one evening as the sun was gently gliding behind the western mountain and casting its gigantic shadows across the vale were such as time can never efface from my memory.

This is still one of the best places in Yellowstone to view bison, with a gorgeous backdrop of open country and wooded mountains. Elk and mule deer are also commonly seen, and the reintroduction of wolves has added another dimension to wildlife viewing. The valley contains several small ponds created when the retreating glaciers left large blocks of ice that formed "kettles." Erratic glacial boulders are scattered along the way. There are campgrounds at Slough Creek and Pebble Creek and very good fishing in Slough Creek, too. But look out for one other critter: the ubiquitous ground squirrels that dart into the road, playing chicken with your tires.

Yellowstone River Picnic Area

Picnic areas don't generally merit a mention, but this one—1.5 miles east of Tower Junction on the Northeast Entrance Road—is an exception

YELLOWSTONE

because of its proximity to a grand view. A two-mile trail takes off from here for Grand Canyon of the Yellowstone River. The hike is easy and provides a good chance to see bighorn sheep, but be careful to stay away from the canyon rim. For a loop hike (four miles round-trip), continue to the Specimen Ridge Trail, where you turn left and follow it back to your starting point.

Slough Creek Area

Slough Creek Campground is a favorite of fly-fishers who come here to try for the area's acclaimed cutthroat trout. The **Slough Creek Trail** starts at the campground and is one of the more distinctive in the park. The trail—actually a wagon road—makes for a delightful and gentle day hike through Douglas fir forests and open meadows. It continues all the way to the park boundary, 11 miles north of the campground, and is used for access to Silver Tip Ranch. This is the only way into the ranch, and because no motor vehicles are allowed you may meet folks on a horse-drawn wagon during your hike. Day hikers often go up the road as far as the first meadow, a distance of eight miles round-trip.

Yellowstone Association Institute

The nonprofit Yellowstone Association Institute teaches many classes out of Lamar Valley's historic Buffalo Ranch, approximately 10 miles east of Tower Junction. To augment the park's small wild herd, bison were brought here in 1902 from private ranches. The bison stayed in pens at night and were herded during the day. After 1915, they were allowed to roam freely in summer, although all of the park's bison were rounded up and driven here for winter. After 1938, the roundups ended, but the bison were fed hay every winter in Lamar Valley. Finally in 1952, even this practice was halted and the bison were allowed to roam throughout the park. The historic buildings are worth a look, or better still, take one of the institute's excellent classes. Get details at 307/344-2294, www.yellowstoneassociation.org.

Specimen Ridge

Just east of the historic Buffalo Ranch is a turnout across from Specimen Ridge, where explorers discovered the standing trunks of petrified trees that had been buried in volcanic ash and mudflows some 50 million years ago. Over the centuries, the trunks literally turned to stone as silica entered the wood. The process was repeated over the centuries as new forests gradually developed atop the volcanic deposits, only to be buried by later flows. Scientists have found 27 different forests on top of each other, containing walnut, magnolia, oak, redwood, and maple—evidence that the climate was once more like that of today's Midwestern states. Erosion eventually revealed the trees, many of which are still standing. This is one of the largest areas of petrified trees known to exist.

There is no trail to the petrified forest, but during summer rangers lead hikes into the area. Check at the Mammoth Visitor Center for upcoming treks. Mark Marschall's *Yellowstone Trails* provides a description of the 1.5-mile route if you want to try it on your own. A lesser-known petrified forest in the northwest corner of Yellowstone is accessible via U.S. Hwy. 191.

Wolf Watching

Between the Slough Creek and Pebble Creek Campgrounds, wolf aficionados fill roadside turnouts each morning and evening, waiting patiently for members of the Druid Peak Pack to appear. Bring your binoculars and spotting scope! During the wolf denning season, the Park Service prohibits parking or walking along certain stretches of the road, but two turnouts are available.

Northeast Entrance

At the east end of Lamar Valley, the road continues northeast up Soda Butte Creek and between the steep rocky cliffs of **Barronette Peak** (10,404 feet) and **Abiathar Peak** (10,928 feet). Stop at **Soda Butte,** where you'll find a substantial travertine mound similar to those at Mammoth. Although the springs are no longer very active, the air still reeks of hydrogen sulfide, the "rotten egg" gas. South of Soda Butte and several miles up a backcountry trail is **Wahb Springs,** found within Death Gulch. Here poisonous gases are emitted from the ground, killing animals in the vicinity. Early explorers reported finding dead bears that had been overcome by the fumes. Less than one mile north of Soda Butte is a pullout where a half-mile trail leads to pretty **Trout Lake.** It's a nice afternoon break from the crowds elsewhere in Yellowstone.

North of Pebble Creek Campground, the road squeezes through beautiful **Icebox Canyon,** past Barronette Peak, and into the (unburned) lodgepole pine forests. It follows the creek all the way to the edge of the park, crossing into Montana two miles before the park border. The **Northeast Entrance Station** is a classic log building built in 1935 and now designated a National Historic Landmark. The twin towns of Silver Gate and Cooke City (see Gateway Towns later in this chapter) are just up the road.

A fine day hike starts from the Warm Creek Picnic Area, 1.5 miles west of the entrance station. The trail climbs 1,100 feet in 1.5 miles before dropping into flower-filled mountain meadows along Pebble Creek. If you continue more than two miles you'll need to ford the creek, which can be deep before late summer. Backpackers use this trail for longer trips into the area; see Into the Backcountry for details.

Tower Fall

TOWER JUNCTION TO CANYON

Roosevelt Lodge

Lying at the junction of the roads to Canyon, Mammoth, and Lamar Valley, Roosevelt Lodge was built in 1920 and named for Pres. Theodore Roosevelt, who camped a few miles to the south during his 1903 visit. A lifelong supporter of Yellowstone, Roosevelt helped push through legislation that clamped down on the rampant destruction of park wildlife early in the 20th century.

The Roosevelt area is a favorite of families, wolf-watchers, and anglers, many of whom return year after year. The main building has the rough-edged flavor of a hunting lodge and a peacefulness that you won't find at Old Faithful, Canyon, or Mammoth. Inside are two large stone fireplaces, and the porch out front has comfortable rocking chairs that fill each evening. Folks plop their feet on the rail, nurse a beer, and watch the evening roll in. Heavenly. Rustic cabins—most built in the 1920s—provide simple accommodations, and Roosevelt has a restaurant and little gift shop/general store, along with horseback rides. It's also the only place in Yellowstone to offer wagon rides and Old West cookouts; call well ahead for reservations.

Lost Lake Trail starts behind Roosevelt Lodge and climbs through forested hills to the lake, where you can either return back via the Roosevelt Horse Trail or contour along the hillside to the Petrified Tree parking area, where another path loops back to the lodge, a distance of four miles.

Stop at the overlook to **Calcite Springs,** two miles southeast of the junction, where a walkway provides dramatic views into the canyon of the Yellowstone River, with steaming geothermal activity far below. The cliff faces contain a wide strip of columnar basalt, some of which overhangs the highway just to the south.

Tower Fall

On summer afternoons the parking lot at Tower Fall fills with cars as folks stop to see Tower Creek plummeting 132 feet before joining the Yellowstone River. The towerlike black rocks of the area are made of volcanic basalt. Nearby are a campground and a Yellowstone General Store. Tower Fall overlook is just a couple hundred paved feet from the parking area, or you can follow the path one-half mile down the switchbacks to the canyon bottom, where the vista is far more impressive and a rainbow is sometimes visible. Be prepared to get wet in the spray! A ford of the Yellowstone River—used by Bannock Indians in the 19th century—is just one-quarter mile away. For more than a hundred years, a huge boulder stood atop Tower Fall; the water and gravity finally won in 1986.

Dunraven Pass and Mt. Washburn

Continuing southward, the road climbs along Antelope Creek and eventually switchbacks up the aptly named Mae West Curve. The North Fork Fire swept through this country in 1988, but the area is now verdant with new trees, grasses, and flowers. **Dunraven Pass** (8,859 feet) is named for the Earl of Dunraven, who visited the park in 1874 and whose widely read book *The Great Divide* brought Yellowstone to the attention of wealthy European travelers. This is the highest point along any park road, even higher than the three other places where the road crosses the Continental Divide! Look for whitebark pines near the road, and be sure to stop just south of here for a view across to the distant Grand Canyon of the Yellowstone.

For an outstanding day hike, climb **Mt. Washburn,** a 10,243-foot peak with commanding vistas in all directions. The two trails up the mountain both gain about the same elevation (1,400 feet) and are around six miles round-trip. The most popular route begins from the often full parking lot at Dunraven Pass and heads up from the south side. A few miles north of the pass, the old Chittenden Road turns off and leads to another access point; drive the first mile up this road to a large parking area and then hike—or mountain-bike—to the summit of Washburn from the north side. Many wildflowers bloom in midsummer, and bighorn sheep may be seen right along the trail. Bring warm clothes and rain gear because conditions on top may be much cooler and windier than below.

GRAND CANYON OF THE YELLOWSTONE

Yellowstone is best known for its geysers and animals, but for many visitors the Grand Canyon is the park's most memorable feature. This 20-mile-long canyon ranges from 1,500 to 4,000 feet across and has colorful yellow, pink, orange, and buff cliffs that drop as much as 1,200 feet on either side. The river itself tumbles abruptly over two massive waterfalls, sending up a roar that's audible for miles along the rims. Grand Canyon is accessible by road from both the north and south sides, with equally amazing views. The lodgepole pine forests around here escaped the fires of 1988.

Carving a Canyon

After the massive volcanic eruptions some 650,000 years ago, rhyolite lava flows came through what is now the Grand Canyon. The flows eventually cooled, but geothermal activity within the rhyolite weakened the rock with hot steam and gasses, making it susceptible to erosion. Over the centuries, a series of glaciers blocked water upstream, each time creating a lake. As each glacier retreated it undammed the stream, allowing the water in the lake to empty suddenly. The weakened rhyolite was easily eroded by these periodic floods of water and glacial debris, thus revealing pastel yellow and red canyon walls colored by the thermal activities. The **Lower Falls** are at the edge of the thermal basin, above rock that was not weakened by geothermal activity. The **Upper Falls** are at a contact point between hard rhyolite that does not erode easily and a band of rhyolite that contains more easily eroded volcanic glass. Today the canyon is eroding more slowly, having increased in depth just 50 feet over the last 10,000 years.

Canyon Village

Canyon Village on the north rim is a forgettable shopping mall in the wilderness, complete with a visitors center, various stores and eating places, a post office, a gas station, cabins, lodges, and a campground. It's a good place to come on a rainy

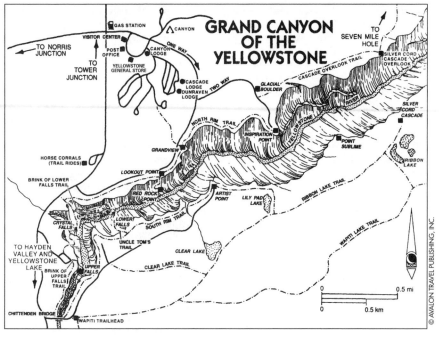

summer afternoon when the kids are starting to scream for ice cream. Horseback rides are available less than one mile south of here. Step into **Canyon Visitor Center,** 307/242-2550, for park information or to see the natural-history exhibits. Hours are daily 8 A.M.–7 P.M. Memorial Day through September, and daily 9 A.M.–6 P.M. until mid-October. It's closed in winter. A revamped and larger visitors center here should be completed in 2004.

North Rim Vistas

A one-way road takes visitors to a series of extremely popular overlooks along the north rim of Grand Canyon of the Yellowstone. Farthest east is **Inspiration Point,** where the views of the canyon and Lower Falls are, well, inspirational. **North Rim Trail** leads along the rim from Inspiration Point up to Chittenden Bridge, three miles away. Some sections of this scenic and nearly level path are paved. Just a couple hundred feet up from Inspiration Point, be sure to look for a 500-ton boulder deposited by a glacier during

the glaciation that ended 15,000 years ago. It originated in the Beartooth Mountains at least 30 miles north of here and was carried south atop a moving river of ice.

The five-mile-long **Seven Mile Hole Trail** takes off near this boulder, providing fantastic views for the first mile or so, minus the crowds at Inspiration Point. Look for **Silver Cord Cascade,** a thin ribbon of water dropping over the opposite wall of the canyon, but be careful not to go too close to the very loose edge. It's a very long way down! The trail switchbacks steeply to the Yellowstone River, passing odoriferous thermal areas en route. Many anglers come to Seven Mile Hole (it's seven miles downriver from Lower Falls) while other folks come to relax along the river. Save your energy for the strenuous 1,400-foot climb back up. Three campsites are available near the base of the trail for those who want to make this an overnight hike (permit required).

The one-way road continues westward to overlooks at **Grandview** and **Lookout Point.** From

Lookout Point, a half-mile trail drops several hundred feet to **Red Rock Point** for a closer view of Lower Falls. Farthest west along the one-way North Rim Road is the trail to the **Brink of the Lower Falls.** The trail is one-half-mile long and paved, descending 600 feet to a viewing area where you can peer over the edge as the water plummets in a thunderous roar over the 308-foot precipice (twice the height of Niagara Falls). This is probably the most breathtaking sight in Yellowstone, but if you suffer from vertigo don't even think about looking over the brink! Just south of where the one-way road rejoins the main highway is a turnoff to the **Brink of the Upper Falls,** where a short walk takes you to a less dramatic but still beautiful view of the 109-foot-high Upper Falls.

A party of prospectors wandered north into this country in 1867, following the Yellowstone River downstream without suspecting the canyon below. A. Bart Henderson wrote in his diary of strolling down the river and being

very much surprised to see the water disappear from my sight. I walked out on a rock & made two steps at the same time, one forward, the other backward, for I had unawares as it were, looked down into the depth or bowels of the earth, into which the Yellow plunged as if to cool the infernal region that lay under all this wonderful country of lava and boiling springs.

South Rim Vistas

The south rim is lined with additional dramatic views into Grand Canyon. Cross the Chittenden Bridge over the Yellowstone River (otters are sometimes seen playing in the river below) and continue one-half mile to Uncle Tom's parking area, where a short trail leads to views of the Upper Falls and Crystal Falls. More unusual is **Uncle Tom's Trail,** which descends 500 feet to Lower Falls. The trail is partly paved, but it's steep and includes 328 metal steps before you get to the bottom—good exercise if you're in shape. It was named for "Uncle" Tom Richardson who, with the help of wooden ladders and ropes, led paying tourists

to the base of the falls around the turn of the 20th century. Because there was no bridge, Uncle Tom also rowed his guests across the river near the present Chittenden Bridge. After his permit was revoked in 1903, visitors had to make do on their own.

One mile beyond Uncle Tom's parking area, the road ends at the parking area for **Artist Point,** the most famous—and crowded—of all Grand Canyon viewpoints. A short paved path leads to an astoundingly beautiful spot where one can look upriver to the Lower Falls or down the opposite direction into the canyon. Look for thermal activity far below. The point is apparently where artist Thomas Moran painted some of his famous watercolors. Avoid the crowds and afternoon thunderstorms by getting here early in the morning; it's almost always deserted at sunrise.

South Rim Trail begins at the Chittenden Bridge and continues for two miles along the rim to Artist Point, providing more viewpoints en route. The least-traveled part of this trail continues eastward from Artist Point, providing an amazingly quick escape from the mob scene at Artist Point, as well as a chance to see the kaleidoscopically colored canyon, hear the roar of the river from far below, and watch for squirrels and birds. But be careful to stay away from the edge where the rocks are loose. It's doubtful that anyone could survive such a fall, and I once came dangerously close to testing that postulate. The trail continues to Lilly Pad Lake, where you can follow the **Ribbon Lake Trail** to a pair of lakes. From here, a spur path leads to a hill that provides a wonderful view of the canyon and Silver Cord Cascade. With a drop of 1,200 feet, Silver Cord is the highest falls in Yellowstone. Also nearby are two campsites for those wanting to spend a night on the rim of the canyon; see Into the Backcountry for camping details. From the Artist Point parking area to Ribbon Lake, it's four miles round-trip. A variety of other trails on the South Rim provide alternate starting points and possible loop hikes to the Ribbon Lake area. (As an aside, the old trail to Point Sublime has been closed because of unsafe conditions along the canyon rim.)

CANYON TO LAKE JUNCTION

Hayden Valley

Just a few miles south of Canyon, the country abruptly opens into beautiful Hayden Valley, named for Ferdinand V. Hayden, leader of the 1871 expedition into Yellowstone. Reaching eight miles across, this relatively level part of the park was once occupied by an arm of Yellowstone Lake. The sediments left behind by the lake, along with glacial till, do not hold sufficient water to support trees. As a result, the area is occupied primarily by grasses, forbs, and sage. This is one of the best areas in the park to see wildlife, especially bison and elk. The Yellowstone River wanders across Hayden Valley, and streams enter from various sides. The waterways are excellent places to look for Canada geese, trumpeter swans, pelicans, and many kinds of ducks. Although they are less common, grizzly bears sometimes can be found feeding in the eastern end of the valley. Because of the bears, hikers need to be especially cautious when tramping through the grasses and shrubs, where it is easy to surprise a bear or to be likewise surprised. On the north end of Hayden Valley, the road crosses **Alum Creek,** named for its highly alkaline water, which could make anything shrink. In the horse-and-buggy days, Yellowstone wags claimed that a man had forded the creek with a team of horses and a wagon but came out the other side with four Shetland ponies pulling a basket!

Mud Volcano Area

Shortly after the road climbs south out of Hayden Valley, it passes one of the most interesting of Yellowstone's many thermal basins. On the east side of the road, a turnout overlooks **Sulphur Caldron,** where a highly acidic pool is filled with sulfur-tinted waters and the air is filled with the odor of hydrogen-sulfide gas. Directly across the road is the Mud Volcano area, where a two-thirds-mile loop trail provides what could be a tour through a bad case of heartburn. Pick up a Park Service brochure (50 cents) from the box for descriptions of all the bizarre features here. The area is in a constant state of flux

as springs dry up or begin overflowing, killing trees in their path. **Churning Caldron** is a frothing pool where periodic jets send superheated water into the air. Just up the trail is one of the most interesting features, **Black Dragons Caldron,** where an explosive spring blasts constantly through a mass of boiling black mud. The wildest place at Mud Volcano is **Dragon's Mouth,** which the Park Service notes is named for "the rhythmic belching of steam and water shooting from the cavernous opening." It's easy to imagine the fires of hell not far below this spring. The waters are 180°F. During winter (and often in summer), the Mud Volcano area is a good place to see elk or bison.

Along the Yellowstone

South of Mud Volcano, the road parallels the Yellowstone River. At **LeHardy Rapids** a boardwalk provides an overlook where early summer visitors see blush-red spawning cutthroats. In late summer, this part of the Yellowstone River is a very popular fly-fishing spot—some call it the finest stream cutthroat fishing in the world—and a good place to view ducks and swans. Earlier in the year, it's open only to the bears that gorge on the cutthroats. By the way, the Yellowstone River, which begins at Yellowstone Lake, is the longest free-flowing (undammed) river in the Lower 48.

YELLOWSTONE LAKE

When first-time visitors see Yellowstone Lake, they are stunned by its magnitude. The statistics are impressive: 110 miles of shoreline, 20 miles north to south and 14 miles east to west, with an average depth of 139 feet and a maximum depth of 390 feet. Yellowstone Lake can seem like a sheet of glass laid to the horizon at one moment and just a half hour later be a roiling ocean of whitecaps and wind-whipped waves. These changeable waters can be dangerous to those in canoes or small boats; several people have drowned, including experienced park rangers. The water is covered by ice at least half of the year, and breakup does not come until late May or early June. Even in summer, water

YELLOWSTONE

temperatures are often only in the 40s. David Folsom, who was part of an exploration party traveling through the area in 1869, described Yellowstone Lake as an

inland sea, its crystal waves dancing and sparkling in the sunlight as if laughing with joy for their wild freedom. It is a scene of transcendent beauty which has been viewed by few white men, and we felt glad to have looked upon it before its primeval solitude should be broken by the crowds of pleasure seekers which at no distant day will throng its shores.

Fishing Bridge

The area around famous Fishing Bridge (built in 1937) was for many years a favorite place to catch cutthroat trout. Unfortunately, these same fish are a major food source for grizzlies, and this area is considered some of the most important bear habitat in Yellowstone. Conflicts between bears and humans led to the death of 16 grizzlies here. To help restore trout populations and to provide food for the grizzlies, the Park Service banned fishing from Fishing Bridge in 1973 and tried to move the developments to the Grant Village area. Lobbying by folks from Cody (worried lest they lose some of the tourist

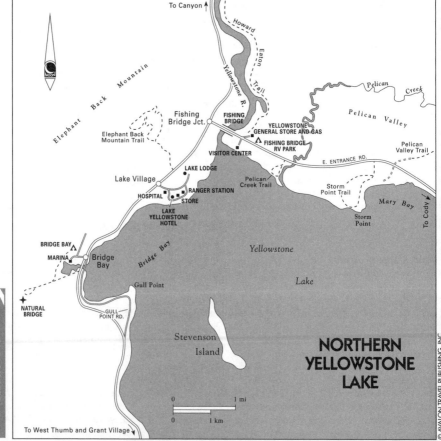

YELLOWSTONE

Yellowstone Lake near Bridge Bay

traffic) kept some of the facilities at Fishing Bridge from closing. Remaining facilities include an RV park, Yellowstone General Store, and gas station. **Fishing Bridge Visitor Center,** 307/242-2450, houses exhibits of birds, animals, and geology. It's open daily 8 A.M.–7 P.M. Memorial Day to early September, and daily 9 A.M.–6 P.M. for the rest of September. It's closed the remainder of the year. The bridge itself is still a popular stopping point and a good place to see large cutthroat trout in the shallows. For a nice loop hike, take **Elephant Back Mountain Trail,** which begins one mile south of Fishing Bridge Junction. This three-mile (round-trip) trail climbs 800 feet in elevation through dense lodgepole forests to panoramic views across Yellowstone Lake and into Pelican Valley.

Lake Yellowstone Hotel

Lake Yellowstone Hotel, the oldest extant park hostelry, was built in 1889–1891 by the Northern Pacific Railroad and originally consisted of a simple boxlike structure facing Yellowstone Lake. The hotel was sold to Harry Child in 1901, and two years later Robert Reamer—the architect who designed Old Faithful Inn—was given free rein to transform this into a more attractive place. Hard to believe that the same architect could create a grand log masterpiece and a sprawling Southern colonial mansion with distinctive ionic columns in the same park! Lake Yellowstone Hotel is the second-largest wood-framed building in North America and requires 500 gallons of paint each year to keep it in shape. During the 1960s and '70s the hotel fell into disrepair under the management of General Host Corporation, and in disgust, the Park Service bought out the concession and leased it to another company. Major renovations in the 1980s transformed the dowdy old structure into a luxurious grand hotel with much of the charm it had when Pres. Calvin Coolidge stayed here in the 1920s.

Today, Lake Yellowstone Hotel is one of the nicest places to stay in the park, with fine vistas out over the lake and comfortable quarters. Relax with a drink in the sunlit **Sun Room** while a pianist or a string quartet provides the atmosphere. Free 45-minute historic **tours of Lake Yellowstone Hotel** are given Monday–Friday at 5:30 P.M. from early June to late September. The hotel also houses a restaurant, gift shop, and snack bar.

Be sure to take a walk along the lakeshore out in front of the hotel, where the Absaroka Range forms a backdrop far to the east. The highest mountain is Avalanche Peak (10,566 feet). Almost due south is the 10,308-foot summit of Mt. Sheridan, named for Gen. Philip Sheridan, a longtime supporter of expanding the park to include the Tetons. Watch for the big white pelicans catching fish on the lake.

Just east of Lake Yellowstone Hotel is the **Lake Ranger Station,** built in 1922–1923 and now on the National Register of Historic Places. Inside the octagonal main room you will find a massive central fireplace, exposed log rafters, and rustic light fixtures. A short walk away is **Lake Lodge,** another rustic log structure that houses a reasonably priced cafeteria with grand windows fronting the lake. A Yellowstone General Store stands nearby, and dozens of plain cabins are behind it.

To West Thumb

The highway south from Lake Junction to West Thumb follows the lakeshore nearly the entire distance. A campground and boat harbor are at **Bridge Bay,** along with a ranger station, marina, and store. Stop here for hour-long boat tours of Yellowstone Lake, offered several times a day throughout the summer, or for guided fishing trips and boat rentals.

For an enjoyable day hike, visit **Natural Bridge,** a 51-foot-high span of rock that was carved by the waters of Bridge Creek. The three-mile (round-trip) trail starts from the marina parking lot. The last part of the way into Natural Bridge is along a paved road that was open to cars until recently. Cyclists can ride bikes to Natural Bridge on a separate trail that starts south of the marina.

Back on the main road, keep your eyes open for Canada geese and trumpeter swans as you drive south. **Gull Point Drive,** a two-mile-long side road, offers views of **Stevenson Island** just offshore; farther south, **Frank Island** and tiny **Dot Island** become visible. The small **Potts Hot**

Springs Basin, just north of West Thumb, is named for fur trapper Daniel T. Potts, one of the first white men to explore the Yellowstone country. His travels here in 1826 were described the following year in a Philadelphia newspaper article. It was perhaps the first published mention of Yellowstone Lake and the hot springs.

EAST ENTRANCE ROAD

Heading east from Fishing Bridge, the road follows the shore of Yellowstone Lake past country that escaped the fires of 1988. Three miles east of the bridge are Indian Pond—popular with birders—and the trailhead for **Storm Point Trail.** This pleasant three-mile (round-trip) loop trail is essentially level and goes past a large colony of yellow-bellied marmots before reaching Storm Point, where waves often pound against the rocks. The trail is often closed in spring and early summer because of grizzlies, and mosquitoes may make a June or July trip less enjoyable. North of here, Pelican Valley is considered important grizzly habitat and is closed to all overnight camping year-round. Even daytime use is not allowed until July 4, and then only between 9 A.M. and 7 P.M. Before venturing out on the Storm Point Trail or into Pelican Valley, check at the Lake Ranger Station for current bear information. The half-mile-long **Pelican Creek Nature Trail** starts one mile east of Fishing Bridge and provides an easy hike to a beach along Yellowstone Lake. Much of the way is on boardwalk over a marshy area.

At **Steamboat Point** the road swings out along the shore, providing excellent views across the lake and of a noisy fumarole. For an even better view (don't miss this one!), take the **Lake Butte Overlook** road, which continues one mile to a small parking area 1,000 feet above the lake. This is a fine place to watch sunsets and to get a feeling for the enormity of Yellowstone Lake. Back on the main highway and heading east, Yellowstone Lake is soon behind you and visible in only a few spots as the road climbs gradually, passing scenic **Sylvan Lake,** a nice place for picnics. Just up the road is tiny Eleanor Lake (little more than a puddle) and the trail to 10,566-

foot **Avalanche Peak.** This two-mile-long unmarked trail begins across the road on the east side of the creek and climbs steeply. It emerges from the forest halfway up, with the top gained via a scree slope. At the summit, you can see most of the peaks in the Absarokas and in the Tetons 70 miles away, but snow is present on top until mid-July.

Immediately east of Eleanor Lake, the main road climbs to 8,530-foot **Sylvan Pass,** flanked by Hoyt Peak on the north and Top Notch Peak to the south. Steep scree slopes drop down both sides. East of Sylvan Pass, the road descends quickly along Middle Creek (a tributary of the Shoshone River), providing good views to the south of Mt. Langford and Mt. Doane. **East Entrance Ranger Station** was built by the army in 1904. For many years, the road leading up to Sylvan Pass from the east took drivers across Corkscrew Bridge, a bridge that literally looped over itself as the road climbed steeply up the narrow valley. The road continues eastward to Cody through beautiful Wapiti Valley; see the Bighorn Basin chapter for details.

Into the Backcountry

Most Yellowstone visitors act as though they were chained to their cars with a hundred-yard tether—as if by getting away from their vehicles they might miss some other sight down the road. For the 2 percent or so who *do* abandon their cars, Yellowstone has much to offer beyond the spectacular geysers and canyons for which it is famous. Although many parts of the Yellowstone backcountry are heavily visited, regulations keep the sense of wildness intact by separating campsites and limiting the number of hikers. If you head out early or late in the season, you'll discover solitude just a few miles from the traffic jams.

Much of Yellowstone consists of rolling lodgepole (or burned lodgepole) forests. With a few exceptions, anyone looking for dramatic alpine scenery would probably be better off heading to Grand Teton National Park, the Beartooth Mountains, or the Wind River Mountains. The Yellowstone backcountry is still enjoyable to walk through, however, and many trails lead past waterfalls, geysers, and hot springs. Besides, this is one of the finest places in America to view wildlife—including bison, elk, grizzlies, and wolves—in a setting other than a zoo.

Most Yellowstone visitors act as though they were chained to their cars, but the 2 percent or so of visitors who abandon their cars find that Yellowstone has much to offer beyond the spectacular geysers and canyons for which it is famous.

Before August, when they start to die down, you should also be ready for the ubiquitous mosquitoes. Ticks are a nuisance from mid-March to mid-July in lower elevation parts of Yellowstone. The fires of 1988 created some problems for backcountry hikers, but trails have all been cleared, and hikers will get a good chance to see how the land is recovering.

Day Hikes

This section covers multiday backcountry hikes, but many hikers just head out on day outings, many of which are described in the Exploring the Park section of this chapter. Every part of the park has something different to offer day-hikers, but notable ones include the Dogshead and Lewis Channel trails to Shoshone Lake, Yellowstone Lake Overlook Trail near West Thumb, Lone Star Geyser Trail, various trails (some paved) in the Old Faithful area, Mystic Falls Trail (accessed from Biscuit Basin), the Fairy Falls Trail in Midway Geyser Basin, trails to Bunsen Peak and Osprey Falls (south of Mammoth), Beaver Ponds and Sepulcher Mountain Trails (from Mammoth), Yellowstone River Picnic Area Trail (near Tower Junction), Slough

Creek Trail (from Slough Creek Campground), Lost Lake Trail (from Roosevelt Lodge), Mt. Washburn trails, North Rim, Seven Mile Hole, and South Rim, and Ribbon Lake trails in the Canyon area, Elephant Back Mountain Trail near Fishing Bridge, Natural Bridge Trail near Bridge Bay, and the Storm Point Trail on Lake Yellowstone. All of these are described in previous sections, or you can pick up day-hike pamphlets and detailed hiking books from park visitors centers.

Rules and Regulations

The Park Service maintains more than 300 campsites in the Yellowstone backcountry, most of which have pit toilets and fire rings, along with storage poles to keep food from bears. Hikers may stay only at designated campsites. Wood fires are not allowed in many areas and are discouraged elsewhere, so be sure to have a gas stove for cooking. Bear-management areas have special regulations; they may be for day-use only, include seasonal restrictions, or specify minimum group sizes. Pets are not allowed on the trails within Yellowstone, and special rules apply for those coming in with horses, mules, burros, and llamas. Because of wet conditions and the lack of forage, no stock animals are permitted before July.

A free **backcountry-use permit** is required of each overnight party and is available in person from various Yellowstone ranger stations and visitor scenters within 48 hours of your hike. Because of the popularity of backcountry trips, you should make reservations before your arrival in the park. Unfortunately, the Park Service has taken a lesson from the IRS and makes the process as complex as bureaucratically possible. Try to follow me here. Reservations cost $20 per trip, and the reservation forms are available from the Backcountry Office, P.O. Box 168, Yellowstone National Park, WY 82190, 307/344-2160. Campsite reservation requests must be mailed in, using these forms; reservations are not accepted by phone, fax, or over the web (but they have a printable version on the park website, www.nps.gov/yell).

You'll receive a confirmation notice by return mail and will exchange the notice for a permit when you get there; the permit must be obtained in person at a ranger station within 48 hours of your first camping date. Before receiving your permit, you will be given a lengthy rundown on what to expect and what precautions to take, and you'll be shown a bear-safety video. The ranger stations are open seven days a week June–August, generally from 8 A.M. to 4:30 P.M.

For backcountry rules, bear safety tips, and suggestions for hiking and horsepacking, pick up (or find on the web) Yellowstone's *Backcountry Trip Planner,* which shows locations of campsites throughout the park and provides detailed information on wilderness access and precautions. You may want to also pick up or request the free park pamphlet *Beyond Road's End.*

Those interested in horsepacking or llama trips should contact the park at 307/344-7381, www.nps.gov/yell, for a list of outfitters authorized to operate in Yellowstone. The outfitters offer everything from day trips to weeklong adventures deep into the backcountry.

More Information

Following is a description of a few two- to four-day backcountry hikes covering various parts of Yellowstone. The park has more than 1,000 miles of trails, so this is obviously a tiny sampling of the various hiking options.

Before you head out you will probably want to look over your hiking options. Two excellent source books are *Yellowstone Trails,* by Mark Marschall (Yellowstone Association, www.yellowstoneassociation.org), and *Hiking Yellowstone National Park,* by Bill Schneider (Globe Pequot Press, www.falconbooks.com). Get them from park gift shops or visitors centers, which also sell topographic park maps. The best maps are those produced by Trails Illustrated; these feature all of the major trails and show the severity of burn from the 1988 fires—a considerable help when planning hiking trips.

NORTH YELLOWSTONE TRAILS

Sportsman Lake Trail and Electric Peak

The land west of Mammoth is some of the most rugged in Yellowstone, with several peaks topping 10,000 feet. Several trails cut westward across this country, one of the most interesting being the 24-mile-long Sportsman Lake Trail. The route begins at Glen Creek Trailhead five miles south of Mammoth and follows Glen Creek (a good place to see elk in autumn) for four miles before crossing into the Gardner River drainage. Along the way, a short spur trail leads to pretty Cache Lake. Considerably more challenging is a second side trip, the climb up 10,992-foot **Electric Peak,** the tallest mountain in this corner of Yellowstone. Many folks camp near Electric Peak and spend a day climbing. It's eight miles round-trip and you gain 3,000 feet on the way up, but the trail becomes harder to follow the higher you climb. See a park trail guidebook for details and precautions on this hike. It is possible to day-hike to the top of Electric Peak from the Glen Creek Trailhead, but it's not recommended unless you have a masochistic streak, have done a lot of hiking, and are in great shape.

Beyond the side trail to Electric Peak, Sportsman Lake Trail crosses the Gardner River twice, and there are no bridges. The water can be dangerously deep early in the summer, so this hike is generally done in August or September. After you ford the river, the trail climbs to Electric Divide (watch for bighorn sheep) and then drops steeply to Sportsman Lake and down along pretty Fan Creek to the Fawn Pass Trailhead on U.S. Hwy. 191. Because this is a one-way hike you will need to set up some sort of vehicle shuttle. Another problem is bears. This country overflows with grizzly activity, and a party size of four or more is recommended for travel here. Off-trail travel is prohibited in some areas; see the Park Service for details.

Black Canyon of the Yellowstone

For an early-summer backpacking trip, it's hard to beat this 19-mile trek along the northern edge of Yellowstone. Start at the Hellroaring Trailhead, 3.5 miles west of Tower, and follow the Yellowstone River Trail in a steep descent to the river, 600 feet below. A suspension bridge crosses the river, and from here on you remain on the north side all the way to Gardiner. One ford at Hellroaring Creek can be dangerous before August, but it can be avoided if you hike a mile or so upstream to a stock bridge crossing. After this point, the hike alternates between high ridges overlooking Black Canyon of the Yellowstone and quieter stretches where the trail drops down along the edge of the water. Dramatic Knowles Falls is a highlight. The trail is in good condition, but you may find it hot and dry in midsummer.

Pebble Creek and Bliss Pass Trails

Pebble Creek Trail cuts through a section of Yellowstone that is far away from the geysers and canyons for which the park is famous. The crowds don't come here, but the country is some of the nicest mountain scenery to be found. The trail connects with the Northeast Entrance road at both ends, making access easy. You can start from either end, but if you begin at Warm Creek Picnic Area (1.5 miles west of the entrance station), you get to the high meadows quicker. From the picnic area the trail climbs 1,100 feet in the first 1.5 miles, but beyond this it's all downhill. The best time to hike this trail is in late summer, when the water levels are lower (there are four fords) and the mosquitoes have abated. Hikers are treated to abundant alpine flowers and grand mountain scenery along the way, with the chance to see moose or elk in the meadows.

For a longer alternative hike, follow Pebble Creek Trail 5.5 miles from the picnic area and then turn west onto **Bliss Pass Trail.** The path crosses Pebble Creek (quite deep until late summer) before climbing 1,400 feet over Bliss Pass and then dropping down 2,700 feet to Slough Creek Trail. From here it is an easy walk to Slough Creek Campground. Total distance from the Warm Creek Picnic Area to Slough Creek Campground is 20 miles. The easy Slough Creek Trail is described as a day hike in the Northeast Entrance Road section.

SOUTH YELLOWSTONE TRAILS

Shoshone Lake

The largest lake in the Lower 48 without direct road access, Shoshone Lake is probably the most visited part of Yellowstone's backcountry. Its shoreline is dotted with more than two dozen campsites, but most of these fill on midsummer nights with hikers, canoeists, and kayakers. Because of the lake's popularity, reserve well ahead for a summertime campsite. On-water access is via Lewis Lake and the Lewis River Channel. Anglers come to fish in the channel or lakes; Shoshone Lake has good numbers of brown, lake, and brook trout, all of which were planted here. Hikers access Shoshone Lake primarily from the DeLacy Creek Trailhead on the north side between West Thumb and Old Faithful, or from the east side via Dogshead Trailhead. A 22-mile trail circles Shoshone Lake, although it is away from the shoreline much of the distance. You may see moose or elk and are certain to meet clouds of mosquitoes before August. The finest lake vistas come from the east side, where the trail follows the lakeshore for four miles. On the west end of the lake, hikers will find **Shoshone Geyser Basin,** an area filled with small geysers, beautiful pools, and bubbling mud pots. Most of the lake escaped the 1988 fires, but trails from the east side (via Dogshead Trailhead) traverse burned stands of lodgepole.

Heart Lake

The Heart Lake area is another extremely popular backcountry and day-hiking area, offering easy access, a pretty lake, hot springs, and impressive mountain vistas. **Heart Lake Trail** begins just north of Lewis Lake (six miles south of Grant Village). The trail is fairly easy, climbing slowly through unburned forests for the first five miles and then following Witch Creek down past burned forests to Heart Lake, eight miles from the trailhead. Witch Creek is fed almost entirely by the hot springs and geysers scattered along it.

Near the Heart Lake patrol cabin the trail splits. Continue straight ahead another 26 miles to eventually reach the isolated and challenging Thorofare Trail on the southeast end of Yellowstone Lake; getting there requires fording the Yellowstone River, which may be waist deep even in late summer. For something a bit less remote, turn right and hike one-half mile to the **Mt. Sheridan Trail,** which heads west and climbs 2,800 vertical feet in three miles. Reaching the 10,308-foot summit will certainly leave you winded. A fire lookout at the top provides views across Yellowstone Lake and south to the Tetons.

At the base of Mt. Sheridan and just to the north is a small thermal area that contains **Rustic Geyser** (eruptions to 50 feet, but irregular) and **Columbia Pool,** among other attractions. Be very careful when walking here because of the overhanging rim at the pool edge.

Although many people simply hike to Heart Lake for an overnight trip, one could take many longer hikes out of here, including into the remote Thorofare (described later). A complete loop around the lake is approximately 34 miles round-trip but requires two Snake River fords that are at least to your knees in late July; check with the rangers for flow levels. The Heart Lake area is prime grizzly habitat and is closed until the first of July. Do not take chances in this country!

Bechler River

The southwest portion of Yellowstone is known as Cascade Corner, a reference to its many tall waterfalls; more than half of the park's falls are here. This scenic and wild country escaped the fires of 1988 and is popular with anglers. Primary access is from either the Bechler Ranger Station (pronounced BECK-ler) or the Cave Falls Trailhead, both of which are well off the beaten path and must be reached via Cave Falls Road from the Idaho side. It's 22 miles in from Ashton, Idaho, the last 10 on a gravel road. As an alternative, **Grassy Lake Road** provides a narrow and rough gravel connection to Cave Falls Road. Grassy Lake Road begins at Flagg Ranch Resort near Yellowstone's South Entrance; see a good map for the exact route.

All hikers must register at the Bechler Ranger Station, even if they are heading out from Cave Falls Trailhead, three miles farther down the road.

Cave Falls is a wide but not particularly tall drop along the Falls River. It's named for a cave on the west end of the waterfall. The Forest Service's **Cave Falls Campground** ($10) is open mid-May through August.

A spiderweb of trails cuts across the Bechler country, leading to many waterfalls and past several hot springs. One popular hike goes from Bechler Ranger Station to the Old Faithful area, a distance of 30 miles; its downhill much of the way if you do this in reverse by starting at Old Faithful. From Bechler Ranger Station the trail cuts across expansive Bechler Meadows and then up narrow Bechler Canyon, passing Colonnade, Ouzel, and Iris Falls along the way. Many people stop overnight at Three River Junction to enjoy the hot springs–warmed water. Beyond this point, the trail punches over the Continental Divide and then runs west of Shoshone Lake to Lone Star Geyser and the trailhead at Kepler Cascades. It's best to hike this route in August or September after the Bechler River drops enough to be more safely forded. This also allows time for the meadows to dry out a bit (watch out for leeches) and for the mosquitoes to quiet to a dull roar. For the long trek between Bechler Ranger Station and Old Faithful you will need to set up some sort of vehicle shuttle, but shorter in-and-out loop trips could be created by reading the various Yellowstone hiking guides and studying topographic maps.

The Thorofare

If any part of Yellowstone deserves the title untamed wilderness, it has to be the Thorofare. Situated along Two Ocean Plateau and cut through by the upper Yellowstone River, this broad expanse of unroaded country reaches from Yellowstone Lake into the Teton Wilderness south of the park. This is *the* most remote country anywhere in the Lower 48; at its heart you'd need to hike 30 miles in any direction to reach a road. Because of the distances involved, many people choose to traverse the Thorofare via horseback. There is

considerable grizzly activity in this area, so various restrictions are in place. In addition, some major river crossings are impassable until late summer. Access to the Thorofare is via Heart Lake Trail (described previously), the Thorofare Trail, or through Teton Wilderness within Bridger-Teton National Forest.

The **Thorofare Trail** begins at Nine Mile Trailhead on the East Entrance Road and hugs the shore of Yellowstone Lake for the first 17 miles. This stretch was spared from the fires of 1988 and provides some incredible opportunities to watch sunsets over the lake, particularly from campsites near Park Point. The trail continues along Southeast Arm and then follows the broad Thorofare Valley upstream beside the Yellowstone River (great fishing). There are several difficult creek and river crossings before you reach the Thorofare Ranger Station at mile 32, but this is not even the halfway point! Civilization is another 36 miles away. To get there, the often muddy South Boundary Trail heads west over the Continental Divide, through four difficult creek or river fords, through forests burned in the 1988 fires, and past Snake Hot Springs before finally ending at the South Entrance Station.

Needless to say, trips into the Thorofare are only for those with a lot of stamina and extensive backcountry experience. Shorter variations are possible, of course, but most involve hiking in and out the same way. Check at the Lake Ranger Station for conditions in the Thorofare and study Yellowstone hiking guides before even considering a big trip here. It's spectacular and remote country, but that means you're on your own much of the time.

One way to cut nine miles off your hike into the Thorofare is by a boat ride across Yellowstone Lake. The folks at Bridge Bay Marina, 307/344-5217, can drop you off at a few campsites on the east side, but this is a pricey option. Contact the Park Service's Backcountry Office at 307/344-2160 to find out which campsites are accessible by motorboat. These sites tend to fill up fast, so you'll need to reserve well ahead.

Other Summer Recreation

FISHING

In the early years of the park, fish from Yellowstone Lake were a specialty at the various hotels, and because there was no limit on the take, up to 7,500 pounds of fish were caught each year. After commercial fishing was halted, park policy shifted to planting nonnative species. But by the 1970s, Yellowstone Lake had been devastated by overfishing, and new regulations were needed. Beginning in 1973, bait fishing was banned, Fishing Bridge was closed to anglers, and catch-and-release rules were put into place. Increased fish populations have been a boon for wildlife, especially grizzlies, bald eagles, and osprey. Because of these regulations, Yellowstone National Park has an almost mythical status when it comes to fishing. Each year some 75,000 visitors spend time fishing in the park. The most commonly caught fish in Yellowstone are cutthroat, rainbow, brown, lake, and brook trout, along with mountain whitefish. Montana grayling are found at only a few small lakes within the park, most notably Grebe Lake. All native species in the park—including Montana grayling, cutthroat trout, and mountain whitefish—are now catch-and-release only. Fishing regulations are complex and are described in a booklet available at park visitors centers or on the web at www.nps.gov/yell.

The Yellowstone River is still considered one of the best places in the world to catch cutthroat trout, and the Madison River is a justifiably famous fly-fishing river with a wide range of conditions. Yellowstone Lake is where the lure anglers go to catch cutthroats and lake trout. Beginners may have luck in the Gallatin River, but they're less likely to do well in the Firehole River, where the fish are smart and wary. Peaceful Slough Creek in the northeast corner of Yellowstone is filled with fat rainbows and cutthroats, attracting fly-fishers from around the globe.

Several good books—available in local stores and visitors centers—provide tips on fishing Yellowstone waters. Try one of the following: *Bud*

Lilly's Guide to Fly Fishing the New West, by Bud Lilly and Paul Schullery (Portland, OR: Frank Amato Publications); *Yellowstone Fishes; Ecology, History, and Angling in the Park,* by John Varley and Paul Schullery (Stackpole Books; www.stackpolebooks.com); or *Fishing Yellowstone,* by Richard Parks (Globe Pequot Press; www.falconbooks.com).

Trouble in Paradise

The last decade was not at all kind to aquatic ecosystems in Yellowstone as a series of diseases and nonnative threats appeared. Perhaps the greatest threat comes from lake trout (Mackinaw), a species that had been illegally planted either accidentally or intentionally in the 1980s or earlier. Lake trout were first discovered in Yellowstone Lake in 1994, and studies have since revealed that many thousands of them now inhabit the lake. A highly aggressive and long-lived species, lake trout feed on and compete with the prized native cutthroat, threatening to devastate the population. (The average lake trout eats 80–90 cutthroat trout per year in Yellowstone.) Cutthroat spawn in the shallow waters of the lake's tributary streams, where they are caught by grizzly bears, bald eagles, and other animals. Lake trout spawn in deeper waters that are inaccessible to predators, so fewer cutthroat and more lake trout could have an impact on grizzlies and eagles. Eradication of the lake trout is virtually impossible, but the Park Service has used gill nets to catch thousands of them. There are no size or possession limits on lake trout caught in Yellowstone Lake or Heart Lake, but any lake trout you catch in these lakes must be kept and shown to rangers to help determine the population size.

Another problem is threatening trout, especially rainbow trout, throughout the Rockies. **Whirling disease,** a devastating parasite-caused disease, has seriously hurt populations of rainbow trout in parts of the Madison River outside Yellowstone. The disease was discovered in Yellowstone Lake cutthroats in 1998, and there are fears that it could spread to other lakes and rivers in the park. It is spread in part when mud or water is brought in from contaminated areas on waders, boats, and boots. Be sure to clean up thoroughly with a bleach solution before entering or leaving an area. Get details on whirling disease at www.whirlingdisease.org.

As if the other problems weren't enough, **New Zealand mud snails** were discovered in park waters in 1995. These miniscule snails (natives of New Zealand) are now in the Firehole, Gibbon, Madison, and Snake Rivers, where they can form dense colonies on aquatic plants and streambed rocks, crowding out native aquatic insects that are a food source for fish.

Fishing Regulations

In most parts of Yellowstone, the fishing season extends from Memorial Day weekend to the first Sunday of November, but check the regulations for specifics. Hayden Valley and some other areas are entirely closed to fishing, and only artificial lures and flies are allowed in the park. Lead cannot be used. All native species in the park—Montana grayling, cutthroat trout, and mountain whitefish—are catch-and-release only. Barbless hooks are preferable for catch-and-release fishing because they cause less damage and are easier to remove. Some rivers, including the Madison River, the Firehole River, and the Gibbon River (downstream from Gibbon Falls) are open only to fly-fishing.

Anglers don't need a state fishing license but must obtain a special Yellowstone National Park permit, available from visitors centers, ranger stations, and Yellowstone General Stores, plus fishing shops in surrounding towns. The adult **fishing fee** is $10 for a 10-day permit or $20 for a season permit. Kids ages 12–15 get permits for free, and younger children do not need a permit. Park visitors centers and ranger stations have copies of current fishing regulations.

BOATING

Bridge Bay Marina runs hour-long scenic **boat tours** of Yellowstone Lake ($9.25 adults, $5 ages 2–11) several times a day in the summer, providing a fine introduction to the area. Also avail-

able at the marina are **guided fishing trips** ($55–72 an hour for up to six people) and **boat rentals** ($7.50 per hour for a 16-foot rowboat; $30 per hour for a 18-foot motorboat with a 40-horsepower outboard).

The best Yellowstone Lake fishing is from boats rather than from the shoreline. If you're bringing your own boat or canoe to Yellowstone, pick up a park boat permit at the Lake Ranger Station or Grant Village Visitor Center. Boat slips are available at Bridge Bay Marina for $12–18 per night. All streams are closed to watercraft, with the exception of the Lewis River Channel between Shoshone and Lewis Lakes. Motorboats are allowed only on Lewis Lake and parts of Yellowstone Lake.

Sea Kayaking

Several companies offer guided sea kayak trips in the park. **Snake River Kayak & Canoe School,** 307/733-9999 or 800/529-2501, www.snake riverkayak.com, leads a variety of trips on Yellowstone Lake, starting with three-hour sunset tours ($75 per person) and half-day paddles in the West Thumb area ($165 per person), all the way up to eight-day paddling trips that leave the crowds behind as you explore the lake; these cost $1,095 per person, all-inclusive. They also guide sea kayaking tours of Lewis and Shoshone Lakes, and have a full range of kayaking classes (taught in Jackson and Grand Teton National Park).

Jackson Hole Kayak School, 307/733-2471 or 800/733-2471, www.jhkayakschool.com, has day tours of Yellowstone Lake or Lewis Lake for $150 per person. They also offer three-day tours of Yellowstone Lake for $680 per person, and three-day tours of Lewis and Shoshone Lakes for $600 per person. The overnight trip prices include transportation from Jackson, kayaking and camping gear, supplies, and all meals.

O.A.R.S., 209/736-4677 or 800/346-6277, www.oars.com, offers half-day sea kayak trips from Grant Village for $60 adults or $40 kids. In addition, they guide multiday trips to the quiet south and southeast arms of Lake Yellowstone. Adult rates are $525 for three days or $637 for four days. Tents and sleeping bags are available for rent, or bring your own.

BICYCLING

Cycling provides a unique way to see Yellowstone up close. Unfortunately, park roads tend to be narrow shoulders and traffic is heavy, making for dangerous conditions. These problems are exacerbated early in the year by high snowbanks, so bikes are not allowed on certain roads. Call 307/344-7381 for current road conditions.

If you're planning a cycling trip through Yellowstone, be sure to wear a helmet and high-visibility clothing. A bike mirror also helps. If you want to avoid some of the hassles and don't mind spring conditions, visit the park between late March and the third Friday in April, when motorized vehicles are usually prohibited from entering the park (except for park administrative vehicles). During this period, cyclists are allowed to ride only on the stretch between the West Entrance and Mammoth Hot Springs; other roads are closed to cycling because they're being plowed. Fall is also a good time to ride because traffic is much lighter than in summer. The best times to ride in summer are in the morning before traffic thickens or late in the afternoon before the light begins to fade and you become less visible to motorists.

Where to Ride

The best main park roads to ride (less traffic or better visibility and shoulders) are the following sections: Mammoth to Tower, Tower to Cooke City, Canyon to Lake, and Lake to Grant Village. Bikes are not allowed on backcountry trails or boardwalks inside Yellowstone. Several relatively short but fun mountain-bike rides are available around the park, including the paved trail from Old Faithful to Morning Glory Pool (two miles), the partly paved trail to Lone Star Geyser in the Old Faithful area (two miles), Fountain Flat Drive (six miles) to the vicinity of Midway Geyser Basin, the old Chittenden Road up Mt. Washburn (three miles each way, but gaining 1,400 feet on the way up), Bunsen Peak Road near Mammoth (six miles and steep in places), the Old Gardiner Road from Mammoth to Gardiner (five miles), and Blacktail Plateau Drive (seven miles) east of Mammoth. Of these routes, cars are allowed only on the Old Gardiner Road and Blacktail Plateau Drive, but traffic is light on these two.

Bike Rentals and Tours

Unfortunately, there are no bike rentals inside Yellowstone or Gardiner, although they are available in the surrounding towns of West Yellowstone, Jackson, and Cody. **Backroads,** 800/462-2848, www.backroads.com, has six-day multisport trips into Yellowstone and Grand Teton that include biking, hiking, rafting, and kayaking. These are offered as either camping trips ($1,200 per person including meals) or trips where you stay at local inns ($2,200 per person including meals). Contact the Park Service for a list of other permitted bicycle-tour operators.

TRAIL RIDES

Summertime **horseback rides** are available from the corrals at Mammoth Hot Springs, Canyon Village, and Roosevelt Lodge. These cost $25 for one hour or $37 for a two-hour ride. Kids must be at least eight years old and 48 inches tall, and there is a 250-pound weight limit, much to the relief of the horses. Roosevelt also has **stagecoach rides** ($7 adults, $6 ages 2–11) several times a day in the summer. In addition, **Old West dinner cookouts** at Roosevelt combine a horseback or wagon ride with a filling steak dinner.

For details on trail rides, contact Xanterra Parks & Resorts, 307/344-7311, www.travelyellowstone.com. Several outfitters provide backcountry pack trips inside Yellowstone; get a list from Park Service visitors centers or at 307/344-7381, www.nps.gov/yell.

HOT SPRINGS

Many people are disappointed to discover that there are no places in Yellowstone where you can soak in the hot springs. Not only is it illegal, but it can also be dangerous because temperatures often approach boiling and bathers can cause severe damage to these surprisingly fragile natural wonders. Legal bathing pools are found in cold-water streams that have hot springs feeding into them. You're not allowed to enter the source pool or stream itself. Families often stop for a swim in the Firehole River along Firehole Canyon Drive near Madison. The Park Service doesn't encourage this, and there are no lifeguards, so parents need to watch children closely.

Thirty miles north of Yellowstone in the little burg of Pray, Montana, is **Chico Hot Springs.** If you're staying in the Mammoth Hot Springs area of Yellowstone, a side trip to Chico may be worthwhile. The large outdoor pool is a great place to relax, the gourmet restaurant serves some of the best dinners anywhere around, and the classic old hotel is a favorite. Details at 406/333-4933 or 800/468-9232, www.chicohotsprings.com.

Winter in Yellowstone

Winter transforms Yellowstone into an extraordinarily beautiful place where the fires and brimstone of hell meet the bitter cold and snow of winter. The snow often averages four feet in depth but can exceed 10 feet on mountain passes. The snow is usually quite dry, although late in the season conditions deteriorate as temperatures rise. Early in the winter or after major storms, backcountry skiing can be difficult because of the deep powder. Temperatures are generally in the 10–25°F range during the day, while nights frequently dip below zero. (The record is –66°F, recorded on February 9, 1933.) Winds can make these temperatures feel even colder, so visitors should come prepared for extreme conditions.

The thermal basins are a real wintertime treat. Hot springs that are simply colorful pools in summer send up billows of steam in the winter, coating nearby trees with thick layers of ice and turning them into "ghost trees." The geysers put on astounding displays as boiling water meets frigid air; steam from Old Faithful can tower 1,000 feet into the air! Bison and elk gather around the hot springs, soaking up the heat and searching for dried grasses, and bald eagles are

Bison trudge through the snow along the Firehole River near Old Faithful.

YELLOWSTONE

often seen flying over the heated waters of Firehole River. The bison are perhaps the most interesting to watch as they swing their enormous heads from side to side to shovel snow off the grass. Grand Canyon of the Yellowstone is another place transformed by the snow and cold. Although the water still flows, the falls are surrounded by tall cones of ice, and the canyon walls lie under deep snow. A good resource on winter access to Yellowstone is *Yellowstone Winter Guide* by Jeff Henry (www.roberts-rinehart.com).

HISTORICAL WINTER USE

During Yellowstone's first 75 years as a park, winter visitation was almost unknown. The only people in the park were caretakers who spent months at a time with no contact with the world outside. This began to change in 1949, when snow-plane tours were first offered from the West Entrance. The planes skimmed over the surface and could only hold two people—the driver and a passenger—so visitation barely topped 30 people that winter. In 1955, snowcoaches were permitted to come into Yellowstone, and more than 500 people visited, although few stayed overnight.

Snowmobiling Changes Everything

The first snowmobilers arrived in 1963, when the machines were still a novelty. As snowmobiling became increasingly more popular, communities around Yellowstone benefited economically and began promoting the park as a winter wonderland. In the winter of 1971–1972 the Park Service began encouraging snowmobile use by grooming the roads and opening Old Faithful Snow Lodge (it has since been replaced by a much nicer building of the same name). By the end of that winter, more than 25,000 people had visited. Since then, winter use has rocketed; today, more than 140,000 people visit Yellowstone each winter, and the park admits more snowmobiles than all other national parks combined. Prior to 2003, as many as 1,600 snowmobiles flooded into Yellowstone on busy days, spewing choking blue smoke that created localized pollution and sometimes sickened park em-

ployees working at entrance stations. While these numbers pale in comparison to summer visitation, environmentalists worry that snowmobilers and skiers could adversely affect the park's wildlife at a time when the animals are already under great stress.

In the heavy snow winter of 1996–1997 large numbers of bison moved out of Yellowstone, some of them along the groomed snowmobile road out the west side of the park. Nearly 1,100 bison were killed that year as part of Montana's effort to protect cattle from brucellosis. The slaughter precipitated a lawsuit by the Fund for Animals that forced the Park Service to rethink its winter-use policies. To address the effects of snowmobiles and other uses, the Park Service under President Clinton attempted to ban snowmobiles from the park. Industry groups and others successfully fought the closure, with support from the snowmobile-friendly Bush administration. New rules are now in place, allowing a maximum of 1,100 snowmobiles daily, and mandating that cleaner and quieter machines with four-stroke engines be used for rentals. (Private owners of snowmobiles won't be required to have four-stroke machines until 2004–2005.) The regulations also require that 80 percent of snowmobilers must be led by commercial guides.

ROADS

Most of Yellowstone's roads officially close to cars on the Monday after the first Sunday in November and remain shut down all over except for the 56 miles between Mammoth and Cooke City. Roads don't open for cars again until sometime between mid-May and early June. The roads are groomed for snowmobiles and snowcoaches from mid-December to mid-March. The rest of the winter you'll only find skiers and park personnel on the roads. During winter, the most popular (and crowded) times to visit Yellowstone are around Christmas and New Year's and over the Presidents' Day weekend in February. If you plan to arrive at these times, make lodging reservations six months to a year in advance. The rest of the winter, you should probably reserve at least three months ahead.

ACCOMMODATIONS

During winter only two places offer lodging inside the park. **Mammoth Hot Springs Hotel,** on the north end of the park, is the only accommodation accessible by road and has ski and snowshoe trails nearby, while the recently built **Old Faithful Snow Lodge and Cabins** puts you close to the geysers and many miles of ski trails. Each has a restaurant, lounge, gift shop, and rentals of skis and snowshoes. Mammoth has a couple of advantages over Old Faithful: far fewer snowmobiles so it's much quieter, and road access to the Lamar Valley where wolves, bison, and elk are major attractions. You might even see a pack of wolves take down an elk. Lodging prices and seasons are described in Yellowstone Accommodations.

A wide variety of package trips are offered in winter, from two-night specials to a version that encompasses three nights at Old Faithful, three nights at Mammoth, breakfasts and lunches, skis and snowshoes, hot tub use, ice skating, and snowcoach tours. Mammoth also offers Sunday breakfast buffets and special dinners, along with ice skate and hourly hot tub rentals. Get details on winter lodging options in the park from Xanterra Parks & Resorts, 307/344-7311, www.travelyellowstone.com.

Just south of Yellowstone in the Rockefeller Parkway is **Flagg Ranch Resort,** 307/543-2861 or 800/443-2311, www.flaggranch.com, where you'll find modern cabins that are open in winter. See the Grand Teton National Park chapter for specifics on Flagg Ranch. It's another 55 miles from Flagg Ranch to Jackson, a wintertime base for many Yellowstone visitors. On the east side of Yellowstone, lodging is available just outside the park at Pahaska Teepee and other lodges in the Wapiti Valley area; see the Bighorn Basin chapter for details. Other accommodations (described in the Yellowstone Gateway Town sections) can be found just outside the park in the towns of West Yellowstone, Gardiner, Cooke City, and Silver Gate.

The only wintertime camping place is Mammoth Campground, where temperatures are milder and the snow lighter.

SERVICES

Only the Mammoth and Old Faithful visitors centers are open during winter. Free ranger-led activities include evening programs at Mammoth and Old Faithful. Check the winter edition of *Yellowstone Today* for details, or find it on the web at www.nps.gov/yell.

Xanterra Parks & Resorts, 307/344-7311, www.travelyellowstone.com, offers a variety of guided ski and snowmobile tours and provides wildlife bus or van tours; call for details. In addition, the Yellowstone Association Institute, 307/344-2294, www.yellowstoneassociation.org, has outstanding winter classes.

The Mammoth Clinic, 307/344-7965, is open weekdays (except Wednesday afternoons) in the winter for medical emergencies.

Supplies and Warming Huts

The Yellowstone General Store at Mammoth is open for groceries and supplies year-round, but only meals and gas are available at Old Faithful. Warming huts are located at Old Faithful, Madison Junction, Canyon, West Thumb, Fishing Bridge, and Indian Creek (south of Mammoth Hot Springs). All contain restrooms and snack machines (except Indian Creek and West Thumb), and all are open 24 hours (except for Old Faithful, where other facilities are available). The huts at Madison and Canyon also have snack bars selling hot chili or soup. Park rangers are often at the warming huts during the middle of the day.

SNOWCOACHES

The easiest and most enjoyable way to get into Yellowstone in the winter is on the ungainly snowcoaches—machines that look like something the Norwegian Army might have used during World War II. Most were actually built by a Canadian company, Bombidier. They can be noisy, and the windows fog up (hence the spray bottles of antifreeze). But despite their ancient condition and spartan interiors, these beasts still work well and can carry 10 passengers, gear (two suitcases per person), and skis.

YELLOWSTONE

You will also see (or ride in) several other over-snow vehicles, including vans on tracks.

Snowcoach Tours

A variety of snowcoach tours are provided by Xanterra Parks & Resorts, 307/344-7311, www.travelyellowstone.com. All snowcoach tours and transportation are half-price for kids ages 2–11 and free for toddlers. Adult per-person rates to Old Faithful are $102 round-trip from Flagg Ranch (where the plowing ends just south of Yellowstone), $92 round-trip from West Yellowstone, and $97 round-trip from Mammoth. They also provide tours most days from Mammoth to Canyon for $92 round-trip, and Old Faithful to Canyon for $97 round-trip.

Shorter snowcoach tours depart two or three times a week from Old Faithful for the Firehole River/Fountain Flats area (three hours; $24 round-trip) and West Thumb Geyser Basin (three hours; $24). Three-hour winter wildlife bus tours to the Lamar Valley ($21) depart from Mammoth on Wednesdays, providing a good opportunity to see wolves. Also available from Mammoth is a daybreak bus tour (3.5 hours; $21 with a continental breakfast). Children under 12 are half-price, and kids under two are free on all snowcoach trips. See following description for combination snowcoach and cross-country skiing trips. For any of these trips, be sure to make reservations well in advance.

During the winter, **Alltrans/Gray Line,** 307/733-4325 or 800/443-6133, www.jacksonholealltrans.com, has daily bus runs from Jackson to Flagg Ranch for $40 one-way, arriving in time to meet the snowcoach departures for Yellowstone. Reservations are required.

Yellowstone Alpen Guides, 406/646-9591 or 800/858-3502, www.yellowstoneguides.com, leads snowcoach tours from West Yellowstone. All-day trips are $97 ($89 seniors, $77 kids) to Grand Canyon of the Yellowstone, or $87 ($79 seniors, $66 kids under 12) to the Old Faithful area. Guests on the latter run have an option of getting dropped at Biscuit Basin, where they can ski to Old Faithful and meet the rest of the group for the return trip. Special snowcoach-and-guided-ski tours are $109 per person. Also available is a three-night package trip that includes two nights in West Yellowstone, a night at Old Faithful Snow Lodge, and two days of wildlife snowcoach tours for $395 per person.

Buffalo Bus Touring Co., 406/646-9564 or 800/426-7669, www.yellowstonevacations.com, also operates snowcoach vans from West Yellowstone, with tours to Old Faithful for $84 adults or $64 kids.

For a truly unique experience, book a trip with another West Yellowstone–based company, **Yellowstone Expeditions,** 406/646-9333 or 800/728-9333, www.yellowstoneexpeditions.com. They run converted vans jacked up above tracks and skis and have a remote base camp near Canyon that is perfect for those who want to really explore Yellowstone in winter. Guests stay in eight heated tent cabins, with two yurts providing a central kitchen and dining/social area. These overnight trips start at $1,400 for two people for three nights and four days, up to $2,280 for two people for seven nights and eight days. The price includes lodging, food, bedding, round-trip transportation from West Yellowstone to the base camp near Canyon, and backcountry ski guides. Ski and snowshoe rentals are extra. Days are spent skiing or snowshoeing in the Canyon area or along trails around Hayden Valley, Norris, or Mt. Washburn. The camp sauna is perfect after a long day in the backcountry. This is the only overnight accommodation at the Canyon area during the winter. Recommended.

SKIING AND SNOWSHOEING

Cross-country skis and snowshoes provide the finest ways to see Yellowstone in the winter. Rent them from Old Faithful Snow Lodge or Mammoth Hot Springs Hotel. Both places also provide lessons and guided tours for groups or individuals. The towns surrounding Yellowstone also have shops that rent skis and snowshoes. The Old Faithful area is the center for skiing within Yellowstone, with trails circling the Upper Geyser Basin and leading to nearby sights. You'll find similar ski trails (marked but not groomed) in the Tower Fall, Canyon, Northeast, and Mammoth areas. Get free ski-trail maps at the visitors centers.

Old Faithful Snow Lodge is open in winter, providing an excellent base for day trips into nearby areas or for a snowcoach tour of the park.

Skiers and snowshoers sometimes assume that they can't possibly cause problems for Yellowstone's wildlife, but studies show that elk and bison often move away from skiers, which forces the animals to expend energy they need to survive through the bitterly cold winters. It's best to stay on the trails and to keep from skiing into areas where elk or bison may be disturbed by your presence. For more on skiing and winter visitation in the park, see Jeff Henry's *Yellowstone Winter Guide* (www.roberts-rinehart.com), or *Winter Tales and Trails: Skiing, Snowshoeing and Snowboarding in Idaho, the Grand Tetons and Yellowstone National Park* by Ron Watters (Great Rift Press).

Shuttles and Tours

Xanterra Parks & Resorts, 307/344-7311, www.travelyellowstone.com, operates **skier shuttles** ($12.50 round-trip) from Mammoth eastward by van to Blacktail Plateau and Tower Junction, or southward by snowcoach to Golden Gate and Indian Creek. From these last two many folks choose to ski back to Mammoth because it's mostly downhill. A similar snowcoach shuttle is available from Old Faithful to Fairy Falls Trailhead or the Continental Divide area for $11. In these last two trips you ski back to the Snow Lodge on your own; the Continental Divide run is eight miles long and primarily downhill.

Skiers will also appreciate the van service offered between Mammoth and Cooke City ($59 round-trip), where you're given all day to ski into the beautiful Absaroka Mountains. In addition, Xanterra has all-day Grand Canyon snowcoach-and-guided-ski tours ($99 round-trip) twice a week from Old Faithful and once weekly from Mammoth. **Afternoon ski-daddles** are guided five-hour ski tours from Old Faithful to Fairy Falls or DeLacey Creek. They're offered twice a week and cost $35.

Guided snowshoe tours ($27 with snowshoes provided) are offered from Old Faithful twice weekly and Mammoth once a week. They last three hours and are a great way to explore the country. Besides these concessioner-run tours, park naturalists sometimes lead ski trips from Old Faithful to nearby sights. Stop by the visitors center for details.

Safety on Skis

Yellowstone's roads are heavily traveled by snowmobiles and snowcoaches, making for all sorts of potential conflicts. Be sure to keep to the right while skiing. Most trails are identified by orange metal markers on the trees. If you're planning a backcountry trip, pick up a use permit from one of the ranger stations. A thorough understanding of winter camping and survival is imperative before you head out on any overnight trip, and avalanche safety classes are a wise investment of your time.

Before heading into backcountry areas, get avalanche-safety information from the **Avalanche Advisory Hotline** in Bozeman, 406/587-6981, www.gomontana.com/avalanche. The recording does not cover the entire park, but it does include the Washburn Range and areas near Cooke City and West Yellowstone. It's updated daily in the winter.

SNOWMOBILES

Nearly three-quarters of all winter visitors to Yellowstone enter the park on snowmobiles, and it isn't uncommon to meet long lines of machines ripping down the roads at any time of the day, disrupting Yellowstone's pristine winter silence. Despite the fact that the five national forests surrounding Yellowstone have many hundreds of miles of groomed trails and thousands of square miles of terrain open to the machines, Yellowstone's 180 miles of roads have become the focus of this mechanized winter onslaught.

Practicalities

If you really *must* come into Yellowstone by snowmobile, please show a few courtesies and precautions. In particular, stay on the roads and stay well away from the bison and elk commonly found along or on the roads. This is a highly stressful time of the year for them already, without being harassed by a steady stream of machines. If they stop in the middle of the road, wait for them to move, don't try to make them move. Also, if skiers are on the road, slow down and give them a wide berth as you pass. The speed limit (45 mph) is enforced, and one of the most bizarre Yellowstone sights is a park ranger waiting in a speed trap with his radar gun, ready to catch speeding sleds. Park regulations now require that all rental snowmobiles must be the cleaner and quieter four-stroke machines, but private owners have until the winter of 2004–2005 to get four-stroke machines. The new regulations also require that 80 percent of snowmobilers must be led by commercial guides.

Snowmobiles are available for rent from all four sides of the park, with most snowmobilers coming in from West Yellowstone, where prices are usually a bit lower and access is quicker. Expect to pay $100–150 per day, including clothing and helmet, for a machine or $140–190 for a guided tour. The machines can also be rented at Mammoth and Old Faithful inside the park. You'll need a valid driver's license to drive snowmobiles into Yellowstone. Contact chamber of commerce offices in West Yellowstone, Jackson, or Cody for a listing of snowmobile rental companies. You can purchase gas inside the park at Mammoth Hot Springs, Canyon, Fishing Bridge, and Old Faithful.

Camping

Tent camping in Yellowstone's early days left a bit to be desired. One 1884 tourist noted that during the height of summer, "the principle upon which the beds are populated is said to be the addition of visitors so long as they may arrive, or until the occupants 'go for their guns.' The plan is simple, and relieves the authorities of responsibility." It's still crowded in the park, but at least guns are prohibited today!

Camping is available at a dozen sites scattered along the Yellowstone road network. Most of these campsites are open from at least Memorial Day to mid-September, but only Mammoth Campground remains open throughout the year. Generators are allowed in more than half of the campgrounds but can only be used between 8 A.M. and 8 P.M. Roadside or parking-lot camping is prohibited, and rangers vigorously enforce this.

Reservations are available—and advised—for five concessioner-managed campgrounds: Bridge Bay Campground, Canyon Campground, Grant Village Campground, Madison Campground, and Fishing Bridge RV Park. Contact Xanterra Parks & Resorts for reservations (no extra charge) at 307/344-7311, www.travelyellowstone.com. The other seven (Park Service-managed) campgrounds inside Yellowstone are available on a first-come, first-camped basis with no reservations. You can pay with cash, checks, or credit cards.

During July and August, virtually all campsites in Yellowstone fill *before noon,* so get there early or reserve a space in advance! The busiest weekends are—not surprisingly—around Fourth of July and Labor Day, but Yellowstone's most popular campgrounds fill up even in late fall and early summer. Call the Park Service at 307/344-2114 for a recording noting which campgrounds are currently full.

Bridge Bay Campground
This camping area is adjacent to the Bridge Bay Marina on the north side of Lake Yellowstone and also near a ranger station and store. Meals are available at Lake Yellowstone Hotel and Lake Lodge, just a few miles from here. This campground fills quickly most summer days. Generators are permitted, and it has flush toilets and a dump station. The campground is open late May to mid-September and costs $15. Contact Xanterra Parks & Resorts, 307/344-7311, www.travelyellowstone.com, for reservations (highly recommended). Group sites are also available.

Canyon Campground
This exceptionally popular camping area is close to the dramatic overlooks at Grand Canyon of the Yellowstone. A park visitors center, Yellowstone General Store, restaurant, cafeteria, post of-

fice, gas station, and other lodging are a short walk away. Not surprisingly, the campground fills early most summer days. It has coin-operated washers and dryers, showers ($3 per person), flush toilets, and a dump station. Generators are permitted. Canyon Campground is open June to early September and costs $15. Contact Xanterra Parks & Resorts, 307/344-7311, www.travelyellowstone.com, for reservations (highly recommended).

Fishing Bridge RV Park

Located on the north end of Yellowstone Lake, this campground is open only to hard-sided RVs, with a 40-foot maximum length. No tents, pop-ups, or other campers that bears might break into easily are allowed. Sites with full hookups cost $29 for up to four people, and generators are permitted. Bathhouses have showers ($3 per person), flush toilets, and coin-operated washers and dryers. Dining is available a few miles away at Lake Yellowstone Hotel and Lake Lodge. The RV Park is open mid-May through September and fills early most days. Contact Xanterra Parks & Resorts, 307/344-7311, www.travelyellowstone.com, for reservations (highly recommended).

Grant Village Campground

Located near the south end of Yellowstone Lake and 19 miles southeast of Old Faithful, this campground fills early and offers woodsy sites. It has showers nearby ($3 per person), flush toilets and coin-operated washers and dryers, and a dump station. Generators are permitted. Nearby are restaurants, a park visitors center, and a general store. The campground is open late June–September and costs $15. Contact Xanterra Parks & Resorts, 307/344-7311, www.travelyellowstone.com, for reservations (highly recommended). Group sites are available.

Indian Creek Campground

This quiet campground generally fills late in the day, but is just eight miles south of Mammoth, where you'll find food and other services. No generators, and it has vault toilets. It sits alongside pretty Indian Creek and is open early June to mid-September. The 73 sites go for $10 each. No reservations.

Lewis Lake Campground

Located on the southeast end of Lewis Lake, this campground is the southernmost in the park. It fills early and is open late June to early November. It has vault toilets, and a boat ramp is nearby. Campsites are $10. Food and other services are available at Grant Village to the north or Flagg Ranch to the south. No reservations.

Madison Campground

Located 16 miles north of Old Faithful, this is the closest campground to Yellowstone's most famous attraction. West Yellowstone is 14 miles to the west. The campground is near the confluence of the Gibbon, Madison, and Firehole Rivers and makes a fine base for exploring all of the park's main attractions. Madison fills early in the day throughout summer. Generators are allowed, and the campground has flush toilets and a dump station. It's open May to late October and costs $15. Contact Xanterra Parks & Resorts, 307/344-7311, www.travelyellowstone.com, for reservations (highly recommended).

Mammoth Campground

This very popular campground is near a residential area and along the busy park road, but is just a short walk from the hot springs, visitors center/museum, shops, horseback rides, and eating places in Mammoth. Generators are permitted and road traffic can be noisy, so this isn't the most peaceful spot. It has flush toilets and is the only park campground that remains open year-round. The cost is $12. No reservations.

Norris Campground

One of Yellowstone's most dramatic geyser basins is just one-quarter mile away from Norris Campground. The campsites fill early most days, and the campground has flush toilets. Food and supplies are available at Canyon Village, 12 miles east of Norris. Generators are permitted, and the campground is open early May through September. The cost is $12. No reservations.

Pebble Creek Campground

This campground makes a good base for wildlife watching in Lamar Valley and for exploring the scenic Icebox Canyon area. It's located in a quiet corner of the park, seven miles from the Northeast Entrance. Food and limited supplies are available at Tower Fall and Roosevelt. Pebble Creek Campground has vault toilets and is open June through September. Campsites are $10. No reservations.

Slough Creek Campground

This campground is especially popular with anglers who come here to fly-fish for cutthroat trout and with wildlife enthusiasts who watch the bison, elk, and wolves of Lamar Valley. Good local hiking is nearby, too. Food and limited supplies are available at Tower Fall and Roosevelt. The campground is open late May through October and has vault toilets. Campsites are $10. No reservations.

Tower Fall Campground

Located close to this dramatic waterfall on Tower Creek, this campground has 32 sites and vault toilets. Limited groceries and supplies are available at the nearby general store, with meals at Roosevelt. The campground is open mid-May through September. Campsites cost $10. No reservations.

OTHER CAMPING OPTIONS

When everything else is packed, folks head to campgrounds on surrounding Forest Service and Grand Teton National Park lands or to private campgrounds and motels in the gateway towns. All are described elsewhere in this book. The farther you get from Yellowstone, the more likely you are to find space. If you reach Nebraska, you should have no trouble at all. Campers can take showers ($3 per person) at Old Faithful Lodge, Grant Village, Fishing Bridge RV Park, and Canyon Village Campground.

Hotels, Lodges, and Cabins

Yellowstone accommodations range from extremely basic cabins with four thin walls starting at $40, up to luxury suites that will set you back $400. Following a fine old Park Service tradition, the rooms do not have TVs, and most lack phones. What they do offer is the chance to relax in comfortable accommodations and explore the magical world outside. Most are open early June to mid-September, with additional winter lodging at Mammoth Hot Springs Hotel and the Old Faithful Snow Lodge. Several hundred more motels and other places to stay operate outside park boundaries in the towns of Jackson, Cody, West Yellowstone, Gardiner, and Cooke City.

Xanterra Parks & Resorts is Yellowstone's lodging concessioner. For reservations, call 307/344-7311, or visit them online at www.travelyellowstone.com. **Make Yellowstone lodging reservations six months ahead** for the park's prime hotels, or you may find that the only rooms available are in Grant Village, the laughing stock of park lodges. Those traveling with small children should also request

cribs when making reservations. Special wheelchair-accessible (ADA-compliant) rooms are available at most of the park's cabins and hotels. (As an aside, several web-based companies purport to make reservations for hotels and lodges inside Yellowstone, but all of these charge a service fee. Save yourself money and hassles by just going direct to Xanterra.)

At the turn of the 20th century, most visitors to Yellowstone stayed in park hotels rather than roughing it on the ground. Three of these wonderful old lodging places remain: Old Faithful Inn, Lake Yellowstone Hotel, and Mammoth Hot Springs Hotel. Standard motel rooms can be found at Grant Village. In addition, three nicer places opened in the 1990s: the Old Faithful Snow Lodge and two small lodges at Canyon Village. All told, more than 2,200 rooms and cabins provide overnight accommodations in Yellowstone.

Not all lodging options inside the park are nearly as pleasant, however. Hundreds of simple boxes are clustered in the Lake, Mammoth, Old

Faithful, and Roosevelt areas. Most of these cabins offer a roof over your head, simple furnishings, and communal showers, but the more expensive cabins are considerably nicer, and two of them even include private hot tubs. Fortunately, prices are fairly reasonable for all of the cabins.

Lodging rates are listed for two people; children under age 12 stay free. Add $10 per person for additional older kids or adults in the hotel rooms or cabins. Prices may be lower in May when snow still covers much of the park. Also available are a variety of winter and summer package deals that include lodging, tours, hikes, and more. Especially noteworthy are the two- to five-day **Lodging and Learning** packages that combine tours, educational activities, and hikes led by naturalist-guides from the Yellowstone Association Institute, with accommodations in park hotels, plus breakfasts and lunches. Get details at 307/344-2294, www.yellowstone association.org.

Rates listed are without tax, which is 6 percent on the south half of the park (inside Teton County—including Old Faithful, Grant Village, and Lake Village) and 8 percent on the north half (inside Park County—including Roosevelt, Mammoth Hot Springs, and Canyon Village).

CANYON VILLAGE

The centrally located **Canyon Lodge** is just one-half mile from Grand Canyon of the Yellowstone, one of the park's premier attractions. The main lodge is part of a late-1950s complex of ugly structures built around a large parking lot. The area has all the charm of an aging shopping mall from an era when bigger meant better. The lodge itself covers the space of a football field and houses a dining room, cafeteria, lounge, and snack shop, but no guest rooms.

Cabins

Behind the lodge in the trees (at least the setting is peaceful), the road circles past three sprawling clusters of cabins, all with private baths. You'll find 540 cabins here. The most basic "pioneer" units start at $56 d and aren't much to look at

outside but are actually fairly roomy and comfortable inside. Two newer types of cabins are available at Canyon: the "frontier" units for $79 d and the "western" cabins for $112 d.

Lodges

Providing far better accommodations are two 1990s additions: **Dunraven Lodge** and **Cascade Lodge.** Rooms at both of these attractive log- and rock-trimmed structures are furnished with rustic lodgepole pieces and have two double beds and private baths. Rooms in the lodges cost $123 d. The cabins and lodges at Canyon are open June to mid-September.

GRANT VILLAGE

The southernmost lodging in Yellowstone, Grant Village offers accommodations in condo-type units from the 1980s, with exceptional parking-lot views from the rooms. These buildings would be completely out of place in *any* national park, especially Yellowstone. Six hideously ugly lodge buildings contain proletarian motel-type units for $90 s or d, and slightly nicer rooms for $101 s or d. All of these have two double beds and private baths, and several wheelchair-accessible rooms are available. A park visitors center and campground are in the area, along with a variety of concessioner facilities, including a restaurant, waterside café, general store, lounge, snack shop, and gift shop. Grant Village is open from late May–September and has 300 units.

LAKE VILLAGE

The Lake Village area has a full range of lodging options for travelers.

Lake Yellowstone Hotel

This fascinating Southern Colonial-style building delivers a magnificent view across Yellowstone Lake. Begun in 1889, the building expanded and changed over the decades to yield its current configuration of 158 guest rooms. The hotel has been lovingly restored and exudes a grandeur and charm rarely found today. It's the sort of place where Fred Astaire and Ginger Rogers

YELLOWSTONE

The Lake Yellowstone Hotel is the second largest wood-framed building in North America.

would feel comfortable dancing—if they were still alive.

The Lake's inviting hotel rooms all contain updated furnishings, private baths, and in-room phones. Standard units cost $157 d on the backside or $167 d facing the lake, and a delightfully spacious two-bedroom suite is the most elaborate (and most expensive) accommodation in the park at $392 for four people. For the best vistas, ask for a third-floor room on the lake side when making your reservations.

Downstairs is a good restaurant (reservations required for dinner), along with a fast-food eatery; the cafeteria at Lake Lodge is only a short walk away. The real treat at Lake Yellowstone Hotel is the **Sun Room,** where rows of windows front the lake. The room's ambience is further enhanced by period wicker furnishings and evening chamber music or classical piano. It's a great place to sip a martini or write a postcard. The hotel is open mid-May to early October.

Annex and Cabins

Out back is the **Lake Yellowstone Hotel Annex,** where the recently refurbished rooms cost $107 d.

No view, but each room has two double beds, phones, a bath, and pleasant furnishings.

Also behind Lake Yellowstone Hotel are more than a hundred rather dingy old boxes from the 1950s, each with two double beds. These have been jammed together in row after identical row to create the **Lake Yellowstone Hotel Cabins.** Fortunately, they're fairly reasonable ($83 d), and cabin guests can pretend they're traveling on a more ample budget by spending time in the hotel dining room and the Sun Room. Lake Yellowstone Hotel Cabins all contain two double beds and private baths, and they're open mid-May to early October.

Lake Lodge Cabins

A short distance east of Lake Yellowstone Hotel is **Lake Lodge.** Built in the 1920s, this archetypal log building has a gracious lobby containing two stone fireplaces, rustic furnishings, an open ceiling where the supporting log trusses and beams are visible, and a delightful front porch. One end of the building houses a large and reasonably priced cafeteria with picture windows framing Lake Yellowstone, and the other end contains a recreation hall for employees. Lodging options at Lake Lodge are not nearly as gracious, consisting of plain-vanilla "pioneer" cabins from the 1920s and '30s, each with a double bed and private bath for $51 d, and a bit more comfortable "western" cabins built in the 1950s and '60s that include two double beds and private baths with showers for $112 d. The 186 cabins at Lake Lodge are open mid-June to late September. Guests here often walk over to the nearby Lake Yellowstone Hotel for fine dining and the chance to relax in the Sun Room.

MAMMOTH HOT SPRINGS

The rambling **Mammoth Hot Springs Hotel** sits in the northwest corner of Yellowstone near park headquarters in the settlement of Mammoth. Built in 1937 (one wing was constructed in 1911 and the original hotel was built even earlier), the hotel has 222 rooms in a variety of configurations. Elk are a common sight on the grounds, and in the fall the bulls' bugling may wake you in the morning. There's live piano music downstairs in the map room most summer evenings as a counterpoint to the elk songs. (The room is named for a distinctive map of the United States crafted from 16 types of wood; it's on the northern wall.) Also just off the lobby is a gift shop. Just steps away are Park Service headquarters, the fine Albright Visitor Center and other historical buildings, along with places to eat and buy groceries, gas, and trinkets.

Hotel rooms are comfortable but modest at Mammoth. Several rooms on each floor provide low-cost accommodations ($65 d) with communal baths down the hall, but most have two beds and private baths ($90 d); ask for a corner room with windows if available. The hotel also houses two luxury suites ($261 d). The hotel is open early May to early October and late December to early March. Rates are the same in summer and winter, but early-season discounts are available. In the winter, "getaway packages" are a better bet, including one that provides two nights' lodging, two breakfasts, hot tub access, ice skates, skis, and a skier drop-off starting at $232 for two people. Hot tubs are available on an hourly basis during winter, offering a great way to relax after a day of cross-country skiing. Mammoth Hotel and Old Faithful Snow Lodge offer the only wintertime hotels inside the park.

the cabins at Mammoth Hot Springs

YELLOWSTONE

Cabins

Behind the hotel are 116 cabins, including budget units ($54 d) with a shared bathhouse, and delightful "frontier" cottages (from $86 d) with small porches and private baths. Most of these accommodations were built in 1938, and all contain two double beds. Some are duplex units that can be joined for families or friends traveling together. Dozens of ground squirrels populate the grounds, providing endless entertainment for the kids. Two units also have private outdoor hot tubs and are the nicest cabins in Yellowstone ($135 d). The cabins are open from early May to early October.

OLD FAITHFUL

The Old Faithful area contains a plethora of lodging options, including two large hotels—Old Faithful Inn and Old Faithful Snow Lodge—and several dozen cabins.

Old Faithful Inn

Built in 1903–1904, the timeless Old Faithful Inn (described in the Exploring the Park section of this chapter) is easily the most delightful place to stay inside Yellowstone—if not in all of America. I wouldn't trade it for a thousand Hiltons. If you're able to get a room here during your visit to the park, do so; you certainly won't regret it! The hotel contains 327 guest rooms to suit all budgets. Even those staying in the simplest rooms here will enjoy the five-star lobby with its towering stone fireplace, the old-fashioned writing tables, cushy overstuffed chairs, a classy bar and restaurant, and evening piano music.

Most rooms in the original section of the hotel are cramped spaces with a brass double bed, dresser, in-room sink, bare-bulb lighting, older carpets, log walls, and communal baths down the hall; these go for $69 d. Of the cheap rooms, the best ones (these are often reserved a year ahead) are the dormer rooms on the second floor—particularly room 229—but those who stay there must walk past folks in the lobby to take a shower! Many other types of rooms are available throughout this sprawling hotel. The attractively appointed midrange rooms ($92 d) are comfortable and contain two double beds,

phones, and tub baths with colorful tiles. Premium rooms vary in price from $113 to $164 d depending in part on whether they face the geyser, but personally I don't think they are much better than the midrange units. If you have the money, rent a suite for $334 d. When booking, ask for a room or suite in the East Wing facing the geyser if possible. Good choices include numbers 2002, 2010, 2012, 2014, and 2016; all have notable views of Old Faithful Geyser. Old Faithful Inn is open early May to mid-October, but a major preservation project starting in 2003 may shorten the season somewhat in the fall.

Old Faithful Lodge Cabins

Although it is an attractively rustic building that would be a major focal point almost anywhere else, Old Faithful Lodge is overshadowed by its grand neighbor, Old Faithful Inn. The lodge does not contain guest rooms but houses a large cafeteria (open for lunch and dinner only), recreation hall, gift shop, bake shop, ice cream stand, espresso cart, and showers. Unlike the inn, the lodge has enormous windows that face the geyser, providing those eating in the cafeteria with dramatic views of the eruptions. The lodge's massive fir logs and stone pillars add to a feeling of permanence. Behind and beside Old Faithful Lodge are approximately 130 moderately priced but cramped cabins. These contain older (but functional) furnishings, and most have two beds. The simplest budget units share communal bathhouses and cost just $40 d; they're the cheapest rooms in Yellowstone and just a few steps from Old Faithful. Slightly nicer (but still small) cabins have one or two beds and private baths, and cost $65 d. There is even a pair of handicapped-accessible cabins here. The cabins at Old Faithful Lodge are open mid-May to mid-September.

Old Faithful Snow Lodge

Completed in 1999, the 100-room Old Faithful Snow Lodge provides accommodations in both summer and winter (Mammoth Hot Springs Hotel is Yellowstone's only other wintertime hotel). Both inside and out, Snow Lodge evokes the spirit of "parkitecture" from the early 1900s. The building blends the past and present, with timbers (recycled from old buildings), hardwood floors, a central stone fireplace, custom-designed overstuffed couches, and wrought-iron accents, along with all the modern conveniences you expect from a fine hotel—unless you're expecting TVs, which no park hotels contain. Rooms are beautifully appointed and comfortable, and all have private baths. The hotel also houses a restaurant, snack shop, lounge, and gift shop, along with a ski shop and snowmobile rentals in winter. Rates are $134 d.

In addition to the hotel, 34 four-plex Snow Lodge Cabins are available behind the building, costing $112 d. Built in 1989, these **Western Cabins** have standard motel furnishings, with two double beds and a full bath. In addition, duplex **Frontier Cabins** provide simple accommodations with bath for $68 d. The Snow Lodge and Cabins are open early May through October and mid-December to early March. Rates are the same in summer and winter, but early-season discounts are available. During winter, "getaway packages" are a better bet, including one that provides two nights' lodging, two breakfasts, skis, a round-trip snowcoach ride to Old Faithful, and a skier drop-off starting at $470 for two people.

ROOSEVELT LODGE

Located at the junction of the roads to Canyon, Mammoth, and Lamar Valley, this is *the* place to escape the crowds and return to a quieter and simpler era. Roosevelt Lodge is decidedly off the beaten path to the major Yellowstone sights, and that suits folks who stay here just fine. Named for Pres. Theodore Roosevelt—perhaps the most conservation-minded president ever—the lodge has the well-worn feeling of an old dude ranch, and many families treat it as such. More than a few folks book cabins for several weeks at a stretch, enjoying the wolf-watching, fly-fishing, horseback and wagon rides, and barbecue cookout dinners. (Cookouts book up six months ahead, so reserve your space when you make a Roosevelt Lodge reservation.)

The main lodge features two large stone fireplaces, a family-style restaurant with notable meals, a lounge, a gift shop, a little general store, and a big front porch with old-fashioned rocking chairs. Surrounding it are 82 utilitarian cabins, most of which were built in the 1920s. Most basic—and just a step up from camping—are the "Roughrider" cabins, with one,

© DON PITCHER

The cabins at Roosevelt Lodge are a good place to escape the crowds.

two, or three beds, a writing table, and a wood-stove (the only ones in any Yellowstone lodging). These cabins share a communal bathhouse, cost $48 for up to six guests, and fill up quickly. Call far ahead to reserve one of these classics! The same price will also get you larger cabins without the woodstove (but still no private bath). Nicer "frontier" cabins with hardwood floors, one or two double beds, and private baths go for $86 d. All of these cabins can get stuffy in midsummer, and the windows lack screens. Two of the Roosevelt cabins are wheelchair-accessible. The Roosevelt Lodge and cabins are open early June to early September.

Food

RESTAURANTS

You'll find good restaurants at Mammoth Hot Springs, Lake Yellowstone Hotel, Old Faithful Inn, Old Faithful Snow Lodge, Grant Village, Roosevelt Lodge, and Canyon Lodge. All of these are open for three meals a day throughout the summer, and the Snow Lodge also opens for the winter season (mid-Dec. to early Mar.).

The enormous **Old Faithful Inn Dining Room** is easily the nicest of these eating options, with impressive all-you-can-eat breakfast and lunch buffets, plus a dinner menu that stars prime rib, halibut, chicken, steaks, and pork chops ($15–20 entrées). The cozy lounge serves single-malt scotches, tequilas, and cognacs, with a backdrop of etched-glass windows.

Another excellent choice is the **Lake Yellowstone Hotel Dining Room,** with breakfast buffets, a lunch that features blackened salmon wrap and good salads, plus dinner selections such as shrimp cocktails, beef tenderloin, or rack of lamb.

Meals in other restaurants throughout the park are also reasonably priced and quite good. Typical menus include steaks, burgers, seafood, pasta, chicken, and vegetarian dishes. The filling breakfasts and chocolate pecan pie at **Mammoth Hot Springs Dining Room** are noteworthy, and **Roosevelt Lodge Dining Room** emphasizes down-home carnivore fare such as barbecue ribs, country fried steaks, sandwiches, chili, and fried chicken. The dinner menu at **Grant Village Dining Room** includes huckleberry chicken, ribeye steak, polenta lasagna, prime rib, and trout. They also have a substantial breakfast buffet. The building is one of the newer ones in the park, with a bland exterior but big windows facing the lake (although trees obscure the view). **Obsidian Dining Room** at the Snow Lodge has a fun Western flair. In addition to an extensive breakfast menu, the restaurant serves specialty burgers, steaks, and seafood.

Dinner reservations are _required_ in the summer at Old Faithful Inn Dining Room (307/545-4999), Lake Yellowstone Hotel Dining Room (307/242-3899), and Grant Village Dining Room (307/242-3499), and they should be made before your arrival. For a dinner table at Old Faithful Inn, reserve a week ahead if you want a choice of seating times.

CAFETERIAS AND FAST FOOD

Yellowstone has always catered to families, and several park cafeterias provide dependably good food for decent prices. Your kids' noise will almost certainly be drowned out by racket from the rest of the hoi polloi (I'm speaking from experience here). Of particular note are **Lake Lodge Cafeteria** and **Old Faithful Lodge Cafeteria,** both of which are housed in grand stone-and-timber buildings with tall windows. Lake Lodge faces Lake Yellowstone, and Old Faithful Lodge faces the geyser. Less distinguished are **Canyon Lodge Cafeteria**—with a 1960s design that hasn't aged well—and the **Grant Village Lake House.** At the latter, big windows open onto Yellowstone Lake (great for sunsets), and you can graze a pasta and salad bar in the evenings or order a pizza. In addition to these options, you'll find snack shops or delis selling burgers, vegieburgers, sandwiches, espresso, and ice cream in Mammoth, Old Faithful, Lake, and Canyon.

Many of the park's **Yellowstone General Stores** have food services of the burger, fries, and milkshake variety, and can put together box lunches for a to-go meal.

OLD WEST COOKOUT

The Old West wagon cookouts at Roosevelt Lodge's are a longtime family favorite and so popular that you'll need to make reservations at least six months in advance of your visit. These events take place every evening from early June to early September, and you either hop onboard the horse-drawn wagons or astride a horse for a saunter into history. Cookouts take place in Pleasant Valley, three miles from the lodge, and include cowboy music, a campfire, and a big buffet dinner of steak, baked beans, coleslaw, potato salad, corn, corn muffins, watermelon, apple cobbler, and beverages. Top it off with a cup of cowboy coffee. No discounts are given for vegetarians, but they can make substitutions if you notify them in advance. Covered seating is available in case of rain.

Wagon rides last 1.5 hours round-trip, and cost $32 adults, $20 ages 5–11, or free for younger kids. Horseback riders can choose either a one-hour trail ride and meal at $43 adults, $33 ages 8–11, or a two-hour trail ride that costs $53 adults or $43 kids. Make reservations at 307/344-7311, www.travelyellow stone.com. If you're in the area and don't have a reservation, ask to get on the waiting list. You might get lucky and have someone cancel at the last minute.

LOUNGES

Just because you're in a national park doesn't mean you can't tip back a gin and tonic. **Bear Pit Lounge** inside Old Faithful Inn is a fine place for a drink in the evening, with etched-glass panels depicting bear characters.

Beverage service is also available on the upstairs mezzanine and the outside deck facing Old Faithful. Another good place for a drink is **Firehole Lounge** at the nearby Old Faithful Snow Lodge.

Lake Yellowstone Hotel's aptly named **Sun Room** fills a large wing of the lobby and is surrounded on three sides by picture windows. It exudes a casual elegance, making this a wonderful spot to while away the hours reading a book, writing postcards, or just listening to the piano tunes with a drink in your hand.

Smaller bars are located off the dining rooms at Mammoth Hot Springs, Roosevelt Lodge, Lake Lodge, Grant Village, and Canyon Lodge. The little corner bar at Mammoth has the only public TV inside Yellowstone; none of the in-park hotel rooms have televisions.

GROCERIES AND SUPPLIES

The park's 11 Yellowstone General Stores are located at Mammoth, Canyon, Old Faithful, Fishing Bridge, Grant Village, Lake, and Roosevelt. Each outlet has its own personality, and several of these—most notably the Lower Basin store at Old Faithful and the ones at Lake and Fishing Bridge—are grand old log structures. The Mammoth general store is another historic structure, here for nearly a century.

In addition to groceries, beer, and liquor, these stores sell a variety of merchandise, clothing, souvenirs, film and photo supplies, T-shirts, and accessories. Featured items include locally made arts and crafts, and they even offer interpretive programs. The larger ones also have popular soda fountains with burgers, shakes, and other fast food. General stores at Canyon and Old Faithful deliver the best selection, and the Mammoth store is open year-round. The others are generally open mid-May through September. The stores are managed by Delaware North Park Services, www.yellowstonegeneralstores.com.

Getting Around

BY CAR

Yellowstone's roads were long a source of irritation to travelers. Much of the roadbed was built at the turn of the 20th century, when horses and carriages were the primary means of travel. Increasing traffic and larger vehicles contributed to deterioration of park roads, as did stretched-thin park maintenance budgets. By the early 1990s many miles of park roads were pockmarked with bone-jarring potholes. Yellowstone is now at the tail end of a massive road reconstruction program, and each summer you'll find a different section undergoing rebuilding, so be ready for delays somewhere during your journey. In 2003 and 2004, most of the attention will be on the roads between Canyon and Roosevelt and between Madison and Norris. This may mean delays of up to 30 minutes at times. Fortunately, all this work means that the roads are vastly better than they were just a few years ago. Check with the park for the latest on the road situation and this year's construction delays, or see the free park newspaper.

The **speed limit** on all park roads is a strictly enforced 45 mph, although during summer you're not likely to approach this speed because long lines of traffic form behind monstrous RVs. **Gas stations** are located at Old Faithful, Canyon Village, Mammoth Hot Springs, Fishing Bridge, Grant Village, and Tower Junction, while repair services are available at all of these except Mammoth Hot Springs and Tower Junction. Additional service stations can be found in the surrounding towns.

Seasonal Access

Most roads in Yellowstone close on the Monday after the first Sunday in November and usually open again by mid-May. Plowing begins in early March, and the roads reopen in sections. The roads connecting Mammoth to West Yellowstone open first, and Dunraven Pass is plowed last. Note that spring storms may cause closures or restrictions on some park roads; get the latest from entrance stations or visitors centers. Only the road between Mammoth and Cooke City is kept plowed all winter long. The roads are groomed for snowmobiles (snow conditions permitting) by mid-December. If you're planning a trip early or late in the season, contact the park for current road conditions; 307/344-7381, www.nps.gov/yell.

PARK TOURS

During summer, most people come into Yellowstone in private cars or RVs, but there *are* other ways of getting around. For many people, an interpretive bus tour provides a quick overview of the park while leaving the driving to an expert. This is especially true for RVers who can park at Fishing Bridge RV Park or Bridge Bay Campground and don't need to worry about driving on narrow park roads.

In-Park Tours

From mid-May to late September, **Xanterra Parks & Resorts,** 307/344-7311, www.travel yellowstone.com, offers full-day bus tours from Canyon Lodge, Lake Hotel, Old Faithful Inn, Fishing Bridge RV Park, Bridge Bay Campground, and Grant Village. Tours of either the upper or lower loops are $38 adults or $17 ages 12–16 (free for younger kids). A longer Grand Loop tour (not recommended unless you're into sensory overload and more than 10 hours of riding around) costs $42 adults or $20 teens. The Grand Loop tour is only available from Mammoth or Gardiner.

Xanterra also offers **Lamar Valley wildlife excursions** that originate from Canyon Lodge, Bridge Bay, Lake Yellowstone Hotel, or Fishing Bridge RV Park and cost $30 adults or $13 teens. These last three or four hours and provide an opportunity to catch a glimpse of wolves. In addition, amateur photographers may want to join a professionally taught **Photo Safari** provided several times a week out of Old Faithful Inn and Lake Yellowstone Hotel;

$40 adults for four hours, or $23 for teens. All-day trips to **Mt. Washburn** from Bridge Bay Campground, Lake Yellowstone Hotel, Fishing Bridge RV Park, or Canyon Lodge are $34 adults, $16 teens.

Also available are three-hour **Firehole Basin** tours ($19 adults, $9 teens), and two-hour **Hayden Valley twilight tours** (a top time to find bears) for $14 adults or $8 teens. One of the most distinctive tour offerings is to ride a classic canvas-topped **1937 Yellowstone bus** on sunset tours around Lake Yellowstone. The vehicle gets almost as much attention as the scenery during these fun trips back in time. They cost $17 adults or $8.50 teens.

Other Bus Tours

Upper or lower loop tours are available out of West Yellowstone from **Buffalo Bus Touring Co.,** 406/646-9564 or 800/426-7669, www .yellowstonevacations.com, and **Gray Line,** 406/646-9374 or 800/523-3102, www.grayline yellowstone.com. The latter is a couple of bucks cheaper at $38 adults or $25 kids.

Additional Yellowstone tours leave out of Cody ($60) aboard **Powder River Transportation/Coach USA,** 307/527-6316 or 800/527-6316, and from Jackson ($80) aboard **Alltrans/ Gray Line,** 307/733-4325 or 800/443-6133, www.jacksonholealltrans.com. Those without vehicles can use Gray Line tours for access to the parks; the bus can pick you up at many places along the road system, but you'll need to schedule this in advance. This is not a separate service from the Gray Line tours; instead the regular tour bus stops, meaning that you get a portion of the tour at the same time.

4x4 Stage, 406/848-2224 or 800/517-8243, offers by-request connections around the park and to surrounding communities. Call 24 hours ahead for reservations. **Karst Stage,** 406/388-2293 or 800/287-4759, www.karststage.com,

has wintertime transportation between the Bozeman airport and Mammoth Hot Springs.

Specialized Tours

In addition to traditional classes, the Yellowstone Association Institute, 307/344-2294, www.yellowstoneassociation.org, also offers a popular series of **Lodging and Learning** packages. These two- to five-day programs blend education, recreation, and comfortable lodging. Naturalist-guides from the Association lead excursions, and participants are provided with accommodations in park hotels, plus breakfasts and lunches. The programs include special ones for families, winter ski treks, winter wildlife, and one that emphasizes hiking. For the private touch, the Institute has **Educational Adventures,** tours in which a wildlife biologist travels with you in your own vehicle. They're sort of like having your own personal trainer for Yellowstone wildlife.

Operated by the highly respected Teton Science School, **Wildlife Expeditions,** 307/733-2623 or 888/945-3567, www.tetonscience.org /wildlife, leads a variety of wildlife-viewing safaris throughout the region, including multiday wildlife tours into Yellowstone.

For a listing of licensed tour operators offering wildlife, natural history, and photography tours in the park, contact the Park Service at 307/344-738, www.nps.gov/yell. Other good companies and individuals offering guided tours of the area include: **Callowishus Park Touring Company,** 307/733-9521, www.callowishus.com; **Jackson's Hole Adventure,** 307/654-7849 or 800/392-3165, www.jacksonholeadventure.com; **Tory and Meredith Taylor,** 307/455-2161; **Upstream Anglers and Outdoor Adventures,** 307/739-9443 or 800/642-8979, www.upstreamanglers.com; and **Yellowstone Country Adventures,** 406/994-0422, www.yellowstone country-adventures.com.

Other Practicalities

Complete details on park entrance fees, visitors centers, and sights are provided in the Exploring the Park section of this chapter.

VACATION PLANNING

If you're planning a trip to Yellowstone, call the park at 307/344-7381 to request a copy of their *Yellowstone Guide.* It provides detailed up-to-date information on hiking and camping, fishing, services, road construction, safety issues, park highlights, and lots more. The same information (and much more) is available online at www.nps.gov/yell.

Several print and online sources provide unofficial information on Yellowstone. One of the better private sources is the Lander-based *Yellowstone Journal,* 307/332-2323 or 800/656-8762, www.yellowstonepark.com. The publication comes out five times a year and is sold in stores inside and around the park. A good freebie publication is called simply *Yellowstone Park,* published annually by the *Billings Gazette,* and available online at www.billingsgazette.com. You'll find it in regional visitors centers outside the park. Also check out the web-only **Yellowstone Traveler,** www.yellowstoneparktraveler.com, maintained by Circumerro Publishing.

RANGER-NATURALIST PROGRAMS

Park naturalists lead slide shows, films, guided walks, kids' programs, campfire talks, and other activities at the campgrounds and visitors centers. These are always favorites of visitors, and on summer days you can choose from more than two dozen different Yellowstone activities, all of which are free. Get a complete listing in the *Yellowstone Today* paper you receive upon entering the park, or online at www.nps.gov/yell. Evening slide programs are also offered in winter at Mammoth and Old Faithful. For a more in-depth look at the park, take a class through the Yellowstone Association Institute, www.yellowstoneassociation.org, or join one of their popular **Lodging and Learning Packages.**

TRAVELING WITH CHILDREN

Yellowstone is a major family destination in summer, and visiting the park has become something of a rite of passage for middle-class American families (along with thousands of European and Japanese families). Families will especially appreciate the woodsy campgrounds, the inexpensive but simple cabins, and the reasonable cafeteria meals that are available around the park. Most lodges and hotels have cribs for those traveling with infants. Of special interest to kids ages 5–12 is the **Junior Ranger Program** ($3), in which children attend a nature program, hike a trail, and complete other activities. They're rewarded with an official Junior Ranger patch and are sworn in. It's always a big hit, but your kids may later try to arrest you if you get too close to an elk.

ACCESSIBILITY

Disabled visitors to Yellowstone will find that the park is making a concerted effort to provide accessible facilities, although they have a long way to go. Most of the major tourist areas, including Old Faithful, have at least some paths that are paved, and accessible accommodations can be found at Canyon, Grant Village, Old Faithful, and Lake. Accessible campsites are also available throughout the park. For details, call 307/344-2018 to request a copy of the *Visitor Guide to Accessible Features in Yellowstone National Park,* or find the same information on the web at www.nps.gov/yell.

SUPPORTING THE PARK

The **Yellowstone Association,** 307/344-2289, www.yellowstoneassociation.org, is a nonprofit organization that assists with education, research, publishing, and book sales inside the park. The organization also teaches classes through the Yellowstone Association Institute.

The **Yellowstone Park Foundation** is another nonprofit group that works with the National Park Service by providing funds for projects and programs that would not be otherwise supported. Their biggest project is to help raise the $15 million needed for a new visitors center at Old Faithful. All funding comes from individuals and corporations, not from the government. Contact the foundation at 406/586-6303, www .ypf.org, for more details.

SHOPPING AND GIFTS

Nearly every road junction in Yellowstone has some sort of general store, gas station, or gift shop. **Yellowstone General Stores** are especially interesting because they tend to be in rustic old log structures and staffed by friendly retired folks and fresh college kids. The stores are being modernized but still retain the historic charm from past eras. Here you'll find all of the standard tourist supplies and gifts, plus groceries, snack bars, booze, camping equipment, books, fishing supplies, and locally made arts and crafts. The largest general stores are located at Old Faithful and Canyon.

The **Old Faithful Inn Gift Shop** is well worth a visit, with a good selection of items from apparel to artwork. It often has book signings and guest presentations during summer. **The Shop at Old Faithful Lodge** has artists in residence creating paintings or pottery (for sale, of course). Additional gift shops can be found in the other hotel

YELLOWSTONE ASSOCIATION

Founded in 1933, the nonprofit Yellowstone Association assists in educational, historical, and scientific programs. The organization publishes several natural-history publications and provides funds to produce trail leaflets and park newspapers, along with the excellent *Yellowstone Science* magazine. In addition, the association manages book sales at visitors centers, funds park exhibits and research, and otherwise assists the park in educating the public. The group is probably best known for the **Yellowstone Association Institute,** operating out of the historic Buffalo Ranch in Lamar Valley.

Instructors at the institute lead more than 100 different natural-history and humanities classes in the summer, along with several others in winter. Most of these last 2–5 days and typically cost around $60 per day—a real bargain. Courses cover the spectrum from wolf ecology to horsepacking and provide a great way to learn about this wonderful wild place. Class size is small; most classes contain 10–15 students. Participants typically stay at the Buffalo Ranch in comfortable log cabins ($22 per person per night) and cook meals in the shared kitchen.

In addition to these classes, the Yellowstone Association Institute also offers a **Lodging and Learning Program,** two- to five-day packages that blend education, recreation, and lodging. Naturalist-guides from the Association lead small-group excursions (13 people max), and participants are provided with accommodations in park hotels, plus breakfasts and lunches. Their *Yellowstone for Families* program is especially popular, with a mix of activities for both kids and parents over four days: animal tracking, wildlife watching, photography, painting, hiking, and more.

For folks who really want the personalized touch (and can afford it), the Institute has **Educational Adventures,** private tours in which a wildlife biologist travels with you in your vehicle for 6–8 hours, providing an introduction to park wildlife and ecology.

Membership in the Yellowstone Association starts at $30 per year and is tax-deductible. Members get discounts on classes taught by the Yellowstone Association Institute and can sign up early. They also receive quarterly newsletters and discounts for purchases of items sold by the Association. For details and a listing of classes and books on the park, contact the Yellowstone Association Institute at 307/344-2294, www.yellow stoneassociation.org.

complexes at Lake Lodge, Mammoth Hot Springs, Roosevelt Lodge, Canyon Lodge, and Grant Village.

MONEY

You'll discover **ATMs** at most of the settled areas, including Old Faithful Inn, Old Faithful Snow Lodge, Fishing Bridge, Lake Yellowstone Hotel, Mammoth Hot Springs Hotel, Mammoth General Store, Canyon General Store, Canyon Lodge, and Grant Village. Park lodges and hotels are able to provide a limited **currency exchange** for international travelers Monday–Friday 8 A.M.–5 P.M.

MEDICAL SERVICES

For medical emergencies 24 hours a day, the park manages **Lake Hospital,** 307/242-7241, an acute-care facility with 10 beds. It's open late May to mid-September; also here are a clinic and pharmacy. Outpatient services are available both here and at the **Old Faithful Clinic,** 307/545-7325, open mid-May to mid-October. Open weekdays year-round, the **Mammoth Hot Springs Clinic,** 307/344-7965, has a physician available. Call 911 for emergencies.

CLEANING UP

In summer, find coin-operated **washers and dryers** at Fishing Bridge RV Park, Canyon Village Campground, and Grant Village Campground. **Public showers** ($3) are at Fishing Bridge RV Park, Lake Lodge, Old Faithful Lodge, Grant Village, and Canyon Village Campground.

OTHER SERVICES

For a complete directory of the many other Yellowstone visitor services, see *Yellowstone Today,* which you receive upon entering the park. You can also download a copy off the web from the Yellowstone site, www.nps.gov/yell.

A year-round **post office** is located in a 1930s-era stone building at Mammoth Hot Springs, and seasonal post offices can be found at Old Faithful, Lake Village, Canyon Village, and Grant Village.

Check the visitors centers for a schedule of **church services.** Process film (prints only) in **one-hour film labs** at Old Faithful, Canyon, and Fishing Bridge. **Cell phone** users will find spotty service in many parts of Yellowstone, but your phone will probably work in the country around Old Faithful, Lake, and Mammoth (and possibly elsewhere).

Working in Yellowstone

During summer, both the National Park Service and private concessioners provide several thousand jobs in Yellowstone. These positions rarely last more than six months. You can find much more about Yellowstone jobs—both public and private—by heading to www.nps.gov/yell /technical/jobs on the web.

PARK SERVICE JOBS

Yellowstone National Park hires more than 300 seasonal employees each year, but many more people apply, so the competition is stiff for new hires. Most seasonals start out as a park ranger (leading naturalist walks, working in entrance stations, etc.) or laborer (building trails, cleaning campgrounds and restrooms, etc.), but more specialized positions are available in the fields of natural resources or law enforcement. Seasonals typically make $10–12 per hour, with housing taken out of this pay. You must be a U.S. citizen to be employed by the Park Service. Although there is a national register for seasonal rangers, specific vacancy announcements come out when jobs are available, and you will need to apply within the specified time frame and meet all qualifications. For details on seasonal park service jobs, call Yellowstone's human resources office at 307/344-2052, or visit www.usajobs.opm.gov for a listing of park jobs. The Department of Interior's site, www.doi.gov/hrm/jobs.html, has additional job info.

YELLOWSTONE

VOLUNTEER POSITIONS

Unpaid volunteers do many jobs in Yellowstone and other national parks, and it isn't necessary to be a U.S. citizen to do volunteer work. The Park Service operates a **Volunteers in Parks** (VIP) program at Yellowstone that includes more than 300 people each year. To join the ranks of the employed but unpaid, call the park's VIP coordinator at 307/344-2039, or visit the volunteer website: www.nps.gov/volunteer.

A national nonprofit organization, the New Hampshire–based **Student Conservation Association** (SCA), 603/543-1700, www.sca-inc.org, provides workers for Yellowstone who do a wide range of activities, from trail maintenance to answering visitors' questions. Volunteers get most expenses paid. Contact SCA for details.

CONCESSIONER JOBS

The park has two primary concessioners, Xanterra Parks & Resorts and Delaware North Parks Service, along with the smaller Yellowstone Park Service Stations. Most employees of these companies are college students (who live in dorm-style accommodations), retired folks (who live in their RVs), or young people from other countries (including many from Poland, Czech Republic, Russia, Finland, and other European nations). Don't expect high pay; entry-level positions start at around $6 per hour, with meals and lodging deducted from this paltry sum. A good overall website for concessioner jobs inside Yellowstone is www.coolworks.com/yell.htm.

Xanterra

Xanterra Parks & Resorts is in charge of lodging, restaurants, bus tours, boat rentals, horse rides, several campgrounds, and similar services within the park. They are also the largest park and resort management company in the nation, with concessioners in such diverse spots as Everglades National Park and Grand Canyon National Park. The company hires more than 3,000 people each summer in Yellowstone. For more information and an application, call 307/344-5324, or head to their website: www.ynpjobs.com. It's best to apply

---

GREATER YELLOWSTONE COALITION

The primary environmental group involved with protecting Yellowstone and the surrounding public lands is the Greater Yellowstone Coalition, based in Bozeman, Montana. This private nonprofit organization is involved in all sorts of environmental issues within the 10-million-acre Greater Yellowstone Ecosystem, including such hot-button issues as logging, mining, winter use, and bison management. It represents some 8,000 members and publishes a quarterly newsletter detailing various issues. Annual membership costs $25; contact the organization by calling 406/586-1593, or find it on the web at www.greateryellowstone.org.

---

early in the year (Dec.–Jan.) for summer jobs. The more competitive winter positions often go to those with previous work experience in the park.

Delaware North

In 2002 the National Park Service terminated its contract with Hamilton Stores, a company that had operated in Yellowstone since 1915. The end of this era has led to some much-needed changes, and the 11 stores (now called Yellowstone General Stores) are all being updated and modernized. The new concessioner is Delaware North Parks Service, with regional offices in Bozeman, Montana. The company employs around 750 folks seasonally in Yellowstone, with another 35 as year-round managers. Many of the seasonals are retirees who bring their RVs along for private accommodations. If you can start in April or May, you're considerably more likely to be hired.

For employment information and applications, contact Delaware North Human Resources at Attn: Human Resources, Delaware North Park Services, 707 Bridger Dr., Suite C, Bozeman, MT 59715, 406/586-7593, www.yellowstonegeneralstores.com.

Service Stations

The third concessioner is **Yellowstone Park Service Stations,** the folks who pump Conoco gas and wash your windshield. Get hiring information at 406/848-7333, www.ypss.com.

Gateways to Yellowstone

Yellowstone National Park is most commonly entered via one of several Wyoming or Montana towns. From the south, people generally arrive from the energetic town of Jackson, detailed in an earlier chapter. Described in this chapter are four Montana towns that act as park gateways: West Yellowstone, which predictably enough is immediately west of Yellowstone; Gardiner, at the northwest gate just a few miles from Mammoth Hot Springs; and the twin towns of Cooke City and Silver Gate just beyond the Northeast Entrance to Yellowstone. Also described are two Wyoming towns: Cody, which provides access through Wapiti Valley to Yellowstone's East Entrance, and the Wind River Valley town of Dubois on the east side of Togwotee Pass.

For points to the east and south—including the towns of Lander, Pinedale, Alpine, and Afton—see my *Moon Handbooks Wyoming*. Nearby towns in Montana, including Red Lodge, Bozeman, Billings, and Livingston, are fully covered in *Moon Handbooks Montana,* by W. C. McRae and Judy Jewell. See Don Root's *Moon Handbooks Idaho* for coverage of Island Park, Swan Valley, and the scoop on the tater state. Avalon Travel Publishing (www.moon.com) publishes all three of these books.

Cooke City, Montana

West Yellowstone, Montana

West Yellowstone (elev. 6,650) is the definitive Western tourist town. With a year-round population of only 1,000 (three times that in the summer) but more than 50 places to stay, it's pretty easy to see what makes the West Yellowstone cash registers ring. The West Entrance gate—most popular of all Yellowstone entrances—lies just a couple hundred feet away. "West," as the town is known locally, isn't particularly attractive, and in the 1990s a major development added several corporate hotels and other ugly additions to an already crowded mix of restaurants, motels, T-shirt stores, and gift shops.

West Yellowstone may be decidedly middlebrow, but the surrounding land is anything but, with Gallatin (GAL-a-tin) National Forest lying north and west, Caribou-Targhee National Forest just a few miles to the south, and Yellowstone National Park just a few feet to the east. It's just a couple of miles east from West Yellowstone to the Wyoming border, and the Idaho border lies only nine miles west.

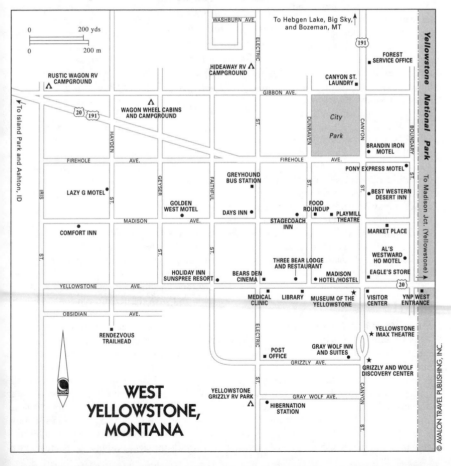

WEST YELLOWSTONE, MONTANA

HISTORY

In 1907, the Union Pacific Railroad completed laying tracks for its Oregon Short Line to the western border of Yellowstone. The following summer, Yellowstone Special trains began rolling in from Salt Lake City, dropping tourists for their stagecoach tours of the park. A small town—West Yellowstone—quickly developed on the margins of the park, providing lodging, meals, and tourist trinkets. After World War II, interest in rail travel declined and more people came to Yellowstone by automobile. Although the last passengers stepped off the train in 1960, the Union Pacific's historic stone depot and neighboring buildings still stand; they now house a museum, library, police station, jail, medical clinic, and other offices.

West Yellowstone may be decidedly middle-brow, but its surroundings are anything but. Gallatin National Forest lies north and west, Caribou-Targhee National Forest is a few miles to the south, and Yellowstone National Park just a few feet to the east.

The West Yellowstone area was rocked by a devastating magnitude-7.5 earthquake on August 17, 1959. One of the most powerful temblors ever recorded in the Lower 48 states, the quake cracked Hebgen Dam and caused a massive landslide (estimated at more than 80 million tons of debris!) that generated a 20-foot-high tsunami and created Earthquake Lake. Twenty-eight people died, and the geysers and hot springs of Yellowstone were dramatically affected for years.

SIGHTS

Museum of the Yellowstone

The **Museum of the Yellowstone,** 124 Yellowstone Ave., 406/646-1100, www.yellowstone historiccenter.org, is a stone-and-log structure from the railroad days that served for decades as the town's train depot. Entrance is $6 adults, $4 students and kids, and $15 families; free for kids under three. The museum is open daily 8:30 A.M.–7 P.M. (until 10 P.M. in the summer) from mid-May to mid-October; closed the rest of the year. Inside are exhibits on the history of park transportation (including railroads and stagecoaches), the 1959 Hebgen Lake earthquake, the fires of 1988, and wildlife displays, including "Old Snaggletooth" the grizzly and an enormous cave bear skull. Videos and movies about Yellowstone are shown in the theater, and the museum offers 45-minute free walking tours at noon and 4 P.M. daily in the summer, along with afternoon nature or history talks most days. Also here is a good collection of regional books for sale. Out front is a grand old park bus that was last used in 1959.

Right next door is another wonderful stone structure (built in 1925) that served until the late 1950s as an elegant Union Pacific Dining Lodge. The building has a spacious dining hall containing an enormous fireplace, a 45-foot-tall vaulted ceiling, and handmade light fixtures. Also worth a look-see is an **Oregon Short Line Railroad car** housed at the Holiday Inn Sunspree Resort, 315 Yellowstone Avenue. Built in 1903, the railroad car has been beautifully restored with antiques.

Grizzly and Wolf Discovery Center

In the early 1990s, a massive $50 million project covering 67 acres transformed (some might prefer the term decimated) the town of West Yellowstone. Included are a grizzly and wolf theme park, an IMAX theater, three major hotels, cabins, a restaurant, fast-food joints, an RV park, and a post office. The centerpiece is the **Grizzly and Wolf Discovery Center,** 201 S. Canyon St., home to 10 Alaskan and Canadian grizzlies and seven captive-born gray wolves. Not all of the bears are visible at any given time, but visitors are bound to see at least one in the pseudo-natural habitat. The center is open daily all year 8 A.M. to dusk. Entrance costs $8.50 adults, $8 seniors, $4 ages 5–12, free for kids under five. This center attracts throngs of visitors and photographers who might otherwise never see a grizzly or wolf, and there's always a staff member out to answer any questions. The center remains controversial, however. Scientists note that the bears here are genetically distinct from those in Yellowstone, and anyone who has spent time around grizzlies in the wild will be dismayed to see them in captivity, even in a facility less oppressive than traditional zoos. The folks at Grizzly and Wolf Discovery Center counter that all these bears were either raised in captivity or were "problem" bears that would almost certainly have been killed had they not been moved here. In addition to the bears and wolves, the center has wildlife exhibits (including a walk-in bear den), bear safety tips (I recommend not entering bear dens), a 40-minute video on bears, plus the obligatory gift shop. Get details at 406/646-7001 or 800/257-2570, www.grizzlydiscoveryctr.com.

Yellowstone IMAX Theatre

Directly in front of the Grizzly and Wolf Discovery Center is the **Yellowstone IMAX Theatre,** 406/646-4100 or 888/854-5862, where you can watch the big-budget production of *Yellowstone* on the 60- by 80-foot screen; other movies typically are on wolves, bears, or some other nature or Old West topic. The theater is open daily 9 A.M.–9 P.M. May to mid-October, with reduced hours the rest of the year. Admission costs $8 adults, $6 ages 3–11; free for younger children. The featured attraction is a 35-minute movie that presents Yellowstone history and geology complete with stirring music and a cast of dozens. If you haven't seen IMAX flicks before, hold onto your seat—lots of jaw-dropping scenes here. The movie packs in the crowds on summer days, but the film seems like a Disneylandish version of reality, ignoring many of the things you're likely to see in the park—such as burned forests and crowds of visitors—and putting history into a pretty little box. Reality wasn't—and isn't—quite like this. Even more disconcerting is that this glorification of the park stands right next to the park. To me it symbolizes the make-a-buck attitude that holds Yellowstone up as an attraction while developing a massive complex on its very margin.

Other Sights

Family-run **Eagle's Store,** on the corner of Canyon and Yellowstone, 406/646-9300, is definitely worth a stop. Built in the 1920s, this historic log building contains all of the standard tourist knickknacks, along with quality Western clothing, jewelry, fishing tackle, and a delightful old-fashioned soda fountain open in summer.

Evidence of the powerful 1959 earthquake is still visible north of West Yellowstone along Hebgen Lake. The Forest Service has an **Earthquake Visitor Center;** get there by heading eight miles north on U.S. Hwy. 191 and turning left on U.S. Hwy. 287. Continue another 17 miles west to the center; open daily 8:30 A.M.–6 P.M. from Memorial Day to late September only.

ACCOMMODATIONS

The proximity to Yellowstone makes the town of West Yellowstone an extremely popular stopping place for vacationers in both summer and winter. More than 2,000 rooms are available. It is also a pricey place to stay; only a few places have rooms for less than $65 during the peak seasons. The streets are lined with more than three dozen motels, so I won't try to describe all of them, although you'll find general information and links at the West Yellowstone Chamber website, www.westyellowstonechamber.com. For the printed version, call them at 406/646-7701.

Be aware that during summer everything in West Yellowstone fills up by early afternoon, so get there early or make advance bookings. Motels can even be full on weekends in late September. Reserve a room in March or April for the peak summer season.

Hostel

Budget travelers will be happy to discover the West Yellowstone International Hostel (not affiliated with AYH) in the historic **Madison Hotel,** 139 Yellowstone Ave., 406/646-7745 or 800/838-7745, www.wyellowstone.com /madisonhotel. Now on the National Register of Historic Places, the hotel has friendly owners and a delightfully rustic lobby crowded with deer and moose heads. Presidents Harding and

Hoover stayed here (though it wasn't a hostel at the time, of course). Travelers stay in clean and comfortable bedrooms (three or four beds in each, with bedding provided) that have been furnished with handmade lodgepole furniture. The classic hotel rooms are a delightful mix of old and new, providing the ambience of a place that has been here since 1912. No televisions or phones are provided in the rooms, but they do have a small fridge and microwave for hostelers in the back, plus a TV in the lobby. A computer is available to check your email ($5 per hour). Lodging costs $20 per person in three-bed dorm rooms. Make hostel reservations a few days ahead in midsummer or get here before evening to be sure of a space in the dorms.

In addition to hostel rooms, the hotel has a range of other economical options, starting with a basic room with a bath down the hall and no TV for $26 s or $36 d; or $52 for a room with space for four and a private bath. Behind the hotel is a separate building with standard motel accommodations (private baths and TVs) for $49 d or $75 for a room with three double beds. The Madison Hotel is open late May to early October only.

$50-100

A good budget choice is **Lazy G Motel**, 123 Hayden, 406/646-7586, www.wyellowstone .com/clients/lazyg, where the clean and cozy rooms cost $48-59 s or d. All contain fridges and phones; kitchenettes are $10 extra. Closed in April.

Al's Westward Ho Motel, 16 Boundary St., 406/646-7331 or 888/646-7331, www.wyellow stone.com/alswestwardho, charges $52-66 s or d, and some rooms contain kitchenettes. Open May-Oct., no in-room phones. **Alpine Motel**, 120 Madison Ave., 406/646-7544, is similar: $55 for one bed, $65-67 for two beds, six-person units with kitchens for $95; $5 extra for fridges and microwaves. The Alpine also has a family suite that sleeps six with a full kitchen for $100. No phones or air conditioning. It is open mid-May through October.

Pony Express Motel, 4 Firehole Ave., 406/646-7644 or 800/323-9708, www.yellow stonevacations.com, has a quiet location but no phones; $49 for one bed or $64 for two beds. A kitchenette is $75 for up to four people. A little nicer, but still reasonably priced is another property with the same owners, **City Center Motel**, 408/646-7337 or 800/742-0665, www.yellowstonevacations.com, where rooms are $69 for one queen bed or $89 for two. A community kitchen and indoor hot tub are available for guests.

Wagon Wheel Cabins and Campground, 408 Gibbon, 406/646-7872, www.wyellow stone.com/wagonwheel, has a collection of 10 attractive cabins, most containing full kitchens. The cabins are on large lots surrounded by trees, and each has a barbecue grill and picnic table. Basic "camping cabins" cost $45 d, and a one-bedroom unit starts at $75 d. The largest unit has three bedrooms and a fireplace, and sleeps six for $175. There's a three-night summertime minimum on the larger cabins and a five-night minimum in winter (if they are open). The cabins at Wagon Wheel fill early, so book well ahead. They may be closed in the winter.

Golden West Motel, 429 Madison Ave., 406/646-7778, www.wyellowstone.com/golden west, is a small motel with a dozen well-maintained rooms costing $52-62 s or d; $8 extra for kitchenettes. Closed Nov. and April.

Three Bear Lodge, 217 Yellowstone Ave., 406/646-7353 or 800/646-7353, www.three -bear-lodge.com, is probably best known for its popular restaurant of the same name. The 74-room motel features contemporary rooms, plus four indoor hot tubs and an outdoor pool. A wide variety of rooms are available, starting at $75 for standard rooms, up to $110 for ones that include a jetted tub. Two-room family units are $85-148; the largest sleeps six. Open year-round.

You'll find very good accommodations at **Brandin' Iron Inn**, 201 Canyon St., 406/646-9411 or 800/217-4613 www.yellowstone vacations.com. Rooms cost $89 for one bed or $99 for two, including fridges, a light breakfast, and two indoor hot tubs.

Seven miles west of town, **Lionshead Super 8 Lodge**, 406/646-9584 or 800/843-1991, www.wyellowstone.com/lionshead, has quality rooms, a country setting, plus a sauna and hot tub. Rooms are $92–96 s or d. It's very popular with the retirement crowd, who park RVs in the adjacent campground.

Days Inn, 118 Electric St., 406/646-7656 or 800/548-9551, www.wyellowstone.com/loomis, is a large and modern motel with standard rooms ($87–96 d), along with deluxe suites containing king beds and in-room hot tubs ($101 d). The motel also has a hot tub, saunas, and a small indoor pool that features the star attraction: a 90-foot water slide.

Other moderately priced lodging choices in West Yellowstone with good reputations include **Big Western Pine Motel,** 234 Firehole Ave., 406/646-7622 or 800/646-7622, www.wyellowstone.com/bigwesternpine; **Evergreen Motel,** 229 Firehole Ave., 406/646-7655 or 877/340-9580, www.wyellowstone.com/evergreenmotel; **One Horse Motel,** 216 Dunraven, 406/646-7677 or 800/488-2750, www.onehorsemotel.com; **Roundup Motel/Dude Motor Inn,** 3 Madison Ave., 406/646-7301 or 877/949-7669, www.wyellowstone.com/roundup; **Travelers Lodge,** 225 Yellowstone Ave., 406/646-9561 or 800/831-5741; and **Yellowstone Lodge,** 251 Electric St., 406/646-0020 or 877/239-9298, www.yellowstonelodge.com.

$100 and Up

One of the nicer places in West Yellowstone is **Stage Coach Inn,** filling an entire block at 209 Madison Ave., 406/646-7381 or 800/842-2882, www.yellowstoneinn.com. Rooms go for $99–129 s or d, and include access to a sauna and two hot tubs. The hotel features an impressive Western-style lobby with fireplace, plus a restaurant and heated underground parking.

At **Hibernation Station,** 212 Gray Wolf Ave., 406/646-4200 or 800/580-3557, www.hibernationstation.com, you'll find 40 modern cabins—each a bit different inside—with handmade log furniture and down comforters. Some also contain kitchenettes. Rates start at $99 d for a cabin with a queen bed, or $159 for one that sleeps four and contains a queen-size bunk bed, fireplace, and kitchenette. Families (not on a budget) will appreciate the large condo unit

with room for eight, a full kitchen and dining area, fireplace, and jetted tubs for $269. A big indoor hot tub is available for all guests.

The motel chains have moved into West Yellowstone in a big way. One of the nicest of these is **Comfort Inn,** 638 Madison Ave., 406/646-4212 or 888/264-2466, www.w-yellowstone.com/comfortinn. The featured attraction here is the biggest indoor pool in town, but the motel also has a small exercise room, hot tub, and continental breakfast. Rates are $129 s or d in standard rooms, or $189 for six-person suites.

Best Western Desert Inn, 133 Canyon St., 406/646-7376 or 800/528-1234, www.bestwestern.com, has an indoor pool and hot tub and serves a continental breakfast. Prices fluctuate through the summer and may be higher on weekends and lower on weekdays, but are typically in the $120–145 range.

The large **Gray Wolf Inn & Suites,** 250 S. Canyon, 406/646-0000 or 800/852-8602, www.graywolf-inn.com, features a hot tub, sauna, and a small indoor pool, plus a breakfast buffet. An added attraction, especially in the winter, is the heated underground parking garage. Rates are $109 s or d in standard rooms, $199–239 for one- and two-bedroom suites that come with full kitchens.

The most elaborate place in town is the ludicrously named **West Yellowstone Conference Hotel Holiday Inn Sunspree Resort,** 315 Yellowstone Ave., 406/646-7365 or 888/633-1724, www.yellowstoneholidayinn.com, with spacious rooms, an indoor pool, an exercise room, a sauna, and a hot tub. Standard rooms cost $139 d, two-room family suites are $191 and sleep six, and luxurious executive suites (king bed, jetted tub, and wet bar) run $175–200.

Other good upper-end lodging choices in West Yellowstone include **Best Western Cross Winds Motor Inn,** 201 Firehole Ave., 406/646-9557 or 800/528-1234, www.bestwestern.com; **Marriott Fairfield Inn,** 105 S. Electric St., 406/646-4892 or 800/565-6803, www.wyellostoneinn.com/fairfieldinn; and **Kelly Inn,** 104 S. Canyon St., 406/646-4544

or 800/259-4672, www.wyellowstone.com
/kellyinn.

Guesthouses

There are no B&Bs in West Yellowstone; the
last one was driven out of business in 1999 after
all the new chain motels flooded the local lodging market. Out in the country eight miles west
of town, **Sportsman's High Vacation Rentals,**
406/646-7865, www.yellowstonerental.net, has
six vacation homes and cabins for rent. These
range from a luxurious carriage house (perfect for
a romantic getaway) that sleeps four for $185 per
night, up to a spacious two-story home with
five bedrooms and five baths that sleeps eight
for $315. All of these contain knotty pine inte-
riors, country-style appointments, and full
kitchens. A three-night minimum stay is required in summer.

Local companies renting condos and townhouses include **Yellowstone Townhouses,**
406/646-9331, www.wyellowstone.com/wytown
houses; **Yellowstone Village Rental Condos**
(near Hebgen Lake), 406/646-7335 or 800/276-
7335; and **Lodgepole Townhouse,** 406/646-
0154 or 801/266-3766. A three-night minimum
stay is required for all of these places.

CAMPING

Public Campgrounds

The nearest Park Service camping place is inside
Yellowstone at **Madison Campground,** 14
miles east of West Yellowstone. The cost is $15,
and it's open May to late October. Make reservations (advised) at 307/344-7311, www.travel
yellowstone.com.

Gallatin National Forest has several campgrounds in the West Yellowstone area. The closest camping spot is **Baker's Hole Campground**
($12; open May–Sept.), just three miles north
of West Yellowstone. It's open for RVs and
other hard-sided vehicles only because of bear
problems. Tent campers will need to go north
of town to **Hebgen Lake,** where five different
tenting areas are strung westward along the
lake; closest is the **Lonesomehurst Campground** ($12; open May–Sept.), 12 miles from

West Yellowstone. No reservations are taken
at these Forest Service sites.

The Forest Service maintains four public-use
cabins ($30 a night for four people) in the coun-
try around West Yellowstone. Three of these are
open year-round. The closest is **Basin Station
Cabin,** eight miles west of town. Get details on
Forest Service camping and cabins at 406/823-
6961, www.fs.fed.us/r1/gallatin/recreation.

RV Parks

West Yellowstone has six private campgrounds
right in town, and several more are west or north
of town. Most of the in-town places are just RV
parking lots. Far nicer are two places with shady
trees and quiet sites: **Rustic Wagon Campground,** 634 U.S. Hwy. 20, 406/646-7387,
www.rusticwagonrv.com, ($25 for tents or
$34–36 for RVs); and **Wagon Wheel Cabins
and Campground,** 408 Gibbon Ave., 406/646-
7872, www.wyellowstone.com/wagonwheel, ($24
for tents or $32 for RVs). Noncampers can show-
er at either of these for $5. Rustic is open mid-
April through October, and Wagon Wheel is
open Memorial Day to September.

The other in-town RV parks are **Pony Express RV Park,** 4 Firehole Ave., 406/646-7644 or
800/323-9708, www.yellowstonevacations
.com; **Hideaway RV Campground,** 310 Electric
St., 406/646-9049, www.hideawayrv.com; **Yellowstone Cabins & RV Park,** 504 U.S. Hwy. 20
West, 406/646-9350; and **Yellowstone Grizzly
RV Park,** 210 S. Electric, 406/646-4466,
www.grizzlyrv.com. Two places are west of town
on U.S. Hwy. 20: **Yellowstone Park KOA,**
406/646-7606 or 800/562-7591, www.koa
.com; and **Lionshead Resort/Super 8 Motel,**
406/646-9584 or 800/800-8000, www.wyellow
stone.com/lionshead. The KOA has an outdoor
pool. **Yellowstone Holiday Resort,** 406/646-
4242 or 800/643-4227, www.yellowstoneholi-
day.com, is an RV campground along Hebgen
Lake north of West Yellowstone.

FOOD

West Yellowstone has many restaurants, but prices
are generally higher than in Wyoming towns and

the menu is plebeian, with burgers and fries as the dominant food group. Expect to pay $12–20 for dinner entrées.

Breakfast and Lunch

For omelets, buckwheat pancakes, and other good breakfast, run on over to **Running Bear Pancake House,** 538 Madison Ave., 406/646-7703, but be ready for a long wait in midsummer. Tasty lunches too; open 7 A.M.–2 P.M. only.

Joycee's Baking Company, 29 Canyon St., 406/646-9737, bakes artisan breads and serves focaccia sandwiches and specialty pizzas. Drop by in the morning for a mocha and one of their tasty cinnamon rolls. Open summers only, and closed by 4 P.M. most days.

Ernie's Deli & Bakery, 406 U.S. Hwy. 20 West, 406/646-9467, is the local doughnut shop in the morning, and it makes unbeatable sandwiches for lunch. They'll put together a big box lunch for $7.25 if you're heading into the park and want to leave the sandwiches to the experts. Also try **Picnic Basket,** 311 Canyon, 406/646-1001, for box lunches and sandwiches.

Stop by **Mocha Mammas** (inside Free Heel and Wheel), 40 Yellowstone Ave., 406/646-7744, www.wyellowstone.com/freeheelwheel, for espresso and bagels. Another good espresso destination is **The Book Peddler,** 106 Canyon St., 406/646-9358, www.thebookpeddler.com, where you'll find several tables in the back for bagels and coffee. It's a good place to hang out on a cold winter day. They're open until 10 in the summer.

American

If you're searching for a down-home greasy spoon serving three meals a day, your hunt will end at **Old Town Cafe,** 18 Madison, 406/646-9633. Chicken-fried steaks, biscuits and gravy, buffalo burgers, and hot open-faced sandwiches grace the menu, and pine paneling decorates the walls. Fans of '50s diners will appreciate the simple and filling meals here.

Beartooth BBQ, 118 Madison Ave., 406/646-4252, is a busy walk-up stand with two picnic tables out front and a menu of beef brisket sandwiches, hot dogs, and Friday–Sunday pork

spare ribs. Open seasonally. Just up the street is the local high-schoolers' hangout, the **Dairy Queen.** Pig out cheaply at tiny **Mountain Mike's Cafe,** 38 Canyon, 406/646-9462, which serves all-American faves: burgers, sandwiches, steak, and chicken, plus freshly baked pies for dessert. A few picnic tables sit outback.

Justifiably popular for both lunch and dinner, **Bullwinkles Saloon & Eatery,** 19 Madison Ave. W, 406/646-7974, cranks out steaks, burgers, pork chops, salads, and homemade pastries. Big portions too. **Timberline Cafe,** 135 Yellowstone Ave. (next to the Madison Hotel), 406/646-9349, is another popular family place for breakfast, with a small salad and potato bar, reasonable meals, a kid's menu, and daily specials.

Three Bear Restaurant, 205 Yellowstone Ave., 406/646-7811, is a friendly place with an up-market dinner menu of shrimp, halibut, trout, chicken, and steaks. They have a good salad-and-soup bar, a children's menu, and apple brown Betty à la mode for dessert. Open three meals a day and entirely nonsmoking. Dinner entrées are $12–20.

International

Wild West Pizza, 20 Madison Ave. (next to Strozzi's Bar), 406/646-4400, makes the best local pizzas and calzones. I'm not sure how they came up with the pizza names, but somehow the "Sacajawea" has fresh spinach, feta, kalamata olives, and artichoke hearts! **Pete's Rocky Mountain Pizza,** 104 Canyon St., 406/646-7820, also has pizzas and Italian specialties. They offer free delivery if you just want to eat a pizza in your motel room. **Gusher Pizza and Sandwich Shoppe,** Madison and Dunraven, 406/646-9050, is a family place with fast service, the best Reubens in these parts, and tolerable pizzas (frozen crust, alas). Wednesday is all-you-can-eat spaghetti night.

Chinatown, 100 Madison Ave., 406/646-7088, serves surprisingly authentic Chinese meals, and has $5 lunchtime specials.

Texas Rose Restaurant, 335 U.S. Hwy. 20 West, 406/646-0095, www.texasrosewestyellowstone.com, serves authentic Tex-Mex meals, including vegetarian items and homemade salsa.

They're open until 1 A.M. daily in summer. Drop by on Tuesday nights when the tacos are just 79 cents.

Steaks and More

Coachman Restaurant, downstairs in the Stage Coach Inn, 209 Madison Ave., 406/646-7381 or 800/842-2882, www.yellowstoneinn.com, serves three meals a day, including big traditional breakfasts (great omelets), along with steak, seafood, and pasta for dinner. They also feature a salad bar and a substantial wine list.

The most unusual local eatery is rustic **Eino's Bar,** 406/646-9344, nine miles north of town on U.S. Hwy. 191. It's a cook-your-own steak, burger, and chicken place with a big indoor grill and a motley, hard-drinking crowd. The bar is famous for its bloody Marys and is popular with snowmobilers. Open for lunch and dinner year-round. The patio features a view across Hebgen Lake, and the bar has a big-screen TV and pool tables.

If gourmet meals are your goal, you're probably out of luck in West Yellowstone. Best bet? Drive to Big Sky (57 miles north) for the acclaimed **Lone Mountain Ranch,** 406/995-4644 or 800/514-4644, www.lmranch.com. Several other upscale restaurants are also in the Big Sky area.

Brewpub

Wolf Pack Brewing Co., 139 N. Canyon St., 406/646-7225, www.wolfpackbrewing.com, generally has four German-style beers on draught, including Wapiti Wheat, Old Snaggletooth Scwartzbier, Jim Bridger Marzen, and Lone Mountain Amber. The menu includes pub fare such as bratwursts, sandwiches, and Polish sausages.

Groceries

Market Place, 22 Madison Ave., 406/646-9600, and **Food Roundup Supermarket,** on the corner of Madison and Dunraven, 406/646-7501, are the local grocery stores. Market Place also contains a deli and bakery. For sweet treats, head to **Arrowleaf Ice Cream Parlor,** 29 Canyon St., 406/646-9776. In addition to homemade ice cream, shakes, banana splits, and waffle cones, Ar-

rowleaf serves burgers, chili dogs, and surprisingly good soups.

ENTERTAINMENT

During summer, you can attend lighthearted comedies and musicals for the whole family at **Playmill Theatre,** 124 Madison Ave., 406/646-7757, www.playmill.com. They've been in operation for more than four decades.

Watch flicks at **Bears Den Cinema,** 15 Electric St., 406/646-7777. In addition to the IMAX films described earlier, **Yellowstone IMAX Theatre,** 406/646-4100 or 888/854-5862, shows Hollywood's latest efforts most evenings.

The bar at **Stage Coach Inn,** 209 Madison Ave., 406/646-7381, has live bands Tuesday–Saturday nights, or try **Iron Horse Saloon,** inside the West Yellowstone Conference Hotel at 315 Yellowstone Ave., 406/646-7365. **Lionshead Super 8 Lodge,** seven miles west of town, 406/646-9584, www.wyellowstone.com/lionshead, has square dancing in the summer.

EVENTS

On the second weekend of March, the **Rendezvous Marathon Ski Race,** a nationally known Nordic ski race, attracts hundreds of participants; 406/646-9222, www.rendezvousskitrails.com. The following weekend brings a very different event, the **World Snowmobile Expo,** 406/646-7001, www.snowmobileexpo.com, with races, demos, and other activities.

A fun parade, live music, and fireworks highlight the town's **Fourth of July** festivities, and the **Yellowstone Rod Run** takes place on the first full weekend of August, bringing vintage cars of all types to the oldest such event in the Pacific Northwest. The **Wild West Yellowstone Rodeo** features bareback riding, team roping, saddle bronc riding, bull riding, and more to the rodeo arena on two weekends in July and August. The **Burnt Hole Mountain Man Rendezvous** on the third weekend of August includes arts and crafts, traditional games, tall-tale competitions, and other old-time events.

At the **Yellowstone Film Festival,** 406/646-

1100, www.yellowstonefilmfestival.org, in late September more than 60 films are screened, and you can attend workshops, a tradeshow, and other events.

SUMMER RECREATION
Horses and Bikes

Horseback trail rides and Western cookouts are available from **Parade Rest Guest Ranch,** seven miles north of town, 406/646-7217 or 800/753-5934, www.paraderestranch.com, and **Diamond P Ranch,** seven miles to the west, 406/646-7246. Several other ranches farther afield also offer horseback rides; contact the chamber of commerce for details.

The 30-km Rendezvous Trail System becomes mountain-bike central when summer rolls around. It starts from the southern edge of town; get a map at the visitors center. Rent mountain bikes from **Yellowstone Bicycles,** 132 Madison Ave., 406/646-7815, or **Free Heel and Wheel,** 40 Yellowstone Ave., 406/646-7744, www.wyellowstone.com/freeheelwheel. Free Heel also rents bike trailers, bike racks, and baby joggers; ask about their free daily bike rides.

Fishing

You'll find five different **fly-fishing shops** in town, a reflection of the sport's importance in the Yellowstone area. In business for more than 45 years, **Bud Lilly's Trout Shop,** 39 Madison Ave., 406/646-7801 or 800/854-9559, www .budlillys.com, is the best-known local place, with fishing tackle, clothing, guides, and even a gallery. Also well worth a look are **Arrick's Fishing Flies,** 125 Madison Ave., 406/646-7290, www.arricks.com; **Eagle's Tackle Shop,** 3 Canyon St., 406/646-7521; **Jacklin's Fly Shop,** 105 Yellowstone Ave., 406/646-7336, www .jacklinsflyshop.com, and **Madison River Outfitters,** 117 Canyon St., 406/646-9644, www .flyfishingyellowstone.com. All of these offer guided fishing and equipment.

River Rafting

Three rafting companies run all-day and half-day whitewater trips down the Gallatin River ap-proximately 50 miles north of West Yellowstone (near Big Sky). The rafting season is generally late May–September, and you'll pay around $80 for all day or $40 for a half-day trip. The companies are **Geyser Whitewater Expeditions,** 406/995-4989 or 800/914-9031, www.raftmontana.com; **Montana Whitewater,** 307/763-4465 or 800/799-4465, www.montanawhitewater.com; and **Yellowstone Raft Company,** 406/995-4613 or 800/348-4376, www.yellowstoneraft.com. All three companies also offer sit-on-top kayaks for those who'd rather paddle it themselves. Yellowstone Raft Company also leads trips down the challenging Madison River northwest of West Yellowstone, and Geyser Whitewater has gentle scenic floats for those who'd rather relax.

WINTER RECREATION
Cross-Country Skiing

West Yellowstone is infamous for its bitterly cold winters, when the thermometer can drop to −50°F. Fortunately, it doesn't always stay there, and by March the days have often warmed to a balmy 20°F. In November, West Yellowstone becomes a national center for cross-country skiers, with the U.S. Nordic and biathlon ski teams training here.

Two trail systems provide a wide variety of Nordic skiing conditions. The 30-km **Rendezvous Trail** system (www.rendezvousski trails.com) takes off from the southern edge of town and is groomed with both classical and skating tracks from early November through April. The nine-km **Riverside Trail** begins on the east side of town and leads to the Madison River within Yellowstone National Park. This trail is partially groomed and provides a good opportunity to see bison, elk, and possibly moose; it's closed to skate skiing. You can also ski the snowpacked streets in winter. Find many more places for flat tracking or telemarking in adjacent Yellowstone National Park and the Gallatin and Caribou-Targhee National Forests. Before heading out, get recorded avalanche-safety information from the **Avalanche Advisory Hotline,** 406/587-6981, www.gomontana.com/avalanche. It's updated daily in the winter.

Rent skinny skis from **Bud Lilly's Trout Shop,** 39 Madison Ave., 406/646-7801 or 800/854-9559, www.budlillys.com; or **Free Heel and Wheel,** 40 Yellowstone Ave., 406/646-7744, www.wyellowstone.com/freeheelwheel. Freeheel also rents snowshoes, as does **Yellowstone Rental & Sports,** eight miles west of town on U.S. Hwy. 20, 406/646-9377 or 888/646-9377.

The closest downhill ski and snowboard area is the world-class **Big Sky Resort,** 57 miles north of West Yellowstone, 800/548-4486, www.bigsky resort.com. The resort features 15 lifts and more than 3,500 acres of terrain. You will find excellent cross-country trails at Lone Mountain Ranch near Big Sky.

Dogsledding

For a delightfully different way to explore the Gallatin National Forest backcountry, take a sled dog tour from **Klondike Dreams,** 406/646-5988, www.klondikedreams.com. Half-day tours are $100 per person ($85 kids), and all day is $165 per person ($150 kids), including lunch. Owner Roger Vincent can also shuttle skiers into backcountry cabins by dog sled.

Snowcoach Trips

Yellowstone Alpen Guides, 406/646-9591 or 800/858-3502, www.yellowstoneguides.com, leads snowcoach tours from West Yellowstone. All-day trips are $97 ($89 seniors, $77 kids) to Grand Canyon of the Yellowstone, or $87 ($79 seniors, $66 kids under 12) to the Old Faithful area. Guests on the latter run have an option of getting dropped at Biscuit Basin, where they can ski to Old Faithful and meet up with others. Special snowcoach-and-guided-ski tours are $109 per person. Also available is a three-night package trip that includes two nights in West Yellowstone, a night at Old Faithful Snow Lodge, and two days of wildlife snowcoach tours for $395 per person.

For a truly unique experience, book a winter trip with another West Yellowstone–based company, **Yellowstone Expeditions,** 406/646-9333 or 800/728-9333, www.yellowstoneexpeditions .com. The company has homey tent-cabins at the Canyon area during the winter, with a variety of multinight adventures for skiers.

Snowmobiles

The chamber of commerce trumpets West as the "snowmobile capital of the world," and each day between November and late March hundreds (and sometimes thousands) of snowmobilers show up to roar through Yellowstone's West Entrance or across thousands of acres of adjacent Forest Service lands. On busy days long lines of snowmobiles belch blue smoke into the air while waiting to enter the park.

At least 15 different snowmobile tour and rental companies operate out of West Yellowstone. Rentals run $100–175 per day depending on the type of machine; guided Yellowstone tours are more expensive. Hundreds more folks bring in their own "crotch rockets" to ride on park roads or national forest lands, and many local motels offer snowmobile/lodging packages. The West Yellowstone Chamber of Commerce, 406/646-7701, can provide current snow and trail conditions, a detailed map of local trails, and a listing of companies that rent snowmobiles.

A quieter option is to take a snowcoach tour of Yellowstone from **Yellowstone Alpen Guides,** 555 Yellowstone Ave., 406/646-9591 or 800/858-3502, www.yellowstoneguides.com; or **Yellowstone Expeditions,** 406/646-9333 or 800/728-9333. Tours cost $87–97 per day, and both companies also have multinight trips.

SHOPPING

Many West Yellowstone shops sell the obligatory Yellowstone souvenirs, corny T-shirts, and other items with mass appeal. You'll probably get bored after one or two of these gift shops, but many more await your exploration. Fortunately, the town does have several more distinctive places.

Housed in the Yellowstone Apothecary retail complex at 121 Madison St., **Homeroom,** 406/646-4338, www.yellowstoneshop.com, is the pretend-you're-in-Jackson shop, with a fine selection of Western furnishings, accessories for the home, and gifts.

Seldom Seen Knives, 406/646-4116, www .seldomseenknives.com, at 115 Yellowstone Ave., is worth a look, not only for Steve Hulett's unusual knives, but also for his multicolor wooden letter openers and other locally crafted items, including offbeat fencepost vases.

Books

The Book Peddler, 106 Canyon St., 406/646-9358, www.thebookpeddler.com, is a large and attractive bookstore with an abundance of regional titles. A pleasant café sells espresso, bagels, and pastries in the back. This is a great place to hang with the locals. **Bookworm Books,** 14 Canyon St., 406/646-9736, is another good shop with both new and used titles, including many first editions; it's open nightly until midnight all summer! Check out their collection of vintage Yellowstone tourist antiques, particularly the collectable spoons, plates, and stereo views. The small local **library** is housed in the railroad's old stone dining lodge at 200 Yellowstone Ave., 406/646-9017.

Outdoor Gear

Yellowstone Rental & Sports, 406/646-9377 or 888/646-9377, www.wyellowstone.com /yellowstonerentals, rents a variety of outdoor gear, including tents, sleeping bags, cookstoves, fishing boats, canoes, mountain bikes, baby strollers and car seats, snowshoes, and even backhoes for those who want to dig things up a bit. It's eight miles west of West Yellowstone along U.S. Hwy. 20.

INFORMATION AND SERVICES

The **West Yellowstone Chamber of Commerce,** 30 Yellowstone Ave., 406/646-7701, www.westyellowstonechamber.com, is open daily 8 A.M.–8 P.M. Memorial Day to Labor Day; daily 8 A.M.–5 P.M. in May and Labor Day to October; and Mon.–Fri. 8 A.M.–5 P.M. the rest of the year. The office is also staffed by Park Service employees (406/646-4403) whenever Yellowstone is open. Daily ranger talks are a feature in July and August.

In addition to the Chamber's website, you'll find useful information at www.westyellow stonetraveler.com, maintained by Circumerro Publishing, and Yellowstone Park Net's www .westyellowstonenet.com. Check your email or surf the web at **West Yellowstone Web Works,** 27 Geyser St., 406/646-7006, www.wyellow stone.com, or inside the **Madison Hotel,** 139 Yellowstone Ave., 406/646-7745 or 800/838-7745, www.wyellowstone.com/madisonhotel.

The **Hebgen Lake Ranger District Office** is just north of town on U.S. Hwy. 191/287, 406/646-7369, www.fs.fed.us/r1/gallatin, Pick up maps of Gallatin National Forest, along with an interesting brochure on the Madison River Canyon Earthquake Area.

West Yellowstone's **post office** is at 209 Grizzly Ave., 406/646-7704. You'll find **ATMs** in several local banks, hotels, and other businesses.

Wash clothes at **Canyon Street Laundromat,** 312 Canyon St., 406/646-9733, where you'll also find showers. Other laundry options are **Econo-Mart Laundromat,** 307 Firehole Ave., 406/646-7887, or **Swan Cleaners & Laundromat,** 520 Madison Ave., 406/646-7892.

The **Clinic at West Yellowstone,** 236 Yellowstone Ave., 406/646-7668, takes walk-in patients. It generally has a doctor and physicians assistant on duty and is open Monday–Saturday.

TRANSPORTATION

By Air

Sky West/Delta, 406/646-7351 or 800/453-9417, www.delta.com, has three flights a day to West Yellowstone airport (just north of town) from Salt Lake City June–September. The rest of the year, the closest air service is in Bozeman, Idaho Falls, or Jackson Hole.

By Bus and Taxi

Greyhound, 800/231-2222, www.greyhound .com, has daily summer-only runs between Bozeman and Salt Lake City, with a stop in front of West Yellowstone Office Services at 132 Electric Street.

Community Bus Service, 406/646-7600, provides bus service ($10) between West Yellowstone and Bozeman on Thursdays in summer and Tuesdays and Thursdays in winter. Two companies offer winter shuttles between the Bozeman airport and West Yellowstone: **4x4 Stage,** 406/848-2224 or 800/517-8243, and **Karst Stage,** 406/388-2293 or 800/287-4759, www.karststage.com. The cost is $65 per person round-trip. In summer, both companies have custom shuttles throughout the Yellowstone region, but call 24 hours ahead for reservations.

Yellowstone Taxi, 406/646-1111, provides local transport and private transport to other towns in the region, including Jackson ($115 per person).

By Car

West Yellowstone has some of the highest gas prices in the region; fill up before you get here! Rental cars are available through **Budget** (at the airport), 406/646-7882 or 800/527-0700, www.budget.com; or **Big Sky Car Rentals,** 406/646-9564 or 800/426-7669, www.yellowstonevacations.com. Rates start around $45 per day for a compact.

PARK TOURS

Several companies offer all-day tours of Yellowstone June–September. **Gray Line,** 633 Madison Ave., 406/646-9374 or 800/523-3102, www.graylineyellowstone.com, offers lower loop park tours daily and upper loop tours three times a week for $40 ($36 seniors, $30 kids) plus park entrance fees. They also lead Grand Teton National park tours for $50 from West Yellowstone, along with a wildlife tour that goes through Lamar Valley for $40.

Buffalo Bus Touring Co., 429 Yellowstone, 406/646-9564 or 800/426-7669, www.yellowstonevacations.com, has narrated loop tours of Yellowstone for $38 per person or $25 for kids under 16 (plus the park entrance fee). They do the lower park loop daily and the upper loop on Mondays, Wednesdays, and Fridays. In the winter, they operate snowcoach vans, with tours to Old Faithful for $84 adults, $64 kids.

Yellowstone Tours & Travel, 406/646-9310 or 800/221-1151, www.yellowstone-travel.com, takes smaller groups (maximum 12) on van tours of the park for a bit more: $50 for either loop of the park, $60 for Grand Teton/Jackson Hole.

Yellowstone Alpen Guides, 555 Yellowstone Ave., 406/646-9591 or 800/858-3502, www.yellowstoneguides.com, leads more personalized tours, from day trips to multiday excursions. The company provides the naturalist-guide, and you travel around the park in the company van or your own car.

Gardiner, Montana

The little tourist town of Gardiner, Montana (pop. 800), lies barely outside the northwest entrance to Yellowstone, just three miles from the Wyoming line. The Yellowstone River slices right through town. Park headquarters at Mammoth Hot Springs is just five miles away, and the large warehouses of park concessioner Xanterra Parks & Resorts dominate the vicinity. Gardiner is the only year-round entrance to Yellowstone, and the Absaroka-Beartooth Wilderness lies just north of here. The town sits at an elevation of 5,300 feet—some 900 feet lower than Mammoth—and has warm, dry summers and relatively mild winters.

Gardiner was founded in 1880, and three years later the Northern Pacific Railroad extended a line to the edge of Yellowstone, making the town the first major entryway into the park. A reporter of that era described Gardiner as having "200 hardy souls, with 6 restaurants, 1 billiard hall, 2 dance halls, 4 houses of ill-fame, 1 milk man and 21 saloons." Today, the most distinctive structure in town is the monumental stone park entryway—similar to France's Arc de Triomphe—which was the primary entry point into Yellowstone for many years. Built in 1903, **Roosevelt Arch** was dedicated by Pres. Theodore Roosevelt, a man regarded by many as Yellowstone's patron saint. A tablet above the keystone is inscribed, "For the Benefit and Enjoyment of the People." (The arch was actually built to offset the park visitors' initial disappointment at finding the rather ordinary country in this part of Yellowstone!)

ACCOMMODATIONS

Gardiner has many places to stay, but be sure to reserve ahead in the summer; rooms may be hard to find even in mid-September. Rates plummet after (and before) the gold rush of seasonal tourists; $75 summertime rooms suddenly go for $35!

Under $100

The most basic local accommodations are at **Gardiner Town Motel;** 406/848-7322: $45 s $50 d with no air conditioning, phones, or cable TV.

Yellowstone River Motel, 406/848-7303 or 888/797-4837, www.yellowstonerivermotel.com, is open May–October. Economy rooms in the older building are $55 s or $59 d, while rooms in

Roosevelt Arch, Gardiner

© DON PITCHER

the new addition run $75 s or d. A garden patio overlooks the river, and a family unit with kitchenette is also available.

Jim Bridger Motor Court, 406/848-7371 or 888/858-7508, is a classic Western place with clean and well-kept log cabins built in 1937. Rates are $60 d to $70 for four people; open mid-May to mid-Oct. The three-story **Motel 6,** 406/848-7520 or 800/466-8356, www.motel6.com, has predictable rooms and a view of the parking lot. Summer rates are $70 s or $76 d.

Westernaire Motel, 406/848-7397 or 888/273-0358, www.yellowstonemotel.com, has clean rooms but somewhat dated furnishings. Rooms with one queen bed are $65; those with two queens cost $75. You're likely to see elk hanging out here most of the summer; guess they like the owner's plants better than other places.

Originally built in the 1950s but updated with newer furnishings, **Hillcrest Cottages,** 200 Scott St., 406/848-7353 or 800/970-7353, www.hillcrestcottages.com, has cozy 15 units, all with kitchenettes and picnic tables. Most have showers, but a few contain tubs. No phones. Rates are $76 d, plus $6 per person for up to six. Open May–Sept. **Riverside Cottages,** 406/848-7719 or 877/774-2836, www.riversidecottages.com, is a little place with motel units ($69–79 s or d), cottages ($89–109 d) with full kitchens, and suites (119–129 for up to six). Rooms are updated, and guests will appreciate the gazebo out back that contains a hot tub overlooking the Yellowstone River.

Located on the north end of town next to the rodeo grounds, **Yellowstone Village Inn,** 406/848-7417 or 800/228-8158, www.yellowstonevillageinn.com, has modern rooms for $75–86 s or d, and kitchenette suites for $135–165; the larger suites sleep six. Amenities include an indoor pool, sauna, and light breakfast.

The modern **Best Western by Mammoth Hot Springs,** 406/848-7311 or 800/829-9080, www.bestwestern.com/mammothhotsprings, has an indoor pool, saunas, and a hot tub. Rooms are $95–115 s or d, and suites cost $185. **Super 8 Motel,** 406/848-7401 or 800/800-8000, www.yellowstonesuper8.com, charges $90 s or d, including an indoor pool and continental breakfast.

GATEWAYS

$100 and Up

Absaroka Lodge, 406/848-7414 or 800/755-7414, www.yellowstonemotel.com, is a modern motel with immaculate rooms for $90 s or d, and suites with kitchenettes that cost $100 s or d, or $110 for four people. All rooms have balconies overlooking the Yellowstone River.

Out in the country five miles northwest of Gardiner, **Maiden Basin Inn,** 406/848-7080 or 800/624-3364, www.maidenbasininn.com, is a recently built eight-room lodge with a variety of accommodations. The inn exudes country charm, and rooms start at $100. A two-bedroom townhouse with a full kitchen, living room, and loft rents for $175. The latter sleeps seven people. All rooms have private decks where you can sit on a rocking chair with a view of Electric Peak inside Yellowstone. An outdoor hot tub is available, and a continental breakfast is served in the lobby. The inn is open mid-May to mid-October.

Comfort Inn, 406/848-7536 or 800/228-5150, www.yellowstonecomfortinn.com, charges $99 s or d for contemporary rooms with log furnishings; suites and hot tub rooms are $150. A light breakfast is available in the lobby, and the motel has three indoor hot tubs.

Bed-and-Breakfasts

One of the nicest local places to stay is **Yellowstone Inn B&B,** 406/848-7000 or 800/704-5685, www.yellowstoneinnbandb.com, consisting of a beautifully restored stone house (built in 1903) that has been furnished in a New West style. The three guest rooms cost $85–95 d and have shared or private baths. Out back is a private, two-level cottage with kitchenette for $115 d. A full breakfast is served, and guests will enjoy the outdoor hot tub. Well-behaved kids are welcome.

Also of note is **Yellowstone Suites B&B,** 506 4th St., 406/848-7937 or 800/948-7937, www.wolftracker.com/ys, another stone house that's nearly a century old. Features include Victorian antique furnishings, hardwood floors, a veranda, a hot tub, and full breakfasts. The four guest rooms have shared or private baths and

cost $85–108 s or d; one contains a kitchenette. Kids are welcome.

North Yellowstone B&B, 406/848-7651, www.northyellowstone.com, is a delightful country place, with two modern log cabins located two miles up Jardine Road. The cabins are $85 s or d; $5 per person for additional guests up to six. A full breakfast is served at the main house. No phones and only a tiny TV are provided, but the cabins have private baths, small fridges, and barbecue grills. Outside, weeping willow trees provide shade, and gorgeous sagebrush country heads out in all directions.

Headwaters of the Yellowstone B&B, 406/848-707 or 888/848-7220, www.headwatersbandb.com, is a large and recently built house on five acres of land along the Yellowstone River. It's located one mile north of the Gardiner airport and has four guest rooms and a suite (all $125 s or d), along with two modern cabins with full kitchens ($150 for up to six). All of these rooms have private baths, and the rate includes a full breakfast. Many Yellowstone visitors stay by the week in the cabins; $125 without breakfast.

Guesthouses

Arch House, 406/848-2205, is a historic rock home located just two blocks from the arch entryway into Yellowstone. The two-bedroom guesthouse sleeps up to six and includes a full kitchen, bath, living room with stone fireplace, and dining room. It rents for $125 d, plus $10 each for additional guests up to a maximum of six. The owners run Electric Peak Espresso next door, a good place to start your morning with a jolt of caffeine, and serve a continental breakfast.

Above the Rest Lodge, 406/848-7747 or 800/406-7748, www.abovetherestlodge.com, has five modern and well-appointed cabins less than two miles north of Gardiner up Jardine Road. Smallest is a one-bedroom unit with a spiral staircase and full kitchen; $125 for four people. Largest is a spacious three-bedroom home that sleeps 10 people for $260 per night. All of these have full kitchens and decks facing Yellowstone. Open year-round.

Out-of-Town Accommodations

Mountain Retreat, 406/848-7272 or 800/727-0798, has an older two-bedroom cabin with kitchen. Located in the country 10 miles north of Gardiner, it has no TV or phones; $90 for up to four people.

Slip and Slide Ranch, 406/848-7648, www.slipandslide.com, is 12 miles north of Gardiner. Bed-and-breakfast accommodations are available in the contemporary home, which has three guest rooms, two baths, and a private entrance; $75 d, including a full breakfast. The B&B rooms are available from mid-May to mid-September. If you really want to escape, the ranch also offers a spacious and modern log lodge 2.5 miles in the hills (4WD required). The lodge sleeps five for $150, or up to 12 for $300. A three-night minimum is required, and it is open mid-February to mid-October. The owners are outfitters and use this lodge for hunters in the fall and winter.

Besides lodging in Gardiner, several places are available in Paradise Valley, 20 miles to the north. A good one is **Dome Mountain Cabins and Guest Houses,** 406/333-4361 or 800/313-4868, www.domemountainranch.com, which has B&B cabin accommodations for $95–150 d and full-house rentals available on a weekly basis as corporate retreats. The latter aren't cheap: up to $6,000 for six nights!

Farther away, but worth a visit if you're heading north, is **Chico Hot Springs,** 30 miles north of Gardiner in Pray, Montana. This classic old hotel sits adjacent to a hot-springs-fed pool ($5.75), and the restaurant is an attraction in its own right. Dinner reservations are required. Rooms in the main and lower lodge cost $45–149. A variety of cabins and houses are also available, all the way up to a five-bedroom log home (popular with wedding parties and family reunions) that sleeps 20 for $315 per night. Call 406/333-4933 or 800/468-9232 for more information, or visit www.chicohotsprings.com. The resort also has a café and day spa, along with summertime horseback rides and fly-fishing, and wintertime dog sledding. The saloon swings to live bands on weekends year-round.

CAMPING

Yellowstone National Park's **Mammoth Campground** is five miles up the hill at Mammoth Hot Springs and costs $12. The campground is open year-round but sits close to a busy road. No reservations are taken.

Closer—and more peaceful—is the small **Eagle Creek Campground** ($7; open year-round), less than two miles northeast of Gardiner up the gravel road on the way to Jardine. This Gallatin National Forest campground (www.fs.fed.us/r1/gallatin/recreation) is approximately 500 feet higher than Gardiner, and you will need to bring water from town or treat water from the creek here. Two other Forest Service campgrounds (free; open mid-June through Oct.) are a few miles up Jardine Road.

Park RVs at **Rocky Mountain Campground,** 406/848-7251, www.rockymountaincampground.com, for $26 ($15 for tents); open mid-May to mid-Oct. Showers for noncampers cost $4, and a public laundromat is on the site. Campsites are also available in crowded, along-the-river sites at **Yellowstone RV Park,** 406/848-7496, open May–October on the northwest end of town. Rates are $31 for RVs, $22 for tents.

FOOD

K Bar Club, 406/848-9995, doesn't look like much either outside or inside, but the from-scratch pizzas are very good in this locals' hangout; kids and families are welcome. Also popular with families is **Outlaw's Pizza,** in the Outpost Mall on the northwest end of town, 406/848-7733, for standard pizzas, pasta, and calzone, and a small salad bar.

Town Cafe, 406/848-7322, has sandwiches and burgers. Better food, including a big salad bar, are upstairs in the Town Loft (summer only), where you can enjoy the vistas while you eat. Also downtown is **Sawtooth Deli,** 406/848-7600, with cold and hot subs, grilled sandwiches, soups, salads, and espresso for lunch, or pasta, steaks, chicken, and more for dinner. The covered deck is a favorite hangout. Closed Sun. and Nov.–Apr.

Yellowstone Mine Restaurant, inside the Best Western on the northwest side of town,

406/848-7336, offers good but overpriced meals served in an old-time mine atmosphere. The summertime breakfast buffet is popular, and they have the best steaks around. At **Corral Drive Inn,** 406/848-7627, Helen and her sons serve the biggest, juiciest, and messiest (grab a handful of napkins) hamburgers anywhere around.

Park Street Grill & Café, 406/848-7989, seems out of place in down-home Gardiner. Most of the menu isn't your standard Old West fare, although they do serve steaks and prime rib. Instead, it's Italian food with flare, including such delights as shrimp fra diavolo (large shrimp sautéed with garlic, peppers, and tomatoes served over linguine) or Crazy Mt. Alfredo with chicken breast, soppressata, Italian sausage, and hot peppers. Meals come with a big house salad, and the atmosphere is rustic elegance. Park Street Grill is open for dinners only ($12–21 entrées) and is closed in the off-season.

Shop for groceries, fresh baked goods, and deli items at **Food Farm,** 406/848-7524, across the river on the northwest end of town. For a sweet treat, step into **Electric Peak Espresso and Ice Cream,** 406/848-2205; it's close to the arch on Park Street.

EVENTS AND ENTERTAINMENT

The big annual event in town is the **Gardiner Ranch Rodeo,** which comes around the third weekend of June. Other **NRA rodeos** come to Gardiner two or three times a month in May, June, and July. End summer with a blast at **Buffalo Days,** held the Friday before Labor Day and featuring live music, dancing, and plenty of barbecued buffalo, beef, and pork. Look for live bands on some weekends at the **Two-Bit Saloon,** 406/848-7743.

RIVER RAFTING

During summer, three rafting companies offer whitewater trips from Gardiner down the Yellowstone River. **Yellowstone Raft Company,** 406/848-7777 or 800/858-7781, www.yellowstoneraft.com, has been running trips since 1978. Other good companies are **Montana**

Whitewater, 307/763-4465 or 800/799-4465, www.montanawhitewater.com; and **Wild West Rafting,** 406/848-2252 or 800/862-0557, www.wildwestrafting.com.

The rapids in this stretch of the Yellowstone River are relatively gentle, in the Class II–III range, and the featured attractions are half-day eight-mile trips or all-day 17-mile trips. Expect to pay around $31 adults, $21 kids for three-hour trips, or $66 adults, $46 kids for a full-day voyage. Yellowstone Raft Company and Montana Whitewater both have a variety of other options, such as sit-on-top kayaks, and other river trips, including down the Gallatin River near Big Sky. Wild West offers scenic float trips in Paradise Valley north of Gardiner (same prices). In addition to these companies, several two-bit operators also run whitewater trips each summer, but ask around to get an idea of their reputation before signing up.

OTHER RECREATION

There are two fly-fishing shops in Gardiner: **Park's Fly Shop,** 406/848-7314, and **Big Sky's Flies and Guides,** 107 S. 2nd St., 406/848-9998 or 888/315-3789, www.bigskyflies.com. During the winter, Park's also rents cross-country skis.

For horseback rides and backcountry pack trips, contact **Wilderness Connection,** 406/848-7287, www.wilderness-connection.com, or **Rendezvous Outfitters,** 406/848-7697 or 800/565-7110.

Mountain Biking

No local companies rent mountain bikes, but if you bring your own there are a pair of fine biking options. The Old Gardiner Road to Mammoth gains 900 feet in a distance of five miles and makes for a fun ride back down. Also worth a ride is the old road to Livingston, a gravel road that follows the west side of the Yellowstone River out of Gardiner. It starts near the arch and passes an interesting old cemetery with century-old graves a few miles up.

SHOPPING

Silvertip Bookstore, 501 Scott St., 406/848-2225, sells new and used titles and serves espres-

Cooke City and Silver Gate, Montana 259

GATEWAYS

so and smoothies. You'll also find a choice of Western books, along with espresso coffee, downtown on Park Street at **High Country Trading,** 406/848-7707.

Yellowstone Gallery & Frameworks, 406/848-7306, www.yellowstonegallery.com, is an excellent place for quality pottery, jewelry, paintings, and photography. Also worth a look downtown is **Off the Wall Gallery,** 406/848-7775.

Flying Pig Camp Store, 406/848-7510, www.flyingpigcampstore.com, sells quality outdoor gear, and has rental computers to check your email.

The portion around Gardiner is lower in elevation and covered with forests, while farther east are the alpine peaks of the Beartooth Mountains.

The **post office** is on the north end of town along U.S. Hwy. 89, 406/848-7579. Get fast cash at the ATM inside the Exxon station just north of the river or from the First Interstate Bank on the northwest end of town. Wash clothes at **Arch Laundrette,** next to High Country Trading on Park Street. Wash clothes at **Arch Laundrette,** next to High Country Trading on Park Street. Both Yellowstone Village Inn and Rocky Mountain Campground also have washers and driers available to the public.

INFORMATION AND SERVICES

The **Gardiner Chamber of Commerce,** 222 Park St., 406/848-7971, www.gardinerchamber .com, has local information and is open Monday–Friday 9 A.M.–4 P.M., and Saturday–Sunday 10 A.M.–2 P.M. May–September, and Tuesday–Thursday 10 A.M.–4 P.M. the rest of the year. If the office is closed, check the information kiosk on the north end of town for maps, brochures, and events.

The **Gardiner District Office** of Gallatin National Forest, 406/848-7375, www.fs.fed.us /r1/gallatin, has maps and information on the 930,584-acre **Absaroka-Beartooth Wilderness.**

TRANSPORTATION AND TOURS

Based in Bozeman, **4x4 Stage,** 406/848-2224 or 800/517-8243, offers taxi service throughout the Yellowstone area, including into Gardiner. Call 24 hours ahead for reservations. Livingston-based **V.I.P. Taxi,** 406/222-0200 is also available.

From mid-May through September, **Xanterra Parks & Resorts,** 307/344-7311, www.travel yellowstone.com, operates full-day bus tours of Yellowstone out of Gardiner. Rates are $42 adults, $20 ages 12–16, and free for kids under 12; park entrance fees are extra. These are a bit grueling because you leave at 8:30 A.M. and don't get back until 6:15 P.M.

Cooke City and Silver Gate, Montana

Shortly after you exit Yellowstone's northeast corner along U.S. Hwy. 212, the road widens slightly as it passes through two settlements: Silver Gate and the larger Cooke City, Montana. The towns are just three miles apart and almost within spitting distance of the Wyoming line. The area code—406—is larger than the combined population of both settlements! Although they depend on tourism, these quiet, homespun places lack the hustle and bustle of West Yellowstone and have a more authentic feel. No leash laws exist here, so you're likely to see dogs sleeping on the sidewalks or wandering lazily down the middle of the road. Most establishments are built

of log, befitting the mining heritage of this area. Silver Gate even has a building code that requires all structures to be of log or rustic architecture—it's the only municipality in the country with such a code. Pilot and Index Peaks are the prominent rocky spires visible along the highway east of Cooke City. Dramatic Amphitheater Peak juts out just south of Silver Gate.

During winter, the road is plowed all the way from Gardiner, through the northern part of Yellowstone, and into Cooke City, making this a popular staging area for snowmobilers and skiers heading into the Beartooth Mountains. East of Cooke City, the Beartooth Highway across

10,947-foot Beartooth Pass is closed by the first of November (often earlier) and doesn't open again until late May.

HISTORY

The town of Cooke City was first called Shoo-Fly, but the name was changed in honor of Jay Cooke Jr., a promoter of the Northern Pacific Railroad. The promised railroad never materialized, but the name stuck. Cooke City had its start in 1882 when the boundaries of the Crow Reservation were shifted to the east, opening this area to mining. A small gold rush ensued, and by the following summer, Cooke City had grown to hold several hundred miners, along with two smelters, two sawmills, and a cluster of businesses. At its peak, the town was also home to 13 saloons. As with many 19th-century mining towns, the population of Cooke City had wild swings, with up to 1,000 people at one time, but just 20 souls a few years later. The isolation, modest gold and silver strikes, and high transportation costs (no railroad was ever built into the settlement) kept mining from ever really booming. Today fewer than a hundred people live in Cooke City year-round, but the population triples with the arrival of summer residents.

The town of Silver Gate has a briefer history. The land here was first homesteaded in the 1890s, but the town didn't appear until 1932 when John Taylor and J. J. White founded it as a haven for summer residents looking for a home close to Yellowstone. Only a handful of folks live here in the winter, but that swells to 100 or so when the long days of summer return.

The country around Silver Gate and Cooke City was torched in the Storm Creek Fire of 1988, leaving charred hills just a couple hundred feet to the north and prompting alterations in the road signs to read "Cooked City." Today, tourism is the ticket to ride for both Cooke City and Silver Gate. In summer the towns are crowded with folks en route to (or from) Yellowstone. Both Soda Butte Lodge and Miners Saloon in Cooke City have one-armed bandits with slot-machine poker and keno gambling. In the fall, hunters head into the surrounding mountains, and when the snow flies, the snowmobiles come out of hibernation.

Reminders of the mining era abound in the surrounding country, but not all of it is benign. Reclamation ponds catch toxic runoff from some of these old mines.

SIGHTS

It's hard to miss the red **Cooke City General Store,** 406/838-2234, one of the oldest buildings in the area. Built in 1886, this classic country market sells groceries, quality T-shirts, and gifts that include Indian jewelry and imported items from all over the globe. They also have Yellowstone and Wyoming fishing licenses. Open summers only. Across the street is another summertime place that is well worth a look, **Blain Gallery,** 406/939-2474, features original watercolors by Mary Blain, along with pottery, baskets, and photographs.

© DON PITCHER

downtown Cooke City

COOKE CITY ACCOMMODATIONS

Cooke City and Silver Gate have quite a few old-fashioned motels and cabins that provide a delightful Old West feeling. As with other towns surrounding Yellowstone, advance reservations are always a good idea in midsummer or midwinter.

Cabins

Three miles east of Cooke City, **Big Moose Resort**, 406/838-2393, www.cookecitybigmoose .com, has rustic cabins, a small store, and gas pumps, all open June–October, and December–March. The seven cabins contain older furnishings and private baths; two include kitchenettes. Rates start at $55 d, up to $65 for a four-person cabin with kitchenette.

Right across the road, **Big Bear Lodge**, 406/838-2267, www.sandersbigbearlodge.com, is primarily a fishing lodge but offers nightly accommodations throughout the year. Guests stay in six older but well-kept log cabins, each of which has two double beds. Rates are $55–65 d, and breakfasts are available in the main lodge for an extra $6.50 per person. The lodge is a popular destination for fly-fishing enthusiasts, who come here on three- to six-night package trips that include lodging, meals, and guided horseback rides and fishing. Anglers head into backcountry areas inside Yellowstone, returning each evening to the lodge. In winter, Big Bear is a popular overnight rest stop for skiers and snowmobilers.

Antler's Lodge, 406/838-2432, www.yellowstonelodges.com, charges $50–70 for a range of cabins, some that include kitchens and lofts. It's open late May–September. **Absaroka Cabins**, 406/838-2018, rents out three modern cabins with kitchenettes. These cost $73 d, or $83 for four people, and are open year-round.

Beartooth Plateau Lodge, 406/445-2293 or 800/253-8545, www.beartoothoutfitters .com, is a comfortable log home with space for six people. It has a full kitchen and bath with clawfoot tub; open June–Sept. The house rents for $85 d, plus $10 for each additional person. The owners also run Beartooth Plateau Outfitters, next door.

Located 4.5 miles north of Cooke City up a jeep/hiking trail, the Forest Service's **Round Lake Cabin** sleeps four, and costs just $25. It's open July to mid-September and mid-December through March. For details, call 406/848-7375, or visit www.fs.fed.us/r1/gallatin/recreation.

Motels

You'll find spacious, clean, and comfortable rooms and cabins at **High Country Motel**, 406/838-2272. Rates are $55–78, including some units with kitchenettes. Open all year, and recommended. **Hoosier's Motel**, 406/838-2241, has good rooms for $65 s or d; open mid-May to mid-Oct. **Alpine Motel**, 406/838-2262 or 888/838-1190, www.ccalpinemotel.com, is also open all year and has rooms for $58–68 s or d. They have two apartment-style units with two bedrooms and a full kitchen for $85 d, plus $10 per person (maximum of six).

With 32 guest rooms on two floors, **Soda Butte Lodge**, 406/838-2251 or 800/527-6462, www.cookecity.com, is the largest lodging place in the area. The hotel contains one of the best restaurants in these parts (Prospector), and guests are welcome to use the small indoor pool and hot tub. Rooms with king beds cost $75, those with two queens are $80, and family suites are $130 for up to six guests. Open year-round.

Elk Horn Lodge, 406/838-2332, www.bear tooths.com/elkhorn, has attractive and spotless motel rooms ($52 s or $57 d) and two cabins ($67 d or $77 for four guests). Open year-round.

SILVER GATE ACCOMMODATIONS

Range Riders Lodge, 406/838-2359, is a classic two-story log building with a bar downstairs and rooms above. Rates are reasonable—$35–50 d—but no phones or TVs are provided, and the bath is a few steps down the hall. The original 1930s furniture is still here. Range Riders is open Memorial Day to Labor Day.

Silver Gate Cabins, www.silver-gate-cabins
.com, features eigh`t attractive log cabins from the
1930s that contain kitchenettes and cost $57–75
s or d. Also here are five motel units for $42–68
s or d. Outside, you'll find barbecue grills, volleyball and horseshoes, and a playground for
kids. It's open June–September; call 406/838-
2371 in the summer, or 307/733-3774 in winter.

Grizzly Lodge, 406/838-2219, www.yellow-
stonelodges.com, is a century-old log building
right on the river and close to the Yellowstone
border. Guests stay in a variety of rooms (including
kitchenettes, two-bedroom units, and rooms with
lofts) inside the lodge for $50–75. Also here are a
sauna and hot tub. Open Memorial Day to Oct.

CAMPING

Heading east from Cooke City, you'll find four
forest service campgrounds ($8; open mid-July to
mid-Sept.) within 10 miles of town. Closest is
Soda Butte Campground, just one-half mile
from town; another mile to the east is **Colter
Campground.** Get details at 406/848-7375,
www.fs.fed.us/r1/gallatin/recreation.

Park RVs ($20) in Cooke City at **Big Moose
Resort,** 406/838-2393, www.cookecitybig
moose.com; open only in the summer. Showers
are available from Soda Butte Lodge (Cooke
City) for $5.

FOOD

Inside Cooke City's Soda Butte Lodge, **Prospector Restaurant,** 406/838-2251, is well known
for prime rib cooked to perfection, but it's also
open for breakfast and lunch. Also here is the
Ore House Saloon, with sports on the TV and
video poker and keno machines to take your
money. Everything at Soda Butte Lodge is open
year-round.

Cooke City Bike Shack, 406/838-2412,
cranks out espresso coffees and is a great place to
meet locals. **Bistro Cafe,** in Cooke City,
406/838-2160, serves standard American fare
for lunch, but dinner is when this authentically
French bistro shines, with quality steaks, veal,
lamb, and fish. Entrées are $13–21.

Beartooth Cafe, in Cooke City, 406/838-
2475, has good sandwiches for lunch, dinners
that star free-range Angus beef steaks, and more
than 100 kinds of beer. They serve breakfast on
weekends and are open summers only. Next door
is **Buns 'N Beds,** 406/838-2030, with year-
round deli sandwiches, soups, and salads. Also in
Cooke City, **The Grizzly Pad,** 406/838-2161,
has reasonable prices, three meals a day, and locally famous milk shakes, burgers, and fries.

In peaceful Silver Gate, **Log Cabin Cafe,**
406/838-2367, is a consistent favorite, with well-
prepared trout, pasta, barbecued beef, steaks,
and homemade soups. Open in the summer and
fall only. Cooke City's **Miner's Saloon,** 406/838-
2214, is a classic Old West bar where the stools
are filled with locals and tourists. Pull the handles
on the one-armed bandits, or try a game of pool,
foosball, or air hockey. The menu includes surprisingly good pizzas and burgers.

For groceries and supplies, head to Cooke City
General Store (described under Sights) or **Summit
Provisions** in Silver Gate, 406/838-2248.

ENTERTAINMENT AND EVENTS

Drinking is the most popular recreational activity in these parts, but **Range Riders Lodge** in Silver Gate, 406/838-2359, also has live country
music on weekends all summer. The twin towns
have a fun **Fireman's Picnic and 4th of July
fireworks,** and Silver Gate is home to **Shake-
speare in the Parks** in late August. Summer
wraps up with a **Chili Cookoff and Open Con-
tainer Golf Tournament** over Labor Day weekend. Sounds dangerous.

RECREATION

Yellowstone is less than four miles away, and it's
the obvious site for recreation in the Cooke
City–Silver Gate area during the summer. The
Absaroka-Beartooth Wilderness is accessible
from Cooke City and various points to the east
along the gorgeous Beartooth Highway. One of
the more unusual sights is **Grasshopper Glacier,**
eight miles north of Cooke City and 4,000 feet
higher. The glacier contains the remains of a

swarm of locusts that was apparently caught in a snowstorm while flying over the mountains.

Summertime horseback rides, pack trips into the Absaroka-Beartooth Wilderness, and guided fly-fishing expeditions are provided by several local outfitters: **Beartooth Plateau Outfitters,** 406/445-2328 or 800/253-8545, www.beartoothoutfitters.com; **Castle Creek Outfitters,** 406/838-2301; **Skyline Guide Service,** 406/838-2380 or 877/238-8885, www.flyfishyellowstone.com; and **Stillwater Outfitters,** 406/855-0016, www.stillwater outfitters.com.

Bikes and Skis

Cooke City Bike Shack, 406/838-2412, www.cookecitybikeshack.com, is a hub for the outdoor adventure crowd. The friendly owner Bill Blackford is a jack of all trades, running the espresso machine one minute and fixing a bike or selling outdoor gear the next. In the winter he rents snowshoes, backcountry skis, avalanche transceivers, and other supplies, and guides tele-marking and cross-country ski trips; $95 per person for an all-day trek. Backcountry skiers and snowboarders who want to head out on their own can catch a five-mile snowmobile ride ($15 per person) into the high country at Daisy Pass, gaining 2,100 feet of elevation along the way. This makes for a great day of skiing and a fun downhill run back to town.

Snowmobiling

Cooke City has become a hub for winter sports. Pick up a map of groomed cross-country ski trails and snowmobile routes from local businesses. The area consistently ranks among the top snow-mobiling destinations in America. Snowmobile rentals (and summertime ATV rentals) are available from **Cooke City Exxon,** 406/838-2244, and **Yamaha Shop,** 406/838-2231 or 800/527-6462. The local snowmobile club grooms approximately 60 miles of trails in the surrounding mountains; call 406/838-2272 for information. Be sure to also call the **Avalanche Advisory Hotline** at 406/838-2341 for the latest on back-country conditions before heading out, or check the website: www.mtavalanche.com.

INFORMATION AND SERVICES

The **Cooke City-Silver Gate Chamber of Commerce,** 406/838-2495, has a small summertime visitors center in Cooke City. It's generally open daily 11 A.M.–5 P.M. June to mid-September. When it's closed, drop by High Country Motel or Elk Horn Lodge for local information. Put away your cell phone in Cooke City and Silver Gate; there's no service here. If you're heading here from other areas, fill your tank because gas prices here are some of the highest in the region.

Despite its remoteness, you'll discover three (count 'em) **ATMs** in Cooke City. The town also has a laundromat.

Based in Bozeman, **4x4 Stage,** 406/848-2224 or 800/517-8243, offers by-request connections around the park and to surrounding communities, including to Cooke City and Silver Gate. Call 24 hours in advance for reservations.

Shoshone National Forest

Shoshone National Forest encompasses more than 2.4 million acres and extends along a 180-mile strip from the Montana border to the Wind River Mountains. Sagebrush dominates at the lowest elevations, but as you climb, lodgepole, Douglas fir, Engelmann spruce, and subalpine fir cover the slopes. Above 10,000 feet, the land opens into alpine vegetation and barren rocky peaks. The **Shoshone National Forest Supervisor's Office** is in Cody at 808 Meadow Lane, 307/527-6241, www.fs.fed.us/r2/shoshone. Get information and forest maps there or from ranger stations in Cody, Dubois, and Lander.

HISTORY

Shoshone is America's oldest national forest. On March 30, 1891, Pres. Benjamin Harrison signed a proclamation creating Yellowstone Park Timberland Reserve adjacent to Yellowstone National Park. At first this title meant very little, but in 1902 Pres. Theodore Roosevelt appointed rancher and artist A. A. Anderson to control grazing and logging and catch poachers. His strong management almost got him lynched. Three years later under Gifford Pinchot, the forest reserves were transferred to the Department of Agriculture and renamed national forests. The land was renamed Shoshone National Forest in 1908.

RECREATION

More than half of Shoshone National Forest lies inside wilderness boundaries; the Absaroka-Beartooth, North Absaroka, and Washakie Wilderness Areas cover much of the country east of Yellowstone National Park, while the Wind River Mountains contain the Fitzpatrick and Popo Agie Wildernesses (see the Wind River Mountains Country chapter for more on these areas). Part of the credit for the surprising expanse of wilderness areas on the national forest goes to Buffalo Bill. By bringing people into the area to hunt, fish, and explore, he helped create what one author called a "dude's forest." In ad-

dition, the Buffalo Bill Dam (which he vociferously supported) prevented logs from being sent down the North Fork of the Shoshone River and thus made logging less important.

More than 1,500 miles of trails offer hiking and horseback access to much of this country. Shoshone has more than 50 campgrounds, most costing $5–10 per night during summer. Once the water has been shut off for winter (generally Oct.–Apr.), you can camp for free but will have to haul out your own trash. Space is generally available even at the busiest times of year. In addition, free dispersed camping is possible at undeveloped sites throughout the forest, with the exception of heavily traveled U.S. Hwy. 14/16/20, where you must be one-half mile off the road.

Although they are uncommon, black bears roam throughout the forest, and grizzlies are found within the northern portions, including the North Absaroka and Washakie Wilderness Areas. Be sure to take the necessary bear precautions anywhere in the backcountry. Bears also sometimes wander into campgrounds along U.S. Hwy. 14/16/20 near Yellowstone National Park. Actually, you are more likely to encounter mosquitoes, deer flies, and horse flies in midsummer, so be sure to bring insect repellent.

NORTH ABSAROKA WILDERNESS

The 350,488-acre North Absaroka Wilderness is one of the lesser-known wild places in Wyoming. It abuts Yellowstone National Park to the west and is bordered by the Sunlight Basin and Beartooth Highways to the north and U.S. Hwy. 14/16/20 to the south. North Absaroka Wilderness is primarily used by hunters who arrive on horseback. The few hikers here tend to be quite experienced with backcountry travel and willing to tolerate the lack of trail signs and the steep and frequently washed-out paths. Much of the wilderness is relatively inaccessible, and snow may be present on passes until mid-July.

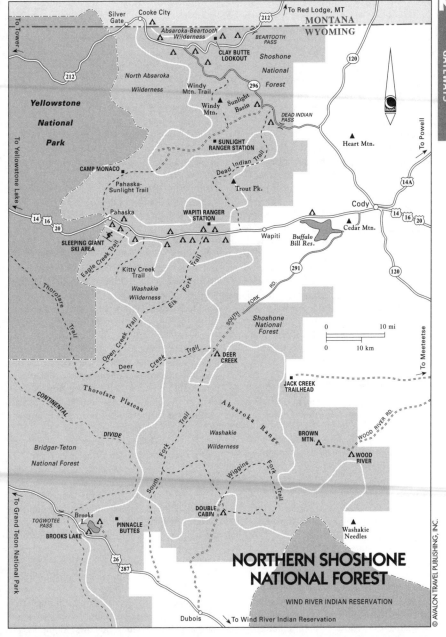

NORTHERN SHOSHONE
NATIONAL FOREST

WIND RIVER INDIAN RESERVATION

© AVALON TRAVEL PUBLISHING, INC.

Ask at the ranger stations for current trail conditions, and be sure to get topographic maps before heading out. Large populations of grizzly and black bears, bighorn sheep, moose, and elk are found in the Absaroka Mountains, and golden eagles are a common sight. The tough landscape is of volcanic origin, and the topsoil erodes easily, turning mountain creeks into churning rivers of mud after heavy summer rainstorms.

Hikes

The enormous 1988 Clover-Mist Fire that began in Yellowstone burned through a large portion of the North Absaroka Wilderness, but the land is recovering as young trees and other plants become established. Some areas were also replanted following the fire. Many hikers begin from trailheads near the Crandall Ranger Station along the Chief Joseph Scenic Highway. The **North Crandall Trail** is the most popular, a 16-mile hike up the North Fork of Crandall Creek. It is primarily used by horsepackers and offers great views of Hurricane Mesa along the way. Another popular wilderness path is **Pahaska-Sunlight Trail,** an 18-mile trek that begins at Pahaska Campground on U.S. Hwy. 14/16/20 and heads north through historic Camp Monaco to Sunlight Basin.

WASHAKIE WILDERNESS

Covering 704,529 acres, Washakie Wilderness is one of the largest chunks of wild land in Wyoming. Named for Shoshone Chief Washakie, it lies between U.S. Hwy. 14/16/20 (the road connecting Yellowstone and Cody) and U.S. Hwy. 26/287 (Dubois area). To the west are Yellowstone National Park and Teton Wilderness. The Washakie is a land of deep narrow valleys, mountains of highly erodible volcanic material, and steplike buttes. The mountains—a few top 13,000 feet—are part of the Absaroka Range. About half of the land is forested. One of the unique features of Washakie Wilderness is a petrified forest, a reminder of the region's volcanic past.

Hikes

There are numerous trails through the Washakie Wilderness, but most require that you either return the same way or end at a location far from your starting point. Several trails stretch into Yellowstone National Park and are popular with extended horsepacking trips. The most popular Washakie Wilderness hikes are from U.S. Hwy. 14/16/20 in Wapiti Valley. Most folks use them for short day hikes or horseback rides rather than attempting longer backcountry treks.

Kitty Creek Trail leaves from the Kitty Creek summer home area, nine miles east of Yellowstone. Low-clearance vehicles will need to park along the highway. The trail follows the creek past two large scenic meadows to Flora Lake, 6.5 miles and 2,500 feet higher. This is the shortest hike in the area and one of the most popular.

The 21-mile-long **Elk Fork Trail** starts at Elk Fork Campground and crosses Elk Creek several times en route to remote Rampart Pass at nearly 11,000 feet. It is steep and rocky in the higher elevations. West of the Continental Divide you enter the Teton Wilderness. For the really ambitious, the Open Creek and Thorofare Trails continue on into Yellowstone National Park.

Deer Creek Trail departs from the free Deer Creek Campground, 42 miles southwest of Cody on State Hwy. 291 (South Fork Rd.). The trail switchbacks very steeply uphill at first and after two miles reaches an attractive waterfall. Continue another eight miles from here to the Continental Divide and the Thorofare portion of the Teton Wilderness. This is probably the quickest route into this remote country and is popular with both horsepackers and hikers.

South Fork Trail takes off from the South Fork Guard Station across the creek from Deer Creek Campground. (Take a signed spur road to get there.) It climbs up along South Fork Creek to Shoshone Pass on the Continental Divide (9,858 feet). From here you can continue on several trails to the south, rambling over three more passes to eventually reach Double Cabin Campground, 27 miles north of Dubois. Another long hike into Washakie Wilderness leaves from this campground and follows the **Wiggins Fork Trail** up into a connecting series of paths: Absaroka, Nine Mile, East Fork, and Bug Creek Trails. It ends back at Double Cabin Campground. Total length is 60 miles. Along the way you're likely to see hundreds of elk in the high country as well as bighorn sheep. You won't see many other hikers.

SUNLIGHT BASIN

The **Chief Joseph Scenic Highway** (State Hwy. 296) is a 46-mile route through a magnificent Wyoming landscape. Popularly known as Sunlight Basin Road, it is paved and most of it remains open year-round, providing access for backcountry skiers and snowmobilers to the beautiful Beartooth Pass area. (An eight-mile portion between Cooke City, Montana, and Pilot Creek, Wyoming, is not plowed in the winter. It typically opens by early May.) Chief Joseph Highway begins 17 miles north of Cody off State Hwy. 120, with Heart Mountain prominent to the southeast, and climbs sharply up from the dry east side, passing a brilliant red butte en route to **Dead Indian Pass,** named for an incident during an 1878 fight between Bannocks and the U.S. Army. After the battle, Crow scouts found a wounded old Bannock warrior here. They killed and scalped him, burying the body under a pile of rocks. Other tales claim that the name came from the body of an Indian propped up as a ruse to trick the army during Chief Joseph's attempted escape to Canada in 1877. Chief Joseph *did* lead the Nez Perce through this country, avoiding the cavalry by heading up Clarks Fork Canyon, a route the army had considered impassable. An overlook on top of Dead Indian Pass provides a panoramic vista of the rugged mountains and valleys below. The river forms a boundary between the volcanic Absarokas to the south and the granitic Beartooth Mountains to the north.

Indians weren't the only ones killed in this era. In 1870, two miners, Marvin Crandall and T. Dougherty, headed into the Upper Clarks Fork following reports of gold in the area. When they failed to meet up with other miners, a search party was sent out. The searchers were themselves attacked by Indians, but they later found the bodies of Crandall and Dougherty—scalped and decapitated, with their heads atop mining picks. In a perverse bit of humor, tin

cups sat in front of each skull and the right hand of each man held a spoon. The men had apparently been killed while eating and the bodies were left as a warning against further white exploration of the area.

West of the overlook, the road switchbacks down hairpin turns into remote and beautiful Sunlight Basin. The name came about in the 1840s. Fur trappers worked this area for beaver and discovered a place flooded with light, but it was so remote that "the only thing that can get into this valley most of the year is sunlight." Today it is considerably more accessible but still just as beautiful. A gravel side road leads seven miles up the valley to **Sunlight Ranger Station,** built in 1936 by the CCC. It's open summers only. This is some of the finest elk winter range anywhere and the home of several scenic old guest ranches (described later).

Back on the main road, a bridge—highest in Wyoming at 300 feet above Sunlight Creek—spans deep, cliff-walled **Sunlight Gorge.** Sorry, no bungee jumping allowed. The highway then continues northwest past Cathedral Cliffs and through a scenic ranching and timbering valley, offering views into the deep gorge that belongs to the Clarks Fork of the Yellowstone River. In some sections, sheer cliffs tower 1,200 feet above the water. Part of the area burned by the 1988 Clover-Mist Fire is visible near **Crandall Ranger Station.** This area also contains the only large herd of mountain goats in Wyoming. Eventually you reach the junction with U.S. Hwy. 212, the Beartooth Highway (see Beartooth Mountains section for a description of this beautiful route).

Camping and Hiking

The Forest Service's Lake Creek, Hunter Peak, and Dead Indian Campgrounds ($5–10; open mid-May through Sept.) are found along Chief Joseph Scenic Highway. **Dead Indian Trail** (just uphill from Dead Indian Campground) goes two miles to a fine overlook into Clarks Fork Canyon. Also of interest is **Windy Mountain Trail** which climbs 10,262-foot Windy Mountain. It starts from a trailhead four miles east of the Crandall Ranger Station (interesting old log buildings here), is approximately seven miles one-way, and gains 3,700 feet in elevation. Windy Mountain can also be climbed from the other side near the Sunlight Ranger Station. Trailheads into the North Absaroka Wilderness are at the Crandall Ranger Station and beyond the Little Sunlight Campground (free; open year-round) on Forest Rd. 101.

River Running

Clarks Fork of the Yellowstone River (named for William Clark, of the Lewis and Clark expedition) is Wyoming's only designated Wild and Scenic River. Experienced kayakers will find a couple of great stretches of class IV–V whitewater in the upper Clarks Fork; however, use considerable caution because there are several big drops. Be sure to pull out before dangerous Box Canyon, which is considered unrunnable. Find more class IV waters farther down the river. Check with the Forest Service for specifics. Below the rapids are quieter stretches. Based in Cody, **Red Canyon River Trips,** 1374 Sheridan Ave., 307/587-6988 or 800/293-0148, www.imt.net/~rodeo/raft.html, leads gentle float trips down a scenic 12-mile section of the Clarks Fork. The half-day trip costs $50 per person and is offered from late May to early August.

Accommodations

In the heart of beautiful Sunlight Basin, **Seven D Ranch,** 307/587-9885, www.7dranch.com, is a family-oriented guest ranch offering horseback rides, cookouts, fly-fishing, hiking, and pack trips, and something parents will really appreciate: free child care for tots during riding periods, along with a special program for older kids. The setting is spectacular—it's where some of the Marlboro ads were shot—and the cabins are comfortable and cozy. Weekly all-inclusive rates are $3,020 for two people. The ranch has space for a maximum of 32 guests. Open early June to mid-Sept.; adults only in Sept.

K Bar Z Guest Ranch, 307/587-4410, www.agonline.com/kbarz, is off the Chief Joseph Scenic Highway in the Crandall Creek area. Nightly log cabin accommodations are available for $85 d, or two people can stay for six nights for

$1,700, all-inclusive (horseback rides, Yellowstone sightseeing, backcountry pack trips, and guided fishing trips). A hot tub and sauna are waiting at the end of a long day. The ranch is open year-round, and features fall hunting and winter snowmobile adventures. A maximum of 30 guests can stay here.

Hunter Peak Ranch, 4027 Crandall Rd., 307/587-3711, www.nezperce.com/ranchhp .html, is on the banks of the upper Clarks Fork River and offers lodging in rustic log cabins or motel-style rooms. Unlike most dude ranches, this one operates on an à la carte basis. Lodging is $90–100 d per night or $560 d per week, with extra charges for meals, horseback rides, and pack trips. The main lodge was built from hand-hewn logs in 1917. Open year-round.

Also in Sunlight Basin, **Elk Creek Ranch,** 307/587-3902 (summers) or 207/384-5361 (winters), www.elkcreekranch.com, provides a unique co-ed opportunity for teenagers to gain a wide range of ranching and wilderness skills. Ranch stays ($2,900 per person all-inclusive for a four-week session) include lots of time on horseback and the opportunity to train horses, build cabins, cut hay, and learn other ranch work. The backpacking adventures ($2,800 per person all-inclusive for a four-week session) give kids plenty of time in the backcountry, where they learn a range of outdoor and mountain-climbing skills. Two month-long sessions are offered each summer with a maximum of 30 kids at a time.

Bluebird Condos, 307/527-6589, www.tct west.net/~jim, is near the Clark Fork bridge, 24 miles from Yellowstone and 42 miles from U.S. 120. One large unit is available with six beds and a full kitchen. It rents for $90 s or d, plus $20 for each additional guest.

Other Services

The little settlement called **Painter** is 21 miles southeast of Cooke City on Chief Joseph Hwy. and right along the Clarks Fork River. Here you'll find a general store and gas pumps, along with year-round RV hookups ($15) at **Painter Estates RV Resort,** 307/527-5248. Open May–Nov. Not far away is the seasonal **Cary Inn Restaurant,** 307/527-5510, serving three meals a day.

SOUTH FORK AREA

South Fork Road heads southwest from Cody and follows the South Fork of the Shoshone River for 42 miles to the edge of the Washakie Wilderness (described later). It's a beautiful drive through definitive Western country with tree-covered mountains and the rich valley below. During winter, the South Fork area has one of the largest collections of frozen waterfalls in the Lower 48, with more than 200 world-class multipitch climbs. Ice climbers are here all winter, and the **Water Fall Ice Roundup** takes place each February. Get details at www.southforkice.com.

Accommodations

The **Double Diamond X Ranch,** 307/527-6276 or 800/833-7262, www.ddxranch.com, is an excellent family-oriented dude ranch near the South Fork River, 34 miles southwest of Cody. The ranch covers only 200 acres, but it is surrounded by Shoshone National Forest land. Guests take part in horseback rides, trout fishing, hiking, cookouts, and day trips to Cody. The kid's program is one of the best around, with entertaining and educational activities every day, and the ranch brings in professional entertainers several times a week. There's space for up to 36 guests. Facilities include remodeled log cabins—some dating to 1914—and lodge accommodations, plus an indoor pool and hot tub. Meals are noteworthy. All-inclusive rates are $3,700 for two people for six nights; open mid-Apr.–Oct.

Bison Willy's Bunkhouse, 307/587-0629, www.bisonwillys.com, is open from mid-October through mid-April, and is primarily used by ice climbers. The hostel has two co-ed sleeping rooms with bunk space for 12 people at $22 each, plus a kitchenette and showers. You'll need to bring your own sleeping bag. It is located on Double Diamond X Ranch and houses dude ranch workers in summer. The cabin is part of the American Alpine Club's national hut system, and members get a discount. Guided ice climbs may be available.

Rustler's Roost Guest House, 307/587-8171 or 800/667-6352, www.rustlersroost.homestead.com/guesthouse.html, is a small furnished house with a deck overlooking the South Fork, plus a full kitchen and outdoor hot tub. It sleeps four for $100.

BEARTOOTH MOUNTAINS

Spectacular Beartooth Highway (U.S. Hwy. 212) connects Cooke City and Yellowstone National Park with the historic mining town of Red Lodge, Montana. Along the way, it passes through the Beartooth Mountains on a road built by the CCC in the 1930s. Some have called this the most scenic route in America. If you like alpine country, towering rocky spires, and a landscaped dotted with small lakes and scraggly trees, you're going to love this drive. A small corner (23,750 acres out of a total of 945,334 acres) of the **Absaroka-Beartooth Wilderness** lies in Wyoming just north of the highway—the rest is right across the Montana border.

Over the Top

A national scenic byway, Beartooth Highway sails across a high plateau and then over the twin summits of **Beartooth Pass**—the east summit is 10,936 feet, and a short distance farther is the west summit at 10,947 feet. A scenic overlook at west summit provides views of the Absarokas to the south and west, the Beartooths to the north, and Bighorn Basin to the east. Majestic rock faces rise in all directions, the most obvious being Beartooth Mountain (its sharp point resembles the tooth of a bear), Pilot Peak, and Index Peak. This is the highest highway pass in Wyoming and one of the highest in North America.

As the road enters Montana, it passes Beartooth Mountain and begins a rapid elevator ride down folded ribbon curves into the resort town of Red Lodge. On top, keep your eyes open for moose, mule deer, mountain goats, bighorn sheep, marmots, and pikas. Be ready for strange weather at this elevation, including snow at any time of year. The highway is closed with the first heavy snowfall (generally in September) and doesn't get going until mid-July. The flowers don't really get going until mid-July.

Twin Lakes Ski Area sits near the Wyoming–Montana border and provides Olympic ski

Beartooth Pass area, Shoshone National Forest

training for teens in June and July. South of the summit is the appropriately named Top of the World Store (see the description under Camping and Supplies in this chapter), and another mile or so farther south is the turnoff to an old fire lookout tower at **Clay Butte,** where you'll discover horizon-to-horizon views of the surrounding countryside. A narrow gravel road climbs three miles to the tower, perched at an elevation of 9,811 feet. The small visitors center here is staffed July to mid-September.

Camping and Supplies

There are four developed campgrounds (all $8–10; open July to Labor Day) along this stretch of U.S. Hwy. 212, and more once you drop into Montana. **Beartooth Lake** and **Island Lake** Campgrounds border alpine lakes. In addition, dispersed camping is allowed for free once you get off the main roads. Grizzlies inhabit this country, so be sure to store your food safely.

Top of the World Store, 307/899-2482, sits along the highway between the two Forest Service campgrounds. It's a popular stopping point for cyclists and other travelers over the pass. The

general store has a limited selection of food and gifts, plus gas pumps, three motel rooms ($30 d), and a handful of RV spaces ($14) with hookups. The store and motel generally open in late May and close in mid-October. They reopen for winter weekends January–March when the area is a snowmobile destination (but no lodging in winter).

Hiking

The open country at this elevation is dotted with whitebark pines and Engelmann spruce, and it delivers marvelous cross-country hiking opportunities. Anglers should bring a fishing pole to take a few casts for the brook, cutthroat, and rainbow trout in the alpine lakes. Two major trail systems are found in the High Lakes area.

The **Beartooth High Lakes Trail**—actually a series of trails—connects Island Lake, Beartooth Lake, Beauty Lake, and many smaller alpine ponds and puddles. A good place to start is from the boat ramp at Island Lake; see topographic maps for specific routes. This is a very popular late-summer area for day hiking or for access to the Beartooth Wilderness. Be sure to bring a compass, topo map, and warm clothes before heading out on a day hike; the weather can close in very quickly at this elevation, and afternoon thunderstorms are frequent. Always be aware of lightning activity when hiking in this exposed country.

Beartooth Loop National Recreation Trail is just two miles east of Beartooth Pass. This 15-mile loop traverses alpine tundra and passes several lakes and a century-old log stockade of unknown origins.

Wapiti Valley/North Fork

Wapiti Valley provides one of the most popular and scenic routes into or out of Yellowstone National Park, connecting Cody with the park's East Entrance. Pres. Theodore Roosevelt came here often and called it "the most scenic 50 miles in the U.S." The valley is bisected by the North Fork of the Shoshone River, which U.S. Hwy. 14/16/20 parallels for the entire 50 miles from Yellowstone to Cody. Heading east out of Yellowstone, the highway drops through high forests and past an array of volcanic pinnacles and cliffs as the country becomes drier and more open. Cottonwoods line the gradually widening river, and Douglas firs intermix with sage, grass, and rock at lower elevations. Trailheads provide access to two backcountry areas that border the highway: North Absaroka Wilderness and Washakie Wilderness. After a major reconstruction in the late 1990s, the road is in excellent condition the entire distance from Cody to Yellowstone.

Wapiti Valley (the tourism promoters have recently started promoting it as "**East Yellowstone Valley**") is dotted with lodges, dude ranches, and resorts, many of which offer family-style meals, barbecue cookouts, horseback rides, pack trips, fishing, hiking, river rafting, and other outdoor recreation. If you aren't staying on an all-inclusive plan, most of these perks will cost extra, and some—such as meals or horseback rides (around $20 for one hour or $45 for a half-day)—are often available to both guests and the general public. The lodges generally do not have TVs or phones in the rooms, but most will provide transportation from Cody on request. Those Wapiti lodges and guest ranches that are open in winter are favorite bases for snowmobiling and cross-country skiing. Get additional information on Wapiti Valley at 307/587-9595, www.yellowstone-lodging.com.

On the western end of the valley are Shoshone National Forest campgrounds and hiking trails. The fishing is great in the river, and at Buffalo Bill Reservoir on the eastern end of Wapiti Valley.

Wapiti Valley provides one of the most popular and scenic routes into or out of Yellowstone National Park, connecting Cody with the park's East Entrance. Pres. Theodore Roosevelt called it "the most scenic 50 miles in the U.S."

PAHASKA TEPEE

Less than three miles from Yellowstone's East Entrance (48 miles west of Cody), Pahaska Tepee was built in 1904 to house Buffalo Bill's guests and others on their way to the park. Pahaska (pronounced pa-HAZ-ka) was Buffalo Bill's nickname, a Crow Indian word meaning "Long Hair."

The original Pahaska Tepee is a two-story log building that contains a few of Buffalo Bill's original items, including an old buffalo skull over the stone fireplace and several flags that were given to him. Although it is no longer used and in need of major repairs, the main lodge is open for fascinating free tours on weekdays during the summer. The bar inside Pahaska Tepee is small but contains a stunning Thomas Molesworth chandelier crafted in 1938; it's said to be worth $2 million. Look around for other furnishings from Molesworth and a beautiful stained-glass window.

On one of Buffalo Bill's many hunting treks with European royalty, he led the Prince of Monaco into the North Fork country. **Camp Monaco,** 15 miles up the Pahaska-Sunlight Trail from Pahaska Tepee, was named in his honor. Unfortunately, the old spruce tree inscribed with the words "Camp Monaco" was killed when the Clover-Mist Fire burned through here in 1988.

Pahaska Tepee Resort has a mix of old and new cabins and small A-frame motel rooms; summer rates start at $90 d in a small housekeeping cabin up to $450 for a two-bedroom condo (two-night minimum for this one). Wintertime guests can use the outdoor hot tub. Also here are a restaurant, gift shop, gas pumps, and limited supplies. Pahaska is open year-round. In winter the road is not plowed beyond Pahaska, and the lodge becomes a popular place to rent snowmobiles and cross-country skis for trips into Yellowstone. Contact Pahaska at 307/527-7701 or 800/628-7791, www.pahaska.com.

SKIING AND SNOWBOARDING

Just four miles from Yellowstone's East Gate, **Sleeping Giant Ski Area** is a small family skiing and snowboarding hill with a chairlift and T-bar providing a 500-foot vertical rise. Lifts operate mid-December to early April, and tickets cost $20 adults, $10 kids under 12. Nordic skis, alpine skis, and snowboards are available for rent. For details, contact them at 307/587-4044 (Shoshone Lodge), www.skisleepinggiant.com, or get the ski report at 307/587-7669 (24 hours).

Also based here is **North Fork Nordic Trails,** with more than 50 km of groomed cross-country ski trails for both classical and skate skiing. No charge, and the grooming is generally completed in time for the weekend rush of skiers. Trails cover a widely varied terrain along the river and right to the edge of Yellowstone National Park. Call Shoshone Lodge at 307/527-4044 for specifics.

DOWN THE ROAD

Below Sleeping Giant Ski Area the road passes a whole series of delightfully weird volcanic rock formations. Signs point out several of the most obvious. Stop at the **Firefighters' Memorial,** which honors 15 firefighters who were killed nearby in the Blackwater Fire of 1937. The picnic area here has a special pond for anglers with disabilities.

Pahaska Tepee was built in 1904 and is open for tours in the summer.

Eight miles farther east is the historic **Wapiti Ranger Station.** Built in 1903, it was the nation's first Forest Service ranger station. Just a few hundred feet away and right along the highway is **Wapiti Wayside Visitor Center,** 307/587-3925, open Mon.–Fri. 8 A.M.–8 P.M. and Sat.–Sun. 8:30 A.M.–5 P.M. between Memorial Day and Labor Day; closed the rest of the year. Pull in for details on local camping and recreation opportunities, and watch the informative video on safety in bear country. Check the board for recent bear sightings. A few miles to the west (not marked and on an old section of the highway) is Mummy Cave, where a 10,000-year-old mummified body was discovered in 1957.

Next up is a parking area at **Holy City,** an impressive group of dark red volcanic rocks with the North Fork of the Shoshone River cutting away at their base. Try to pick out Anvil Rock, Goose Rock, and Slipper Rock here. The highway leaves Shoshone National Forest and then passes the scattered settlement called **Wapiti**—an Indian word meaning "elk"—20 miles east of Cody. As you might guess, a large elk herd winters in this valley. An unusual volcanic rock ridge near here is locally called Chinese Wall. The eastern half of the road between Cody and Yellowstone passes through this broad and fertile valley; it's quite a change from the rock-lined route to the west. On the east end, the road borders Buffalo Bill Reservoir (see Buffalo Bill State Park) before plunging through three tunnels on the descent into Cody.

CAMPING

Nine different Shoshone National Forest campgrounds provide rustic accommodations along the North Fork of the Shoshone River. Most of these are open mid-May through September (some remain open through October) and cost $5–10 per site; no reservations are taken. All sites have picnic tables, fire rings, potable water, and outhouses. In areas where bears are a problem, the campgrounds also contain bearproof food-storage boxes. All of these Forest Service campgrounds are on the west half of the 50-mile stretch of highway between Cody and Yellowstone. Of

these, **Big Game Campground** is closest to Cody at 25 miles to the west, and **Three Mile Campground** is closest to the park, just three miles from Yellowstone's East Gate. Get details on public campgrounds from the Forest Service's Wapiti Wayside Visitor Center (described previously). Dispersed camping outside designated campsites is not allowed anywhere between Cody and Yellowstone along U.S. Hwy. 14/16/20.

Two campgrounds are within Buffalo Bill State Park, described later. Also mentioned are two Wapiti Valley lodges that have RV campgrounds: Green River Inn and Yellowstone Valley Inn.

UPPER NORTH FORK RANCHES

More than 20 lodges, motels, and guest ranches line the road between Yellowstone and Cody. Lodging places west of the midpoint between Cody and Yellowstone are in the more secluded and wooded canyon country of the upper North Fork of the Shoshone River. These places are listed as follows, arranged by their distance from downtown Cody on U.S. Hwy. 14/16/20, starting with those nearest the East Entrance to Yellowstone. Places east of the midpoint between Cody and Yellowstone are situated in the broad and beautiful Wapiti Valley and are typically visible from the highway. Pahaska Tepee—the closest lodge to Yellowstone—is described earlier in this chapter.

Shoshone Lodge

Located 46 miles west of Cody (four miles east of Yellowstone), Shoshone Lodge, 307/587-4044, www.shoshonelodge.com, is a classic mountain lodge with rustic log cabins and home-cooked meals served in the main lodge. The cabins have been updated with Western furnishings, and they range in size from one to three rooms; some contain kitchens. Nightly lodging rates start at $100 d or $110 for four guests, although the nicest cabins are considerably more expensive (up to $260 for a three-bedroom cabin that sleeps six). Horseback rides are available, and Shoshone Lodge is open mid-May to October. The owners also run Sleeping Giant Ski Area, directly across the road.

Crossed Sabres Ranch

Established in 1898, Crossed Sabres Ranch, 307/587-3750, www.crossedsabres.com, 42 miles west of Cody (eight miles east of Yellowstone), has a beautiful historic lodge, plus space for 40 guests in modernized two-bedroom cabins with log furniture and Western décor. After a day of horseback riding, hiking, river rafting, square dancing, or exploring Yellowstone, guests can relax with an evening cookout or soak in the hot tub. All-inclusive weekly packages are $1,990 for two people; open June to mid-September.

Goff Creek Lodge

Stay in deluxe log cabins at Goff Creek Lodge, 307/587-3753 or 800/859-3985, www.goff creek.com, 40 miles west of Cody (10 miles east of Yellowstone). Cabins are offered on either a nightly basis ($95 d) with activities and meals extra, or by the week ($1,880 for two people) on an all-inclusive basis. Goff Creek is open May to mid-October. A variety of outdoor adventures fill the bill here, including horseback rides, pack trips, fly-fishing, and chuck wagon cookouts. All of these options, including meals at the restaurant, are also open to the general public.

Elephant Head Lodge

Forty miles west of Cody (10 miles east of Yellowstone), Elephant Head Lodge, 307/587-3980, www.elephantheadlodge.com, is a no-frills dude ranch with a gracious main lodge built in 1910. Guests stay in 13 modernized cabins, all with private baths and most with decks. Because of its proximity to the park, Elephant Head makes a good base for exploring Yellowstone. Peak-season lodging-only rates are $110 d per day. The largest cabin—it's actually more like a luxury apartment—sleeps eight people comfortably and has a full kitchen; $170. All-inclusive packages with lodging, meals, and horseback rides are $250 for two people per day. Elephant Head's restaurant is open for breakfast and dinner and is locally famous for steaks, pork chops, and other carnivorous fare. It's a frequent destination for Cody folks looking for an evening out. Horseback rides are also available for both guests and the general public. The ranch is open mid-May through September.

Absaroka Mountain Lodge

Find old-time hospitality and adventure at Absaroka Mountain Lodge, 307/587-3963, www.absarokamtlodge.com, 38 miles west of Cody (12 miles east of Yellowstone). Guests stay in comfortable log cabins with private baths and dine in the historic main lodge, built in 1910. Nightly rates start at $76–108 for one bed, up to $145–155 for a two-bedroom cabin that sleeps eight. Their package plan includes lodging, three meals a day, and four hours per day of horseback rides for $135 per person per day. Open May–Sept. Trail rides and meals are also available to folks who aren't staying here.

Blackwater Creek Ranch

Thirty-five miles west of Cody (15 miles east of Yellowstone), Blackwater Creek Ranch, 307/587-5201 or 888/243-1607, www.black watercreekranch.com, is a fine place to relax amid the natural beauty of the area. Featured attractions include horseback rides, trout fishing, hiking, games, barbecues, and plenty of kid activities. The gracious log cabins contain fireplaces, and meals are served in the modern Old West–style lodge. Also here are an outdoor pool, a large hot tub, and a game room with billiards and table tennis. All-inclusive one-week stays cost $2,400 for two people, and the ranch is open May–September.

UXU Ranch

A classic Western dude ranch, UXU Ranch, 307/587-2143 or 800/373-9027, www.uxuranch.com, is 33 miles west of Cody (17 miles east of Yellowstone). It offers horseback riding, hiking, fly-fishing, mountain biking, and day trips to Yellowstone and Cody. Guests stay in comfortable cabins containing private baths and porches; some also have fireplaces or gas stoves. After a day of trail riding, you can relax in the big hot tub or visit with new friends in the main lodge. Special children's activities and nature talks are available, and the gourmet meals are memorable. All-inclusive six-night stays cost $2,750 for two people, or four people can stay in the luxurious Hollister cabin (featured in *Architectural Digest*) for $6,100. The ranch is open June–September.

Bill Cody Ranch

Located halfway between Cody and Yellowstone (25 miles in either direction), Bill Cody Ranch, 307/587-6271 or 800/615-2934, www.bill codyranch.com, has graceful log cabins, a comfortable lodge, horseback rides, creekside cookouts, and trout fishing. All-inclusive stays are $270 for two people per night; lodging-only rates are $115 d. Looking for more room and privacy? The guest ranch is open May–September. They also rent out a comfortable fully furnished home with space for 10 guests at $365 per day; three-night minimum stay for the house. Meals, chuck wagon cookouts, and horseback rides are also offered to those not staying at Bill Cody Ranch.

Rimrock Dude Ranch

Twenty-five miles west of Cody (25 miles east of Yellowstone), Rimrock Dude Ranch, 307/587-3970, www.rimrockranch.com, is a classic place with creekside log cabins, horseback riding, backcountry pack trips, a large swimming pool, river rafting, hearty family-style meals, and grand mountain country. Pack trips into the mountains are a special favorite. In the winter, this is a popular destination for snowmobilers; the ranch rents snowmobiles and leads tours into Yellowstone. Summertime weekly rates are $2,700 for two people, all-inclusive. Rimrock is open May to mid-September and December–March.

LOWER WAPITI VALLEY ACCOMMODATIONS

The places listed are east of the midpoint between Yellowstone and Cody, in the broad and open portion of Wapiti Valley; those listed under Upper North Fork Accommodations are west of the midpoint, in the more secluded and wooded canyon country.

Built in 1922, **Trail Shop Inn & Cafe,**

307/587-3741, www.trailshopinn.com, 23 miles west of Cody (27 miles east of Yellowstone), sits off the road and along the North Fork Shoshone River. Rustic cabins with private baths are $80 s or d. Open May–Sept.

Green Creek Inn and RV Park, 307/587-5004 or 877/587-5004, www.greencreekinn.com, 22 miles west of Cody (28 miles east of Yellowstone), has roadside motel rooms for $55–65 d; add $5 per person for additional guests. RV sites (no tents) are $17, but they lack showers or a restroom! Open mid-Apr. to mid-Nov.

Stay in modern log cabins at **DNR Ranch at Rand Creek,** 307/527-7176 or 888/412-7335, www.dnrranch.com, 19 miles west of Cody (31 miles east of Yellowstone). Small cabins cost $95 for up to four guests; the largest can sleep eight for $163. All-inclusive stays are also available; a full week is $2,000–3,000 for two people, including horseback rides, lodging, and breakfast and dinner daily. Built in 1905, DNR Ranch's main lodge is the oldest building in the area. The ranch is open May–December. Trail rides are also offered to folks who are not staying here.

Rocking D River Ranch, 17 miles west of Cody (33 miles east of Yellowstone), 307/587-8329 www.rockingd-riverranch.com, has off-the-road lodging in a loft cabin, bunkhouse, sheepwagon, or tepee. Meals are available upon request. **Wapiti Lodge & Steak House,** 18 miles west of Cody (32 miles east of Yellowstone), 307/587-6659, is "downtown" Wapiti, with a bar, restaurant, and post office in the same building. The restaurant is closed Mondays and Tuesdays but open all year. Breakfast is served until 3 P.M.

At **Yellowstone Valley Inn,** 307/587-3961 or 877/587-3961, www.yellowstonevalleyinn .com, 18 miles west of Cody (32 miles east of Yellowstone), small cabins are $69 d, motel rooms cost $79–125 d, tent spaces are $15, and RV sites with full hookups run $25. The inn sits right on the North Fork Shoshone River and has a restaurant, lounge, and laundromat. Open May–Nov.

Streamside Inn, 307/587-8242 or 800/285-1282, www.wtp.net/streamside, is 15 miles west of Cody (35 miles east of Yellowstone) near the east end of Buffalo Bill Reservoir. Modern motel rooms go for $70 s or $74 d, including a continental breakfast. Kitchenettes are $10 extra. Campers can pitch a tent for $15, and RV hookups cost $25. Guests have access to the large outdoor pool and horseback rides are offered. The inn is open May–October.

Red Pole Ranch, 307/587-5929 or 800/326-5929, www.redpoleranch.com, 11 miles west of Cody (39 miles east of Yellowstone), has eight updated log cabins starting for $75 d, up to $125 for one that sleeps six and has a full kitchen. Open May–Sept.

BUFFALO BILL STATE PARK

Six miles west of Cody on U.S. Hwy. 14/16/20, **Buffalo Bill Reservoir** is a popular place for local boaters and fishermen. Buffalo Bill State Park, 307/587-9227, http://wyoparks.state.wy.us, encompasses the reservoir and includes two campgrounds ($12 for nonresidents or $6 for Wyoming residents; open May–Sept.) on the north shore. Day use of the park is $4 for nonresident vehicles or $2 for those with Wyoming plates. **Cody Country Outdoors** operates a general store near the main entrance to the park and has groceries, bait and tackle, skiff rentals, and guided charters; 307/527-7999.

Atop the dam, the impressive **Buffalo Bill Dam visitor center,** 307/527-6076, www.bbdvc.org, has historical displays and jaw-dropping views into the canyon, which plummets 350 feet below you. The center is open daily 8 A.M.–8 P.M. May–September; closed the rest of the year. Even if it's closed, stop for the view over the dam.

Fishing is good for rainbow, cutthroat, brown, and Mackinaw trout in Buffalo Bill Reservoir. The lake also offers some of the finest windsurfing conditions anywhere, with nearly constant 30 mph winds; *Outside* magazine once rated it among the country's 10 best spots. The water's cold: You'll need a wetsuit until mid-June.

History

In 1899, Buffalo Bill Cody acquired the rights to build canals and irrigate some 60,000 acres of land near the new town of Cody. With passage of the Reclamation Act of 1902, the project was taken over by the Reclamation Service and an enormous concrete-arch dam was added to provide water. The 328-foot-high dam was begun in 1904 and required five years to finish. It cost nearly $1 million and when finally completed was the tallest dam in the world. Seven men died along the way, including a chief engineer, and the first two contractors were forced into bankruptcy as a result of bad weather, floods, engineering difficulties, and labor strife. A lack of sand and crushed gravel forced them to manufacture it from granite, and 200-pound boulders were hand-placed into the concrete to save having to crush more gravel.

Originally named Shoshone Dam, the impoundment was renamed in honor of Buffalo Bill in 1946. A hydroelectric plant and a 25-foot addition to the top were completed in 1993, bringing the total dam height to 353 feet and increasing water storage by 50 percent. The dam irrigates more than 93,000 downstream acres through the Shoshone Reclamation Project, making it one of the only Wyoming irrigation schemes that actually benefits the state's farmers to a large extent.

Cody

The city of Cody (pop. 8,800, elev. 5,095) marks the transition point between the forested mountains of northwest Wyoming and the sage-covered plains of Bighorn Basin. It's a favorite stopping place for Yellowstone tourists. The park is just 54 miles due west of downtown, and other magnificent country spreads in all directions—the Beartooth Mountains and Sunlight Basin to the north, the Absaroka Range and Wapiti Valley to the west and south. Established as an agricultural and tourism center, Cody retains both roles today, although tourism seems to be gaining in importance with each passing year. The town is one of the few places in Wyoming that continued to prosper throughout the 1990s; only Jackson Hole exceeds Cody as a tourism center. Not surprisingly, both are gateways to the national parks that dominate northwest Wyoming. Cody is also home to several midsize companies, including oil, mining, and logging operations. One of the biggest employers (after the hospital, the school district, and Wal-Mart) makes—I kid you not—ear tags for livestock.

Cody has several attractions, including the justly famous Buffalo Bill Historical Center, along with Trail Town and other local sights. The Shoshone River flows right through town, providing the opportunity for scenic float trips. Lots of events crowd the summer calendar, from nightly rodeos and shoot-outs to parades and powwows; biggest of all is the annual Cody Stampede in July. The town also takes pride in a long list of artists that includes Charles Cary Rumsey and Harry Jackson. Famed abstract expressionist Jackson Pollock was born here but achieved his reputation in New York and never returned to his birthplace.

HISTORY

Just west of Cody—past the Wal-Mart, RV parks, fireworks stands, and gas stations—are the Absaroka Mountains, named for the Native Americans who first lived here. They called themselves the Absaroka, or "Children of the

Large Beaked Bird." Whites interpreted this as crow, and the natives have been called Crow Indians ever since. Explorer John Colter passed through this region in 1808 while recruiting Indians to supply beaver furs. When Colter returned to the semblance of civilization called Fort Manual Lisa, everyone laughed at his tales of a spectacular geothermal area along the "Stinkingwater River." Soon everyone was calling it

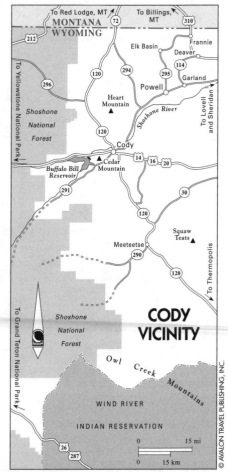

CODY VICINITY

GATEWAYS

"Colter's Hell." But the geysers were real, and they still steam along the Shoshone (formerly the Stinkingwater) just west of present-day Cody. Other mountain men came later, followed by miners who found copper and sulfur in Sunlight Basin. The first real settler in the area was a Prussian, Otto Franc, who developed a large cattle spread at the famous Pitchfork Ranch. (Franc is said to have helped finance the Wyoming Stock Growers during the Johnson County War. He was later murdered, and some blamed men affiliated with the homesteaders.)

Because of desertlike conditions, Bighorn Basin was one of the last parts of Wyoming to be settled, and most of the towns did not spring up until the 1890s, when passage of the Carey Act brought a flood of irrigation speculators, investors, and farmers. In 1895, William F. "Buffalo Bill" Cody and two partners began plans for the Shoshone Land and Irrigation Company, with headquarters along the Shoshone River just west of the present city of Cody. Cody had spent much time in the Bighorn Basin, guiding parties of wealthy sportsmen, and was convinced that a combination of tourism and irrigated farming could transform this desert land. Officially founded in 1896, the name Cody was a natural choice for this new settlement. At the urging of Buffalo Bill, the Chicago, Burlington, & Quincy Railroad arrived in 1901, bringing in thousands of tourists who continued west up Shoshone Canyon to Yellowstone by stagecoach. Between 1904 and

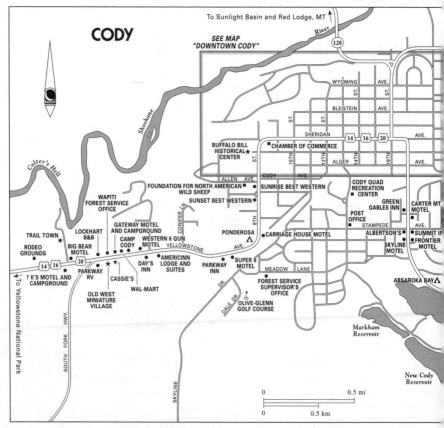

1909, construction of massive Buffalo Bill Dam employed hundreds of workers, and the reservoir later provided water to irrigate farmland in Bighorn Basin. Tourism is still a cornerstone of Cody's economy, fueled both by its status as an entry point into the park, and also because of the world famous Buffalo Bill Historical Center. Oil was first discovered near Cody in 1904, and Park County remains an important oil producer. Other local businesses include a wallboard manufacturing plant, a lumber mill, and a producer of ranch products. As in Cody's earliest days, tourism is a cornerstone of Cody's economy, fueled both by its status as an entry point into the park, and the presence of the world-famous Buffalo Bill Historical Center.

© AVALON TRAVEL PUBLISHING, INC.

BUFFALO BILL CODY

For many people today, the name "Buffalo Bill" brings to mind a man who helped slaughter the vast herds of wild bison that once filled the West. But William F. Cody cannot be so easily pigeonholed, for here was one of the most remarkable men of his or any other era—a man who almost single-handedly established the aura of the "Wild West." More than 800 books—many of them the dime-store novels that thrilled generations of youngsters—have been written about Cody. In many of these, the truth was stretched far beyond any semblance of reality, but the real life of William Cody contains so many adventures and plot twists that it seems hard to believe one person could have done so much.

Young Cody

Born to an Iowa farm family in 1846, William Cody started life as had many others of his era. His parents moved to Kansas when he was six, but his abolitionist father, Isaac Cody, soon became embroiled in arguments with the many slaveholders. While defending his views at a public meeting, Isaac Cody was stabbed in the back and fled for his life. When a mob learned of his father's whereabouts, the eight-year-old Will Cody rode on his first venture through enemy lines, galloping 35 miles to warn of the impending attack. Three years later, when Isaac Cody died of complications from the stabbing, 11-year-old Will Cody became the family's breadwinner. There were four other children to feed. Will quickly joined the company of Alexander Majors, running dispatches between army supply wagons and giving his $40 monthly wages to his mother. In Cody's autobiography he claimed to have killed his first Indian on this trip, an action that gave him the then-enviable title "youngest Indian slayer of the plains."

On his first long wagon trek west, the army supply wagons were attacked by Mormon zealots who took all the weapons and horses, forcing Cody to walk much of the thousand miles back to his Kansas home. It was apparently on this walk that Cody met Wild Bill Hickok. At Wyoming's Fort Laramie, young Will sat in awe as famed scouts Jim Bridger and Kit Carson reminisced about their adventures. The experience was a turning point in Cody's life; he resolved to one day become a scout. Cody's next job offered excellent training: he became a rider for the Pony Express. At just 15 years of age he already was one of the finest riders in the West and a crack shot with a rifle. On one of his Pony Express rides, Cody covered a total of 320 miles in just 21 hours and 40 minutes—the longest Pony Express ride ever. The Civil War had begun, and at age 18 Cody joined the Seventh Kansas Regiment, serving as a scout and spy for the Union Army.

After the Civil War, Will Cody tried his hand at the hotel business and then briefly joined Gen. George Custer as a scout before returning to Kansas to do a little land speculating along the route of the newly built railroad. Cody and a partner bought land and laid out a town that they named Rome. For a short while it boomed. One day a man appeared in Rome, offering to take over the town while leaving Cody with only a small portion of the place he had founded. Thinking it was only intimidation from a shady operator, Cody laughed at the man, not knowing that he was president of the railroad's townsite company. The railroad quickly chose another townsite, and three days later all the inhabitants of Rome moved east to the new site, taking their buildings with them. Cody was left with a worthless patch of land.

Buffalo Hunter and Scout

In 1867, Cody found work hunting buffalo to supply fresh meat for the railroad construction crews, a job that soon made him famous as "Buffalo Bill" and paid a hefty $500 per month. With 75 million bison spread from northern Canada to Mexico, and herds so vast that they took many days to pass one point, it seemed impossible that they could ever be killed off. Cody was one of the best hunters in the West; in just eight months, he slaughtered 4,280 buffalo, often saving transportation by driving the herd toward the camp and dropping them within sight of the workers. Cody's name lives on in the jingle: "Buffalo Bill, Buffalo Bill; never missed and never will; always aims and shoots to kill; and the company pays his buffalo bill . . ."

After this stint, Cody finally got the job he wanted—chief scout for the U.S. Army in the West, a job packed with excitement and danger. Conflicts with Indians had reached a fever pitch as more and more whites moved into the last Indian strongholds. Cody worked as scout for Gen. Philip Sheridan, providing information on the Indians' movements, leading troops in pursuit of the warriors, and joining in the battles, including one in which he supposedly killed Chief Tall Bull. His men considered Buffalo Bill good luck because he managed to keep them out of ambushes.

During the Indian campaigns, the writer/preacher/scoundrel Ned Buntline began writing of Cody's exploits for various New York papers, giving Buffalo Bill his first taste of national acclaim. Soon Buntline had cranked out several romantic novels loosely based on Cody's adventures. America had a new national hero. European and Eastern gentry began asking Cody to guide them on buffalo hunts. On the trips, Cody referred to them as "dudes" and to his camps as "dude ranches"—perhaps the first time anyone had used the terms for such hunters. One of Wyoming's most unusual businesses had begun. Cody's incredible knowledge of the land and hunting impressed the men, but they were stunned to also discover in him a natural showman. In 1872, the Grand Duke Alexis of Russia came to the United States and was guided by Cody on a hunt that made national headlines and brought even more fame to the 26-year-old. On a trip to New York in 1872, Cody met Buntline again and watched a wildly distorted theater production called Buffalo Bill. Amazingly, Cody adjusted quickly to the new surroundings. Dressed in the finest silk clothes but with his long scout's hair under a Western hat, Cody suddenly entered the world of high society.

In a short while, Cody was on the stage himself, performing with Ned Buntline and fellow scout Texas Jack in a play called Scouts of the Plains. Although meant to be serious, the acting of all three proved so atrocious that the play had audiences rolling in the aisles with laughter. A New York reviewer called the play "so wonderfully bad it was almost good. The whole performance was so far aside of human experience, so wonderful in its daring feebleness, that no ordinary intellect is capable of comprehending it." Audiences packed the theaters for weeks on end. But Cody was suddenly called back west, for the Sioux were again on the warpath.

Shortly after Cody had returned to guide Gen. Eugene Carr's forces, they learned of the massacre of Custer's men at the Battle of the Little Big Horn. In revenge, Carr's men set out to pursue Indians along the border between Nebraska and Wyoming. Under Cody's guidance, they surprised a group of warriors at War Bonnet Creek. Cody shot the chief, Yellow Hand, and immediately scalped him, raising the scalp above his head with the cry "first scalp for Custer!" (Cody later claimed that he scalped the chief because he was wearing an American flag as a loincloth and had a lock of yellow hair from a white woman's scalp pinned to his clothing.) The Sioux immediately fled. If Cody had been famous before, this event propelled him to even more acclaim. It became the grist for countless dime-store novels and was embellished in so many ways over the years that the true story will never be known.

The Wild West Show

Buffalo Bill's days in the real Wild West were over, and he returned to staging shows, eventually starting his famed Wild West extravaganza. This was unlike anything ever done before—an outdoor circus that seemed to transport all who watched to the frontier. One newspaper remarked that Cody had "out-Barnumed Barnum." There were buffalo stampedes, cowboy bronc riding, Indian camps, a Deadwood stage and outlaws, crack shooting by Annie Oakley, and, of course, Buffalo Bill. At its peak in the late 1890s, the show made Cody more than a million dollars in profit each year.

Amazingly, Sitting Bull and Buffalo Bill became good friends. Cody, who had earlier bragged of his many Indian killings, changed his attitude, eventually saying, "In nine cases out of 10 when there is trouble between white men and Indians, it will be found that the white man is responsible." Cody's other attitudes also continued to evolve. He criticized the buffalo hunters of the 1870s and 1880s for their reckless slaughter, and he later became an ardent supporter of game preserves and limitations on hunting seasons.

The Wild West Show became one of the most popular events anywhere in America and Europe, attracting crowds of up to 40,000 people. Queen Victoria was a special fan (although rumors of an affair are probably false). At the peak of his fame around the turn of the 20th century, Buffalo Bill was arguably the world's best-known man. Cody, however, continued to drink heavily. One day, an obviously drunken Buffalo Bill insisted that his cowboys ride Monarch, a massive and dangerous bison in the entourage. When they refused in front of thousands of spectators, Cody himself climbed on top and was immediately thrown to the ground. He spent the next two weeks in a hospital. For the next decade the show continued to tour but gradually lost its novelty as other forms of entertainment, especially movies, came along. Cody used his money to buy the 40,000-acre TE Ranch in northwestern Wyoming near Yellowstone National Park. For him the Bighorn Basin was paradise. The town that he helped establish here was named Cody in his honor, and he backed the massive Shoshone irrigation project.

A Sad Farewell

Unfortunately, Buffalo Bill seemed to have no comprehension of how to save his wealth. He was a notoriously soft touch and would give money to almost anyone who asked. As his fortune slipped away and his show became more dated, Cody was finally forced to join up with H. H. Tammen, the crooked owner of the Denver Post. Tammen used the aging Cody's fame to attract people to his own circus. He forced Cody's Wild West Show into bankruptcy in 1913, sold off all of the incredible collection of historical artifacts that had been amassed over the years, and left workers to find their own way home. Buffalo Bill was heartbroken but, still trusting Tammen (or in desperation), agreed to join his circus almost as a sideshow act.

Three years later, Cody died while visiting his sister in Denver and was buried on Lookout Mountain near Denver. Cody had wanted to be buried on Cedar Mountain above the town of Cody, but even this wish was denied by Tammen, who apparently paid Cody's widow Louisa $10,000 for the privilege of choosing the burial site (and to use the funeral parade to the burial site as an advertisement for his circus troop). When rumors came that folks from Wyoming intended to dig up Cody's body and take it back to its rightful burial place, Tammen had tons of concrete dumped on top of the grave. Louisa Cody went on to outlive not only her husband but also all four of her children. She ended up caring for her four grandchildren.

Despite the unhappy ending to Buffalo Bill's life, there are few individuals who lived such a diverse and adventure-filled life and who could count so many people as their friends, from the lowliest beggar to the richest king. Cody's life spanned one of the most remarkable eras in American history, and his impact on American culture is still felt today, not just in the image of the West that he created, which lives on in hundreds of Western movies, but also in the Boy Scouts (an organization inspired partly by his exploits), in the city of Cody, and even in the dude ranches that dot Wyoming.

Late in life, Cody was asked how he wanted to be remembered. He replied: "I don't want to die and have people say 'Oh, there goes another old showman.' When I die I want the people of Wyoming who are living on the land that has been made fertile by my work and expenditure to remember me. I would like people to say, 'This is the man who opened up Wyoming to the best of civilization.'"

BUFFALO BILL HISTORICAL CENTER

Each year, more than 220,000 people visit Cody's main attraction, the Buffalo Bill Historical Center (BBHC). The center actually houses five separate museums covering Buffalo Bill, the Plains Indians, Western art, firearms, and natural history, plus a research library, the boyhood home of Buffalo Bill, and two sculpture gardens. This is the largest and most impressive museum in Wyoming and the finest Western museum in the world. Nowhere else in America is such a major museum located in a town with so few people. The late author James Michener once labeled the BBHC "the Smithsonian of the

West," and his term is even truer today with the addition of a natural-history wing in 2002. The museum's collection focuses—not surprisingly—on the Western frontier and includes thousands of artifacts and works of art, culture, and natural history spread throughout more than 300,000 square feet of space.

History
The original Buffalo Bill Museum opened in 1927 in what is now the chamber of commerce log cabin. Opening in 1959, the Whitney Gallery of Western Art formed a nucleus for the current museum location; later additions included the Buffalo Bill Museum, the Plains Indian Museum, and the Cody Firearms Museum. A new natural-history museum is under development and should open early in the 21st century.

Practicalities
Buffalo Bill Historical Center, 307/587-4771 or 800/227-8483, www.bbhc.org, is open year-round. In the busy summer season from June through mid-September, it's open daily 7 A.M.–8 P.M. At other times, hours are reduced: daily 8 A.M.–5 P.M. mid-September through October; daily 10 A.M.–5 P.M. in April; and daily 8 A.M.–8 P.M. in May. From November through March the museum is open Tuesday–Sunday 10 A.M.–3 P.M. Closed Thanksgiving, Christmas, and New Year's Day.

Admission costs $15 adults, $13 seniors, $6 students 18 and older, and $4 ages 6–17. Children under six get in free. The admission is good for two days, and it may well take you two days to explore this massive collection! Tours are generally offered only for school groups and VIPs, but the Historical Center often has summertime demonstrations, and the helpful docents can provide additional info.

On the Museum Grounds
Before heading inside, stop to view Buffalo Bill's **boyhood home,** a tiny yellow building built in 1841 by Isaac Cody. The house stood in LeClarie, Iowa, for almost a century. In 1933 it was sawed in half, loaded on two railcars, and hauled to Cody to be reassembled and refurbished. The house is on

your left as you face the museum. Flanking the museum on the opposite side is *The Scout*, a dramatic, larger-than-life statue of larger-than-life Buffalo Bill. This huge bronze piece was created by New York sculptor Gertrude Vanderbilt Whitney and was unveiled in 1924. Her family later donated 40 acres of surrounding land to the Buffalo Bill Museum. Directly in front of the historical center are three colorfully painted **tepees,** a treat for kids. Once you enter the museum, ask for directions to the **Visitor's Lounge,** where a 10-minute orientation video provides a good introduction. Just inside the entrance on the left is a magnificent feathered cape made in 1839 by a Mesquakie woman from the Great Lakes area; don't miss it.

Buffalo Bill Museum

The Buffalo Bill Museum is a real joy. In it, the life of Buffalo Bill Cody is briefly sketched with all sorts of memorabilia from his Wild West Show, including the famous Deadwood Stage, silver-laden saddles, enormous posters, furniture, guns, wagons, and clothing. Be sure to look for "Lucretia Borgia," the Springfield rifle that helped William Cody gain his nickname. Also here are some of the gifts given to Buffalo Bill by European heads of state—including a fur carriage robe from Czar Alexander II—and by Wild Bill Hickok and Sitting Bull. Original film footage from the Wild West Show runs continuously, offering a fascinating and sometimes unintentionally comical glimpse into the past. Amazingly choreographed marching soldiers, fake Indian battles, sign-language conversations, and bucking broncos make it easy to see how the Wild West Show helped inspire Western movies.

Whitney Gallery of Western Art

The Whitney Gallery contains a stunning collection of masterworks by such Western artists and sculptors as Charles Russell, Frederic Remington, Carl Bodmer, George Catlin, Thomas Moran, Albert Bierstadt, Alfred Jacob Miller, Edgar Paxson, N. C. Wyeth, and others. The studios of Frederic Remington and W. H. D. Koerner have been re-created, and Gertrude Vanderbilt Whitney's *The Scout* is visible from a large window on the north end. The collections of both "cowboy artist" Charles Russell and Frederic

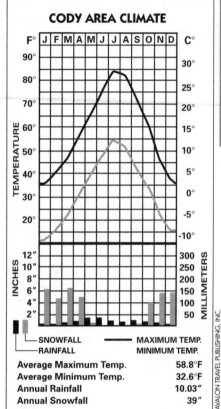

CODY AREA CLIMATE

Average Maximum Temp.	58.8°F
Average Minimum Temp.	32.6°F
Annual Rainfall	10.03"
Annual Snowfall	39"

Remington—best known for his paintings of battles during the Indian wars—are the most complete here; the museum has more than a hundred of each man's paintings. Next to the Whitney Gallery is the **Joseph Henry Sharp Garden,** where you'll find his "Absarokee Hut" filled with the painter's paraphernalia.

The **Kriendler Gallery of Contemporary Western Art** is upstairs from the entrance to the Whitney Gallery and contains a diverse collection of pieces, including several with a delightfully whimsical twist. Well worth the detour.

Plains Indian Museum

The largest exhibition space in the historical center encloses the Plains Indian Museum, with items from the Sioux, Cheyenne, Blackfeet, Crow, Arapaho, Shoshone, and Gros Ventre tribes. At first it may seem incongruous that a museum featuring the man once called the "youngest Indian slayer of the plains" should include so much about the culture of Indians, but Cody's later maturity forced him to the realization that Indians had been severely mistreated and that their culture was of great value. His Wild West Shows re-created some semblance of that lost society, if only for show. Some of the more important items here were given to Buffalo Bill by various Indian performers over the years, and the collection of artifacts is now one of the finest in America.

On exhibit are an extraordinary painted buffalo robe from 1890 that depicts the Battle of Little Big Horn, elaborately decorated baby carriers, ghost-dance dresses, beaded arrow quivers, dance shields (including a Gros Ventre shield from 1700), leather garments, war bonnets, ceremonial pipes, and even a Pawnee grizzly claw necklace. One of the more unusual items is Lone Dog's Winter Count, with figures representing a 71-year sequence of events affecting the Sioux; it was created in 1877. The Hitatsa earth lodge is another highlight. One easy-to-miss area is the special exhibitions gallery downstairs and to the left of the Crow tepee village display. The exhibits change but are always well worth viewing. On the other side of the tepees is a room containing computers and additional displays.

Walking through this remarkable collection always leaves me with mixed emotions. I'm impressed at the beauty of the items and their historical and cultural significance, but saddened by the way all museums—of necessity—remove things from their environment and create a visually enticing setting, but one that is devoid of the living, breathing people who created these objects. If only we could step back into the past to see how life really was, dirt and all.

Draper Museum of Natural History

This newest addition to the BBHC opened in 2002 to rave reviews. The $17-million facility covers 55,000 square feet, with state-of-the-art exhibits on the Greater Yellowstone Ecosystem and

the integral role of humans. Guests begin at a pair of cabins, one of which serves as a naturalist's field station. The other serves as a classroom (of sorts), with a seismograph and computer stations to learn about glaciers, volcanoes, and other natural forces. The main section of the Draper descends along a spiraling path through a giant rotunda, with exhibits describing alpine areas, forests, meadows, and lowland plains ecosystems in the Yellowstone landscape. It's like taking a virtual safari through the area. Multidisciplinary exhibits invite interaction, with lots of kid-friendly audio and video stations, a walk-in beaver lodge, a wolf den, a prairie dog colony, and much more. The winding path ends at a colorful tile map of the Yellowstone ecosystem and an exhibition of children's art.

Cody Firearms Museum

The Cody Firearms Museum houses one of the most comprehensive collections of American firearms in the world, including everything from 16th-century matchlocks to self-loading semiautomatic pistols. This is one museum where the men outnumber the women. Start your visit by viewing "Lock, Stock, & Barrel," a 10-minute video that describes the history of guns and how they work; it's interesting even for those of us who consider the proliferation of guns a national menace. In fact, the entire firearms collection is remarkably informative and well worth taking time to view.

The museum now contains more than 5,000 weapons, but these aren't just rows of guns in glass cases. Some of the more unusual items include a 10-shot repeating flintlock rifle made for the New York Militia around 1825 and a 17th-century windlass crossbow. There are all sorts of displays to explore, including a colonial gun shop, a Western stage station, an early-1900s firearms factory, and a truly extraordinary collection of embellished arms. One of the most lavish is an intricately carved flintlock sporting carbine presented by Empress Elizabeth I of Russia to King Louis XV of France. The Boone and Crockett Club's collection of trophy animal heads is here, including an elephant-sized moose housed in a re-created hunting lodge. Take the elevator to the basement for even more gun displays. All told, this museum houses more implements of destruction and mayhem than you're likely to see at an NRA convention.

Additional Exhibits

Downstairs from the Buffalo Bill Museum is a spacious gallery used for special exhibitions (always worth a look), along with the **Harold McCracken Research Library,** open Monday–Friday 8 A.M.–noon and 1–5 P.M. May–October. The library houses 250,000 historical photos and 15,000 books, including more than 300 volumes about Buffalo Bill—mostly dime novels and comic books.

Other spaces to view include the **Photography Gallery** near the entrance to the Draper, with changing exhibits, and **Ranch and Range,** a collection of wonderful photos taken by Charles Beldon on the Pitchfork Ranch in the 1930s.

Other facilities at the Buffalo Bill Historical Center include an outstanding **gift shop and bookstore,** plus a café for light meals. Head to the sculpture garden for a lunchtime buffalo

burger or Polish dog at the **Western cookout** beneath the aspen trees.

Activities and Events

During summer you'll find a wide range of demonstrations every day, including wool-spinning demonstrations, historical talks, cowboy singing, storytelling, and various lectures. Get a brochure at the front desk for today's activities. The **Larom Summer Institute in Western American Studies** is an in-depth two-week history course with two sessions offered each June. Contact the museum for details.

The BBHC plays host to many annual events, including Cowboy Songs and Range Ballads in April, the Plains Indian Powwow in mid-June, and the Old West Show & Auction, also in June. See Events section for details on these and other museum activities.

OTHER SIGHTS

Trail Town

Point your horses toward the mountains and head 'em two miles west of Cody to a unique collection of historic buildings at Trail Town, 307/587-5302.

historic buildings at Trail Town, Cody

The site is open daily 8 A.M.–8 P.M. mid-May through September only; $5 entrance (free for kids under 13). Trail Town is the creation of Bob Edgar, the man who discovered Mummy Cave—one of the most important archaeological finds in the West—in 1957. Edgar purchased the old Arland and Corbett trading post, and then began dragging in other historic Wyoming cabins. Some were transported whole, others were disassembled and then put back together at Trail Town. Currently the site holds 26 buildings dating from 1879 to 1901, plus 100 wagons.

For those who love history, Trail Town is an incredible treasure trove without the fancy gift shops and commercial junk that tag along with most such endeavors. This is the real thing, low-key and genuine. Probably the most famous building here is an 1883 cabin from the Hole-in-the-Wall country that Butch Cassidy and the Sundance Kid used as a rendezvous spot. Also at Trail Town is the oldest saloon (another hang-out of the gang) from this part of Wyoming, complete with bullet holes in the door, and a cabin where Jim White—one of the most famous buffalo hunters—was murdered in 1879. The log home of Crow Indian scout Curley stands along main street, too. (Curley was the only one of General Custer's command who escaped alive from the Battle of the Little Big Horn.) Be sure to step inside **Museum of the Old West,** a more recent log cabin filled with artifacts that include a black hearse, rifles found at Indian battlefield sites, arrowheads, beaded necklaces, a cradleboard, and items from the fur traders. Look above the display cases for what may be the most significant discovery, a dugout canoe that was found buried along the Yellowstone River in Montana. It might have belonged to a trapper but is remarkably similar to the ones used by Lewis and Clark. They buried canoes while heading west, planning to dig them up on their return trip. The wood dates to that era; could this be one they left behind?

The bodies of buffalo hunter Jim White and several other historic figures have been reinterred in a small graveyard at Trail Town. One of the most interesting of these is Belle Drewry, a prostitute known as "The Woman in Blue."

After bouncing around several 19th-century mining towns, she ended up in the lawless and now-abandoned town of Arland, located northwest of Meeteetse. One night in 1897 she shot a cowboy to death during a dance. The following night his outlaw friends took retribution by murdering her. Belle was buried in the blue dress that she always wore. Also buried in the cemetery is **John "Liver Eating" Johnston,** the mountain man portrayed by Robert Redford in the movie *Jeremiah Johnston.* Those who have seen the film will be surprised to learn that Johnston died in 1900 at the Old Soldiers' Home in Los Angeles! Friends sent him there by train from Montana when his health deteriorated, but he only spent a month in California before his death at the age of 76. After the movie came out, schoolchildren in Los Angeles helped promote moving Johnston's body closer to his mountain home. Nearly 2,000 people showed up for the reburial in 1974, including Robert Redford. A memorial to explorers John Colter and Jim Bridger also

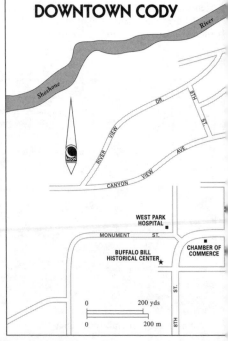

DOWNTOWN CODY

stands near the graveyard. The historic buildings, artifacts, and graves at Trail Town provide a fine counterpoint to the glitzier Buffalo Bill Historical Center.

Irma Hotel

Pick up a copy of the *Cody Historic Walking Tour* brochure ($2) at the visitors center for an informative introduction to local buildings and their history. One of the most engaging stories is about the Irma Hotel, named for Buffalo Bill Cody's daughter. It was built in 1902 to house tourists arriving by train and was one of three way stations to Yellowstone that Cody built. The luxurious saloon has a French-made cherrywood back bar given to Buffalo Bill by Queen Victoria. The queen spent $100,000 to have it built—no doubt helping to fuel rumors of a romance between her and Buffalo Bill. Many famous people have gathered at the bar over the years.

The **Cody Gunslingers** perform in front of the Irma Monday–Friday June–September.

Cody was established long after the era of gunfights in the streets, so this isn't particularly authentic, but it does attract a crowd each evening. The gunfight officially starts at 6 P.M., but the first 15 minutes or so are typically wasted on ads for local businesses. You know you're in America when the advertising even delays a gunfight! Call 307/587-4221 for details on the gunslingers.

Harry Jackson Art Museum

Cody's most famous living artist, Harry Jackson, has a large gallery at 602 Blackburn Avenue. It doesn't look like much outside, but inside you'll discover an amazing diversity of works, covering the palette from abstract expressionist paintings, dark World War II pieces, collages, and cubist studies to his more recent paintings and sculptures (many of which contain distinctively painted surfaces). His other sculptures include the monumental *Sacajawea* at the Buffalo Bill Historical Center and *Horseman* in Beverly

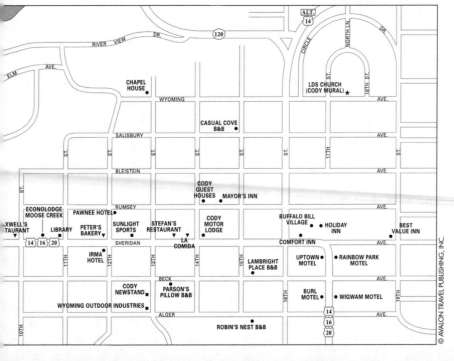

Hills. Jackson's pieces have been exhibited throughout the United States and in Italy, where his works are cast. Now something of a living legend, Jackson divides his time between Cody and Italy. All bronzes (but not his paintings) displayed here are for sale, but they're only for serious art patrons willing to spend thousands of dollars—a 10-foot painted Sacagawea goes for $400,000. The gallery is typically open Monday–Friday 8 A.M.–5 P.M., but call 307/587-5508 for the latest, or visit them virtually at www.harryjackson.com. Entrance costs $4.

Art Galleries

The **Buffalo Bill Historical Center** (described previously) houses an excellent gift shop with art prints, Indian jewelry, and reproductions of bronze sculptures. Next to the chamber of commerce office at 836 Sheridan Avenue is the **Cody Country Art League,** 307/587-3597, www.codyart.vcn.com, displaying paintings, sculptures, photos, and crafts for sale. They also offer workshops and juried art shows.

Simpson Gallagher Gallery, 1161 Sheridan Ave., 307/587-4022, www.sggfineart.com, is one of the best in Cody, with works that go well beyond the standard Western clichés. Just down the street is **Wyoming Artisans,** 307/527-7000, a cooperative where everything is made in Wyoming, including paintings, pottery, lamps, jewelry, and carvings. Of less interest but possibly worth a peek are two shops with predictable artworks: **Big Horn Gallery,** 1167 Sheridan Ave., 307/587-6762, www.bighorngalleries.com, and **Kilian Gallery,** 1361 Sheridan Ave., 307/527-5380.

Old West Miniature Village

Cody has an abundance of offbeat attractions, from talking sheep to sanctified ceilings. The most unusual—and actually worth a visit—is **Old West Miniature Village and Museum** (a.k.a. Tecumseh's Trading Post), 142 W. Yellowstone Ave., 307/587-5362, www.imt.net/~rodeo/mini.html. Owner Jerry Fick has spent decades creating an enormous diorama that offers a truncated version of Wyoming and Montana history. The term "kitsch" quickly enters your head when you step in-

side, but you've got to appreciate the effort that went into creating thousands of hand-carved figures and an array of miniature villages. Of considerably more interest is his collection of artifacts that includes a knife from the Battle of Little Bighorn, old-time cowboy garb, the bow and arrows that belonged to Geronimo, and many Plains Indian artifacts. Entrance is $3, and the collection is open daily 8 A.M.–8 P.M. May–September; call for winter hours.

Counting Sheep

The **Foundation for North American Wild Sheep** has its national headquarters just south of Buffalo Bill Historical Center at 720 Allen Ave., 307/527-6261, www.fnaws.org. A favorite of wealthy trophy hunters, this nonprofit group funds wild sheep research and conservation. The place is a bit bizarre, with oversized bronze rams and a recording that plays out front even when nobody's around. The building is open Monday–Friday 8 A.M.–5 P.M.

Yet More Sights

Cedar Mountain, the 7,889-foot-tall summit overlooking Cody from the west, is where Buffalo Bill had wanted to be buried. A winding 4WD trail climbs to the top, but there's no public access at present. Also here is **Spirit Mountain Cave,** one of the first national monuments ever designated (1909). A lack of interest caused the designation to be withdrawn, but the caverns are still on public land. Spelunkers can get permission to enter from the BLM office in Cody.

Southeast of Cody near Beck Lake is the **Wyoming Vietnam Veterans Memorial,** a black granite memorial modeled after the one in Washington. It contains the names of 137 Wyoming men who were killed or declared missing in action.

If you're really desperate for something to do, visit the **Cody Murals** on the domed ceiling of the Latter-day Saints (Mormon) church at 1719 Wyoming Avenue. Tours are available daily during summer; call 307/587-3290. No, it isn't the Sistine Chapel. The mural (painted in 1951) offers a rosy-tinted version of Mormon Church history and the Bighorn Basin pioneers.

ACCOMMODATIONS

The tourist town of Cody is jam-packed with places to stay, but be ready to pay more than anyplace in Wyoming except Jackson Hole. Budget accommodations are nonexistent during the summer, although rates plummet with the first cold nights of fall. The town doesn't have a hostel, but one is definitely needed! Most of the year, finding lodging in Cody is not a problem as long as you check in before 4 P.M., but during July and August you should reserve a week ahead—and longer for the Cody Stampede in early July.

Cody Area Central Reservations, 307/587-0200 or 888/468-6996, www.wyvacation.com, makes reservations for many local motels, mountain lodges, and B&Bs at no additional charge. It's a good one-stop place to plan your trip to the Cody and Jackson Hole area. In addition to these places, you will find many dude ranches and lodges in the mountain country around Cody; these are described previously in the Wapiti Valley/North Fork, Sunlight Basin, and South Fork Area sections.

Under $50

Cody's least expensive place to stay is also its oldest: the **Pawnee Hotel,** 1032 12th St., 307/587-2239. Built in 1900, the hotel contains 22 refurbished rooms, including four with clawfoot bathtubs. Rates start at $28 s or $34 d with a shared bath down the hall. Rooms with private baths are $32–38s or $42–48 d, and a four-person suite is $48. The owner is very accommodating.

$50–100

Stay in attractive log cabins from the 1920s at **Carriage House Motel,** 1816 8th St., 307/587-2572 or 800/531-2572. The cabins are small and don't have phones, but they have been lovingly remodeled. Rates are $50'60 for one bed, $70 for two beds, or $90 for a two-room suite that sleeps five. Open May–Oct.

Frontier Motel, 1801 Mountain View Dr., 307/527-7119 or 800/707-4940, is a good bargain place with small rooms and dated—but clean—furnishings. Rates start at $54 s or $56 d,

or $84 for two queen beds. Kitchenette units (no dishes) are $84 d. Across the road is **Skyline Motel,** 1919 17th St., 307/587-4201 or 800/843-8809, which also has older furnishings, but the rooms are large and there's a big heated outdoor pool, plus a fenced play area for children. Rates are $50 s, $60 d, or $68–76 for four.

Rainbow Park Motel, 1136 17th St., 307/587-6251 or 800/710-6930, is an older motel with clean, well-kept rooms for $54 s or $67 d; kitchenettes cost $5 extra.

Uptown Motel, 1562 Sheridan Ave., 307/587-4245, is a 10-unit motel with well-maintained rooms; $59 for one queen bed or $69 for two. Half the rooms contain microwaves and fridges.

Gateway Motel and RV Park, 203 Yellowstone, 307/587-2561, has basic motel rooms (some with kitchenettes) for $60–70 d. Rustic cabins (built in 1946) are $60–70 d. No phones are provided in the rooms or cabins, but guests can use the computer in the lobby to check their email. Gateway is open May–September.

Big Bear Motel, 139 W. Yellowstone Ave., 307/587-3117 or 800/325-7163, www.bigbear motel.com, is an older place with dated rooms for $65 s or $70 d. No phones in the rooms, but there's a large outdoor pool. Open May–Oct.

Buffalo Bill Cody's historic **Irma Hotel,** 1192 Sheridan Ave., 307/587-4221 or 800/745-4762, www.irmahotel.com, has a great downtown location and all the ambience you could want. It's the real thing—a classic Old West hotel. The eight suites in the original building ($93 s or $100 d) provide updated rooms, or stay in the far less noteworthy motel rooms in the annex for $67 s or $74 d. Be sure to ask about the ghost (of Buffalo Bill?) that supposedly haunts the rooms. **Best Value Inn,** 1807 Sheridan Ave., 307/587-4258 or 888/315-2378, www.bestvalueinn.com, has a quiet off-the-main-drag location. Rooms are $64–91 s or d.

Carter Mountain Motel sits atop the hill near Albertson's at 1701 Central Ave., 307/587-4295, www.kswope.vcn.com, and features nicely maintained rooms. Standard units (some with fridges) are $69–79 s or d. Suites with full kitchens are $95–149; the largest can sleep nine. A very good moderately priced option is **Summit Inn,** 1714 Stampede Ave., 307/587-4040 or 800/587-9008, with 17 modern rooms—all with two queen beds—for $79 s or d. Open May–Sept.

The appropriately named **Burl Inn,** 1213 17th St., 307/587-2084 or 800/388-2084, features a unique decor that includes handcrafted burled wood beds and lamps, along with velvet paintings. The rooms are large and clean: $85 s or $90 d for standard rooms, or $105 d for the honeymoon suite with a king bed and jetted tub. Closed Nov.–Jan.

Parkway Inn, 720 W. Yellowstone Ave., 307/587-4208 or 800/707-4940, www.park wayinncody.com, is a comfortable older place with remodeled rooms costing $88 for one bed or $98 for two. Amenities include an outdoor pool and continental breakfast. Open June–Sept. The hotel is owned by Kit Cody, Buffalo Bill's grandson.

Cody Motor Lodge, 1455 Sheridan Ave., 307/527-6291 or 800/340-2639, features large rooms for $89–92 s or d, and two suites (one has a kitchen) for $135 d or $150 for five people.

$100 and Up

Green Gables Inn, 1636 Central Ave., 307/587-6886 or 800/707-4940, is an attractive new two-story motel on the south side of Cody. Standard rooms are $100 s or d, and suites run $125 for up to six guests. A continental breakfast is served each morning. Open May–Oct.

Best Western Sunrise, 1407 8th St., 307/587-5566 or 800/528-1234, www.bestwestern.com /sunrisemotorinn, is another comfortable place, with an outdoor pool and continental breakfast for the guests. Rates are $89–110 s or d. Open May to mid-Oct. **Super 8 Motel,** 730 W. Yellowstone Ave., 307/527-6214 or 800/800-8000, www.super8.com, has typical chain-motel rooms for a steep $89–149 s or d. **Days Inn,** 524 W. Yellowstone Ave., 307/527-6604 or 800/325-2525, www.daysinn.com, offers rooms for $105 s or $115–125 d, and features an indoor pool, hot tub, and continental breakfast.

EconoLodge Moose Creek, 1015 Sheridan Ave., 307/587-2221 or 800/424-6423, www .econolodge.com, has newly refurbished rooms

just a couple of blocks from the Buffalo Bill Historical Center. Smaller rooms with one queen bed are $118 s or d, and large rooms with two beds cost $128 for four guests. Amenities include an indoor pool and continental breakfast.

Buffalo Bill Village Resort consists of three separate operations that total nearly 350 rooms: Holiday Inn, Comfort Inn, and Buffalo Bill Village Resort. All three are located in the heart of Cody at 1701 Sheridan Avenue and share the same phone numbers and website: 307/587-5555 or 800/527-5544, www.blairhotels.com /bbv. Guests at all three facilities can use the outdoor heated pool and small fitness center at the Holiday Inn and are welcome to join the free wine and champagne reception each evening. **Holiday Inn at Buffalo Bill Village Resort,** includes 189 attractively decorated rooms for $129–159 s or d. Priority club members get nicer rooms at no extra charge, and you can sign up when you register. **Comfort Inn at Buffalo Bill Village Resort** charges $129–149 s or d, including a light breakfast. The most distinctive of this Cody lodging triumvirate is **Buffalo Bill Village Resort,** which consists of 83 cozy log cabins. These cabins were built in the 1920s to house workers and their families for nearby Buffalo Bill Dam. The cabins were later moved here and have since been updated to include phones, TVs, private baths, and air-conditioning. Small cabins have a queen or king bed for $109. Family cabins ($139–159) have two bedrooms with three or four double beds. The cabins are open May to mid-October.

One of the nicest chain motels in town, **Kelly Inn,** 307/527-5505 or 800/635-3559, www.kellyinns.com, is one mile east of Cody at 2513 Greybull Highway. The spacious standard rooms are $92 s or $110 d, six-person family rooms with fridges and microwaves go for $145, and rooms with hot tubs cost $145 d. Also here are a sauna and hot tub. A light breakfast is available in the lobby. You'll find fine motel accommodations at **Best Western Sunset,** 1601 8th St., 307/587-4265 or 800/624-2727, www.bestwestern.com/sunsetmotorinn, where the rooms are $109'129 s or d. Amenities include indoor and outdoor pools, a hot tub, playground, and fitness facility.

AmericInn Lodge and Suites, 508 Yellowstone Ave., 307/587-7716 or 800/634-3444, www.americinn.com, is one of the newest places to stay in Cody and offers some of the nicest rooms. All are large, with standard rooms (king or two queen beds) for $139 d, and luxurious suites (some with jetted tubs and fireplaces) for $160–210. Other amenities include an indoor pool, hot tub, and sauna, plus a light breakfast.

Guesthouses, Cabins, and Apartments

Families may want to stay in one of 20 nicely furnished homes, cottages, apartments, and lodges managed by **Cody Guest Houses,** 307/587-6000 or 800/587-6560, www.codyguesthouses.com. Prices start at $99 d for a small cottage, up to $350 for a luxurious three-bedroom lodge in Wapiti Valley.

Cosy Cody Cottages, 307/587-9253, www .cosycodycottages.com, has two cottages located at 1403 and 1405 Rumsey Avenue. Rates are $100 d ($110 for four guests), and both places contain private baths, full kitchens, and laundry facilities.

Moose Alley Lodging, 307/587-6159 or 877/511-4438, www.moosealleylodging.com, is a studio apartment with a full kitchen; $99 d. Located 30 miles north of Cody and near the little settlement of Clark along U.S. 120, **Cabins by the Creek,** 307/587-6074 or 800/377-7255, www.codyvacationproperties.com, rents two quaint cabins for $155 d, including an outdoor hot tub.

Bed-and-Breakfasts

Several historic buildings are now part of the Cody B&B scene, offering a taste of the genteel past. **Parson's Pillow B&B,** 1202 14th St., 307/587-2382 or 800/377-2348, www.cruising -america.com/parsonspillow, is probably one of the most interesting and enjoys a good central location. Completed in 1902, the building served for many years as a Methodist-Episcopal Church. Today it's a cozy and well-maintained B&B with antique furnishings, five guest rooms, private baths, and full breakfasts; $85–95 s or d. Kids

older than age five are accepted and will appreciate the room with bunk beds.

Built in 1924, **Lambright Place B&B,** 1501 Beck Ave., 307/527-5310 or 800/241-5310, www.lambrightplace.com, was originally a farmhouse. Three rooms in the large main house are available for $90–95 d, and a separate cottage/bunkhouse with a Western theme sleeps five for $140. All rooms have private baths, and the breakfasts are memorable. Kids are welcome, and the bunkhouse works well for families.

Also recommended is **Robin's Nest B&B,** 1508 Alger Ave., 307/527-7208 or 866/723-7797, www.robinsnestcody.com. On a quiet street just a few blocks from the heart of town, this 1928 brick and frame home features a relaxing and shady backyard, a large living room, and three guest rooms with private baths; $100 d. Most unique is the treehouse suite, situated on an upstairs porch. A full breakfast is served each morning, and well-behaved kids are accepted.

For lodging in a classic Cody home, stay at **The Mayor's Inn,** 1413 Rumsey Ave., 307/587-0887 or 888/217-3001, www.mayorsinn.com, built in 1909 by Frank Houx, the town's first mayor. In 1997 it was moved to the present site and restored to its original opulence. The four guest rooms ($95–205 d) include private baths with jetted tubs, down comforters, terrycloth robes, and heated floors. The nicest room has a king bed and jetted tub. A full breakfast is served each morning; no young children allowed. Also available is a separate cottage with full kitchen for $80 (no breakfast). In addition to lodging, Mayor's Inn also serves gourmet dinners Friday–Sunday evenings with a limited menu. Reservations are required.

Casual Cove B&B, 1431 Salisbury, 307/587-3622 or 866/559-7444, www.casualcove.com, is a renovated 1908 home with three guest rooms, all with private baths. Room rates are $60–70 s or d, including a full breakfast. No kids under age six are permitted.

Lockhart B&B Inn, 109 Yellowstone, 307/587-6074 or 800/377-7255, www.codyvacation properties.com, has seven guest rooms with private baths and a country decor. Rates are $95–100 d, including a full breakfast and access to a treat-filled refrigerator. Kids are welcome, and the B&B

GATEWAYS

CAROLINE LOCKHART

The West overflows with famous men, but women sometimes get unjustly shunted aside in the accolades. One of the most interesting was Caroline Lockhart (1871–1962), a woman who began her career as an actress but turned quickly to journalism as a writer for a Boston newspaper. Using the pen name "Suzette," she became one of the country's first female newspaper reporters. The job led her into all sorts of adventures, from entering a circus cage with a lion that had killed his trainer the previous day to testing the Boston Fire Department's new fire nets by jumping out of a fourth-story hotel window. When she heard of a "Home for Intemperate Women" where the women were being severely mistreated, Caroline decided to investigate by posing as a derelict. She got her story all right, but it took considerable convincing from her editor to get her out. "Release!" shouted the matron running the house. "We can't! She's not cured yet." One of Lockhart's most lasting impacts was the creation of Mother's Day. Although Anna Jarvis came up with the concept, Caroline Lockhart made it a reality by tirelessly promoting the idea in the newspapers.

In 1904, Lockhart took a bold step. After an interview with Buffalo Bill Cody in the town named for him, she decided to move to Wyoming. She purchased the local newspaper, the *Cody Enterprise*, and quickly made a name for herself as a crusader against prohibition and "game hogs" (hunters who killed everything in sight). She also founded the Cody Stampede, the big annual event in Bighorn Basin. Lockhart authored seven novels, including *The Lady Doc*, a book that managed to ruffle local feathers with its too-close-to-the-truth descriptions of real-life Cody people. Despite this controversy, her witty, humorous, and insightful writing gained a national reputation.

In 1925, she sold the *Cody Enterprise* and acquired a ranch that eventually included 7,000 acres of land along the Bighorn River north of Lovell, dividing her time between her Cody home (now the Lockhart Bed and Breakfast) and her ranch. She died at the age of 92. Today her old ranch lies within Bighorn Canyon National Recreation Area.

is open May to mid-November. The home once belonged to the writer Caroline Lockhart; see the Special Topic "Caroline Lockhart" to learn more about her life.

Cody Guest Houses maintains three delightful B&Bs in the Cody area, all with a full breakfast. These include Victorian House B&B, Angel's Keep B&B, and Heart 2 Heart Bed, Barn and Breakfast. For details on any of these, call 307/587-6000 or 800/587-6560, or find more on the web at www.codyguesthouses.com. **Victorian House B&B** is a beautiful three-bedroom home with private baths and an indoor hot tub. Rates are $135–185 d for individual rooms, or $450 for the entire six-person house. **Angel's Keep B&B** is housed within a restored 1930s church and has two rooms for $95–105 d. Located on a ranch seven miles north Cody, **Heart 2 Heart Bed, Barn and Breakfast** has two bedrooms with a shared bath for $85 d.

CAMPING

The closest public campground ($12 for non-residents, or $6 for Wyoming residents) is 11 miles west in Buffalo Bill State Park. Find many more campgrounds ($5–10) in Shoshone National Forest; the nearest is 28 miles west of Cody in the upper North Fork.

Private Campgrounds

You'll find eight private RV park/campgrounds in Cody. Rates range widely: $20–30 for RVs, or $10–18 for tents. The two best ones are **Ponderosa Campground,** 1815 8th St., 307/587-9203, open mid-Apr. to mid-Oct.; and **7 K's RV Park,** 232 W. Yellowstone Ave., 307/587-5890, open May–Sept. Both of these have shade trees, and Ponderosa also has tepees ($21) and basic cabins ($34). **Cody KOA,** two miles east on U.S. Hwy. 14/16/20, 307/587-2369 or 800/562-8507, www.koa.com, opened in 1964 as the first franchised KOA. Rates are $24–30 for tents and $30–39 for RVs. Open May–September, with an outdoor pool, free pancake breakfast, and rodeo shuttle, and simple cabins for $44–56 d. **Camp Cody,** 415 W. Yellowstone Ave., 307/587-9730 or 888/231-2267, has RV hookups for $18 and tent spaces for $12.50. It's open year-round and includes an outdoor pool.

Other park-it spots (around $10–12 for tents or $15–20 for RVs) include **Gateway Motel and RV Park,** 203 W. Yellowstone Ave., 307/587-2561; **Rivers View RV Park,** 109 W. Yellowstone Ave., 307/587-6074 or 800/377-7255, www.codyvacationproperties.com; **Parkway RV Campground** 132 W. Yellowstone Ave., 307/527-5927 or 800/484-2365, ext. 3881; and **Absaroka Bay RV Park,** U.S. Hwy. 14/16/20 South, 307/527-7440 or 800/557-7440. You can also park RVs at several of the Wapiti Valley lodges (described previously), including **Green Creek Inn and RV Park** and **Yellowstone Valley Inn.** Noncampers can take showers for $5 at Gateway Campground, 7 K's RV Park, or Ponderosa Campground.

FOOD

Because Cody is a tourist town, it's no surprise to find many fine places to eat, covering the spectrum from buffalo burgers to Chinese won tons. Of course, Cody also has all of the Wyoming standards—Taco John's, Subway, Quizno's, McDonald's, Taco Bell, and more.

Breakfast and Lunch

Hang out with the farmers over breakfast or lunch at **Our Place,** 148 W. Yellowstone, 307/527-4420. The coffee is still just 25 cents. **Cody Coffee Company & Eatery,** 1702 Sheridan Ave., 307/527-7879, has espresso, pastries, soups, and deli sandwiches.

Peter's Bakery, 1191 Sheridan Ave., 307/527-5040, bakes breads, cookies, bagels, and turnovers. It's a great place for sub sandwiches, soups, burgers, and more. You won't want to go back to Subway after this; the bread they use is made from scratch, not pulled from the freezer. On weekday evenings, they also have mix-and-match pasta dishes.

Patsy Ann's Pastry & Ladle, 1243 Beck Ave., 307/527-6297, creates good sandwiches, homemade soups, and pastries (including great sticky buns). **Sunset House Restaurant,** 1651 8th St., 307/587-2257, is a casual family spot for lunch, and it also features breakfast and dinner buffets.

Anyone traveling with young children will appreciate **Mustard's Last Stand,** 1276 Sheridan Ave., 307/527-4147, where 21 varieties of hot dogs are the predominant menu item.

Dinner

Proud Cut Saloon, 1227 Sheridan Ave., 307/587-7343, is a fine old-time Wyoming bar and restaurant offering unusual sandwiches at lunchtime and outstanding steak and prime rib for dinner. It's the real thing, with a rustic Old West decor. **Irma Hotel,** 1192 Sheridan Ave., 307/587-4221, www.irmahotel.com, is a longtime favorite of locals for lunch and dinner, but the food is nothing special. Drop by in the morning for their big breakfast buffet.

Tommy Jacks Cajun Grill, 1134 13th St., 307/587-4917, serves tasty gumbo, seafood, steaks, and other meals in a smoke-free atmosphere. **Bubba's Bar-B-Que,** 512 Yellowstone Ave., 307/587-7427, is one of a small chain of Bubba's, with the original in Jackson. It has the best salad bar in town, big breakfasts, and inexpensive ribs, steak, or chicken for dinner.

In existence since 1922, **Cassie's Supper Club,** 214 Yellowstone Ave., 307/527-5500, www.cassies.com, is famous locally for its steaks, prime rib, and shrimp. The Wednesday lunchtime Mexican specials attract a crowd.

Besides these dinner options, several Wapiti Valley/North Fork lodges (described early in this chapter) serve outstanding meals and attract both locals and tourists. A couple of notable ones are **Elephant Head Lodge,** 307/587-3980, www.elephantheadlodge.com; **Goff Creek Lodge,** 307/587-3753 or 800/859-3985, www.goffcreek.com; and **Wapiti Lodge & Steak House,** 307/587-6659.

Eclectic

The ever-popular **Maxwell's Fine Food & Spirits,** 937 Sheridan Ave., 307/527-7749, dishes up homemade lunches that include sandwiches, pasta, and salads. It's a bright and friendly setting, with a patio for sunny days, and a small bakery/coffeeshop. The dinner menu features pasta, seafood, chicken, beef, and vegetarian dishes. Closed Sunday.

Stefan's Restaurant, 1367 Sheridan Ave., 307/587-8511, is an enjoyable place with a diverse menu available three meals a day. Dinner entrées are unconventional takes on such favorites as steaks, baby back ribs, Kung Pao chicken, and shrimp scampi. The atmosphere is a bit upscale but not stuffy. Be sure to save room for the luscious desserts.

Also of note is **The Mayor's Inn,** 1413 Rumsey Ave., 307/587-0887 or 888/217-3001, www.mayorsinn.com, where gourmet dinners are served Friday–Sunday evenings in a quaint Victorian setting. The limited menu changes every week; reservations required.

International

In the heart of town, **La Comida,** 1385 Sheridan Ave., 307/587-9556, serves excellent Mexican food for reasonable prices. Take in the local scene from the outside patio. On the west side of town, **Zapata's,** 1362 W. Yellowstone Ave., 307/527-7181, offers New Mexican–style meals and good margaritas.

For decent Chinese food—including a lunch buffet and family-style dinners—visit **Hong Kong Restaurant,** 1201 17th St., 307/587-6420. **Dragon Wall Buffet,** 225 Yellowstone Ave., 307/587-8899, has all-you-can-eat buffets for both lunch ($6.50) and dinner ($9.50).

Pizza Hut, 736 Yellowstone Ave., 307/527-7819, has predictable pizzas and lunch buffets. Other pizza options are Maxwell's Fine Food & Spirits (for the gourmet version; described earlier) and **Pizza on the Run,** 1310 Sheridan Ave., 307/587-5550, for the nothing-special variety.

Groceries and Specialty Foods

Cody's grocers include an **Albertson's,** on the south side of Cody at 1825 17th St., 307/527-7007, and a big **Wal-Mart SuperCenter,** on the west end at 321 Yellowstone Ave., 307/527-4673. For natural foods and Wyoming-made gifts, head to **Whole Foods Trading Co.,** 1239 Rumsey, 307/587-3213. **Wyoming Buffalo Company,** 1280 Sheridan Ave., 307/587-8708 or 800/453-0636, specializes in buffalo jerky, salami, sausage, and fresh meat, with a variety of gift packages. Stop in for a free sample.

EVENTS AND ENTERTAINMENT

Summer is a busy time in Cody, with special events nearly every weekend. Cody calls itself "Rodeo Capital of the World," and it packs the calendar with nightly summertime rodeos, plus the famous Cody Stampede. The rodeo grounds are one mile west of town on U.S. Hwy. 14/16/20.

Cody Nite Rodeo

After nearly 60 years of operation, the Cody Nite Rodeo is still one of the best in a state filled with rodeos. Shows begin at 8:30 P.M. nightly June–August and always attract a crowd. The best performances take place Friday and Saturday nights, when you'll see events sanctioned by the Professional Rodeo Cowboys Association (PRCA). A crowd favorite is the calf scramble, starring kids from the stands. Tickets cost $12 adults and $6 children; free for kids under six. For top-of-the-action seats, be sure to get there early and follow the signs to the "buzzards roost" section ($2 extra). Get rodeo details at 307/587-5155 or 800/207-0744, www.codystampederodeo.org.

Cody Stampede

Independence Day sets the stage for Cody's main event, the Cody Stampede, held July 1–4. Established in 1922, it attracts thousands of visitors from all over the nation. Parade fans are treated to one each morning (including a kiddie parade), with dozens of marching bands, mountain men, vintage autos, floats, cowboys, and tons of free candy. Special PRCA rodeo performances, a street dance, art shows, running events, fireworks, and a carnival complete the schedule. Get details at 307/587-5155 or 800/207-0744, www.cody stampederodeo.org.

More Events

At 6 P.M. each summer evening, the **Cody Gunslingers** perform downtown at the Irma Hotel. The mock gunfights are Western-style entertainment. They're worth a look if you haven't seen one before, but still corny and quite out of character for settled-down Cody.

Cowboy Songs and Range Ballads is a

unique Western musical festival held the second weekend of April at the Buffalo Bill Historical Center. You'll hear true cowboy music (not country-and-western), along with poetry and stories from cowboys, ranchers, musicians, and folklorists. Get details at 307/587-4771, www.bbhc.org/events.

Held in the Robbie Powwow Garden in front of the Buffalo Bill Historical Center in late June, the **Plains Indian Powwow** attracts several hundred participants from all over the Rockies and Canada vying for $10,000 in prize money. It includes daylong singing and dancing in tribal regalia and various dance competitions. Visitors can purchase Indian arts and crafts and taste Indian tacos and fry bread. Contact the BBHC for specifics: 307/587-4771, www.bbhc .org/events.

The **Old West Show & Auction** in mid-June offers a chance for collectors to purchase quality old cowboy gear. It's considered the finest such event in the nation and attracts a wealthy crowd. Get details at 307/587-9014, www.codyold west.com. The **Yellowstone Jazz Festival** in mid-July brings both regional and national jazz groups; details at www.yellowstonejazz.com.

The **Buffalo Bill Art Show & Sale** in mid-September is the largest art event of the year, with exhibitions, a symposium, receptions, and an auction; 307/587-5002 or 888/598-8119, www.buffalobillartshow.com.

Music and Entertainment

The downtown City Park band shell is the place to be for Friday evening **Concerts in the Park** in July and August. These free musical performances—in a variety of genres—start at 6 P.M. **Cassie's,** 214 Yellowstone Ave., 307/527-5500, www.cassies.com, has Wednesday night country swing dance lessons, along with country-and-western and mellow rock tunes nightly throughout the summer. Hang around the bar long enough and you can join in that old Cassie's favorite, barroom brawling.

Park Drive In, on the east end of Big Horn Dr., 307/587-2712, is one of the few drive-in theaters left in Wyoming. Open Thurs.–Sun. only. For the indoor version, head to **Cody The-**atre,** 1171 Sheridan Ave., 307/587-2712, or the fourplex version: **Big Horn Cinemas,** 2525 Big Horn Ave., 307/587-8009.

RECREATION
River Rafting

One of the most popular summertime activities in Cody is floating the class I and II Shoshone River. Beware, however, that even with these mild conditions, you should plan on getting soaked in the rapids. Expect to pay around $22 adults ($20 kids) for a six-mile run that lasts 90 minutes, or $30 adults ($28 kids) for a 13-mile (three-hour) float. For details, contact **Wyoming River Trips,** 233 Yellowstone Hwy., 307/587-6661 or 800/586-6661, www. wyomingrivertrips.com; **River Runners,** 1491 Sheridan Ave., 307/527-7238 or 800/535-7238, www.imt.net/~rodeo/rrunners.html; or **Red Canyon River Trips,** 1374 Sheridan Ave., 307/587-6988 or 800/293-0148, www.imt.net /~rodeo/raft.html.

Founded in 1978, Wyoming River Trips is the most experienced company in Cody. Red Canyon River Trips is newer, but the guides are very experienced and use smaller rafts for a more personalized trip. Both Wyoming River and Red Canyon offer inflatable kayak trips for those who want to run the rapids on their own power. In addition, Red Canyon leads scenic float trips down the Clarks Fork ($50); see Sunlight Basin for details.

If you want to try rafting or kayaking on your own, you'll find several miles of technical class IV water with some class V drops below the dam and above DeMaris Springs. Above the dam are stretches of class I and II water with good access from the main highway. Ask locally for flow conditions before heading out because snowmelt and dam releases can dramatically affect water levels. The rafting companies offer half-day whitewater trips down the North Fork above the reservoir for $55 per person including lunch. These trips only run late May–July, when the water level is high.

Most rafters put in three miles west of Cody off Demaris Street. Just upstream from the put-in point is DeMaris Springs, a part of **"Colter's Hell"** that is on private property and not open to the public. The area was once far more active, with hot springs bubbling out of the river and sulfurous smoke rising all around. People actually died from the poisonous gas. Today the geothermal activity has lessened, but the air still smells of sulfur and small hot springs color the cliff faces. Miners worked over nearby hillsides in search of sulfur; the diggings are still apparent. It's also pretty obvious why they first called this the Stinkingwater River.

Horse and Wagon Rides

Horseback rides are available from **Cedar Mountain Trail Rides,** 307/527-4966, located one mile west of the rodeo grounds; and **Buffalo Bill's Trail Rides,** at the Cody KOA one mile east of the airport, 307/587-2369 or 800/562-8507, www.koa.com. Hour-long trail rides are $20. Many of the lodges in Wapiti Valley (described previously) also offer horseback rides. Get a complete listing of Cody-area outfitters and guides from the chamber of commerce, and a list of permitted outfitters from local Forest Service offices.

Each August, horse enthusiasts join in a week-long trip called **High Country Trail Ride.** Most folks bring their own horse, but rentals are also available. The route takes participants through Sunlight Basin, with overnight camping, a support staff, veterinarians, catered meals, and entertainment beneath the circus tent. Call 307/527-7468 for details.

If you just want to see wild horses, contact **Red Canyon Wild Mustang Tours,** 307/587-6988 or 800/293-0148, www.imt.net/~rodeo/mustang.html.

More Recreation

The newly built **Cody Quad** is an impressive recreation center on the south side of town at 1402 Heart Mountain St., 307/587-0400. It houses a large indoor pool, hot tub, wading pool, basketball and racquetball courts, an indoor track, and exercise machines. Nonresident rec center passes are $10 adults, $5 kids. Next door is the **Victor J. Riley Arena and Com-**munity Events Center, 307/587-1400, which serves as a summertime convention center and winter ice rink.

Wheel Fun Rentals, 1390 Sheridan Ave., 307/587-4779, www.wheelfunrentals.com, rents a variety of offbeat peddle-powered vehicles, including fringe-topped surreys. I can't imagine pedaling around in these contraptions—at least not without a mask—but tourists seem to love them. Wheel Fun also rents mountain bikes and rollerblades. **Cody Bike Tours,** 307/587-9520, www.codybiketours.com, guides backroads cycling trips in the area.

The 18-hole **Olive Glenn Golf and Country Club,** 802 Meadow Lane, 307/587-5308, is a PGA championship course with a complete golf shop and upscale restaurant. Families enjoy playing **miniature golf** at the downtown city park, 307/587-3685. It's open summers only.

Outdoor Gear

For quality backcountry equipment, especially if you travel by horse, be sure to drop by **Wyoming Outdoor Industries,** 1231 13th St., 307/527-6449 or 800/725-6853. You won't find Gore-Tex jogging bras here, just tough equipment for backcountry use (especially horsepacking), including folding woodstoves, pack saddles, bear-resistant panniers, and wall tents. They also have a mail-order catalog.

Sunlight Sports, 1251 Sheridan Ave., 307/587-9517, is the largest outdoors shop in town, with tents, climbing equipment, clothes, topographic maps, and more, all housed within a classic building with hardwood floors and a tin ceiling. Sunlight Sports also rents cross-country and downhill skis, snowboards, and snowshoes during the winter and is the place to get details on ice climbing in the South Fork area.

North Fork Anglers, 1438 Sheridan Ave., 307/527-7274, www.northforkanglers.com, has anything you might need for fly-fishing, including a full-service retail shop, professional fishing guides, and fly-tying clinics. **Sierra Trading Post,** 1402 8th St., 307/578-5802, has an outlet store in the large log building across from the Buffalo Bill Historical Center.

SHOPPING

As you might expect from a tourist town, Cody has more than its share of shops dealing in clunky jewelry, crass T-shirts, and fake Indian trinkets. Fortunately, it's also home to several places with a bit more class.

Cody Rodeo Company, 1291 Sheridan Ave., 307/587-5913, www.codyrodeocompany.com, has a big selection of cowboy hats and also sells Western wear, rodeo memorabilia, and decorative items in a playful setting. Get fancy Western duds at **Custom Cowboy Shop,** 1286 Sheridan Ave., 307/527-7300. **Corral West Ranchwear,** 1625 Stampede Ave., 307/587-4493, www.corralwest.com, has inexpensive Western wear.

Traditions West Antique Mall, 1131 Sheridan Ave., 307/587-7434, and **Old West Antique Mall,** 1215 Sheridan Ave., 307/587-9014, are good places to look for Western antiques.

Stop by the local consignment shops for deals on Western-style kids' clothes: **Mommie and Me** 1012 12th St., 307/587-1131, and **Olive and Sweet Pea,** 1272 Sheridan Ave., 307/587-3647.

New books are available from **Cody Newsstand,** 1121 13th St., 307/587-2843, and **The Thistle,** 1243 Rumsey, 307/587-6635. Cody Newsstand also has one of the best magazine selections in Bighorn Basin. **Wyoming Well Book Exchange and Oilfield Supply,** 1902 E. Sheridan Ave., 307/587-4249, has the oddest combination in town: bodice-buster novels and oil-drilling equipment!

INFORMATION AND SERVICES

Get local information from the **Cody Country Chamber of Commerce,** 836 Sheridan Ave., 307/587-2297 or 800/393-2639, www.cody chamber.org. Hours are Monday–Saturday 8 A.M.–6 P.M. and Sunday 10 A.M.–3 P.M. Memorial Day to Labor Day, and Monday–Friday 8 A.M.–5 P.M. the rest of the year. This log building housed the original Buffalo Bill Museum from 1927 to 1969 and was built as a replica of Cody's TE Ranch. It's on the Na-

tional Register of Historic Places. A regional tourism organization, **Park County Travel Council,** is also based here, providing publications (call 800/393-2639) and web information (www.yellowstone.org) to travelers heading through Cody, Powell, Meeteetse, and Wapiti Valley. Another good source for Cody information is **Cody Wyoming Net,** www .codywyomingnet.com.

The **BLM's Cody Field Office** is at 1002 Blackburn Ave., 307/578-5900, www.wy.blm .gov. The Forest Service has two local offices: the **Shoshone National Forest Supervisor's Office,** 808 Meadow Lane, 307/527-6241, www .fs.fed.us/r2/shoshone, and the smaller **Wapiti Ranger District Office,** 203 W. Yellowstone, 307/527-6921.

The **Park County Library,** 1057 Sheridan Ave., 307/587-6204, has regional titles and computers for Internet access.

Cody's **West Park Hospital,** 707 Sheridan Ave., 307/527-7501 or 800/654-9447, www .westparkhospital.org, is the largest in Bighorn Basin and one of the finest in the state. The hospital's **Urgent Care Clinic,** 702 Yellowstone Ave., 307/587-7207, is open daily and evenings. No appointment needed.

Get fast cash at **ATMs** scattered throughout Cody, including one inside the Buffalo Bill Historical Center and another in the Wal-Mart SuperCenter.

Wash clothes at **Eastgate Laundry,** next to Albertson's at 1813 17th St., 307/587-5355; and **Quick Coin-Op Laundromat,** 930 12th St., 307/587-6519.

TRANSPORTATION

Yellowstone Regional Airport (www.flyra.com) is just east of town on U.S. Hwy. 14/16/20. **Sky-West/Delta,** 307/587-9740 or 800/221-1212, www.delta.com, has daily flights to Salt Lake City, while **Great Lakes Aviation,** 307/432-7000 or 800/554-5111, www.greatlakesav.com, has daily service to Denver and Rock Springs. **Spirit Mountain Aviation,** 307/587-6732, offers scenic flights and charter service.

Phidippides Shuttle Service, 307/527-6789

or 866/527-6789, www.phidpdes.com, provides shuttle vans to the airport in Billings, Montana.

Rent cars at the airport from Budget, Hertz, or Thrifty. See the "Rental Car Contacts" Special Topic in the On the Road chapter.

Buses from **Powder River Transportation/Coach USA,** 307/682-0960 or 800/442-3682, stop at Kelly Inn, 2513 Greybull Highway, providing service north to Billings, Montana, east to Rapid City, South Dakota, and south to Denver. They stop in most Bighorn Basin towns, and serve much of central and eastern Wyoming.

TOURS

The **Cody Trolley,** 307/527-7043, www.cody trolleytours.com, takes you on an informative hour-long tour of town (and up to Buffalo Bill Dam) for $11. These tours are offered several times a day in summer.

During summer, daily tours of Yellowstone National Park—$60 adults, $54 seniors, and $30 kids—are available through **Powder River Tours/Coach USA,** 307/527-3677 or 800/442-3682. These tours cover either the southern park loop or the northern portion, and two-day tours that include the whole shebang are $110 adults,

$99 seniors, and $55 kids. You can stay overnight in Yellowstone and return on a later bus for no extra charge (on a space-available basis) or transfer to Gray Line buses to reach Jackson (307/733-4325 or 800/443-6133, www.jacksonholealltrans.com) or West Yellowstone (406/646-9374 or 800/523-3102, www.gray lineyellowstone.com).

For a more personalized trip, call **Grub Steak Expeditions,** 307/527-6316 or 800/527-6316, www.grubsteaktours.com. It leads 12-hour auto tours of the park, along with visits to Sunlight Basin, Wapiti Valley, and the South Fork. One-day tours cost $300 for two people, plus $100 for each additional guest. These tours are popular with families looking for a unique perspective on the park, and some are led by the co-owner, a retired Yellowstone park ranger. **Yellowstone Expedition Services,** 307/587-5452 or 888/808-7990, www.yellowstoneparktours.com, also offers customized auto tours into Yellowstone with a maximum of six people per group.

Wildlife biologist Sean Sheehan leads **Wyoming Nature Tours,** 307/527-6306, www.wyoming-naturetours.com, with natural-history trips throughout the Big Horn Basin, including to Bighorn Canyon.

Dubois

Approaching Dubois (pop. 1,000, elev. 6,917 feet) from either direction, you drive through the extraordinary red, yellow, and gray badlands that set this country apart. The luxuriant Wind River winds its way down a narrow valley where horses graze in the irrigated pastures and old barns and newer log homes stand against the hills, while the tree-covered Absaroka and Wind River Mountains ring distant views. The town of Dubois consists of a long main street that makes an abrupt elbow turn and then points due west toward the mountains. The many log buildings and snatches of wooden sidewalks give the place an authentic frontier feel. Locals live in cabins, trailer homes, and simple frame houses. Dubois weather is famously mild; warm Chinook winds often melt

any snow that falls. Grand scenery reigns in all directions. Snowmobilers, hunters, and anglers have discovered that Dubois provides a good place to relax in Wyoming's "banana belt" while remaining close to the more temperamental mountains. The area basks in an average of 300 days of sunshine each year. By the way, Dubois is pronounced DU-boys; other pronunciations will reveal your tenderfoot status. Locals sometimes jokingly call it "Dubious."

HISTORY

Dubois began in the 1880s when pioneer ranchers and more than a few rustlers, including Butch Cassidy, settled in the area, followed by Scandinavian hand-loggers who cut lodgepole for railroad ties. The town that grew up along the juncture of Horse Creek and the Wind River was first known as Never Sweat, but when citizens applied for a post office the Postal Service refused to allow the name and suggested Dubois instead—the name of an Idaho senator who just happened to be on the Senate committee that provided funding for the post office.

Like many edge-of-the-mountain towns, Dubois is in transition. For most of its existence, it served as a logging and ranching center. In 1987, the Louisiana Pacific sawmill shut down, throwing many loggers and millworkers onto the unemployment rolls. Loggers blamed environmentalists and the Forest Service for sharply reducing the timber available; environmentalists countered that the company was simply using the reductions as an excuse to close an aging mill. After everyone ran out of mud to sling, they decided to look at what Dubois had to offer and discovered that, lo and behold, they just happened to be sitting in an almost-undiscovered recreational and retirement gold mine. In the 1990s the town leapt full force into the tourism business. The transformation of Dubois to a visitor-oriented economy certainly has its downside—elaborate "trophy" log summer homes are beginning to overrun the lush pastures on both ends of town—but so far this pretty little place has been spared the onslaught of "industrial tourism." Stay tuned.

> *Snowmobilers, hunters, and anglers have discovered that Dubois provides a good place to relax in Wyoming's "banana belt" while remaining close to the more temperamental mountains.*

SIGHTS

National Bighorn Sheep Center

The National Bighorn Sheep Interpretive Center, 907 W. Ramshorn, 307/455-3429 or 888/209-2795, www.bighorn.org, houses displays on desert bighorn, Rocky Mountain bighorn, stone sheep, and Dall sheep. The museum details how the population was brought back from the brink of extinction, and it in-

cludes fine hands-on exhibits and interactive displays on how bighorns live. Also here is a diorama of a Sheepeater Indian trap and mounted specimens around a 16-foot-high central "mountain." A theater shows videos on bighorn sheep and other topics, and a gift shop sells books and other items. The center is open daily 9 A.M.–8 P.M. Memorial Day to Labor Day, and daily 9 A.M.–5 P.M. the rest of the year. Entrance costs $2 adults, 75 cents kids under 12, or $5 families.

The center offers **wildlife tours** of the Whiskey Basin Habitat Area just west of town. These four-hour van-and-hiking trips cost $25 for adults or $10 for kids and include binoculars and spotting scopes to view the animals. During winter the focus is on bighorn sheep, while summertime visitors take nature hikes and look for birds. Reservations are required; call the center for details, or visit their website. The center also has brochures describing self-guided tours of Whiskey Basin and the **Spence/Moriarity Wildlife Habitat Management Area** east of Dubois.

Dubois Museum

The Dubois Museum, 909 W. Ramshorn (next door to the Bighorn Sheep Center), 307/455-2284, www.windriverhistory.org, is open daily 9 A.M.–5 P.M. Memorial Day to mid-September, and Tuesday–Saturday 10 A.M.–4 P.M. the rest of the year. Entrance is $1 adults or 50 cents kids under 12. The small museum houses a handful of exhibits on the Sheepeater Indians, with other displays on ranch life, geology, and wildlife. Be sure to check out the hilarious photo of 1930s movie star Tim McCoy teaching golf to a rather skeptical group of Shoshone Indians! Out front are seven historic log cabins and an old gas station, all containing interesting displays.

Other Attractions

Just west of Dubois is a signed turnoff to a

GATEWAYS

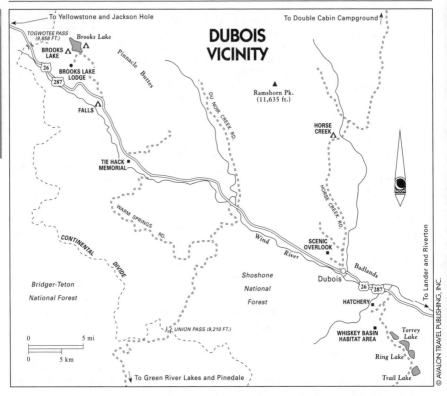

© AVALON TRAVEL PUBLISHING, INC.

scenic overlook. The gravel road climbs sharply (no RVs) for approximately one mile to the viewpoint, where displays note the surrounding peaks. Enjoy marvelous views of 11,635-foot Ramshorn Peak from here. **Rocky Mountain bighorn sheep** crowd the Dubois area in the winter. Many are visible on the hills just south of town, with hundreds more gathered in the Whiskey Basin Habitat Area, five miles east and described earlier.

The magnificent badlands on both sides of Dubois, but especially to the east, are well worth exploring. The BLM maintains a fascinating **Badlands Interpretive Trail** up Mason Draw, 2.4 miles northeast of town. Pick up a booklet describing the trail at the visitors center. Depending on your route, the hike should take an hour or two to complete.

Rock hounds will find all sorts of petrified

wood, agates, and other colorful rocks up the Wiggins Fork and Horse Creek drainages; ask at the chamber of commerce for directions.

One thing you certainly would not expect to find in Dubois is a training center for lawyers, but famed Wyoming attorney Gerry Spence has one on his Thunderbird Ranch east of town. His nonprofit (!) **Trial Lawyers College** puts some 50 lawyers through an intense four-week session each summer, with mock trials and professional actors; 307/455-2389, www.triallawyerscollege .com. Watch your step with all these lawyers around Dubois!

ACCOMMODATIONS

Dubois makes an excellent stopping point on the way to Yellowstone and Grand Teton National Parks, with lodging prices well below those in Jackson Hole. All places are open year-round unless noted otherwise.

Under $50

If you're looking for quietude, head three miles east of town to **Riverside Inn & Campground,** 307/455-2337 or 877/489-2337, www.dte world.com/riversideinn, where the motel rooms (some with microwaves and fridges) are $30–35 s or $40–49 d. Guests have fishing access to a private stretch of the river. Riverside is open May–November.

Right on the river, **Wind River Motel,** 519 W. Ramshorn, 307/455-2611 or 877/455-2621, www.wyoming.com/~dtewindriver, has a mix of rustic cabins, motel rooms, and suites for $30–75 s or d. Some rooms contain kitchenettes.

$50 and Up

Branding Iron Inn, 401 Ramshorn, 307/455-2893 or 800/341-8000, www.brandingiron inn.com, has cozy and well-maintained duplex log cabins that were built in the 1940s. Rates are $35–80 s or d; kitchenettes cost $10 extra. Out back are corrals for folks traveling with horses.

One-half mile east of Dubois, **Chinook Winds Mountain Lodge,** 307/455-2987 or 800/863-0354, has a variety of rooms. Riverside motel units are $40–65 s or d and contain small fridges. Cabins with full kitchens cost $65–85 d. The Wind River is right out the back door. They're open mid-May to mid-October.

Trail's End Motel, 511 Ramshorn, 307/455-2540 or 888/455-6660, www.trailsendmotel .com, has recently remodeled rooms starting for $48 s or $52 d. The nicer rooms ($72–138 d) have decks facing the Wind River and include in-room fridges and microwaves. An exercise room is also available.

A fine riverside place is **Black Bear Country Inn,** 505 W. Ramshorn, 307/455-2344 or 800/873-2327, www.blackbearcountryinn.com, where rooms cost $40–60 s or d, including fridges and microwaves. A kitchenette apartment sleeps up to seven people for $95. The motel is open mid-May through October.

Find attractive accommodations at the largest motel in town, **Stagecoach Motor Inn,** 103

Ramshorn, 307/455-2303 or 800/455-5090, www.dteworld.com/stagecoach. Rates are $52 s or $62–68 d, including use of an outdoor pool; kitchenettes cost $80–98 and sleep four to six. King suites are $80 d. Families will appreciate the outdoor pool, hot tub, and shady backyard play area.

For historic rooms, stay at **Twin Pines Lodge & Cabins,** 218 Ramshorn, 307/455-2600 or 800/550-6332, www.dteworld.com/twinpines. Built in 1934 and listed on the National Register of Historic Places, the lodge has modern and rustic cabins for $55 s or $60–65 d, with fridges and VCRs in all, plus microwaves in some units.

Two miles west of town is **Super 8 Motel,** 307/455-3694 or 800/800-8000, www.super8 .com, where the rooms are $55–71 s or $59–81 d, including access to a hot tub. Nearby is **Bald Mountain Inn,** 307/455-2844 or 800/682-9323, www.baldmountaininn.com, where spacious motel rooms cost $64–74 s or d; add $7 for kitchenette units. Bring your fishing pole;

© DON PITCHER

the badlands near Dubois

302 Gateways to Yellowstone

the Wind River is just out back. Closed Apr. to mid-May.

Bed-and-Breakfasts

Jakey's Fork Homestead, 307/455-2769, www.frontierlodging.com, has B&B accommodations in a delightful century-old homestead four miles east of town. It's close to the bighorn sheep refuge in Whiskey Basin and offers extraordinary views of both the Wind River Mountains and nearby badlands. Birdwatchers will find a host of feathered friends in the trees and marsh. Be sure to ask owner Irene Bridges about Butch Cassidy's encounter with Indians nearby. Guests can stay in the modern home or a rustic sod-covered cabin. A sauna and hot tub bathtub are available, and the rooms have shared baths. A full breakfast is served, and children will enjoy the toy-filled playroom. Rates are $70–85 d in the house or $105–125 d ($20 extra for four people) in the cabin.

Just two blocks from downtown Dubois is **The Stone House B&B,** 207 S. 1st St., 307/455-2555, www.duboisbnb.com. Inside this stately home are two guest rooms ($50 s or $55 d) with shared baths, along with a basement suite ($70 d) that has a private bath. Adjacent is a three-room cottage for $80 d or $100 for four people. A full breakfast is served each morning, and the sitting room faces Whiskey Mountain, a good place to watch for bighorn sheep. Open May–October.

Dude Ranches

Quite a few dude ranches/mountain lodges are found in the Dubois area. Five are described as follows, and another five places are described in the Over Togwotee Pass section of this chapter.

Ten miles out East Fork Rd., **Lazy L&B Ranch,** 307/455-2839 or 800/453-9488, www.lazylb.com, is a century-old ranch offering creekside log cabins, horseback riding, overnight pack trips, cowboy poetry and songs, a swimming pool, hot tub, stocked fishing ponds, kids' programs, volleyball and pool, fly-fishing, and a rifle range. The ranch's horseback-riding program is excellent, and guests can choose trips through the badlands or high into the mountains. Lazy L&B is open June–Sep-

tember, with all-inclusive weekly rates of $2,300 for two people. The ranch also operates **Bear Basin Wilderness Camp,** www.bearbasin camp.com, a great base from which to explore the Washakie Wilderness. A maximum of eight guests stay in wall tents.

Sixteen miles north of Dubois in gorgeous Dunoir Valley, **Absaroka Ranch,** 307/455-2275, www.dteworld.com/absaroka, has all of the typical guest ranch offerings: horseback riding, guided fly-fishing, hiking, and cookouts. The ranch accommodates just 18 guests and emphasizes the personal touch. It is surrounded by national forest land and has a comfortable main lodge (built in 1910), attractively restored log cabins, and a redwood sauna. The ranch is open mid-June to mid-September. All-inclusive weekly rates are $2,600 for two people.

Bitterroot Ranch, 307/455-2778 or 800/545-0019, www.ridingtours.com/wyoming.htm, emphasizes horseback riding for experienced riders; each guest gets to ride several different horses. The owners breed Arabian horses and offer cross-country jumping courses, pack trips, cattle drives, fly-fishing, and kids' programs. Both French and German are spoken here, attracting an international clientele. The ranch is open June–September and has space for 32 guests in a dozen cabins. All-inclusive weekly rates are $3,100 for two people. The owners also run Equitors, www.equitours.com, a travel agency that sets up horseback rides all over the globe.

South of Dubois in beautiful Jakeys Fork Canyon, **CM Ranch,** 307/455-2331 or 800/455-0721, www.cmranch.com, is one of Wyoming's oldest dude ranches; it's been here since 1927. The ranch offers dramatic badlands topography and a variety of fossils, making it a favorite of geologists (and amateur rock hounds). Trails lead into the adjacent Fitzpatrick Wilderness, a destination for horseback trips. Fishing is another popular activity, and a fishing guide is available. The immaculate lodge buildings have space for 60 guests, and kids love the big outdoor pool. All-inclusive weekly rates at this delightful old-time ranch are $2,200–2,400 for two people. The ranch is owned by the Kemmerer family, whose ancestors founded the town of Kemmerer,

Wyoming. The Kemmerers also own Jackson Hole Mountain Resort.

Operating as a dude ranch since 1920, **T-Cross Ranch,** 307/455-2206, www.ranch web.com/tcross, is 15 miles north of Dubois near Horse Creek, and is open mid-June through September. Surrounded by the Shoshone National Forest, this remote ranch has weekly accommodations at $2,400 for two people, including horseback riding, all meals, activities for kids, trout fishing, and a hot tub. Backcountry pack trips and other activities are also available. Lodging is in eight comfortable log cabins, and the main lodge has a massive stone fireplace and spacious front porch.

CAMPING

The closest public camping spot is **Horse Creek Campground** ($5; open late May–Sept.), 12 miles north of Dubois on Horse Creek Road.

Circle-Up Camper Court, 225 W. Welty, 307/455-2238, charges $17 for tents (some shade), $26 for RVs, and $25 for basic cabins. Kids love the tepees for $20. Folks not camping here pay $4 for showers. Open year-round, this is one of Wyoming's better private campgrounds. You can also park RVs ($18–20) or pitch tents ($15) at **Riverside Inn & Campground,** three miles east of town, 307/455-2337 or 877/489-2337, www.dteworld.com/riversideinn. Open May–November.

FOOD

Breakfast and Lunch

Popular with both locals and tourists, **Cowboy Cafe,** 115 E. Ramshorn, 307/455-2595, has good home-style breakfasts with big helpings of biscuits and gravy. For a real artery-clogger, try the steak and eggs.

Ramshorn Bagel and Deli, 202 E. Ramshorn, 307/455-2400, serves bagels, sandwiches, and espresso for breakfast and lunch. **Village Cafe/Daylight Donuts,** 515 W. Ramshorn, 307/455-2122, offers doughnuts and coffee in the morning and pizza and fried chicken dinners when evening rolls around.

Fine Dining

Cafe Wyoming, 106 E. Ramshorn, 307/455-3828, sits back from the street along Horse Creek. The food is distinctive and creative, with a lunch and dinner menu that changes every week. They always have pastas, chicken, seafood, sandwiches, and vegetarian specials, along with a couple of house favorites: broiled ribeye with bleu cheese sauce, and Cajun broiled catfish. There's a diverse wine list, and dinner entrées run $13–21. Reservations are highly recommended. The café is closed Sundays and Mondays, during April, and mid-October to mid-November. House-made sauces are available in the café or online at www.howlingwolfsauce.com.

Line Shack Lodge, 307/455-3232 or 888/266-4695, www.lineshack.com, serves three meals a day with daily specials but is best known for Friday night prime rib dinners. They're located at the top of Union Pass, 13 scenic miles west of Dubois. The saloon here has live bands in the winter, when this is a very popular snowmobile destination.

American

Bernie's Cafe, next to the Super 8 at 1408 Warm Springs Dr., 307/455-2115, opens at 6 A.M. each morning, and it doesn't close until 10 P.M. You'll find down-home cooking, fast service, and all-American meals for reasonable prices. It's a favorite of families.

Rustic Pine Steakhouse, 119 E. Ramshorn, 307/455-2772, is a carnivore's delight, with prime rib on Friday and Saturday nights; open for dinner only.

Get malts and sundaes from the old-time soda fountain inside the **Dubois Drugstore,** 126 E. Ramshorn, 307/455-2300. **The Really Wild Bunch Grill & Bar,** 112 E. Ramshorn, 307/433-3670, www.pinnacle buttes.com, is a downtown place with a covered front porch for streetside dining.

Groceries and Bakeries

Get groceries at **Ramshorn Food Farm,** 610 W. Ramshorn, 307/455-2402. For pastries, breads, and tasty hardtack made from an old Swedish recipe, stop by **Circle-Up Camper Court,** 225 W. Welty, 307/455-2238.

ENTERTAINMENT

Dubois is a hopping place during the summer, especially on weekends. Find country-and-western bands at **Rustic Pine Tavern,** 119 E. Ramshorn, 307/455-2430, and **Outlaw Saloon,** 204 W. Ramshorn, 307/455-2387. The Rustic Pine is a classic Western bar with elk and moose heads, plenty of old wood, and a pool table. Check out the ashtrays, which note, "God spends his vacation here." The famous Tuesday night **square dances** bring in dudes from local ranches in July and August. You may want to avoid this night if you don't want to be overwhelmed with fellow visitors.

EVENTS

The **International Pedigree Stage Stop Sled Dog Race** (IPSSSDR) stops here. See the Jackson chapter for more info.

The Dubois **Spur Spangled Celebration** on Fourth of July weekend is the biggest local event, with an ice-cream social, parade, rodeo, Western barbecue, fireworks, and rubber-ducky races down the river. In mid-July, **Dubois Museum Day** is a folk art festival with Indian dancing, frontier crafts demonstrations, and lectures. Another mid-July event is the **Badlands Classic Mountain Bike Race,** with 12- and 16-mile bike courses.

A **National Art Show** comes to town on the last week of July, attracting both professionals and amateurs. Also don't miss the always popular Dubois firefighter's **Buffalo Barbecue,** held the second Saturday of August. Get specifics on these and other events from the Dubois Chamber of Commerce, 307/455-2556.

Budding musicians should check out the **Greater Yellowstone Music Camp** in late June, with nationally known instructors, concerts, and jam sessions in acoustic blues and swing for guitar, fiddle, and bass players. Get details at 307/455-3748, www.greateryellowstone musiccamp.com.

SUMMER RECREATION

Dubois sits at the confluence of the Wind River and Horse Creek, and both streams provide good trout fishing right in town. Hot springs keep the Wind River flowing all year. See the visitors center for descriptions of local fishing holes and for brochures from local outfitters who offer pack trips and horseback rides.

The nine-hole **Antelope Hills Golf Course,** 307/455-2888, is on the western end of Dubois. Rent mountain bikes from **Bob's Bike Corral,** 124 E. Ramshorn St., 307/455-3193.

WINTER RECREATION

The Absarokas and Wind River Mountains around Dubois are crowded with **snowmobilers** during winter, and several places rent "sleds" in town and nearby. Don't expect peace and quiet with all of these machines roaring through the backcountry! More than 300 miles of trails head out in all directions, with the Union Pass area a particular focus.

For something quieter, **cross-country skiers** will find trails near Falls Campground and Brooks Lake (both 23 miles west of town) and Cowboy Village Resort at Togwotee (40 miles west) and in backcountry wilderness areas off-limits to snowmobiles. **Dogsled** trips are popular winter diversions and are detailed in the Over Togwotee Pass section.

SHOPPING

Teddy Bear Shoppe, inside the Black Bear Country Inn, 505 W. Ramshorn, 307/455-2344 or 800/873-2327, www.blackbearcountryinn .com, has more then 500 different teddy bears on display and for sale. It's touted as the largest selection of teddy bears in the West. Don't let your three-year-old know about this place!

Trapline Gallery, 120 E. Ramshorn, 307/455-2800, sells Indian-crafted beadwork, jewelry, and artwork, as well as furs. **Tukadeka Traders/Horse Creek Gallery,** 104 E. Ramshorn, 307/455-3345, has an impressive collection of antique trade beads for sale, along with tacky antler carvings and Indian trinkets. A few doors down is a nice bookshop, **Two Ocean Books,** 128 E. Ramshorn, 307/455-3554. **Water Wheel Gift Shop,** 113 E. Ramshorn, 307/455-2112, also carries a selection of Wyoming titles.

Purchase stylish Western wear inside the historic **Welty's General Store,** 113 W. Ramshorn, 307/455-2377. The hours are haphazard. Be sure to ask them about Butch Cassidy's priceless old pistol, although you won't be able to see it because it's locked away.

For fishing supplies, head to **Wind River Fly Shop,** 116 E. Ramshorn, 307/455-2140, or **Whiskey Mountain Tackle,** 1418 Warm Springs Dr., 307/455-2587.

INFORMATION AND SERVICES

The **Dubois Chamber of Commerce,** 616 W. Ramshorn, 307/455-2556, www.duboiswyoming .org, is open Monday–Saturday 9 A.M.–7 P.M., Sunday noon–5 P.M. Memorial Day to Labor Day, and Monday–Friday 9 A.M.–5 P.M. the rest of the year. Ask for a self-guided tour map of

old logging flumes, tie-hack cabins, and other historic structures.

Stop by the Shoshone National Forest **Wind River Ranger District** office at 1403 W. Ramshorn (one mile west of town), 307/455-2466, www.fs.fed.us/r2/shoshone, for maps of Shoshone and Bridger-Teton National Forests and information on local trails. They also have a listing of local horsepacking outfitters. See the chapter on Bighorn Basin for more on the Washakie Wilderness. The Fitzpatrick Wilderness is described in the Wind River Mountains section.

Dubois does not have a hospital, but the **Dubois Medical Center,** 706 Meckem, 307/455-2516, has nurse practitioners. Wash clothes at the **Laundromat** at 410 W. Ramshorn (across from Branding Iron Motel).

Check your email or surf the web for free at the new **Dubois Library,** 201 1st St., 307/455-2032, www.fremontcountylibraries.org; or for a fee at **Cyber Cafe,** 116 E. Ramshorn, 307/455-4011.

Trail's End Motel, 307/455-2540 or 888/455-6660, www.trailsendmotel.com, provides shuttle van service to the airports in Jackson or Riverton.

Dubois Vicinity

Anyone who loves the outdoors will discover an abundance of pleasures around Dubois. There's good fishing for rainbow, cutthroat, brown, and brook trout in Wind River and for rainbow, brook, and Mackinaw trout in the many alpine lakes. You'll also see lots of deer, elk, and bighorn sheep. Hikers and horse-packers will find hundreds of miles of Forest Service trails in the area. Photographers love the brilliantly colored badlands that frame Dubois on both the east and west sides. Each winter, hundreds of snowmobilers climb on their "sleds" and cross-country skiers strap on their "boards" to enter the world of deep powder in the Absarokas.

HORSE CREEK AREA

Horse Creek Road heads north from Dubois, with scenic views of the Absarokas and nearby

badland country. Several dude ranches are in the area. **Horse Creek Campground** ($5; open late May–Sept.) is 12 miles north. Forest Road 504 continues another five miles, providing access to the Washakie Wilderness via Horse Creek Trail. Forest Road 508 splits off near Horse Creek Campground and leads another 17 miles to **Double Cabin Campground** ($5; open late May–Sept.). Several trails head into the wilderness from here; the most popular are Frontier Creek Trail and the Wiggins Fork Trail. You'll find remnants of a petrified forest six miles up the Frontier Creek Trail, but they have been rather picked over by illegal collectors. (It's unlawful to remove petrified wood from a wilderness area. Please leave pieces where you find them.) For other Washakie Wilderness trails information, ask at the Dubois Ranger Station.

UNION PASS

The first road across the Absarokas headed through Union Pass southwest of Dubois. The pass forms a divide between the waters of the Columbia, Colorado, and Mississippi Rivers and marks the boundary of the Absaroka, Wind River, and Gros Ventre Mountain Ranges. Near the pass are an interpretive sign and a nature trail through a flower-filled meadow. Union Pass Road (gravel) leaves U.S. Hwy. 26/287 eight miles northwest of Dubois and climbs across to connect with State Hwy. 352 north of Pinedale. A major reconstruction project has dramatically improved the road in recent years, and the road is kept open year-round, providing a beautiful over-the-mountains connection between Pinedale and Dubois.

A scenic 20-mile side road begins a few miles up Union Pass Road, heads along Warm Springs Creek, and eventually reconnects with U.S. Hwy. 26/287. Find fantastic views of the Absaroka and Wind River Ranges along this route. The remains of an old tie-hack logging flume are visible, and a warm spring (85°F) flows into the creek.

Accommodations and Food

The Union Pass area is popular with mountain-bikers, cross-country skiers, and hordes of wintertime snowmobilers. The center of all this frenzy is **Line Shack Lodge,** located five miles up the road near the 8,600-foot summit, 307/455-3232 or 888/266-4695, www.lineshack.com. The modern 15,000-square-foot lodge has a wonderful setting, with an inviting interior, windows facing the mountains, and a deck that's especially popular for summertime weddings. Guests stay in 18 suites, all with two queen beds, hot tubs, fridges, microwaves, and VCRs. Most of these cost $75 d in summer or $120 d in winter, but two larger suites also have a queen futon, private deck, and stone fireplace for $100 d in summer or $150 d in winter. Extra guests are $30 per person (free for kids), but various package deals are offered if you want to add in meals, snowmobile rentals in winter, or ATV rentals and horseback rides in the summer. Peak season is January and February, when you'll need to book a room one year in advance! The Line Shack has a full-service restaurant that gets packed with folks from Dubois for their Friday night prime rib and salad bar ($11). The saloon has live music December–February, and there's a snowmobile shop on the grounds.

One-quarter mile downhill from Line Shack is **The Sawmill,** 307/455-2171 or 866/472-9645, www.thesawmill.org, with condo-style rooms ($75 d) and two-level suites ($110 d). A separate bunkhouse (popular with snowmobilers on a budget) has nine beds that go for $35 per person, including access to a large hot tub. A restaurant and bar are on the premises, and snowmobile rentals are available.

Over Togwotee Pass

The enjoyable drive west from Dubois first cuts through the colorful badlands, playing tag with the Wind River as it begins a long ascent to 9,658-foot Togwotee Pass (pronounced TOE-go-tee). The pass is named for a subchief under Chief Washakie. Togwotee was one of the last independent Sheepeater Indians—a branch of the Shoshones—and the man who led a U.S. government exploratory expedition over this pass in 1873. He even guided Pres. Chester Arthur on his month-long visit to Yellowstone in 1883.

Togwotee Pass is one of the most scenic drives imaginable, with Ramshorn Peak peeking down from the north for several miles until the road plunges into dense lodgepole forests (Shoshone National Forest) with lingering glimpses of the Pinnacle Buttes. At the crest it emerges into grass-, willow-, and flower-bedecked meadows with Blackrock Creek winding through. Whitebark pine and Engelmann spruce trees cover the nearby slopes. As the highway drops down the western side into the Bridger-Teton National Forest, another marvelous mountain range— the Tetons—dominates the horizon in dramatic fashion. Snow lies along the roadsides until early July; notice the high posts along the road used by snowplows. Togwotee Pass is a complete shock after all the miles of sagebrush and grassland that control the heartland of Wyoming. It's like entering another world—one of cool, forested mountains and lofty peaks instead of the arid land with horizonwide vistas.

PINNACLE BUTTES AND BROOKS LAKE

Dominating the view along U.S. Hwy. 26/287 for perhaps 15 miles are the castlelike Pinnacle Buttes. Twenty-three miles west of Dubois, you'll come to the turnoff to Brooks Lake, elevation 9,100 feet. Take it, even if you don't plan on camping here. A five-mile gravel road leads to the cliff-rimmed lake, and a clear creek flows east and south from here. The Forest Service's excellent **Pinnacles** and **Brooks Lake** Camp-

grounds are along the lakeshore and cost $10 per night; open mid-June to mid-Sept. Facing the lake is historic Brooks Lake Lodge (see the description in the Jackson Hole chapter).

Back on the main highway, you'll want to stop at **Falls Campground** (also $6; open June to mid-Sept.). Here, Brooks Creek tumbles into a deep canyon. Catch impressive views of **Brooks Creek Falls** along the short trail beginning from the parking lot. In winter, cross-country skiers will find an easy but ungroomed ski trail that heads out two miles from here. **Wind River Lake** is another five miles up the hill, just below the pass. It's a gorgeous place for picnics and fishing, with deep blue water and the sharp cliffs of Pinnacle Buttes behind. There's even a wheelchair-accessible float for anglers.

MOUNTAIN LODGES AND DUDE RANCHES

Sixteen miles west of Dubois is **Mackenzie Highland Ranch,** 307/455-3415, where accommodations are offered in a variety of cabins and other rustic buildings. The simplest cabins share a bathhouse and cost $45–90 for up to four people. Nicer cabins with kitchens and private baths are $135–215 for four guests, and the finest is a modern four-bedroom home (it sleeps eight) with two baths and a full kitchen for $245. There's a three-night minimum stay. This isn't an all-inclusive dude ranch, but trail rides, meals, ATV rentals, and guided fishing trips are offered in the summer, and the ranch is a base for snowmobilers, skiers, dog mushers, and hunters at other times of the year. A portion of Mackenzie Highland Ranch is used for lepidopterology research each summer, with graduate-level classes offered through Sam Houston State University. This unique program is run by professor Karölis Bagdonas, a specialist in moths and butterflies; he discovered the vital importance of moths in the diet of Yellowstone grizzlies.

Crooked Creek Ranch, 307/455-3035 or 888/238-2647, www.crookedcreek-gr.com, is 16 miles from Dubois along Union Pass Road. In summer, the ranch has horseback rides, ATV rentals, hiking, and fishing. In winter it's the haunt of snowmobilers; the Continental Divide Snowmobile Trail is very close. The ranch rents snowmobiles, sells gas, and has a restaurant, lounge, and convenience store. Guests stay in modern log cabins for $75 s or $150 d.

In the mountains 18 miles west of Dubois, **Triangle C Dude Ranch,** 307/455-2225 or 800/661-4928, www.trianglec.com, was established as the first tie-hack camp in the region and now operates as a summertime guest ranch and wintertime snowmobiling and cross-country skiing center. In summer, the main emphasis is horseback riding, but guests will also enjoy fishing, hiking, children's activities, wagon rides, and evening entertainment. Weekly rates are $3,400 for two people. The ranch is open Memorial Day to Labor Day for summer fun, plus mid-December through March for snowmobiling.

Twenty miles west of Dubois is **Pinnacle Buttes Lodge and Campground,** 307/455-2506 or 800/934-3569, www.pinnaclebuttes.com, where motel rooms are $65 s or $70 d, and cabins with kitchenettes (but no TVs) go for $75–160. The cabins and motel rooms sleep four people each. You'll also find a restaurant

with home-cooked meals, an outdoor pool, hot tub, and camping spaces ($10 for tents, $19 for RVs). Open year-round, with snowmobile rentals in the winter.

See the Jackson Hole chapter for information on **Brooks Lake Lodge**—on the lake of the same name—and **Cowboy Village Resort at Togwotee**—a few miles west of Togwotee Pass.

DOGSLEDDING

Washakie Outfitting, 307/733-3602 or 800/249-0662, www.dogsledwashakie.com, leads trips from Brooks Lake Lodge. On these trips, Iditarod veteran Billy Snodgrass offers half-day ($140 adults, $90 kids), all-day ($210 adults, $115 kids), overnight ($450 adults, $280 kids), and trips that combine time behind the dogs with time on a snowmobile.

Continental Divide Dogsled Adventures, 307/739-0165 or 800/531-6874, www.dogsledadventures.com, also leads dogsled tours in the Brooks Lake area, starting with a half-day trip that costs $175 for adults or $80 for kids. A variety of longer trips are available, including a three-night adventure where you stay overnight in a surprisingly comfortable yurt; $1,920 per person, with meals. All trips include round-trip transportation from Jackson.

Resources

Suggested Reading

Note: Several of the following books are now out of print. You can find many of them in regional libraries, or check the web for special orders or rare book auctions. Websites like www.amazon.com, www.barnesandnoble.com, and others will also search used bookstores for out-of-print titles.

Regional Titles

Birkby, Jeff. *Touring Montana and Wyoming Hot Springs.* Guilford, CT: Globe Pequot Press (Falcon), www.falconbooks.com, 1999.

Blackstone, D. L., Jr. *Traveler's Guide to the Geology of Wyoming.* Laramie, WY: Geological Survey of Wyoming, www.wsgsweb.uwyo.edu, 1988. An excellent overview of Wyoming's geological history and how to see it in today's landscapes.

Graham, Kenneth L. *Camping Wyoming and the Black Hills.* Guilford, CT: Globe Pequot Press (Falcon), www.falconbooks.com, 2001.

Graham, Kenneth Lee. *Fishing Wyoming.* Guilford, CT: Globe Pequot Press (Falcon), www .falconbooks.com, 1998. A 300-page tome that goes far beyond the standard coverage of Yellowstone and Jackson Hole.

Herrero, Stephen. *Bear Attacks: Their Causes and Avoidance.* Guilford, CT: The Lyons Press, www.lyonspress.com, 2002. An authoritative volume on the lives of bears and staying safe in their country.

Kilgore, Gene. *Gene Kilgore's Ranch Vacations.* Emeryville, CA: Avalon Travel Publishing, www.travelmatters.com, 2001. The definitive guide to dude and guest ranches in Wyoming and the rest of North America. Includes detailed, up-to-date descriptions of the best places to be a city-slicker cowboy.

Largeson, David R., and Darwin R. Spearing. *Roadside Geology of Wyoming.* Missoula, MT: Mountain Press Publishing Co., www.mountain-press.com, 1988. Wyoming is perhaps the most geologically interesting of all the states. This is an invaluable road guide for anyone wanting to know more about geology without resorting to dense textbooks.

McClure, Michael. *Camping Wyoming.* Atlantic City, WY: WigRaf Publishing, www.campwyo.com, 1999. An amazingly detailed guide to virtually every possible Wyoming camping spot.

Parent, Laurence. *Scenic Driving Wyoming.* Guilford, CT: Globe Pequot Press (Falcon), www.falconbooks.com, 1997. The best and most complete guide to scenic roads in Wyoming.

Petersen, David. *Among the Elk.* Flagstaff, AZ: Northland Publishing, www.northlandpub.com, 1988. The story of wapiti, with outstanding photos by Alan D. Carey. Out of print.

Phillips, Wayne. *Central Rocky Mountain Wildflowers: Including the Greater Yellowstone Ecosystem.* Guilford, CT: Globe Pequot Press (Falcon), www.falconbooks.com, 1999.

Retallic, Ken. *Flyfisher's Guide to Wyoming.* Gallatin Gateway, MT: Wilderness Adventures Press, 1998. An excellent guide; particularly helpful for anglers headed to Yellowstone.

Schneider, Bill. *Bear Aware: Hiking and Camping in Bear Country.* Guilford, CT: Globe Pequot/Falcon, www.falconbooks.com, 2001. A handy pocket-size book that is easy to read and up to date.

Travsky, Amber. *Mountain Biking Wyoming.* Guilford, CT: Globe Pequot Press (Falcon), www.falconbooks.com, 1999.

Onward Travel

The following is a shameless promotion for other Moon Handbooks (www.moon.com) covering the region. All of these are authoritative guides for their respective states or regions.

McRae, W. C., and Judy Jewell. *Moon Handbooks Montana.* Emeryville, CA: Avalon Travel Publishing, 2002.

Metzger, Stephen. *Moon Handbooks Colorado.* Emeryville, CA: Avalon Travel Publishing, 2002.

Pitcher, Don. *Moon Handbooks Wyoming.* Emeryville, CA: Avalon Travel Publishing, 2003.

Root, Don. *Moon Handbooks Idaho.* Emeryville, CA: Avalon Travel Publishing, 2001.

Weir, Bill, and W. C. McRae. *Moon Handbooks Utah.* Emeryville, CA: Avalon Travel Publishing, 2001.

Jackson Hole and Grand Teton National Park

Good, John M., and Kenneth L. Pierce. *Interpreting the Landscape: Recent and Ongoing Geology of Grand Teton and Yellowstone National Parks.* Moose, WY: Grand Teton Natural History Association, www.grandtetonpark.org, 1996. This attractive book has the latest geologic research on the parks and presents it in an understandable format with excellent illustrations.

Love, J. D., and John C. Reed, Jr. *Creation of the Teton Landscape: the Geologic Story of Grand Teton National Park.* Moose, WY: Grand Teton Natural History Association, www.grandtetonpark.org, 1995. A small but authoritatively detailed guide to the geology of Jackson Hole and the Tetons.

History

Betts, Robert B. *Along the Ramparts of the Tetons: The Saga of Jackson Hole, Wyoming.* Boulder, CO: University Press of Colorado, www.upcolorado.com, 1978. A substantial, detailed, and beautifully written book about the history of Jackson Hole.

Burt, Nathaniel. *Jackson Hole Journal.* Norman, OK: University of Oklahoma Press, www.oupress.com, 1983. Tales of growing up as a dude in Jackson Hole. Contains some very amusing stories.

Hayden, Elizabeth Wied, and Cynthia Nielsen. *Origins, A Guide to the Place Names of Grand Teton National Park and the Surrounding Area.* Moose, WY: Grand Teton Natural History Association, www.grandtetonpark.org, 1988. A guide to the obscure sources for place names in Grand Teton.

Huidekoper, Virginia. *The Early Days in Jackson Hole.* Boulder, CO: University Press of Colorado, www.upcolorado.com, 1978. Filled with more than 100 photos from old-time Jackson Hole. Out of print.

Righter, Robert W. *Crucible for Conservation: The Creation of Grand Teton National Park.* Boulder, CO: University Press of Colorado, www.upcolorado.com, 1982. The story of how the Tetons were spared through a half-century battle.

Ringholz, Raye C. *Little Town Blues: Voices from the Changing West.* Salt Lake City, UT: Gibbs-Smith Publisher, www.gibbs-smith.com, 1992. A cautionary note on the consequences of unbridled growth, this important small book visits several small towns in the West, including Jackson, where the rural qualities and beauty that attract visitors are being inundated by tourism and development.

Thompson, Edith M., and William Leigh Thompson. *Beaver Dick: The Honor and the Heartbreak.* Laramie, WY: Jelm Mountain Press, 1982. A touching historical biography of Beaver Dick Leigh, one of the first white men to settle in Jackson Hole. Out of print.

Natural History

Carrighar, Sally. *One Day at Teton Marsh.* Lincoln, NE: University of Nebraska Press, www.unp.unl.edu, 1979. A classic natural history of life in a Jackson Hole marsh. Made into a movie by Walt Disney. Out of print.

Clark, Tim W. *Ecology of Jackson Hole, Wyoming: A Primer.* Salt Lake City, UT: Paragon Press, www.paragon-press.com, 1981. An excellent scientific introduction to ecological interrelationships within Jackson Hole. Out of print.

Murie, Margaret, and Olaus Murie. *Wapiti Wilderness.* Boulder, CO: University Press of Colorado, www.upcolorado.com, 1986. The lives of two of America's most-loved conservationists in Jackson Hole and their work with elk.

Raynes, Bert. *Birds of Grand Teton National Park and the Surrounding Area.* Moose, WY: Grand Teton Natural History Association, www.grandtetonpark.org, 1984. A guide to local birds. Out of print.

Shaw, Richard J. *Plants of Grand Teton and Yellowstone National Parks.* Salt Lake City, UT: Wheelwright Press, 1981. Photos and descriptions of the most commonly found plants in the parks.

Travsky, Amber. *Mountain Biking Jackson Hole.* Guilford, CT: Globe Pequot Press (Falcon), www.falconbooks.com, 2001. Thirty-one rides in Jackson Hole, Grand Teton National Park, and surrounding areas.

Recreation

Carter, Tom. *Day Hiking Grand Teton National Park.* Garland, TX: Dayhiking Press, 1993. A pocket-size guide to 15 day-treks in the park.

Dufy, Katy, and Darwin Wile. *Teton Trails.* Moose, WY: Grand Teton Natural History Association, www.grandtetonpark.org, 1995. A useful guide to more than 200 miles of trails in the park.

Jackson, Reynold G. *A Climber's Guide to the Teton Range.* Seattle, WA: Mountaineers Books, www.mountaineerbooks.org, 1996. The definitive (415 pages!) climbing guide for the Tetons.

Prax, Brian, and Mark Schultheis. *The Book: Guide to Mountain Biking in the Jackson Hole Area.* Jackson, WY: Prax Photography and Productions, 2001. This spiral-bound book is the most complete guide to local cycling options, and includes coverage on Teton Valley.

Rossiter, Richard. *Teton Classics: 50 Selected Climbs in Grand Teton National Park.* Guilford, CT: Globe Pequot Press (Falcon), www.falconbooks.com, 1994. A small and nicely illustrated guide to 50 climbing routes in the Tetons.

Schneider, Bill. *Best Easy Day Hikes Grand Teton.* Guilford, CT: Globe Pequot Press (Falcon), www.falconbooks.com, 1999.

Schneider, Bill. *Hiking Grand Teton National Park.* Guilford, CT: Globe Pequot Press (Falcon), www.falconbooks.com, 1999.

Stone, Robert. *Day Hikes in Grand Teton National Park and Jackson Hole.* Guilford, CT: Globe Pequot Press (Falcon), www.falconbooks.com, 2000.

Viola, Bob, and Thomas Turiano. *Jackson Hole Ski Guide.* Guilford, CT: Globe Pequot Press (Falcon), www.falconbooks.com, 1998.

Watters, Ron. *Winter Tales and Trails: Skiing, Snowshoeing and Snowboarding in Idaho, the*

Grand Tetons and Yellowstone National Park. Pocatello, ID: Great Rift Press, 1997. A book that combines lucid writing on the area's rich history with guides to winter trails. More than 350 pages of details from an expert in the field.

Woods, Rebecca. *Jackson Hole Hikes.* Jackson, WY: White Willow Publishing, 1999. An excellent guide that includes trails in Grand Teton National Park and surrounding national forest areas. Easy to use and informative.

Yellowstone National Park

Note: Several natural history and geology books encompass both Yellowstone and Grand Teton National Parks. See the preceding section on Jackson Hole and Grand Teton National Park for additional titles with overlapping coverage.

Geology

Bryan, Scott. T. *The Geysers of Yellowstone.* Boulder, CO: University Press of Colorado, www.upcolorado.com, 1995. The definitive guide to more than 400 geysers and other geothermal features in Yellowstone.

Fritz, William J. *Roadside Geology of the Yellowstone Country.* Missoula, MT: Mountain Press Publishing Co., www.mountainpress.com, 1986. All of the park roads are covered in this easy-to-follow Yellowstone geology primer.

Schreier, Carl. *Yellowstone's Geysers, Hot Springs and Fumaroles.* Moose, WY: Homestead Publishing, 1987. An attractive small book filled with color photos and brief descriptions.

History

Bartlett, Richard A. *Yellowstone: A Wilderness Besieged.* Tucson, AZ: University of Arizona Press, www.uapress.arizona.edu, 1989. The history of Yellowstone and the fight to prevent its destruction by railroad magnates, concessioners, and others.

Haines, Aubrey L. *Yellowstone Place Names: Mirrors of History.* Boulder, CO: University Press of Colorado, www.upcolorado.com, 1996. For the Trivial Pursuit enthusiast; 318 pages of detailed descriptions with every possible name from every obscure corner of Yellowstone.

Haines, Aubrey L. *The Yellowstone Story: A History of Our First National Park.* Boulder, CO: University Press of Colorado, www.upcolorado.com, 1996. A definitive two-volume history of the park. Volume one (history up to the park's establishment) is the most interesting.

Janetski, Joel C. *Indians of Yellowstone Park.* Salt Lake City, UT: University of Utah Press, www.upress.utah.edu, 1987. A general overview of the earliest settlers in Yellowstone and later conflicts with incoming whites.

Milstein, Michael. *Yellowstone Album: 125 Years of America's Best Idea.* Billings, MT: The Billings Gazette, www.billingsgazette.com, 1996. A delightful book filled with historical photographs, along with photos of postcards, souvenirs, and other tourist artifacts.

Schreier, Carl (ed.). *Yellowstone: Selected Photographs 1870–1960.* Moose, WY: Homestead Publishing, 1989. An outstanding collection of historical photographs from the park.

Natural History

Craighead, Frank J. *Track of the Grizzly.* San Francisco, CA: Sierra Club Books, www.sierraclub.org, 1982. The life of grizzlies in Yellowstone, by one of the most famous bear researchers.

Krakell, Dean, II. *Downriver: A Yellowstone Journey.* San Francisco, CA: Sierra Club Books, www.sierraclub.org, 1987. An extraordinarily moving journey down the magnificent Yellowstone River.

McEneaney, Terry. *Birds of Yellowstone.* Boulder, CO: Roberts Rinehart, www.roberts-rinehart.com, 1988. A guide to Yellowstone birds and where to find them.

Reese, Rick and Terry Tempest Williams. *Greater Yellowstone: The National Park and Adjacent Wildlands.* Helena, MT: American Geographic Publishing, 1991. An attractive book with considerable information on ecological conditions in one of the Lower 48's largest intact ecosystems. Out of print.

Schullery, Paul (ed.). *Yellowstone Bear Tales.* Boulder, CO: Roberts Rinehart Publishers, www.roberts-rinehart.com, 1991. First-person stories of bear encounters from a range of travelers—including President Theodore Roosevelt—between 1880 and 1950.

Schullery, Paul. *Searching for Yellowstone.* New York: Houghton Mifflin Co., www.hmco.com, 1997. An eloquently written book by a long-time park ranger whose knowledge of the park goes far beyond the hype. Must-reading for anyone who cares about Yellowstone.

Scott, Douglas M., and Suvi A. Scott. *Wildlife of Yellowstone and Grand Teton National Parks.* Salt Lake City, UT: Wheelwright Press, 1990. A brief descriptive guide to Yellowstone and Grand Teton critters.

Shaw, Richard J. *Wildflowers of Yellowstone and Grand Teton National Parks.* Salt Lake City, UT: Wheelwright Press, 1992. Color photos and short descriptions of more than 100 wildflowers in the Greater Yellowstone Ecosystem.

Wuerthner, George. *Yellowstone: A Visitor's Companion.* Mechanicsburg, PA: Stackpole Books, 1992, www.stackpolebooks.com. A detailed guide to the natural history of Yellowstone.

Recreation

Bach, Orville E., Jr. *Hiking the Yellowstone Backcountry.* San Francisco, CA: Sierra Club Books, www.sierraclub.org, 1998. A pocket-size guide to hiking, canoeing, biking, and skiing in the park.

Butler, Susan Springer. *Scenic Driving Yellowstone and Grand Teton National Parks.* Guilford, CT: Globe Pequot Press (Falcon), www.falconbooks.com, 1999.

Carter, Tom. *Day Hiking Yellowstone.* Garland, TX: Dayhiking Press, 1991. A pocket-size guide to 20 day-treks, coordinated with the Trails Illustrated topographic maps.

Charlton, Robert E. *Yellowstone Fishing Guide.* Ketchum, ID: Lost River Press, 1995. A detailed guide to fishing in the park. Leaves no trickle unfished.

Henry, Jeff. *Yellowstone Winter Guide.* Boulder, CO: Roberts Rinehart Publishers, www.roberts-rinehart.com, 1998. A detailed guide to visiting Yellowstone in the winter; especially good for cross-country skiers.

Lilly, Bud, and Paul Schullery. *Bud Lilly's Guide to Fly Fishing the New West.* Portland, OR: Frank Amato Publications, 2000. The authoritative fishing source from the father of Western trout fishing.

Marschall, Mark C. *Yellowstone Trails: A Hiking Guide.* Yellowstone National Park, WY: The Yellowstone Association, www.yellowstoneassociation.org, 1999. An excellent, up-to-date, and detailed guidebook to the park's 1,000 miles of hiking trails.

Nelson, Don. *Paddling Yellowstone and Grand Teton National Parks.* Guilford, CT: Globe Pequot Press (Falcon), www.falconbooks.com, 1999.

Olsen, Ken, Dena Olsen, Steve Scharosch, and Hazel Scharosch. *Cross-Country Skiing Yellowstone Country.* Guilford, CT: Globe Pequot Press (Falcon), www.falconbooks.com,

1994. Detailed descriptions of 200 miles of ski trails in and near the park, including helpful trail profiles.

Parks, Richard. *Fishing Yellowstone*. Guilford, CT: Globe Pequot Press (Falcon), www.falconbooks.com, 1998. One of several authoritative guides, this one provides details on fly- and lure fishing, along with descriptions of more than 100 sites.

Schneider, Bill. *Hiking Yellowstone National Park*. Guilford, CT: Globe Pequot Press (Falcon), www.falconbooks.com, 1997. Clear maps and helpful trail profiles make this the most useful book for anyone heading out on Yellowstone hiking routes. Contains descriptions of more than 100 trails.

Schmidt, Jeremy, and Steven Fuller. *Yellowstone Grand Teton Road Guide: The Essential Guide for Motorists*. Jackson, WY: Free Wheeling Travel Guides, 1998. A pocket-sized guide to the roads of the two parks, with accurate, up-to-date information.

Stone, Robert. *Day Hikes in Yellowstone National Park and Jackson Hole*. Guilford, CT: Globe Pequot Press (Falcon), www.falconbooks.com, 2000.

Tawney, Robin. *Family Fun in Yellowstone National Park*. Guilford, CT: Globe Pequot Press (Falcon), www.falconbooks.com, 2001.

Varley, John D., and Paul D. Schullery. *Yellowstone Fishes: Ecology, History, and Angling in the Park*. Mechanicsburg, PA: Stackpole Books, www.stackpolebooks.com, 1998. The comprehensive guide to the fish of Yellowstone, written by two authorities in the field.

Cody and Shoshone National Forest

Cook, Jeannie (ed.). *Buffalo Bill's Town in the Rockies: A Pictorial History of Cody, Wyoming*. Cody, WY: Park County Historical Society, 1996. A photographic visit to Cody's interesting past.

James, H. L. *Scenic Driving the Beartooth Highway*. Guilford, CT: Globe Pequot Press (Falcon), www.falconbooks.com, 1997.

Rosa, Joseph G., and Robin May. *Buffalo Bill and His Wild West*. Lawrence, KS: University Press of Kansas, www.kansaspress.ku.edu, 1989. One of the newer books on Buffalo Bill, with a somewhat revisionist take on his life and times. Rich in detail on Cody's Wild West show.

Russell, Don. *The Lives and Legends of Buffalo Bill*. Norman, OK: University of Oklahoma Press, www.oupress.com, 1979. The most complete biography on the life of Buffalo Bill Cody.

Schneider, Bill. *Hiking the Beartooths*. Guilford, CT: Globe Pequot Press (Falcon), www.falconbooks.com, 2001.

Internet Resources

Yellowstone National Park
www.nps.gov/yell
A fine starting point for any exploration of the Yellowstone area.

Grand Teton National Park
www.nps.gov/grte
This official Park Service site has an abundance of background information about Grand Teton.

National Elk Refuge
http://nationalelkrefuge.fws.gov
This website details Jackson Hole's famous refuge with its picturesque sleigh rides among the elk.

U.S. Forest Service
www.fs.fed.us
This federal agency manages land within several national forests in the Greater Yellowstone Ecosystem. These include Bridger-Teton National Forest, www.fs.fed.us/btnf, Ashley National Forest (Flaming Gorge National Recreation Area) www.fs.fed.us/r4/ashley, Shoshone National Forest, www.fs.fed.us/r2/shoshone, and Caribou-Targhee National Forest, www.fs.fed.us/r4/caribou.

Wyoming Division of Tourism and State Marketing
www.wyomingtourism.org
The state's tourism site has everything you'd expect in the way of an interactive visitors center and much more.

Wyoming Department of Transportation
www.wyoroad.info
This website has updated road conditions, webcams, and details on road construction projects.

Wyoming Public Radio
http://uwadmnweb.uwyo.edu/wpr
A good starting place for information on public radio around Wyoming.

Wyoming State Trails Program
http://wyotrails.state.wy.us/trails
Check out this website for details on hiking, biking, cross-country skiing, snowmobile trails, Volksmarch, and other trails around the Wyoming.

Wyoming Homestay & Outdoor Adventures
www.wyomingbnb-ranchrec.com
Better known as WHOA, this organization maintains links to several dozen bed-and-breakfasts, dude ranches, guest cabins, and other distinctive lodging options.

Wyoming Game and Fish Department
http://gf.state.wy.us
Head to this website for details on fishing licenses and seasons, along with current issues affecting fish. You can even download application forms.

Wyoming Fishing Network
www.wyomingfishing.net
An exceptionally useful online source for Wyoming anglers.

Wyoming Outfitters and Guides Association
www.wyoga.org
Interested in a backcountry pack trip? Visit this website to find outfitters for the area you plan to visit.

Dude Ranchers' Association
www.duderanch.org
This national organization's helpful homepage has links to the websites of 30 different Wyoming guest ranches.

National Museum of Wildlife Art
www.wildlifeart.org

This large Jackson museum exhibits the works of many internationally recognized artists.

Jackson Hole Chamber of Commerce
www.jacksonholechamber.com

This website is a fine starting point for travel to Jackson, with a multitude of weblinks to local businesses.

Grand Targhee Ski Resort
www.grandtarghee.com

This resort on the west side of the Tetons is a favorite of powderhounds.

Jackson Hole Gallery Association
www.jacksonholearts.com

A great web source for more than two dozen Jackson art galleries.

Jackson Hole Mountain Resort
www.jacksonhole.com

The big one, this is the primary ski and snowboard destination in Jackson Hole.

Snow King Resort
www.snowking.com

Jackson's town hill, this small ski area is accessible and surprisingly challenging.

Jackson Hole Traveler
www.jacksonholetraveler.com

This private website is nicely designed and packed with useful information and links.

West Yellowstone Chamber of Commerce
www.westyellowstonechamber.com

The most complete web source for West Yellowstone, Montana.

Gardiner Chamber of Commerce
www.gardinerchamber.com

Details on the little edge-of-Yellowstone town of Gardiner, Montana.

Buffalo Bill Historical Center
www.bbhc.org

Cody's famous museum now covers an incredible 300,000 square feet, making it easily the most impressive museum in the region.

Park County Travel Council
www.yellowstone.org

This regional tourism agency has a great website for travelers heading into Cody.

Dubois Chamber of Commerce
www.duboiswyoming.org

This is the best web source for information on the Dubois area.

Index

CONSERVATION/ WILDERNESS AREAS

EVENTS

GALLERIES/ART MUSEUMS

HIKING/BACKPACKING

TOURS/GUIDES

M Index

Acknowledgments

The second edition of *Moon Handbooks Yellowstone & Grand Teton* has gained a bit of bulk (and hopefully some muscle), and now offers substantially more regional coverage than its sister title, *Moon Handbooks Wyoming*. It would be impossible to thank all of the people who helped me with this update, but several individuals deserve applause.

A special thank you goes to the following chamber of commerce and visitors center people who helped open doors to their hometowns or reviewed my manuscript for problems. Three folks from the Jackson Hole Chamber of Commerce provided a wealth of regional information and bent over backward to assist in my research for this book: Jesse O'Connor, Chris Hansen, and Jon Mobeck. As always, Claudia Wade of the Park County Travel Council came through in flying colors, as did Lee Anne Ackerman of the Cody Chamber of Commerce. Suzy Hahn of the Cooke City-Silver Gate Chamber of Commerce provided the lowdown on that pretty corner of Montana, and Jeanne Miyoshi of the Teton Valley Chamber of Commerce detailed the west side of the Tetons.

The following hard-working Forest Service employees assisted with my updates: Megan Lyons Bogle from Caribou-Targhee National Forest, Linda Meriglino from Bridger-Teton National Forest, and Gordon K. Warren from Shoshone National Forest.

I also wish to thank Rick Hoeninghausen of Xanterra Parks & Resorts, Judith Blair of Blair Hotels in Cody, and the staff of the Wort Hotel in Jackson for their generous assistance. This book was shepherded through the production process by my editor, Amy Scott. Thanks to her and the rest of the gang at Avalon Travel Publishing for getting this book into your hands.

I offer a very special thanks to my wife, Karen Shemet, and our children, Aziza and Rio, for keeping me grounded while I researched and wrote this book.

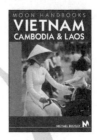

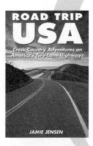

U.S. ~ Metric Conversion

1 inch	= 2.54 centimeters (cm)
1 foot	= .304 meters (m)
1 yard	= 0.914 meters
1 mile	= 1.6093 kilometers (km)
1 km	= .6214 miles
1 fathom	= 1.8288 m
1 chain	= 20.1168 m
1 furlong	= 201.168 m
1 acre	= .4047 hectares
1 sq km	= 100 hectares
1 sq mile	= 2.59 square km
1 ounce	= 28.35 grams
1 pound	= .4536 kilograms
1 short ton	= .90718 metric ton
1 short ton	= 2000 pounds
1 long ton	= 1.016 metric tons
1 long ton	= 2240 pounds
1 metric ton	= 1000 kilograms
1 quart	= .94635 liters
1 US gallon	= 3.7854 liters
1 Imperial gallon	= 4.5459 liters
1 nautical mile	= 1.852 km

To compute Celsius temperatures, subtract 32 from Fahrenheit and divide by 1.8. To go the other way, multiply Celsius by 1.8 and add 32.

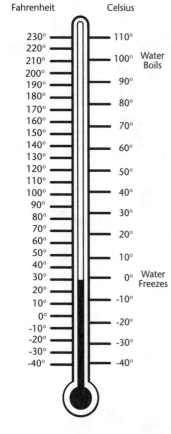

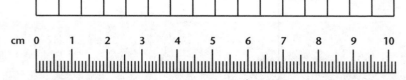